# THE SOCIOLOGY OF RELIGION

GARLAND LIBRARY OF SOCIOLOGY
(VOL. 18)

GARLAND REFERENCE LIBRARY
OF SOCIAL SCIENCE
(VOL. 612)

# GARLAND LIBRARY OF SOCIOLOGY
## General Editor: Dan A. Chekki

1. *Conflict and Conflict Resolution: A Historical Bibliography*
   by Jack Nusan Porter
2. *Sociology of Sciences: An Annotated Bibliography of Invisible Colleges, 1972–1981*
   by Daryl E. Chubin
3. *Race and Ethnic Relations: An Annotated Bibliography*
   by Graham C. Kinloch
4. *Friendship: A Selected, Annotated Bibliography*
   by J. L. Barkas
5. *The Sociology of Aging: An Annotated Bibliography and Sourcebook*
   by Diana K. Harris
6. *Medical Sociology: An Annotated Bibliography, 1972–1982*
   by John G. Bruhn, Billy U. Philips, and Paula L. Levine
7. *The Clinical Sociology Handbook*
   by Jan M. Fritz
8. *Issues in the Sociology of Religion: A Bibliography*
   by Anthony J. Blasi and Michael W. Cuneo
9. *The Influence of the Family: A Review and Annotated Bibliography of Socialization, Ethnicity, and Delinquency, 1975–1986*
   by Alan C. Acock and Jeffrey M. Clair

10. *Jewish Family Issues: A Resource Guide*
    by Benjamin Schlesinger
11. *Social Stratification: An Annotated Bibliography*
    by Graham C. Kinloch
12. *Psychocultural Change and the American Indian: An Ethnohistorical Analysis*
    by Laurence French
13. *Social Support and Health: An Annotated Bibliography*
    by John G. Bruhn, Billy U. Philips, Paula L. Levine, and Carlos F. Mendes de Leon
14. *Sociology of Sport: An Annotated Bibliography*
    by Paul Redekop
15. *The Sociology of Mental Illness: An Annotated Bibliography*
    by Richard K. Thomas
16. *Dimensions of Communities: A Research Handbook*
    by Dan A. Chekki
17. *The Sociology of Work: A Critical Annotated Bibliography*
    by Parvin Ghorayshi
18. *The Sociology of Religion: An Organizational Bibliography*
    by Anthony J. Blasi and Michael W. Cuneo

# THE SOCIOLOGY OF RELIGION
## *An Organizational Bibliography*

Anthony J. Blasi
Michael W. Cuneo

GARLAND PUBLISHING, INC. • NEW YORK & LONDON
1990

**Library of Congress Cataloging-in-Publication Data**

Blasi, Anthony J.
    The sociology of religion ; an organizational bibliography
Anthony J. Blasi, Michael W. Cuneo.
      p.  cm. — (Garland library of sociology ; vol. 18) (Garland
reference library of social science ; vol. 612)
    ISBN 0–8240–2584–9 (alk. paper)
    1. Religion and sociology—Bibliography.  2. Religions—
Bibliography.  3. Sects—Bibliography.  4. Cults—Bibliography.
I. Cuneo, Michael W.  II. Title.  III. Series.  IV. Series: Garland
reference library of social science ; v. 612.
Z7831.B54   1990
[BL60]
016.3066—dc20
                        90–40684
                          CIP

Printed on acid-free, 250-year-life paper
Manufactured in the United States of America

# CONTENTS

Preface of the General Editor     xv

Preface     xix

Introduction     xxiii

List of Abbreviations     xxix

### PART I: ASIAN TRADITIONS

Chapter One: *Hindu*     3
    General     3
    Ananda Marga     9
    Divine Light Mission     9
    Hare Krishna     11
    Healthy-Happy-Holy Organization     13
    Meher Baba     13
    Pattini     14
    Radhasoami     14
    Rajneesh     14
    Ramakrishna     15
    Vedanta     15
    Yoga     15

Chapter Two: *Buddhist*     17
    General     17
    India (Ancient)     17
    South Asia     18
    Southeast Asia and Pacific     19
    Sri Lanka     21
    Western     23

Modern Sects and Movements                      24
Soka Gakkai (Nichiren Shoshu)                   25
Theravada                                       26
Zen                                             27
Chapter Three: *Other Asian*                    29
   Chinese                       29
   Jain                          30
   Parsi                         30
   Shinto                        30
   Sikh                          31


PART II: HEBREW, JEWISH, AND ISLAMIC TRADITIONS

Chapter Four: *Hebrew*                          35
Chapter Five: *Jewish*                          39
   General                       39
   Africa                        43
   Asia                          43
   Australia                     44
   Canada                        44
   Europe                        46
   Great Britain                 48
   Israel                        50
   Latin America                 53
   United States                 53
   Black Hebrew Nation           67
   Hasidic                       68
   Lubavichter                   69
   Sephardic                     69
Chapter Six: *Islamic*                          71
   General                       71
   Algeria                       77
   Egypt                         77
   Morocco                       78
   Other African                 79
   Southeast Asia and Pacific    79
   South Asia                    81
   Middle East                   84
   West                          84

Black Muslim                                                86
Ismaili                                                    87
Mouride                                                    88
Shi'ite                                                    88

PART III: CHRISTIAN: EARLY AND LITURGICAL TRADITIONS

Chapter Seven: *Early Christian*                           93
Chapter Eight: *Orthodox and Other Eastern*               97
    General                            97
    Orthodox (U.S.A.)                  97
    Coptic                             98
    Ethiopian Orthodox                 98
    Greek Orthodox                     98
    Russian Orthodox                   99
    Serbian Orthodox                  100
    Syrian Orthodox                   101
    Ukrainian Orthodox               101
Chapter Nine: *Roman Catholic: Historical and Contemporary*
    *Perspectives*                    103
    General                           103
    Catholic Action                   108
    Catholic Clergy                   109
    Catholic Traditionalist           111
    Charismatic Movement              112
    Jansenist                         118
    Mariology                         119
    Modernist Crisis                  120
    Religious Orders and Congregations 120
    Second Vatican Council            125
Chapter Ten: *Roman Catholic: United States of America*   129
    Works, 1930–1949                  129
    Works, 1950–1959                  131
    Works, 1960–1969                  137
    Works, 1970–1979                  149
    Works, 1980-1989                  168

Chapter Eleven: *Roman Catholic: International Studies*   181
    Africa   181
    Australia and New Zealand   182
    Pacific and East Asia   183
    India   184
    Sri Lanka   185
    Europe (General)   185
    Austria   186
    Belgium   186
    France   187
    Germany   191
    West Germany   192
    Hungary   193
    Italy   193
    Malta   196
    Netherlands   196
    Norway, Sweden   198
    Poland   198
    Spain   199
    Switzerland   202
    Yugoslavia   202
    Great Britain   202
    Northern Ireland   205
    Ireland   205
    North America   207
    Canada   207
    Latin America (General)   214
    Mexico   217
    Argentina   218
    Bolivia, Ecuador, Peru, Uruguay, Venezuela   219
    Brazil   220
    Chile   224
    Colombia   226
    Paraguay   226
    Guatemala   227
    Nicaragua   227
    Other Central American and Caribbean   228

Chapter Twelve: *Anglican*    231
   Church of England    231
   Church of Ireland    234
   Anglican Church of Canada    234
   Episcopal (U.S.A.)    236
   Africa, Australia, Latin America    240

PART IV: CHRISTIAN: REFORMATION TRADITIONS

Chapter Thirteen: *Protestant: General and Historical Studies*    243
   Reformation    243
   Europe    243
   Canada    244
   U.S.A.    244
   Latin America (General)    249
   Mexico    249
   Brazil and Chile    250
   Argentina    251
   Colombia, Guatemala, Nicaragua, Uruguay    252
   Asia    252
Chapter Fourteen: *Lutheran*    253
   Germany, Hungary    253
   West Germany    253
   Finland    254
   Sweden    254
   Canada, Australia    255
   Latin America    255
   U.S.A. (General)    255
   United Lutheran Church in America    258
   Lutheran Church in America    259
   American Lutheran Church    260
   Lutheran Church—Missouri Synod    261
   Norwegian Lutheran Church in America    262
Chapter Fifteen: *Calvinist*    263
   Calvinist (General)    263
   Netherlands    264
   South Africa    264
   France    265
   Australia    265

Great Britain .................................................... 266
Northern Ireland ................................................ 266
Ireland (Presbyterian) .......................................... 267
Latin America (Presbyterian, Christian and Missionary
    Alliance) .................................................. 267
Puritan (U.S.A.) ................................................ 267
Congregationalist (U.S.A.) ...................................... 267
Presbyterian (U.S.A.) ........................................... 269
United Presbyterian Church (U.S.A.) ............................. 271
Reformed Church in America ...................................... 274
Christian Reformed Church (U.S.A.) .............................. 275
Dutch Reformed, German Reformed (U.S.A.) ........................ 275
Chapter Sixteen: *Anabaptist* ................................... 277
Anabaptist (General and Historical) ............................. 277
Amish ........................................................... 278
Hutterite ....................................................... 279
Mennonite (Russia, France) ...................................... 280
Mennonite (Latin America) ....................................... 281
Mennonite (North America) ....................................... 281
Chapter Seventeen: *Baptist* .................................... 289
Great Britain ................................................... 289
Europe .......................................................... 289
Soviet Union .................................................... 290
Australia, India ................................................ 290
Canada .......................................................... 290
U.S.A. (General) ................................................ 291
America Baptist Convention ...................................... 293
Southern Baptist (U.S.A.) ....................................... 295
Chapter Eighteen: *Methodist* ................................... 301
General ......................................................... 301
Great Britain ................................................... 301
Canada, Australia ............................................... 303
Latin America ................................................... 304
African Methodist Episcopal Church .............................. 304
U.S.A. (General) ................................................ 304
The Methodist Church (U.S.A.) ................................... 307
United Methodist Church (U.S.A.) ................................ 307

Chapter Nineteen: *Holiness and Pentecostal*     311
    Holiness Religion (General)     311
    Holiness (Church of God—Anderson, Indiana)     312
    Holiness (Father Divine)     312
    Holiness (Church of the Nazarene)     313
    Pentecostal (General)     313
    Pentecostal (Italy, France)     318
    Pentecostal (Great Britain)     318
    Pentecostal (General Latin American)     319
    Pentecostal (Brazil)     319
    Pentecostal (Chile)     320
    Pentecostal (Colombia, Mexico, Puerto Rico)     321
    Pentecostal (U.S.A.—General)     322
    Pentecostal Church of God in America     323
    United Pentecostal Church (U.S.A.)     323
    Assembly of God (U.S.A.)     323
    Full Gospel Businessmen's Fellowship International     324
    Snake Handling     324
Chapter Twenty: *Independent Protestant Traditions*     325
    Waldensian     325
    Moravian     325
    Brethren (United, Evangelical United, Exclusive)     326
    Quaker     326
    Pietist     328
    Salvation Army     328
    Adventist (Irvingite, Millerite)     329
    Adventist (Jehovah's Witnesses)     329
    Seventh-day Adventist     333
    Adventist (Christadelphian)     335
    Christian Science     335
    Communitarian     337
    Disciples of Christ     338
    Churches of Christ     339
    Mainline Merger (United Church of Canada)     340
    Mainline Merger (United Church of Christ)     341
    Mainline Merger (Uniting Church in Australia)     343
    Jesus Movement (Miscellaneous)     343
    Jesus Movement (Children of God [or Family of Love])     348
    African Independent (Miscellaneous)     349

African Independent (Apostolic Church of John Maranke) 350
African Independent (Kimbangu) 351
Japanese Independent (Mukyokai) 351
Russian Origin (Doukhobor) 351
Russian Origin (Molokan) 352
British Independent (Oxford Group Movement) 352
British Independent (New Testament Church
   of God, Levellers) 352
American Independent (Miscellaneous) 353
American Independent (Jews for Jesus) 353
American Independent (Polish National Catholic Church) 353
Chapter Twenty-one: *Protestant: Theological and Ideological
   Alignments* 355
Liberal Protestant (Miscellaneous) 355
Liberal Protestant (Social Gospel) 356
Liberal Protestant (Unitarian) 357
Liberal Protestant (YMCA) 358
Fundamentalist Protestant 358
Evangelical (U.S.A.) 364
Evangelical (France, Latin America) 367
Evangelical (Billy Graham Crusade) 367
Conservative Protestant (General) 369
Conservative (Canada, Australia) 369
Conservative (U.S.A.) 370
Moral Majority 374

## PART V: INDEPENDENT TRADITIONS

Chapter Twenty-two: *Mormon* 379
Works, 1937–1949 379
Works, 1950–1959 380
Works, 1960–1969 382
Works, 1970–1979 384
Works, 1980–1989 388
Aaronic Order 393
Morrisites 393

xii

Chapter Twenty-three: *New Religions*    395
    est    395
    Human Potential Movement    395
    New Thought    396
    Occult    396
    People's Temple (Jonestown)    398
    Satanism    400
    Scientology    400
    Spiritualism (General)    402
    Spiritualism (Australia, Philippines)    402
    Spiritualism (Ghana)    402
    Spiritualism (Great Britain)    402
    Spiritualism (Brazil)    403
    Spiritualism (Mexico)    404
    Spiritualism (Puerto Rico)    404
    Spiritualism (U.S.A.)    405
    Synanon    405
    Theosophy    406
    Transcendental Meditation    406
    UFO Cult    407
    Unification Church    408
    Miscellaneous    414
Chapter Twenty-four: *Little Traditions and Third-World*
    *Syncretisms*    415
    Africanist Religion in Brazil    415
    Umbanda    416
    Candomblé    418
    Antoniens    418
    Jamaa    418
    Bhils    419
    Cargo Cults    419
    Ghost Dance    420
    Rastafarian    420
    Voodoo    421
    Tonghak    422
    Miscellaneous    422
Chapter Twenty-Five: *Other Independent Traditions*    424
    Gnostic (Ancient)    424
    Freemasonry    424

Swedenborg 425
Shakers 425
Oneida 426
Baha'i 426
Monotheism and Polytheism 427

Author Index 429
Subject Index 453

xiv

# PREFACE OF THE GENERAL
# EDITOR

The increasing rate of change in recent years poses some bewildering and complex problems for modern societies. Issues such as abortion, euthanasia, inequality and injustice, poverty, discrimination, human rights, and nuclear armaments and war have undercurrents of religious controversy. Community leaders and legislators are frequently confronted with public debates and controversies on a wide spectrum of social problems that have some relevance to religion and morals. Among young people and among members of small religious and quasi-religious movements, the winds of change are blowing.

Religious beliefs and practices have been a universal feature of all societies. According to Emile Durkheim every society needs a religion. Religion takes many forms and plays different roles. It can be a solid foundation for social cohesiveness of a society or it can be a powerful source of tension and conflict between groups. Religion as a set of symbolic forms relates humans to the ultimate conditions of their existence. The experiences of misfortune, suffering, and death give rise to profound questions about the meaning of it all. Religious symbols provide a context of meaning where these experiences can be dealt with when other forms of explanation and problem solution have failed.

The study of religion as it relates to other institutions of society is central to the sociology of religion. Sociologists are interested in studying how religion is organized and how it affects our behavior in family life, economic achievement, and political and cultural activities. Sociologists also examine the belief systems developed by people in different circumstances and how religious beliefs change over time as circumstances change. Sociologists of religion have asked important questions such as: What are the social functions of religion? Is today's world becoming less religious? Can organized religion influence large-scale social action and societal change? Sociologists have long been fascinated with the way belief systems seem to change the course of history and influence the character and development of nations.

A common assumption today is that religion is becoming less and less important in modern industrial societies. However, not all sociologists share this view. Despite widespread secularization in modern societies, there is evidence that people continue to express a belief in some supernatural reality that is beyond the forces of nature and physical laws. Recent public opinion polls in the United States suggest a rising tide of religious interest. Nevertheless, there are inconsistencies and contradictions: levels of morality and ethics tend to remain low; hunger is a reality for the poor; and levels of self-esteem are low for many persons.

In the 1980's there was a renewed interest in religion and its role in public life. Religious cultures and themes tend to mold the nature of collective life and serve as a basis for public moral dialogue. Changes since the 1960's have significantly altered long established relations between religion and culture. Traditional distinctions between the religious and secular are being blurred. The changing character of religious pluralism in America includes, among others, a decline of the liberal establishment and a resurgence of conservative religious and moral interests. For some observers, Moral Majority, prolife groups, charismatic renewal, new quasi-religious cults and sects, anti-nuclear coalitions—all are embodied in American religion. American democratic ideals and especially the general pattern of changing roles for women have also, it appears, changed the ideological and social structure of American religion.

There seems to be a common belief that science and religion are incompatible. Increasing emphasis on materialism, the growth of science, and the secularization process are not considered to be conducive to religiosity. However, the lack of adequate understanding of religion by many seems to be the root cause of several intergroup conflicts. There is a need to maintain a balance between the religious and scientific view of life, for as Albert Einstein remarked, "Science without religion is lame, religion without science is blind."

This reference volume is a continuation of the authors' earlier work, *Issues in the Sociology of Religion* (1986), published in our Sociology Series. The present volume includes studies of both the great and little religious traditions of the world as well as new religions and cults that have emerged in contemporary societies. One of the characteristic features of this book is that it provides information that might help the user to make longitudinal and ecological connections among various studies of the same and different entities and to identify the trends of research.

Furthermore, it highlights a significant presence of specific religious traditions or denominations in the national, regional, and local contexts. The efforts to prepare a fairly comprehensive, well-organized, and up-to-date scholarly resource by Anthony J. Blasi and Michael W. Cuneo deserve appreciation by those interested in religious studies and by those involved in religious organizations. This encyclopedic volume should serve as an important research tool for serious students of religion.

DAN A. CHEKKI
University of Winnipeg

# PREFACE

The present volume is designed as a scholarly resource complementary to our earlier bibliography, *Issues in the Sociology of Religion* (Garland, 1986). Whereas the 1986 bibliography organizes entries by the major thematic issues of the sociology of religion, this one does so by the names of specific religious traditions and organizations. Its purpose is to give students of religion generally and sociologists in particular convenient access to the impressively rich and far-flung literature that has been generated by the sociological study of religion.

The five major divisions of the volume reflect the broadly cross-cultural scope of its contents. The first part consists of three chapters that list studies of the great Asian traditions, including the classical Hindu and Buddhist faiths and their variegated descendants. The three chapters of the second part feature sociological accounts of various aspects of the Hebrew, Jewish, and Islamic traditions. The third part, the volume's most extensive, contains six chapters, one dedicated to studies of early Christianity, three to those of Roman Catholicism, and one each to studies of Anglican and Byzantine Christianity respectively. Part IV includes nine chapters, each differently focused on denominations and movements which belong, if sometimes only peripherally, to the Reformation family of Christian traditions. The final and residual part is composed of four chapters diversely dedicated to studies of syncretistic phenomena, the so-called new religions, and other religions not quite so new, such as the Mormon and Baha'i.

In order to locate works pertaining to a religious tradition or organization of specific research interest, the user is advised to consult either the Table of Contents or the Subject Index. If interested in studies of a religion in a particular geographical region, such as Islam in the Middle East or Methodism in Great Britain, it is likewise recommended that the user refer to the Table of Contents or Subject Index for easy location of the appropriate bibliographic entries. The volume otherwise conforms closely to the format of our 1986 bibliography. Each entry is numbered according to its order of appearance in the text. The volume's several hundred cross-listed entries are accompanied by notations that direct the user to a specific numbered entry for full bibliographic information. Multiple entries by one author under the same heading appear in chronological order by date of publication. The user who is interested in the works of a particular scholar should consult the Author Index.

The volume includes several kinds of entry: books, journal articles, essays from anthologies or collections, as well as M.A. theses and Ph.D. dissertations that have been cited in the published literature. Celebrated classics which were first published in languages other than English are cited only in their English translation. Other works not originally in English are recorded in their language of first publication and in translation. There are numerous entries of French, German, Italian, Portuguese, and Spanish works in addition to English ones. The volume covers the literature up to and including 1988 and part of 1989, excluding theses and dissertations that have never been cited, convention proceedings, textbooks, and unpublished meeting papers.

The research method closely approximates that employed for our 1986 bibliography. Entries have been taken from the principal journals in the field—*Sociological Analysis* and *Social Compass*. Additional entries have been selected from two major interdisciplinary journals—the *Journal for the Scientific Study of Religion* and the *Review of Religious Research*. A knowledge of monographs in the field and an examination of book reviews in the journals led to more entries. In addition, an unsystematic exposure to general sociological journals resulted in the inclusion of further articles and books. Finally, previously published bibliographic essays were consulted; these often defined the field broadly, necessitating a cautious selectiveness. These bibliographic works include the annual update that appears in *Social Compass* (Belgium); *Social Scientific Study of Religion: A Bibliography*, by Morris I. Berkowitz and J.E. Johnson (Pittsburgh: University of Pittsburgh Press, 1967); *Sociologie du Christianisme:*

*Bibliographie Internationale (1900–1961)*, by Hervé Carrier and Emile Pin (Rome: Presses de l'Université Grégorienne, 1964); *Sociologia de la Religión y Teología, Estudio Bibliográfico*, by the Instituto Fe y Secularidad (Madrid: Ed. Cuadernos para el Dialogo, 1975, 1978); and *La Religion au Canada: bibliographie annotée des travaux en sciences humaines des religions, 1945–1970/ Religion in Canada: Annotated Inventory of Scientific Studies of Religion, 1945–1972*, by Stewart Crysdale and Jean-Paul Montminy (Québec: Presses de l'Université Laval, 1974).

The volume's principal criteria of inclusion are that a work be identifiably sociological in design and, of course, that it involve the examination of at least some aspect of one or more religious traditions. Where disciplinary boundaries are blurred, as is occasionally the case with the sociology of religion on the one hand and theology and anthropology on the other, the decision whether or not to include a particular work has been a matter of our considered judgment.

The bibliography is relatively inclusive, within limitations of space and, perhaps more telling, limitations of its authors' scholarly purview. Despite our gesture toward cross-cultural comprehensiveness, the volume is heavily weighted in favor of works of a North American provenance, a circumstance obviously reflective more of residential contingency than the productivity of scholars outside of Canada and the United States. Living and working as we do in North America simply has given us far greater exposure to North American scholarship than to that from elsewhere. This geographic imbalance is vividly documented in the chapters on Roman Catholicism, with the section on Catholicism in the United States running generously to more than four hundred numbered entries and that on Catholicism in Belgium totalling a mere thirteen. The various chapters on Protestantism are likewise composed preponderantly of entries that represent studies of North American phenomena. It seems unimaginable, for example, that the three entries given for Baptists in Great Britain would be exhaustive of the applicable literature. The same might be said of the relatively sparse listings for European Lutheranism.

Nevertheless, we hope others agree that such occasional disproportion is more than redeemed by the over-all value of the volume as a research tool. Even where it cannot claim exhaustiveness, the bibliography is at the very least a useful starting point for those interested in canvassing the scholarly literature pertinent to a given religious tradition or organization.

If sometimes biased in favor of Canadian and especially American studies, the volume is more often a reliable guide to the field's main tours of research. The entries on the Roman Catholic Church in the United States, for example, are quantitative indication of the very considerable scholarly resources that have been expended by American sociologists toward investigation of matters involving parochial education, the priesthood, and the impact of the Second Vatican Council upon American Catholicism. The sections on international Catholicism show that European scholars have been comparatively more concerned with examining along more broadly societal lines the changing relationship of the church with other cultural institutions. Also noteworthy, and something again reflected by the distribution of entries, is how investigation of new religious movements, particularly in this regard the Unification Church, served throughout the 1970s and 80s to reinvigorate the sociology of religion and to enliven its theoretical spirit.

We express gratitude to the many friends and colleagues who encouraged us in this undertaking. We are particularly and deeply grateful to Margaret Cuneo, for supporting the project from its inception, lending it her intellectual guidance throughout, and preparing the final manuscript. The final stages of research were greatly assisted by a faculty publication grant provided by Fordham University.

# INTRODUCTION

In order to enhance its value as a research tool, we have annotated many of the volume's more than three thousand numbered entries. Annotations are generally provided except in cases where works were not directly accessible to us or in others where the titles of works are sufficiently clear so as to render annotation redundant. The annotations include information that might help the user to make longitudinal and ecological connections between different studies of the same religious entity, to set up comparisons between different entries, and to identify the genre of research represented by the various studies.

## LONGITUDINAL CONNECTIONS

Perhaps no information conveyed by the annotations is so critical as that concerning the historical period upon which any given study is focused. Such information enables the user to identify in at least a preliminary way the particular population under investigation. A study of the pre-monarchy Hebrews is concerned quite obviously with a sociologically identifiable population significantly different from one of the post-exile Hebrews. And perhaps even more graphically, studies of, let us say, first-century Christians on the one hand and contemporary charismatics on the other are hardly of the same religious movement.

The continuities across time that are reflected by the maintenance of traditional religious symbols and texts are also sociological realities, but realities which join different populations. This is clearly so when two studies focus on separate historical epochs, but it is also the case across smaller units of time. Findings about a denomination by studies only ten years apart may not be about the *same* people. Such findings must be interpreted in light of different kinds of population change, or changes in the attributes of the same people.

The time that a study reflects is manifestly important when a religious entity is also an immigrant one. Over time, an immigrant group may move from a marginal position in its host society to a more central position. Correspondingly, it may acquire and master the resources needed to institutionalize its religious distinctiveness. Alternatively, such distinctiveness may be jettisoned as an immigrant group grows increasingly comfortable with the symbolic universe of its host society. In light of this dynamic, therefore, it is exceedingly important that previous studies concerning the religion of immigrant groups be located in time.

Upward mobility is also something to be taken into consideration regarding the changes that may occur over time to the religiosity of social groups, immigrant or otherwise. As a group ascends the status ladder, the role played by religion in its social presence is not likely to remain unchanged. It is, of course, important here to distinguish between the cultural status and political standing of a religion itself on the one hand and that of its members on the other. A religion may be marginal to a particular cultural world, but its members economically secure and politically powerful. Or a religion may be culturally central and its members poor and powerless. There are, for example, influential Greek Orthodox Christians in the United States and poor Catholics in Ireland, rich and poor Muslims alike in Indonesia, and also both influential and powerless Jews in Israel. A religion as a cultural system may undergo upward mobility while many or most of its members do not, or conversely it may remain tangential to the dominant society while at least part of its membership attains success within the reigning stratification system. All of these possibilities once again highlight the importance of situating previous studies of a religious entity within an appropriate historical context.

Something else to keep in mind are the contextual fluctuations to which religious organizations are frequently subject. As the import of a musical note in a score changes according to whether the note appears in a melody line or in a chordal structure, so the cultural import of a religious organization varies according to its historical context. A religion in a given area may at one point in time exert a decisive—perhaps even monopolistic—influence, at a subsequent date find itself in competition with other religions of equal claim to cultural legitimacy, and still later perhaps be branded as deviant. The cultural career of the United Church of Canada is instructive in this regard. With an irreparably shrunken membership, the United Church has been demoted in the course of only several decades from "Canada's denomination" to a minority faith of only residual political influence, though it has not, at least yet, been relegated to the status of a mere cultural curiosity. The storied decline of Roman Catholicism in Quebec makes the same point perhaps even more vividly. And as is illustrated by the rising fortunes of Asian religious traditions in Canada, this process may also occur in the opposite direction.

## ECOLOGICAL CONNECTIONS

For a variety of reasons, it is important to know where given studies have been conducted, and this is something that the annotations attempt to clarify whenever appropriate. (Sometimes there are enough studies of a particular tradition or denomination to warrant organizing the entries under geographically specific subheadings.) The most obviously relevant consideration is national context; a given religion may command popular allegiance and political power in one nation and yet be a persecuted minority in another.

Beyond national contexts, there are reasons at times for an interest in local environments. In the case of a community study, for example, one may need to know what previous studies have revealed about the community's religious organizations. Or it may be that a particular religious organization has a significant presence in only a few specific communities. Or that a study has been conducted in a particular community that is somehow idiosyncratic in terms of the broader national context. The possibility of the local distinctiveness of a religious entity is especially relevant to the interpretation of participant-observation studies, which are themselves usually tied to specific localities.

Between the national and local levels, the regional level is also sometimes of importance. Within some nations identifiable ethnic and subnational groups are concentrated according to region; Canada is a striking example of this, but Great Britain, Nigeria, India, the Soviet Union, Belgium, and Sudan also come to mind. The religions associated with subnational groups may vary in their social significance from one part of the nation to another. Similarly, there may be regional variations in the significance of religions quite independently of ethnic or subnational group distributions. For example, fundamentalist groups located in the southern United States may contribute to the dominant culture, but elsewhere in the nation they may evince strident opposition toward it. Or, by way of typological illustration, Mormonism is a conventional church in Utah and parts of Idaho, but in other states it may possess characteristics distinctive of a religious cult. This kind of variation suggests that the social scientist should not assume that a nationwide sample is always or necessarily superior to a smaller one of narrower scope. What kind of representativeness is of most merit depends upon the research interests at hand; the annotations and headings provided throughout the volume are intended to serve such interests.

When reviewing the empirical literature of any field in sociology, one should be attuned to the comparability and incomparability of different studies. It is not terribly fruitful to report in mechanical fashion that Smith 1980 found X positively correlated with Y and Jones 1980 did not, if Smith and Jones were reporting findings from geographically incomparable data bases. Human organizations are not like chemical reagents; different *samples* of them cannot be expected to have identical attributes. Both time and place may indicate variable contexts that affect the character of the organizations in which a researcher has an interest.

## GENRES OF INQUIRY

It frequently occurs in the sociology of organizations that different kinds of research technique yield different results. Organizations—religious or otherwise—usually have leadership élites with backgrounds and views quite unlike those of their general memberships. Participant-observation studies of strategically placed subgroups, historical documentary studies, content analyses of speeches and publications, and interviews of major figures may lead to conclusions different from those yielded by interview or questionnaire data derived from representative membership samples.

Similarly, there are often significant discrepancies between "attitudes" as revealed in questionnaires on the one hand and ethnographic data from field work on the other; "attitudes" are sometimes mere verbalizations that are set aside in the face of real events. The different kinds of inquiry often complement one another by

xxvi

presenting different and possibly contrary pictures. Accordingly, the annotations frequently specify the kind of research that is behind any given study. The user may wish to seek out overlapping studies of different genres of research, or perhaps she or he may find that some religious organization remains to be investigated by a particular technique.

# ABBREVIATIONS

The use of abbreviations is kept to a minimum in order to enhance the ease with which the bibliography can be used. Thus only the following journals and reference sources are abbreviated:

JSSR    *Journal for the Scientific Study of Religion*
RRR     *Review of Religious Research*
SA      *Sociological Analysis. A Journal in the Sociology of Religion*
SC      *Social Compass* (English and French)
DA      *Dissertation Abstracts* (followed by the volume, issue number, and page where a given dissertation is summarized)

# PART I
# ASIAN TRADITIONS

# 1
## Hindu

*GENERAL*

1. Adams, Bert N. "Urban Skills and Religion: Mechanisms for Coping and Defense Among the Ugandan Asians." SOCIAL PROBLEMS 22,1 (1974): 28-42.

   A sample of 190 Hindu and 104 Ismaili Muslim Asians in Kampala. Ugandan Asians were under pressure in 1971, causing many of them to leave the country. Religiosity reduces anxiety or insecurity, but it is accompanied by feelings of fatalism. Asians of high socio-economic status and with local investments saw themselves as more vulnerable but also as better able to cope.

2. Aggarwal, P.C. CASTE, RELIGION AND POWER: AN INDIAN CASE STUDY. Delhi: Sri Ram Center for Industrial Relations, 1971.

3. Allen, M.R. "Kumari or Virgin Worship in Kathmandu Valley." CONTRI-BUTIONS TO INDIAN SOCIOLOGY 10,2 (1976): 293-316.

   Based on 1973-74 field work in Kathmandu Valley, Nepal.

4. Ambroise, Yvon. "Hindu Religious Movements: A Sociological Perspective." JOURNAL OF DHARMA 7,4 (1982): 358-373.

   Eighteenth to twentieth century movements in India.

5. Ambroise, Yvon. "The Hindu Concept of Space and Time Structuring the Day to Day Life of Man." SC 29,4 (1982): 335-348.

   The Hindu vision considers the world in terms of life and non-life, not of a dichotomy between sacred and profane.

6. Appadurai, Arjun, and Carol Appadurai Breckenridge. "The South Indian Temple, Authority, Honour and Redistribution." CONTRIBUTIONS TO INDIAN SOCIOLOGY 10,2 (1976): 187-211.

   Based on 1973-74 field work at the Sri Minaksi-Sundaresvarar Temple, Mandurai (Tamil Natu), and the Sri Parthasarathi Svami Temple, Madras City.

3

7. Babb, Lawrence A. THE DIVINE HIERARCHY: POPULAR HINDUISM IN CENTRAL INDIA. New York: Columbia University Press, 1975.

8. Batra, S.M. THE PLACE OF LIVESTOCK IN THE SOCIAL AND ECONOMIC SYSTEM OF A VILLAGE IN HARYANA. Unpublished Ph.D. dissertation, University of Delhi, 1981.

9. Batra, S.M. "The Sacredness of the Cow in India." SC 33,2-3 (1986): 163-175.

   Textual origins, historical development, modern significance.

10. Bharati, Agehananda. "Ritualistic Tolerance and Ideological Rigour: The Paradigm of the Expatriate Hindus in East Africa." CONTRIBUTIONS TO INDIAN SOCIOLOGY 10,2 (1976): 317-339.

11. Carstairs, G.M. THE TWICE-BORN: A STUDY OF A COMMUNITY OF HIGH-CASTE HINDUS. London: Hogarth Press, 1957.

12. Chaudhuri, B. THE BAKRESHWAR TEMPLE: A STUDY ON CONTINUITY AND CHANGE. Delhi: Inter-Indian Publications, 1981.

13. Datta, Jatindra Mohan. "Geographical Distribution of the Brahmans in India." MODERN REVIEW 103,4 (1958): 318-320.

14. Datta, Jatindra Mohan. "Influence of Religious Beliefs on the Geographical Distribution of Brahmans in Bengal." MAN IN INDIA 42,2 (1962): 89-103.

    Mostly data from 1931.

15. Dumont, Louis. "World Renunciation in Indian Religions." CONTRIBUTIONS TO INDIAN SOCIOLOGY 4 (1960): 33-62.

16. Franda, Marcus F. MILITANT HINDU OPPOSITION TO FAMILY PLANNING IN INDIA. American Universities Field Staff XVI, No. 11, Sept. 1972.

17. Gandhi, Raj S. "The Caste-joint Family Axis of Hindu Social System, the Ethos of Hindu Culture and the Formation of Hindu Personality." SOCIOLOGUS 24,1 (1974): 56-64.

18. Gellner, David. "Max Weber, Capitalism and the Religion of India." SOCIOLOGY 16,4 (1982): 526-543.

19. Gladstone, J.W. "Caste, Religion and People's Movements in Kerala with Particular Reference to South Kerala." RELIGION AND SOCIETY 32,1 (1985): 24-35.

    Nineteenth to twentieth centuries.

20. Gupta, Krishna P. RELIGIOUS EVOLUTION IN PRE-MODERN ASIA: A COMPARATIVE STUDY OF K'ANG YU-WEI AND VIVEKANANDA. Unpublished Ph.D. dissertation, Harvard University, 1977.

21. Harper, Edward B. "Ritual Pollution as an Integrator of Caste and Religion." In E.B. Harper (ed.), RELIGION IN SOUTH ASIA. Seattle: University of Washington Press, 1964.

   Religious belief not only reinforces caste but integrates by making the several castes interdependent.

22. Heesterman, J.C. "Householder and Wanderer." CONTRIBUTIONS TO INDIAN SOCIOLOGY 15 (1981): 251-271.

23. Hertel, Bradley R. "Some Dimensions of Sanskritization: Belief, Practice and Egalitarianism Among Hindus of the Gangetic Plain." JSSR 12,1 (1973): 17-32. See "Errata," JSSR 12,2 (1973): 225; Carolyn Henning Brown, "Comment," JSSR 13,2 (1974): 223-224; and B.R. Hertel, "Reply," JSSR 13,2 (1974): 225-227.

   Survey data from Northern India. Ritual is more common among those of higher social status while belief in the supernatural is stronger among those of lower social status.

24. Hertel, Bradley R. "Church, Sect, and Congregation in Hinduism: An Examination of Social Structure and Religious Authority." JSSR 16,1 (1977): 15-26.

   The popular notion that the Brahman's power derives wholly from birth is rejected in favor of the view that at birth Brahmans inherit only the *potential* for religious authority and that maintenance of their power requires Brahman priests to heed the wishes of their congregations.

25. Houtart, François. RELIGION ET MODES DE PRODUCTION PRECAPITALISTES. Bruxelles: Editions de l'Université des Bruxelles, 1980.

   Historical sociology of religious origins. Chapter 4 looks at the origins of Hinduism, in the context of the establishment of the Aryans and the emergence of the caste system. Chapter 5 focuses on Kerala up to modern times.

26. Houtart, François, and Geneviève Lermercinier. "Religion and Castes – South India. An Introduction. Religion et castes – L'Inde du Sud. En guise d'introduction." SC 28,2-3 (1981): 145-162.

   The Indian caste structure cannot be understood apart from the religious factor. But one must situate the cast phenomenon itself in the specific economic and social conditions which produce its meaning.

27. Indradeva, Shrirama. "La doctrine du Karma dans une perspective sociologique." DIOGENES 140 (1987): 141-154.

   Historical overview, focusing on ancient origins.

28. Jain, S.P. "Religion, Caste, Class and Education in a North Indian Community." SOCIOLOGY AND SOCIAL RESEARCH 53,4 (1969): 482-489.

   Interview data from a mid-sized town of northwest India.

29. Jeffrey, Robin. "Religious Symbolisation of the Transition from Caste to Class: The Temple-entry Movement in Travancore, 1860-1940." SC 28,2-3 (1981): 269-291.

Historical material pertaining to a society in southern India.

30. Juyal, B.N. "The Politics of Untouchability in Uttar Pradesh." RELIGION AND SOCIETY (India) 21,3 (1974): 62-81.

31. Kantowsky, Detlef. "Die Fehlkonzeption von Max Webers Studie über <Hinduismus und Buddhismus> in Indien: Ursachen und Folgen." ZEITSCHRIFT FÜR SOZIOLOGIE 14 (1984): 466-474.

32. Lemercinier, Geneviève. "Kinship Relationships and Religious Symbolism among the Clans of Kerala during the Sangan Period (First Century A.C.)." SC 26,4 (1979): 461-489.

33. Lemercinier, Geneviève. "Relationships between Means of Production, Caste and Religion. The Case of Kerala between the 13th and the 19th Century." SC 28,2-3 (1981): 163-199.

34. Lewy, Guenter. RELIGION AND REVOLUTION. New York: Oxford University Press, 1974.

Chapter 12 reviews the Hindu nationalist movement; Chapter 13 focuses on Gandhi's contribution to Indian independence.

35. Lynch, Owen M. "Pilgrimage with Krishna, Sovereign of the Emotions." CONTRIBUTIONS TO INDIAN SOCIOLOGY 22,2 (1988): 171-194.

Based on 1980-82 participant-observation, interview, and historical data, in and pertaining to Mathura, India.

36. Madan, T.N. "Religious Ideology in a Plural Society: The Muslims and Hindus of Kashmir." CONTRIBUTIONS TO INDIAN SOCIOLOGY 6 (1972): 106-141.

Based on field work in Utrassu-Umanagri. Each group holds both an ideological and a practical view of the other.

37. Mahar, Pauline Moller. "Changing Caste Ideology in a North Indian Village." JOURNAL OF SOCIAL ISSUES 14,4 (1958): 51-65.

Interviews in a village, Khalapur, in northwestern Uttar Pradesh, focusing on the ways Hindu villagers reconcile the new constitutional rights of former untouchables with their traditional caste ideology.

38. Mahar, Pauline Moller. "A Ritual Pollution Scale for Ranking Hindu Castes." SOCIOMETRY 23 (1960): 292-306.

Offers a revised method for measuring caste ranking.

39. Mahar, Pauline Moller. "Changing Religious Practices of an Untouchable Caste." ECONOMIC DEVELOPMENT AND CULTURAL CHANGE 8,3 (1960): 279-287.

6

Study of the Chuhra (Cuhras), a group of untouchable sweeper-scavengers, after the 1950 Indian constitution abolished untouchability.

40. Michael, S.M. "The Politicization of the Ganapati Festival." In Mahipal Bhuriya and S.M. Michael (eds.), ANTHROPOLOGY AS A HISTORICAL SCIENCE - ESSAYS IN HONOR OF STEPHEN FUCHS. Indore: Sat Prakashan, 1984. Reprinted in SC 33,2-3 (1986): 185-197.

Late nineteenth-century stratagem to unify Hindus in the face of Muslims.

41. Mies, Maria. "Das indische Dilemma. Neo-Hinduismus, Modernismus und die Probleme der wirtschaftlichen Entwicklung." In R. König (ed.), ASPEKTE DER ENTWICKLUNGSSOZIOLOGIE. KÖLNER ZEITSCHRIFT FÜR SOZIOLOGIE UND SOZIALPSYCHOLOGIE, SONDERHEFT, 13. Köln und Opladen: Westdeutscher Verlag, 1969, pp. 163-181.

42. Mishra, S.N. "Surplus Cattle in India: A Critical Survey." SOCIOLOGICAL BULLETIN 22,2 (1973): 297-308.

There is no apparent economic rationality in maintaining the surplus.

43. Mishra, S.N. LIVESTOCK PLANNING IN INDIA. New Delhi: Vikas, 1978.

44. Nandy, S.K. "A Critique of Max Weber's Conception of the Ethic of India." VISVABHARATI QUARTERLY 32 (1966-67): 277-304.

45. Pillai, Mary. "The Non-Brahmin Movement and Desacralization." SC 29,4 (1982): 349-368.

Historical material on Tamil-Nadu.

46. Rösel, J.A. "Über die soziale Gewalt von Wirklichkeitsbildern. Das sanskritistische Indienbild und seine Verwirklichung. Am Beispiel der Indien-Studie Max Webers." INTERNATIONALES JAHRBUCH FÜR RELIGIONSSOZIOLOGIE 9 (1975): 45-76.

47. Roy, Prodipto. "The Sacred Cow in India." RURAL SOCIOLOGY 20,1 (1955): 8-15.

The prohibition of animal slaughter is favored by a minority in India.

48. Sachchidananda. "Emergent Scheduled Caste Elite in Bihar." RELIGION AND SOCIETY 21,3 (1974): 55-61.

1971-72 interview data from educated members of the former untouchable castes.

49. Sharma, Arvind. "What is Hinduism? A Sociological Approach." SC 33, 2-3 (1986): 177-183.

To define the Hindu religious phenomenon, one cannot begin with a doctrine but must first identify the Hindu people. Hinduism is the religious expression of the Hindu people.

50. Sharma, Arvind. "New Hindu Religious Movements in India." In
    James A. Beckford (ed.), NEW RELIGIOUS MOVEMENTS AND RAPID SOCIAL
    CHANGE. Newbury Park, California: Sage, 1986, pp. 220-239.

    Application of a tripartite typology to three representative
    movements: Ramana Maharshi, Sathya Sai Baba, and Hare Krishna.

51. Sharma, Ursula M. "The Immortal Cowherd and the Saintly Carrier.  An
    Essay in the Study of Cults." SOCIOLOGICAL BULLETIN 19,2 (1970):
    137-152.

    1966-67 field work in Kangra District in the Himalayan region, on
    cults of two saints - Baba Balak Nath and Baba Ludru.  The former is
    commercial and dependent on impersonal relationships;  the latter
    not commercial but dependent on personal relationships with the
    Mahant (chief official of the cult).

52. Sharma, Ursula M. "Public Shrines and Private Interests: The Symbol-
    ism of the Village Temple." SOCIOLOGICAL BULLETIN 23,1 (1974): 71-92.

    Field work in a Himalayan village, focusing on why Hindu shrines are
    seldom used for worship though accorded great significance.

53. Srinivas, Mysore N. RELIGION AND SOCIETY AMONG THE COORGS.  Oxford:
    Clarendon Press, 1952.  See also RELIGION AND SOCIETY AMONG THE COORGS
    OF SOUTH INDIA.  New York: Asia Publishing House, 1965.

54. Srinivasa Rao, G.S.S. "The Relevance of Neo-Vedanta for an Ethos of
    Development in India." RELIGION AND SOCIETY (India) 20,4 (1973):
    34-41.

    Review of neo-Vedanta thought:  Roy, Dayananda, Vivekananda, Gandhi,
    Tagore, Radhakrishnan.

55. Stackhouse, Max L. "The Hindu Ethic and the Ethos of Development:
    Some Western Views." RELIGION AND SOCIETY (India) 20,4 (1973): 5-33.

    Review of the literature, from Max Weber onward.

56. Stern, Henri. "Religion et société en Inde selon Max Weber: Analyse
    critique de l'Hindouisme et du Bouddhisme." SOCIAL SCIENCE
    INFORMATION 10,6 (1971): 69-112.

57. Subramaniam, K. BRAHMIN PRIEST OF TAMIL NADU. New York: Halsted,
    1975.

58. Tambiah, S.J. "The Renouncer: His Individuality and His Community."
    CONTRIBUTIONS TO INDIAN SOCIOLOGY 15 (1981): 299-320.

59. Thapar, Romila. "Householders and Renouncers in the Brahmanical and
    Buddhist Traditions." CONTRIBUTIONS TO INDIAN SOCIOLOGY 15 (1981):
    273-298.

60. Utrecht, Ernst. "Religion and Social Protest in Indonesia." SC 25,
    3-4 (1978): 395-418.

Both Islam and Hindu religion have been involved in social protest in Indonesia.

61. Weber, Max. THE RELIGION OF INDIA. THE SOCIOLOGY OF HINDUISM AND BUDDHISM, translated and edited by Hans H. Gerth and Don Martindale. New York: Free Press, 1958.

62. Wilson, Jim. "Text and Context in Fijian Hinduism: Uses of Religion." RELIGION. JOURNAL OF RELIGION AND RELIGIONS 5,1 (1975): 53-68.

1972-73 questionnaire data from ethnic Indian students at the University of the South Pacific, focusing on the use they make of Hindu texts.


*ANANDA MARGA*

63. Kuner, Wolfgang. SOZIOGENESE DER MITGLIEDSCHAFT IN DREI NEUEN RELIGIÖSEN BEWEGUNGEN. Frankfurt am Main: Peter Lang, 1983.

Application of an alienation scale and a life process scale.

64. Kuner, Wolfgang. "New Religious Movements and Mental Health." In Eileen Barker (ed.), OF GODS AND MEN. NEW RELIGIOUS MOVEMENTS IN THE WEST. Macon, Georgia: Mercer University Press, 1983, pp. 303-308.

Administration of the Minnesota Multiphase Personality Inventory to German members of the Unification Church, the Children of God, and Ananda Marga.


*DIVINE LIGHT MISSION*

65. Armstrong, Paul F. TAKING KNOWLEDGE: A SOCIOLOGICAL APPROACH TO THE STUDY OF MEDITATION AND THE DIVINE LIGHT MISSION. Unpublished Ph.D. dissertation, Essex University, 1978.

66. Bromley, David G., and Anson D. Shupe, Jr. STRANGE GODS. THE GREAT AMERICAN CULT SCARE. Boston: Beacon, 1981.

67. Chagnon, Roland. TROIS NOUVELLES RELIGIONS DE LA LUMIERE ET DU SON: LA SCIENCE DE LA SPIRITUALITE, ECKANKAR, LA MISSION DE LA LUMIERE DIVINE. Montréal: Les Editions Paulines, 1985.

68. Derks, Frans, and Jan M. van der Lans. "Subgroups in Divine Light Mission Membership: A Comment on Downton." In E. Barker (ed.), OF GODS AND MEN [volume cited in item 64], pp. 303-308.

Points to changes in kinds of member over time.

69. Downton, James V., Jr. SACRED JOURNEY: THE CONVERSION OF YOUNG AMERICANS TO DIVINE LIGHT MISSION. New York: Columbia University Press, 1979.

70. Downton, James V., Jr. "An Evolutionary Theory of Spiritual Conversion and Commitment: The Case of Divine Light Mission." JSSR 19,4 (1980): 381-396.

The conversion process to Divine Light Mission is shown to be gradual rather than dramatic. Research data is drawn from interviews.

71. DuPertuis, Lucy Guyn. COMPANY OF TRUTH: MEDITATION AND SACRALIZED INTER-ACTION AMONG WESTERN FOLLOWERS OF AN INDIAN GURU. Unpublished Ph.D. dissertation, University of California at Berkeley, 1983. [DA 45:3 A, p. 952]

72. DuPertuis, Lucy. "How People Recognize Charisma: The Case of Darshan in Radhasoami and Divine Light Mission." SA 47,2 (1986): 111-124.

Discusses the recognition of charisma as an active, conscious social process involving the confirmation of belief through non-cognitive alterations of perception.

73. Foss, Daniel A., and Ralph W. Larkin. "Worshiping the Absurd: The Negation of Social Causality Among the Followers of Guru Maharaj Ji." SA 39,2 (1978): 157-164.

Former participants in the 1960s youth counterculture were seen to turn to Divine Light Mission in the absence of the plausibility of the former youth culture or acceptability of conventional society. Based on participant observation.

74. Khalsa, Kirpal Singh. "New Religious Movements Turn to Worldly Success." JSSR 25,2 (1986): 233-247.

In contrast to the Healthy-Happy-Holy Organization and the Vajradhatu Church, Divine Light Mission did not venture into entrepreneurial and professional activities.

75. Messer, Jeanne. "Guru Maharaj Ji and the Divine Light Mission." In Charles Y. Glock and Robert N. Bellah (eds.), THE NEW RELIGIOUS CONSCIOUSNESS. Berkeley: University of California Press, 1976, pp. 52-72.

General account written by a devotee.

76. Pilarzyk, Thomas. "The Origin, Development, and Decline of a Youth Culture Religion: An Application of Sectarianization Theory." RRR 20,1 (1978): 23-43.

The development of the Divine Light Mission shows that cults are inherently fragile social institutions which are constrained from effective institutionalization by internal factors. In a pluralistic environment, DLM was constrained by doctrinal precariousness, the unique locus of its leadership, and problems generating and sustaining consistent commitment among its members.

77. Pilarzyk, Thomas J., and Lakshmi Bharadwaj. "What is Real? The Failure of the Phenomenological Approach in a Field Study of the Divine Light Mission." HUMANITY AND SOCIETY 3,1 (1979): 16-34.

Suggests the need for greater self-awareness on the part of field researchers studying Divine Light Mission.

78. Price, Maeve. "The Divine Light Mission as a Social Organization." SOCIOLOGICAL REVIEW 27,2 (1979): 279-296.

Examines the various constraints which militated against the organizational success of DLM.

*HARE KRISHNA*

79. Breckwoldt, R. "The Hare Krishna Movement in Australia." AUSTRALIAN AND NEW ZEALAND JOURNAL OF SOCIOLOGY 9,2 (1973): 70-71.

Participant-observation study with interviews, 1971-72 in Sydney, Australia.

80. Bromley, David G. "Hare Krishna and the Anti-cult Movement." In David G. Bromley and Larry D. Shinn (eds.), KRISHNA CONSCIOUSNESS IN THE WEST. Lewisburg, Pennsylvania: Bucknell University Press, 1988, pp. 47-59.

 * Bromley, D.G., and A.D. Shupe, Jr. STRANGE GODS. Cited above as item 66.

81. Carey, Seán. "The Hare Krishna Movement and Hindus in Britain." NEW COMMUNITY 10,3 (1983): 477-486.

Background of the movement; its presence in Great Britain since 1969. Case studies of devotees, based on 1981-82 field work.

82. Daner, Francine J. "Conversion to Krishna Consciousness: The Transformation from Hippie to Religious Ascetic." In Roy Wallis (ed.), SECTARIANISM: ANALYSES OF RELIGIOUS AND NON-RELIGIOUS SECTS. London: Peter Owen, 1975, pp. 53-69.

Cases of conversion, chosen to typify the experience.

83. Daner, Francine J. THE AMERICAN CHILDREN OF KRSNA. A STUDY OF THE HARE KRSNA MOVEMENT. New York: Holt, Rinehart and Winston, 1976.

Based on field work in temples in New York, Boston, West Virginia, Houston, London, Paris, and Amsterdam. Life histories demonstrate self-degradation rituals and establishment of new identities in the course of conversion and entrance into Krishna temples.

84. Holmes, Barbara. "Status Hierarchy and Religious Sanctions: A Report on the Krishna Cult." HUMAN MOSAIC 7 (1974): 31-45.

Field study of a local house temple in an unspecified location in the U.S.A.

85. Johnson, Gregory. COUNTER CULTURE IN MICROCOSM: AN ANALYSIS OF THE HARE KRISHNA MOVEMENT. Unpublished Ph.D. dissertation, Harvard

University, 1974.

86. Johnson, Gregory. "The Hare Krishna in San Francisco." In C.Y. Glock and R.N. Bellah (eds.), THE NEW RELIGIOUS CONSCIOUSNESS [volume cited in item 75], pp. 31-51.

1971 life history data, as well as interview and participant-observation information from the early 1970s.

87. Judah, J. Stillson. "The Hare Krishna Movement." In Irving I. Zaretsky and Mark P. Leone (eds.), RELIGIOUS MOVEMENTS IN CONTEMPORARY AMERICA. Princeton: Princeton University Press, 1974, pp. 463-478.

General description of the movement.

88. Judah, J. Stillson. HARE KRISHNA AND THE COUNTERCULTURE. New York: Wiley-Interscience, 1974.

89. Levasseur, Martine. ETHNOGRAPHIE D'UNE SECTE: L'ASSOCIATION INTERNA-TIONALE POUR LA CONSCIENCE DE KRISHNA. Paris: Editions Lidis, 1985.

90. O'Brien, Leslie N. "Some Defining Characteristics of the Hare Krishna Movement." AUSTRALIAN AND NEW ZEALAND JOURNAL OF SOCIOLOGY 9,2 (1973): 72-73.

1972 literature analysis, participant-observation study, interviews, questionnaire; Melbourne, Australia.

91. O'Brien, Leslie N. "A Case Study of the Hare Krishna Movement." In Alan Black and Peter Glasner (eds.), PRACTICE AND BELIEF. STUDIES IN THE SOCIOLOGY OF AUSTRALIAN RELIGION. Sydney: Allen and Unwin, 1983, pp. 134-153.

1972 participant observation, analysis of documentary evidence, and interview data from Melbourne.

92. Rochford, E. Burke, Jr. "Recruitment Strategies, Ideology, and Organization in the Hare Krishna Movement." SOCIAL PROBLEMS 29,4 (1982): 399-410. Reprinted in E. Barker (ed.), OF GODS AND MEN [volume cited in item 64], pp. 283-302.

Survey of over 200 American devotees shows that opportunistic exploitation of local conditions, rather than ideology or structure, has been responsible for the growth of the movement in the U.S.A.

93. Rochford, E. Burke, Jr. HARE KRISHNA IN AMERICA. New Brunswick, New Jersey: Rutgers University Press, 1985.

94. Rochford, E. Burke, Jr. "Dialectical Processes in the Development of Hare Krishna: Tension, Public Definition, and Strategy." In David G. Bromley and Phillip E. Hammond (eds.), THE FUTURE OF NEW RELIGIOUS MOVEMENTS. Macon, Georgia: Mercer University Press, 1987, pp. 109-122.

Focus on developments in the United States.

95. Rochford, E. Burke, Jr. "Factionalism, Group Defection, and Schism in the Hare Krishna Movement." JSSR 28,2 (1989): 162-179.

Based upon 1980 participation observation in Los Angeles; study of Kirtan Hall, a short-lived organization in the Hare Krishna tradition.

96. Whitworth, John, and Martin Shiels. "From across the Black Water: Two Imported Varieties of Hinduism." In Eileen Barker (ed.), NEW RELIGIOUS MOVEMENTS: A PERSPECTIVE FOR UNDERSTANDING SOCIETY. New York: Mellen, 1982, 155-172.

General description of the International Society for Krishna Consciousness, and the Ramakrishna Vedanta Society.

97. Wright, Stuart A. LEAVING CULTS: THE DYNAMICS OF DEFECTION. Washington: Society for the Scientific Study of Religion, 1987.

Data from current and former members of the Unification Church, Hare Krishna, and Children of God.

## HEALTHY-HAPPY-HOLY ORGANIZATION

  * Khalsa, Kirpal Singh. "New Religious Movements Turn to Worldly Success." Cited above as item 74.

98. Tobey, Alan. "The Summer Solstice of the Healthy-Happy-Holy Organization." In C.Y. Glock and R.N. Bellah (eds.), THE NEW RELIGIOUS CONSCIOUSNESS [volume cited in item 75], pp. 5-30.

1973 questionnaire and observation data from an annual festival for which many adherents gathered.

## MEHER BABA

99. Anthony, Dick, and Thomas Robbins. "The Meher Baba Movement: Its Affect on Post-adolescent Social Alienation." In I.I. Zaretsky and M.P. Leone (eds.), RELIGIOUS MOVEMENTS IN CONTEMPORARY AMERICA [volume cited in item 87], pp. 479-511.

Participant-observation study during 1970 at the Meher Spiritual Center in Myrtle Beach, South Carolina. Focus is from the perspective of youth culture; the Center is seen as an expressive community.

100. McGee, Michael. "Meher Baba - The Sociology of Religious Conversion." GRADUATE JOURNAL 9,1-2 (1976): 43-71.

Based on field work undertaken during 1967 and following years in Chapel Hill, North Carolina. Background and observations.

101. Robbins, Thomas. "Eastern Mysticism and the Resocialization of Drug Users: The Meher Baba Cult." JSSR 8,2 (1969): 308-317.

The cult served as a "half-way house" between the drug culture and reassimilation into conventional society.

102. Robbins, Thomas. CONTEMPORARY "POST-DRUG" CULTS: A COMPARISON OF TWO GROUPS. Unpublished Ph.D. dissertation, University of North Carolina, 1973. [DA 35:1 A, p. 588]

Comparison of two 1960s countercultural youth religions - a Meher Baba community and a Jesus People community.

*PATTINI*

103. Hiatt, Lester R. "The Pattini Cult of Ceylon: A Tamil Perspective." SC 20,2 (1973): 231-249.

104. Obeyesekere, Gananath. "The Goddess Pattini and the Lord Buddha. Notes on the Myth of the Birth of the Deity." SC 20,2 (1973): 217-229.

Examines the symbolization of purity and impurity in two nativity myths.

*RADHASOAMI*

* DuPertuis, Lucy. "How People Recognize Charisma: The Case of Darshan in Radhasoami and Divine Light Mission." Cited above as item 72.

105. Juergensmeyer, Mark. "Radhasoami as a Trans-national Movement." In Jacob Needleman and George Baker (eds.), UNDERSTANDING THE NEW RELIGIONS. New York: Seabury, 1979, pp. 190-200.

General discussion, based on prior observation and familiarity with movement literature. Approaches Radhasoami as a transnational movement.

*RAJNEESH*

106. Carter, Lewis F. "The 'New Renunciates' of the Bhagwan Shree Rajneesh: Observations and Identification of Problems of Interpreting New Religious Movements." JSSR 26,2 (1987): 148-172.

The focus is on research problems caused by the dispersed and mobile followers of Rajneesh, with their variation in commitment, linked communal groups, multiple corporate identities, and ideological inconsistencies.

107. Latkin, Carl A., Richard A. Hagan, Richard A. Littman, and Norman D. Sundberg. "Who Lives in Utopia? A Brief Report on the Rajneeshpuram Research Project." SA 48,1 (1987): 73-81.

Members of the disbanded community were young, mostly white, well-educated, and from middle-class and upper-middle-class backgrounds. Psychological data indicate healthy self-perceptions.

108. Pace, Enzo. "Pilgrimage as Spiritual Journey: An Analysis of

Pilgrimage using the Theory of V. Turner and the Resource Mobilization Approach." SC 36,2 (1989): 229-244.

109. Palmer, Susan J. "Charisma and Abdication: A Study of the Leadership of Bhagwan Shree Rajneesh." SA 49,2 (1988): 119-135.

110. Wallis, Roy, and Steve Bruce. "Religion as Fun? The Rajneesh Movement." Chapter 8 in SOCIOLOGICAL THEORY, RELIGION AND COLLECTIVE ACTION. Belfast: The Queen's University, 1986.

*RAMAKRISHNA*

111. Carey, Seán. A SOCIOLOGICAL STUDY OF THE RAMAKRISHNA MISSION IN GREAT BRITAIN. Unpublished Ph.D. dissertation, University of Newcastle-upon-Tyne, 1981.

112. Gupta, Krishna P. "Religious Evolution and Social Change in India: A Study of the Ramakrishna Mission Movement." CONTRIBUTIONS TO INDIAN SOCIOLOGY 8 (1974): 25-50.

Focus on the late nineteenth-century revival centering around Ramakrishna and Vivekananda.

113. Schneiderman, Leo. "Ramakrishna: Personality and Social Factors in the Growth of a Religious Movement." JSSR 8,1 (1969): 60-71.

The Ramakrishna movement owed much of its initial strength to its fusion of an archaic, traditionalist rhetoric with a 'modern' set of meliorative goals.

*VEDANTA*

114. Damrell, Joseph. SEEKING SPIRITUAL MEANING. THE WORLD OF VEDANTA. Beverly Hills, California: Sage, 1977.

Participant-observation study, centered in California.

* Whitworth, John, and Martin Shiels. "From across the Black Water: Two Imported Varieties of Hinduism." Cited above as item 96.

*YOGA*

115. Glick, Steven. AN ANALYSIS OF THE CHANGE PROCESS IN THE GURU-DISCIPLE RELATIONSHIP. Unpublished Ph.D. dissertation, Temple University, 1982.

116. Hillery, George A., Jr., and Paula C. Morrow. "The Monastery as a Commune." INTERNATIONAL REVIEW OF MODERN SOCIOLOGY 6,1 (1976): 139-154.

Presents indices of interaction intensiveness and attitudes of commitment, freedom, aliention, and anomie, from a variety of monasteries

15

and communes, including a Yoga commune in the U.S.A.

117. Parsons, Arthur S. "Yoga in a Western Setting: Youth in Search of Religious Prophecy." SOUNDINGS 57 (1974): 222-235.

1972 participant-observation study of a group which formed around Kundalini Yoga classes in Boston.

118. Sinha, Manju, and Braj Sinha. "Ways of Yoga and the Mechanisms of Sacralization." In Hans Mol (ed.), IDENTITY AND RELIGION. INTERNATIONAL CROSS-CULTURAL APPROACHES. Beverly Hills, California: Sage, 1978, pp. 133-150.

Application of the identity-theory of Hans Mol to traditional yoga materials.

119. Wilson, Stephen R. "In Pursuit of Energy: Spiritual Growth in a Yoga Ashram." JOURNAL OF HUMANISTIC PSYCHOLOGY 22,1 (1982): 43-56.

Participant-observation study at Kripalu Yoga Ashram in Pennsylvania, describing how the guru-disciple relationship and the structure of the ashram foster personal and spiritual growth among the residents.

120. Wilson, Stephen R. "Becoming a Yogi: Resocialization and Deconditioning as Conversion Processes." SA 45,4 (1984): 301-314.

Participant-observation study illustrates two related kinds of conversion. Socialization is the learning of group roles and norms. Deconditioning is the elimination of problematic lines of action acquired in the socialization process.

# 2
# Buddhist

121. Bechert, Heinz. "Einige Fragen der Religionssoziologie und Struktur des südasiatischen Buddhismus." In J. Matthes (ed.), BEITRÄGE ZUR RELIGIONSSOZIOLOGISCHEN FORSCHUNG/ESSAYS ON RESEARCH IN THE SOCIOLOGY OF RELIGION. INTERNATIONALES JAHRBUCH FÜR RELIGIONS-SOZIOLOGIE 4. Köln, Opladen: Westdeutscher Verlag, 1968, pp. 251-295.

    Historical sociological overview; comments on Max Weber's THE RELIGION OF INDIA [item 61].

122. Kolm, Serge Christophe. "Marxisme et Bouddhisme." CAHIERS INTERNATIONAUX DE SOCIOLOGIE 31,77 (1984): 339-360.

    Examines thematic parallels and differences between the two philosophies.

123. Obeyesekere, Gananath. "Theodicy, Sin and Salvation in a Sociology of Buddhism." In Edmund R. Leach (ed.), DIALECTIC IN PRACTICAL RELIGION. London: Cambridge University Press, 1968, pp. 7-40.

    Conceptual clarification, using Max Weber as a point of departure.

124. Strenski, Ivan. "Lévi-Strauss and the Buddhists." COMPARATIVE STUDIES IN SOCIETY AND HISTORY 22,1 (1980): 3-22.

    Examines similarities in the respective world views of Claude Lévi-Strauss and Buddhism.

125. Tambiah, S.J. "Buddhism and This-worldly Activity." MODERN ASIAN STUDIES 7,1 (1973): 1-20.

    Departures from Max Weber's analyses; includes sections on Sri Lanka, Thailand, and Japan.

*INDIA (ANCIENT)*

126. Chakravarti, Uma. "The Social Philosophy of Buddhism and the Problem

of Inequality." SC 33,2-3 (1986): 199-221.

Discusses social context and philosophers' response in the sixth century B.C.E.

127. Darian, Jean C. "Social and Economic Factors in the Rise of Buddhism." SA 38,3 (1977): 226-238.

Buddhism better satisfied the political and economic needs of rulers and the economic and status needs of merchants than did earlier Hinduism.

* Houtart, François. RELIGION ET MODES DE PRODUCTION PRECAPITALISTES. Cited above as item 25.

128. Houtart, François, and Geneviève Lemercinier. THE GREAT ASIATIC RELIGIONS AND THEIR SOCIAL FUNCTIONS. Louvain-la-Neuve: Centre de Recherches Socio-Religieuse, 1980.

* Kantowsky, Detlef. "Die Fehlkonzeption von Max Webers Studie über <Hinduismus und Buddhismus> in Indien: Ursachen und Folgen." Cited above as item 31.

129. Sharma, Arvind. "How and Why did Women in Ancient India become Buddhist Nuns?" SA 38,3 (1977): 239-251.

The concept of relative deprivation is applied to available literary materials about why women in India became nuns within the first few centuries of the Buddhist movement.

* Weber, Max. THE RELIGION OF INDIA. Cited above as item 61.


SOUTH ASIA

130. Bopegamage, A. "Status Seekers in India. A Sociological Study of the Neo-Buddhist Movement." ARCHIVES EUROPEENNES DE SOCIOLOGIE 20,1 (1979): 19-39.

The neo-Buddhist movement in India (1930-69) represented a conversion of largely former Mahar untouchables in Maharashtra state. Data from 1969-70, from 1,334 Mahar and 1,689 neo-Buddhist households in Maharashtra, show that conversion was often motivated by desire for higher status.

131. Ch'en, Kenneth. "Chinese Communist Attitudes towards Buddhism in Chinese History." CHINA QUARTERLY 22 (1965): 14-30.

Review of the accounts given by communist historians.

132. Fiske, Adele M. "Religion and Buddhism among India's New Buddhists." SOCIAL RESEARCH 36,1 (1969): 123-137.

Analysis of 1966-67 interview data in India suggests the conversion of former untouchables to Buddhism is religious insofar as the desire to assert one's human dignity is religious.

133. Greenwold, Stephen M. "Monkhood versus Priesthood in Newar Buddhism."
In Christolph von Fürer-Haimendorf (ed.), CONTRIBUTIONS TO THE
ANTHROPOLOGY OF NEPAL. Warminister: Aris and Phillips, 1974, pp. 129-
149.

General description based on a twenty-two-month field study.

134. Greenwold, Stephen M. "Buddhist Brahmans." ARCHIVES EUROPEENNES DE SOCI-
OLOGIE 15,1 (1974): 101-123. See Anne Vergati Stahl, "Comment," 16,2
(1975): 310-316; and S. Greenwold, "Reply," 18,1 (1977): 194-197.

1970-72 observations in Nepal. Buddhism in interaction with Hinduism
has a hereditary clergy, a temple-based financial and social structure,
and an adherence to the caste system, all recasting parallel Hindu
institutions.

135. Houtart, François. "Buddhism and Politics in South East India."
SOCIAL SCIENTIST (India) 5,3 (1976): 3-22; 5,4 (1976): 30-45.

   * Thapar, Romila. "Householders and Renouncers in the Brahmanical and
   Buddhist Traditions." Cited above as item 59.

136. Toffin, Gérard. "Les aspects religieux de la royauté Néwar au Népal."
ARCHIVES DE SCIENCES SOCIALES DES RELIGIONS 48,1 (1979): 53-82.

Assesses the linkage between religion and kingship among the Newars, a
highly hinduized Nepalese population.

*SOUTHEAST ASIA AND PACIFIC*

137. Akahoshi, Hidefumi. "Hongwanji in Rural Japan and Cosmopolitan
Hawaii." SOCIAL PROCESS IN HAWAII 26 (1963): 80-82.

138. Brohm, John F. BURMESE RELIGION AND THE BURMESE RELIGIOUS REVIVAL.
Unpublished Ph.D. dissertation, Cornell University, 1957. [DA 17:8,
p. 1644]

1953 village study in the Central Plain area; suggests contrasts with
urban phenomena in Rangoon. The government's support of the revival
is part of a genuine development in the urban setting, occasioned by
contact with the West.

139. Condominas, Georges. "Notes sur le Bouddhisme populaire en milieu
rural lao." ARCHIVES DE SOCIOLOGIE DES RELIGIONS 25 (1968): 81-110;
26 (1968): 111-150.

Studies the relationship between popular Buddhism and agricultural
development in five Laotian villages.

140. Coughlin, R.J. "Some Social Features of Siamese Buddhism." ASIA 2,7
(1952): 403-408.

141. Evers, Hans-Dieter. "The Buddhist Shanga in Ceylon and Thailand. A Comparative Study of Formal Organizations in Two Non-industrial Societies." SOCIOLOGUS 18,1 (1968): 20-35.

Based on 1964-66 field work in then Ceylon, and Thailand.

142. Gheddo, P. CATTOLICI E BUDDISTI NEL VIETNAM. IL RUOLO DELLE COMUNITA RELIGIOSE NELLA CONSTRUZIONE DELLE PACE. Firenze: Ed. Vellechi, 1968.

143. Keyes, Charles F. "Buddhism and National Integration in Thailand." JOURNAL OF ASIAN STUDIES 30,3 (1971): 552-553.

For over a century, the Thai government encouraged as a matter of national policy the unification of Theravada Buddhist groups. This was achieved structurally when the various clergy were brought into a single organizational framework.

144. Lewy, Guenter. "Militant Buddhist Nationalism: The Case of Burma." JOURNAL OF CHURCH AND STATE 14 (1972): 19-41. Revised version in G. Lewy, RELIGION AND REVOLUTION [item 34], pp. 324-345.

145. Ling, T.O. "Buddhist Factors in Population Growth and Control. A Survey based on Thailand and Ceylon." POPULATION STUDIES 23 (1969): 53-60.

Buddhism is found to be indirectly responsible for high fertility rates.

146. Marliere, M. ETUDE D'UN GROUPE DE TROIS MONASTERES BOUDDHIQUES SIS A THONBURI (THAILANDE). ESSAI DE SOCIOGRAPHIE BOUDDHIQUE. Geneva: Droz, 1977.

147. Mendelson, E. Michael. "Religion and Authority in Modern Burma." WORLD TODAY 16,3 (1960): 110-118.

148. Mendelson, E. Michael. "Buddhism and the Burmese Establishment." ARCHIVES DE SOCIOLOGIE DES RELIGIONS 9,17 (1964): 85-95.

The 'Buddhist Revival' sponsored by U Nu in Burma's early years of independence was an attempt on the part of the political authority to strengthen its ascendency over the Buddhist *Sangha* (Order of Monks).

149. Mendelson, E. Michael. SANGHA AND STATE IN BURMA: A STUDY OF MONASTIC SECTARIANISM AND LEADERSHIP. Ithaca, N.Y.: Cornell University Press, 1975.

150. Morioka, Kiyomi. "Préférence pour le mariage non-mixte parmi les Amidistes <Shin> du bouddhisme japonais." SC 17,1 (1970): 9-20.

Case study of a Japanese village showing Shin-Amidist endogamy to be a sign of the integration of religious faith into daily life.

151. Mulder, J.A. Niels. "Merit. An Investigation of the Motivational Qualities of the Buddhist Concept of Merit in Thailand." SC 16,1 (1969): 109-120.

On the whole, the economy of merit-making provides Thai society with a model that stresses the usefulness of saving, investing, and achievement. Merit therefore can become a value that is potentially conducive to economic growth.

152. Piker, Steven. "The Problem of Consistency in Thai Religion." JSSR 11,3 (1972): 211-229.

Based on 1962-63 and 1967-68 ethnographic evidence from the Province of Ayuthaya, some 50 miles north of Bangkok.

153. Sarkisyanz, Manuel. BUDDHIST BACKGROUNDS OF THE BURMESE REVOLUTION. The Hague: Nijhoff, 1965.

154. Sarkisyanz, Manuel. "Messianic Folk-Buddhism as Ideology of Peasant Revolts in Nineteenth and Early Twentieth-century Burma." RRR 10,1 (1968): 32-38.

Discusses the symbiotic connection between political radicalism and religious millenarianism in turn-of-century Burma.

155. Spiro, Melford. BUDDHISM AND SOCIETY -- A GREAT TRADITION AND ITS BURMESE VICISSITUDES. London: Allen and Unwin, 1971.

156. Tamney, Joseph B. "Chinese Family Structure and the Continuation of Chinese Religions." ASIAN PROFILE 6 (1978): 211-217.

1970 questionnaire data from ethnic Chinese students at the University of Singapore and Nanyang University.

157. Wichmann, Arthur A. "Burma: Agriculture, Population and Buddhism." AMERICAN JOURNAL OF ECONOMICS AND SOCIOLOGY 24,1 (1965): 71-83.

Buddhist thought constitutes an imposing obstacle to the population control policies needed for long-term economic development in Burma.

158. Wichmann, Arthur A. "Buddhism, Economic Development, and Neutralism in Burma." SOUTHWESTERN SOCIAL SCIENCE QUARTERLY 46,1 (1965): 20-27.

Based on readings of Pali texts.

*SRI LANKA*

159. Ames, Michael M. "Westernization or Modernization? The Case of Sinhalese Buddhism." SC 20,2 (1973): 139-170.

Western symbolic forms are related accidentally, but not essentially, to modernization in Sri Lanka.

160. Evers, Hans-Dieter. "Die soziale Organisation der singhalesischen Religion." KÖLNER ZEITSCHRIFT FÜR SOZIOLOGIE UND SOZIALPSYCHOLOGIE 16,2 (1964): 314-326.

Description of three roles: the Buddhist monk (Bhikkhu), the priest of the gods (Kapurala), and the exorcist (Edura). The spheres of the three form a coherent total phenomenon rather than reflecting separate sects.

* Evers, Hans-Dieter. "The Buddhist Shanga in Ceylon and Thailand. A Comparative Study of Formal Organizations in Two Non-industrial Societies." Cited above as item 141.

161. Fernando, Charlie. "How Buddhists and Catholics of Sri Lanka See Each Other -- A Factor Analytic Approach." SC 20,2 (1973): 321-332.

    1970 data from a survey, subjected to factor analysis.

162. Fernando, Tissa. "Buddhist Leadership in the Nationalist Movement of Ceylon: The Role of the Temperance Campaign." SC 20,2 (1973): 333-336.

163. Gombrich, Richard. "Le clergé bouddhiste d'une circonscription kandienne et les élections générales de 1965." SC 20,2 (1973): 257-266.

164. Houtart, François. "Les fonctions sociales de la symbolique religieuse chez les Bouddhistes à Sri Lanka." ARCHIVES DE SCIENCES SOCIALES DES RELIGIONS 37 (1974): 23-41.

    Examines Buddhist expressions in three areas of Singhalese society: rural regions, cities, and political surroundings.

165. Kalansuriya, A.D.P. "Empirical Buddhism: A Novel Aspect of Sinhalese Buddhism Made Explicit." SC 25,2 (1978): 251-265.

    Criticizes P.A.S. Saram and other scholars for conceptualizing from a no-longer-existent form of Buddhism rather than from empirically evident lines of conduct.

* Ling, T.O. "Buddhist Factors in Population Growth and Control. A Survey based on Thailand and Ceylon." Cited above as item 145.

166. Malalgoda, Kitsiri. "The Buddhist-Christian Confrontation in Ceylon, 1800-1880." SC 20,2 (1973): 171-200.

* Obeyesekere, Gananath. "The Goddess Pattini and the Lord Buddha. Notes on the Myth of the Birth of the Deity." Cited above as item 104.

167. Pathirana-Wimaladharma, Kapila. "Some Observations on the Religious Festivals, Village Rituals and the Religiosity of the Sinhala Rural Folk in the N.C.P. Ceylon." SC 20,2 (1973): 267-285.

    Study of a dry zone, the North Central Province. Consonant with economic changes that development occasions, there is a parallel process of rationalization in the religious attitudes and conduct of the peasants.

168. Sarachandra, Ediriweera R. "Traditional Values and the Modernization of a Buddhist Society: The Case of Ceylon." In Robert N. Bellah (ed.), RELIGION AND PROGRESS IN MODERN ASIA. New York: Free Press, 1965.

The Buddhism of the religious élite emphasizes a non-theistic cult of knowledge for progress. The common man needs a theistic-polytheistic hierarchy for magical recourse.

169. Saram, P.A.S. "Weberian Buddhism and Sinhalese Buddhism." SC 23,4 (1976): 355-382.

Examines the relationship between Buddhism and popular religion in Sri Lanka. Assesses the impact of Weberian sociology upon the study of Buddhism, and proposes a new approach to the study of Buddhism in Sri Lanka.

170. Saram, P.A.S. "Bouddhisme et société à Sri Lanka." REVUE INTERNATIONALE DES SCIENCES SOCIALES 29,2 (1977): 338-349. See also "Buddhism and Society in Modern Sri Lanka." INTERNATIONAL SOCIAL SCIENCE JOURNAL 29,2 (1977): 313-323.

General historical discussion, framed in terms of Buddhist doctrine, the feudal church, Buddhism as separate from the feudal order, Buddhist culture, and Buddhism amidst modern politics.

171. Seneviratne, H.L. "L'ordination bouddhiste à Ceylon." SC 20,2 (1973): 251-256.

The Buddhist ordination rite in eighteenth-century Ceylon is claimed to have two kinds of symbolic meaning, one internal to the rite and the other related to the legitimation of royal power.

172. Smith, Donald E. "The Sinhalese Buddhist Revolution." In Donald E. Smith (ed.), SOUTH ASIAN POLITICS AND RELIGION. Princeton: Princeton University Press, 1966.

173. Wilson, Howard A. "An 'Anatomy' of the Buddhist Renaissance in Ceylon in the Work of K.N. Jayatilleke." SC 20,2 (1973): 201-215.

174. Yalman, Nur. "On the Meaning of Food Offering in Ceylon." SC 20,2 (1973): 287-302.


*WESTERN*

   * Akahoshi, Hidefumi. "Hongwanji in Rural Japan and Cosmopolitan Hawaii." Cited above as item 137.

175. Hasegawa, Charles. "The Hongwanji Buddhist Minister in Hawaii: A Study of an Occupation." SOCIAL PROCESS IN HAWAII 26 (1963): 73-79.

Study of ministers of the Nishi Hongwanji, or Jodo Shinshu, in Hawaii. Data from denominational reports and inventory of ministers' duties.

176. Horinouchi, Isao. AMERICANIZED BUDDHISM: A SOCIOLOGICAL ANALYSIS OF A PROTESTANTIZED JAPANESE RELIGION. Unpublished Ph.D. dissertation, University of California, Davis, 1973. [DA 34:7 A, p. 4429]

Historical analysis (1898-1973) of Jodo Shinshu, with particular
focus upon the Sacramento church. Based upon interviews, participant
observation, and documentary analysis.

177. Kashima, Tetsuden. BUDDHISM IN AMERICA: THE SOCIAL ORGANIZATION OF AN
ETHNIC RELIGIOUS INSTITUTION. Westport, Connecticut: Greenwood Press,
1977.

178. Mullins, Mark R. "The Organizational Dilemmas of Ethnic Churches: A
Case Study of Japanese Buddhism in Canada." SA 49,3 (1988): 217-233.

Examines the problem of religious leadership in an ethnic religious
organization that has a highly assimilated membership but is dependent
upon a religious body in the 'old country' for almost all of its
leaders.

179. Mullins, Mark R. RELIGIOUS MINORITIES IN CANADA: A SOCIOLOGICAL STUDY
OF THE JAPANESE EXPERIENCE. Lewiston, New York: Edwin Mellen Press,
1988.

180. Patrick, John W. "Personal Faith and the Fear of Death among Divergent Religious Populations." JSSR 18,3 (1979): 298-305.

Focuses upon Buddhist, Congregationalist, and Southern Baptist congregations in Honolulu. Fear of death is found to be positively related
to extrinsic religion among Christian respondents only.

181. Spencer, Robert F. JAPANESE BUDDHISM IN THE UNITED STATES, 1940-1946.
Unpublished Ph.D. dissertation, University of California, Berkeley,
1946.

182. Spencer, Robert F. "Social Structure of a Contemporary Japanese-
American Buddhist Church." SOCIAL FORCES 26,3 (1948): 281-287.

Description of a congregation in a California university town,
affiliated with the Nishi-Hongwanji branch of the Shin denomination.

183. Tajima, Paul J. JAPANESE BUDDHISM IN HAWAII: ITS BACKGROUND, ORIGIN,
AND ADAPTATION TO LOCAL CONDITIONS. Unpublished M.A. thesis,
University of Hawaii, 1935.


*MODERN SECTS AND MOVEMENTS*

184. Agena, Masako, and Eiko Yoshinaga. "Daishi-Do - A Form of Religious
Movement." SOCIAL PROCESS IN HAWAII 7 (1941): 15-20.

Description of a folk-religious variation of Shingon Buddhism among
first-generation Japanese in Hawaii.

 * Khalsa, Kirpal Singh. "New Religious Movements Turn to Worldly
Success." Cited above as item 74.

185. Moroto, Aiko. CONDITIONS FOR ACCEPTING A NEW RELIGIOUS BELIEF: A CASE

STUDY OF MYOCHIKAI MEMBERS IN JAPAN. Unpublished M.A. thesis, University of Washington, Seattle, 1976.

186. Obeyesekere, Gananath. "The Cult of Huniyan: A New Religious Movement in Sri Lanka." In J.A. Beckford (ed.), NEW RELIGIOUS MOVEMENTS AND RAPID SOCIAL CHANGE [volume cited as item 50], pp. 197-219.

Account of developments in Columbo in the 1960s.

187. Watanabe, Eimi. "Rissho Kosei-kai: A Sociological Observation of its Members, their Conversion and their Activities." CONTEMPORARY RELIGIONS IN JAPAN 9 (1968): 75-151.

Features 1968 interviews, focusing on reasons for joining this Japanese Buddhist sect.

188. Yama, Evelyn K., and Agnes M. Niyekawa. "Chowado." SOCIAL PROCESS IN HAWAII 16 (1952): 48-58.

Study of a Japanese Shingon Buddhist sect whose headquarters had been relocated to Honolulu from Japan.

*SOKA GAKKAI (NICHIREN SHOSHU)*

189. Babbie, Earl R. "The Third Civilization: An Examination of Soka-gakkai." RRR 7,2 (1966): 101-121. Reprinted in Charles Y. Glock (ed.), RELIGION IN SOCIOLOGICAL PERSPECTIVE: ESSAYS IN THE EMPIRICAL STUDY OF RELIGION. Belmont, California: Wadsworth, 1973, pp. 235-260.

Examines the factors which may affect the success of Soka Gakkai, a world-proselytizing Buddhist group based in Japan.

190. Blacker, C. "Le Soka-Gakkai japonais. L'activisme politique d'une secte bouddhiste." ARCHIVES DE SOCIOLOGIE DES RELIGIONS 9,17 (1964): 63-67.

191. Dator, James A. "The Soka Gakkai: A Socio-political Interpretation." CONTEMPORARY RELIGIONS IN JAPAN 6,3 (1965): 205-242.

The Soka Gakkai is a value-creating action group, which places its members in networks of action which give rise to and reinforce faith. It has a controversial presence in the Japanese political world.

192. Gonzáles de Zarate, Roberto M. "Soka Gakkai: Una religión del valor." RAZON Y FE 171 (1965): 53-66.

193. Hashimoto, Hideo, and William McPherson. "Rise and Decline of Soka-gakkai: Japan and the United States." RRR 17,2 (1976): 82-92.

Traces the sect's evolution from the unconventional to the conventional.

194. Holtzapple, Vicki Rea. SOKA GAKKAI IN MIDWESTERN AMERICA: A CASE

STUDY OF A TRANSPOSITIONAL MOVEMENT. Unpublished Ph.D. dissertation, Washington University, 1977. [DA 38:12 A, p. 7415]

Participant-observation study in a midwestern American city, in which movement elite and local members were in conflict over recruitment practices.

195. Hourmant, Louis. "Ascèse, rationalité, modernité en contexte oriental: Le bouddhisme de la Soka Gakkai." SC 36,1 (1989): 83-94.

196. Oh, John Kie-Chang. "The Nichiren Shoshu in America." RRR 14,3 (1973): 169-177.`

A series of random-sample surveys conducted among Buddhists in Los Angeles, Chicago, and New York, indicates that relatively youthful, fairly well-educated Americans are embracing Nichiren Shoshu.

197. Shupe, Anson. "Militancy and Accommodation in the Third Civilization: The Case of Japan's Soka Gakkai Movement." In Jeffrey K. Hadden and Anson Shupe (eds.), PROPHETIC RELIGIONS AND POLITICS. New York: Paragon House, 1986, pp. 235-253.

198. Snow, David A. THE NICHIREN SHOSHU BUDDHIST MOVEMENT IN AMERICA: A SOCIOLOGICAL EXAMINATION OF ITS VALUE ORIENTATION, RECRUITMENT EFFORTS AND SPREAD. Unpublished Ph.D. dissertation, University of California, Los Angeles, 1976. [DA 37:8 A, p. 5374]

Participant observation and analysis of movement literature. Focus is on recruitment activities.

199. Snow, David A. "A Dramaturgical Analysis of Movement Accommodation: Building Idiosyncrasy Credit as a Movement Mobilization Strategy." SYMBOLIC INTERACTION 2,2 (1979): 23-44.

Consideration of the strategy of gaining acceptance as an idiosyncratic entity.

200. Snow, David A. "Organization, Ideology, and Mobilization: The Case of Nichiren Shoshu of America." In D.G. Bromley and P.E. Hammond (eds.), THE FUTURE OF NEW RELIGIOUS MOVEMENTS [volume cited in item 94], pp. 153-172.

1974-75 participant-observation study in Los Angeles, supplemented by a review of the movement's literature.

*THERAVADA*

201. Bechert, Heinz. BUDDHISMUS, STAAT UND GESELLSCHAFT IN DEN LÄNDERN DES THERAVADA-BUDDHISMUS. Wiesbaden: Otto Harrassowitz, 1967.

202. Houtart, François. "Theravada Buddhism and Political Power -- Construction and Destructuration of its Ideological Function." SC 24,2-3 (1977): 207-246.

Discusses the rise of little vehicle Buddhism in Ceylon, Burma, Thailand, Indonesia, Laos, Cambodia, and Vietnam, when these were tributary societies. Transformations occurred with feudalism, and destructuration with colonization by Europeans.

203. Silber, Ilana Friedrich. "'Opting Out' in Theravada Buddhism and Medieval Christianity." RELIGION 15 (1985): 251-277.

*ZEN*

204. Preston, David L. "Becoming a Zen Practitioner." SA 42,1 (1981): 47-55.

Discusses the role of meditation in processes of conversion to Zen.

205. Preston, David L. "Meditative Ritual Practice and Spiritual Conversion-Commitment: Theoretical Implications based on the Case of Zen." SA 43,3 (1982): 257-270.

Proposes theoretical accounts for the transformation undergone by converts in the process of acquiring a new role and learning a new symbol system.

206. Preston, David L. THE SOCIAL ORGANIZATION OF ZEN PRACTICE: CONSTRUCT-ING TRANSCULTURAL REALITY. New York: Cambridge University Press, 1988.

Participant-observation study of two Zen groups (Los Angeles and San Diego); 1980 and 1984 interviews.

207. Tipton, Steven M. "New Religious Movements and the Problem of a Modern Ethic." In Harry M. Johnson (ed.), RELIGIOUS CHANGE AND CONTINUITY. SOCIOLOGICAL PERSPECTIVES. San Francisco: Jossey-Bass, 1979, pp. 286-312. Also in SOCIOLOGICAL INQUIRY 49,2-3 (1979): 286-312.

The Zen portion of the article is based on ten 1976 interviews conducted in the San Francisco area.

208. Tipton, Steven M. GETTING SAVED FROM THE SIXTIES. Berkeley: University of California Press, 1982.

Interpretive study which includes research on the Pacific Zen Center.

209. Wise, David T. DHARMA WEST: A SOCIAL-PSYCHOLOGICAL INQUIRY INTO ZEN IN SAN FRANCISCO. Unpublished Ph.D. dissertation, University of California at Berkeley, 1972.

# 3
## Other Asian

*CHINESE*

210. Freiberg, James W.  "The Taoist Mind: A Case Study in a 'Structure of Consciousness'."  SA 36,4 (1975): 304-322.

   Discusses major elements of the Taoist world view in ancient China and the role played by them in structuring Taoist notions of ontology, spirit, and action.

211. Freiberg, James W.  "L'idéologie, l'état et la conflit des classes dans les 'religions' de la chine ancienne."  L'HOMME ET LA SOCIETE 41-42 (1976): 197-232.

   Reconceptualization in class terms of the orthodoxy/heterodoxy (Confucian/Tao) conflict.

212. Granet, Marcel.  THE RELIGION OF THE CHINESE PEOPLE, translated by Maurice Freedman.  New York: Harper and Row, 1976.

213. Hong, Lawrence K.  "The Association of Religion and Family Structure: The Case of the Hong Kong Family."  SA 33,1 (1972): 50-57.

   Studies the meaning of the 'ancestral cult' by reference to a 1968 sample of Hong Kong families.

214. Molloy, Stephen.  "Max Weber and the Religion of China: Any Way Out of the Maze?"  BRITISH JOURNAL OF SOCIOLOGY 31,3 (1980): 377-400.

   * Tamney, Joseph B.  "Chinese Family Structure and the Continuation of Chinese Religions."  Cited above as item 156.

215. Weber, Max.  THE RELIGION OF CHINA: CONFUCIANISM AND TAOISM, translated by Hans H. Gerth.  Glencoe: The Free Press, 1951.

216. Zingerle, A.  MAX WEBER UND CHINA. HERRSCHAFTS- UND RELIGIONS- SOZIOLOGISCHE GRUNDLAGEN ZUM WANDEL DER CHINESISCHEN GESELLSCHAFT. Berlin: Duncker und Humbolt, 1972.

217. Caillat, Colette. "L'ascétisme chez les Jains." ARCHIVES DE SOCIOLOGIE DES RELIGIONS 18 (1964): 45-53.

218. Gandhi, Raj S. "The Rise of Jainism and its Adoption by the Vaishyas of India: A Case Study in Sanskritisation and Status Mobility." SC 24,2-3 (1977): 247-260.

219. Naveskar, Balwant. CAPITALISTS WITHOUT CAPITALISM: THE JAINS OF INDIA AND THE QUAKERS OF THE WEST. Westport, Connecticut: Greenwood, 1971.

220. Sangave, Vilas A. JAINA COMMUNITY: A SOCIAL SURVEY. Bombay: Popular Prakashan, 1959.

*PARSI*

221. Kennedy, Robert E., Jr. "The Protestant Ethic and the Parsis." AMERICAN JOURNAL OF SOCIOLOGY 68,1 (1962): 11-20. Also in Neil J. Smelser (ed.), READINGS ON ECONOMIC SOCIOLOGY. Englewood Cliffs: Prentice-Hall, 1965, pp. 16-26.

The traditional Zoroastrian value of commercial rationality has been carried through to the modern Parsees.

*SHINTO*

222. Bellah, Robert N. TOKUGAWA RELIGION. Glencoe: The Free Press, 1957.

Suggests that Bushido discipline is largely the basis for the vitality of the modern Japanese economy, serving a purpose similar to what Protestant worldliness did for Western capitalism.

223. Ehrentraut, A. "Symbols of Heritage: The Restoration of Shinto Shrines." ISUKUBA JOURNAL OF SOCIOLOGY 13 (1988): 61-73.

224. Morioka, Kiyomi. "The Impact of Suburbanization on Shinto Belief and Behavior." SC 17,1 (1970): 37-65.

Suburbanization diminishes the importance of shrines which have a merely local appeal.

225. Saniel, Josefa M. "The Mobilization of Traditional Values in the Modernization of Japan." In R.N. Bellah (ed.), RELIGION AND PROGRESS IN MODERN ASIA [volume cited in item 168], pp. 114-132.

The Meiji oligarchs used traditional Shintoist and Confucian beliefs (especially beliefs pertaining to the divinity of the emperor and familism) to motivate and organize modernization.

226. Takayama, K. Peter. "Revitalization Movement of Modern Japanese Civil Religion." SA 48,4 (1988): 328-341.

Many government leaders believe Japan needs to restore the sacred Shinto symbols that once gave Japanese a strong national identity and cosmic unity.

## SIKH

227. Ahluwalis, Gasbir S. "Anti-feudal Dialectic of Sikhism." SOCIAL SCIENTIST (India) 2,8 (1974): 22-26.

228. Ballard, Roger, and Catherine Ballard. "The Sikhs: The Development of South Asian Settlements in Britain." In James L. Watson (ed.), BETWEEN TWO CULTURES: MIGRANTS AND MINORITIES IN BRITAIN. Oxford: Basil Blackwell, 1977, pp. 21-56.

Historical-sociological overview; based in part on 1970-75 research in Leeds.

229. Madan, T.N. "Secularisation and the Sikh Religious Tradition." SC 33,2-3 (1986): 257-273.

Ironically, their stance has come to conflict with a more modern kind of secularization, one which has separated faith and politics again.

# PART II
# HEBREW, JEWISH, AND
# ISLAMIC TRADITIONS

# 4
# Hebrew

230. Bardis, Panos. "Main Features of the Ancient Hebrew Family." SOCIAL SCIENCE 38,3 (1963): 168-183.

231. Berger, Peter L. "Charisma and Religious Innovation: The Social Location of Israelite Prophecy." AMERICAN SOCIOLOGICAL REVIEW 28,6 (1963): 940-950.

Recent biblical scholarship forces a revision of Weber's interpretation of prophetic charisma in Israel. The prophets were not isolated individuals opposed to the established religion of the priests but were themselves closely related to certain cultic offices.

232. Causse, Antonin. DU GROUPE ETHNIQUE A LA COMMUNAUTE RELIGIEUSE: LE PROBLEME SOCIOLOGIQUE DE LA RELIGION D'ISRAEL. Paris: Alcan, 1937.

233. Ferguson, Douglas W. "The Changing Social Meanings of Sacrifices in Jewish Worship: An Historical Overview." SOCIOLOGICAL FOCUS 17,3 (1984): 211-221.

234. Fischoff, Ephraim. MAX WEBER AND THE SOCIOLOGY OF RELIGION WITH SPECIAL REFERENCE TO JUDAISM. Unpublished Ph.D. dissertation, New School for Social Research, 1950.

235. Gottwald, Norman K. "Sociological Method in the Study of Ancient Israel." In Martin J. Buss (ed.), ENCOUNTER WITH THE TEXT. Philadelphia: Fortress, 1979, pp. 69-81.

236. Gottwald, Norman K. THE TRIBES OF YAHWEH. Maryknoll, N.Y.: Orbis, 1979.

Focus is on the Hebrew invasion, settlement, and conquest of Palestine.

237. Guttmann, J. "Max Webers Soziologie des Antiken Judentums." MONATSCHRIFT FÜR GESCHICHTE UND WISSENSCHAFT DES JUDENTUMS 69 (1925): 195-223.

238. Holstein, May A. "Max Weber and Biblical Scholarship." HEBREW UNION COLLEGE ANNUAL 46 (1975): 159-179.

* Houtart, François. RELIGION ET MODES DE PRODUCTION PRECAPITALISTES. Cited above as item 25.

239. Kimbrough, S.T. "Une conception sociologique de la religion d'Israël: L'oeuvre d'Antonin Causse." REVUE D'HiSTOIRE ET DE PHILOSOPHIE RELIGIEUSES 49 (1969): 313-330.

Expresses appreciation for the work of Antonin Causse (b. 1877), a principal French specialist in the Hebrew Bible during the first half of the twentieth century.

240. Kippenberg, H.G. RELIGION UND KLASSENBILDUNC IM ANTIKEN JUDÄA. EINE RELIGIONSSOZIOLOGISCHE STUDIE ZUM VERHALTNIS VON TRADITION UND GESELLSCHAFTLICHER ENTWICKLUNG. Göttingen: Vandenhoeck and Ruprecht, 1978.

241. Lang, Graeme. "Oppression and Revolt in Ancient Palestine: The Evidence in Jewish Literature from the Prophets to Josephus." SA 49,4 (1989): 325-342.

242. Lurje, M. STUDIEN ZUR GESCHICHTE DER WIRTSCHAFTLICHEN UND SOZIALEN VERHÄLTNISSE IM ISRAELITISCH-JÜDISCHEN REICHE. Giessen: Alfred Töpelmann, 1927.

243. Malamat, Abraham. "Tribal Societies: Biblical Genealogies and African Lineage Systems." ARCHIVES EUROPEENNES DE SOCIOLOGIE 14 (1973): 126-136.

The Israelite tribal genealogies are shown to be of utmost significance in unravelling the dynamics of the settlement process in Palestine, and for elucidating the complex anatomy of a particular tribal make-up. The same seems true for the various African lineage systems and their respective societies.

244. Martindale, Don. "Priests and Prophets in Palestine." In Don Martindale (ed.), SOCIAL LIFE AND CULTURAL CHANGE. Princeton: Van Nostrand, 1962, pp. 239-307.

Historical overview of changing forms of Israelite society, the changing roles of priests and prophets, and Israelite social thought and civilization.

245. May, Herbert G. "A Sociological Approach to Hebrew Religion." JOURNAL OF BIBLE AND RELIGION 12,2 (1944): 98-106.

A review of the literature as it stood almost a half-century ago.

246. More, D.R. HEBREW MARRIAGE: A SOCIOLOGICAL STUDY. New York: Philosophine Library, 1953.

247. Petersen, David L. "Max Weber and the Sociological Study of Ancient Israel." In H.M. Johnson (ed.), RELIGIOUS CHANGE AND CONTINUITY [volume cited in item 207], pp. 117-149. Also in SOCIOLOGICAL INQUIRY 49,2-3 (1979): 117-149.

248. Raphaël, Freddy. "Max Weber et le judaisme antique." ARCHIVES EUROPEENNES DE SOCIOLOGIE 11,2 (1970): 297-336.

249. Raphaël, Freddy. "Les Juifs en tant que peuple paria dans l'oeuvre de Max Weber." SC 23,4 (1976): 397-426.

250. Rodd, Cyril S. "On Applying a Sociological Theory to Biblical Studies." JOURNAL FOR THE STUDY OF THE OLD TESTAMENT 19 (1981): 95-106.

251. Rogerson, J.W. "The Use of Sociology in Old Testament Studies." VETUS TESTAMENTUM 36, 1983 Salamanca Congress Supplement. Leiden: E.J. Brill, 1985, pp. 245-256.

252. Schiper, I. "Max Weber on the Sociological Basis of the Jewish Religion." JEWISH JOURNAL OF SOCIOLOGY 1,2 (1959): 250-260.

253. Schluchter, Wolfgang (ed.) MAX WEBERS STUDIE ÜBER DAS ANTIKE JUDENTUM: INTERPRETATION UND KRITIK. Frankfurt: Suhrkamp/KNO, 1981.

254. Theophane, M. "Family Customs in the Old Testament." AMERICAN CATHOLIC SOCIOLOGICAL REVIEW 16,3 (1955): 198-210.

255. Wax, Murray. "Ancient Judaism and the Protestant Ethic." AMERICAN JOURNAL OF SOCIOLOGY 65,5 (1960): 449-455.

Argues that the attitude of Hebrew religion toward magic, time, and personal identity anticipated the Protestant Ethic.

256. Weber, Max. ANCIENT JUDAISM, translated by Hans H. Gerth and Don Martindale. New York: The Free Press, 1952.

257. Wilson, Robert R. SOCIOLOGICAL APPROACHES TO THE OLD TESTAMENT. Philadelphia: Fortress, 1984.

258. Winter, J. Alan. "Immanence and Regime in the Kingdom of Judah: A Cross-disciplinary Study of a Swansonian Hypothesis." SA 44,2 (1983): 147-162.

Belief in the immanence of a high god is hypothesized to prevail in a society whose government is an absolute monarchy transcending local interests. Evidence from the Davidic dynasty supports the hypothesis.

259. Zeitlin, Irving M. ANCIENT JUDAISM. BIBLICAL CRITICISM FROM MAX WEBER TO THE PRESENT. Cambridge, England: Polity Press, 1984; New York: Basil Blackwell, 1984.

# 5
## Jewish

*GENERAL*

260. Azaria, Régine. "'Intégrisme Juif'? ou la norme impossible." SC 32,4 (1985): 429-448.

The concept of integrism does not seem to apply to Jewish phenomena.

261. Baron, Raphael R. "The Measurement of Religious Observance amongst Jews." JEWISH JOURNAL OF SOCIOLOGY 6,1 (1964): 81-90.

Statistical problems of definition, collection, and analysis: indicators of individual observance and communal religious statistics.

262. Bauer, Julien. "Israël et ses significations pour le Judaïsme religieux." LES CAHIERS DU CENTRE DE RECHERCHES EN SOCIOLOGIE RELIGIEUSE 3 (1980): 83-104.

The modern state of Israel has religious significance for some religious Jews.

263. Bok, Willy, and Usiel Schmelz (eds.) DEMOGRAPHIE ET IDENTITES JUIVES DANS L'EGLISE CONTEMPORAINE. Actes du 2e Colloque sur la vie juive dans l'Europe Contemporaine. Bruxelles: Institut de Sociologie de l'Université Libre de Bruxelles, Editions de l'Université, 1972.

264. Brenner, Reeve R. THE FAITH AND DOUBT OF HOLOCAUST SURVIVORS. New York: Macmillan, 1980.

265. Etzioni-Halevy, Eva, and Zvi Halevy. "The 'Jewish ethic' and the 'Spirit of Achievement'." JEWISH JOURNAL OF SOCIOLOGY 19,1 (1977): 49-66.

Review of American, British, and Russian studies. Concept of chosen people is proposed as a source of self-esteem, feeling of obligation, and achievement-motivation.

266. Finkelstein, Louis. THE PHARISEES: THE SOCIOLOGICAL BACKGROUND OF THEIR FAITH, 2 volumes. Philadelphia: Jewish Publication Society of America, 1938.

267. Fishman, Aryei. "Judaism and Modernization: The Case of the Religious Kibbutzim." SOCIAL FORCES 62 (1983): 9-31.

The strong modernization potential of Judaism is illustrated by reference to the orthodox kibbutz federation in Israel.

268. Fishman, Aryei. "The Religious Kibbutz: A Note on the Theories of Marx, Sombart, and Weber on Judaism and Economic Success." SA 50,3 (1989): 281-290.

Uses the orthodox kibbutzim as a standard for evaluating theories regarding Judaism's ability to stimulate high economic performance.

269. Guttmann, J. "Die Juden und das Wirtschaftsleben." ARCHIV FÜR SOZIALWISSENSCHAFT UND SOZIALPOLITIK 36 (1912): 149-212.

Review essay on Werner Sombart's DIE JUDEN UND DAS WIRTSCHAFTSLEBEN.

270. Horowitz, Irving L. "The Jews and Modern Communism: The Sombart Thesis Reconsidered." MODERN JUDAISM 6 (1986): 13-25.

Considers anew the complex relationship between Judaism and the respective economic spirits of capitalism and socialism.

271. Houtart, François, and Geneviève Lemercinier. LE JUIFS DANS LA CATACHESE. ETUDES SUR LA TRANSMISSION DES CODES RELIGIEUX. Bruxelles: Editions Vie Ouvrière, 1972.

272. Krausz, Ernest. "Le facteur religieux dans la formation de l'identité juive." REVUE INTERNATIONALE DE SCIENCES SOCIALES 29,2 (1977): 272-283. See also "The Religious Factor in Jewish Identification." INTERNATIONAL SOCIAL SCIENCE JOURNAL 29,2 (1977): 250-260.

Secondary analysis of American, Israeli, and British data. Secular Judaism compensates for the decline in Jewish religion.

273. Lavender, Abraham. "Jewish Intermarriage and Marriage to Converts: The Religious Factor and the Ethnic Factor." JEWISH SOCIOLOGY AND SOCIAL RESEARCH 2 (1976): 17-22.

274. Lazerwitz, Bernard. "Religiosity and Fertility: How Strong a Connection?" CONTEMPORARY JEWRY 5,1 (1980): 56-63.

275. Loewe, Raphael. "Defining Judaism: Some Ground-clearing." JEWISH JOURNAL OF SOCIOLOGY 7,2 (1965): 153-175.

276. Löwy, Michaël. "Pour une sociologie de la mystique juive: A propos et autour du 'Sabbataï Sevi' de Gershom Scholem." ARCHIVES DE SCIENCE SOCIALES DES RELIGIONS 57,1 (1984): 5-14.

Examines the specific historic and economic conditions which fostered the growth of Sabbatianism, the popular movement which traversed the entire Jewish diaspora in the middle of the seventeenth century.

277. Memmi, A., W. Ackermann, N. Zobermann, and S. Zobermann. "Pratique

religieuse et identité juive." REVUE FRANÇAISE DE SOCIOLOGIE 14,2 (1973): 242-270.

Religious observances and beliefs express Jewish consciousness differently for Ashkenazic and Sephardic Jews.

278. Mirsky, Norman B. (ed.) UNORTHODOX JUDAISM. Columbus: Ohio State University Press, 1978.

279. Moles, Abraham A., and Tamar Grunewald. "Altérité et identité vues par le psycho-sociologue. Une étude trans-culturelle du Judaïsm." SC 18,3 (1971): 357-373.

Finds variation in semantic differential responses between Jewish and non-Jewish German-language respondents.

280. Ohrenstein, Roman A. "Economic Thought in Talmudic Literature in the Light of Modern Economics." AMERICAN JOURNAL OF ECONOMICS AND SOCIOLOGY 27,2 (1968): 185-196.

The talmudic literature contains the constituent elements of a quantitative theory of money.

281. Rabi, W. "Modes et indices d'identification juive." SC 18,3 (1971): 337-356.

Traces the transformation from a religious to a secular identity.

282. Raphaël, Freddy. "Judaism and Secularization." SC 18,3 (1971): 399-412.

283. Raphaël, Freddy. "Le Juif et le Diable dans la civilisation de l'Occident." SC 19,4 (1972): 549-566.

284. Rivkin, Ellis. "The Internal City. Judaism and Urbanization." JSSR 5,2 (1966): 225-240.

Historical analysis; first century C.E.

285. Rudy, Zvi. "Bermerkungen zu einer Soziologie des jüdischen Volkes." KÖLNER ZEITSCHRIFT FÜR SOZIOLOGIE UND SOZIALPSYCHOLOGIE 21,1 (1969): 1-15.

The complex history of the Jewish people offers many research possibilities: ethnic dispersion, identity maintenance, introversion, etc.

286. Ruppin, S.A. DIE JUDEN DER GEGENWART. EINE SOCIALWISSENSCHAFTLICHE STUDIE. Berlin: S. Calvary, 1904. See also THE JEWS OF TO-DAY, translated by Margery Bentwick. New York: Henry Holt, 1913.

287. Ruppin, S.A. SOZIOLOGIE DER JUDEN. Volume I: DIE SOZIALE STRUKTUR DER JUDEN; Volume II: DER KAMPF DER JUDEN UM IHRE ZUKUNFT. Berlin: 1930,1931.

288. Ruppin, S.A.  LES JUIFS DANS LE MONDE MODERNE. SOCIOLOGIE, POPULATION, MIGRATION, ECONOMIE, SIONISME, ANTISEMITISME.  Paris: Payot, 1934.

289. Saldarini, Anthony J.  PHARISEES, SCRIBES AND SADDUCEES IN PALESTINIAN SOCIETY: A SOCIOLOGICAL APPROACH.  Wilmington: Michael Glazier, 1988.

290. Scharf, Betty R.  "Durkheimian and Freudian Theories of Religion: The Case of Judaism."  BRITISH JOURNAL OF SOCIOLOGY 21,2 (1970): 151-163.

   The relative scarcity of Jewish schisms and heresy fits the thesis that a small, not quite insulated community will not engender sufficient anomie to spark rebellion against traditional authority.

291. Schlesinger, Benjamin.  "The Jewish Family and Religion."  JOURNAL OF COMPARATIVE FAMILY STUDIES 5,2 (1974): 27-36.

   Investigates familism in the Jewish religious tradition.

292. Sharot, Stephen.  "Minority Situation and Religious Acculturation: A Comparative Analysis of Jewish Communities."  COMPARATIVE STUDIES IN SOCIETY AND HISTORY 16,3 (1974): 329-354.

   Although the differences between Judaism and the environmental religions were initially greater in China and India than in the Middle East and Europe, the syncretism of the eastern religions contributed to the much greater loss of Jewish distinctiveness in the Orient.

293. Sharot, Stephen.  JUDAISM. A SOCIOLOGY.  New York: Holmes and Meier, 1976.

294. Sharot, Stephen.  "Jewish Millenarianism: A Comparison of Medieval Communities."  COMPARATIVE STUDIES IN SOCIETY AND HISTORY 22,3 (1980): 394-415.

   Although some of the general explanations of millennial movements are relevant to Jewish millenarianism, no one theory accounts for all the cases. Disruption and relative deprivation account for some cases.

295. Sharot, Stephen.  MESSIANISM, MYSTICISM, AND MAGIC: A SOCIOLOGICAL ANALYSIS OF JEWISH RELIGIOUS MOVEMENTS.  Chapel Hill, North Carolina: University of North Carolina Press, 1982.

296. Smith, Anthony D.  "Nationalism and Religion. The Role of Religious Reform in the Genesis of Arab and Jewish Nationalism."  ARCHIVES DE SCIENCE SOCIALES DES RELIGIONS 35 (1973): 23-44.

   While the transition from religion to nationalism could be discerned clearly in the case of the Jews, most Arabs in the early 1970s remained attached to a religion which elevated their ethnic status.

297. Sombart, Werner.  DIE JUDEN UND DAS WIRTSCHAFTSLEBEN.  Leipzig: Duncker und Humbolt, 1911.

298. Steinberg, Stephen.  "Reform Judaism: The Origin and Evolution of a

'Church Movement'." JSSR 5,1 (1965): 117-129. Reprinted in C.Y. Glock (ed.), RELIGION IN SOCIOLOGICAL PERSPECTIVE [volume cited in item 189], pp. 221-234.

Historical sociological study of the emergence of Reform Judaism in response to the inability of Orthodoxy to adapt to the modern world.

299. Vajda, Georges. "Le rôle et la signification de l'ascétisme dans la religion juive." ARCHIVES DE SOCIOLOGIE DES RELIGIONS 18 (1964): 35-43.

Although not accorded decisive emphasis, religious asceticism is congenial to the tradition of rabbinic Judaism.

## AFRICA

300. Attal, Robert. "Tunisian Jewry during the Last Twenty Years." JEWISH JOURNAL OF SOCIOLOGY 2,1 (1960): 4-15.

Discusses political troubles during and after Nazi occupation, and emigration to Israel after World War II.

301. Attal, Robert. "The Statistics of North African Jewry." JEWISH JOURNAL OF SOCIOLOGY 5,1 (1963): 27-34.

Accessibility of data in official yearbook of Morocco and Tunisia; inaccessibility in official data of Algeria, where Jews were classified as 'French' since 1870.

302. Chouraqui, André. "North African Jewry Today." JEWISH JOURNAL OF SOCIOLOGY 1,1 (1959): 58-68.

303. Willner, Dorothy, and Margot Kohls. "Jews in the High Atlas Mountains of Morocco: A Partial Reconstruction." JEWISH JOURNAL OF SOCIOLOGY 4,2 (1962): 207-241.

Reconstruction of life in the High Atlas Mountains during 1950-54; based on interviews conducted in Israel after a 1954 migration.

## ASIA

304. Feitelson, Dina. "Aspects of the Social Life of Kurdish Jews." JEWISH JOURNAL OF SOCIOLOGY 1,2 (1959): 201-216.

Reconstruction of life ways in Iraq before a 1951 mass exodus to Israel; use of 1953-54 interviews conducted in Israel.

305. Nathan, Naphtali. "Notes on the Jews of Turkey." JEWISH JOURNAL OF SOCIOLOGY 6,2 (1964): 172-189.

Overview of schools, social services, communities, economic life, press, languages, and cultural life.

306. Smythe, H.H., and T. Gershuny. "Jewish Castes of Cochin India."

SOCIOLOGY AND SOCIAL RESEARCH 41,2 (1956): 108-114.

Traditionally, different Jewish castes did not worship together or socialize across caste lines. The younger generation is beginning to change this.

307. Strizower, Schifra. "Jews as an Indian Caste." JEWISH JOURNAL OF SOCIOLOGY 1 (1959): 43-57. Reprinted in Louis Schneider (ed.), RELIGION, CULTURE AND SOCIETY. New York: Wiley, 1964, pp. 220-232.

Descriptive analysis of the Indian Jews up to the 1950s; based on modern population data, interviews, and traditions.

*AUSTRALIA*

308. Mol, J.J. (Hans) "A Collation of Data about Religion in Australia." SC 14,2 (1967): 117-132.

309. Taft, Ronald, and Geulah Solomon. "The Melbourne Jewish Community and the Middle East War of 1973." JEWISH JOURNAL OF SOCIOLOGY 16,1 (1974): 57-73.

1973 interview data focusing on attitudes of Melbourne Jews toward the 1967 and 1973 wars in the Middle East, revealing disapproval of Australia's neutrality in 1973.

*CANADA*

310. Bauer, Julien. "Jewish Communities, Jewish Education and Quebec Nationalism." SC 31,4 (1984): 391-407.

311. Driedger, Leo. "Jewish Identity: The Maintenance of Urban Religious and Ethnic Boundaries." ETHNIC AND RACIAL STUDIES 3,1 (1980): 67-88.

Examines the extent to which Jews in Winnipeg, Manitoba, maintain boundaries with residential segregation, institutional completeness, cultural identity, and social distance.

312. Foote, Raymond L. THE FREDERICTON JEWISH COMMUNITY: A STUDY IN CLASS, STATUS AND RELIGION. Unpublished M.A. thesis, University of New Brunswick, 1967.

313. Frideres, James S., and Jay E. Goldstein. "Jewish-Gentile Inter-marriage: Definitions and Consequences." SC 21,1 (1974): 69-84.

Data from a western Canadian community suggest an absence of negative consequences for children of their parents' exogamy.

314. Gillis, A. Ronald, and Paul C. Whitehead. "Halifax Jews: A Community within a Community." In Jean Leonard Elliott (ed.), IMMIGRANT GROUPS. Scarborough: Prentice-Hall, 1971, pp. 84-94.

Examines the minority group status of Jews in Halifax.

315. Gutwirth, Jacques. "The Structure of a Hassidic Community in Montreal." JEWISH JOURNAL OF SOCIOLOGY 14,1 (1972): 43-62.

Belzer Hasidim of Montreal compared with a similar community in Antwerp; post-World War II (largely Hungarian) immigrant communities.

316. Kallen Latowsky, Evelyn. THREE TORONTO SYNAGOGUES: A COMPARATIVE STUDY OF RELIGIOUS SYSTEMS IN TRANSITION. Unpublished Ph.D. dissertation, University of Toronto, 1969.

Based on 1967 telephone interviews with members and participant observation; examines trends toward conservatism and a heightened Jewish identification.

317. Kallen, Evelyn. "Synagogues in Transition: Religious Revival or Ethnic Survival?" In Stewart Crysdale and Les Wheatcroft (eds.), RELIGION IN CANADIAN SOCIETY. Toronto: Macmillan, 1976, pp. 278-288.

Extract from a 1969 dissertation; focus on Toronto. The author uses the name Latowsky on the title page of the dissertation.

318. Kallen, Evelyn. SPANNING THE GENERATIONS: A STUDY IN JEWISH IDENTITY. Don Mills, Ontario: Longman Canada, 1977.

Data on adult members of three north Toronto synagogues from 1966-69 field work and a telephone survey; data on Jewish youth in Toronto from a 1970-72 questionnaire administered to a random sample of Jewish youth in Toronto.

319. Lazar, Morty M. "The Role of Women in Synagogue Ritual in Canadian Conservative Congregations." JEWISH JOURNAL OF SOCIOLOGY 20,2 (1978): 165-171.

Ritual involvement of women permitted but not compelled, resulting in less than fully equal participation. Responses from 21 Canadian Conservative congregations.

320. Rose, Albert (ed.) A PEOPLE AND ITS FAITH: ESSAYS ON JEWS AND REFORM JUDAISM IN A CHANGING CANADA. Toronto: University of Toronto Press, 1959.

321. Rosenberg, Louis. "The Demography of the Jewish Community in Canada." JEWISH JOURNAL OF SOCIOLOGY 1,2 (1959): 217-233.

Canadian census data, 1831-1958, including language, occupations, and demographic variables on Jews.

322. Shaffir, William. "Hassidic Jews and Quebec Politics." JEWISH JOURNAL OF SOCIOLOGY 25,2 (1983): 105-118.

Examination of the reaction of Montreal's two largest Hasidic groups - the Lubavitcher and the Tasher - to the political climate in Quebec during the emergence of Quebec nationalism in the 1970s.

323. Bachi, Roberto. "The Demographic Development of Italian Jewry from the Seventeenth Century." JEWISH JOURNAL OF SOCIOLOGY 4,2 (1962): 172-191.

324. Bensimon, Doris. "Aspects de l'abandon de la pratique religieuse en milieu juif français. Résultats préliminaires d'une inquête." SC 18,3 (1971): 413-425.

A small study of French Jews, demonstrating the difficulty of maintaining Jewish religious practices in the diaspora and in a secularized society. The abandonment of religious practice does not indicate a loss of Jewish identity under such circumstances.

325. Bensimon, Doris, and Françoise Lautman. "Aspects religieux et culturels des mariages entre juifs et chrétiens en France." ETHNIES 4 (1974): 91-116.

1970 survey of 145 mixed (Jewish/Christian) couples in Paris.

326. Bok, Willy. "Entrelacs du religieux et du laic dans les milieux juifs de Belgique." RECHERCHES SOCIOLOGIQUES 16,3 (1985): 333-346.

Overview of Jewish communities and organizations in Belgium.

327. Bronsztejin, Szyja. "The Jewish Population in Poland in 1931." JEWISH JOURNAL OF SOCIOLOGY 6,1 (1964): 3-29.

328. Bronsztejin, Szyja. "A Questionnaire Inquiry into the Jewish Population of Wroclaw." JEWISH JOURNAL OF SOCIOLOGY 7,2 (1965): 246-275.

329. Cohen, Martine. "Renouveaux religieux et individualisme: Le cas du catholicisme et du judaisme en France." SC 36,1 (1989): 33-50.

330. Della Pergola, Sergio. ANATOMIA DELL'EBRAISMO ITALIANO. CARATTERISTICHE DEMOGRAFICHE, ECONOMICHE, SOCIALI, RELIGIOSE E POLITICHE DI UNA MINORANZA. Roma: Beniamino Carucci Ed., 1976.

331. Dunn, Stephen P. "The Roman Jewish Community: A Study in Historical Causation." JEWISH JOURNAL OF SOCIOLOGY 2,2 (1960): 185-201.

Data from a sample of Jewish families in Rome.

332. Engleman, Uriah Z. "Intermarriage among Jews in Switzerland, 1888-1920." AMERICAN JOURNAL OF SOCIOLOGY 34 (1928): 516-523.

Rate of exogamy increased during this period.

333. Ginsberg, Morris. "A Review of the European Jewish Communities Today and Some Questions for Tomorrow." JEWISH JOURNAL OF SOCIOLOGY 6,1 (1964): 118-131.

334. Halevi, H.S. "The Demography of Jewish Communities in Eastern Europe." JEWISH JOURNAL OF SOCIOLOGY 2,1 (1960): 103-109.

Events before and during World War II drastically reduced the Jewish presence in Russia, Poland, Lithuania, and Estonia.

335. Joffe, Natalie F.  "The Dynamics of Benefice among East European Jews."  SOCIAL FORCES 27,3 (1949): 238-247.

Based on interviews conducted in the late 1940s with Jewish immigrants to the U.S.A.

336. Karady, Victor.  "Les conversions des Juifs de Budapest après 1945."  ACTES DE LA RECHERCHE EN SCIENCES SOCIALES 56 (1985): 58-62.

337. Karady, Victor.  "Juifs et Luthériens dans le système scolaire hongrois."  ACTES DE LA RECHERCHE EN SCIENCES SOCIALES 69 (1987): 67-85.

338. Krajzman, Maurice.  "L'image des Juifs et du judaisme dans les manuels d'histoire belges."  REVUE DE L'INSTITUT DE SOCIOLOGIE (Belgium) 1 (1974): 103-132.

339. Ladrière, Paul, and Stéphane Mosès.  "Le Judaïsme dans la culture de l'Europe moderne: avant propos."  ARCHIVES DE SCIENCES SOCIALES DES RELIGIONS 60,1 (1985): 5-10.

General introduction to an issue of the ARCHIVES dedicated to the theme of Judaism in modern European culture.

340. Lestchinsky, Jacob.  "Aspects of the Sociology of Polish Jewry."  JEWISH SOCIAL STUDIES 28,4 (1966): 195-211.

Overview, beginning 1772.

341. Levitte, Georges.  "Impressions of French Jewry Today."  JEWISH JOURNAL OF SOCIOLOGY 2,2 (1960): 172-184.

Observes a high degree of assimilation.

342. Nove, Alec.  "Jews in the Soviet Union."  JEWISH JOURNAL OF SOCIOLOGY 3,1 (1961): 108-120.

Discusses antisemitism and discrimination after the revolution.

343. Raphaël, Freddy.  "La représentation de la mort chez les Juifs d'Alsace."  ARCHIVES DE SCIENCES SOCIALES DES RELIGIONS 39 (1975): 101-117.

Mortuary rites performed by the Jews of Alsace serve to affirm the messianic hope of resurrection in the Promised Land.

344. Scholem, Gerschom.  "Les derniers kabbalistes d'Allemagne."  ARCHIVES DE SCIENCES SOCIALES DES RELIGIONS 60,1 (1985): 9-26.

Explores the elective affinity between kabbalistic mysticism and zionism in eighteenth-century Germany.

345. Silbermann, Alphons.  "Aspekte der öffentlichen Vermittlung der Judentumgeschichte."  SCHWEIZERISCHE ZEITSCHRIFT FÜR SOZIOLOGIE 9,3

(1983): 639-653.

1982 data from West Germany on the meaning of 'Jews' and 'Judaism' for Jews and non-Jews.

346. Tapia, Claude. "North African Jews in Belleville." JEWISH JOURNAL OF SOCIOLOGY 16,1 (1974): 5-23.

Discusses a mostly Tunisian immigrant group in a district of Paris, not successfully integrated into the wider society.

347. Tapia, Claude. "Propositions méthodologiques pour l'étude des comportements religieux - Communautés et pratiques religieuses dans le judaïsme français." ARCHIVES DE SCIENCES SOCIALES DES RELIGIONS 44,1 (1977): 93-101.

Based on research conducted among the Jews who settled in France after the Maghreb countries gained their independence.

348. Tint, Herbert. "The Jews of France." JEWISH JOURNAL OF SOCIOLOGY 1,1 (1959): 127-131.

Review article on Pierre Aubery's MILIEUX JUIFS DE LA FRANCE CONTEM-PORAINE (Paris: Plon, 1957).

349. Vetulani, Adam. "The Jews in Medieval Poland." JEWISH JOURNAL OF SOCIOLOGY 4,2 (1962): 274-294.

350. Yaari, Abraham. "Ner Tamid Societies in Poland and Lithuania." JEWISH SOCIAL STUDIES 21,2 (1959): 118-131.

Examines seventeenth and eighteenth-century Jewish organization.

*GREAT BRITAIN*

351. Brotz, Howard. "The Position of the Jews in English Society." JEWISH JOURNAL OF SOCIOLOGY 1,1 (1959): 94-113.

352. Cohen, Stuart A. "The Reception of Political Zionism in England: Patterns of Alignment among the Clergy and Rabbinate, 1895-1904." JEWISH JOURNAL OF SOCIOLOGY 16,2 (1974): 171-185.

353. Freedman, Maurice. "The Jewish Population of Great Britain." JEWISH JOURNAL OF SOCIOLOGY 4,1 (1962): 92-102.

Discusses difficulties in establishing a demographic description.

354. Krausz, Ernest. "An Anglo-Jewish Community: Leeds." JEWISH JOURNAL OF SOCIOLOGY 3,1 (1961): 88-106.

An examination of the organizational pattern and structure of the third largest Jewish community in Britain.

355. Krausz, Ernest. "Occupation and Social Advancement in Anglo-Jewry."

JEWISH JOURNAL OF SOCIOLOGY 4,1 (1962): 82-90.

Overview based on a review of previously published studies.

356. Krausz, Ernest. LEEDS JEWRY: ITS HISTORY AND SOCIAL STRUCTURE. Cambridge: Heffer, 1964.

357. Krausz, Ernest. "The Edgeware Survey: Demographic Results." JEWISH JOURNAL OF SOCIOLOGY 10,1 (1968): 83-100.

1963 survey on the outskirts of London.

358. Krausz, Ernest. "The Edgeware Survey: Occupation and Social Class." JEWISH JOURNAL OF SOCIOLOGY 11,1 (1969): 75-96.

359. Krausz, Ernest. "The Edgeware Survey: Factors in Jewish Identification." JEWISH JOURNAL OF SOCIOLOGY 11,2 (1969): 151-164.

360. Lipman, V.D. "Synagogal Organization in Anglo-Jewry." JEWISH JOURNAL OF SOCIOLOGY 1,1 (1959): 80-93.

Discusses democratization and reorganization, 1845-1890.

361. Lipman, V.D. "Trends in Anglo-Jewish Occupations." JEWISH JOURNAL OF SOCIOLOGY 2,2 (1960): 202-218.

Shows a Jewish concentration in characteristically immigrant occupations.

362. Lipman, V.D. "Social Topography of a London Congregation: The Bayswater Synagogue, 1863-1963." JEWISH JOURNAL OF SOCIOLOGY 6,1 (1964): 69-74.

Based on membership lists of Bayswater Synagogue.

363. Sharot, Stephen. "Secularization, Judaism and Anglo-Jewry." SOCIOLOGICAL YEARBOOK OF RELIGION IN BRITAIN 4 (1972): 121-140.

364. Sharot, Stephen. "Religious Change in Native Orthodoxy in London, 1870-1914: Rabbinate and Clergy." JEWISH JOURNAL OF SOCIOLOGY 15,2 (1973): 167-187.

Shows contrasts with continental Europe.

365. Sharot, Stephen. "Native Jewry and the Religious Anglicanization of Immigrants in London: 1870-1905." JEWISH JOURNAL OF SOCIOLOGY 16,1 (1974): 39-56.

British Jews promoted the anglicanization of Jewish immigrants.

366. Sharot, Stephen. "The British and American Rabbinate: A Comparison of Authority Structures, Role Definitions and Role Conflicts." SOCIOLOGICAL YEARBOOK OF RELIGION IN BRITAIN 8 (1975): 139-158.

367. Sharot, Stephen. "Instrumental and Expressive Elites in a Religious

Organization: The United Synagogue in London." ARCHIVES DE SCIENCE SOCIALES DES RELIGIONS 43,1 (1977): 141-155.

Tests the fruitfulness of Amitai Etzioni's theory of elite structures by applying it to a Jewish organization formed in 1870.

368. Steinberg, Bernard. "Jewish Schooling in Great Britain." JEWISH JOURNAL OF SOCIOLOGY 6,1 (1964): 52-68.

Historical overview since 1656.

*ISRAEL*

369. Aviad, Janet. RETURN TO JUDAISM. RELIGIOUS RENEWAL IN JERUSALEM. Chicago: University of Chicago Press, 1983.

Study of the conversion of secular Jews to Orthodox Judaism in Jerusalem, especially youth in the 1970s.

370. Bachi, Roberto, and Judah Matras. "Contraception and Induced Abortions among Jewish Maternity Cases in Israel." THE MILBANK MEMORIAL FUND QUARTERLY 40,2 (1962): 207-229.

1959-60 incidence rates are lower for religiously observant women.

371. Capitanchik, David B. "Religion and Politics in Israel." JEWISH JOURNAL OF SOCIOLOGY 27,1 (1985): 29-35.

Discussion of the role of religion in Israeli politics, with a review of some of the literature.

372. Cohen, Percy S. "Alignments and Allegiances in the Community of Shaarayin in Israel." JEWISH JOURNAL OF SOCIOLOGY 4,1 (1962): 14-37.

Study of a Yemeni community within a wider municipal unit (field work, interviews, questionnaire data). Focuses on change stimulated by increased contact with the wider society.

373. Dashefsky, Arnold, and Bernard Lazerwitz. "The Role of Religious Identification in North American Migration to Israel." JSSR 22,3 (1983): 263-275.

Early 1970s data in U.S.A. from those contemplating migration to Israel and from returnees. Religious identification played a role in migration to Israel, but other factors determined decisions to return to the United States.

374. Deshen, Shlomo A. "The Ethnic Synagogue: A Pattern of Religious Change in Israel." In S.N. Eisenstadt (ed.), THE INTEGRATION OF IMMIGRANTS FROM DIFFERENT COUNTRIES OF ORIGIN IN ISRAEL. Jerusalem: Magnes Press, 1969, pp. 66-73.

375. Deshen, Shlomo. "The Varieties of Abandonment of Religious Symbols." JSSR 11,1 (1972): 33-41.

Study of ethnic synagogues in Israel.

376. Etzioni, Amitai. "Kulturkampf ou coalition - le cas d'Israel."
REVUE FRANÇAISE DE SCIENCES POLITIQUES 8 (1958): 311-331.

Consideration of the religious political parties in Israel, 1949-53.

377. Etzioni-Halevy, Eva, and Rina Shapira. "Jewish Identification of
Israeli Students: What Lies Ahead?" JEWISH SOCIAL STUDIES 37 (1975):
251-266.

1966-67 and 1969 questionnaire data from Tel Aviv University students
(before and after the Six Day War).

* Fishman, Aryei. "Judaism and Modernization: The Case of the Religious
Kibbutzim." Cited above as item 267.

378. Gabovitch, B. "Les kibboutsim d'inspiration religieuse." ARCHIVES
DE SOCIOLOGIE DES RELIGIONS 2 (1956): 98-101.

379. Glanz, David, and Michael I. Harrison. "Varieties of Identity Transformation: The Case of the Newly Orthodox Jews." JEWISH JOURNAL OF
SOCIOLOGY 20,2 (1978): 129-141.

Field data and interviews from English-speaking Jews in Jerusalem who
enrolled in institutions designed for the newly Orthodox. The identity
transformations were insufficiently radical to be termed 'conversions'.

380. Hartman, Moshe. "Pronatalistic Tendencies and Religiosity in Israel."
SOCIOLOGY AND SOCIAL RESEARCH 68,2 (1986): 247-258.

Survey of married urban Israeli women up to the age of 55.

381. Katz, Elihu. "Culture and Communication in Israel: The Transformation
of Tradition." JEWISH JOURNAL OF SOCIOLOGY 15,1 (1973): 5-21.

Israeli national sample.

382. Krausz, Ernest, and Mordechai Bar-Lev. "Varieties of Orthodox
Religious Behaviour: A Case Study of Yeshiva High School Graduates
in Israel." JEWISH JOURNAL OF SOCIOLOGY 20,1 (1978): 59-74.

1975 questionnaire data from graduates of 22 Israeli schools.

383. Liebman, Charles S. "Religion and Political Integration in Israel."
JEWISH JOURNAL OF SOCIOLOGY 17,1 (1975): 17-27.

Overview within a civil religion framework.

384. Liebman, Charles S. "Extremism as a Religious Norm." JSSR 22,1
(1983): 75-86.

When extremism is the norm, moderation requires explanation. Application to some Israeli phenomena.

385. Liebman, Charles S., and Eliezer Don-Yehiya. CIVIL RELIGION IN ISRAEL:

POLITICAL CULTURE AND TRADITIONAL JUDAISM IN THE JEWISH STATE.
Berkeley: University of California Press, 1983.

386. Liebman, Charles S., and Eliezer Don-Yehiya. RELIGION AND POLITICS IN
ISRAEL. Bloomington: Indiana University Press, 1984.

387. Matras, Judah. "Religious Observance and Family Formation in Israel:
Some Intergenerational Changes." AMERICAN JOURNAL OF SOCIOLOGY 69
(1964): 464-475.

Religious observance is inversely related to family planning regard-
less of intergenerational changes.

388. Rubin, Nissan. "Death Customs in a Non-religious Kibbutz: The Use of
Sacred Symbols in a Secular Society." JSSR 25,3 (1986): 292-303.

Ideologically-motivated founders of a secular kibbutz created non-
religious ceremonial customs for death. But as ideological fervor
waned, some religious customs began to reappear.

389. Schiff, Garry S. TRADITION AND POLITICS - THE RELIGIOUS PARTIES OF
ISRAEL. Detroit: Wayne State University Press, 1977.

390. Shaffir, William. "The Recruitment of *baalei tshuvah* in a Jerusalem
Yeshiva." JEWISH JOURNAL OF SOCIOLOGY 25,1 (1983): 33-46.

1979-80 field study, using observation, interviews, and a review of
primary literature.

391. Sharot, Stephen, Hannah Ayalon, and Eliezer Ben-Rafael. "Secularization and the Diminishing Decline of Religion." RRR 27,3 (1986): 193-
207.

Study of four ethnic subgroups of Jews in Israel: Moroccan, Iraqi,
Polish, and Rumanian.

392. Shokeid, Moshe. "From Personal Endowment to Bureaucratic Appointment:
The Transition in Israel of the Communal Religious Leaders of Moroccan
Jews." JSSR 19,2 (1980): 105-113.

Observations of Moroccan rabbis in Israel.

393. Tabory, Ephraim. A SOCIOLOGICAL STUDY OF THE REFORM AND CONSERVATIVE
MOVEMENTS IN ISRAEL. Unpublished Ph.D. dissertation, Bar-Ilan
University, Ramat-Gan, Israel, 1980.

394. Tabory, Ephraim. "State and Religion: Religious Conflict among Jews
in Israel." JOURNAL OF CHURCH AND STATE 23,2 (1980): 275-283.

395. Tabory, Ephraim, and Bernard Lazerwitz. "Americans in the Israeli
Reform and Conservative Denominations: Religiosity under an Ethnic
Shield?" RRR 24,3 (1983): 177-187.

Most American Jewish migrants to Israel seek a fuller Jewish life;
few join Reform or Conservative congregations in Israel. Those who do

are committed to a liberal religious orientation and take pride in their American ethnic cultural identity, which they see as innovative and progressive.

396. Weissbrod, Lilly. "Gush Emunim Ideology - From Religious Doctrine to Political Action." MIDDLE EASTERN STUDIES 18,3 (1982): 265-275.

Role of a group of Jewish religious youths, led by Rabbi Kuk Junior, in establishing controversial settlements on the West Bank of the Jordan in the 1970s.

397. Weissbrod, Lilly. "Religion as National Identity in a Secular Society." RRR 24,3 (1983): 188-205.

Discusses the emergence of a religious rather than secular national identity in Israel.

## LATIN AMERICA

398. Centro de Estudios Cristianos. ASPECTOS RELIGIOSOS DE LA SOCIEDAD URUGUAYA. Montevideo: Centro de Estudios Cristianos, 1965.

Jews, Protestants, and Catholics in Uruguay are ranked by education.

399. Dulfano, Mauricio J. "Anti-semitism in Argentina. Patterns of Jewish Adaptation." JEWISH JOURNAL OF SOCIAL STUDIES 31,2 (1969): 122-144.

Renewed antisemitism in Argentina, with the Zionist movement as the current target, has reinforced Jewish insularity.

400. Horowitz, Irving L. "The Jewish Community of Buenos Aires." JEWISH JOURNAL OF SOCIOLOGY 4,2 (1962): 147-171. Also in JEWISH SOCIAL STUDIES 24,4 (1962): 195-222.

Demography, occupational structure, organizations, and cultural context.

401. Lerner, Natan. "A Note on Argentine Jewry Today." JEWISH JOURNAL OF SOCIOLOGY 6,1 (1964): 75-80.

Focuses upon problem of antisemitism.

402. Meisel, Tovye. "The Jews of Mexico." YIVO ANNUAL OF JEWISH SOCIAL SCIENCE 2,3 (1948): 295-312.

Demography, economic structure, education.

403. Rosenwaike, Ira. "The Jewish Population of Argentina. Census and Estimate, 1887-1947." JEWISH SOCIAL STUDIES 22,4 (1960): 195-214.

## UNITED STATES

404. Allinsmith, Wesley, and Beverly Allinsmith. "Religious Affiliation and Politico-economic Attitude." PUBLIC OPINION QUARTERLY 12 (1948):

377–389.

1945–46 U.S. sample; denominational categories.

405. Bannan, Rosemary S. "The Other Side of the Coin: Jewish Student Attitudes toward Catholics and Protestants." SA 26,1 (1965): 21–29.

Survey in high schools in a midwestern city in the United States.

406. Bardis, Panos. "Familism among Jews in Suburbia." SOCIAL SCIENCE 36,3 (1961): 190–196.

Interview data from a sample of 80 Jewish couples from a suburb of a major midwestern metropolis in the U.S.A.

407. Barron, Milton L. "The Incidence of Jewish Intermarriage in Europe and America." AMERICAN SOCIOLOGICAL REVIEW 11,1 (1946): 6–13.

Data from Derby, Connecticut, and review of the literature on Jewish-gentile intermarriage in Europe, Canada, and the United States. There is no evidence of an increasing rate of exogamy for Jews.

408. Blass, Jerome H. "Role Preferences among Jewish Seminarians." SA 38,1 (1977): 59–64.

Provides cross-denominational comparison.

409. Blau, Joseph L. "Alternatives within Contemporary American Judaism." In William G. McLoughlin and Robert N. Bellah (eds.), RELIGION IN AMERICA. Boston: Beacon, 1968, pp. 299–311.

410. Blau, Joseph L. JUDAISM IN AMERICA: FROM CURIOSITY TO THIRD FAITH. Chicago: University of Chicago Press, 1976.

411. Bock, Geoffrey E. THE JEWISH SCHOOLING OF AMERICAN JEWS: A STUDY OF NON-COGNITIVE EDUCATIONAL EFFECTS. Unpublished Ed.D. dissertation, Harvard University, 1976. [DA 37:7 A, p. 4628]

U.S. sample – National Jewish Population Survey.

412. Braude, Lee. "The Rabbi: Some Notes on Identity Clash." JEWISH SOCIAL STUDIES 22,1 (1960): 43–52.

Interviews with 17 rabbis – 7 Reform, 6 Conservative, 4 Orthodox – focusing on conflicting role expectations.

413. Braude, Lee. "Professional Autonomy and the Role of the Layman." SOCIAL FORCES 39,4 (1961): 297–301.

Interviews with 24 Chicago-area rabbis, interpreted with the concepts of 'license' and 'mandate.' License is a role acquisition, mandate an authority over others. As lay people acquire formerly rare license qualifications, rabbis seek mandates, largely as counsellors with skills in applied psychology.

414. Brodbar-Nemzer, Jay. "The Contemporary American Jewish Family." In

Darwin L. Thomas (ed.), THE RELIGION AND FAMILY CONNECTION: SOCIAL
SCIENCE PERSPECTIVES. Provo, Utah: Religious Studies Center, Brigham
Young University, 1988, pp. 66-87.

415. Brownstein, Henry H.  CHANGE IN THE FUNCTION OF SOCIAL INSTITUTIONS:
THE CASE OF THE SYNAGOGUE.  Unpublished Ph.D. dissertation, Temple
University, 1977.  [DA 38:4 A, p. 2355]

Interview data from functionaries, especially rabbis, of 39 synagogues
in the Philadelphia metropolitan area, as well as documentary research.
Findings emphasize the diversity of change trajectories.

416. Burnham, Kenneth E., John F. Connors III, and Richard C. Leonard.  "Religious Affiliation, Church Attendance, Religious Education and Student
Attitudes toward Race."  SA 30,4 (1969): 235-244.

A college student sample.  Catholics were less tolerant of blacks than
Protestants, the latter slightly less tolerant than Jews;  those
claiming no religion were most tolerant.

417. Carlin, Jerome E., and Saul H. Mendlovitz.  "The American Rabbi: A
Religious Specialist Responds to Loss of Authority."  In Marshall
Sklare (ed.), THE JEWS: SOCIAL PATTERNS OF AN AMERICAN GROUP.  Glen-
coe, Illinois: Free Press, 1960, pp. 377-414.

418. Cavan, Ruth Shonle.  "Jewish Student Attitudes toward Interreligious
and Intra-Jewish Marriage."  AMERICAN JOURNAL OF SOCIOLOGY 76,6
(1971): 1064-1071.

1966 university-student data from two middle-west U.S. institutions.
Reform Jews were more willing to enter interfaith marriages than were
Conservative Jews.

419. Christopherson, Victor A., and James Walters.  "Response of Protestants, Catholics, and Jews Concerning Marriage and Family Life."
SOCIOLOGY AND SOCIAL RESEARCH 43,1 (1958): 16-22.

Questionnaire data from white, single, female undergraduate students,
aged 18-23 and beyond the freshman year, who were asked about interfaith dating and marriage, relationships with their families, sex
roles in the family, and desired family size.

420. Cohen, Steven M.  "The Impact of Jewish Education on Religious Identification and Practice."  JEWISH SOCIAL STUDIES 36,3-4 (1974): 316-
326.

1969 questionnaire data from Jewish students at Columbia University,
on eight Jewish practices in the home and four anticipated observances.  Formal Jewish education had little impact but rather correlated
with measures of Jewish identity and knowledge of Hebrew.

421. Dashefsky, Arnold, and Irving M. Levine.  "The Jewish Family: Continuity and Change."  In William V. D'Antonio and Joan Aldous (eds.),
FAMILIES AND RELIGIONS. CONFLICT AND CHANGE IN MODERN SOCIETY.

Beverly Hills, California: Sage, 1983, pp. 163-190.

The focus is on Jewish family life in the United States, approached from a longitudinal perspective.

422. Dashefsky, Arnold, and Howard M. Shapiro. ETHNIC IDENTIFICATION AMONG AMERICAN JEWS: SOCIALIZATION AND SOCIAL STRUCTURE. Lexington, Mass.: Lexington (Heath), 1974.

423. Dukar, Abraham G. "Notes on Culture of American Jewry." JEWISH JOURNAL OF SOCIOLOGY 2,1 (1960): 98-102.

American culture is primary, Jewish secondary.

424. Elazar, Daniel J. "Patterns of Jewish Organization in the United States." In Ross P. Scherer (ed.), AMERICAN DENOMINATIONAL ORGANIZA-TION. A SOCIOLOGICAL VIEW. Pasadena, California: William Carey Library, 1980, pp. 130-149.

425. Elazar, Daniel J., and Rela Geffen Monson. "The Synagogue Havurah - An Experiment in Restoring Adult Fellowship to the Jewish Community." JEWISH JOURNAL OF SOCIOLOGY 21,1 (1979): 67-80.

1975 survey of U.S. rabbis representing all branches of Judaism. Havurot (small fellowship communities) existed in 20% of congregations, especially in the West, in suburbs, and among Reform and Conservative congregations.

426. Engleman, Uriah Z. "The Jewish Synagogue in the United States." AMERICAN JOURNAL OF SOCIOLOGY 41 (1935): 44-51.

427. Engleman, Uriah Z. "Jewish Statistics in the U.S. Census of Religious Bodies (1850-1936)." JEWISH SOCIAL STUDIES 9,2 (1947): 127-174.

428. Featherman, David L. "The Socioeconomic Achievement of White Religio-ethnic Subgroups: Social and Psychological Explanations." AMERICAN SOCIOLOGICAL REVIEW 36,2 (1971): 207-222.

Data from male respondents from native, white, two-child families in seven U.S. metropolitan areas, 1957-67.

429. Friedman, Norman L. "Jewish or Professorial Identity? The Prioriza-tion Process in Academic Situations." SA 32,3 (1971): 149-157.

Responses of American Jewish academics about whether to work on Yom Kippur.

430. Furman, Frida Kerner. "Ritual as Social Mirror and Agent of Cultural Change: A Case Study in Synagogue Life." JSSR 20,3 (1981): 228-241.

Case study of a Reform synagogue with focus upon two culturally disparate rituals.

431. Furman, Frida Kerner. BEYOND YIDDISHKEIT. THE STRUGGLE FOR JEWISH IDENTITY IN A REFORM SYNAGOGUE. Albany, N.Y.: State University of

New York Press, 1987.

1978 ethnographic study in a western metropolis in the U.S.

432. Gans, Herbert J. "American Jewry: Present and Future." COMMENTARY 21 (1956): 422-430, 555-563.

433. Gephart, Jerry C., Michael A. Siegel, and James E. Fletcher. "A Note on Liberalism and Alienation in Jewish Life." JEWISH SOCIAL STUDIES 36,3-4 (1974): 327-329.

Questionnaire data from Salt Lake City Jews, on the proposed merger of Reform and Conservative congregations. Opposition expressed by Reform males.

434. Glassner, Barry, and Bruce Berg. "How Jews Avoid Alcohol Problems." AMERICAN SOCIOLOGICAL REVIEW 45,4 (1980): 647-664.

Data from a detailed study of Jews in an American community highlight informal social control.

435. Glazer, Nathan. "The Jewish Revival in America." COMMENTARY 20 (1955): 493-499; 21 (1956): 17-24.

Part 1 reviews sociological aspects of the revival; Part 2 religious aspects.

436. Glazer, Nathan. AMERICAN JUDAISM. Chicago: University of Chicago Press, 1957.

437. Gockel, Galen L. "Income and Religious Affiliation: A Regression Analysis." AMERICAN JOURNAL OF SOCIOLOGY 74,6 (1969): 632-647. See Sidney Goldstein, "Comment," pp. 647-649; and G.L. Gockel, "Reply," p. 649.

1962 U.S. sample of male household heads. Focus is on income, occupation, and education.

438. Goldscheider, Calvin. "Nativity, Generation and Jewish Fertility." SA 26,3 (1965): 137-147.

Interview data from Providence, Rhode Island.

439. Goldscheider, Calvin. "Fertility of the Jews." DEMOGRAPHY 4 (1967): 196-209.

Review of previous studies, focusing in particular on twentieth-century Providence, Rhode Island.

440. Goldstein, Sidney. "The Roles of an American Rabbi." SOCIOLOGY AND SOCIAL RESEARCH 38,1 (1953): 32-37.

Examines multiple professional roles, as well as conflicting role expectations.

441. Goldstein, Sidney. "Socioeconomic Differentials among Religious

Groups in the U.S." AMERICAN JOURNAL OF SOCIOLOGY 74,6 (1969): 612-631.

U.S. Bureau of the Census data, 1957.

442. Goldstein, Sidney, and Calvin Goldscheider. JEWISH AMERICANS: THREE GENERATIONS IN A JEWISH COMMUNITY. Englewood Cliffs, N.J.: Prentice-Hall, 1968.

443. Gordon, Leonard, and John W. Hudson. "Emergent White Protestant Student Perception of Jews." JSSR 9,3 (1970): 235-238.

Administration of a survey at Arizona State University, designed to show stereotyping.

444. Gould, Julius. "American Jewry - Some Social Trends." JEWISH JOURNAL OF SOCIOLOGY 3,1 (1961): 55-73.

Literature review.

445. Greeley, Andrew M. "The Religious Behavior of Graduate Students." JSSR 5,1 (1965): 34-40.

N.O.R.C. data (U.S.) of 1961 college graduates who were in top 12 graduate schools.

446. Greeley, Andrew M. "The 'Religious Factor' and Academic Careers: Another Communication." AMERICAN JOURNAL OF SOCIOLOGY 78,5 (1973): 1247-1255.

1969 survey of professors in the United States. Tables compare Protestant, Catholic, and Jewish representations by age group, productivity, and attitudes.

447. Harrison, Michael I., and Bernard Lazerwitz. "Do Denominations Matter?" AMERICAN JOURNAL OF SOCIOLOGY 88,2 (1982): 356-377.

Data from a U.S. national survey of Jews show that denominational differences are substantial and more influential within this highly educated and acculturated minority than commonly assumed.

448. Heilman, Samuel C. SYNAGOGUE LIFE. A STUDY IN SYMBOLIC INTERACTION. Chicago: University of Chicago Press, 1973.

Participant-observation study in a northeastern American city.

449. Heilman, Samuel C. "The Gift of Alms: Face-to-face Almsgiving among Orthodox Jews." URBAN LIFE AND CULTURE 3,4 (1975): 371-395.

Based on participant observation in an urban Orthodox synagogue.

450. Heilman, Samuel C. "Inner and Outer Identities: Sociological Ambivalence among Orthodox Jews." JEWISH SOCIAL STUDIES 39,3 (1977): 227-240.

Modern Orthodox Jews, sharing an outer identity with more tradition-

ally Orthodox counterparts, differ from the latter in their inner
identity.

451. Heilman, Samuel C. "Constructing Orthodoxy." In Thomas Robbins and
Dick Anthony (eds.), IN GODS WE TRUST. New Brunswick, N.J.: Transaction, 1981, pp. 141-157.

Reinterpretation is a mechanism of cultural adaptation.

452. Heilman, Samuel C., and Steven M. Cohen. COSMOPOLITANS AND PAROCHIALS.
MODERN ORTHODOX JEWS IN AMERICA. Chicago: University of Chicago
Press, 1989.

Discusses the strategic adaptation of Orthodox Jews to the cosmopolitan situation of modernity.

453. Helmreich, William B. THE WORLD OF THE YESHIVA. AN INTIMATE PORTRAIT
OF ORTHODOX JEWRY. New York: Free Press, 1982.

1974-75 participant-observation study in a New York City yeshiva, and
1976 interviews with respondents from 22 different yeshivas (n=179).

454. Herberg, Will. PROTESTANT-CATHOLIC-JEW. Garden City, N.Y.: Doubleday, 1955.

455. Herberg, Will. "Integration of the Jew into America's Three-religion
Society." JOURNAL OF CHURCH AND STATE 5,1 (1963): 27-40.

456. Himmelfarb, Harold S. THE IMPACT OF RELIGIOUS SCHOOLING: THE EFFECTS
OF JEWISH EDUCATION UPON ADULT RELIGIOUS INVOLVEMENT. Unpublished
Ph.D. dissertation, University of Chicago, 1974. [DA 36:1 A, p. 551]

Sample of Jewish adults in the Chicago metropolitan area.

457. Himmelfarb, Harold S. "Measuring Religious Involvement." SOCIAL
FORCES 53,4 (1975): 606-618.

Factor analysis of data gathered from a sample of Jewish adults in
Chicago. In contrast to Christianity, behavioral rather than
ideational dimensions account for most of the total variance in
religious involvement.

458. Himmelfarb, Harold S. "The Interaction Effects of Parents, Spouse and
Schooling: Comparing the Impact of Jewish and Catholic Schools."
SOCIOLOGICAL QUARTERLY 18,4 (1977): 464-477.

Survey of Chicago area Jews. The main effect of Jewish schooling
seems to be an accentuation in adulthood of the religiosity of one's
parents.

459. Himmelfarb, Harold S. "The Non-linear Impact of Schooling: Comparing
Different Types and Amount of Jewish Education." SOCIOLOGY OF EDUCA-
TION 50,2 (1977): 114-129.

Survey of Chicago area Jews. Supplementary Jewish schooling seems not to have much of a lasting impact.

460. Himmelfarb, Harold S. "Agents of Religious Socialization among American Jews." SOCIOLOGICAL QUARTERLY 20,4 (1979): 477-494.

Path model of religious socialization, applied to data from a Chicago sample of Jewish adults. Parental influences tend to be more indirect than direct, mainly channeling other influences. Religious schooling has both substantial direct and indirect effects. Adult experiences are often more important than childhood ones in the socialization process.

461. Himmelfarb, Harold S. "The Study of American Jewish Identification: How it is Defined, Measured, Obtained, Sustained and Lost." JSSR 19,1 (1980): 48-60.

Review of recent research trends.

462. Himmelfarb, Harold S., and R. Michael Loar. "National Trends in Jewish Ethnicity: A Test of the Polarization Hypothesis." JSSR 23,2 (1984): 140-154.

National Jewish Population Study data (U.S.). The polarization hypothesis holds that young Orthodox have increased Jewish identification and their non-Orthodox counterparts decreased. Results show that Orthodoxy has held membership across generations more successfully, but that no differences in strength of identification have occurred by age within membership categories.

463. Homola, Michael, Dean Knudsen, and Harvey Marshall. "Religion and Socio-economic Achievement." JSSR 26,2 (1987): 201-217.

1972-80 N.O.R.C. (U.S.) surveys.

464. Homola, Michael, Dean Knudsen, and Harvey Marshall. "Status Attainment and Religion: A Reevaluation." RRR 29,3 (1988): 242-258.

1972-80 N.O.R.C. (U.S.) data.

465. Jacks, Irving. "Attitudes toward Interfaith Heterosexual Socializing in a Group of Jewish Teenagers." RRR 9 (1968): 182-188.

Based upon 1965 questionnaire data; sample consists of 225 Jewish teenagers in a middle-sized city in Pennsylvania.

466. Kelly, James R. "The Spirit of Ecumenism: How Wide, How Deep, How Mindful of Truth?" RRR 20,2 (1979): 180-194.

New Jersey survey of ministers, priests, and rabbis; wide support for ecumenism in general, but little reading of literature from outside one's own denomination; disagreement over what issues are really divisive.

467. Kramer, Judith R., and Seymour Leventman. CHILDREN OF THE GILDED GHETTO. New Haven: Yale University Press, 1961.

468. Lasker, Arnold A. "Motivations for Attending High Holy Day Services."
JSSR 10,3 (1971): 241-248.

1967 sample from three Conservative synagogues in one locality, and
respondents of Orthodox and Reform persuasions. Jewish identity was
found to be an important reason.

469. Laumann, Edward O. "The Social Structure of Religious and Ethno-
religious Groups in a Metropolitan Community." AMERICAN SOCIOLOGICAL
REVIEW 34,2 (1969): 182-197.

1966 Detroit-area interviews with a sample of native-born white men,
aged 21-64. Focus is on communality among various religious-ethnic
groupings. Some denominational labels are not comparable to those
used in other studies.

470. Lavender, Abraham. "Studies of Jewish College Students: A Review and
a Replication." JEWISH SOCIAL STUDIES 39,1-2 (1977): 37-52.

1949 and 1971 University of Maryland Jewish student surveys.

471. Lazerwitz, Bernard. "Religion and Social Structure in the United
States." In L. Schneider (ed.), RELIGION, CULTURE AND SOCIETY [volume
cited in item 307], pp. 426-439.

1957-58 U.S. data, civilian population aged 21 and over; education,
occupation, income, worship service attendance, social participation;
some cross-tabulations; 8 denominational categories.

472. Lazerwitz, Bernard. "Contrasting the Effects of Generation, Class,
Sex, and Age on Group Identification in the Jewish and Protestant
Communities." SOCIAL FORCES 49,1 (1970): 50-59.

Both Protestant and Jewish upper-status younger members reject
traditional acts and beliefs but maintain an interest in improved
religious education for their children and in religio-ethnic
organizations. 1966-67 Chicago-area interview data.

473. Lazerwitz, Bernard. "The Community Variable in Jewish Identification." JSSR 16,4 (1977): 361-369.

Data from the National Jewish Population Survey (U.S., 1970-72) show
locality of residence as an important variable correlated with
strength of identity.

474. Lazerwitz, Bernard. "Past and Future Trends in the Size of American
Jewish Denominations." JOURNAL OF REFORM JUDAISM 26,3 (1979): 77-83.

Based on the 1971 National Jewish Population Survey.

475. Lazerwitz, Bernard. "Jewish-Christian Marriages and Conversion."
JEWISH SOCIAL STUDIES 43,1 (1981): 31-46.

Based on the 1971 National Jewish Population Survey.

476. Lazerwitz, Bernard, and Michael Harrison. "American Jewish Denomina-

tions: A Social and Religious Profile." AMERICAN SOCIOLOGICAL REVIEW 44,4 (1979): 656-666.

Data from the National Jewish Population Survey. Ranking of denominations by level of religious and ethnic identification: Orthodoxy, Conservative Judaism, Reform, none. Differences in socioeconomic status have been reduced; tendency of earlier generations toward Orthodoxy remain.

477. Lazerwitz, Bernard, and Michael Harrison. "A Comparison of Denominational Identification and Membership." JSSR 19,4 (1980): 361-367.

Data from National Jewish Population Survey.

478. Levine, Betty C. "Religious Commitment and Integration into a Jewish Community in the United States." RRR 27,4 (1986): 328-343.

Jewish religious commitment furthers integration into a local Jewish community (Indianapolis sample).

479. Liebman, Charles S. "Changing Social Characteristics of Orthodox, Conservative and Reform Jews." SA 27,4 (1966): 210-222.

New York metropolitan area census-tract data for new synagogues and synagogue expansions are used to show that socioeconomic status differences among Jewish denominations have not narrowed; however, the S.E.S. span of each denomination has widened.

480. Liebman, Charles S. THE AMBIVALENT AMERICAN JEW: POLITICS, RELIGION AND FAMILY IN AMERICAN JEWISH LIFE. Philadelphia: Jewish Publication Society of America, 1973.

481. Liebman, Charles S. DECEPTIVE IMAGES: TOWARD A REDEFINITION OF AMERICAN JUDAISM. New Brunswick, N.J.: Transaction, 1988.

482. Lowi, Theodore. "Southern Jews: The Two Communities." JEWISH JOURNAL OF SOCIOLOGY 6,1 (1964): 103-117.

Study of one town in the Deep South, having an 'old' Jewish community of southern background and a 'new' one of northern background.

483. McMurray, Martha. "Religion and Women's Sex Role Traditionalism." SOCIOLOGICAL FOCUS 11,2 (1978): 81-95.

1964 female respondents in a N.O.R.C. (U.S.) sample of college and university students.

484. Mayer, Albert J., and Harry Sharp. "Religious Preference and Worldly Success." AMERICAN SOCIOLOGICAL REVIEW 27,2 (1962): 218-227.

1954-59 greater-Detroit samples. With sufficient controls of background factors, it is shown that the economic achievements of Catholics, mainstream Protestants, and Jews are comparable.

485. Mayer, Egon. "Jewish Orthodoxy in America: Towards the Sociology of a Residual Category." JEWISH JOURNAL OF SOCIOLOGY 15,2 (1973): 151-165.

Suggests that Orthodox never have conceived themselves as a cognitive minority.

486. Mayer, Egon. FROM SUBURB TO SHTETL: THE JEWS OF BORO PARK. Philadelphia: Temple University Press, 1979.

1972-73 community study in the Boro Park area of Brooklyn, New York.

487. Mayer, Egon. LOVE AND TRADITION: MARRIAGE BETWEEN JEWS AND CHRISTIANS. New York: Plenum, 1985.

Review of previous studies, and some original data from religiously mixed couples.

488. Mayer, John E. JEWISH-GENTILE COURTSHIPS. AN EXPLORATORY STUDY OF A SOCIAL PROCESS. Glencoe: Free Press, 1961.

Interviews with religiously-mixed couples who at first were reluctant to cross ethnic lines.

489. Mechanic, David. "Religion, Religiosity, and Illness Behavior: The Special Case of the Jews." HUMAN ORGANIZATION 22,3 (1963): 202-208.

Data from university students at two institutions. Jewish students, especially those of upper-class background, exhibit higher rates of illness behavior.

490. Mueller, Charles W. "Evidence on the Relationship between Religion and Educational Attainment." SOCIOLOGY OF EDUCATION 53,3 (1980): 140-152.

1973-78 N.O.R.C. (U.S.) data. Religion in which respondents were raised is used as a variable, rather than current religion. No substantial religious effects, beginning with the 1908 birth cohort.

491. Mueller, Charles W., and Weldon T. Johnson. "Socioeconomic Status and Religious Participation." AMERICAN SOCIOLOGICAL REVIEW 40,6 (1975): 785-800.

1970 U.S. adult sample. Socioeconomic status and religious participation correlate positively but weakly only for Protestants, especially males. They correlate negatively for Jews.

492. Newman, William M., and Peter L. Halvorson. "American Jews: Patterns of Geographic Distribution and Change, 1952-1971." JSSR 18,2 (1979): 183-193.

American Jews moved to new areas within the United States, but remained overwhelmingly metropolitan and concentrated in the most pluralistic parts of the nation.

493. O'Dea, Thomas F. "The Changing Image of the Jew and the Contemporary Religious Situation: An Exploration of Ambiguities." In Charles H. Stember et al. (eds.), JEWS IN THE MIND OF AMERICA. New York: Basic, 1966, pp. 302-322. Reprinted in Thomas F. O'Dea, SOCIOLOGY AND THE STUDY OF RELIGION. THEORY, RESEARCH, INTERPRETATION. New York:

Basic, 1970, pp. 155-179.

A consideration of U.S. survey data in the context of the sweep of Western history.

494. Piazza, Thomas. "Jewish Identity and the Counterculture." In C.Y. Glock and R.N. Bellah (eds.), THE NEW RELIGIOUS CONSCIOUSNESS [volume cited in item 75], pp. 245-264.

1970-71 University of California, Berkeley, freshman male sample.

495. Pinsky, Irving I. A FOLLOW-UP STUDY OF THE GRADUATES OF ONE OF THE OLDEST EXISTING AMERICAN JEWISH DAY SCHOOLS: THE RABBI JACOB JOSEPH SCHOOL. Unpublished Ph.D. dissertation, Western Reserve University, 1961.

496. Pollack, George. GRADUATES OF JEWISH DAY SCHOOLS: A FOLLOW-UP STUDY. Unpublished Ph.D. dissertation, Western Reserve University, 1961.

497. Polsky, Howard W. "A Study of Orthodoxy in Milwaukee: Social Characteristics, Beliefs, and Observances." In M. Sklare (ed.), THE JEWS: SOCIAL PATTERNS OF AN AMERICAN GROUP [volume cited in item 417], pp. 325-335.

1955-56 interview data.

498. Reissman, Leonard. "The New Orleans Jewish Community." JEWISH JOURNAL OF SOCIOLOGY 4,1 (1962): 110-123.

Demographic and attitudinal data from a sample of known Jewish households show three subcommunities.

499. Rhodes, A. Lewis, and Charles B. Nam. "The Religious Context of Educational Expectations." AMERICAN SOCIOLOGICAL REVIEW 35,2 (1970): 253-267.

1965 U.S. sample of teenage whites, focusing on plans to attend college. Categories are Jewish, Catholic, Baptist, and other Protestant.

500. Robbins, Richard. "American Jews and American Catholics: Two Types of Social Change." SA 26,1 (1965): 1-17. See Thomas F. O'Dea, "Comment," SA 26,1 (1965): 18-20; Jacob Neusner, "Comment," SA 26,3 (1965): 166-168; and R. Robbins, "Reply," SA 26,3 (1965): 168-170.

Comparison of the respective trajectories of the two groupings.

501. Roof, Wade Clark. "Socioeconomic Differentials among White Socioreligious Groups in the United States." SOCIAL FORCES 58,1 (1979): 280-289. See Andrew M. Greeley, "Comment," 59,3 (1981): 824-830; and W.C. Roof, "Reply," 59,3 (1981): 831-836.

1972-76 N.O.R.C. (U.S.) data. Nine denominational categories, with ethnic subsamples of Catholics.

502. Rosen, Bernard C. "Minority Group in Transition: A Study of Adoles-
     cent Religious Conviction and Conduct." In M. Sklare (ed.), THE JEWS:
     SOCIAL PATTERNS OF AN AMERICAN GROUP [volume cited in item 417], pp.
     336-346.

     1950-51 data from youth in Philadelphia and Elmira, New York.

503. Rosenthal, Erich. "The Jewish Population of the United States: A
     Demographic and Sociological Analysis." In Bernard Martin (ed.),
     MOVEMENTS AND ISSUES IN AMERICAN JUDAISM. Westport, Connecticut:
     Greenwood Press, 1978, pp. 25-62.

     Review of data, mostly 1957-70.

504. Rosenwaike, Ira. "The Utilization of Census Tract Data in the Study
     of the American Jewish Population." JEWISH SOCIAL STUDIES 25,1
     (1963): 42-56.

     Illustrative study using 1935 Cincinnati, Ohio (Hamilton County) data,
     making comparisons with 1940 federal census data.

505. Rubinstein, Judah. "Jewish Day of Atonement Census Studies." RRR 5
     (1963): 30-39.

     Provides a rationale and assessment of the Yom Kippur survey in
     Cleveland.

506. Rudavsky, David. "Religion and Religiosity in American Jewish Life."
     JOURNAL OF EDUCATIONAL SOCIOLOGY 33,6 (1960): 314-320.

     1953 sample of Conservative synagogue officials and board members.

507. Sandberg, Neil C. JEWISH LIFE IN LOS ANGELES: A WINDOW ON TOMORROW.
     Lanham, Maryland: University Press of America, 1986.

     Interview data from a sample of Los Angeles-area Jewish households
     (mid-1970s).

508. Schmidt, Nancy J. "An Orthodox Jewish Community in the United States:
     A Minority within a Minority." JEWISH JOURNAL OF SOCIOLOGY 7,2
     (1965): 176-206.

     1960-62 ethnography of a community associated with an Orthodox Torah
     school.

509. Shapiro, Howard M. "Jewish Identification and Intellectuality: A Two
     Generation Analysis." SA 33,4 (1972): 230-238.

     Sample of Jewish males in St. Paul, Minnesota. Older respondents
     evinced a positive correlation between strength of Jewish identity and
     scores on the 'thinking introversion' scale of the Omnibus Personality
     Inventory.

510. Shapiro, Howard M., and Arnold Dashefsky. "Religious Education and
     Ethnic Identification: Implications for Ethnic Pluralism." RRR 15,2
     (1974): 93-102.

Argues that Jewish education furthers Jewish identity.

511. Sharot, Stephen. "The Three-generations Thesis and the American Jews." BRITISH JOURNAL OF SOCIOLOGY 24,2 (1973): 151-164.

Review of previous studies; contrary to W. Herberg's thesis, the third generation of American Jews did not return to traditional ethnic religion.

* Sharot, Stephen. "The British and American Rabbinate: A Comparison of Authority Structures, Role Definitions and Role Conflicts." Cited above as item 366.

512. Sklare, Marshall. CONSERVATIVE JUDAISM: AN AMERICAN RELIGIOUS MOVEMENT. Glencoe: Free Press, 1955.

513. Sklare, Marshall. "The Sociology of the American Synagogue." SC 18,3 (1971): 375-384.

The synagogue is necessary for Jewish identity in the United States in a way that it is not in Israel.

514. Sklare, Marshall. "Jewish Religion and Ethnicity at the Bicentennial." MIDSTREAM: A MONTHLY JEWISH REVIEW 21,9 (1975): 19-28.

515. Slotkin, J.S. "Adjustment in Jewish-Gentile Intermarriages." SOCIAL FORCES 21,2 (1942): 226-230.

Interview study of the adjustment of intermarried couples in Chicago.

516. Steinberg, Bernard. "Jewish Education in the United States: A Study in Religio-ethnic Response." JEWISH JOURNAL OF SOCIOLOGY 21,1 (1979): 5-35.

Historical overview.

517. Steinberg, Stephen. "The Anatomy of Jewish Identification: A Historical and Theoretical View." RRR 7,1 (1965): 1-8.

Concludes that Jewish identity in the United States has been severely weakened by secularization.

518. Steinberg, Stephen. "The Changing Religious Composition of American Higher Education." In C.Y. Glock (ed.), RELIGION IN SOCIOLOGICAL PERSPECTIVE [volume cited in item 189], pp. 102-116.

1969 sample of faculty in U.S. institutions of higher education, supplemented with other data.

519. Steinberg, Stephen. THE ACADEMIC MELTING POT. CATHOLICS AND JEWS IN AMERICAN HIGHER EDUCATION. New York: McGraw-Hill, 1974.

1969 Carnegie Commission Survey on Faculty and Student Opinion data; the data on college and university faculty in 303 U.S. institutions are the principal focus.

520. Stryker, Robin. "Religio-ethnic Effects on Attainments in the Early Career." AMERICAN SOCIOLOGICAL REVIEW 46,2 (1981): 212-231.

1975 follow-up survey of 1957 white high school seniors in Wisconsin, with a Milwaukee subsample, focusing on subsequent education and first job. Categories established by religious and ethnic identities.

521. Warner, W. Lloyd, and Leo Srole. "Assimilation or Survival: A Crisis in the Jewish Community of Yankee City." In M. Sklare (ed.), THE JEWS: SOCIAL PATTERNS OF AN AMERICAN GROUP [volume cited in item 417], pp. 347-356. Also in W. Lloyd Warner and Leo Srole, THE SOCIAL SYSTEM OF AMERICAN ETHNIC GROUPS. New Haven: Yale University Press, 1945, pp. 205-217.

Discussion of events which occurred in the 1930s.

522. Warren, Bruce L. "Socioeconomic Achievement and Religion: The American Case." SOCIOLOGICAL INQUIRY 40,2 (1970): 130-155.

Based on two 1960 U.S. surveys.

523. Weisbrod, Aviva, Martin F. Sherman, and Nancy C. Sherman. "Values as a Function of Religious Commitment in Judaism." JOURNAL OF SOCIAL PSYCHOLOGY 110 (1980): 101-107.

Research in Baltimore on 15 couples from each of three groups - two Orthodox and one Reform.

524. York, Aaron. VOLUNTARY ASSOCIATIONS AND COMMUNAL LEADERSHIP AMONG JEWS OF THE UNITED STATES. Unpublished Ph.D. dissertation, Bar-Ilan University, Ramat-Gan, Israel, 1979.

525. Young, Pauline V. "The Reorganization of Jewish Family Life in America: A Natural History of the Social Forces Governing the Assimilation of the Jewish Immigrant." SOCIAL FORCES 7,2 (1928): 238-244.

General characterization, with some quotations.

526. Zelan, Joseph. "Religious Apostasy, Higher Education, and Occupational Choice." SOCIOLOGY OF EDUCATION 41,4 (1968): 370-379.

1958 N.O.R.C. (U.S.) data from arts and science graduate students, containing a high proportion (25%) of religious 'nones', 80% of whom had been raised in a religion. The pattern is accentuated in elite colleges. Data are presented by religious background.


*BLACK HEBREW NATION*

527. Singer, Merrill. SAINTS OF THE KINGDOM: GROUP EMERGENCE, INDIVIDUAL AFFILIATION, AND SOCIAL CHANGE AMONG THE BLACK HEBREWS OF ISRAEL. Unpublished Ph.D. dissertation, University of Utah, 1979. [DA 40:12 A, p. 6339]

528. Singer, Merrill. "Life in a Defensive Society: The Black Hebrew

Israelites." In Jon Wagner (ed.), SEX ROLES IN CONTEMPORARY AMERICAN COMMUNES. Bloomington, Indiana: Indiana University Press, 1982, pp. 45-81.

Focus on male domination in the Black Hebrew Israelites. 1977-78 participant-observation data collected in Dimona, Arad, and Mitzpe Ramon, all in Israel.

529. Singer, Merrill. "The Social Context of Conversion to a Black Religious Sect." RRR 30,2 (1988): 177-192.

Open-ended life-history interviews with a sample of Black Hebrews in Israel, apparently in 1978.

## HASIDIC

530. Berger, Alan L. "Hasidism and Moonism: Charisma in the Counter-culture." SA 41,4 (1981): 375-390.

Suggests modifications of Weber's conceptualization of charisma, in light of evidence from the Unification Church and from the Hasidim.

531. Bosk, Charles L. "Cybernetic Hasidism: An Essay on Social and Religious Change." SOCIOLOGICAL INQUIRY 44,2 (1974): 131-144.

Hasidism had the advantage of flexibility in its competition with Rabbinism and Messianism in the Jewish communities of eighteenth-century Poland.

532. Bosk, Charles L. "The Routinization of Charisma: The Case of the Zaddik." In H.M. Johnson (ed.), RELIGIOUS CHANGE AND CONTINUITY [volume cited in item 207], pp. 150-167. Also in SOCIOLOGICAL INQUIRY 49 (1979): 150-167.

Historical sociology, using eighteenth and nineteenth-century phenomena.

533. Gutwirth, Jacques. VIE JUIVE TRADITIONELLE: ETHNOLOGIE D'UNE COMMUN-AUTE HASSIDIQUE. Paris: Les Editions de Minuit, 1970.

534. Gutwirth, Jacques. "Les Communautés Hassidiques, sources et trésors pour la sociologie religieuse de la judaïcité." SC 18,3 (1971): 385-397.

The transformation of Hasidism from its Ukrainian mystical origins to its present forms is suggestive for sociological inquiry.

  * Gutwirth, Jacques. "The Structure of a Hassidic Community in Montreal." Cited above as item 315.

535. Gutwirth, Jacques. "Hassidim et judaïcité à Montréal." RECHERCHES SOCIOGRAPHIQUES 14,3 (1973): 291-326.

Unlike other Jews in Montreal, the Hasidim did not opt for Anglophone culture or for Zionism.

536. Pinsker, Sanford. "Piety as Community: The Hasidic View." SOCIAL
RESEARCH 42,2 (1975): 230-246.

Study of the Lubavitcher Hasidim of Crown Heights, Brooklyn, and the
Satmar Hasidim of Williamsburg, Brooklyn.

537. Poll, Solomon. THE HASIDIC COMMUNITY OF WILLIAMSBURG: A STUDY IN THE
SOCIOLOGY OF RELIGION. New York: Schocken, 1969.

538. Sharot, Stephen. "Hasidism and the Routinization of Charisma." JSSR
19,4 (1980): 325-336.

The spread of Hasidism in eastern Europe, late eighteenth and early
nineteenth centuries, is related to the routinization of charisma in
dynasties of *zaddikim*.

539. Zylberberg, Jacques. "Nationalisation et dénationalisation: Le cas
des collectivités sacrales excentriques." SC 31,4 (1984): 409-426.

Consideration of the Jehovah's Witnesses, the Hasidim, and Catholic
Pentecostals in Quebec, Canada.

*LUBAVITCHER*

540. Bauer, Julien. "De la déviance religieuse: Le sous-système hassidique
à Montréal." LES CAHIERS DE RECHERCHES EN SCIENCES DE LA RELIGION 5
(1984): 235-260.

By gaining influence among Montreal Jews, the Lubavitcher risk losing
their specificity.

541. Shaffir, William. LIFE IN A RELIGIOUS COMMUNITY: THE LUBAVITCHER
CHASSIDIM IN MONTREAL. Toronto: Holt, Rinehart and Winston of Canada,
1974.

Participant-observation and interview study, beginning in 1967.

542. Shaffir, William. "Witnessing as Identity Consolidation: The Case of
the Lubavitcher Chassidim." In H. Mol (ed.), IDENTITY AND RELIGION
[volume cited in item 118], pp. 39-57.

Based on participant-observation study in Montreal.

543. Singer, M. "The Use of Folklore in Religious Conversion: The Chasidic
Case." RRR 22,2 (1980): 170-185.

Folklore contributes to the attraction, attachment, and resocialization of the neophyte.

*SEPHARDIC*

544. Elazar, Daniel J. THE OTHER JEWS: THE SEPHARDIM TODAY. New York:
Basic Books, 1989.

# 6
## Islamic

545. Abaza, Mona, and Georg Stauth. "Occidental Reason, Orientalism, Islamic Fundamentalism: A Critique." INTERNATIONAL SOCIOLOGY 3,4 (1988): 343-364.

546. Alexander, Daniel. "Is Fundamentalism an Integrism?" SC 32,4 (1985): 373-392.

    Examines parallels and differences between fundamentalism in Anglo-Saxon countries, Latin integrism, and militant Muslim movements.

547. Arjomand, Said Amir (ed.) FROM NATIONALISM TO REVOLUTIONARY ISLAM. Albany, New York: State University of New York Press, 1984.

548. Arjomand, Said Amir. "Social Change and Movements of Revitalization in Contemporary Islam." In J.A. Beckford (ed.), NEW RELIGIOUS MOVE-MENTS AND RAPID SOCIAL CHANGE [volume cited in item 50], pp. 87-112.

    Discusses the development of communications media and transportation, urbanization, the spread of literacy and education, and tendencies toward national integration.

549. Arjomand, Said Amir. "The Emergence of Islamic Political Ideologies." In James A. Beckford and Thomas Luckmann (eds.), THE CHANGING FACE OF RELIGION. Newbury Park, California: Sage, 1989, pp. 109-123.

550. Austruy, Jacques. L'ISLAM FACE AU DEVELOPPEMENT ECONOMIQUE. Paris: Ed. Ouvrières, 1961.

551. Baccouche, Hachemi. "Dans les pays musulmans: Retour ou recours au sacré?" RECHERCHES SOCIOLOGIQUES 13,1-2 (1982): 131-137.

    Examines religious revival and the permeation of everyday life by Islam.

552. Balic, Smail. "Das Offenbarungsverständnis und der islamische Integralismus." SCHWEIZERISCHE ZEITSCHRIFT FÜR SOZIOLOGIE 9,3 (1983): 717-724.

Modern interpretations of the Koran and other sources thus far have emphasized political rather than spiritual aspects of life, and form rather than content.

553. Bellah, Robert N. "Islamic Tradition and the Problems of Moderniza-
     tion." In R.N. Bellah, BEYOND BELIEF. ESSAYS IN A POST-TRADITIONAL
     WORLD. New York: Harper and Row, 1970, pp. 146-167.

554. Bellah, Robert N. "Islam and the Challenge of Modernity." In Joachim
     Matthes (ed.), INTERNATIONALES JAHRBUCH FÜR RELIGIONSSOZIOLOGIE 6.
     Opladen: Westdeutscher Verlag, 1970, pp. 65-82.

555. Berque, Jacques. "Islam et socialisme." In SOCIOLOGIE DE LA <CON-
     STRUCTION NATIONALE> DANS LES NOUVEAUX ETATS. Bruxelles: Institut
     de Sociologie, 1968, pp. 15-29. Also in REVUE INTERNATIONALE DE
     SOCIOLOGIE 2-3 (1967): 201-215.

556. Berque, Jacques. "Introduction." SC 25,3-4 (1978): 301-313.

     Observations on the relative neglect accorded Islam by social scien-
     tists of religion.

557. Bouhdiba, A. LA SEXUALITE EN ISLAM. Paris: Presses Universitaires
     de France, 1975.

558. Carré, Olivier. "<Intégrisme islamique?>" SC 32,4 (1985): 413-420.

     Discusses parallels between modernizing socialist regimes and Islamic
     protest movements.

559. Charnay, Jean-Paul. "Le marxisme et l'Islam." ARCHIVES DE SOCIOLOGIE
     DES RELIGIONS 10 (1960): 133-146.

     A bibliographic essay.

560. Charnay, Jean-Paul. "Jeux de miroirs et crises de civilisations.
     Réorientations du rapport Islam-Islamologie." ARCHIVES DE SOCIOLOGIE
     DES RELIGIONS 33 (1972): 135-174.

     Critical appraisal of Western Islamic scholarship.

561. Charnay, Jean-Paul. "Préalables épistémologiques a une sociologie
     religieuse de l'Islam." ARCHIVES DE SCIENCES SOCIALES DES RELIGIONS
     37 (1974): 79-86.

     Warns against Western ethnocentrism in the sociological study of Islam.

562. Charnay, Jean-Paul. SOCIOLOGIE RELIGIEUSE DE L'ISLAM. Paris:
     Sindbad, 1977.

563. Chelhod, Joseph. INTRODUCTION A LA SOCIOLOGIE DE L'ISLAM: DE L'ANI-
     MISME A L'UNIVERSALISME. Paris: Editions P. Maisonneuve, 1958.

564. Chelhod, Joseph. "Pour une sociologie de l'Islam." REVUE D'HISTOIRE

ET DE PHILOSOPHIE RELIGIEUSES 40,4 (1960): 367-382.

565. Dobretsberger, Josef. "Les problèmes d'adaptation en Islam. Religion et société industrielle dans les pays mahométans." SC 14,4 (1967): 273-283.

566. Durán, Khálid. "The 'Golden Age Syndrome' - Islamist Medina and Other Historical Models of Contemporary Muslim Thought." SCHWEIZERISCHE ZEITSCHRIFT FÜR SOZIOLOGIE 9,3 (1983): 703-716.

   Seventh-century Medina and alternatives such as Mecca serve as precedent-setting models for contemporary Muslim thought.

567. Eccel, A. Chris. RAPIDLY INCREASING SOCIETAL SCALE AND SECULARIZATION: A CENTURY OF HIGHER MUSLIM EDUCATION AND THE PROFESSIONS IN EGYPT. Unpublished Ph.D. dissertation, University of Chicago, 1978. [DA 39:6 A, p. 3850]

   Historical study of increasing societal complexity as a cause of disruption in religious institutions.

568. Eccel, A. Chris. "The Differential Socio-religious Impact of the Definition of Religious Elites in Christianity and Islam." SC 31,1 (1984): 105-123.

   A critique of E. Gellner [item 573] and development of an etiological argument to account for the respective roles of religious elites in Islam and Christianity.

569. Fathi, Asghar. "The Islamic Pulpit as a Medium of Political Communication." JSSR 20,2 (1981): 163-172.

   Historical analysis reveals the centrality of the Islamic pulpit for the communication of socio-political issues throughout the Muslim world.

570. Freund, Wolfgang S. "Religionssoziologische und sprachstrukturelle Aspekte des Entwicklungsproblems in der islamischen Welt." In Günter Dux, Thomas Luckmann, and Joachim Matthes (eds.), INTERNATIONALES JAHRBUCH FÜR RELIGIONSSOZIOLOGIE 7. Opladen: Westdeutscher Verlag, 1971, pp. 105-125.

   Examines the inner-worldly ethic of Islam and its relationship to the Arabic language.

571. Gandhi, Raj S. "The Economic Ethic of Islam." SOCIOLOGUS 26,1 (1976): 66-75.

   Portrayal of an economic ethic, purportedly based on the Koran.

572. Gardet, Louis. LA CITE MUSULMANE: VIE SOCIALE ET POLITIQUE, second revised edition. Paris: J. Vrin, 1954.

573. Gellner, Ernest. "A Pendulum Swing Theory of Islam." ANNALES MAROCAINES DE SOCIOLOGIE 1 (1968): 5-14. Reprinted in Roland Robertson

(ed.), SOCIOLOGY OF RELIGION. New York: Penguin, 1969, pp. 127-138.

Argues that fragmented tribal groups within Islam make more concessions to the worldly order than do central forms of Islam, despite the latter's greater identification with the larger community.

574. Hamès, Constant. "Deux aspects du fondamentalisme islamique." ARCHIVES DE SCIENCES SOCIALES DES RELIGIONS 50,2 (1980): 177-190.

Discusses tension between reformism and fundamentalism in the contemporary Muslim world.

575. Henry, Paget. "Indigenous Religions and the Transformation of Peripheral Societies." In J.K. Hadden and A. Shupe (eds.), PROPHETIC RELIGIONS AND POLITICS [volume cited in item 197], pp. 123-150.

General discussion featuring as examples the Rastafarians, Liberation Theology, and Islamic revivalism.

576. Hermassi, Elbaki. "Politics and Culture in the Middle East." SC 25,3 -4 (1978): 445-464.

The nation state is a foreign innovation in the context of Islam and other critical factors of middle-east culture.

577. Iqbal, S.M. "Political Thought in Islam." SOCIOLOGICAL REVIEW 1,3 (1908): 249-261.

578. Kedourie, Elie. "Islam and Orientalists: Some Recent Discussions." BRITISH JOURNAL OF SOCIOLOGY 7,3 (1956): 217-225.

579. Lemercinier, Geneviève. "Aspects sociologiques de la genèse de l'Islam." SC 25,3-4 (1978): 359-369.

Islam began as a social protest movement with a strong egalitarian component, but generated new religious meanings and roles when it achieved political power.

580. Levy, Reuben. THE SOCIAL STRUCTURE OF ISLAM. New York: Cambridge University Press, 1957.

581. Lewy, Guenter. "Changing Conceptions of Political Legitimacy: Abandonment of Theocracy in the Islamic World." In David Spitz (ed.), POLITICAL THEORY AND SOCIAL CHANGE. New York: Aldine-Atherton, 1967, pp. 91-116.

  * Lewy, Guenter. RELIGION AND REVOLUTION. Cited above as item 34.

582. Marthelot, Pierre. "L'Islam et le développement. Essai sur quelques publications récentes." ARCHIVES DE SOCIOLOGIE DES RELIGIONS 14 (1962): 131-138.

Particular attention is accorded GEOGRAPHIE ET RELIGIONS by P. Deffontaines (Paris: Gallimard, 1948).

583. Montague, Joel. "Islam et planning familial. La fin du commencement." CULTURES ET DEVELOPPEMENT 7,1 (1975): 131-140.

Overview of a debate.

584. Rodinson, Maxime. "La vie de Mahomet et le problème sociologique des origines de l'Islam." DIOGENES 20 (1957): 37-64.

585. Rodinson, Maxime. "Mahomet et les origines de l'Islam." CAHIERS RATIONALISTES 164 (1957): 173-183.

586. Rodinson, Maxime. "Sociology of Islam." ANNEE SOCIOLOGIQUE (1960): 362-374.

Review of a number of recent books.

587. Rodinson, Maxime. "Une étude sur l'Islam." ARCHIVES DE SOCIOLOGIE DES RELIGIONS 15 (1963): 137-143.

Review essay on W. Montgomery Watt's ISLAM AND THE INTEGRATION OF SOCIETY (London: Routledge and Kegan Paul, 1961).

588. Rodinson, Maxime. "Le poids de l'Islam sur le développement économique et social." FRERES DU MONDE 33,1 (1965): 9-20.

589. Rodinson, Maxime. MAHOMET. Paris: Ed. du Seuil, 1968.

590. Rodinson, Maxime. ISLAM E CAPITALISMO. Torino: Einaudi, 1968. See also ISLAM AND CAPITALISM, translated by Brian Pearce. Austin: University of Texas Press, 1978.

591. Rodinson, Maxime. MARXISME ET MONDE MUSULMAN. Paris: Seuil, 1972.

592. Rosenthal, Erwin I.J. ISLAM IN THE MODERN NATIONAL STATE. London: Cambridge University Press, 1965.

593. Saiedi, Nader. "What is Islamic Fundamentalism?" In J.K. Hadden and A. Shupe (eds.), PROPHETIC RELIGIONS AND POLITICS [volume cited in item 197], pp. 173-195.

594. Shaktir, Moin. "Status of Women: Islamic View." SOCIAL SCIENTIST (India) 4,7 (1976): 70-75.

Review of the teachings of Mohammed.

595. Shariati, Ali. ON THE SOCIOLOGY OF ISLAM. Berkeley, 1979.

596. Siddique, Sharon. "Conceptualizing Contemporary Islam: Religion or Ideology?" ANNUAL REVIEW OF THE SOCIAL SCIENCES OF RELIGION 5 (1981): 203-223.

597. Simson, Uwe. "Der Islam: ein Träger politischer Ideen?" SCHWEIZERISCHE ZEITSCHRIFT FÜR SOZIOLOGIE 9,3 (1983): 677-686.

Claims that there exists no connection between religious and social codes in Islam. Islam has been used for post hoc legitimation, and hence cannot be used for predictive purposes by social scientists.

598. Simson, Uwe. "Islam, legitimität und entwicklung." ÖSTERREICHISCHE ZEITSCHRIFT FÜR SOZIOLOGIE 11 (1986): 120-128.

599. Tamney, Joseph B. "Church-State Relations in Christianity and Islam." RRR 16,1 (1974): 10-18.

Questionnaire data from university students in the Philippines, Indonesia, and Singapore, 1969-70. Muslims favor cooperation between religion and the state. Catholics hold no consistent position, varying between national samples and even within them. Protestants in Indonesia accept that nation's model of church-state cooperation, but they do so less in Singapore.

600. Tibi, Bassam. "Die gegenwärtige politische Revitalisierung des Islam: Eine religionssoziologische Bedeutung." SCHWEIZERISCHE ZEITSCHRIFT FÜR SOZIOLOGIE 9,3 (1983): 677-686.

Islamic symbolism has been used against rapid social change. But the idea of al-nizam al-Islami (the Islamic system) as an alternative to existing secular structures has no basis in Islamic sacred sources and has actually been adopted from the West.

601. Tomasi, Luigi. "Il mondo islamico oggi." AGGIORNAMENTI SOCIALI 37,7 (1987): 533-552.

602. Turner, Bryan S. WEBER AND ISLAM. A CRITICAL STUDY. London: Routledge and Kegan Paul, 1974.

603. Turner, Bryan S. "Islam, Capitalism and the Weber Theses." BRITISH JOURNAL OF SOCIOLOGY 25,2 (1974): 230-243.

Critique of Weber's analyses of Islam.

604. Turner, Bryan S. "Orientalism, Islam and Capitalism." SC 25,3-4 (1978): 371-394.

Argues that Orientalism is not a fruitful model for conceptualizing the historic relationship between Islamic societies and capitalism.

605. Turner, Bryan S. "Une interprétation des représentations occidentales de l'Islam." SC 31,1 (1984): 91-104.

Argues that Western scholarship of Islam has been characteristically invidious and ideological.

606. Waardenburg, Jacques. "Official and Popular Religion in Islam." SC 25,3-4 (1978): 315-341.

The tension which exists between normative and popular Islam has not been experienced by Muslims as a failure of their religion but rather as an indication of human weakness.

607. Waardenburg, Jacques. "The Puritan Pattern in Islamic Revival Movements." SCHWEIZERISCHE ZEITSCHRIFT FÜR SOZIOLOGIE 9,3 (1983): 687-702.

On the basis of recent Islamic revival movements, a 'puritan' ideal type of ethos is proposed.

608. Watt, W. Montgomery. ISLAM AND THE INTEGRATION OF SOCIETY. London: Routledge and Kegan Paul, 1961.

609. Zubaida, Sami. "Economic and Political Activism in Islam." ECONOMY AND SOCIETY 1,3 (1972): 308-338.

Discusses the reasons underlying the failure of the urban Muslim bourgeoisie to achieve political dominance and autonomy.


## ALGERIA

610. Faouzi, Adel. "Islam, réformisme et nationalisme dans la résistance à la colonisation française en Algérie (1830-1930)." SC 25,3-4 (1978): 419-432.

Argues that Islam obscured class consciousness by legitimating first the colonial government and subsequently the nationalist movement.

611. Gellner, Ernest. "The Unknown Apollo of Biskra: The Social Base of Algerian Puritanism." GOVERNMENT AND OPPOSITION 9 (1974): 277-310.

Discusses contrasting styles of Islamic religious life, especially in Algeria from the late nineteenth century to the present.

612. Gendarme, René. "La résistance des facteurs socio-cultures au développement économique. L'exemple de l'Islam en Algérie." REVUE ECONOMIQUE (1959): 220-236.

Formulates the argument that Islamic religion and culture retard the development of capitalism. Uses as points of departure the ideas of Sombart, Weber, Hauser, and Tawney.

613. Hadj-sadok, Mohammed. "De la théorie à la pratique des prescriptions de l'Islam en Algérie contemporaine." SC 25,3-4 (1978): 433-443.

From the eighth century to the nineteenth, Sharia (canon law) was the legal system in Algeria. The French colonization created a parenthesis of 132 years. Since 1962 the Algerian government has insisted upon the Muslim character of the nation, but it has not yet returned completely to Sharia. The government has preferred to take into account the teachings of history and to use modern methods.


## EGYPT

614. Austruy, Jacques. STRUCTURE ECONOMIQUE ET CIVILISATION: L'EGYPTE ET LE DESTIN ECONOMIQUE DE L'ISLAM. Paris, 1960.

615. Bayyumi, Muhammad Ahmad M. THE ISLAMIC ETHIC OF SOCIAL JUSTICE AND THE SPIRIT OF MODERNIZATION: AN APPLICATION OF WEBER'S THESIS TO THE RELATIONSHIP BETWEEN RELIGIOUS VALUES AND SOCIAL CHANGE IN MODERN EGYPT. Unpublished Ph.D. dissertation, Temple University, 1976. [DA 37:4 A, p. 2240]

Focuses upon the Muslim Brotherhoods in modern times.

616. Berger, Monroe. ISLAM IN EGYPT: SOCIAL AND POLITICAL ASPECTS OF POPULAR RELIGION. Cambridge: Cambridge University Press, 1970.

617. Davis, E. "Islamic Radicalism in Egypt." In Said Amir Arjomand (ed.), FROM NATIONALISM TO REVOLUTIONARY ISLAM. Albany, New York: State University of New York Press, 1984.

618. Gilsenan, Michael. "Some Factors in the Decline of the Sufi Orders in Modern Egypt." MUSLIM WORLD 57,1 (1967): 11-18.

Review of the literature; general discussion.

619. Gilsenan, Michael. SAINT AND SUFI IN MODERN EGYPT. AN ESSAY IN THE SOCIOLOGY OF RELIGION. Oxford: Clarendon, 1973.

620. Gilsenan, Michael. "L'Islam dans l'Egypte contemporaine: Religion d'Etat, religion populaire." ANNALES 35,3-4 (1980): 598-614.

Argues that Islam legitimated the state and army until the defeat of 1967, after which efforts to use religion to support the state have only created opposition.

621. Ibrahim, Saad Eddin. "Anatomy of Egypt's Militant Islamic Groups: Methodological Note and Preliminary Findings." INTERNATIONAL JOURNAL OF MIDDLE EAST STUDIES 12,4 (1980): 423-453.

622. Ibrahim, Saad Eddin. "Egypt's Islamic Militancy Revisited." In J.K. Hadden and A. Shupe (eds.), PROPHETIC RELIGIONS AND POLITICS [volume cited in item 197], pp. 353-361.


MOROCCO

623. Clément, Jean-François. "Mouvements islamiques et représentation de l'Islam dans la Tensift." In Ernest Gellner and Jean-Claude Vatin (eds.), ISLAM ET POLITIQUE AU MAGHREB. Paris: Editions du CNRS, 1981, pp. 57-90.

Interview material from three centers, placed in a broad historical context.

624. Gellner, Ernest. "The Far West of Islam." BRITISH JOURNAL OF SOCIOLOGY 9,1 (1958): 72-82.

Review of STRUCTURES SOCIALES DU HAUT-ATLAS, by Jacques Berque.

625. Gellner, Ernest. SAINTS OF THE ATLAS. London: Weidenfeld and

Nicolson, 1969;  Chicago: University of Chicago Press, 1969.

626. Hagopian, Elaine C.  "Islam and Society Formation in Morocco. Past and Present."  JSSR 3,1 (1963): 70-80.


## OTHER AFRICAN

627. Bel, Alfred.  LA RELIGION MUSULMANE EN BERBERIE: ESQUISSE D'HISTOIRE ET DE SOCIOLOGIE RELIGIEUSE. ETABLISSEMENT ET DEVELOPPEMENT DE L'ISLAM EN BERBERIE DU VIIe AU XXe SIECLE.  Paris: Geuthner, 1938.

628. Creevey, Lucy E.  "Religion and Modernization in Senegal."  In John L. Esposito (ed.), ISLAM AND DEVELOPMENT. RELIGION AND SOCIOPOLITICAL CHANGE.  Syracuse, New York: Syracuse University Press, 1980, pp. 207-221, 252-254.

Presentation of various kinds of data from 1960-1978.

629. Duvignaud, Jean.  ENQUÊTES ET RECHERCHES EN SOCIOLOGIE ISLAMIQUE MEGHREBINE.  Tunis, 1963.

630. Lienhardt, Peter.  "The Mosque College of Lamu and its Social Background."  TANGANYIKA NOTES AND RECORDS 5 (1959): 228-242.

Based on 1958 field work.

631. Martin, B.G.  MUSLIM BROTHERHOODS IN NINETEENTH-CENTURY AFRICA.  Cambridge: Cambridge University Press, 1976.


## SOUTHEAST ASIA AND PACIFIC

632. Alatas, Syed Hussein.  "Some Comments on Islam and Social Change in Malaysia."  In Joachim Matthes (ed.), INTERNATIONALES JAHRBUCH FÜR RELIGIONSSOZIOLOGIE 5.  Opladen: Westdeutscher Verlag, 1969, pp. 133-140.

633. Cayrac-Blanchard, Françoise.  "Evolution politique de l'Islam en Indonésie."  PROJET 140 (1979): 1281-1286.

634. Fistié, Pierre, and Patricia Sockeel-Richarté.  "L'Islam et le politique en Malaysia."  PROJET 140 (1979): 1287-1293.

Overview of developments after 1957.

635. Hirikoshi, Hiroko.  "Islamic Scholasticism, Social Conflicts and Political Power. Corporate and Non-corporate Features of Muslim Learned Men in West Java."  SC 31,1 (1984): 75-89.

Examines historical fluctuations in the social leadership provided by the *ulama* in West Java.

636. Kessler, Clive S.  "Islam, Society and Political Behaviour: Some

Comparative Implications of the Malay Case." BRITISH JOURNAL OF
SOCIOLOGY 23,1 (1972): 33-50.

Examines ideal versus actual political culture in Islamic settings,
with particular focus on the Pan-Malayan Islamic Party in Kelantan,
Malaysia.

637. Mintz, Jeanne S. MOHAMMED, MARX AND MARHAEN: THE ROOTS OF INDONESIAN
SOCIALISM. New York: Praeger, 1965.

638. Peacock, James L. MUSLIM PURITANS: REFORMIST PSYCHOLOGY IN SOUTHEAST
ASIA ISLAM. Berkeley: University of California Press, 1978.

639. Regan, Daniel. "Islam, Intellectuals and Civil Religion in Malaysia."
SA 37,2 (1976): 95-110.

During emergencies a temporary civil religion emerges as an alternative to consociational politics of accommodation, but the idea of a
national integration through a lasting civil creed has yet to take
root.

640. Regan, Daniel. "Islam as a New Religious Movement in Malaysia." In
J.A. Beckford and T. Luckmann (eds.), THE CHANGING FACE OF RELIGION
[volume cited in item 549], pp. 124-146.

641. Rodgers, Susan. "Islam and the Changing of Social and Cultural
Structures in the Angkola Batak Homeland." SC 31,1 (1984): 57-74.

For the majority of the Angkola population, on Sumatra, the symbols
and ritual practices of Islam combine in ingenious ways with indigenous adat belief and practice. This process has created a sturdy
synthesis that has joined itself to the major symbols of the Indonesian nation.

642. Tamney, Joseph B. "Muslim and Christian Attitudes toward Fasting in
Southeast Asia." RRR 19,1 (1977): 3-15.

Though Muslims value fasting more highly than do Christians, they are
increasingly inclined to accord it this-worldly meaning.

643. Tamney, Joseph B. "Established Religiosity in Modern Society: Islam
in Indonesia." SA 40,2 (1979): 125-135.

Interviews with residents of Java, aged 16-40. Community size is
negatively related to Islamic religiosity but education is positively
related to it.

644. Tamney, Joseph B. "Modernization and Religious Purification: Islam in
Indonesia." RRR 22,2 (1980): 207-217.

1975 interviews with residents of Java, aged 16-40. Education and
community size are related to the decline of folk religion and to a
net increase in the proportion of Muslims who are active religious
purists. Modernization favors purification, not because modern people
reject syncretism but because they abandon magical practices.

645. Tamney, Joseph B. "Functional Religiosity and Modernization in Indonesia." SA 41,1 (1980): 55-65.

1975 interviews with residents of Java, aged 16-40, who belonged to two ethnic groups - Javanese and Sundanese. Resort to religion in the course of making decisions increased with education and urbanization.

646. Tamney, Joseph B. "Islamic Popularity: The Case of Indonesia." SOUTHEAST ASIAN JOURNAL OF SOCIAL SCIENCES 15,1 (1987): 53-65.

Islam's popularity is related to the negative qualities of alternative systems (e.g., the backwardness of folk culture, the foreignness of Christianity).

* Utrecht, Ernst. "Religion and Social Protest in Indonesia." Cited above as item 60.

647. Utrecht, Ernst. "The Muslim Merchant Class in the Indonesian Social and Political Struggles." SC 31,1 (1984): 27-55.

Examines recent conflict between the Muslim merchant class and the military government.

648. Van Dijck, Cees. "Islam and Socio-political Conflicts in Indonesian History." SC 31,1 (1984): 5-25.

From the end of the thirteenth century, Islam has been a source of inspiration and legitimation for expansionist rulers, ambitious pretenders, exploited peasants, rising merchants, mystics, and even Marxists.


*SOUTH ASIA*

649. Ahmad, Aziz. "Problems of Islamic Modernism, with Special Reference to Indo-Pakistan Sub-continent." ARCHIVES DE SOCIOLOGIE DES RELIGIONS 23 (1967): 107-116.

A fully secularized state is antipathetic to Islamic ideals.

650. Ahmad, Imtiaz. "The Muslim Electorate and Election Alternatives in Uttar Pradesh." RELIGION AND SOCIETY 21,2 (1974): 55-77.

Study of the 1974 state election.

651. Camps, Arnulf. "Some Aspects of the Religious Crisis of Islam in West Pakistan." SC 9,3 (1962): 221-237.

The difficulty of adapting to the modern world is exacerbated by the large number of sects and the predominance of popular religion.

652. Camps, Arnulf. "Searching after the Straight Path. The Role of the Religious Leader, the Pir, in the Islam of West Pakistan." SC 11,6 (1964): 23-28.

Use of previous studies, and a 1960 field study.

653. Chopra, Suncet. "Problems of the Muslim Minority in India." SOCIAL
SCIENTIST 5,2 (1976): 67-77.

654. Eberhard, Wolfram. "Modern Tendencies in Islam in Pakistan."
SOCIOLOGUS 10,2 (1960): 139-152.

Examines tensions among Sunni, Shia, Ismaili, and Qadiani, over the
nature of the new Pakistani state.

655. Eister, Allan W. "Perspectives on the Functions of Religion in a
Developing Country: Islam in Pakistan." JSSR 3,12 (1964): 227-238.

1960 data from 52 villages in 29 areas; 450 respondents. Focuses on
the openness of Islam toward religious nonconformity and change.

656. Ellickson, Jean. "Islamic Institutions: Perception and Practice in
a Village in Bangladesh." CONTRIBUTIONS TO INDIAN SOCIOLOGY 6 (1972):
53-65.

Based on 1968-69 field work in the village of Shaheenpur in then East
Pakistan.

657. Gaborieau, Marc. "Muslims in the Hindu Kingdom of Nepal." CONTRIBU-
TIONS TO INDIAN SOCIOLOGY 6 (1972): 84-105.

Based on observations in the mid-1960s; determination of the status
of a non-Hindu group in Nepal.

658. Gaborieau, Marc. "Le culte des saints chez les musulmans au Népal
et en Inde du nord." SC 25,2-3 (1978): 477-494.

The cult of the saints gives individuals and groups opportunities to
express their particularism. The role played by the saints for the
Muslims is strikingly similar to that played by local divinities for
the Hindus.

659. Gaborieau, Marc. "Le Pakistan: Etat des musulmans ou état musulman?"
PROJET 140 (1979): 1273-1280.

Overview of the issue of established Islam.

660. Gaborieau, Marc. "Typologie des spécialistes religieux chez les
musulmans du sous-continent indien: Les limites de l'islamisation."
ARCHIVES DE SCIENCES SOCIALES DES RELIGIONS 55,1 (1983): 29-51.

Discusses the discontinuity between normative tradition and actual
practice in India and other Muslim societies.

661. Gaborieau, Marc. "Hiérarchie sociale et movements de réformes chez
les Musulmans du sous-continent Indien." SC 33,2-3 (1986): 237-256.

Despite Islam's official egalitarianism, Muslim society in India may
be characterized as a truncated caste system.

&ast; Jain, S.P. "Religion, Caste, Class and Education in a North Indian Community." Cited above as item 28.

662. Jai Singh, Herbert. "Indian Muslims and the Challenge of Modernity." RELIGION AND SOCIETY 29,4 (1982): 62-86.

663. Kanwar, Mahfooz A. "Traditional vs. Modern Trends in Pakistan: A Muslim Society in Transition." SC 18,2 (1971): 263-277.

Observations based on 1968-69 interviews in what was then West Pakistan.

664. Krishna, Gopal. "Piety and Politics in Indian Islam." CONTRIBUTIONS TO INDIAN SOCIOLOGY 6 (1972): 142-171.

A historical sociological overview.

665. Krishna, Gopal. "Islam, Minority Status and Citizenship: Muslim Experience in India." ARCHIVES EUROPEENES DE SOCIOLOGIE 27,2 (1986): 353-368.

General discussion of the post-independence situation.

666. Lindholm, Charles. "Paradigms of Society: A Critique of Theories of Castes among Indian Muslims." ARCHIVES EUROPEENES DE SOCIOLOGIE 26,1 (1985): 131-141.

&ast; Madan, T.N. "Religious Ideology in a Plural Society: The Muslims and Hindus of Kashmir." Cited above as item 36.

667. Mauroof, Mohamed. "Aspects of Religion, Economy, and Society among the Muslims of Ceylon." CONTRIBUTIONS TO INDIAN SOCIOLOGY 6 (1972): 66-83.

Based on 1967-68 and 1970 field work.

668. Momin, A.R. "Conflict of Law and Religion in Contemporary India. A Study of the Supreme Court Verdict Relating to Muslim Law." SC 33, 2-3 (1986): 223-237.

Study of a 1985 decision in which the meaning of 'wife' was at issue.

669. Robinsom, Francis. "Islam and Muslim Society in India." CONTRIBUTIONS TO INDIAN SOCIOLOGY 17,2 (1983): 185-203.

670. Samaraweera, Vivaya. "Some Sociological Aspects of the Muslim Revivalism in Sri Lanka." SC 25,3-4 (1978): 465-475.

Attributes the self-identity of the Muslim minority in Sri Lanka to a turn-of-the-century revivalist movement.

671. Sharma, S.L., and R.N. Srivastava. "Institutional Resistance to Induced Islamization in a Convert Community: An Empirical Study in Sociology of Religion." SOCIOLOGICAL BULLETIN 16,1 (1967): 69-80.

The conversion of the Meos of the Mewat region (India) to Islam has produced an amalgam of Hindu and Muslim religiosity. An organized effort to purge the Meos of Hindu customs has resulted in anomie.

672. Wilber, Donald N. "The Structure and Position of Islam in Afghanistan." MIDDLE EAST JOURNAL 6,1 (1952): 41-48.

General description, based on 1951 interviews.


## MIDDLE EAST

673. Charârâ, Waddâ. "L'Islam libanais en miettes." SC 35,4 (1988): 637-644.

Argues that a union of Muslim factions around Islam is not the recipe for a revived Lebanese state.

674. Haddad, Juliette. "Sacré et vie quotidienne. Perspectives sur une société arabo-musulmane moderne." SC 29,4 (1982): 311-333.

Focus is on the Jordanian population in the regions of Karak and Aqaba. Once nomads, these people now experience settled lives and formal education. Islamic beliefs are retained while pre-islamic ones tend to be abandoned.

675. Shadid, Mohammed, and Rick Seltzer. "Growth in Islamic Fundamentalism: The Case of Palestine." SA 50,3 (1989): 291-298.

Based on interviews conducted with 3,306 Palestinians living in the West Bank and Gaza Strip.

676. Smith, Peter. BABI AND BAHA'I RELIGIONS: FROM MESSIANIC SHI'ISM TO A WORLD RELIGION. New York: Cambridge University Press, 1987.

Discussion of Babi, a nineteenth-century Islamic movement in Iran.

677. Souryal, Sam S. "The Religionization of a Society: The Continuing Application of Shariah Law in Saudi Arabia." JSSR 26,4 (1987): 429-449.

Saudi Arabia, which uses sharia law, has lower crime rates than neighboring countries which do not use it.

678. Yalman, Nur. "Islamic Reform and the Mystic Tradition in Eastern Turkey." ARCHIVES EUROPEENES DE SOCIOLOGIE 10,1 (1969): 41-60.

Focuses upon the Alevi, a reformed sect in eastern Turkey in which Muslim mysticism has remained vibrant.


## WEST

679. Andezian, Sossie. "Pratiques féminines de l'Islam en France." ARCHIVES DE SCIENCES SOCIALES DES RELIGIONS 55,1 (1983): 53-66.

Examines the role played by female immigrants in maintaining and spreading the observance of Islam in France.

680. Barclay, Harold B. "A Lebanese Community in Lac La Biche, Alberta."
In J.L. Elliott (ed.), IMMIGRANT GROUPS [volume cited in item 314],
pp. 66-83.

Examines the extent to which this Lebanese community has been able to
perpetuate its Muslim tradition.

681. Bastide, Roger. "L'Islam noir au Brésil." HESPERIS. ARCHIVES
BERBERES ET BULLETIN DE L'INSTITUT DES HAUTES ETUDES MAROCAINES 39
(1952): 373-382.

Studies historical and ethnological traces of Islam among Brazilian
blacks.

682. Dassetto, Felice, and Albert Bastenier. "Organisations Musulmanes de
Belgique." RECHERCHES SOCIOLOGIQUES 16,3 (1985): 347-358.

Examines the adaptation of recent Muslim immigrants to Belgium.

683. Datunashvili, I.I. "Description du niveau actuel de la religiosité
dans les régions de Belokany, Zakataly et Kakhi." SC 21,2 (1974):
121-126.

Early 1960s study of religious life in three regions of the Azerbaid-
jan SSR, where dominant religion is Sunnite Islam; particular
attention paid to informal religious structures as reflected in the
cult of healing saints and funerary ritual.

684. Fauset, Arthur. "Moorish Science Temple of America." In J.M. Yinger
(ed.), RELIGION, SOCIETY AND THE INDIVIDUAL. New York: Macmillan,
1957.

Examines the Moorish Science Temple of America; case study of a lower-
class sect as a moral community under duress, to the point of almost
literal brotherhood and sisterhood.

685. Haddad, Yvonne, and Adair T. Lummis. ISLAMIC VALUES IN THE UNITED
STATES. A COMPARATIVE STUDY. New York: Oxford University Press, 1987.

686. Hamès, Constant. "Islam et structures sociales chez les immigrés
Soninké en France." SC 26,1 (1979): 87-98.

Among the Mauritanian Soninké immigrants in France, a social category,
the *moodi*, are depositaries of religious knowledge. Religious
activity includes the Muslim teaching as provided by the *moodi*, and
certain magical practices. Because of the institution of the *moodi*,
Islam is making advances among the Soninké, except for the practices
of *ramadan*. Islam also helps the Soninké maintain their community
identity amidst French society.

687. Schiffauer, Werner. "Religion und Identität. Eine Fallstudie zum
Problem der Reislamisierung bei Arbeitsemigranten." SCHWEIZERISCHE
ZEITSCHRIFT FÜR SOZIOLOGIE 10,2 (1984): 485-516.

Based on a single interview with a female Turkish migrant and member of the Nurcu movement in West Germany.

688. Weibel, Nadine.  "Le renouveau islamique: Regards sur une communauté de prière à Strasbourg."  SCHWEIZERISCHE ZEITSCHRIFT FÜR SOZIOLOGIE 9,3 (1983): 757–774.

Personal observation study of a middle-class student prayer group, including some immigrant workers, which began as a prayer meeting and eventually led to the purchase of a building (1982) for a mosque.  The community is organized in part around a rejection of occidental influences.


## BLACK MUSLIM

689. Beynon, Erdmann D.  "The Voodoo Cult among Negro Migrants in Detroit." AMERICAN JOURNAL OF SOCIOLOGY 43 (1938): 894–907.

Analyzes cultist movement, early form of Black Muslimism, in terms of race consciousness and concern over status.

690. Burns, W. Haywood.  "Black Muslims in America: A Reinterpretation." RACE 5,1 (1963): 26–37.

691. Edwards, Harry.  "Black Muslim and Negro Christian Family Relationships."  JOURNAL OF MARRIAGE AND FAMILY 30,4 (1968): 604–611.

Analysis of 14 Nation of Islam and 14 lower-class black Christian families; notes tendency of the former toward middle-class values and conduct.

692. Kaplan, Howard M.  "The Black Muslims and the Negro American's Quest for Communion."  BRITISH JOURNAL OF SOCIOLOGY 20,2 (1969): 164–177.

A communion based on hostility toward whites is the foundation of the Black Muslim movement's attractiveness for potential joiners.  The fluidity of communions explains the fluctuation of the movement's appeal.

693. Laue, James H.  "A Contemporary Revitalization Movement in American Race Relations: The Black Muslims."  SOCIAL FORCES 42,3 (1964): 315–323.

Based on participant observation, analysis of primary documentary sources and media presentations, and dialogue with students and movement leaders.

694. Lincoln, C. Eric.  THE BLACK MUSLIMS OF AMERICA.  Boston: Beacon, 1961.

695. Lincoln, C. Eric.  "The Black Muslims as a Protest Movement."  In Arnold M. Rose (ed.), ASSURING FREEDOM TO THE FREE.  Detroit: Wayne State University Press, 1964, pp. 220–240.

Historical overview from the movement's origins in 1930.

696. Maesen, William A. "Watchtower Influences on Black Muslim Eschatology." JSSR 9,4 (1970): 321-326.

Black Muslim leaders appear to have been influenced in the early 1930s by eschatological teachings of the Jehovah's Witnesses.

697. Mamiya, Laurence H. "From Black Muslim to Bilalian: The Evolution of a Movement." JSSR 21,2 (1982): 138-152.

Examines the occurrence of schism along class lines in the Black Muslim movement.

698. Monteil, Vincent. "La Religion des <Black muslims>." ESPRIT 32,331 (1964): 601-629.

Historical overview and review of the scholarly literature.

699. Parenti, Michael J. "The Black Muslims: From Revolution to Institution." SOCIAL RESEARCH 31,2 (1964): 175-194.

Interprets collective self-help as a step toward cultural accommodation.

700. Watson, G. Llewellyn. "Social Structure and Social Movements: The Black Muslims in the U.S.A. and the Ras-Tafarians in Jamaica." BRITISH JOURNAL OF SOCIOLOGY 24,2 (1973): 188-204.

Focuses on similarities between the two movements.

701. Young, T.R., and Paul Chassy. "La restauration d'une identité: Les <Black Muslims>." CAHIERS INTERNATIONAUX DE SOCIOLOGIE 51 (1971): 277-289.

Argues that the Black Muslim movement gave to its adherents a reinvigorated and unspoiled self-image.

## ISMAILI

* Adams, Bert N. "Urban Skills and Religion: Mechanisms for Coping and Defense among the Ugandan Asians." Cited above as item 1.

702. Bocock, Robert J. "The Ismailis in Tanzania: A Weberian Analysis." BRITISH JOURNAL OF SOCIOLOGY 22,4 (1971): 365-380.

Examines the role of the Aga Khan in introducing an Asian Muslim group in Tanzania to rational capitalism during the era of British administration.

703. Clarke, Peter B. "The Imam of the Ismailis." SOCIOLOGICAL YEARBOOK OF RELIGION IN BRITAIN 8 (1975): 125-138.

In the Ismaili community the Imam is conceived by most as the historical expression of the divine sovereignty and the sign or assurance of salvation.

704. Clarke, Peter B. "The Ismailis: A Study of Community." BRITISH
JOURNAL OF SOCIOLOGY 27,4 (1976): 484-494.

1972-74 study of a community of Ismailis in London, after the 1972
expulsion of Ismailis from Uganda.

*MOURIDE*

705. Bergmann, Herbert. "Die Bruderschaft der Muriden – Eine funktionale
Analyse. Einige Aspekte des Islam im Senegal." SOZIALE WELT 19,2
(1968): 150-171.

706. Cruise O'Brien, Donal B. THE MOURIDES OF SENEGAL. Oxford: Clarendon,
1971.

707. Cruise O'Brien, Donal B. SAINTS AND POLITICIANS. ESSAYS IN THE
ORGANIZATION OF A SENEGALESE PEASANT SOCIETY. Cambridge: Cambridge
University Press, 1975.

708. Cruise O'Brien, Donal B. "A Versatile Charisma. The Mouride Brotherhood 1967-1975." ARCHIVES EUROPEENNES DE SOCIOLOGIE 18,1 (1977): 84-
106.

Revising conclusions in his 1971 book on the Mouride Brotherhood of
Senegal, in which he had predicted the demise of the movement, the
author observes that though no longer estate managers, political
brokers, or capitalists, movement devotees have become bosses of
peasants' trade unions.

709. Monteil, Vincent. "Une confrérie musulmane: Les Mourides du Sénégal."
ARCHIVES DE SOCIOLOGIE DES RELIGIONS 14 (1962): 77-102.

Descriptive presentation based on archival research and documentary
analysis.

*SHI'ITE*

710. Alidoost-Khaybari, Yadollah. RELIGIOUS REVOLUTIONARIES: AN ANALYSIS
OF THE RELIGIOUS GROUP'S VICTORY IN THE IRANIAN REVOLUTION OF 1978-79.
Unpublished Ph.D. dissertation, University of Michigan, 1981. [DA
42:2 A, p. 867]

711. Arjomand, Said Amir. "Religion, Political Action and Legitimate
Domination in Shi'ite Iran: Fourteenth to eighteenth centuries A.D."
ARCHIVES EUROPEENNES DE SOCIOLOGIE 20,1 (1979): 59-109.

Historical account of the secularization of government first by means
of a separate political apparatus in the Islamic empire and then by
means of the sectarian Shi'ite religion.

712. Arjomand, Said Amir. "The Shi'ite Hierocracy and the State in Pre-Modern Iran: 1785-1890." ARCHIVES EUROPEENNES DE SOCIOLOGIE 12,1 (1981): 40-78.

713. Arjomand, Said Amir. "The Ulama's Traditionalist Opposition to Parliamentarianism: 1907-1909." MIDDLE EASTERN STUDIES 17,2 (1981): 174-190.

714. Arjomand, Said Amir. "Shi'ite Iran and the Revolution in Iran." GOVERNMENT AND OPPOSITION. A JOURNAL IN COMPARATIVE POLITICS 16,3 (1981): 293-316.

715. Arjomand, Said Amir. THE SHADOW OF GOD AND THE HIDDEN IMAM: RELIGION, POLITICAL ORDER, AND SOCIETAL CHANGE IN SHI'ITE IRAN FROM THE BEGINNING TO 1890. Chicago: University of Chicago Press, 1984.

716. Arjomand, Said Amir. "Traditionalism in Twentieth Century Iran." In S.A. Arjomand (ed.), FROM NATIONALISM TO REVOLUTIONARY ISLAM [volume cited in item 617].

717. Awada, Hassam. "Le Liban et le flux islamiste." SC 35,4 (1988): 645-673.

The movement to establish an Islamic state, in imitation of the Iranian, in Lebanon contradicts the pluralist nature of the Lebanese population.

718. Braswell, George W., Jr. A MOSAIC OF MULLAHS AND MOSQUES: RELIGION AND POLITICS IN IRANIAN SHI'AH ISLAM. Unpublished Ph.D. dissertation, University of North Carolina, 1975. [DA 37:3 A, p. 1654]

Discussion of popular versus government-sponsored Shia Islam under the Shah.

719. Jacobs, Norman. "La religion et le développement économique: Le cas de l'Iran." ARCHIVES DE SOCIOLOGIE DES RELIGIONS 15 (1963): 43-48.

Argues that religious culture provided an impetus for economic development in the Iran of the late 1950s.

720. Kimmel, Michael S., and Rahmat Tavakol. "Against Satan: Charisma and Tradition in Iran." In Ronald M. Glassman and William H. Swatos, Jr. (eds.), CHARISMA, HISTORY, AND SOCIAL STRUCTURE. Westport, Connecticut: Greenwood, 1986, pp. 101-112.

Contextualizes the 1979 revolution.

721. Richard, Yann. "Le rôle du clergé: Tendances contradictoires du chi'isme iranien contemporain." ARCHIVES DE SCIENCES SOCIALES DES RELIGIONS 55,1 (1983): 5-28.

Discusses controversy over clerical power in Iran since the 1979 revolution.

722. Richard, Yann. "Le intégrisme islamique en Iran." SC 32,4 (1985): 421-428.

'Revolutionary traditionalism' more appropriately describes the recent movement in Iran than do the terms 'integrism' or 'fundamentalism.'

723. Sicking, T. RELIGION ET DEVELOPPEMENT: ETUDE COMPAREE DE DEUX VILLAGES LIBANAIS. Beirut: Dar el-Machreq Sarl Editeurs, 1985.

724. Skocpol, Theda. "Rentier State and Shi'a Islam in the Iranian Revolution." THEORY AND SOCIETY 11,3 (1982): 265-283.

Discusses the social anatomy of the Iranian revolution.

725. Thaiss, Gustav. "The Bazaar as a Case Study of Religion and Social Change." In Ehsam Yar-Shatar (ed.), IRAN FACES THE SEVENTIES. New York: Praeger, 1971.

# PART III
# CHRISTIAN: EARLY AND
# LITURGICAL TRADITIONS

# 7

## Early Christian

726. Bergmann, Werner. "Das frühe Mönchtum als soziale Bewegung." KÖLNER
ZEITSCRIFT FÜR SOZIOLOGIE UND SOZIALPSYCHOLOGIE 37,1 (1985): 30-59.

Considers early Egyptian and Syrian Christian monasticism as countercultural movements.

727. Blasi, Anthony J. "Role Structures in the Early Hellenistic Church."
SA 47,3 (1986): 226-248.

Use of the literary stratum of the New Testament known as 'Q' to
identify typical acts, roles, and statuses of the users, audiences,
and mentioned third parties associated with the texts.

728. Blasi, Anthony J. EARLY CHRISTIANITY AS A SOCIAL MOVEMENT. Bern and
New York: Peter Lang, 1988.

Application of the social movement model to the first 50 years of
Christianity (35-85 C.E.). Evidence gained from literary analysis is
compared to new religious movements of the twentieth century.

729. Funk, Aloys. STATUS UND ROLLEN IN DEN PAULUSBRIEFEN. EINE INHALTS-
ANALYTISCHE UNTERSUCHUNG ZUR RELIGIONSSOZIOLOGIE. Innsbruck:
Tyrolia-Verlag, 1981.

Content analysis of the authentic Pauline letters to ascertain the
distribution of roles between the sexes and the Jewish vs. Greek
identity of the customary distribution in each of the churches
addressed by the letters.

730. Gager, John G. KINGDOM AND COMMUNITY. THE SOCIAL WORLD OF EARLY
CHRISTIANITY. Englewood Cliffs, New Jersey: Prentice-Hall, 1975.

731. Hadot, Jean. "Contestation socio-religieuse et apocalyptique dans
le judéo-christianisme." ARCHIVES DE SOCIOLOGIE DES RELIGIONS 24
(1967): 35-47.

An overview of major research challenges for the sociological scholar
of primitive Christianity.

* Houtart, François. RELIGION ET MODES DE PRODUCTION PRECAPITALISTES. Cited above as item 25.

732. Judge, Edwin A. THE SOCIAL PATTERN OF CHRISTIAN GROUPS IN THE FIRST CENTURY. London: Tyndale, 1960.

733. Kee, Howard Clark. CHRISTIAN ORIGINS IN SOCIOLOGICAL PERSPECTIVE. Philadelphia: Westminster, 1980.

734. Kreissig, Heinz. "Zur sozialen Zusammensetzung der frühchristlichen Gemeinden im ersten Jahrhundert u.z." EIRENE. STUDIA GRAECA ET LATINA 6 (1967): 91-100.

Examines references to social stratification in early Christian literature.

735. Kyrtatas, Dimitris. "Prophets and Priests in Early Christianity: Production and Transmission of Religious Knowledge from Jesus to John Chrysostum." INTERNATIONAL SOCIOLOGY 3,4 (1988): 365-384.

736. Lampe, Peter. DIE STADTRÖMISCHEN CHRISTEN IN DEN ERSTEN BEIDEN JAHRHUNDERTEN. Tübingen: Mohr, 1988.

737. Laub, F. "Sozialgeschichtlicher Hintergrund und ekklesiologische Relevanz der neutestamentlichfrühchristlichen Haus- und Gemeinde-Tafelparaenese - ein Beitrag zur Soziologie des Frühchristentums." MÜNCHENER THEOLOGISCHE ZEITSCHRIFT 37 (1986): 249-271.

738. MacDonald, Margaret Y. THE PAULINE CHURCHES. A SOCIO-HISTORICAL STUDY OF INSTITUTIONALIZATION IN THE PAULINE AND DEUTERO-PAULINE WRITINGS. Cambridge: Cambridge University Press, 1988.

739. Malherbe, Abraham J. SOCIAL ASPECTS OF EARLY CHRISTIANITY, second enlarged edition. Philadelphia: Fortress, 1983.

740. Malina, Bruce J., and Jerome H. Neyrey. CALLING JESUS NAMES. THE SOCIAL VALUE OF LABELS IN MATTHEW. Sonoma, California: Polebridge, 1988.

741. Meeks, Wayne A. THE FIRST URBAN CHRISTIANS. THE SOCIAL WORLD OF THE APOSTLE PAUL. New Haven: Yale University Press, 1983.

Focus on Corinth.

742. Oakman, Douglas E. JESUS AND THE ECONOMIC QUESTIONS OF HIS DAY. Lewiston, New York: Edwin Mellen Press, 1986.

743. Petersen, Norman R. REDISCOVERING PAUL: PHILEMON AND THE SOCIOLOGY OF PAUL'S NARRATIVE WORLD. Philadelphia: Fortress, 1985.

744. Richter, Philip J. "Recent Sociological Approaches to the Study of the New Testament." RELIGION 14 (1984): 77-90.

745. Schoenfeld, Eugen. "Justice: An Illusive Concept in Christianity." RRR 30,3 (1989): 236-245.

746. Schreiber, Alfred. DIE GEMEINDE IN KORINTH. Münster: Aschendorff, 1977.

747. Scroggs, R. "The Sociological Interpretation of the New Testament: The Present State of Research." NEW TESTAMENT STUDIES 26 (1980): 164-179.

748. Stark, Rodney. "The Class Basis of Early Christianity: Inferences from a Sociological Model." SA 47,3 (1986): 216-225.

Argues that early Christianity, as a cult rather than a sect, was not a proletarian movement.

749. Theissen, Gerd. "Theoretische Probleme religionssoziologischer Forschung und die Analyse des Urchristentums." NEUE ZEITSCHRIFT FÜR SYSTEMATISCHE THEOLOGIE UND RELIGIONSPHILOSOPHIE 16,1 (1974): 35-56.

750. Theissen, Gerd. "Die Tempelweissagung Jesu: Prophetie im Spannungsfeld von Stadt und Land." THEOLOGISCHE ZEITSCHRIFT 32 (1976): 144-158. Reprinted in G. Thiessen, STUDIEN ZUR SOZIOLOGIE DES URCHRISTENTUMS [item 753], pp. 142-159.

751. Theissen, Gerd. "<Wir haben alles verlassen> (Mc X, 28): Nachfolge und soziale Entwurzelung in der jüdisch-palestinischen Gesellschaft des 1. Jahrhundrerts N. Chr." NOVUM TESTAMENTUM 27 (1977): 161-196. Reprinted in G. Thiessen, STUDIEN ZUR SOZIOLOGIE DES URCHRISTENTUMS [item 753], pp. 106-141.

752. Theissen, Gerd. SOCIOLOGY OF EARLY PALESTINIAN CHRISTIANITY, translated by John Bowden. Philadelphia: Fortress, 1978.

753. Theissen, Gerd. STUDIEN ZUR SOZIOLOGIE DES URCHRISTENTUMS. WISSENSCHAFTLICHE UNTERSUCHUNGEN ZUM NEUEN TESTAMENT 19. Tübingen: Mohr, 1979.

754. Theissen, Gerd. THE SOCIAL SETTING OF PAULINE CHRISTIANITY. ESSAYS ON CORINTH. Philadelphia: Fortress, 1982.

755. Watson, Francis. PAUL, JUDAISM AND THE GENTILES. A SOCIOLOGICAL APPROACH. Cambridge: Cambridge University Press, 1986.

756. Wiefel, Wolfgang. "Erwägungen zur soziologischen Hermeneutik urchristlicher Gottesdienstformen." KAIROS 14,1 (1972): 36-51.

# 8
## Orthodox and Other Eastern

*GENERAL*

757. Müller-Armack, Alfred. RELIGION UND WIRTSCHAFT. GEISTESGESCHICHTLICHE HINTERGRÜNDE UNSERER EUROPÄISCHEN LEBENSFORM. Stuttgart: W. Kohlhammer, 1959.

758. Papaderos, Alexander. "Orthodoxy and Economy: A Dialogue with Alfred Müller-Armack." SC 22,1 (1975): 33-66.

    Critique of a widespread view, shared by the German scholar Müller-Armack, that Byzantine culture was exclusively other-worldly and therefore not supportive of this-worldly economic development.

759. Runciman, S. THE ORTHODOX CHURCHES AND THE SECULAR STATE. Auckland: Oxford University Press, 1971.

760. Savramis, Demosthenes. ZUR SOZIOLOGIE DES BYZANTINISCHEN MÖNCHTUMS. Leiden: Brill, 1962.


*ORTHODOX (U.S.A.)*

761. Donus, Robert B. "Greek-Americans in a Pan-Orthodox Parish: A Sociologist's View." ST. VLADIMIR'S THEOLOGICAL QUARTERLY 18,1 (1974): 44-52.

    Sample of Greek members of an ethnically-mixed Orthodox church in Bergenfield, New Jersey, focusing on aspects of religiosity.

762. Kayal, Philip M. "Eastern Orthodox Exogamy and 'Triple' Melting Pot Theory: Herberg Revisited." ST. VLADIMIR'S THEOLOGICAL QUARTERLY 25,4 (1981): 239-257.

    Examination of marriage statistics in northeastern American Orthodox dioceses.

  * Laumann, Edward O. "The Social Structure of Religious and Ethnoreligious Groups in a Metropolitan Community." Cited above as item 469.

* Mayer, Albert J., and Harry Sharp. "Religious Preference and Worldly Success." Cited above as item 484.


COPTIC

763. Assad, Maurice M. "The Coptic Church and Social Change in Egypt." INTERNATIONAL REVIEW OF MISSION 61,242 (1972): 117-129.

764. Wakin, Edward. A LONELY MINORITY: THE MODERN STORY OF EGYPT'S COPTS. New York, 1963.


ETHIOPIAN ORTHODOX

765. Göricke, Fred, and Friedrich Heyer. "The Orthodox Church of Ethiopia as a Social Institution." In G. Dux and T. Luckmann (eds.), BEITRÄGE ZUR WISSENSOZIOLOGIE. BEITRÄGE ZUR RELIGIONSSOZIOLOGIE, Bd. 10. Opladen: Westdeutscher Verlag, 1976, pp. 181-241.

766. Hoben, Allan. "Traditional Amhara Society." In A. Tuden and L. Plotnicov (eds.), SOCIAL STRATIFICATION IN AFRICA. New York: Free Press, 1970.

The Ethiopian Orthodox see heaven as a hierarchical arrangement, much like the social order of their world. Order and legitimate control are religiously valued. The church is subservient to the state, often getting real authority from it. The emperor is considered to be the elect of God.


GREEK ORTHODOX

767. Goussidis, Alexandre. "Analyse statistique et sociographique des ordinations dans l'Eglise de Grèce entre 1950 et 1969." SC 22,1 (1975): 107-148.

The chief source of ordinations in the Church of Greece lies in the socially lower stratum of the population belonging to areas as yet untouched by modern civilization.

768. Hadzimichali, Nectaire. "L'Eglise Orthodoxe grècque et le messianisme en Afrique." SC 22,1 (1975): 85-95.

The introduction of Orthodoxy in twentieth-century Africa did not come from an organized mission but from the historical encounter of Greek orthodox messianism with its African homologue. The Greek tradition of a close link between religion and nation highlighted the meaning of struggles for independence, especially in Uganda and Kenya. In Zaire, on the other hand, Orthodoxy entered only after independence, and was received favorably because of correspondence between its messianism and that inspired by the prophetic movement of Simon Kimbangu.

769. Jioultsis, Basil. "Religious Brotherhoods: A Sociological View."

SC 22,1 (1975): 67-84.

Brotherhoods began to develop in the eighteenth century because of the inability of the church to meet people's spiritual needs; micro-sociological account.

770. Kokosalakis, Nikos. "Religion and Modernization in 19th-Century Greece." SC 34,2-3 (1987): 223-241.

The specificity of contemporary Greek culture and society cannot be understood without analysis of the nineteenth-century relations between religion and politics in Greece.

771. Kourvetaris, George A., and Betty A. Dobratz. "An Empirical Test of Gordon's Ethclass Hypothesis among Three Ethnoreligious Groups." SOCIOLOGY AND SOCIAL RESEARCH 61,1 (1976): 39-53.

Questionnaire data from Greek Orthodox, Italian Catholic, and Swedish Lutheran couples in a midwest United States city. The couples confined their primary group relations to persons of their own ethnicity and class, more than chance would determine.

772. Mantzaridis, George. "New Statistical Data concerning the Monks of Mount Athos." SC 22,1 (1975): 97-106.

1959-74 data on 20 monasteries on Mount Athos.

773. Millett, David. "The Orthodox Church: Ukrainian, Greek and Syrian." In J.L. Elliott (ed.), IMMIGRANT GROUPS [volume cited in item 314], pp. 47-65.

Examines the early and contemporary status of the Orthodox Church in Canada.

* Mol, J.J. (Hans) "A Collation of Data about Religion in Australia." Cited above as item 308.

774. Saloutos, Theodore. "The Greek Orthodox Church in the United States and Assimilation." INTERNATIONAL MIGRATION REVIEW 7,4 (1973): 395-407.

History of the gradual abandonment of an effort to maintain Greek national identity.

775. Savramis, Demosthenes. DIE SOZIALE STELLUNG DER PRIESTER IN GRIECHEN-LAND. Leiden: Brill, 1968.

*RUSSIAN ORTHODOX*

776. Fireside, Harry. ICON AND SWASTIKA: THE RUSSIAN ORTHODOX CHURCH UNDER NAZI AND SOVIET CONTROL. Cambridge, Massachusetts: Harvard University Press, 1971.

777. Fireside, Harry. "The Russian Orthodox Church under Nazi Occupation,

1941-1944." AMERICAN BEHAVIORAL SCIENTIST 17,6 (1974): 884-908.

There was a grass-roots religious revival during the German occupation on the Eastern front, which the Germans attempted to use for their own purposes. The participants seemed to be seeking a third way - neither Soviet nor Nazi.

778. Fletcher, W.C. "Underground Orthodoxy. A Problem in Political Control." CANADIAN SLAVONIC PAPERS 12,4 (1970): 363-394.

779. Fletcher, W.C. THE RUSSIAN ORTHODOX CHURCH UNDERGROUND, 1917-1970. London: Oxford University Press, 1971.

780. Greil, Arthur L., and David Kowalewski. "Church-state Relations in Russia and Nicaragua: Early Revolutionary Years." JSSR 26,1 (1987): 92-104.

781. Konstantinov, D. "Orthodoxy and the Younger Generation in the U.S.S.R." THE WORLD YEARBOOK OF RELIGION 1 (1969): 871-885.

782. Lane, Christel O. "Russian Piety among Contemporary Russian Orthodox." JSSR 14,2 (1975): 139-158.

Practice seems the most central element of religiosity for contemporary Russian Orthodox.

783. Murvar, Vatro. "Russian Religious Structures. A Study in Persistent Church Subservience." JSSR 7,1 (1968): 1-22.

784. Robbins, Thomas. "Religious Mass Suicide before Jonestown: The Russian Old Believers." SA 47,1 (1986): 1-20.

Late seventeenth, early eighteenth-century Russian 'Old Believers' committed suicide in contexts of catastrophic collective events at hermitages or monasteries. Discusses parallels and divergences with the Jonestown phenomenon.


*SERBIAN ORTHODOX*

785. Fahey, Frank J., and Djuro J. Vrga. "The Anomic Character of a Schism. Differential Perception of Functions of the Serbian Orthodox Church by Two Feuding Factions." RRR 12,3 (1971): 177-185.

The 1963 schism in the Serbian Orthodox Church in the U.S.A. was based in part on the anomie of post-World War II immigrants who experienced status degradation in the general society and within the church.

786. Ribeyrol, Monette, and Dominique Schnapper. "Cérémonies funéraires dans la Yougoslavie orthodoxe." ARCHIVES EUROPEENNES DE SOCIOLOGIE 17,2 (1976): 220-246.

The Serbian Orthodox tradition in Yugoslavia was shaken, but not destroyed, when the communist government attempted to impose secular funerary ceremonials.

787. Vrga, Djuro J. "Perception et interprétation subjective des causes de la division religieuse. Une analyse des discordances ethno-religieuses des immigrants." SC 18,2 (1971): 247-261.

788. Vrga, Djuro J., and Frank J. Fahey. "The Relationship of Religious Practices and Beliefs to Schism." SA 31,1 (1970): 46-55.

The two groups in the 1963 schism of the Serbian Orthodox Church in the U.S.A. did not differ in belief or practice but in recency of migration, educational achievement, status mobility in the U.S., and political party affiliation.

789. Vrga, Djuro J., and Frank J. Fahey. "Political Ideology and Religious Factionalism." JSSR 10,2 (1971): 111-113.

The religiously dissenting group in the 1963 schism of the Serbian Orthodox Church in the U.S.A. was found to be predominantly Republican; this group evidently hoped for more relief through the more manifest anti-communism of the Republicans than through the social ameliorative policies of the Democrats.

790. Vrga, Djuro J., and Frank J. Fahey. "Status Loss as a Source of Ethno-religious Factionalism." JSSR 10,2 (1971): 101-110.

Study following a 1963 schism in the Serbian Orthodox Church in the U.S.A. Strains and conflicts in an immigrant ethnic group develop because a significant number but not all members experience a drastic discrepancy between their social standing in the native country and their achieved status in the adopted society.

## SYRIAN ORTHODOX

791. Houtart, François. "L'implantation portugaise au Kerala et ses effets sur l'organisation sociale et religieuse des Syriens et sur le système des castes." SC 28,2-3 (1981): 201-235.

History of the Portuguese attempt to impose the Latin rite, and of the Syrian-Indians' religious regrouping in non-caste structures which resemble castes.

 * Millett, David. "The Orthodox Church: Ukrainian, Greek and Syrian." Cited above as item 773.

## UKRAINIAN ORTHODOX

 * Millett, David. "The Orthodox Church: Ukrainian, Greek and Syrian." Cited above as item 773.

792. Sánchez Cano, José. "La nacionalidad y la consagración conciliar en la Iglesia Ortodoxa Ucraniana." REVISTA ESPAÑOLA DE LA OPINION

PUBLICA (Spain) 31 (1973): 239-311.
Historical overview, medieval to modern.

# 9

## Roman Catholic: Historical and Contemporary Perspectives

*GENERAL*

793. Blasi, Anthony J. "Sociological Implications of the Great Western Schism." SC 36,3 (1989): 311-325.

    Fourteenth to fifteenth-century Catholicism.

794. Briefs, Goezt. "The Disputes between Catholicism and Liberalism in the Early Decades of Capitalism." SOCIAL RESEARCH 4,1 (1937): 52-73.

795. Bromley, David G., and Anson D. Shupe. "The Tnevnoc Cult." SA 40,4 (1979): 361-366.

    Reminiscent of the famous Nacerima study by Horace Miner.

796. Dann, Graham M.S. "Religious Belonging in a Changing Catholic Church." SA 37,4 (1976): 283-297.

    Depicts twentieth-century change of Catholicism from a uniform bureau-cratic model to a pluriform model of religious belonging. The latter model allows for analyses of decentralization, ecumenism, interest groups, parties, and conflict in the Catholic Church.

797. Dann, Graham M.S. "The Catholic Church and Models of Socio-religious Change: An Appraisal." SA 39,3 (1978): 189-202.

    Presents four analytical models for the study of contemporary Catholi-cism: typological, dimensional, evolutionary, and political.

798. Deluz, Christiane. "Pèlerins à Jérusalem à la fin du Moyen-Age." SC 36,2 (1989): 159-173.

    Fourteenth to sixteenth centuries.

799. Donovan, John D. "The Social Structure of the Parish." In C.J. Nuesse and Thomas J. Harte (eds.), THE SOCIOLOGY OF THE PARISH. AN INTRODUCTORY SYMPOSIUM. Milwaukee: Bruce, 1951, pp. 75-99.

800. Fedele, Marcello. "Ideologia cattolica e società borghese." CRITICA

SOCIOLOGICA 17 (1971): 34-57.

Christian theory can condemn the historic forms of capitalism while retaining the latter's basic theoretical framework of agreement between worker and employer.

801. Fichter, Joseph H. "The Profile of Catholic Religious Life." AMERICAN JOURNAL OF SOCIOLOGY 58 (1952): 145-150.

Religious practice is found to vary by age and sex.

802. Gabriel, Karl, and Franz-Xaver Kaufmann (eds.) ZUR SOZIOLOGIE DES KATHOLIZISMUS. Mainz: Matthias-Grünwald-Verlag, 1980.

803. Greeley, Andrew M. "After Secularity: The Neo-Gemeinschaft Society: A Post-Christian Postscript." SA 27,3 (1966): 119-127.

Portrays Catholicism in movement from *Gemeinschaft* toward *Gesellschaft*.

804. Grumelli, Antonio. SOCIOLOGIA DEL CATTOLICESIMO. Rome: Editrice Ave, 1965. See also SOCIOLOGIA DEL CATOLICISMO. Barcelona: Ins. Catl. de Estudios Sociales, 1968.

805. Hégy, Pierre. L'AUTORITE DANS LE CATHOLICISME CONTEMPORAIN, DU SYLLABUS A VATICAN II. Paris: Beauchesne, 1975.

806. Hégy, Pierre. "The Invisible Catholicism." SA 48,2 (1987): 167-176.

Data from a French survey and three other surveys show strong correlations with traditional items characteristic of pre-Vatican II subculture. This model of a visible institutional church is rejected in the French sample. Social involvement and rejection of the doctrine of the two realms appear to be the major characteristics of an 'invisible Catholicism.'

807. Hoc, Joseph M. N.-H. THE SYSTEM OF CONTROLLED DECENTRALIZATION OF THE CATHOLIC CHURCH. Unpublished Ph.D. dissertation, Stanford University, 1961. [DA 22,2 A, p. 668]

808. Honigsheim, Paul. "Soziologie der Scholastik." In Max Scheler (ed.), VERSUCHE ZU EINER SOZIOLOGIE DES WISSENS. München and Leipzig: Duncker and Humbolt, 1924, pp. 302-307.

809. Houtart, François. "Sociologie de la paroisse comme assemblée eucharistique." SC 10,1 (1963): 75-91.

810. Houtart, François. "Conflicts of Authority in the Roman Catholic Church." SC 16,3 (1969): 309-325.

811. Hunt, Chester L. "Catholicism and the Birthrate." RRR 8 (1967): 67-80.

Concludes that the reproductive patterns of Catholics internationally are influenced more by social pressures than by religious teaching.

812. Imse, Thomas P. "Spiritual Leadership and Organizational Leadership. The Dilemma of Being Pope." SC 16 (1969): 275-280.

813. Isambert, François-A. "Autour du Catholicisme populaire: Réflexions sociologiques sur un débat." SC 22,2 (1975): 193-210.

Controversy over liturgical changes suggests analysis using the concept of 'popular religion.'

814. Karcher, Barbara C., Ira E. Robinson, and Jack O. Balswick. "Fichter's Typology and Changing Meanings in the Catholic Church." SA 33,3 (1972): 166-176.

Study of a non-traditional Roman Catholic parish after Vatican II suggests a revision of Fichter's typology of Roman Catholic parishioners.

815. Langrod, George. "Le mécanisme institutionel de l'Eglise catholique abordé sous l'angle de la science administrative." SC 16,2 (1969): 241-254.

816. McSweeney, Bill. ROMAN CATHOLICISM. THE SEARCH FOR RELEVANCE. Oxford: Basil Blackwell, 1980.

A critical assessment of Catholicism's attempt to achieve a *modus vivendi* with the prevailing secular culture.

817. McSweeney, Bill. "Catholic Piety in the Nineteenth Century." SC 34, 2-3 (1987): 203-210.

Argues that the ecclesiocentric piety fostered by the church during the nineteenth century served to insulate Catholics from the influences of the wider society.

818. Morlet, Joël. "L'appartenance religieuse comme voie d'accès à la rationalité moderne: Evolution des militants jacistes des années 1950-60." SC 36,2 (1989): 263-279.

819. O'Dea, Thomas F. "The Role of the Intellectual in Catholic Tradition." DAEDALUS 101 (1972): 151-189. See also "La funzione dell'intellettuale nella tradizione cattolica." COMMUNITA 170 (1973): 166-209.

A social history, beginning generally with the Council of Trent but noting some antecedent influences.

820. Osterrieth, Anne. "Medieval Pilgrimage: Society and Individual Quest." SC 36,2 (1989): 145-157.

821. O'Toole, Roger (ed.) SOCIOLOGICAL STUDIES IN ROMAN CATHOLICISM: HISTORICAL AND CONTEMPORARY PERSPECTIVES. Lewiston, New York: Edwin Mellen, 1989.

822. Pin, Emile. INTRODUCTION A L'ETUDE SOCIOLOGIQUE DES PAROISSES CATHOLIQUES. CRITERES DE CLASSIFICATION ET TYPOLOGIE. Paris: Action

Populaire, 1956.

823. Pin, Emile. LA PAROISSE CATHOLIQUE. LES FORMES VARIABLES D'UN SYSTEME SOCIAL. Rome: Presses Universitaires Gregorienne, 1963.

824. Poulat, Emile. "Trois problèmes pour la sociologie du catholicisme." SC 16,4 (1969): 471-483.

The field is insufficiently supported, theoretically tied to beliefs and practices, and reduced to studying immediate problems as defined by church bureaucracies.

825. Poulat, Emile. "Catholicisme urbain et pratique religieuse." ARCHIVES DE SOCIOLOGIE DES RELIGIONS 29 (1970): 97-116.

A critique of F. Boulard and J. Rémy's PRATIQUE RELIGIEUSE URBAINE ET REGIONS CULTURELLES (Paris: Editions Ouvrières, 1968).

826. Poulat, Emile. "L'Eglise romaine: Le savior et le pouvoir." ARCHIVES DE SCIENCES SOCIALES DES RELIGIONS 37 (1974): 5-21.

Examines the social and political impulsions behind the re-establishment of Thomism by Pope Leo XIII.

827. Poulat, Emile. L'EGLISE EBRANLEE: CHANGEMENT, CONFLIT ET CONTINUITE DE PIE XII A JEAN-PAUL II. Tournai: Castermann, 1980.

828. Rémy, Jean. "Opinion publique, groupes de pression et autorité constituée dans la vie de l'Eglise catholique. Contribution à une théorie de la légitimité religieuse." SC 19,2 (1972): 155-184.

Church governing agencies and public opinion interest groups engage in a social negotiation.

829. Seidler, John. "Contested Accommodation: The Catholic Church as a Special Case of Social Change." SOCIAL FORCES 64,4 (1986): 847-874.

Changes in Catholicism occur in processes of evolutionary updating, religious reconstruction, and power contention. Accident, luck, and key personalities determine the timing of any dramatic changes.

830. Sengstock, Mary C. "Traditional and Nationalist Identity in a Christian Arab Community." SA 35,3 (1974): 201-210.

Analysis of religious and nationalist identity in a Chaldean Iraqi community in Detroit, Michigan. Earlier immigrants' nationalist sentiments were not lost through assimilation; increased nationalist identity of recent immigrants is due in part to an increase in urbanism and bureaucratic participation in the modern Middle East.

831. Servais, Emile, and Joseph Bonmariage. "Sunday Mass Attendance as a Cultural Institution." SC 16,3 (1969): 369-386.

Data from students at Louvain.

* Sicking, T. RELIGION ET DEVELOPPEMENT: ETUDE COMPAREE DE DEUX

VILLAGES LIBANAIS. Cited above as item 723.

\* Silber, Ilana Friedrich. "'Opting Out' in Theravada Buddhism and Medieval Christianity." Cited above as item 203.

832. Spaulding, Kent E. "The Theology of the Pew." RRR 13,3 (1972): 206-211.

833. Spencer, A.E.C.W. "Catholicism and Communication." SC 14,1 (1967): 67-71.

834. Spitzer, Allen. "The Culture Organization of Catholicism." AMERICAN CATHOLIC SOCIOLOGICAL REVIEW 19,1 (1958): 2-12.

Typological approach from an anthropological perspective.

835. Stark, Werner. "The Sociology of Catholicism." BLACKFRIARS 25,414 (1954): 364-374.

836. Stark, Werner. "The Routinization of Charisma: A Consideration of Catholicism." SA 26,4 (1965): 203-211.

Maintains that Weber's model does not apply to Catholicism.

837. Stark, Werner. "The Place of Catholicism in Max Weber's Sociology of Religion." SA 29,4 (1968): 202-210.

Argues that Weber's conceptualization of Catholicism was unduly influenced by contemporary prejudice.

838. Vaillancourt, Jean-Guy. PAPAL POWER. A STUDY OF VATICAN CONTROL OVER LAY CATHOLIC ELITES. Berkeley: University of California Press, 1980.

839. Vallier, Ivan. "Comparative Studies of Roman Catholicism: Dioceses as Strategic Units." SC 16,2 (1969): 147-184.

840. Vallier, Ivan. "The Roman Catholic Church: A Transnational Actor." INTERNATIONAL ORGANIZATION 25,3 (1971): 479-502.

Internal changes have resulted from Catholicism's struggles with competitor institutions (nation states, transnational political movements, other Christian bodies).

841. Vallier, Ivan, and Jean-Guy Vaillancourt. "Catholicism, Laity, and Industrial Society: A Cross-national Study of Religious Change." ARCHIVES DE SOCIOLOGIE DES RELIGIONS 23 (1967): 99-102.

Progress report on a comparative study of the Roman Catholic laity in France, Chile, and the United States.

842. Weigert, Andrew J., and Darwin L. Thomas. "Socialization and Religiosity: A Cross-national Analysis of Catholic Adolescents." SOCIOMETRY 33,3 (1970): 305-326.

Purposive samples from male Catholic schools in New York, St. Paul,

San Juan, and Merida. Dimensions of religiosity are related to adolescents' perception of the control and support received from parents.

843. Weigert, Andrew J., and Darwin L. Thomas. "Secularization: A Cross-national Study of Catholic Male Adolescents." SOCIAL FORCES 49,1 (1970): 28-36.

Adolescent samples from New York City, St. Paul, San Juan, and Merida.

844. Weigert, Andrew J., and Darwin L. Thomas. "Secularization and Religiosity: A Cross-national Study of Catholic Adolescents in Five Societies." SA 35,1 (1974): 1-23.

Weakening of traditional belief in the modernized societies presages changes in the configuration of religiosity within Catholicism.

845. Whyte, John. CATHOLICS IN WESTERN DEMOCRACIES. A STUDY IN POLITICAL BEHAVIOUR. Dublin: Gill and Macmillan, 1981.

846. Young, Barry S., and John E. Hughes. "Organizational Theory and the Canonical Parish." SA 26,2 (1965): 57-71.

Considers the parish as a social system rather than as a normative structure.


*CATHOLIC ACTION*

847. Liénard, Georges, and André Rousseau. "Conflit symbolique et conflit social dans le champ religieux. Propositions théoriques et analyse d'un conflit suscité par l'Action Catholique Ouvrière dans le nord de la France." SC 19,2 (1972): 263-290.

A case study for the analysis of repercussions of social conflict in the religious sphere.

848. McCarthy, M. Laetitia. THE SOCIAL ASPECT OF THE SODALITY SYSTEM AS A PHASE OF CATHOLIC ACTION IN THE CITY OF JOLIET. Unpublished M.A. thesis, Loyola University of Chicago, 1936.

849. Poggi, Gianfranco. "La Chiesa nel mondo moderno e l'appello al laicato. Introduzione ad uno studio sociologico dell'Azione Cattolica." RASSEGNA ITALIANA DI SOCIOLOGIA 3,2 (1962): 239-259.

General analysis of the problems preventing the effectiveness of Catholic Action.

850. Poggi, Gianfranco. IL CLERO DI RISERVA. STUDIO SOCIOLOGICO SULL' AZIONE CATTOLICA ITALIANA DURANTE LA PRESIDENZA GEDDA. Milano: Feltrinelli, 1963.

851. Poggi, Gianfranco. CATHOLIC ACTION IN ITALY: SOCIOLOGY OF A SPONSORED ORGANIZATION. Stanford, California: Stanford University Press, 1967.

852. Potvin, Roland. L'ACTION CATHOLIQUE. SON ORGANISATION DANS L'EGLISE. Québec: Les Presses Universitaires de Laval, 1957.

*CATHOLIC CLERGY*

853. Bogan, R.V. THE LIFE WORLDS OF PRIESTS. A STUDY OF RECENTLY ORDAINED ROMAN CATHOLIC PRIESTS. Unpublished M. Phil. thesis, University of Surrey, 1976.

854. Ference, Thomas P., Fred H. Goldner, and R. Richard Ritti. "Priests and Church. The Professionalization of an Organization." AMERICAN BEHAVIORAL SCIENTIST 14,4 (1971): 507-524.

General overview pointing to the emergence of conflicts which previously had been latent.

855. Fichter, Joseph H. "A Comparative View of the Parish Priest." ARCHIVES DE SOCIOLOGIE DES RELIGIONS 16 (1963): 44-48.

A nation-wide (U.S.A.) survey of 2,183 diocesan parish priests and 2,216 of the their parishioners found that the laity think more highly of the priests than the priests think of themselves.

856. Fichter, Joseph H. "The Myth of the Hyphenated Clergy." THE CRITIC 27,3 (Dec. 1968 - Jan. 1969). Reprinted in Joseph H. Fichter, ORGANIZATION MAN IN THE CHURCH [item 858], pp. 37-53.

Professionalization of the pastoral role renders ambiguous the status of non-pastor clergy.

857. Fichter, Joseph H. "Catholic Church Professionals." THE ANNALS 387 (1970): 77-85.

Fewer people are entering the priestly and religious careers, and many are leaving them. Traditional structures are being revised, and the authoritarian system is giving way to collegiality. A new focus on task-orientation has emphasized professionalization, which in turn has promoted self-fulfillment and relative autonomy.

858. Fichter, Joseph H. ORGANIZATION MAN IN THE CHURCH. Cambridge, Massachusetts: Schenckman, 1974.

859. Kauffmann, Michel. "Regard statistique sur les prêtres qui quittent le ministère." SC 17,4 (1970): 495-502.

Overview based on official data, covering the years 1962-68, from a variety of nations and regions.

860. Moore, John. "The Catholic Priesthood." SOCIOLOGICAL YEARBOOK OF RELIGION IN BRITAIN 8 (1975): 30-60.

An overview of the factors which constitute the contemporary 'crisis' of the Catholic priesthood.

861. Moran, Robert. "Liturgy, Authority and Tradition. Priestly Attitudes and the Age Factor." RRR 10,1 (1969): 73-80.

Illustrates how variables other than age might affect attitudes of Roman Catholic priests toward change in the post-conciliar church.

862. Nebreda, Julián. O RENACER O MORIR: UNA RELEXION SOCIORELIGIOSA SOBRE LA CRISIS VOCACIONAL. Madrid: Instituto Teológico de Vida Religiosa, 1974.

863. Pin, Emile. "The Priestly Function in Crisis." In Karl Rahner (ed.), THE IDENTITY OF THE PRIEST, translated by John Drury. New York: Paulist, 1969, pp. 45-58.

Overview based on previously published studies of the 1960s.

864. Poblete Barth, Renato. CRISIS SACERDOTAL. Santiago de Chile: Ed. del Pacifico, 1965.

865. Schallert, Eugene J., and Jacqueline M. Kelley. "Some Factors Associated with Voluntary Withdrawal from the Catholic Priesthood." LUMEN VITAE 25,3 (1970): 425-460. Also in HOMILETIC AND PASTORAL REVIEW 81 (1970-71): 177-183, 254-267.

Based on 317 interviews with former clergy from throughout the Catholic world, though most conducted in San Francisco; interviews of a large control group of priests.

866. Stewart, James H. "Values, Interests, and Organizational Change: The National Federation of Priests' Councils." SA 34,4 (1973): 281-295.

Based on questionnaires sent to elected delegates in 1970 and 1972. Value-oriented delegates were both more committed to pastoral change and more militant than were their interest-oriented counterparts.

867. Stewart, James H. AMERICAN CATHOLIC LEADERSHIP. A DECADE OF TURMOIL 1966-1976. A SOCIOLOGICAL ANALYSIS OF THE NATIONAL FEDERATION OF PRIESTS' COUNCILS. The Hague: Mouton, 1978.

868. Stewart, James H. "When Priests Began to Bargain." RRR 20,2 (1979): 168-179.

Study of the National Federation of Priests' Councils (U.S.A.); data from two time periods is used to test hypotheses concerning organizational effectiveness and changes in value and interest orientations.

869. Sutter, Jacques. "Vocations sacerdotales et séminaires: Le dépérissement du modèle clérical." ARCHIVES DE SCIENCES SOCIALES DES RELIGIONS 59,2 (1985): 177-196.

A general review of European scholarship in the 1960s and 1970s on the clerical profession.

870. Turner, Donald E. SOME EFFECTS OF BUREAUCRACY UPON PROFESSIONALS WHO WORK IN COMPLEX ORGANIZATIONS: AUTHORITY AND EVALUATION IN THE ROMAN

CATHOLIC CHURCH. Unpublished Ph.D. dissertation, Stanford University, 1971. [DA 32:8 A, p. 4700]

871. Von Deschwanden, Leo. "Eine Rollenanalyse des katholischen Pfarrei-priesters." In J. Matthes (ed.), BEITRÄGE ZUR RELIGIONSSOZIOLOGISCHEN FORSCHUNG/ESSAYS ON RESEARCH IN THE SOCIOLOGY OF RELIGION [volume cited in item 121], pp. 123-157.

Theoretical framework for analyzing the role of the Catholic parish priest.

## CATHOLIC TRADITIONALIST

872. Cuneo, Michael W. CONSERVATIVE CATHOLICISM IN NORTH AMERICA: PRO-LIFE ACTIVISM AND THE PURSUIT OF THE SACRED. Brussels: Pro Mundi Vita, 1987. See also Michael W. Cuneo, LE CONSERVATISME CATHOLIQUE NORD-AMERICAIN, translated by Pierre Delooz. Bruxelles: Pro Mundi Vita, 1987.

Discusses differences between Catholic Conservatism and Catholic Traditionalism against the background of anti-abortion protest in North America.

873. Dinges, William D. CATHOLIC TRADITIONALISM IN AMERICA. A STUDY OF THE REMNANT FAITHFUL. Unpublished Ph.D. dissertation, University of Kansas, 1983. [DA 44:4 A, p. 1116]

Social movement and resource mobilization approach. Use of partici-pant observation, analysis of questionnaire data, and review of primary literature.

874. Dinges, William D. "Catholic Traditionalism." In Joseph H. Fichter (ed.), ALTERNATIVES TO AMERICAN MAINLINE CHURCHES. New York: Rose of Sharon, 1983, pp. 137-158.

Focuses on emerging Traditionalist organizations after the Second Vatican Council.

875. Dinges, William D. "Ritual Conflict as Social Conflict: Liturgical Reform in the Roman Catholic Church." SA 48,2 (1987): 138-157.

Resistance to twentieth-century liturgical reform gives expression to class and interest-group conflict linked to the weakening of Catholic identity in a pluralist society, to a crisis of role status loss among clerical elites, and to the emergence and empowerment of a new know-ledge class within the Church.

876. Dinges, William D. "The Quandary of Dissent on the Catholic Right." In Roger O'Toole (ed.), SOCIOLOGICAL STUDIES IN ROMAN CATHOLICISM [item 821], pp. 107-126.

Focuses upon Catholic Traditionalism, with special attention accorded the schismatic Archbishop Lefebvre.

877. Raboud, I. "Mgr. Lefèbvre et ses fidèles valaisans." SCHWEIZERISCHE
ZEITSCHRIFT FÜR SOZIOLOGIE 9 (1983): 617-638.

## CHARISMATIC MOVEMENT

878. Batiuk, Mary E. UNDERSTANDING CATHOLIC CHARISMATIC COMMUNITY. AN
ETHNOGRAPHIC APPROACH. Unpublished Ph.D. dissertation, Washington
University, St. Louis, 1982. [DA 43:12 A, p. 4045]

Based on participant observation in Living Word Community, in the
American midwest. Dialectical integration of sociological polarities
- rational/irrational, natural/supernatural, individual/community,
autonomy/authority.

879. Bord, Richard J., and Joseph E. Faulkner. "Religiosity and Secular
Attitudes: The Case of Catholic Pentecostals." JSSR 14,3 (1975):
257-270.

Survey of Catholic pentecostals in eight states of the U.S. Religiosity indices are associated only with social attitudes which have
direct implications for doctrinal or church-related considerations.

880. Bord, Richard J., and Joseph E. Faulkner. THE CATHOLIC CHARISMATICS.
THE ANATOMY OF A MODERN RELIGIOUS MOVEMENT. University Park, Pennsylvania: Pennsylvania State University Press, 1983.

Participant observation and interviews, 1967-71 and after 1974, of an
unsystematic nature. 1972-74 systematic study, including questionnaire data from Indiana, Louisiana, Maryland, Michigan, New Jersey,
New York, Pennsylvania, and Wisconsin.

881. Castiglione, Miriam. I NEOPENTECOSTALI IN ITALIA. DAL JESUS MOVEMENT
AI BAMBINI DI DIO. Torino: Claudiana, 1974.

882. Chagnon, Roland. LES CHARISMATIQUES DU QUEBEC. Montréal: Québec/
Amerique, 1979.

883. Charuty, Giordana. "Guérir la memoire. L'intervention rituelle du
catholicisme pentecôtiste français et italien." SC 34,4 (1987): 437-
463.

Ethnographic data on a specialized cure for psychic suffering.
Efficacy does not depend on fixed repetitions of a formal ritual but
on the voluntary evocation of a meaning.

884. Cohen, Martine. "A propos du renouveau charismatique aux Etats Unis."
ARCHIVES DE SCIENCES SOCIALES DES RELIGIONS 59,2 (1985): 197-204.

Critical review of R.J. Bord and J.E. Faulkner's THE CATHOLIC CHARIS-
MATICS. THE ANATOMY OF A MODERN RELIGIOUS MOVEMENT [item 880].

885. Cohen, Martine. "Vers de nouveaux rapports avec l'institution
écclésiastique: L'exemple du Renouveau Charismatique en France."

ARCHIVES DE SCIENCES SOCIALES DES RELIGIONS 62,1 (1986): 61-80.

Although a Catholic protest movement, the charismatic movement in
France does not challenge the church's ultimate legitimacy. The
Catholic hierarchy informally regulates the movement.

* Cohen, Martine. "Renouveaux religieux et individualisme: Le cas du
  catholicisme et du judaisme en France." Cited above as item 329.

886. Connelly, James T. NEO-PENTECOSTALISM: THE CHARISMATIC REVIVAL IN THE
MAINLINE PROTESTANT AND ROMAN CATHOLIC CHURCHES IN THE UNITED STATES.
Unpublished Ph.D. dissertation, University of Chicago, 1977.

887. Cote, Pauline. DE LA PROTESTATION FEMININE: LES FEMMES DANS LE
RENOUVEAU CHARISMATIQUE. Unpublished Thèse de Maîtrise en Science
Politique, Université Laval, 1984.

888. Doutreloux, Albert, and Colette Degive. "Perspective anthropologique
sur un mouvement religieux actuel." SC 25,1 (1978): 43-54.

Based on observations of Belgian prayer groups. The charismatic movement occasions the exercise of control, reinforcing a conservative
social framework.

889. Ebaugh, Helen Rose Fuchs, Kathe Richman, and Janet Saltzman Chafetz.
"Life Crises among the Religiously Committed: Do Sectarian Differences
Matter?" JSSR 23,1 (1984): 19-31.

Based on interviews conducted in Houston, Texas, with Christian
Scientists, Catholic charismatics, and Baha'is. These three groups
define crises similarly but react differently to them.

890. Ebaugh, Helen Rose Fuchs, and Sharron Lee Vaughn. "Ideology and
Recruitment in Religious Groups." RRR 26,2 (1984): 148-157.

Based on 1978 interviews conducted in Houston, Texas, with Christian
Scientists, Catholic charismatics, and Baha'is. Charismatics tend to
recruit actively through casual acquaintances, whereas Christian
Scientists and Baha'is operate through more primary relationships.

891. Fichter, Joseph H. "Liberal and Conservative Catholic Pentecostals."
SC 21,3 (1974): 303-310.

Study of American Catholic pentecostals. Politically liberal respondents were found to have more education, and frequently more Catholic
education, than their conservative compeers.

892. Fichter, Joseph H. THE CATHOLIC CULT OF THE PARACLETE. New York:
Sheed and Ward, 1975.

Questionnaire data from lay participants in the U.S.A.; based on a
sample drawn from a 1972 directory.

893. Griffin, Ronald J. SOCIAL CHANGE, BELIEF, AND PENTECOSTALISM IN THE
ROMAN CATHOLIC CHURCH. Unpublished M.A. thesis, York University, 1976.

[National Library of Canada, Canadian Theses on Microfiche #26628]

1975 questionnaire data from two prayer groups in Saskatoon, Saskatchewan, and two in Toronto, Ontario, with control group samples from
nearby parishes; path analysis of variables, with movement membership
the dependent variable; predictors include traditional belief,
literalism, dogmatism, alienation, age, education, family religious
practice.

894. Hammond, Judith A. A SOCIOLOGICAL STUDY OF THE CHARACTERISTICS AND
ATTITUDES OF SOUTHERN CHARISMATIC CATHOLICS. Unpublished Ph.D.
dissertation, Florida State University, 1975. [DA 36:6 A, p. 4037]

Retrospective questions about deprivations, to explore deprivation as
an antecedent to this kind of religiosity.

895. Harper, Charles L. "Spirit-filled Catholics. Some Biographical
Comparisons." SC 21,3 (1974): 311-324.

Presents four typical cases, 1970-72, suggestive of a model of factors
predisposing participation in the charismatic movement.

896. Harrison, Michael I. THE ORGANIZATION OF COMMITMENT IN THE CATHOLIC
PENTECOSTAL MOVEMENT. Unpublished Ph.D. dissertation, University of
Michigan, 1971. [DA 33:5 A, p. 2513]

1969 study which includes questionnaires, observation, interviews of
leaders, and documentary analysis. Movement participants are compared
to a sample of Catholic students at the University of Michigan.

897. Harrison, Michael I. "Preparation for Life in the Spirit: The Process
of Initial Commitment to a Religious Movement." URBAN LIFE AND
CULTURE 2,4 (1974): 387-414.

Based on observation in Ann Arbor, Michigan, a 1969 questionnaire,
interviews, and an analysis of primary literature.

898. Harrison, Michael I. "Sources of Recruitment to Catholic Pentecostalism." JSSR 13,1 (1974): 49-64.

1969 questionnaire survey in prayer groups in Ann Arbor, East Lansing,
and Flint, Michigan. People are more likely to be drawn to a movement who are exposed to it in person, share its problem-solving perspective, have few social obligations that might conflict with
membership, and have or develop social relationships with members.

899. Harrison, Michael I. "The Maintenance of Enthusiasm: Involvement in a
New Religious Movement." SA 36,2 (1975): 150-160.

Based on similar data sources as reported for item 898.

900. Harrison, Michael I. "Dimensions of Involvement in Social Movements."
SOCIOLOGICAL FOCUS 10,4 (1977): 353-366.

Questionnaire data on participation in Catholic pentecostalism suggest
several distinct modes of behavioral involvement.

901. Harrison, Michael I., and John K. Maniha. "Dynamics of Dissenting Movements within Established Organizations: Two Cases and a Theoretical Interpretation." JSSR 17,3 (1978): 207-224.

Neo-pentecostalism within the Roman Catholic and Episcopal churches provides illustration of dissenting movements which do not separate from their parent bodies.

902. Hégy, Pierre. "Images of God and Man in a Catholic Charismatic Renewal Community." SC 25,1 (1978): 7-21.

Focuses on a new system of devotions which was in process of development in a charismatic renewal community in the New York City area.

903. Heirich, Max. "Change of Heart: A Test of Some Widely-held Theories about Religious Conversion." AMERICAN JOURNAL OF SOCIOLOGY 83,3 (1977): 653-680.

Data can be organized to support various explanations for conversion: stress, previous socialization, and direct social influence. But the evidence falls away when the argument is more carefully organized. It would be more to the point for inquiries to probe the circumstances and procedures for affirming or changing a sense of ultimate grounding, at both individual and social levels.

904. Johnson, C. Lincoln, and Andrew J. Weigert. "An Emerging Faithstyle: A Research Note on the Catholic Charismatic Renewal." SA 39,2 (1978): 165-172.

Random sample from a U.S. mailing list, suggesting that the Catholic charismatic movement was not potentially schismatic. It was an alternative answer to a combination of ethical and psychic deprivations.

905. Keane, Roberta C. FORMAL ORGANIZATION AND CHARISMA IN A CATHOLIC PENTECOSTAL COMMUNITY. Unpublished Ph.D. dissertation, University of Michigan, 1974. [DA 35:11 A, p. 7406]

1967-72 study of the routinization of charisma and the development of oligarchy in a community in Ann Arbor, Michigan.

906. Lane, Ralph, Jr. "Catholic Charismatic Renewal." In C.Y. Glock and R.N. Bellah (eds.), THE NEW RELIGIOUS CONSCIOUSNESS [volume cited in item 75], pp. 162-179.

A general history of the movement, with description of typical prayer meetings based on San Francisco Bay Area observations made circa 1970.

907. Lane, Ralph, Jr. "The Catholic Charismatic Renewal Movement in the United States: A Reconsideration." SC 25,1 (1978): 23-35.

Focus on a community in San Francisco which moved in 1977 to South Bend, Indiana.

908. Laurentin, René. CATHOLIC PENTECOSTALISM, translated by Matthew J.

O'Connell. New York: Doubleday, 1977.

909. Lee, Raymond L., and S.E. Ackerman. "Conflict and Solidarity in a Pentecostal Group in Urban Malaysia." SOCIOLOGICAL REVIEW 28,4 (1980): 809-828.

1977-78 ethnographic and interview data from a Catholic pentecostal group in Bandar Baru, near Kuala Lumpur.

910. McGuire, Meredith B. "An Interpretive Comparison of Elements of the Pentecostal and Underground Church Movements in American Catholicism." SA 35,1 (1974): 57-65.

Study of 16 underground groups, 1969-73, and five Catholic pentecostal groups, 1971-73, in northern New Jersey. There were few socio-economic differences between the two kinds of group, but much difference in their respective social psychologies of responding to ambiguity and change.

911. McGuire, Meredith B. "Toward a Sociological Interpretation of the 'Catholic Pentecostal' Movement." RRR 16,2 (1975): 94-104.

A 1971-74 study of seven Catholic pentecostal prayer groups in northern New Jersey.

912. McGuire, Meredith B. "The Social Context of Prophecy: 'Word-gifts' of the Spirit among Catholic Pentecostals." RRR 18,2 (1977): 134-147.

A 1971-75 study of seven Catholic pentecostal prayer groups in northern New Jersey. The 'gift of prophecy' and related speech roles, along with roles of hearers and controllers of speech, are orchestrated in a way enabling the group leaders to maintain firm control of prayer meetings while creating the semblance of spontaneity and egalitarianism.

913. McGuire, Meredith B. "Testimony as a Commitment Mechanism in Catholic Pentecostal Prayer Groups." JSSR 16,2 (1977): 165-168.

Testimony ('witnessing') is found to be the central commitment mechanism for seven Catholic pentecostal prayer groups in northern New Jersey. Testimony includes acts both of involvement and abandonment.

914. McGuire, Meredith B. PENTECOSTAL CATHOLICS. POWER, CHARISMA, AND ORDER IN A RELIGIOUS MOVEMENT. Philadelphia: Temple University Press, 1982.

Based on 1971-77 qualitative research in northern New Jersey.

915. Macioti, Maria I. "Neo-pentecostali e carismatici." CRITICA SOCIO-LOGICA 43 (1977): 17-38.

General account of the neo-pentecostal and charismatic movements among the urban Italian middle class.

916. Moore, John. "The Catholic Pentecostal Movement." SOCIOLOGICAL

YEARBOOK OF RELIGION IN BRITAIN 6 (1973): 73-90.

Analysis of the origins, development, and social character of a 'cult movement' which has taken root in the highly formal and institutional structure of the Roman Catholic church.

917. Neitz, Mary Jo. SLAIN IN THE SPIRIT: CREATING AND MAINTAINING A RELIGIOUS SOCIAL REALITY. Unpublished Ph.D. dissertation, University of Chicago, 1981. [DA 42:6 A, p. 2893]

918. Neitz, Mary Jo. CHARISMA AND COMMUNITY. A STUDY OF RELIGIOUS COMMITMENT WITHIN THE CHARISMATIC RENEWAL. New Brunswick, New Jersey: Transaction, 1987.

919. Pace, Enzo. "Charismatics and the Political Presence of Catholics." SC 25,1 (1978): 85-99.

Study of the charismatic movement in the Veneto region of Italy. By affirming a sharp division between the public or political and the private sides of life, the movement maintains a continuity with traditional Catholicism and represents a departure from recent political activism.

920. Pin, Emile. "En guise d'introduction: Comment se sauver de l'anomie et de l'aliénation. Jesus People et Catholiques Pentecostaux." SC 21,3 (1974): 227-239.

Discusses suggestive parallels between the two movements.

921. Quebedeaux, Richard. THE NEW CHARISMATICS: THE ORIGINS, DEVELOPMENT, AND SIGNIFICANCE OF NEO-PENTECOSTALISM. Garden City: Doubleday, 1976.

922. Reny, Paul, and Jean-Paul Rouleau. "Charismatiques et sociopolitiques dans l'église catholique au Québec." SC 25,1 (1978): 125-143.

Argues that environmental factors are more important than internal features of the charismatic renewal movement.

923. Ribeiro de Oliveira, Pedro A. "Le renouveau charismatique au Brésil." SC 25,1 (1978): 37-42.

Survey data show that the movement is based not on conversion but rather on the reactivation of Catholic spirituality among the privileged classes.

924. Scorsone, Suzanne Rozell. AUTHORITY, CONFLICT AND INTEGRATION: THE CATHOLIC CHARISMATIC RENEWAL MOVEMENT AND THE ROMAN CATHOLIC CHURCH. Unpublished Ph.D. dissertation, University of Toronto, 1979. [DA 40:12 A, p. 6338]

Study of movement factions, one compatible with the authority structure of Roman Catholicism and one not. The first is represented by the Community of God's Love, in Rutherford, New Jersey; the second by the Word of God community in Ann Arbor, Michigan. Detailed analysis of the influence of the second wing in the Archdiocese of Toronto, Ontario, shows it to be minimal.

925. Séguy, Jean. "La protestation implicite. Groupes et communautés charismatiques." ARCHIVES DE SCIENCES SOCIALES DES RELIGIONS 48,2 (1979): 187-212.

A general review of European scholarship on the Catholic charismatic movement.

926. Thompson, John R. "La participation catholique dans le mouvement du renouveau charimatique." SC 21,3 (1974): 325-344.

Participant-observation study of three prayer groups in southern California. Interpretive framework is provided by Troeltsch's third type - mysticism.

927. Walker, Andrew G. "Sociological and Lay Accounts as Versions of Reality: Choosing between Reports of the 'Charismatic Renewal Movement' amongst Roman Catholics." THEORY AND SOCIETY 2,2 (1975): 211-233.

Argues that there is no principled ground for accepting over any other account a sociological account of the charismatic renewal movement.

928. Westley, Frances R. "Searching for Surrender. A Catholic Charismatic Renewal Group's Attempt to Become Glossolalic." AMERICAN BEHAVIORAL SCIENTIST 20,6 (1977): 925-940.

Study of a small group in Montreal whose members tried but failed to experience glossolalia.

* Zylberberg, Jacques. "Nationalisation et dénationalisation: Le cas des collectivités sacrales excentriques." Cited above as item 539.

929. Zylberberg, Jacques, and Pauline Cote. "La réenchantement du monde: Le cas du pentecôtisme catholique." RECHERCHES SOCIOLOGIQUES 17,2 (1987): 129-144.

930. Zylberberg, Jacques, and Jean-Paul Montminy. "Réproduction socio-politique et production symbolique: Engagement et désengagement des charismatiques catholiques québecois." THE ANNUAL REVIEW OF THE SOCIAL SCIENCES OF RELIGION 4 (1980): 121-148.

Presents a model of church dependency and domination by the state and capital; application to Quebec from 1973 to 1979.


*JANSENIST*

931. Lovell, Terry. "Weber, Goldmann and the Sociology of Belief." ARCHIVES EUROPEENNES DE SOCIOLOGIE 14,2 (1973): 304-323.

Reflections on Lucien Goldmann [item 932] and Max Weber's THE PROTES-TANT ETHIC AND THE SPIRIT OF CAPITALISM.

932. Goldmann, Lucien. LE DIEU CACHE. Paris: Gallimard, 1955. See also THE HIDDEN GOD. A STUDY OF TRAGIC VISION IN THE *PENSEES* OF PASCAL AND THE TRAGEDIES OF RACINE, translated by Philip Thody. London: Routledge and Kegan Paul, 1964; New York: Humanities, 1964.

Argues that there exists a homology of structure between the situation of the *noblesse de robe* and the properties of Jansenism.

## MARIOLOGY

933. Carroll, Michael P. "Visions of the Virgin Mary: The Effect of Family Structures on Marian Apparitions." JSSR 22,3 (1983): 205-221.

A Freudian interpretation.

934. Carroll, Michael P. "The Virgin Mary at LaSalette and Lourdes: Whom Did the Children See?" JSSR 24,1 (1985): 56-74.

Desire for a parental figure is offered as an explanation.

935. Carroll, Michael P. THE CULT OF THE VIRGIN MARY. Princeton: Princeton University Press, 1986.

A psychoanalytic interpretation of various Marian apparitions.

936. Cousin, Bernard. "La dévotion mariale aux XVIIe et XVIIIe siècles en Provence." SC 33,1 (1986): 57-64.

937. Deliège, Robert. "Arockyai Mary, gardienne du village chez les Parayars de l'Inde du Sud." SC 33,1 (1986): 75-89.

The caste system set up cultural barriers which blocked the spread of Catholic doctrine to some nominally Catholic castes. The Parayars retained much of their ancient belief system and remained ignorant of most Catholic dogmas. The Virgin Mary, however, entered into their worship system. In a supernatural world of coarse, cruel and blood-thirsty deities, she stood out as a goddess of kindness and love.

938. DeVallée, Thérèse. "Devotion to the Virgin Mary in Sri Lanka: Letters to Our Lady of Perpetual Succour." SC 33,1 (1986): 65-74.

Devotees, writing letters to a shrine in Colombo, were urban middle-class people in a society characterized by transition to the capitalist mode of production.

939. Fee, Joan L., Andrew M. Greeley, William C. McCready, and Theresa A. Sullivan. YOUNG CATHOLICS. A REPORT TO THE KNIGHTS OF COLUMBUS. Los Angeles: Sadlier, 1981.

1979 questionnaire data on American and Canadian young Catholic adults.

940. Gadille, Jacques. "Lourdes - un pèlerinage à l'échelle de la catholicité: Bilan d'une enquête." SC 36,2 (1989): 175-186.

Features 1984 interviews of visitors to Lourdes.

941. Lopes, Policarpo. "Le pèlerinage à Fatima: Une expression mystique du sacré populaire." SC 36,2 (1989): 187-199.

942. O'Connor, Mary. "The Virgin of Guadalupe and the Economics of Symbolic Behavior." JSSR 28,2 (1989): 105-119.

   * Pace, Enzo. "Pilrimage as Spiritual Journey: An Analysis of Pilgrimage Using the Theory of V. Turner and the Resource Mobilization Approach." Cited above as item 108.

943. Tanoni, Italo. "Le culte marial de la Sainte Maison de Lorette et son évolution." SC 33,1 (1986): 107-138.


## MODERNIST CRISIS

944. Kurtz, Lester R. "The Politics of Heresy." AMERICAN JOURNAL OF SOCIOLOGY 88,6 (1983): 1085-1115.

   Argues that heresy and orthodoxy are complementary aspects of the social process out of which belief systems are articulated. Attributes of heresy are outlined, and the Roman Catholic modernist crisis is examined.

945. Kurtz, Lester R. THE POLITICS OF HERESY: THE MODERNIST CRISIS IN ROMAN CATHOLICISM. Berkeley: University of California Press, 1986.

   A documentary study which examines the role of heresy in the formation of orthodoxy.

946. Lyng, Stephen G., and Lester R. Kurtz. "Bureaucratic Insurgency: The Vatican and the Crisis of Modernism." SOCIAL FORCES 63,4 (1985): 901-922.

   Assesses the value of the concept 'bureaucratic insurgency' (i.e., social movements outside organizations) for understanding the Catholic modernist crisis.

947. Poulat, Emile. "<Modernisme> et <intégrisme>: Du concept polémique à l'irénisme critique." ARCHIVES DE SOCIOLOGIE DES RELIGIONS 27 (1969): 3-28.

   Highlights major themes of the author's HISTOIRE, DOGME ET CRITIQUE DANS LA CRISE MODERNISTE (Paris-Tournai: Casterman, 1962) and INTEGRISME ET CATHOLICISME INTEGRAL (Paris-Tournai: Casterman, 1969).

948. Talar, C.J.T. METAPHOR AND MODERNIST: THE POLARIZATION OF ALFRED LOISY AND HIS NEO-THOMIST CRITICS. Lanham, Maryland: University Press of America, 1988.


## RELIGIOUS ORDERS AND CONGREGATIONS

949. Aquina, Mary. "A Sociological Study of a Religious Congregation of

African Sisters in Rhodesia." SC 14,1 (1967): 3-32.

A historical and sociological study of the Sisters of the Child Jesus of Fort Victoria, an African congregation founded by the Dominican Missionary Sisters.

950. Arbuckle, Gerald. OUT OF CHAOS: REFOUNDING RELIGIOUS CONGREGATIONS. New York: Paulist, 1988.

Anthropological analysis of changes in Roman Catholic religious congregations, using concepts of myth, ritual, and culture drawn from the work of Mary Douglas and Mircea Eliade.

951. Bataillon, Marcel. "D'Erasme à la Compagnie de Jésus. Protestation et intégration dans la Réforme Catholique du XVIe siècle." ARCHIVES DE SOCIOLOGIE DES RELIGIONS 24 (1967): 57-81.

Discusses the strategic role played by the Society of Jesus in the Catholic Reformation of the sixteenth century.

952. Blazowich, A. SOZIOLOGIE DES MÖNCHTUMS UND DER BENEDIKTINERREGEL. Wien: Herder, 1954.

953. Browne, J. Patrick. FACTORS CONTRIBUTING TO A PREFERENCE FOR CHANGE IN DEFINITION OF THE SOCIETY OF ST. SULPICE. Unpublished Ph.D. dissertation, Catholic University of America, 1974. [DA 35:2 A, p. 1231]

Secondary analysis of questionnaire data from the American province.

954. Brunetta, Giuseppe. "Una ricerca socioreligiosa sui Cappuccini." AGGIORNAMENTI SOCIALI 9-10 (1974): 617-632.

955. Calabro, William V. SOME ORGANIZATIONAL DETERMINANTS OF ORIENTATION TO CHANGE: A CASE STUDY OF THE ATTITUDES OF WOMEN RELIGIOUS TO THE CALL FOR AGGIORNAMENTO IN THE CATHOLIC CHURCH. Unpublished Ph.D. dissertation, New York University, 1976. [DA 37:9 A, p. 6067]

New York Metropolitan area study of the Sisters of Charity of St. Vincent de Paul.

956. Carli, R., F. Crespi, and G. Pavan. ANALISI DELL'ORDINE DEI FRATI MINORI CAPPUCCINI. Milan: Etas Kompass, 1974. See also ANALISI DELL'ORDINE DEI FRATI MINORI CAPPUCCINI, METODOLOGIA E DOCUMENTAZIONE. Rome: Laurentianum, 1974.

957. Coser, Lewis. "The Militant Collective: Jesuits and Leninists." SOCIAL RESEARCH 40 (1973): 110-128.

958. Culligan, Martin J. FACTORS THAT INFLUENCE VOCATIONS TO THE VINCEN-TIAN FATHERS. Unpublished M.A. thesis, De Paul University, 1964.

Sample of 192 Vincentian candidates and priests ordained less than 10 years.

959. Curcione, Nicholas R. STRUCTURAL FACTORS AFFECTING CAREER COMMITMENT:
A STUDY OF RECRUITMENT TO THE CLARETIAN PRIESTHOOD. Unpublished Ph.D.
dissertation, University of California, Los Angeles, 1970. [DA 31:5
A, p. 2510]

Questionnaire data on altar boys, non-altar boys, minor seminary
students, and major seminary students. Organizational influences were
found to be less important than primary group influences.

960. De Bonte, Walter. "The Components of the Novitiate. Introduction to
an Inquiry." SC 13,5-6 (1966): 401-414.

961. Dudley, Charles J., and George A. Hillery, Jr. "Freedom and Monastery
Life." JSSR 18,1 (1979): 18-28.

Participant-observation and interview data, 1967-78, and questionnaire
data, 1970-76, from five U.S. Trappist monasteries. Focus is on types
of freedom, alienation, cohesion, and deprivation of freedom.

962. Faase, Thomas P. "Bulwark-Catholics and Conciliar-humanists in the
Society of Jesus." SOCIOLOGICAL QUARTERLY 21,4 (1980): 511-527.

Data from participants in the 1975 32nd General Congregation of the
order, and a sample of non-delegates.

963. Faase, Thomas P. MAKING THE JESUITS MORE MODERN. Washington:
University Press of America, 1981.

1974-75 questionnaire data on participants in the 32nd General
Congregation of the order (legislative leadership meeting).

964. Faase, Thomas P. "International Differences in Value Ranking and
Religious Style among Jesuits." RRR 24,1 (1982): 3-18.

1975 survey research among delegates to the 32nd General Congregation
of the order and a 1% sample of non-delegates, to determine differences in value ranking and religious style.

965. Faase, Thomas P. "Making Jesuits More Modern: Changing Values in a
Changing Religious Order." SOCIAL ACTION 32 (1982): 65-86.

Participant-observation, interview, and questionnaire data from
delegates to the 32nd General Congregation, 1974.

966. Fecher, Con J. LIFE-STYLE AND DEMOGRAPHY OF CATHOLIC RELIGIOUS
SISTERHOODS AND HEALTH OF OTHER RELIGIOUS GROUPS. Dayton, Ohio:
University of Dayton Press, 1975.

967. Francis, E.K. "Toward a Typology of Religious Orders." AMERICAN
JOURNAL OF SOCIOLOGY 55 (1950): 437-449.

968. Gannon, Thomas M. "Catholic Religious Orders in Sociological
Perspective." In R.P. Scherer (ed.), AMERICAN DENOMINATIONAL ORGANIZ-
ATION [volume cited in item 424], pp. 159-193.

Brief historical review of the origins and development of Catholic religious orders, and a summary of some recent empirical research on them.

969. Gannon, Thomas M. "Problem-solving versus Problem-setting: The Case of the Jesuit General Survey." RRR 23,4 (1982): 337-353. See also Carroll J. Bourg, "Comment," 353-356.

970. Goddijn, H.P.M. "The Monastic Community Life in Our Times." SC 12, 1-2 (1965): 101-113.

971. Gundlach, Gustav. ZUR SOZIOLOGIE DER KATHOLISCHEN IDEENWELT UND DES JESUITENORDENS. Freiburg im Breisgau: Herder, 1927.

972. Hill, Michael. THE RELIGIOUS ORDER. London: Heinemann, 1973.

Neo-Weberian analysis of how radical change within religious orders has often been legitimated by appeals to tradition. Application to western monasticism, and to the eighteenth-century Methodist renewal and the nineteenth-century Oxford Movement in the Church of England.

973. Hillery, George A., Jr. "Triangulation in Religious Research: A Sociological Approach to the Study of Monasteries." RRR 23,1 (1981): 22-38.

1967-80 study of eleven Trappist and two Trappistine monasteries in the United States.

 * Hillery, George A., Jr., and Paula C. Morrow. "The Monastery as a Commune." Cited above as item 116.

974. Hostie, Raymond. "Vie et mort des instituts religieux." SC 18,1 (1971): 145-147.

Plan of a study in progress.

975. Hostie, Raymond. VIE ET MORT DES ORDRES RELIGIEUX. APPROCHES PSYCHO-SOCIOLOGIQUES. Paris: Desclée de Brouwer, 1972. See also VIDA Y MUERTE DE LAS ORDENES RELIGIOSAS: ESTUDIO PSICOSOCIOLOGICO. Bilbao: Desclée, 1973.

976. Laloux, Joseph. "Une enquête sur une congrégation religieuse." SC 18,1 (1971): 142-144.

Description of research in progress on the Sisters of Providence.

977. Le Bras, Gabriel. "Les confréries chrétiennes, problèmes et proposi-tions." REVUE HISTORIQUE DE DROIT FRANÇAIS ET ETRANGER 19-20 (1940-1941): 320-363.

978. Mattez, M.T. QUELQUES ASPECTS DU CONTEXTE SOCIOLOGIQUE DE LA VOCATION RELIGIEUSE. Louvain: Université Catholique, 1955.

979. Mehok, William J. "What Do Jesuits Do?" SC 8,6 (1961): 567-574.

1955-59 world-wide occupational distribution.

980. Mehok, William J. "Jesuit Trends." RRR 10 (1969): 177-180.

A short note on the author's JESUIT INTERNATIONAL GEOGRAPHIC ANALYSIS OF TRENDS (Cambridge: The Cambridge Center for Social Studies, 1968).

981. Moulin, Léo. "Pour une sociologie des ordres religieux." SC 10,2 (1963): 145-170.

982. O'Connell, John J. "The Integration and Alienation of Religious to Religious Orders." SC 18,1 (1971): 65-84.

Questionnaire data from scholastics (trainees) in the Wisconsin Province (U.S.A.) of the Society of Jesus.

983. Pin, Emile. "Les instituts religieux apostoliques et le changement socio-culturel." NOUVELLE REVUE THEOLOGIQUE 87,4 (1965): 395-411. Also in Hervé Carrier and Emile Pin, ESSAIS DE SOCIOLOGIE RELIGIEUSE. Paris: Spes, 1967.

General discussion, conceptual framework.

984. Rouleau, Jean-Paul. "Mouvements et ordres religieux aujourd'hui." LES CAHIERS DE RECHERCHES EN SCIENCES DE LA RELIGION 5 (1984): 175-205.

985. Santy, Herman. "The Problems of Female Religious Congregations: Some Force-lines for Sociological Research." SC 16,2 (1969): 255-264.

986. Scarvagliere, Giuseppe. L'INSTITUTO RELIGIOSO COME FATTO SOCIALE. Padova: Ed. Laurenziane, 1973.

987. Schnepp, Gerald J., and John T. Kurz. "Length of Life of Male Religious." AMERICAN CATHOLIC SOCIOLOGICAL REVIEW 14,3 (1953): 156-161.

Data from Society of Mary organizational records on members who died, 1819-1951.

988. Séguy, Jean. "Charisme, sacerdoce, foundation: Autour de L.M. Grignion de Montfort." SC 29,1 (1982): 5-24.

Historical study of the charisma of an eighteenth-century founder of two religious congregations, the Missionaries of the Society of Mary and the Daughters of Wisdom.

989. Thompson, Mary. MODIFICATIONS IN IDENTITY: A STUDY OF THE SOCIALIZA-TION PROCESS DURING A SISTER FORMATION PROGRAM. Unpublished Ph.D. dissertation, University of Chicago, 1963.

990. Verdonk, A.L.T. "Réorientation ou désintégration? Une enquête sociologique sur une congrégation religieuse masculine aux Pays-Bas." SC 18,1 (1971): 123-141.

1967 survey among members of the Netherlands Province of the Holy Family Missionaries.

991. Vollmer, Howard M. "Member Commitment and Organizational Competence in Religious Orders." BERKELEY PUBLICATIONS IN SOCIETY AND INSTITUTIONS 3,1 (1957): 13-26.

Consideration of socialization objectives of orders, from an examination of Benedictine and Jesuit literature.

992. Weigert, Andrew J. "An Emerging Intellectual Group Within a Religious Organization: An Exploratory Study of Change." SC 18,1 (1971): 101-115.

Examines the phenomenon of special students among the Jesuits, 1942-69.

993. Whitley, Cuthbert M. THE REVITALIZATION PROCESS IN RELIGIOUS LIFE: A STUDY OF A BENEDICTINE CONGREGATION. Unpublished Ph.D. dissertation, Catholic University of America, 1977. [DA 38:4 A, p. 2200]

Study of the American Cassinese Federation, comparing 1947 and 1974 profiles.

994. Williams, Drid. "The Brides of Christ." In Shirley Ardener (ed.), PERCEIVING WOMEN. London: Malaby Press, 1975, pp. 105-125.

1971 data from a Carmelite (female discalced) convent in England, focusing on the space and time co-ordinates of the nuns' everyday life.

995. Wittberg, Patricia. "Transformations in Religious Commitment." REVIEW FOR RELIGIOUS 44,2 (1985): 161-170.

Examines changes in commitment mechanisms as religious congregations move from being intentional communities to being voluntary associations.

996. Wittberg, Patricia. "Feminist Consciousness among American Nuns: Patterns of Ideological Diffusion." WOMEN'S STUDIES INTERNATIONAL FORUM 12,5 (1989): 529-537.

Explores the applicability of Philip Converse's model of ideological diffusion to a sample of 25 American nuns.

997. Wittberg, Patricia. "The Dual Labor Market in the Catholic Church: Expanding a Speculative Inquiry." RRR 30,3 (1989): 287-290.

Argues that Catholic nuns are not in the primary labor market when they work for the institutional church, in contrast to their positions in their own schools and hospitals.

998. Wittberg, Patricia. "Non-ordained Workers in the Catholic Church: Power and Mobility among American Nuns." JSSR 28,2 (1989): 148-161.

Examines job dissatisfaction among a sample of 25 American nuns.

*SECOND VATICAN COUNCIL*

999. Aloisi, Michael F. "Vatican II, Ecumenism and a Parsonian Analysis of

Change." SA 49,1 (1988): 17-28.

Vatican II is understood as an attempt to increase the adaptive capacity of the Roman Catholic Church.

1000. Caporale, Rocco. VATICAN II: LAST OF THE COUNCILS. Baltimore: Helicon Press, 1964.

1001. Caporale, Rocco. LES HOMMES DU CONCILE. Paris: Cerf, 1965.

1002. Caporale, Rocco. "The Dynamics of Hierocracy: Processes of Continuity-in-Change of the Roman Catholic System during Vatican II." SA 28,2 (1967): 59-68.

Considers modernization as a function of membership pressure, forms of religious power, and doctrinal reformulation.

1003. Casanova, Antoine. VATICAN II ET L'EVOLUTION DE L'EGLISE. Paris, 1969.

1004. Dulong, Renaud. UNE EGLISE CASSEE. ESSAI SOCIOLOGIQUE SUR LA CRISE DE L'EGLISE CATHOLIQUE. Paris: Ed. Economie et Humanisme, Ed. Ouvrières, 1971.

Develops conceptual models for understanding the 'crisis' of the post-Vatican II church.

1005. Endres, Michael E. "Catholic Marriage Values and Social Change." SA 27,1 (1966): 1-8.

Analysis undertaken in the context of changes wrought by the Second Vatican Council.

1006. Goddijn, H.P.M., and Walter Goddijn. "Concile et sociologie." SC 11,5 (1965): 21-27.

The focus on collegiality at the council suggests a new role for sociological inquiry.

1007. Houtart, François. "Critical Decisions and Institutional Tensions in a Religious Institution: The Case of Vatican II." RRR 9,3 (1968): 131-146.

General reflections; the H. Paul Douglass Lectures for 1967.

1008. Ladrière, Paul. "L'athéisme à Vatican II. De la condamnation du communisme à la négociation avec l'humanisme athée." SC 24,4 (1977): 347-391.

Study of the drafting of the Vatican II statement on atheism.

1009. O'Dea, Thomas F. "The Catholic Crisis: Second Chance for Christianity." In Donald E. Cutler (ed.), THE RELIGIOUS SITUATION. Boston: Beacon, 1968, pp. 288-329.

Reflections written in light of the Second Vatican Council.

1010. O'Dea, Thomas F. THE CATHOLIC CRISIS. Boston: Beacon, 1968.

1011. Scarpati, Rosario. "Aspetti sociologici del concilio ecumenico."
ORIENTIMENTI PASTORALI 13,2 (1963): 22-28. See also "Aspects
sociologiques du Concile Oecuménique." SC 11,5 (1965): 29-35.

1012. Ward, Charles D., and James E. Barrett. "The Ecumenical Council and
Attitude Change among Catholic, Protestant and Jewish College
Students." JOURNAL OF SOCIAL PSYCHOLOGY 74 (1968): 91-96.

October 1965, December 1965, and May 1966 questionnaire data from
introductory psychology students at the University of Maryland.

# 10
## Roman Catholic: United States of America

1013. Abel, Theodore. PROTESTANT HOME MISSIONS TO CATHOLIC IMMIGRANTS. New York: Institute of Social and Religious Research, 1933.

     Interviews with workers at mission centers, and with their clients; questionnaire data, observation, reviews of primary literature, and life histories of mission workers and converts.

   * Allinsmith, Wesley, and Beverly Allinsmith. "Religious Affiliation and Politico-economic Attitude." Cited above as item 404.

1014. Augustine, Dominic. "The Catholic College Man and the Negro." AMERICAN CATHOLIC SOCIOLOGICAL REVIEW 8,3 (1947): 204-208.

     Questionnaire data from male students in one midwestern and two eastern Catholic colleges.

1015. Bowdern, Thomas S. A STUDY OF VOCATIONS: AN INVESTIGATION INTO THE ENVIRONMENTAL FACTORS OF VOCATION TO THE PRIESTHOOD AND THE RELIGIOUS LIFE IN THE UNITED STATES FROM 1919 TO 1929. Unpublished Ph.D. dissertation, Saint Louis University, 1936.

     Detailed cross tabulations on a massive sample of novices and seminarians.

1016. Bowdern, Thomas S. "Letter to the Editor." AMERICA 65 (1941): 410.

     Mentions an important sample limitation in Bowdern [item 1015].

1017. Bowdern, Thomas S. "How Vocations Grow." REVIEW FOR RELIGIOUS 1 (1942): 364-375.

     Summary of Bowdern [item 1015].

1018. Cantril, Hadley. "Education and Economic Compositions of Religious Groups: An Analysis of Poll Data." AMERICAN JOURNAL OF SOCIOLOGY 48 (1943): 574-579.

1939-40 U.S. surveys. Religious affiliation (Protestant, Catholic, other, or none) is cross-tabulated with education and social class, for the nation and for regions of the nation.

1019. Chapman, Stanley H. "The Development of the Catholic Church in New Haven, Connecticut." AMERICAN CATHOLIC SOCIOLOGICAL REVIEW 5,3 (1944): 161-168.

1941-42 data, with comparative information on other denominations in New Haven.

1020. Christina, M. "Study of the Catholic Family through Three Generations." AMERICAN CATHOLIC SOCIOLOGICAL REVIEW 3,3 (1942): 144-153.

Questionnaire data on family background, from 1511 members of 10 female religious communities; respondents are of Irish, German, and American descent.

1021. Gillard, John T. COLORED CATHOLICS IN THE UNITED STATES. Baltimore: Josephite Press, 1941.

1022. Harte, Thomas C. "Catholic Education as a Factor in Catholic Opinion." AMERICAN CATHOLIC SOCIOLOGICAL REVIEW 10,1 (1949): 15-30.

Questionnaire data on moral issues from members of Catholic lay organizations in the United States; representativeness admittedly in doubt.

1023. Kane, John J. "Anti-Semitism among Catholic College Students." AMERICAN CATHOLIC SOCIOLOGICAL REVIEW 8 (1947): 209-218.

Questionnaire data from students in a Catholic college in Philadelphia and its affiliated industrial-relations institute.

1024. Kelly, George A. CATHOLICS AND THE PRACTICE OF THE FAITH. A CENSUS STUDY OF THE DIOCESE OF SAINT AUGUSTINE. Washington: Catholic University of America Press, 1946.

1944 data on background variables and indicators of religious activity; based on interviews.

1025. Kelly, George A., and T. Coogan. "What is our Real Catholic Population?" AMERICAN ECCLESIASTICAL REVIEW 110 (1944): 368-377.

1026. Mang, William. "The Extent of Democratization in Catholic Educational Institutions." AMERICAN CATHOLIC SOCIOLOGICAL REVIEW 2,1 (1941): 57-64.

Review of tuition levels and fathers' occupations of students in 21 Catholic boys' high schools in the north-central U.S.A., 1936-37.

1027. Mihanovich, Clement. "The Mobility of Eminent Catholic Laymen." AMERICAN CATHOLIC SOCIOLOGICAL REVIEW 1,2 (1940): 92-99.

Analysis of data from the 1938-39 AMERICAN CATHOLIC WHO'S WHO.

1028. Mihanovich, Clement, and Eugene Janson. "Social Attitudes of Catholic High School Seniors." AMERICAN CATHOLIC SOCIOLOGICAL REVIEW 7,3 (1946): 170-173.

1945 questionnaire data from seniors in 13 Catholic high schools in St. Louis, on social and moral issues.

1029. Nuesse, C. Joseph. "The Relation of Financial Assessment to Status in a Rural Parish." AMERICAN CATHOLIC SOCIOLOGICAL REVIEW 9,1 (1948): 26-38.

1945 study in a small upper-midwestern U.S. parish.

1030. Robinson, Gilbert K. "The Catholic Birth-rate: Further Facts and Implications." AMERICAN JOURNAL OF SOCIOLOGY 41,6 (1936): 757-766.

Studies the decline of birth rate among Catholic immigrants.

1031. Roche, Richard. CATHOLIC COLLEGES AND THE NEGRO STUDENT. Washington: Catholic University of America Press, 1948.

Questionnaire data from registrars of American Catholic colleges and universities.

1032. Schnepp, Gerald J. LEAKAGE FROM A CATHOLIC PARISH. Unpublished Ph.D. dissertation, Catholic University of America, 1938.

1033. Schnepp, Gerald J. "Nationality and Leakage." AMERICAN CATHOLIC SOCIOLOGICAL REVIEW 3,3 (1942): 154-163.

Data from a census of an urban parish in the eastern United States.

1034. Schnepp, Gerald J. "Economic Status and Leakage." AMERICAN CATHOLIC SOCIOLOGICAL REVIEW 4,2 (1943): 76-92.

Same data source as reported for item 1033.

1035. Stouffer, Samuel A. "Trends in the Fertility of Catholics and Non-Catholics." AMERICAN JOURNAL OF SOCIOLOGY 41,2 (1935): 143-166.

American Catholics had a lower rate of fertility during the period 1919-1933.

1036. Thomas, John L. "The Urban Impact on the American Catholic Family." AMERICAN CATHOLIC SOCIOLOGICAL REVIEW 10,4 (1949): 258-267.

Data on 7000 broken Catholic marriages, from interviews in a diocesan Chancery Court of Separation in a large urban center. Focus is on cited causes of breakup.

*WORKS, 1950-1959*

1037. Abbott, M. Martina. A CITY PARISH GROWS AND CHANGES. Washington: Catholic University of America Press, 1953.

Study of St. John the Baptist Parish, Pittsburgh, Pennsylvania,

131

including a 1949-50 census. Focus is on the changes of the parishioners' places of residence.

1038. Bernard, Raymond. "Some Anthropological Implications of the Racial Admission Policy of the U.S. Sisterhoods." AMERICAN CATHOLIC SOCIOLOGICAL REVIEW 19,2 (1958): 124-133.

Policies of sisters' communities, 1951-57, and population of black sisters as of 1957.

1039. Bowman, Jerome F. A STUDY OF SELECTED SOCIAL AND ECONOMIC FACTORS IN THE FORMATION OF A RELIGIOUS VOCATION. Unpublished M.A. thesis, Loyola University (Chicago), 1958.

Data on 120 midwestern Jesuit candidates.

1040. Bukouski, A.F. "The Stability of the Marriages of Catholic College Students." AMERICAN CATHOLIC SOCIOLOGICAL REVIEW 12,1 (1951): 11-16.

Based on alumni data from five midwestern Catholic colleges.

1041. Burns, M. Sheila. A COMPARATIVE STUDY OF SOCIAL FACTORS IN RELIGIOUS VOCATIONS TO THREE TYPES OF WOMEN'S COMMUNITIES: ABSTRACT OF A DISSERTATION. Washington: Catholic University of America Press, 1957.

1042. Cestello, Bosco D. "Catholics in American Commerce and Industry, 1925 -1945." AMERICAN CATHOLIC SOCIOLOGICAL REVIEW 17,3 (1956): 219-233.

Based on WHO'S WHO volumes.

* Christopherson, Victor A., and James Walters. "Responses of Protestants, Catholics, and Jews Concerning Marriage and Family Life." Cited above as item 419.

1043. Cizon, Francis A. "Interethnic and Interreligious Marriage Patterns in Parish X." AMERICAN CATHOLIC SOCIOLOGICAL REVIEW 15,3 (1954): 244-255.

1923-52 parish record data for a Polish-American parish.

1044. Cross, Robert D. THE EMERGENCE OF LIBERAL CATHOLICISM IN AMERICA. Cambridge: Harvard University Press, 1958.

1045. Curtis, Jack H., Frank Avesing, and Ignatius Klosek. "Urban Parishes as Social Areas." AMERICAN CATHOLIC SOCIOLOGICAL REVIEW 18,4 (1957): 319-325.

Use of St. Louis, Missouri, 1950 census tract data corresponding to parish boundaries; parishes crossing tract boundaries used weighted data from the tracts.

1046. Donovan, John D. THE CATHOLIC PRIEST. A STUDY IN THE SOCIOLOGY OF THE PROFESSIONS. Unpublished Ph.D. dissertation, Harvard University, 1951.

1047. Donovan, John D. "The American Catholic Hierarchy: A Social Profile."

AMERICAN CATHOLIC SOCIOLOGICAL REVIEW 19,2 (1958): 98-112.

1957 questionnaire data from members of the American Catholic hierarchy.

1048. Ellspermann, Camillus. "Knowledge of Catholic Social Teaching among 45 Catholic Industrial Workers." AMERICAN CATHOLIC SOCIOLOGICAL REVIEW 17,1 (1956): 10-23.

1954 questionnaire data from a sample of Catholic workers in a mid-western U.S. industrial town.

1049. Fahey, Frank J. THE SOCIOLOGICAL ANALYSIS OF A NEGRO CATHOLIC PARISH. Unpublished Ph.D. dissertation, University of Notre Dame, 1959.

Study of a black parish in a midwestern city; 1958 interview data.

1050. Fichter, Joseph H. "Urban Mobility and Religious Observance." AMERICAN CATHOLIC SOCIOLOGICAL REVIEW 11,3 (1950): 130-139.

Questionnaire and credit bureau data on 1498 families in a southern U.S. parish, 1939-49.

1051. Fichter, Joseph H. "Institutional Environment and Religious Life." LUMEN VITAE 6,1-2 (1951): 165-172.

Discussion of the institutional and cultural framework for the adolescent, the adult male worker, and the female adult, in St. Mary's parish (Southern Parish).

1052. Fichter, Joseph H. SOUTHERN PARISH: DYNAMICS OF A CITY CHURCH. Chicago: University of Chicago Press, 1951.

1053. Fichter, Joseph H. "The Marginal Catholic: An Institutional Approach." SOCIAL FORCES 32,2 (1953): 167-173.

Data from three parishes in a southern city. Contrasting assumptions, relative morality, anti-authoritarianism, and the dysfunctional parish are related to marginality.

1054. Fichter, Joseph H. SOCIAL RELATIONS IN THE URBAN PARISH. Chicago: University of Chicago Press, 1954.

Data from three parishes are used to explore types of parishioner.

1055. Fichter, Joseph H. PAROCHIAL SCHOOL. A SOCIOLOGICAL STUDY. Notre Dame: University of Notre Dame Press, 1958; Garden City: Doubleday-Anchor, 1964.

Based largely on interviews of parents, teachers, graduates, and students of a parochial elementary school in the 1950s, as well as comparative data collected from teachers attending a summer school session at the University of Notre Dame.

1056. Fichter, Joseph H., and Paul W. Facey. "Social Attitudes of Catholic High School Students." AMERICAN CATHOLIC SOCIOLOGICAL REVIEW 14,2

(1953): 94-106.

1952 questionnaire data from Catholic high school juniors and seniors in Dallas, Shreveport, New Orleans, and Tampa, on social and moral issues.

1057. Foley, Albert S.  GOD'S MEN OF COLOR: THE COLORED CATHOLIC PRIESTS OF THE UNITED STATES, 1854-1954.  New York: Farrar, Straus and Company, 1955.

1058. Fosselman, David H.  "The Parish in Urban Communities."  In C.J. Nuesse and T.J. Harte (eds.), THE SOCIOLOGY OF THE PARISH [volume cited in item 799], pp. 133-153.

Study of a parish in Washington, D.C.

1059. Fosselman, David H.  TRANSITION IN THE DEVELOPMENT OF A DOWNTOWN PARISH.  Washington: Catholic University of America Press, 1952.

Study of a parish in Washington, D.C.

1060. Harte, Thomas J.  "Racial and National Parishes in the United States." In C.J. Nuesse and T.J. Harte (eds.), THE SOCIOLOGY OF THE PARISH [volume cited in item 799], pp. 154-177.

   * Herberg, Will.  PROTESTANT-CATHOLIC-JEW.  Cited above as item 454.

1061. Houtart, François.  "The Religious Practice of Catholics in the United States."  LUMEN VITAE 9,3 (1954): 459-476.

1062. Houtart, François.  "Les paroisses de Chicago."  CHRONIQUE SOCIALE DE FRANCE 63,1 (1955): 77-84.

1063. Houtart, François.  "A Sociological Study of the Evolution of American Catholics."  SC 2,5-6 (1955): 189-216.

Demographic data, with a focus on Chicago;  presents trends up to 1950.

1064. Houtart, François.  ASPECTS SOCIOLOGIQUES DU CATHOLICISME AMERICAIN. VIE URBAINE ET INSTITUTIONS RELIGIEUSES.  Paris: Ouvrières, 1957; New York: Arno, 1978.  See also CATOLICISMO Y SOCIEDAD EN LOS ESTADOS UNIDOS.  Madrid: Taurus, 1959.

Descriptive data on Catholicism in Chicago.

1065. Hynes, Emerson.  "The Parish in the Rural Community."  In C.J. Nuesse and T.J. Harte (eds.), THE SOCIOLOGY OF THE PARISH [volume cited in item 799], pp. 100-132.

1066. Jaeckels, Ronald.  A STUDY OF THE SOCIAL BACKGROUND FACTORS OF SEMIN-ARIANS OF THE WESTERN PROVINCE PREPARING FOR THE PRIESTHOOD IN THE SOCIETY OF THE DIVINE WORD.  Unpublished M.A. thesis, Catholic University of America, 1959.

1067. Jammes, Jean-Marie.  "Statistiques du Catholicisme Américain."

ARCHIVES DE SOCIOLOGIE DES RELIGIONS 3 (1957): 97-120.

1068. Kane, John J. "The Social Structure of American Catholics." AMERICAN CATHOLIC SOCIOLOGICAL REVIEW 16,1 (1955): 23-30.

Review of the literature and analysis of data from the 1953-54 AMERI-CAN CATHOLIC WHO'S WHO.

1069. Kane, John J. CATHOLIC-PROTESTANT TENSIONS IN AMERICA. Chicago: Regnery, 1955.

1070. Kennedy, Robert D. A STUDY IN THE SOCIAL BACKGROUNDS OF PRIESTS AND SEMINARIANS IN THE AMERICAN PROVINCE OF THE OBLATES OF ST. FRANCIS DE SALES. Unpublished M.A. thesis, Catholic University of America, 1954.

1071. Kosa, John, and John F. Nash. "The Social Ascending of Catholics." SOCIAL ORDER 8 (1958): 98-103.

Overview, written at a popular level.

1072. Larson, Richard F. "Measuring 'infinite' values." AMERICAN CATHOLIC SOCIOLOGICAL REVIEW 20,3 (1959): 198-202.

1958 questionnaire data from Seattle archdiocesan priests.

1073. Lipset, Seymour M., and Reinhard Bendix. SOCIAL MOBILITY IN INDUSTRIAL SOCIETY. Berkeley: University of California Press, 1959.

1952 and 1955 national U.S. samples. Among first and second genera-tion immigrants, Protestants are in higher occupational positions. In the third generation, there are no differences.

1074. Liu, William T. A STUDY OF THE SOCIAL INTEGRATION OF CATHOLIC MIGRANTS IN A SOUTHERN COMMUNITY. Unpublished Ph.D. dissertation, Florida State University, 1958. [DA 19:3, p. 592]

Based on 1957-58 questionnaire data.

1075. Mack, Raymond W., Raymond J. Murphy, and Seymour Yellin. "The Protes-tant Ethic, Level of Aspiration, and Social Mobility: An Empirical Test." AMERICAN SOCIOLOGICAL REVIEW 21,3 (1956): 295-300.

Sample consisted of 2205 white males who were salesmen, engineers, and bank officials and clerks. Using chi-square tests on tables, no signifi-cant differences were found between Protestants and Catholics, in cross-generational vertical mobility or in occupational aspiration.

1076. Nuesse, C. Joseph. "Membership Trends in a Rural Catholic Parish." RURAL SOCIOLOGY 22,2 (1957): 123-130.

Study in a midwestern setting, based on annual financial reports of a parish.

1077. O'Dea, Thomas F. "The Catholic Immigrant and the American Scene." THOUGHT 31 (1956): 251-270. Reprinted in T.F. O'Dea, SOCIOLOGY AND THE STUDY OF RELIGION. THEORY, RESEARCH, INTERPRETATION. New York:

Basic, 1970, pp. 69-87.

General background discussion.

1078. O'Dea, Thomas F. THE AMERICAN CATHOLIC DILEMMA. New York: Sheed and Ward, 1958.

1079. Palazzolo, Charles S. CORPUS CHRISTI: A SOCIOLOGICAL ANALYSIS OF A CATHOLIC NEGRO PARISH IN NEW ORLEANS. Unpublished M.A. thesis, Louisiana State University, 1955.

1080. Rossi, Peter H., and Alice S. Rossi. "Background and Consequences of Parochial School Education." HARVARD EDUCATIONAL REVIEW 27,3 (1957): 168-199.

Historical review; 1952-55 data from 'Bay City,' Massachusetts. A combination of religious and ethnic factors led to the founding of parochial schools, but there are few distinctive consequences of attending them.

1081. Scheuer, Joseph F. "Some Parish Population Profiles: Toward the Formulation of Useful Hypotheses in the Sociology of the Parish." AMERICAN CATHOLIC SOCIOLOGICAL REVIEW 17,2 (1956): 131-143.

Reviews ethnic dynamics of two parishes in the Bronx, New York.

1082. Schuyler, Joseph B. NORTHERN PARISH: A SOCIOLOGICAL ANALYSIS OF A RELIGIOUS SOCIAL SYSTEM. Unpublished Ph.D. dissertation, Fordham University, 1956.

1083. Schuyler, Joseph B. "The Parish Studied as a Social System." AMERICAN CATHOLIC SOCIOLOGICAL REVIEW 17,4 (1956): 320-337.

1084. Schuyler, Joseph B. "Potential Elements of Organization and Disorganization in the Parish: As Seen in Northern Parish." AMERICAN CATHOLIC SOCIOLOGICAL REVIEW 18,2 (1957): 98-112.

1955 census of a Bronx, New York, parish.

1085. Schuyler, Joseph B. "Religious Behavior in Northern Parish: A Study of Motivating Values." AMERICAN CATHOLIC SOCIOLOGICAL REVIEW 19,2 (1958): 134-144.

Questionnaire data from a 1955 census of a Bronx, New York, parish.

1086. Schuyler, Joseph B. "Religious Observance Differentials by Age and Sex in Northern Parish." AMERICAN CATHOLIC SOCIOLOGICAL REVIEW 20,2 (1959): 124-131.

Questionnaire data from a 1955 census of a Bronx, New York, parish.

1087. Thomas, John L. "Some Characteristics of Cana Conference Personnel in Chicago." AMERICAN CATHOLIC SOCIOLOGICAL REVIEW 17,4 (1956): 338-349.

1955 questionnaire data, focusing on background variables.

1088. Wagner, Helmut R., Kathryn Doyle, and Victor Fisher. "Religious Background and Higher Education." AMERICAN SOCIOLOGICAL REVIEW 24 (1959): 852-856.

Survey of students at a private eastern U.S. university. Contrary to the pattern observed by Weber in Southern Germany, Catholics did not prefer the B.A. to the B.S. programs in higher proportions than did Protestants.

1089. Zahn, Gordon C. A STUDY OF THE SOCIAL BACKGROUNDS OF CATHOLIC CONSCIENTIOUS OBJECTORS IN CIVILIAN PUBLIC SERVICE DURING WORLD WAR II. Unpublished M.A. thesis, Catholic University of America, 1950.


*WORKS, 1960-1969*

1090. Abramson, Harold J. THE ETHNIC FACTOR IN AMERICAN CATHOLICISM. Unpublished Ph.D. dissertation, University of Chicago, 1969.

1091. Alston, Jon P. "Occupational Placement and Mobility of Protestants and Catholics, 1953-1964." RRR 10,3 (1969): 135-140.

1953-54 and 1963-64 American Institute of Public Opinion poll data. Sample consists of employed white males, 25-54 years of age, who identified themselves as either Protestant or Catholic.

1092. Ammentorp, William, and Brian Fitch. THE COMMITTED: A SOCIOLOGICAL STUDY OF THE BROTHERS OF CHRISTIAN SCHOOLS. Winona, Minnesota: St. Mary's College Press, 1968.

1093. Anderson, Charles H. "Religious Communality among White Protestants, Catholics and Mormons." SOCIAL FORCES 46,4 (1968): 501-508.

Questionnaire data from males in three American cities - one heavily Protestant, one heavily Catholic, one heavily Mormon. Religious preferences were found to be important for all three religious groups in the selection of primary group constituencies.

   * Bannan, Rosemary S. "The Other Side of the Coin: Jewish Student Attitudes toward Catholics and Protestants." Cited above as item 405.

1094. Besanceney, Paul H. "Interfaith Marriages of Catholics in the Detroit Area." SA 26,1 (1965): 38-44.

Data from 1955, 1958, and 1959 Detroit Area Study surveys and from 1961 Michigan marriage records.

1095. Billette, André. "Conversion and Consonance: A Sociology of White American Catholic Converts." RRR 8 (1967): 100-104.

A research note which explores why Protestants embrace Catholicism; data derived from Greeley-Rossi's NORC (Chicago) survey of 2071 white American Catholics and of a control group of 530 Protestants interviewed in 1964.

1096. Blake, Judith. "The Americanization of Catholic Reproductive Ideals."
POPULATION STUDIES 20,1 (1966): 27-43.

Lay Catholic ideal family size is closer to non-Catholic ideals than
to that of the official church. Based on 1943-61 data.

1097. Bressler, Marvin, and Charles F. Westoff. "Catholic Education,
Economic Values and Achievement." AMERICAN JOURNAL OF SOCIOLOGY 69,3
(1963): 225-344.

Argues that Catholic education has no effect on economic values and
achievement.

1098. Burchinal, Lee G., and William F. Kenkel. "Religious Identification
and Occupational Status of Iowa Grooms, 1953-7." AMERICAN SOCIOLOGI-
CAL REVIEW 27,4 (1962): 526-532.

Data from marriages of whites in Iowa, 1953-57. There were few
occupational differences between Catholics and Protestants.

   * Burnham, Kenneth E., John F. Connors III, and Richard C. Leonard.
   "Religious Affiliation, Church Attendance, Religious Education and
   Student Attitudes toward Race." Cited above as item 416.

1099. Carrier, Hervé. "Les catholiques dans la culture américaine." REVUE
DE L'ACTION POPULAIRE 162 (1962): 1091-1102.

1100. Crespi, Irving. "Occupational Status and Religion." AMERICAN
SOCIOLOGICAL REVIEW 28,1 (1963): 131.

1963 U.S. adult Gallup poll sample. Occupational differences between
Protestants and Catholics are found to be minimal.

1101. DeJong, Gordon F., and Joseph E. Faulkner. "The Church, Individual
Religiosity, and Social Justice." SA 28,1 (1967): 34-43.

1964 questionnaire data from introductory sociology students at
Pennsylvania State University, focusing on attitudes toward racial
integration and involvement of the churches in the issue.

1102. Del Grande, Mary V. A STUDY OF THE VALUES OF CATHOLIC HIGH SCHOOL
STUDENTS OF DIFFERING SOCIO-ECONOMIC BACKGROUNDS AND THE RELATIONSHIP
OF THESE VALUES TO THOSE OF THEIR PARENTS. Unpublished Ph.D.
dissertation, St. Louis University, 1960. [DA 20:9, p. 3569]

Survey data seem to indicate that Catholic high schools create differences between lower-class children and their parents.

1103. Dewey, Gerald J. INCONGRUITY AND CONFLICT IN THE PASTORAL ROLE OF
THE CATHOLIC PRIEST: AN INVESTIGATION OF SOCIAL CHANGE. Unpublished
Ph.D. dissertation, University of Notre Dame, 1967. [DA 28:8 A, p.
3270]

Sample is from priests of the Tulsa-Oklahoma City diocese.

1104. Dohen, Dorothy. NATIONALISM AND AMERICAN CATHOLICISM. New York:

138

Sheed and Ward, 1967.

1105. Donovan, John D. "Family Socialization and Faculty Publication: A Study of the Academic Man in the Catholic College." AMERICAN CATHOLIC SOCIOLOGICAL REVIEW 24,2 (1963): 115-126.

Sample of 300 faculty members from 22 Catholic institutions of higher education.

1106. Donovan, John D. THE ACADEMIC MAN IN THE CATHOLIC COLLEGE. New York: Sheed and Ward, 1964.

1960 interview data from 'almost 300' Catholic college professors.

1107. Dougherty, Denis. "Normative Value Differences between Public and Parochial School Adolescents." SA 26,2 (1965): 96-109.

Questionnaire data from public and Catholic school students (8th, 10th, and 12th grades) in Missouri.

1108. Dougherty, Denis. "The Rate of Perseverance to Ordination of Minor Seminary Graduates." SA 29,1 (1968): 35-38.

Examines ordination rates by kinds of educational background of entrants into a midwestern Catholic college-level seminary, 1948-57.

1109. Fay, Leo F. "Student Cathexis of the Structures of Religious Socialization in a Catholic College." SA 29,3 (1968): 136-143.

1966-67 survey at Fairfield University in Connecticut. The socialization structures are deemed ineffective because of their traditional orientation and the critical stance of students toward tradition.

1110. Feagin, Joe R. "Black Catholics in the United States: An Exploratory Analysis." SA 29,4 (1968): 186-192.

Statistical data on black Catholics in the U.S.A.

1111. Femminella, Francis X. "The Impact of Italian Migration on American Catholicism." AMERICAN CATHOLIC SOCIOLOGICAL REVIEW 22,3 (1961): 233-241.

1112. Fichter, Joseph H. RELIGION AS AN OCCUPATION. Notre Dame: University of Notre Dame Press, 1961.

Descriptive data on American Catholic clergy and religious.

1113. Fichter, Joseph H. PRIEST AND PEOPLE. New York: Sheed and Ward, 1965.

1960 survey data of American parish priests and active parish leaders.

1114. Fichter, Joseph H. CATHOLIC PARENTS AND THE CHURCH VOCATION: A STUDY OF PARENTAL ATTITUDES IN A CATHOLIC DIOCESE. Washington: Center for Applied Research in the Apostolate, 1967.

1115. Fichter, Joseph H. AMERICA'S FORGOTTEN PRIESTS. New York: Harper and Row, 1968.

1966 survey of diocesan priests who are neither pastors nor monsignors.

1116. Fox, John T. "The Attitude of Male College Students toward Their Church." AMERICAN CATHOLIC SOCIOLOGICAL REVIEW 24,2 (1963): 127-131.

Development of a scale measuring favorability of stance toward one's church; Catholic respondents more favorable than Protestant respondents; Catholic education did not affect the variable.

1117. Glenn, Norval D., and Ruth Hyland. "Religious Preference and Worldly Success: Some Evidence from National Surveys." AMERICAN SOCIOLOGICAL REVIEW 32,1 (1967): 73-85.

Based on various N.O.R.C. and Gallup polls in the U.S. In the mid-1940s Protestants ranked well above Catholics in income, occupation, and education, but by the mid-1960s the reverse was true, largely because of Catholics' more favorable distribution by region and community size.

1118. Glock, Charles Y., and Rodney Stark. RELIGION AND SOCIETY IN TENSION. Chicago: Rand McNally, 1965.

1963 San Francisco Bay Area survey of churched Christians.

1119. Glock, Charles Y., and Rodney Stark. CHRISTIAN BELIEFS AND ANTI-SEMITISM. New York: Harper and Row, 1966.

1963 San Francisco Bay Area survey of churched Christians.

* Gockel, Galen L. "Income and Religious Affiliation: A Regression Analysis." Cited above as item 437.

* Goldstein, Sidney. "Socioeconomic Differentials among Religious Groups in the U.S." Cited above as item 441.

1120. Grady, L. Augustine, and Robert J. McNamara. "Girls' Attitudes toward Priests and Nuns." In William C. Bier (ed.), WOMAN IN MODERN LIFE. New York: Fordham University Press, 1968, pp. 78-96.

Questionnaire data from female Catholic college students.

1121. Greeley, Andrew M. STRANGERS IN THE HOUSE: CATHOLIC YOUTH IN AMERICA. New York: Sheed and Ward, 1961.

1122. Greeley, Andrew M. SOME ASPECTS OF INTERACTION BETWEEN MEMBERS OF AN UPPER MIDDLE-CLASS ROMAN CATHOLIC PARISH AND THEIR NON-CATHOLIC NEIGHBORS. Unpublished M.A. thesis, University of Chicago, 1961.

1123. Greeley, Andrew M. "Some Aspects of Interaction between Religious Groups in an Upper Middle-class Roman Catholic Parish." SC 9,1-2 (1962): 39-61.

Focuses on intermarriage and other associations between Catholics and non-Catholics in a suburban Chicago parish.

1124. Greeley, Andrew M. RELIGION AND THE COLLEGE GRADUATE. Unpublished Ph.D. dissertation, University of Chicago, 1962.

1125. Greeley, Andrew M. "Anti-intellectualism in Catholic Colleges." AMERICAN CATHOLIC SOCIOLOGICAL REVIEW 23,4 (1962): 350-368. See also Richard A. Lamanna, "Comment," 24,1 (1963): 57-58; and A.M. Greeley, "Reply," 24,2 (1963): 167.

Religious identification associates persons with distinctive institutions and produces a desire to advance the institutional prestige; this gives rise to status-earning performances.

1126. Greeley, Andrew M. "Some Information on the Present Situation of American Catholics." SOCIAL ORDER 13,4 (1963): 9-24.

Review of surveys, 1952-62.

1127. Greeley, Andrew M. RELIGION AND CAREER. New York: Sheed and Ward, 1963.

Based on data from 1961 sample of graduating college students and 1962 sample of graduates.

1128. Greeley, Andrew M. "The Religious Behavior of Graduate Students." JSSR 5,1 (1965): 34-40.

N.O.R.C. (U.S.) data of 1961 graduates from the top ten graduate schools.

1129. Greeley, Andrew M. "Criticism of Undergraduate Faculty by Graduates of Catholic Colleges." RRR 6 (1965): 96-106.

Based on data from a study of June 1961 graduates conducted by the National Opinion Research Center.

1130. Greeley, Andrew M. THE RESISTANT PILGRIM: AMERICAN CATHOLICISM AFTER THE COUNCIL. New York: Sheed and Ward, 1966.

1131. Greeley, Andrew M. "Some Results of Catholic Education in the United States." In Hans Kung (ed.), THE SACRAMENTS. AN ECUMENICAL DILEMMA (CONCILIUM 24). New York: Paulist, 1966, pp. 163-176.

Reports recent N.O.R.C. data.

1132. Greeley, Andrew M. "Religion and Academic Career Plans: A Note on Progress." AMERICAN JOURNAL OF SOCIOLOGY 72,6 (1967): 668-672.

Finds no differences in academic career plans between Catholics and non-Catholics in the United States.

1133. Greeley, Andrew M. FROM BACKWATER TO MAINSTREAM. New York: McGraw-Hill, 1969.

1134. Greeley, Andrew M., and Peter H. Rossi. "Correlates of Parochial School Attendance." SCHOOL REVIEW 72,1 (1964): 52-73.

Based on interviews with a national sample of more than 3500 Catholics between high school age and fifty-seven; finds that attendance at Catholic parochial schools gives a significant boost to church and communion attendance, confession attendance, daily praying, church contributions, religious knowledgeability, and religious orthodoxy.

1135. Greeley, Andrew M., and Peter H. Rossi. THE EDUCATION OF CATHOLIC AMERICANS. Chicago: Aldine, 1966.

Most of the data based on 1963-64 interviews of a national sample of U.S. Catholics by N.O.R.C.

1136. Greeley, Andrew M., with William Van Clere and Grace A. Carroll. THE CHANGING CATHOLIC COLLEGE. Chicago: Aldine, 1967.

1965 open-ended interviews with faculty and students at 19 Catholic and 6 other private colleges and universities.

1137. Greer, Scott. "Catholic Voters and the Democratic Party." PUBLIC OPINION QUARTERLY 25,4 (1961): 611-625.

1956-57 data from a St. Louis metropolitan area sample survey.

1138. Grichting, Wolfgang L. ORGANIZATIONAL STRUCTURE AND CLIMATE: THE CASE OF THE ROMAN CATHOLIC PARISH. Unpublished Ph.D. dissertation, University of Michigan, 1968. [DA 30:2 A, p. 807]

Study of 119 parishes in the Archdiocese of Detroit; interviews of clergy, questionnaires from parishioner sample; typology of attitudes – traditionalism, activism, revisionism, retreatism.

1139. Grichting, Wolfgang L. PARISH STRUCTURE AND CLIMATE IN AN ERA OF CHANGE. A SOCIOLOGIST'S INQUIRY. Washington: C.A.R.A., 1969.

1967 sample of Detroit archdiocesan parishes; subsamples of parishioners and lay leaders.

1140. Haerle, Rudolf K., Jr. "Church Attendance Patterns among Intermarried Catholic: A Panel Study." SA 30,4 (1969): 204-216.

Low rates of church attendance of intermarried Catholics relative to other Catholics reflect patterns set prior to marriage.

1141. Hassenger, Robert. "Varieties of Religious Orientation." SA 25,4 (1964): 189-199.

1963 questionnaire data from a midwestern Catholic women's college.

1142. Hassenger, Robert. "Catholic College Impact on Religious Orientations." SA 27,2 (1966): 67-79.

Data from a Catholic women's college showing no college effect on religious orientation.

1143. Hassenger, Robert. "Portrait of a Catholic Women's College." In R. Hassenger (ed.), THE SHAPE OF CATHOLIC HIGHER EDUCATION. Chicago:

University of Chicago Press, 1967, pp. 83-100.

Historical portrait (1920s and following) of a college in a large midwestern city.

1144. Hassenger, Robert. "The Impact of Catholic Colleges." In R. Hassenger (ed.), THE SHAPE OF CATHOLIC EDUCATION [volume cited in item 1143], pp. 103-161.

Rehearses previously published studies of the subject.

1145. Hassenger, Robert. "The Structure of Catholic Higher Education." In Philip Gleason (ed.), CONTEMPORARY CATHOLICISM IN THE UNITED STATES. Notre Dame: University of Notre Dame Press, 1969, pp. 295-323.

Review of data from the 1960s.

1146. Hong, Lawrence K. "Religious Styles, Dogmatism and Orientations to Change." SA 27,4 (1966): 239-242.

Questionnaire data from students in a Catholic men's college is used to depict different styles of Catholicism.

1147. James, William R. A COMPARATIVE STUDY OF ATTITUDES TOWARD VOCATION TO THE PRIESTHOOD OF EIGHTH-, NINTH- AND TWELFTH-GRADE BOYS. Unpublished M.A. thesis, Catholic University of America, 1961.

Sample of male students in Catholic schools in the diocese of Mobile-Birmingham, Alabama.

1148. Kosa, John, and Cyril O. Schommer. "Religious Participation, Religious Knowledge, and Scholastic Aptitude: An Empirical Study." JSSR 1,1 (1961): 88-97.

Respondents were from an American Catholic undergraduate college. Religious knowledge and participation correlated positively with scholastic aptitude and achievement. A more church-oriented environment is likely to produce higher scores on religious knowledge and participation.

1149. Lamanna, Richard A., and J.J. Coakley. "The Catholic Church and the Negro." In P. Gleason (ed.), CONTEMPORARY CATHOLICISM IN THE UNITED STATES [volume cited in item 1145], pp. 147-194.

Review of previously published data.

1150. Lane, Ralph, Jr. "Research Note on Catholics as a Status Group." SA 26,2 (1965): 110-112.

Why should church attendance be higher among upwardly-mobile Catholics when Catholicism is supposed to militate against values related to upward mobility?

1151. Lane, Ralph, Jr. "The Consequential Dimension of Religiosity among Catholics." SA 27,2 (1966): 94-100.

1963 questionnaire data from the San Francisco Bay Area survey, Catholic subsample. Focus on perceived agreement between respondent and pastor as a variable predictive of believing the church should 'stick to religion.'

* Laumann, Edward O. "The Social Structure of Religious and Ethno-religious Groups in a Metropolitan Community." Cited above as item 469.

* Lazerwitz, Bernard. "Religion and Social Structure in the United States." Cited above as item 471.

1152. Lenski, Gerhard. THE RELIGIOUS FACTOR, revised edition. Garden City: Doubleday, 1963.

1958 interviews from the Detroit Area Study.

1153. Light, Donald W., Jr. "Social Participation in Public and Catholic Schools." RRR 8 (1966): 3-11.

Explores whether Catholic schools have any special effects on their students; data for study were obtained from self-administered questionnaires left at a national sample of Catholic households and completed by adolescents in each family.

1154. Liu, William T. "The Marginal Catholics in the South. A Revision of Concepts." AMERICAN JOURNAL OF SOCIOLOGY 65 (1960): 383-390.

Argues that Catholic immigrants to a southern U.S. city show more anomie than marginality.

1155. Lutterman, Kenneth G. GIVING TO CHURCHES: A SOCIOLOGICAL STUDY OF THE CONTRIBUTIONS TO EIGHT CATHOLIC AND LUTHERAN CHURCHES. Unpublished Ph.D. dissertation, University of Wisconsin, 1962. [DA 23:4, p. 1447]

The lower-class church member gives smaller sums than does the upper-class member, but a higher percentage of income. Local congregations are responsive to contextual status differences and establish conse-quent norms of their own related to church-giving.

1156. McCarrick, Theodore E. THE VOCATION PARISH: AN ANALYSIS OF A GROUP OF HIGH VOCATION-SUPPLYING PARISHES IN THE ARCHDIOCESE OF NEW YORK TO DETERMINE THE COMMON CHARACTERISTICS OF THE VOCATION PARISH. Unpublished Ph.D. dissertation, Catholic University of America, 1963. [DA 24:6, p. 2611]

Data based on major seminarians of the New York Archdiocese.

1157. McNamara, Patrick H. BISHOPS, PRIESTS AND PROPHECY: A STUDY IN THE SOCIOLOGY OF RELIGIOUS PROTEST. Unpublished Ph.D. dissertation, University of California at Los Angeles, 1968. [DA 29:9 A, p. 3235]

A study of protest activity by priests ministering to Mexican-American migrant farm workers in California and South Texas.

1158. McNamara, Patrick H. "Social Action Priests in the Mexican-American

144

Community." SA 29,4 (1968): 177-185.

Analysis of data based on interviews with 13 social-action priests involved with Mexican-American problems in the U.S.

1159. McNamara, Robert J. THE INTERPLAY OF INTELLECTUAL AND RELIGIOUS VALUES. Unpublished Ph.D. dissertation, Cornell University, 1963. [DA 24:2, p. 882]

1961 student samples from undergraduates at Fordham University, University of Notre Dame, Columbia College, and the College of Arts and Sciences at Cornell University.

1160. McNamara, Robert J. "Intellectual Values and Instrumental Religion." SA 25,2 (1964): 99-107.

Based on the same data sources as reported for item 1159.

1161. McNamara, Robert J. "Catholics and Academia." RRR 8 (1967): 81-95.

Discusses the growth in graduate studies at American Catholic universities in the post-World War II era.

1162. McNamara, Robert J. "The Priest-scholar." In R. Hassenger (ed.), THE SHAPE OF CATHOLIC HIGHER EDUCATION [volume cited in item 1143], pp. 203-212.

1163. Madigan, Francis C. "Role Satisfactions and Length of Life in a Closed Population." AMERICAN JOURNAL OF SOCIOLOGY 67,6 (1962): 640-649.

1953-57 data on mortality rates of religious-order priests.

1164. Maiolo, John R., William V. D'Antonio, and William T. Liu. "Sources and Management of Strain in a Social Movement: Some Preliminary Observations." SA 29,2 (1968): 67-78.

Discusses the process by which clearly defined channels for airing and resolving disputes emerged within the Christian Family Movement.

1165. Maloney, Daniel J. AGE DIFFERENCES IN THE PERCEIVED INFLUENCE OF PERSONAL FACTORS ON VOCATION CHOICE. Unpublished M.A. thesis, Catholic University of America, 1963.

Based on data from minor seminarians.

* Mayer, Albert J., and Harry Sharp. "Religious Preference and Worldly Success." Cited above as item 484.

1166. Murphy, Roseanne. A COMPARATIVE STUDY OF ORGANIZATIONAL CHANGE IN THREE RELIGIOUS COMMUNITIES. Unpublished Ph.D. dissertation, University of Notre Dame, 1966. [DA 27:1 A, p. 262]

Interview data from three orders of sisters.

1167. Murphy, Roseanne. "Factors Influencing the Developmental Pace of

Religious Communities." SA 27,3 (1966): 157-169.

Examines the manner in which organizational characteristics of three teaching communities of sisters influence propensities toward change.

1168. Neal, Marie Augusta. VALUES AND INTERESTS IN SOCIAL CHANGE. Englewood Cliffs, N.J.: Prentice-Hall, 1965.

1961 questionnaire data from a sample of Boston archdiocesan priests, focusing on orientations toward values, interests, and change.

1169. Neal, Marie Augusta. "Catholicism in America." In W.G. McLoughlin and R.N. Bellah (eds.), RELIGION IN AMERICA [volume cited in item 409], pp. 312-336.

1170. Neal, Marie Augusta, and Miriam Clasby. "Priests' Attitudes toward Women." In W.C. Bier (ed.), WOMAN IN MODERN LIFE [volume cited in item 1120], pp. 55-77.

Based on a 1961 survey of Boston archdiocesan priests; focus is on priestly stereotyping of women.

1171. O'Dea, Thomas F. "American Catholics and International Life." SOCIAL ORDER 10 (1960): 243-265. Reprinted in T.F. O'Dea, SOCIOLOGY AND THE STUDY OF RELIGION [volume cited in item 1077], pp. 39-68.

Review of factors influencing Catholic views of international relations.

1172. O'Dea, Thomas F. "Catholic Sectarianism: A Sociological Analysis of the so-called Boston Heresy Case." RRR 3 (1961): 49-63. Reprinted in T.F. O'Dea, SOCIOLOGY AND THE STUDY OF RELIGION [volume cited in item 1077], pp. 23-38.

A study of the Feeney schism.

1173. Organic, Harold N. RELIGIOUS AFFILIATION AND SOCIAL MOBILITY IN CONTEMPORARY AMERICAN SOCIETY: A NATIONAL STUDY. Unpublished Ph.D. dissertation, University of Michigan, 1963. [DA 25:1, pp. 679-680]

U.S. sample of males from Christian denominations, whose occupations and whose fathers' occupations were non-agricultural. Protestants show more upward mobility than Catholics. Among Catholics, parochial education correlated positively with upward mobility.

1174. Osborne, William A. "Religious and Ecclesiastical Reform. The Contemporary Catholic Experience in the United States." JSSR 7,1 (1968): 78-86.

Articulation of a thesis that church reform follows the beat of its own drummer.

1175. Potvin, Raymond H., and Thomas K. Burch. "Fertility, Ideal Family-size and Religious Orientation among U.S. Catholics." SA 29,1 (1968): 28-34.

U.S. sample of 1028 married Catholic women. Considers contraceptive practice and fertility as predictors of religious practice.

1176. Potvin, Raymond H., and Charles F. Westoff. "Social Factors in Catholic Women's Choice of a College." SA 28,4 (1967): 196-204.

Questionnaire data from Catholic female students in 45 colleges and universities, focusing on predictors of their choosing Catholic vs. other colleges.

1177. Potvin, Raymond H., and Charles F. Westoff. "Higher Education and the Family Normative Beliefs of Catholic Women." SA 28,1 (1967): 14-21.

Questionnaire data from a sample of freshman and senior women at 46 U.S. colleges and universities; analysis of the Catholic subsample. Selectivity rather than college experience explains differentials in family belief systems of students in public vs. denominational institutions.

1178. Reiss, Paul J. "The Trend in Interfaith Marriages." JSSR 5,1 (1965): 64-67.

Examines the fluctuating rate of religiously mixed marriages in the continental U.S.A. from 1943 onwards.

1179. Reiss, Paul J. "The Catholic College: Some Built-in Tensions." In R. Hassenger (ed.), THE SHAPE OF CATHOLIC HIGHER EDUCATION [volume cited in item 1143], pp. 253-273.

1180. Reiterman, Carl. "Birth Control and Catholics." JSSR 4,2 (1965): 213-233.

Review of 55 years of AMERICA magazine, showing an internal Catholic controversy over contraception.

    * Robbins, Richard. "American Jews and American Catholics: Two Types of Social Change." Cited above as item 500.

1181. Rossi, Peter H., and Andrew M. Greeley. "The Impact of the Roman Catholic Denominational School." SCHOOL REVIEW 72 (1964): 34-51.

Based on interviews with a national sample of more than 3500 Catholics between high-school age and fifty-seven.

1182. Rossi, Peter H., and Alice S. Rossi. "Some Effects of Parochial School Education in America." DAEDALUS 90,2 (1961): 300-328.

Historical overview; data from 1900-1959; additional data from the 'Bay City' study and other previously published reports.

1183. Sampson, Samuel F. A NOVITIATE IN A PERIOD OF CHANGE: AN EXPERIMENTAL CASE STUDY IN SOCIAL RELATIONSHIPS. Unpublished Ph.D. dissertation, Cornell University, 1968. [DA 29:11 A, p. 4118]

Based on one year of field research on a contemplative order in the U.S.

1184. Schommer, Cyril O., John Kosa, and Leo D. Rachiele. "Socio-economic

Background and Religious Knowledge of Catholic College Students."
AMERICAN CATHOLIC SOCIOLOGICAL REVIEW 21,3 (1960): 229-237.

Questionnaire data from entrants to a Catholic college.

1185. Schuyler, Joseph B. NORTHERN PARISH: A SOCIOLOGICAL AND PASTORAL
STUDY. Chicago: Loyola University Press, 1960.

1186. Spaeth, Joe L. "Religion, Fertility, and College Type among College
Graduates." SA 29,3 (1968): 155-159.

Based on 1964 U.S. data from N.O.R.C. In the first three years after
college graduation, graduates of Catholic colleges have more children
than other Catholics, who in turn have more than Protestants, Jews, or
agnostics.

1187. Tarleton, M. Rose. THE RELATION OF PERCEIVED ATTITUDES OF REFERENCE
GROUP MEMBERS TO PERSONAL ATTITUDES TOWARD AND DECISIONS TO ENTER
ROMAN CATHOLIC SISTERHOODS. Unpublished Ph.D. dissertation, Catholic
University of America, 1968. [DA 30:2 A, p. 838]

Study of congruence of self-concept and perceived role, among senior
girls in a Catholic high school in the eastern U.S.A.

1188. Trent, James W., and Jenette Golds. CATHOLICS IN COLLEGE: RELIGIOUS
COMMITMENT AND THE INTELLECTUAL LIFE. Chicago: University of Chicago
Press, 1967.

Based on several data sets, gathered from 1959 to 1963.

1189. Warkov, Seymour, and Andrew M. Greeley. "Parochial School Origins and
Educational Acievement." AMERICAN SOCIOLOGICAL REVIEW 31,3 (1966):
406-414.

Based on a 1960 American survey of 45 scientific, engineering, technical, and other professional occupations. It is suggested that
economic rather than religious factors are responsible for the slower
scientific advancement of parochial school graduates.

1190. Wedge, Rosalma B. THE OCCUPATIONAL MILIEU OF THE CATHOLIC SISTER.
Unpublished Ph.D. dissertation, St. John's University, 1966. [DA 28:8
A, p. 3278]

Based on archival data from the Archdiocese of New York, questionnaire
data from Catholic high-school girls and their parents, a sample
survey of sisters in the New York Archdiocese, and interviews.

1191. Weller, Neil J. RELIGION AND SOCIAL MOBILITY IN INDUSTRIAL SOCIETY.
Unpublished Ph.D. dissertation, University of Michigan, 1963.
[DA 22:1, p. 354]

Sample of Detroit males, 1952-58. Protestants are more likely than
Catholics to attain upper-status non-manual occupations, Catholics
are more likely to have lower-status manual occupations.

1192. Westoff, Charles F., and Raymond H. Potvin. "Higher Education,

148

Religion and Women's Family-size Orientations." AMERICAN SOCIOLOGICAL REVIEW 31,4 (1966): 489-496.

Based on a survey of U.S. women attending colleges and universities. Selectivity rather than attendance at Catholic institutions explains higher family size preference of students at Catholic colleges.

1193. Westoff, Charles F., and Raymond H. Potvin. COLLEGE WOMEN AND FERTILITY VALUES. Princeton: Princeton University Press, 1967.

1194. Wiley, Norbert. "Religious and Political Liberalism among Catholics." SA 28,3 (1967): 142-148.

Survey data from a Catholic university.

1195. Winandy, Donald H. VIEWS OF CATHOLIC EDUCATIONAL LEADERS ON CO-EDUCATION IN INSTITUTIONS OF HIGHER EDUCATION AFFILIATED WITH THE ROMAN CATHOLIC CHURCH IN THE UNITED STATES OF AMERICA. Unpublished Ph.D. dissertation, Florida State University, 1967. [DA 28:7 A, p. 2510]

Questionnaire data from Catholic college and university presidents and their religious superiors show an increasing acceptance of coeducation.

* Zelan, Joseph. "Religious Apostasy, Higher Education, and Occupational Choice." Cited above as item 526.

1196. Zimmer, Basil, and Calvin Goldscheider. "A Further Look at Catholic Fertility." DEMOGRAPHY 3 (1966): 462-470.

Suburbanization seems to be narrowing Protestant-Catholic differentials; based on a sample survey in four metropolitan areas (merged).


*WORKS, 1970-1979*

1197. Abramson, Harold J. "Inter-ethnic Marriage among Catholic Americans and Changes in Religious Behavior." SA 32,1 (1971): 31-44.

Levels of association with the Catholic church vary among ethnic groups. From a national sample of Catholic Americans, the religious behavior of traditionally endogamous ethnic groups is compared with that of exogamous groups.

1198. Abramson, Harold J. "Ethnic Diversity within Catholicism: A Comparative Analysis of Contemporary and Historic Religion." JOURNAL OF SOCIAL HISTORY 4,4 (1971): 359-388. Reprinted in Dolores Liptak (ed.), A CHURCH OF MANY CULTURES: SELECTED HISTORICAL ESSAYS ON ETHNIC AMERICAN CATHOLICISM. New York: Garland, 1988.

Review of Catholic organizational success in Quebec, Germany, Ireland, Poland, Sicily, Mexico, and Puerto Rico, 1949-61, as background for Catholic ethnic groups in the U.S.A.

1199. Abramson, Harold J. ETHNIC DIVERSITY IN CATHOLIC AMERICA. New York:

149

Wiley, 1973.

1963-64 N.O.R.C. (U.S.) data.

1200. Alba, Richard D. "Social Assimilation among American Catholic National-origin Groups." AMERICAN SOCIOLOGICAL REVIEW 41,6 (1976): 1030-1046.

U.S.A. data (1960s) lend support to an assimilationist rather than a pluralist model.

1201. Alba, Richard D., and Ronald C. Kessler. "Patterns of Interethnic Marriage among American Catholics." SOCIAL FORCES 57,4 (1979): 1124-1140.

A 1963 sample of American Catholics, aged 23-57, suggests the declining importance of ethnicity.

1202. Alston, Jon P., Letitia T. Alston, and Emory Warrick. "Black Catholics: Social and Cultural Characteristics." JOURNAL OF BLACK CULTURE 2 (1971): 245-255.

1203. Alvirez, David. "The Effects of Formal Church Affiliation and Religiosity on the Fertility Patterns of Mexican-American Catholics." DEMOGRAPHY 10,1 (1973): 19-36.

Based on 1969 Austin, Texas, interview data from Mexican-American couples.

1204. Apostal, Robert A., and James R. Ditzler. "Research Note: Dogmatism and Attitudes toward Religious Change." SA 32,3 (1971): 180-183.

Survey of adults in a northwestern Minnesota parish.

1205. Becker, Tamar. "Inter-faith and Inter-nationality Attitudinal Variations among Youth toward Self, Family and the Collective." RRR 20,1 (1978): 68-81.

Three sets of data: from Los Angeles, California, public high-school students; Catholic high-school students from the same area; and Israeli high-school students. The cross-national differences were much greater than the intra-national denomination vs. public sample differences.

1206. Blasi, Anthony J. ACOLYTES' PERCEPTIONS AND CHOICE OF THE SACERDOTAL OCCUPATION: A SOCIAL STUDY OF ROLE-TAKING. Unpublished Ph.D. dissertation, University of Notre Dame, 1973. [DA 34:7 A, p. 4421]

Questionnaire data from adolescents in central Missouri, 1973.

1207. Blasi, Anthony J. "Vocations and Perceptions." SA 36,1 (1975): 67-72.

Questionnaire data from adolescents in central Missouri, 1973.

1208. Blasi, Anthony J., Peter J. MacNeil, and Robert O'Neill. "The Relationship between Abortion Attitudes and Catholic Religiosity." SOCIAL

SCIENCE 50,1 (1975): 34-39.

Based on 1974 student questionnaire data from two Catholic colleges in New England.

1209. Bode, Jerry G. "Status and Mobility of Catholics vis-a-vis Several Protestant Denominations: More Evidence." SOCIOLOGICAL QUARTERLY 11,1 (1970): 103-111.

Interview data from a 1967 Nebraska sample.

1210. Boling, T. Edwin. "Sectarian Protestants, Churchly Protestants and Roman Catholics: A Comparison in a Mid-American City." RRR 14,3 (1973): 159-168.

Data from Springfield, Ohio, compare socioeconomic variables, religious attitudes, and religious activity of Catholics, Protestant church members, and Protestant sect members. Catholics resemble Protestant church members in socioeconomic variables and religious attitudes but resemble Protestant sect members in religious practice - for example, attendance and private prayer.

1211. Bouvier, Leon F. THE EFFECT OF CATHOLICISM ON THE FERTILITY OF RHODE ISLAND WOMEN: 1968-1969. Unpublished Ph.D. dissertation, Brown University, 1971. [DA 32:9 A, p. 5351]

Based on 1968-69 interview data from Rhode Island households.

1212. Bouvier, Leon F. "Catholics and Contraception." JOURNAL OF MARRIAGE AND THE FAMILY 34,3 (1972): 514-522.

Based on 1968-69 interviews of Rhode Island housewives. Catholics, other than younger respondents, are more likely to use the natural, or 'rhythm,' method.

1213. Bouvier, Leon F. "The Fertility of Rhode Island Catholics: 1968-1969." SA 34,2 (1973): 124-139.

Representative state-wide samples, 1968-69, show that Catholics exhibit higher fertility expectations than non-Catholics, but that the differences are smaller than in the recent past.

1214. Bouvier, Leon F., and Robert H. Weller. "Residence and Religious Participation in a Catholic Setting." SA 35,4 (1974): 273-281.

Mass attendance of Roman Catholics in Rhode Island varied little from central city to suburbs.

1215. Buetow, Harold A. "The Underprivileged and Roman Catholic Education." JOURNAL OF NEGRO EDUCATION 40,4 (1971): 373-389.

Historical overview, focusing on native American and black education in the U.S.A.

1216. Clemente, Frank. "The Research Productivity of Doctorates in Sociology from Catholic and Non-Catholic Universities." SA 33,2 (1972): 74-80.

Data for doctoral-level sociologists holding membership in the American Sociological Association, 1950-70. Graduates of Catholic Ph.D.-granting departments have lower research productivity, but the difference disappears when confounding independent variables are removed.

1217. Collins, Daniel F. "Black Conversion to Catholicism: Its Implication for the Negro Church." JSSR 10,3 (1971): 209-219.

Examines the background and significance of conversions to Catholicism by southern blacks. Change from communal to individualistic religiosity emerges as a dominant pattern.

1218. Cryns, Arthur G. "Dogmatism of Catholic Clergy and Ex-clergy: A Study of Ministerial Role Perseverance and Open-mindedness." JSSR 9,3 (1970): 239-244.

A study of priests, ex-priests, seminarians, and ex-seminarians, from two metropolitan dioceses.

1219. Curcione, Nicholas R. "Family Influence on Commitment to the Priesthood: A Study of Altar Boys." SA 34,4 (1973): 265-280.

Data from 78 Catholic elementary-school students in Los Angeles.

1220. Dahm, Charles W. AUTHORITY AND CONFLICT IN THE ROMAN CATHOLIC CHURCH: IDEOLOGICAL AND POLITICAL CONSTRAINTS ON DEMOCRATIZATION IN AN AUTHORITARIAN INSTITUTION. Unpublished Ph.D. dissertation, University of Wisconsin, Madison, 1978. [DA 39:8 A, p. 5119]

Focus on the clergy of the Chicago Archdiocese during the tenure of the cardinal archbishop, John Cody, 1965-77.

1221. Dellacava, Frances A. STATUS ABROGATION: A STUDY OF THE FORMER ROMAN CATHOLIC PRIEST. Unpublished Ph.D. dissertation, Fordham University, 1973. [DA 34:1 A, p. 424]

Interview data, not claimed to be representative, suggesting a three-stage status abrogation process.

1222. Dellacava, Frances A. "Becoming an Ex-priest: The Process of Leaving a High-commitment Status." SOCIOLOGICAL INQUIRY 45,4 (1975): 41-49.

1969 and 1970 depth-interview data from 35 ex-priests.

1223. Denhardt, Robert B., and Jerome J. Salomone. "Race, Inauthenticity and Religious Cynicism." PHYLON 33,2 (1972): 120-131.

Examines differences between black and white Catholics' reactions to the stance of their church upon the death of a noted segregationist in Louisiana.

1224. Dixon, Robert C., and Dean R. Hoge. "Models and Priorities of the Catholic Church as Held by Suburban Laity." RRR 20,2 (1979): 150-167.

Survey of three suburban Virginia parishes. Laity had personal and family concerns in mind more than other matters.

1225. Dundon, Mary C. "The Christian Character of Certain Liberal Arts Colleges with a Focus on the Academic Arena." SA 32,2 (1971): 107-119.

Survey of responses of academic deans in Catholic, Protestant, and non-sectarian institutions. Responses from the three groups differed, especially those of the denominational versus non-sectarian groups.

1226. Ebaugh, Helen Rose Fuchs. OUT OF THE CLOISTER. Austin: University of Texas Press, 1977.

1971 questionnaire data from heads of female religious orders in the U.S.A., asking about losses of members; case studies of three orders; interviews with a sample of 'leavers.'

1227. Ebaugh, Helen Rose Fuchs. "Education and the Exodus from Convents." SA 39,3 (1978): 257-264.

1971 survey of female orders in the U.S.; data from major superiors.

1228. Ennis, Joseph G. THE ROLE EXPECTATION OF ROMAN CATHOLIC CAMPUS CHAPLAINS AND ROMAN CATHOLIC UNDERGRADUATES FOR THE ROMAN CATHOLIC CAMPUS CHAPLAIN. Unpublished Ph.D. dissertation, St. John's University, 1975. [DA 36:8 A, p. 5040]

Questionnaire data from chaplains and students in the New York metropolitan area.

1229. Fay, Leo F. "Catholics, Parochial Schools, and Social Stratification." SOCIAL SCIENCE QUARTERLY 55,2 (1974): 520-527.

Questionnaire data from parents of students in 26 parochial schools in Connecticut, Rhode Island, and western Massachusetts. Reasons for sending children to the schools vary by socioeconomic status.

1230. Fay, Leo F. "Differential Anomie Responses in a Religious Community." SA 39,1 (1978): 62-76.

Questionnaire data from an order of nuns whose headquarters is in a large eastern U.S. city.

 * Featherman, David L. "The Socioeconomic Achievement of White Religio-ethnic Subgroups: Social and Psychological Explanations." Cited above as item 428.

1231. Fee, Joan L. "Party Identification among American Catholics, 1972, 1973." ETHNICITY 3,1 (1976): 53-69.

1972-73 N.O.R.C. (U.S.) data show Catholics tending to be Democrats, especially among the older age groups.

1232. Fichter, Joseph H. "High School Influence on Social-class Attitudes." SA 33,4 (1972): 246-252.

Survey of Jesuit high-school students in the U.S.A., 1965 and 1968. A comparison of freshman and senior responses suggests the schools decrease lower-class economic liberalism but increase acceptance of the rights of blacks.

1233. Fox, William S., and Elton F. Jackson. "Protestant-Catholic Differences in Educational Achievement and Persistence in School." JSSR 12,1 (1973): 65-84.

Based on a 1957 U.S. sample. A Protestant advantage appears after the introduction of statistical controls.

1234. Gaede, Stan. "Religious Affiliation, Social Mobility, and the Problem of Causality: A Methodological Critique of Catholic-Protestant Socioeconomic Achievement Studies." RRR 19,1 (1977): 54-62.

1235. Gannon, Thomas M. THE INTERNAL SOCIAL ORGANIZATION AND BELIEF SYSTEM OF AMERICAN PRIESTS. Unpublished Ph.D. dissertation, University of Chicago, 1972.

1236. Gannon, Thomas M. "The Impact of Structural Differences on the Catholic Clergy." JSSR 18,4 (1979): 350-362.

1970-71 N.O.R.C. data on American Catholic priests. The diocesan priesthood appears to have an exchange model of goal integration; the order clergy, an accommodation model.

1237. Gannon, Thomas M. "The Effect of Segmentation in the Religious Clergy." SA 40,3 (1979): 183-196.

Comparisons among respondents belonging to the Order of St. Benedict, Order of St. Francis, Society of Jesus, and Catholic Mission Society of America (Maryknoll), from the 1970 N.O.R.C. survey of U.S. priests.

1238. Garrison, Vivian. "Sectarianism and Psychosocial Adjustment: A Controlled Comparison of Puerto Rican Pentecostals and Catholics." In I.I. Zaretsky and M.P. Leone (eds.), RELIGIOUS MOVEMENTS IN CONTEMPORARY AMERICA [volume cited in item 87], pp. 298-329.

Based on 1966-69 observation, surveys, and interviews in a largely Puerto Rican section of the Bronx, New York.

1239. Gessner, John C. PRIESTLY PERSISTERS AND RESIGNERS: TESTING A FRAMEWORK OF OCCUPATIONAL CHOICE. Unpublished M.A. thesis, University of Notre Dame, 1973.

Data from a 1970 American Catholic priest survey reveal no relationship between age of entry into a seminary and propensity to resign from the ministry, or between age of entry and priestly job satisfaction.

1240. Goldner, Fred H., Thomas P. Ference, and Richard R. Ritti. "Priests and Laity: A Profession in Transition." SOCIOLOGICAL REVIEW MONOGRAPH 20 (1973): 119-137.

Based on 1970 survey data of 986 diocesan priests in a U.S. diocese, spanning the 1939-60 ordination classes. Analyzes the anticipated decline of the clerical status.

1241. Goldner, Fred H., Richard R. Ritti, and Thomas P. Ference. "The Production of Cynical Knowledge in Organizations." AMERICAN SOCIOLOGICAL REVIEW 42,4 (1977): 539-551.

'Cynical knowledge' is an organization member's understanding that presumably altruistic procedures and actions are actually self-serving. A study of the priests of a large U.S. diocese suggests that differences in their beliefs, associated with age, can be explained by an understanding of the role that cynical knowledge plays in an organization dependent upon commitment to altruistic ends.

1242. Greeley, Andrew M. THE CATHOLIC PRIEST IN THE UNITED STATES: SOCIO-LOGICAL INVESTIGATIONS. Washington: U.S. Catholic Conference, 1971.

1970-71 N.O.R.C. data on U.S. Catholic priests.

1243. Greeley, Andrew M. PRIESTS IN THE UNITED STATES: REFLECTIONS ON A SURVEY. New York: Doubleday, 1972.

1244. Greeley, Andrew M. "American Catholics -- Making It or Losing It?" PUBLIC INTEREST 28 (1972): 26-37.

   * Greeley, Andrew M. "The 'Religious Factor' and Academic Careers: Another Communication." Cited above as item 446.

1245. Greeley, Andrew M. "The Sexual Revolution among Catholic Clergy." RRR 14,2 (1973): 91-100.

Dramatic change in attitudes toward birth control and divorce, correlated with age, 'inner direction,' and modern religious values.

1246. Greeley, Andrew M. ETHNICITY, DENOMINATION, AND INEQUALITY. Beverly Hills: Sage, 1976.

1247. Greeley, Andrew M. "Council or Encyclical?" RRR 18,1 (1976): 3-24.

The decline in Catholic orthodoxy and religious devotion is associated with the birth control encyclical.

1248. Greeley, Andrew M. THE AMERICAN CATHOLIC. A SOCIAL PORTRAIT. New York: Basic Books, 1977.

Data from a variety of sources, much of it from N.O.R.C. samples.

1249. Greeley, Andrew M. "The Sociology of American Catholics." ANNUAL REVIEW OF SOCIOLOGY 5 (1979): 91-111.

Review of literature from the 1970s.

1250. Greeley, Andrew M. CRISIS IN THE CHURCH: A STUDY OF RELIGION IN AMERICA. Chicago: Thomas More Press, 1979.

Uses data from previous studies, 1963-77, mostly from the 1970s.

1251. Greeley, Andrew M., William C. McCready, and Kathleen McCourt. CATHO-
LIC SCHOOLS IN A DECLINING CHURCH. Mission, Kansas: Sheed and Ward,
1976.

Based on 1974 re-interviews of respondents who had been identified as
Catholic in the 1973 N.O.R.C. Continuous National Survey (U.S.).

1252. Griffin, John J. AN INVESTIGATION OF THE WORK SATISFACTION OF PRIESTS
OF THE ARCHDIOCESE OF BOSTON. Unpublished Ph.D. dissertation, Boston
College, 1970. [DA 31:6 A, p. 3018]

Based on 1968-69 questionnaire data.

1253. Groat, H. Theodore, Arthur G. Neal, and Evelyn C. Knisely. "Contraceptive Nonconformity among Catholics." JSSR 14,4 (1975): 367-377.

1972 data from 412 white Catholic women, aged 20-44, selected in a
probability sample. Parity relative to desired family size was the
most important predictor of contraceptive nonconformity.

1254. Hall, Douglas T., and Benjamin Schneider. ORGANIZATIONAL CLIMATES AND
CAREERS. THE WORK LIVES OF PRIESTS. New York: Seminar Press, 1973.

1968 interview data from a sample of diocesan priests of the Archdiocese of Hartford, Connecticut.

1255. Hanna, Mary T. CATHOLICS AND AMERICAN POLITICS. Cambridge, Massachusetts: Harvard University Press, 1979.

1256. Heimer, David D. "Abortion Attitudes among Catholic University
Students: A Comparative Research Note." SA 37,3 (1976): 255-260.

Survey of students at a Catholic college in Washington State, compared
to various U.S. poll results.

1257. Henlein, George A., and Robert T. Blackburn. "Faculty Views on Identity and Professionalism for Catholic Colleges and Universities." SA
32,4 (1971): 215-228.

Survey of faculty at 11 Catholic colleges or universities suggests a
trend toward non-sectarian status.

1258. Hoge, Dean R., and Gregory H. Petrillo. "Development of Religious
Thinking in Adolescence: A Test of Goldman's Theories." JSSR 17,2
(1978): 139-154.

Survey of youth in three denominations in Maryland suburbs of Washington, D.C., 1976; respondents were tenth-graders. High-level abstract
thinking about religion is associated with rejection of doctrine,
except among Catholics enrolled in private schools.

1259. Hoge, Dean R., and Gregory H. Petrillo. "Determinants of Church
Participation and Attitudes among High-School Youth." JSSR 17,4
(1978): 359-379.

Data based on interviews with 451 Catholic, Southern Baptist, and

Methodist tenth-graders.

1260. Humphreys, Claire. "Structural Inconsistency and Vocation-related Tension." RRR 16,1 (1974): 31-40.

Study of an order of nuns in western New York State; questionnaire data focusing on occupation-related tension.

1261. Hunt, Larry L., and Janet G. Hunt. "A Religious Factor in Secular Achievement among Blacks: The Case of Catholicism." SOCIAL FORCES 53,4 (1975): 595-605.

1968 interview data from students, grades 3-12, in the Baltimore, Maryland, public school system.

1262. Hunt, Larry L., and Janet G. Hunt. "Black Catholicism and the Spirit of Weber." SOCIOLOGICAL QUARTERLY 17,3 (1976): 369-377.

Examines the association between upward mobility and Catholicism among American blacks.

1263. Hunt, Larry L., and Janet G. Hunt. "Religious Affiliation and Militancy among Urban Blacks: Some Catholic/Protestant Comparisons." SOCIAL SCIENCE QUARTERLY 57 (1977): 821-833.

1964 interview data from black Americans in most regions of the U.S.A.

1264. Hunt, Larry L., and Janet G. Hunt. "Black Catholicism and Occupational Status in Northern Cities." SOCIAL SCIENCE QUARTERLY 58,4 (1978): 657-670.

Late 1960s interview data from black Americans in 15 major northern centers.

1265. Jackson, Elton F., William S. Fox, and Harry J. Crockett, Jr. "Religion and Occupational Achievement." AMERICAN SOCIOLOGICAL REVIEW 35,1 (1970): 48-63.

1957 U.S. national sample. Protestants are more likely than Catholics of the same occupational origin to enter high-status nonmanual occupations, and Catholics more likely to enter low-status nonmanual ones. Protestants are more often sharply upwardly mobile and Catholics more often sharply downwardly mobile. These differences are small but robust.

1266. Jeffries, Vincent, and Clarence E. Tygart. "More on Clergy and Social Issues." JSSR 13,3 (1974): 309-324.

Sample survey of clergy from five denominations in the Los Angeles metropolitan area. Theological position was the best predictor of opinions and activities concerning a variety of social issues.

1267. Johnstone, Ronald L. "Public Images of Protestant Ministers and Catholic Priests: An Empirical Study of Anti-clericalism in the U.S." SA 33,1 (1972): 34-49.

Data from a national sample of American adults, focusing on public images of Catholic, Methodist, and Lutheran clergy. What little anti-clericalism there was existed among Catholics and was directed at Catholic priests.

1268. Jones, Larry A. "Empirical Evidence on Moral Contextualism." RRR 19,3 (1978): 246-252.

Data from survey responses of 1324 Methodist and Catholic laity and clergy. Items eliciting contextualist responses are not symbolically central and appear to involve a specific application of a general rule.

1269. Kaiser, Marvin A. A STUDY OF RETIRED ROMAN CATHOLIC DIOCESAN PRIESTS: A SOCIOLOGICAL ANALYSIS. Unpublished Ph.D. dissertation, University of Nebraska, Lincoln, 1979. [DA 40:2 A, p. 1103]

Interview data from 22 respondents in three mid-western dioceses, with matched data from retirees and non-retirees.

1270. Kelly, Henry E. "Role Satisfaction of the Catholic Priest." SOCIAL FORCES 50,1 (1971): 75-84.

1969 survey of Catholic diocesan clergy in Oklahoma. Role satisfaction is explained by the amount of difference between pre-ordination expectations and post-ordination experiences, and the age of entrance into the seminary (with older ordinands less satisfied).

1271. Kelly, James R. "Relativism and Institutional Religion." JSSR 9,4 (1970): 281-284.

Based on 1968 questionnaire data; investigates the relationship between relativism and some indices of institutional religious practice.

1272. Kelly, James R. "Sources of Support for Ecumenism: A Sociological Study." JOURNAL OF ECUMENICAL STUDIES 8,1 (1971): 1-9.

Based on questionnaire data gathered in Lexington, Massachusetts, during the summer of 1968. Concludes that a person uninterested in either general religious questions or in the secular relevance of the churches is not likely to have an interest in ecumenism.

1273. Kelly, James R. "Who Favors Ecumenism? A Study of Some of the Correlates of Support for Ecumenism." SA 32,3 (1971): 158-169.

Based on 1968 questionnaire data; Roman Catholics who were highly involved in their church and who accepted traditional Christian teachings were more likely than other Catholics to support ecumenism.

1274. Kelly, James R. "The New Roman Church: A Modest Proposal." COMMON-WEAL (December 1971): 222-226.

Discusses the challenges posed by ecumenism and cultural relativism for contemporary American Catholics.

1275. Kelly, James R. "Attitudes toward Ecumenism: An Empirical Investigation." JOURNAL OF ECUMENICAL STUDIES 9,2 (1972): 341-351. Reprinted in Patrick H. McNamara (ed.), RELIGION AMERICAN STYLE. New York: Harper and Row, 1974, pp. 249-258.

1968 questionnaire data indicate points of ecumenical convergence among Catholic and Protestant respondents in Lexington, Massachusetts.

1276. Kelly, James R. "Escaping the Dilemma: Reconciliation and a Communications Model of Conflict." RRR 19,2 (1978): 167-177.

A 1974 questionnaire study conducted among Jewish, Protestant, and Catholic congregations in a northeastern residential suburb.

* Kelly, James R. "The Spirit of Ecumenism: How Wide, How Deep, How Mindful of Truth?" Cited above as item 466.

1277. Kelly, James R., and Avery Dulles. "The Catholic Dilemma." In Charles Van Doren (ed.), BRITANNICA BOOK OF THE YEAR (Special Supplement). New York: Encyclopaedia Britannica, 1977.

Describes changes in the American and universal Roman Catholic Church since the advent of reforms instituted by Vatican Council II.

1278. Klemmack, David L., and Jerry D. Cardwell. "Interfaith Comparison of Multidimensional Measures of Religiosity." PACIFIC SOCIOLOGICAL REVIEW 16,4 (1973): 495-507.

Questionnaire data from students at a southeastern U.S. public university.

1279. Koller, Douglas B. "Belief in the Right to Question Church Teachings, 1958-71." SOCIAL FORCES 58,1 (1979): 290-304.

Finds a pronounced increase in belief in the right to question church teachings, among Detroit Catholics. The magnitude of the change is inversely related to age and directly related to education and church attendance.

1280. Kotre, John N. THE VIEW FROM THE BORDER. A SOCIAL PSYCHOLOGICAL STUDY OF CURRENT CATHOLICISM. Chicago: Aldine-Atherton, 1971.

1968 interviews of graduates of Catholic colleges who were graduate students at the University of Chicago or at Northwestern University. Focus is on the subjects considering themselves still inside their church or not.

* Kourvetaris, George A., and Betty A. Dobratz. "An Empirical Test of Gordon's Ethclass Hypothesis among Three Ethnoreligious Groups." Cited above as item 771.

1281. Koval, John, and Robert Bell. A STUDY OF PRIESTLY CELIBACY. Chicago: National Federation of Priests' Councils, 1970.

1970 survey of American Catholic priests.

1282. Kratcoski, Peter C. "Catholic College Faculties: An Examination of

Their Educational and Professional Attainments and Value Commitments."
SA 32,4 (1971): 199-214.

Survey of faculty of five Catholic colleges. Religious and lay respondents were similar in educational attainments and professional accomplishments, but the former were more committed to specifically Catholic functions of the institutions. Younger lay faculty, lay faculty with higher degrees, and lay faculty with degrees from non-denominational institutions were less committed to specifically Catholic values, but equally committed to more general values of character-building and the general purpose of the institutions.

1283. Lally, John J. "Selection as an Interactive Process: The Case of Catholic Psychoanalysts and Psychiatrists." SOCIAL SCIENCE AND MEDICINE 9,3 (1975): 157-164.

1960 questionnaire data from psychiatrists in New York City; 7% Catholic, 13% Protestant, 62% Jewish, 18% no religion; of those who are also psychoanalysts, the respective figures are 2%, 12%, 62%, and 25%.

1284. Lampe, Philip E. COMPARATIVE STUDY OF THE ASSIMILATION OF MEXICAN AMERICANS: PAROCHIAL SCHOOLS VS. PUBLIC SCHOOLS. Unpublished Ph.D. dissertation, Louisiana State University, 1973. [DA 34:9 A, p. 6145]

1973 questionnaire data from eighth-grade students. Parochial-school students were more assimilated except in self-identification responses.

1285. Lampe, Philip E. "The Acculturation of Mexican Americans in Public and Parochial Schools." SA 36,1 (1975): 57-66.

1973 study of eighth-grade students in San Antonio, Texas.

1286. Lampe, Philip E. "Assimilation and the School System." SA 37,3 (1976): 228-242.

1973 study of eighth-grade students in San Antonio, Texas, comparing assimilation patterns in parochial and public schools.

1287. Lampe, Philip E. "Religion and the Assimilation of Mexican Americans." RRR 18,3 (1977): 243-253.

Extension of the analysis undertaken in item 1286.

1288. Lee, Gary R., and Robert W. Clyde. "Religion, Socioeconomic Status, and Anomie." JSSR 13,1 (1974): 35-47.

1970 data from 191 American Lutheran and 203 Roman Catholic young married couples living in Minnesota. Certain religious variables may be of greater importance than socioeconomic factors as sources of variance in personal normlessness.

1289. Linblade, Zondra G. PATTERN-MAINTENANCE AND INTEGRATION WITHIN A NORMATIVE ORGANIZATION: THE ROMAN CATHOLIC PRIESTHOOD IN THE UNITED STATES. Unpublished Ph.D. dissertation, Loyola University of Chicago, 1976.

* McGuire, Meredith B. "An Interpretive Comparison of Elements of the Pentecostal and Underground Church Movements in American Catholicism." Cited above as item 910.

* McMurray, Martha. "Religion and Women's Sex Role Traditionalism." Cited above as item 483.

1290. McNamara, Patrick H. "Dynamics of the Catholic Church: From Pastoral to Social Concern." In Leo Grebler, Joan W. Moore, and Ralph C. Guzman (eds.), THE MEXICAN AMERICAN PEOPLE. New York: Macmillan-Free Press, 1970, pp. 449-485.

In most of the Southwest, the Catholic Church has been unable to serve as an assimilationist force.

1291. McNamara, Patrick H. "Catholicism, Assimilation and the Chicano Movement: Los Angeles as a Case Study." In Rudolph O. De la Garza, Z. Anthony Kruszewski, and Tomás A. Arciniega (eds.), CHICANOS AND NATIVE AMERICANS: THE TERRITORIAL MINORITIES. Englewood Cliffs, N.J.: Prentice-Hall, 1973, pp. 124-130.

Examines the Archdiocese of Los Angeles as an assimilationist force.

1292. Maher, Joseph A. A STUDY OF THE RELATIONSHIP BETWEEN THE RELIGIOUS ORIENTATION OF ROMAN CATHOLIC PARENTS AND THEIR ATTITUDES TOWARD ROMAN CATHOLIC SCHOOLS. Unpublished Ph.D. dissertation, New York University, 1971. [DA 32:10 A, p. 5632]

Questionnaire data from parents of Catholic elementary-school students in New York City.

1293. Malak, Sharon Jo. "A Study of Catholic College Students' Attitudes toward Abortion." SOCIAL SCIENCE 47 (1972): 229-231.

Questionnaire data from students at a small midwestern Catholic college.

1294. Maranell, Gary M. RESPONSES TO RELIGION. STUDIES IN THE SOCIAL PSYCHOLOGY OF RELIGIOUS BELIEF. Lawrence: University of Kansas Press, 1974.

Clergy sample, and Catholic college student sample; separate data base of interviews with lay Catholics in a southern community.

1295. Moberg, David O., and Jean N. McEnery. "Changes in Church Related Behavior and Attitudes of Catholic Students." SA 37,1 (1976): 53-62.

Based on Marquette University surveys, 1961-1971.

1296. Moberg, David O., and Jean N. McEnery. "Prayer Habits and Attitudes of Catholic Students, 1961-1971." SOCIAL SCIENCE 51,2 (1976): 76-85.

Marquette University surveys, 1961-71. Frequency of prayer diminished; reasons for praying shifted toward an increased desire to converse with God, but the rank order of four reasons for praying remained the same.

1297. Moore, Maurice J. DEATH OF A DOGMA? THE AMERICAN CATHOLIC CLERGY'S VIEWS OF CONTRACEPTION. Chicago: Community and Family Study Center, 1973.

Analysis of data from the N.O.R.C. 1971 study of American Catholic priests.

* Mueller, Charles W., and Weldon T. Johnson. "Socioeconomic Status and Religious Participation." Cited above as item 491.

1298. Munick, Jeanette. UNFORESEEN RETIREMENT: A COMMUNITY OF NUNS IN TRANSITION. Unpublished Ph.D. dissertation, University of Southern California, 1977. [DA 38:10 A, p. 6346]

Ethnography of a residence voluntarily formed by retirees.

1299. Musetto, Andrew P. "Innovators in the Catholic Church." RRR 17,1 (1975): 28-36.

The Catholic Church is composed of significantly different subgroups, with orientation to change and innovation a relevant differentiating variable.

1300. Neal, Marie Augusta. "The Relation between Religious Belief and Structural Change in Religious Orders: Developing an Effective Measuring Instrument." RRR 12,1 (1970): 2-16. See also "The Relation between Religious Belief and Structural Change in Religious Orders: Some Evidence." RRR 12,3 (1971): 153-164.

1967 questionnaire survey of American sisters.

1301. Neal, Marie Augusta. "A Theoretical Analysis of Renewal in Religious Orders in the U.S.A." SC 18,1 (1971): 7-26.

Discusses the importance of a consciousness of social injustice.

1302. Nelsen, Hart M., and Lynda Dickson. "Attitudes of Black Catholics and Protestants. Evidence for Religious Identity." SA 33,3 (1972): 152-165.

1957-69 U.S. Gallup survey data, and 1971 Louisville, Kentucky, survey; black Protestants and Catholics.

1303. Nelson, Joel I., and Charles Simpkins. "Family Size and College Aspirations: A Note on Catholic-Protestant Differences." SOCIOLOGICAL QUARTERLY 14,4 (1973): 544-555.

Survey of Minnesota high-school students. Statistical relationship between family size and college aspirations is higher for Protestants than for Catholics.

1304. Norr, James L. "Religion and Nation Building: The American Case." SOCIOLOGICAL FOCUS 11,4 (1978): 255-269.

Features data for 13 denominations, 1650-1860.

162

1305. O'Brien, Thaddeus J. ATTITUDES OF SUBURBAN ITALIAN-AMERICANS TOWARD THE ROMAN CATHOLIC CHURCH, FORMAL EDUCATION AND THE PAROCHIAL SCHOOL. Unpublished Ph.D. dissertation, University of Chicago, 1972.

1306. O'Connell, Brian J. "Dimensions of Religiosity among Catholics." RRR 16,3 (1975): 198-207.

Data from Catholics in a midwestern American city. The consequential scales must be broken down into individual and social consequences. Individual consequential correlates positively with orthodoxy, devotionalism, and comfort-seeking while social consequential correlates negatively with orthodoxy and comfort-seeking. The relationship between devotionalism and social consequential is curvilinear, with most and least devotional scoring higher. Attitudes on birth control are independent of the other scales.

1307. O'Kane, James. "Economic and Non-economic Liberalism, Upward Mobility Potential and Catholic Working-class Youth." SOCIAL FORCES 48,4 (1970): 499-506.

Examines the relationship between upward mobility potential and the political attitudes of male Catholic working-class adolescents. Mobiles are more liberal than non-mobiles on noneconomic issues, but no relationship occurs with economic issues.

1308. Petersen, James C., and Gary R. Lee. "Religious Affiliation and Social Participation: Differences between Lutherans and Catholics." JOURNAL OF VOLUNTARY ACTION RESEARCH 5,2 (1976): 82-93.

1970 survey of Minnesota respondents reveals that the American Lutheran Church fits more closely than Roman Catholicism the model of a voluntary association.

1309. Peterson, Robert W. STATUS ATTAINMENT PROCESSES IN RELIGIOUS ORGANI-ZATIONS. Unpublished Ph.D. dissertation, University of Wisconsin, Madison, 1976. [DA 37:8 A, p. 5368]

1970-71 N.O.R.C. (U.S.) survey data on Catholic clergy.

1310. Peterson, Robert W., and Richard A. Schoenherr. "Organizational Status Attainment of Religious Professionals." SOCIAL FORCES 56,3 (1978): 794-822.

Seniority and career attributes (attending elite seminaries, receiving advanced degrees, and holding important assignments in the past) are more important predictors of high occupational status of Catholic priests than are background variables. Based on 1970 N.O.R.C. survey of over 3000 U.S. Catholic priests.

1311. Photiadis, John D., and John F. Schnabel. "Religion: A Persistent Institution in a Changing Appalachia." RRR 19,1 (1977): 32-42.

Sample of adult male heads of households in West Virginia. Items reflecting use of religion as a buffer, fundamentalist belief, and religiosity are compared among three denominations - Catholic,

Methodist, and United Evangelical Brethren.

1312. Potvin, Raymond H. "Role Uncertainty and Commitment among Seminary Faculty." SA 37,1 (1976): 45-52.

Survey data from American Catholic priests who staff seminaries reveal that role ambiguity undermines commitment.

1313. Potvin, Raymond H., and Che-Fu Lee. "Catholic College Women and Family-size Preferences: A Reanalysis." SA 35,1 (1974): 24-34.

1964-67 U.S. data. The reanalysis underlines both selectivity and Catholic college effects.

   * Rhodes, A. Lewis, and Charles B. Nam. "The Religious Context of Educational Expectations." Cited above as item 499.

1314. Richardson, James T., and Sandie Wightman Fox. "Religion and Voting on Abortion Reform: A Follow-up Study." JSSR 14,2 (1975): 159-164.

Religious affiliation (Catholic, Mormon) was the most important predictor of how legislators in a western U.S. state legislature would vote on abortion laws.

1315. Rigali, Lucius J. RELIGIOUS COMMITMENT AND SOCIAL INVOLVEMENT IN SELECTED FRANCISCAN PARISHES. Unpublished Ph.D. dissertation, Boston University, 1974. [DA 35:3 A, p. 1748]

Questionnaire data from four parishes in different sections of the U.S. Analysis in terms of communal/associational participation, orthodoxy, devotionalism, class, age, and attitudes toward involvement in social change.

1316. Ritti, Richard R., Thomas P. Ference, and Fred H. Goldner. "Professions and Their Plausibility: Priests, Work, and Belief Systems." SOCIOLOGY OF WORK AND OCCUPATIONS 1,1 (1974): 24-51.

1970 survey of the diocesan priests of a metropolitan American diocese. Focus is on work satisfaction; pastors and curates compared to other professions.

   * Roof, Wade Clark. "Socioeconomic Differentials among White Socio-religious Groups in the United States." Cited above as item 501.

1317. Ryan, M. Desmond. THE CHURCH-SOCIETY RELATIONSHIP: A SURVEY OF THE OPINIONS OF INDIANA CATHOLIC CLERGY. Indianapolis: Indiana Catholic Conference, 1977.

1974-75 survey of Catholic priests in Indiana. Focus is on attitudes about various social issues.

1318. Sampson, Samuel F. CRISIS IN THE CLOISTER. A SOCIOLOGICAL ANALYSIS OF SOCIAL RELATIONSHIPS AND CHANGE IN A NOVITIATE. Norwood, N.J.: Ablex, 1978.

1319. SanGiovanni, Lucinda F.  EX-NUNS. A STUDY OF EMERGENT ROLE PASSAGE. Norwood, N.J.: Ablex, 1978.

1972 intensive interviews with women who left one order of female religious (n = 21).

1320. Schnabel, John F.  VALIDATION OF CONSTRUCTS FOR PREDICTING OCCUPATION- AL ADAPTATIONS.  Unpublished Ph.D. dissertation, University of Notre Dame, 1973.  [DA 33:10 A, p. 5844]

Focus is on adaptations to stress, using a 1970 sample of American Catholic clergy.

1321. Schneider, Louis, and Louis A. Zurcher.  "Toward Understanding the Catholic Crisis: Observations on Dissident Priests in Texas."  JSSR 9,3 (1970): 197-209.

1969 interview and Twenty Statements Test data from San Antonio (Texas) archdiocesan priests who in 1968 called publicly for the resignation of their archbishop.

1322. Schoenherr, Richard A., and Andrew M. Greeley.  "Role Commitment Processes and the American Catholic Priesthood."  AMERICAN SOCIOLOGI- CAL REVIEW 39,3 (1974): 407-426.

1972 N.O.R.C. (U.S.) survey of Catholic priests.  Celibacy appears as the principal issue in commitment to continuation in the priestly role.

1323. Schoenherr, Richard A., and José Pérez Vilarino.  "Organizational Role Commitment in the Catholic Church in Spain and the U.S.A."  In Cornelius Lammers and David Hickson (eds.), ORGANIZATIONS ALIKE AND UNALIKE: INTERNATIONAL AND INTER-INSTITUTIONAL STUDIES IN THE SOCIOL- OGY OF ORGANIZATIONS.  London: Routledge and Kegan Paul, 1979, pp. 346-372.

1970-71 N.O.R.C. (U.S.) survey of Catholic priests and bishops and a contemporaneous survey of priests in Spain.

1324. Schuman, Howard.  "The Religious Factor in Detroit: Review, Replica- tion, and Reanalysis."  AMERICAN SOCIOLOGICAL REVIEW 36,1 (1971): 30- 48.

1966 Detroit Area Study.

1325. Schwartz, David F.  BELIEF AS ASSUMPTIVE SYSTEM: CHANGING CONCEPTION OF CREED, CODE AND CULT AMONG CONTEMPORARY AMERICAN CATHOLIC PRIESTS. Unpublished Ph.D. dissertation, Loyola University of Chicago, 1978.

1326. Schweigardt, Erwin H.  ROLE EXPECTATIONS AND PRACTICES OF DIOCESAN PASTORAL COUNCILS AND DIOCESAN BOARDS OF EDUCATION IN MATTERS OF EDU- CATION IN SELECTED ROMAN CATHOLIC DIOCESES IN THE UNITED STATES. Unpublished Ph.D. dissertation, Catholic University of America, 1972. [DA 33:6 A, p. 2669]

Questionnaire data from 31 dioceses; focus is on organizational conflict.

1327. Seidler, John. REBELLION AND RETREATISM AMONG AMERICAN CATHOLIC
CLERGY. Unpublished Ph.D. dissertation, University of North Carolina,
Chapel Hill, 1972. [DA 33:8 A, p. 4549]

Clergy sample from 136 dioceses, and organizational features of the
dioceses, 1965-70.

1328. Seidler, John. "Priest Resignations in a Lazy Monopoly." AMERICAN
SOCIOLOGICAL REVIEW 44,5 (1979): 763-783.

1971 U.S. survey of diocesan clergy. The focus is on diocesan
attributes related to clergy resignations. As organizations, dioceses
allow internal clerical critics to depart rather than respond to their
criticisms.

1329. Shanabruch, Charles H. THE CHICAGO CATHOLIC CHURCH'S ROLE AS AN
AMERICANIZER, 1893-1928. Unpublished Ph.D. dissertation, University
of Chicago, 1975. [DA 36:7 A, p. 4718]

Documentary study, using several archives.

1330. Sorensen, Andrew A. "Need for Power among Alcoholic and Nonalcoholic
Clergy." JSSR 12,1 (1973): 101-108.

Based on New England snowball samples of Roman Catholic and Episcopal
clergy known to be alcoholics. Clergy with personal, as opposed to
socialized, needs for power are more likely to drink to excess.

1331. Sorensen, Andrew A. ALCOHOLIC PRIESTS: A SOCIOLOGICAL STUDY. New
York: Seabury, 1977.

Based on interview data comparing the careers of 65 alcoholic and 56
non-alcoholic priests.

1332. Stamm, Martin J. THE NEW GUARDIANS OF AMERICAN CATHOLIC HIGHER EDUCA-
TION: AN EXAMINATION OF LAY PARTICIPATION ON THE GOVERNING BOARDS OF
ROMAN CATHOLIC AFFILIATED COLLEGES AND UNIVERSITIES. Unpublished Ph.D.
dissertation, University of Pennsylvania, 1979. [DA 40:3 A, p. 1308]

Examines the extent of 'laicization' of boards, as of 1977. Documentary study and questionnaires from presidents, as well as some interviews. Lay power is seen to be real.

   * Steinberg, Stephen. "The Changing Religious Composition of American
   Higher Education." Cited above as item 518.

   * Steinberg, Stephen. THE ACADEMIC MELTING POT. CATHOLICS AND JEWS IN
   AMERICAN HIGHER EDUCATION. Cited above as item 519.

1333. Struzzo, John A. "Professionalism and the Resolution of Authority
Conflicts among the Catholic Clergy." SA 31,2 (1970): 92-106.

1969 survey of parish and high-school-teaching priests in the Washington, D.C., Archdiocese. Priests with higher levels of preparation are
more likely to oppose traditional norms.

1334. Sweetser, Thomas. THE CATHOLIC PARISH: SHIFTING MEMBERSHIP IN A CHANGING CHURCH. Chicago: Center for the Scientific Study of Religion, 1974.

1335. Szafran, Robert F. "The Distribution of Influence in Religious Organizations." JSSR 15,4 (1976): 339-349.

Examines the distribution of influence in policy making and activity in 85 Roman Catholic dioceses; based on responses of over 3000 diocesan priests.

1336. Traina, Frank J. "Catholic Clergy on Abortion: Preliminary Findings on a New York State Survey." FAMILY PLANNING PERSPECTIVES 6 (1974): 151-156.

1972 sample survey of Catholic priests in New York State; breakdown of data by age, function, diocese, etc.

1337. Wall, David F. PARISH COUNCILS IN THE CATHOLIC CHURCH: PARTICIPATION AND SATISFACTION OF MEMBERS. Unpublished Ph.D. dissertation, Catholic University of America, 1979. [DA 39:9 A, p. 5738]

Questionnaire data from members of randomly selected parish councils in the Baltimore Archdiocese.

   * Warren, Bruce L. "Socioeconomic Achievement and Religion: The American Case." Cited above as item 522.

1338. Watzke, James N. DESOCIALIZATION FROM THE PRIESTHOOD: CRITICAL PROBLEMS OF PERSONAL AND ROLE IDENTITY AMONG THE CATHOLIC RELIGIOUS PROFESSIONALS. Unpublished Ph.D. dissertation, Harvard University, 1971. [DA 33:01, p. 421-A]

Survey of 873 U.S. Catholic ex-clergy who had resigned, 1965-69.

1339. Westhues, Kenneth. THE AMERICAN CATHOLIC WORLD: ITS ORIGINS AND PROSPECTS. Unpublished Ph.D. dissertation, Vanderbilt University, 1970. [DA 31:6 A, p. 3064]

Secularization theory and systems theory. Data from THE OFFICIAL CATHOLIC DIRECTORY, 7 points in time from 1906 to 1968, plus census data. Focus on elementary and secondary schools, rest homes, orphanages, and general hospitals. States are the units of analysis. Importance of minority status, lack of modernization, and ethnicity.

1340. Westhues, Kenneth. "An Alternative Model for Research on Catholic Education." AMERICAN JOURNAL OF SOCIOLOGY 77 (1971): 279-292.

The establishment of Catholic schools arises out of a perception, on the part of the church, of a threatening environment. Demographic and socioeconomic data, using states as units of analysis, demonstrate this.

1341. Westhues, Kenneth. "Stars and Stripes, the Maple Leaf, and the Papal Coat of Arms." CANADIAN JOURNAL OF SOCIOLOGY 3,2 (1978): 245-261.

Discussion of the different positions of the Catholic church in the United States and Canada.

1342. Westoff, Charles F., and Larry Bumpass. "Revolution in Birth Control Practices of United States Roman Catholics." SCIENCE 179 (1973): 41-44.

Data on birth control practices from the 1970 National Fertility Study; comparison with 1955 data.

1343. Westoff, Charles F., and Elise F. Jones. "The End of 'Catholic' Fertility." DEMOGRAPHY 16 (1979): 209-217.

U.S. samples, marriage cohorts 1936-75.

1344. White, Harrison C., Scott A. Boorman, and Ronald L. Breiger. "Social Structure from Multiple Networks." AMERICAN JOURNAL OF SOCIOLOGY 81,4 (1976): 730-780.

Pages 749-754 analyze data presented by S.F. Sampson in item 1183.

1345. Wicks, Jerry W., and Randy L. Workman. "Sex-role Attitudes and the Anticipated Timing of the Initial Stages of Family Formation among Catholic University Students." JOURNAL OF MARRIAGE AND THE FAMILY 40,3 (1978): 505-516.

1976 survey of never-married Catholic students at a private university in California. The more traditional the preferred economic sex roles and the greater the importance placed on the family for providing a secure relationship, the earlier were the plans for marriage and for having the first child.

1346. Wrobel, Paul. OUR WAY. FAMILY, PARISH, AND NEIGHBORHOOD IN A POLISH-AMERICAN COMMUNITY. Notre Dame: University of Notre Dame Press, 1979.

Field-work data, Detroit, early 1970s.

*WORKS, 1980-1989*

1347. Alba, Richard D. "The Twilight of Ethnicity among American Catholics of European Ancestry." ANNALS OF THE AMERICAN ACADEMY OF POLITICAL AND SOCIAL SCIENCE 454 (1981): 86-97.

Examines the apparently rapid assimilation of Catholic ethnic groups in the United States.

1348. Alwin, Duane F. "Religion and Parental Child-rearing Orientations: Evidence of a Catholic-Protestant Convergence." AMERICAN JOURNAL OF SOCIOLOGY 92,2 (1986): 412-440.

1958, 1971, and 1983 data from the Detroit metropolitan area, and 1973-84 N.O.R.C. (U.S.) data, show differences between Protestant and Catholic parental values (e.g., autonomy, obedience) diminishing, with differences within denominations reflecting forms of religious participation.

1349. Blake, Judith. "Catholicism and Fertility: On Attitudes of Young Americans." POPULATION AND DEVELOPMENT REVIEW 10,2 (1984): 329-340.

Based on 1980 N.O.R.C. (U.S.) data from high-school sophomores and seniors. Differences between Catholics, especially practicing Catholics, and others in fertility-related variables persist - expected family size, importance placed on having children, more traditional view of maternal role, less knowledge about birth control.

1350. Browne, J. Patrick, and Timothy J. Lukes. "Women called Catholics: The Sources of Dissatisfaction with the Church, Santa Clara County, California." JSSR 27,2 (1988): 284-290.

Factor analysis produced three clusters of specific attitudes, centering on the church's response to local issues, moral issues, and ideological issues. Local issues are most important in determining women's general satisfaction with the direction of the church.

1351. Brunetta, Guiseppe. "Strutture ecclesiastiche e personale della Chiesa Cattolica negli USA (1915-1985)." AGGIORNAMENTI SOCIALI 36,7-8 (1986): 561-572.

1352. Carroll, Michael P. "Italian Catholicism: Making Direct Contact with the Sacred." In Roger O'Toole (ed.), SOCIOLOGICAL STUDIES IN ROMAN CATHOLICISM [item 821], pp. 27-44.

The 'creative instability' of Italian Catholicism in both Europe and the United States, according to the author, inspires an impulse to innovation which inevitably and inexorably repels religious routinization.

1353. Chadwick, Bruce A. "Catholics and Protestants." In Theodore Caplow et al. (eds.), ALL FAITHFUL PEOPLE: CHANGE AND CONTINUITY IN MIDDLETOWN'S RELIGION. Minneapolis: University of Minnesota Press, 1983, pp. 163-181.

1978 Middletown (Muncie, Indiana) data.

1354. Cieslak, Michael J. "Parish Responsiveness and Parishioner Commitment." RRR 26,2 (1984): 132-147.

Those parishes which most implemented the 'spirit' of Vatican II received greater financial contributions and mass attendance than those which did not.

1355. Coleman, James S., and Thomas Hoffer. PUBLIC AND PRIVATE HIGH SCHOOLS. THE IMPACT OF COMMUNITIES. New York: Basic, 1987.

1980 and 1982 National Center for Education Statistics data, High School and Beyond Study (N.O.R.C.), national sample of high schools. Tables give separate analysis for Catholic high school data.

1356. Coleman, James S., Thomas Hoffer, and Sally B. Kilgore. HIGH SCHOOL ACHIEVEMENT: PUBLIC, CATHOLIC AND PRIVATE SCHOOLS COMPARED. New York: Basic, 1982.

Based for the most part on the same data sources as reported for item 1355.

* Cuneo, Michael W. LE CONSERVATISME CATHOLIQUE NORD-AMERICAIN. Cited above as item 872.

1357. D'Antonio, William V. "The American Catholic Family: Signs of Cohesion and Polarization." JOURNAL OF MARRIAGE AND THE FAMILY 47,2 (1985): 395-405. Reprinted in D.L. Thomas (ed.), THE RELIGION AND FAMILY CONNECTION [volume cited in item 414], pp. 88-106.

Discusses tension between the American quest for autonomy and the traditional Catholic value of obedience.

1358. D'Antonio, William V., and Mark J. Cavanaugh. "Roman Catholicism and the Family." In W.V. D'Antonio and J. Aldous (eds.), FAMILIES AND RELIGIONS [volume cited in item 421], pp. 141-162.

Investigates the impact of religious doctrine and traditions on family structure since ancient times, ethnicity and family in the American Catholic context, and twentieth-century issues.

1359. D'Antonio, William V., James D. Davidson, Dean R. Hoge, and Ruth A. Wallace. AMERICAN CATHOLIC LAITY IN A CHANGING CHURCH. Kansas City: Sheed and Ward, 1989.

Based on a 1987 Gallup survey of adult American Catholics.

1360. De Jong, Judith A., and Donna Coughlan Donovan. "Age-related Differences in Beliefs, Attitudes and Practices of Priests." JSSR 27,1 (1988): 128-136.

1982-84 survey of U.S. diocesan priests. Younger priests participated more in interpersonal religious practices and older priests more in solitary ones. Older priests were more certain about beliefs, younger ones more oriented toward experiences.

1361. Della Fave, L. Richard, and George A. Hillery, Jr. "Status Inequality in a Religious Community: The Case of a Trappist Monastery." SOCIAL FORCES 59,1 (1980): 62-84.

Field study and questionnaire data, 1969 and following; questionnaire distributed in 1972.

1362. Ebaugh, Helen Rose Fuchs. "Leaving the Convent: The Experience of Role Exit and Self-transformation." In Joseph A. Kotarba and Andrea Fontana (eds.), THE EXISTENTIAL SELF IN SOCIETY. Chicago: University of Chicago Press, 1984, pp. 156-176.

Mostly based on interviews of ex-nuns during the 1970s.

1363. Ebaugh, Helen Rose Fuchs. "Leaving Catholic Convents. Toward a Theory of Disengagement." In David G. Bromley (ed.), FALLING FROM THE FAITH. CAUSES AND CONSEQUENCES OF RELIGIOUS APOSTASY. Newbury Park, California: Sage, 1988, pp. 100-121.

Conceptualization of the process, based on a study of convents and ex-nuns conducted in the early 1970s, on an in-depth interview study conducted in 1985, and on the author's experiences prior to 1973.

1364. Ebaugh, Helen Rose Fuchs. BECOMING AN EX: THE PROCESS OF ROLE EXIT. Chicago: University of Chicago Press, 1988.

* Fee, Joan L., Andrew M. Greeley, William C. McCready, and Theresa A. Sullivan. YOUNG CATHOLICS. A REPORT TO THE KNIGHTS OF COLUMBUS. Cited above as item 939.

1365. Fichter, Joseph H. "The Myth of Clergy Burnout." SA 45,4 (1984): 373-382.

A survey of American Catholic priests suggests that only a small minority can be described as having experienced 'burnout.'

1366. Fichter, Joseph H. "The Dilemma of Priest Retirement." JSSR 24,1 (1985): 101-104.

Survey of American Catholic clergy over age 65. Data on commonly reported ailments are given. There seems to be an absence of difficulties adjusting to retirement.

1367. Fichter, Joseph H. THE HEALTH OF AMERICAN CATHOLIC PRIESTS: A REPORT AND A STUDY. Washington: United States Catholic Conference, 1985.

1368. Fichter, Joseph H. "Life-style and Health Status of American Catholic Priests." SC 34,4 (1987): 539-548.

1982 survey of U.S. Catholic priests. The focus is on correlates of good health.

1369. Finke, Roger, and Rodney Stark. "How the Upstart Sects Won America: 1776-1850." JSSR 28,1 (1989): 27-44.

1776 and 1850 data for six denominations; historical interpretation.

1370. Fogarty, John C. THE CATHOLIC PRIEST: HIS IDENTITY AND VALUES. Kansas City: Sheed and Ward, 1988.

1984 survey of Catholic priests in the Diocese of Joliet.

1371. Gallup, George, Jr., and Jim Castelli. THE AMERICAN CATHOLIC PEOPLE. Garden City, N.Y.: Doubleday, 1987.

1372. Gannon, Thomas M. "Episcopato cattolico e politica negli USA degli anni '80." AGGIORNAMENTI SOCIALI 9-10 (1986): 633-644.

1373. Gonzalez Nieves, Roberto O. ECOLOGICAL, ETHNIC AND CULTURAL FACTORS OF CHURCH PRACTICE IN AN URBAN ROMAN CATHOLIC PARISH. Unpublished Ph.D. dissertation, Fordham University, 1984. [DA 46:1 A, p. 266]

Telephone survey of one of the same Bronx parishes studied in 1956 by Joseph F. Scheuer [item 1081].

1374. Gonzalez Nieves, Roberto O., and Michael La Velle. THE HISPANIC CATHOLIC IN THE UNITED STATES: A SOCIO-CULTURAL AND RELIGIOUS PROFILE. New York: Northeast Catholic Pastoral Center for Hispanics, 1985.

1984-85 telephone survey of a sample of Hispanic Catholics in the U.S.

1375. Greeley, Andrew M. THE YOUNG CATHOLIC FAMILY: RELIGIOUS IMAGES AND MARRIAGE FULFILLMENT. Chicago: Thomas More Press, 1980.

1979 data from a sample of married Catholics, aged 18-30.

1376. Greeley, Andrew M. THE RELIGIOUS IMAGINATION. Los Angeles: Sadlier, 1981.

Uses 1979 questionnaire data on U.S. and Canadian young adult Catholics.

1377. Greeley, Andrew M. CATHOLIC HIGH SCHOOLS AND MINORITY STUDENTS. New Brunswick, N.J.: Transaction, 1982.

Analysis of 1980 data collected in The High School and Beyond Study, a representative survey of U.S. high-school students. The analysis used the data subset of minority students attending Catholic high schools.

1378. Greeley, Andrew M. AMERICAN CATHOLICS SINCE THE COUNCIL. AN UNAUTHOR-IZED REPORT. Chicago: Thomas More Press, 1985.

Uses data from previous studies.

1379. Hicks, Thomas H. "A Study of the Background Level of Job Satisfaction, Maturity, and Morale of 'Delayed Vocation' Catholic Priests." RRR 22, 4 (1981): 328-345.

Survey of alumni of a U.S. Catholic seminary for second-career clergy. Demographic variables distinguished this group from a control group of first-career Catholic clergy, but levels of maturity and job satisfaction did not differ.

1380. Hoffer, Thomas, Andrew M. Greeley, and James S. Coleman. "Achievement Growth in Public and Catholic Schools." SOCIOLOGY OF EDUCATION 58,2 (1985): 74-97.

Presents evidence of Catholic education having positive effects on verbal and mathematics achievement.

1381. Hoge, Dean R. CONVERTS, DROPOUTS, RETURNEES: A STUDY OF RELIGIOUS CHANGE AMONG CATHOLICS. New York: Pilgrim Press, 1981.

1979-80 telephone interviews in seven dioceses.

1382. Hoge, Dean R. "Interpreting Change in American Catholicism: The River and the Floodgate." RRR 27,4 (1986): 289-299.

Vatican obstacles to the assimilation of Catholics to American society cause pressures to build up.

1383. Hoge, Dean R. THE FUTURE OF CATHOLIC LEADERSHIP. RESPONSES TO THE

PRIEST SHORTAGE. Kansas City: Sheed and Ward, 1987.

1985 surveys of U.S. Catholic adults, clergy, and college students.

1384. Hoge, Dean R. "Why Catholics Drop Out." In D.G. Bromley (ed.), FALLING FROM THE FAITH [volume cited in item 1363], pp. 81-99.

Review of previously published U.S. findings.

1385. Hoge, Dean R., Raymond H. Potvin, and Kathleen M. Gerry. RESEARCH ON MEN'S VOCATIONS TO THE PRIESTHOOD AND THE RELIGIOUS LIFE. Washington: United States Catholic Conference, 1984.

Mostly C.A.R.A. (U.S.) data for 1968-83, on seminary students.

1386. Hoge, Dean R., Joseph J. Shields, and Mary J. Verdieck. "Changing Age Distribution and Theological Attitudes of Catholic Priests, 1970-1985." SA 49,3 (1988): 264-280.

1985 survey of Roman Catholic priests in the U.S.A. The age distribution shifted toward older age groups, and the ideological profile shifted toward more modern positions.

1387. Hoge, Dean R., Esther Heffernan, Eugene F. Hemrick, Hart M. Nelsen, James P. O'Connor, Paul J. Philibert, and Andrew D. Thompson. "Desired Outcomes of Religious Education and Youth Ministry in Six Denominations." RRR 23,3 (1982): 230-254.

Catholic religious educators gave priority to the students' attainment of moral maturity.

   * Homola, Michael, Dean Knudsen, and Harvey Marshall. "Religion and Socio-economic Achievement." Cited above as item 463.

   * Homola, Michael, Dean Knudsen, and Harvey Marshall. "Status Attainment and Religion: A Reevaluation." Cited above as item 464.

1388. Jensen, Gary F. "Explaining Differences in Academic Behavior between Public-school and Catholic-school Students: A Quantitative Case." SOCIOLOGY OF EDUCATION 59,1 (1986): 32-41.

1973-76 survey data from a Catholic and two neighboring public high schools in a southwest U.S. city. The Catholic school's discipline and rigorous requirements influenced academic behavior.

1389. Kelly, James R. "Catholicism and Modern Memory: Some Sociological Reflections on the Symbolic Foundations of the Rhetorical Force of the Pastoral Letter, 'The Challenge of Peace.'" SA 45,2 (1984): 131-144.

Examines the cultural and theological background of the reception accorded a controversial pastoral letter issued by the American Catholic bishops on the nuclear arms race.

1390. Kelly, James R. "Roman Catholic Catechists and Their Ecumenical Attitudes." RRR 25,4 (1984): 379-386.

Data from a 1982 survey of Roman Catholic educators in the U.S. show strongly pro-ecumenical attitudes.

1391. Kelly, James R. "Toward Confidence: Catholic Social Thought in North America." SOCIAL THOUGHT (Spring 1984): 59-74.

Discusses the manner in which Catholic social thought remains, in the United States and elsewhere, a strategically-placed carrier of the Western humanist tradition in politics and economics.

1392. Kelly, James R. "Residual or Prophetic? The Cultural Fate of Roman Catholic Sexual Ethics of Abortion and Contraception." SOCIAL THOUGHT (Spring 1986): 3-18.

Discusses how the Catholic teaching on abortion and contraception might profitably be linked to a wider context of political and economic egalitarianism.

1393. Kelly, James R. "Ecumenism and Abortion: A Case Study of Pluralism, Privatization and the Public Conscience." RRR 30,3 (1989): 225-235.

Documents how abortion has been perhaps the most ecumenically-resistant issue faced by the Roman Catholic and Protestant churches in the United States.

1394. Kim, Gertrud. "Roman Catholic Organization since Vatican II." In R.P. Scherer (ed.), AMERICAN DENOMINATIONAL ORGANIZATION [volume cited in item 424], pp. 84-129.

General discussion, followed by data on church attendance and religious specialists for the U.S.A.

1395. LaMagdeleine, Donald R. "U.S. Catholic Church-related Jobs as Dual Labor Markets: A Speculative Inquiry." RRR 27,4 (1986): 315-327. See also Patricia Wittberg, "Comment," 30,3 (1989): 287-290; and D.R. LaMagdeleine, "Reply," 30,3 (1989): 291-294.

1396. Lee, Valerie E., and Anthony S. Bryk. "Curriculum Tracking as Mediating the Social Distribution of High School Achievement." SOCIOLOGY OF EDUCATION 61,2 (1988): 78-94.

Comparisons of Catholic and public high school students' mathematics achievement. Catholic schools were more likely to assign college prep tracks to students, eliciting more achievement and aspiration in many cases than would be predicted by background variables alone.

1397. Leege, David C., Michael R. Welch, and Thomas A. Trozzolo. "Religiosity, Church Social Teaching, and Sociopolitical Attitudes: A Research Note on Marital Homogamy as Social Context for U.S. Catholics." RRR 28,2 (1986): 118-128.

Catholic sample from 1977, 1978, and 1980 N.O.R.C. (U.S.) data. Notes a slight tendency for heterogamous Catholics to conform more closely than homogamous Catholics to church teaching on justice and peace.

1398. Lopez Pulido, Alberto. RACE RELATIONS WITHIN THE AMERICAN CATHOLIC

CHURCH: AN HISTORICAL AND SOCIOLOGICAL ANALYSIS OF MEXICAN AMERICAN CATHOLICS. Unpublished Ph.D. dissertation, University of Notre Dame, 1989.

Historical sociology, focusing on the diocese of San Diego in the modern era.

1399. McAuley, E. Nancy, and Moira Mathieson. FAITH WITHOUT FORM: BELIEFS OF CATHOLIC YOUTH. Kansas City: Sheed and Ward, 1986.

1983 questionnaire data (Gallup poll) from high-school seniors at 10 Catholic schools in the Archdiocese of Washington, D.C.

1400. McNamara, Patrick H. "American Catholicism in the Mid-eighties: Pluralism and Conflict in a Changing Church." ANNALS OF THE AMERICAN ACADEMY OF POLITICAL AND SOCIAL SCIENCES 480 (1985): 63-74.

American Catholicism shows mixed signs of decline and vitality. A pluralist model seems relevant - with continuing individualism in belief and practice, institutional conflict, and loss of authority.

1401. Marcum, John P., and Mary Radosh. "Religious Affiliation, Labor Force Participation and Fertility." SA 42,4 (1982): 353-362.

1965 National Fertility Survey (U.S.) data. Catholic fertility rate among women who left the work force resembles that of women who never entered the work force.

1402. Mickey, Thomas J. "Social Order and Preaching." SC 27,4 (1980): 347-362.

Data from 32 American Catholic parishes, showing responses to homilies.

1403. Moberg, David O., and Dean R. Hoge. "Catholic College Students' Religious and Moral Attitudes, 1961-1982: Effects of the Sixties and Seventies." RRR 28,2 (1986): 104-117.

Marquette University surveys, 1961, 1971, 1982. Immense change in a liberal direction 1961-71; lesser change in the reverse direction 1971-82.

  * Mueller, Charles W. "Evidence on the Relationship between Religion and Educational Attainment." Cited above as item 490.

1404. Neal, Marie Augusta. CATHOLIC SISTERS IN TRANSITION. FROM THE 1960s TO THE 1980s. Wilmington, Delaware: Michael Glazier, 1984.

1967 and 1980 questionnaire data from American female religious.

1405. Nelsen, Hart M. "Religious Conformity in an Age of Disbelief: Contextual Effects of Time, Denomination, and Family Processes upon Church Decline and Apostasy." AMERICAN SOCIOLOGICAL REVIEW 46,5 (1981): 632-640.

Questionnaire data from students, grades 4-8, in public and Catholic schools in southern Minnesota.

175

1406. Noell, Jay. "Public and Catholic Schools: A Reanalysis of 'Public and Private Schools.'" SOCIOLOGY OF EDUCATION 55,2-3 (1982): 123-132.

Reanalysis of data used in item 1356: 1980 U.S. sample of high-school sophomores and seniors, reading and mathematics achievement tests. Higher scores among Catholic school students can be predicted by self-selection factors and need not be attributed to the school experiences.

1407. Peck, Gary R. "Black Radical Consciousness and the Black Christian Experience: Toward a Critical Sociology of Afro-American Religion." SA 43,2 (1982): 155-169.

Critical review of the literature on black Catholic-Protestant differences.

1408. Penning, James M. "Changing Partisanship and Issue Stands among American Catholics." SA 47,1 (1986): 29-49.

N.O.R.C. data (U.S.), 1972-74, 1976-78, 1980-83. Notes a growing political conservatism on the part of American Catholics.

1409. Perrin, Robin D. "American Religion in the Post-aquarian Age: Values and Demographic Factors in Church Growth and Decline." JSSR 28,1 (1989): 75-89.

Mean member ages and number of children born to members of 14 denominations; 1972-85 N.O.R.C. (U.S.) data.

1410. Petersen, Larry R., and K. Peter Takayama. "Local/Cosmopolitan Theory and Religiosity among Catholic Nuns and Brothers." JSSR 22,4 (1983): 303-315.

1981 questionnaire data from nuns and brothers in the diocese of Memphis, Tennessee.

1411. Petersen, Larry R., and K. Peter Takayama. "Religious Commitment and Conservatism: Toward Understanding an Elusive Relationship." SA 45,4 (1984): 354-371.

1981 western Tennessee sample of 1036 adult Catholics.

1412. Petersen, Larry R., and K. Peter Takayama. "Community and Commitment among Catholics: A Test of Local/Cosmopolitan Theory." SOCIOLOGICAL QUARTERLY 25,1 (1984): 92-112.

1981 sample of Catholics in west Tennessee. Localism has affected religious beliefs and played a limited role in mediating the effects of education, size of home town, and length of residence. It has little effect on behavioral religiosity.

1413. Philibert, Paul J., and Dean R. Hoge. "Teachers, Pedagogy and the Process of Religious Education." RRR 23,3 (1982): 264-285.

1979-80 survey of parents and religious educators in six U.S. denominations; profiles of preferred pedagogical method and teacher qualities, correlated with educational objectives.

1414. Richardson, James T. "The 'Old Right' in Action: Mormon and Catholic Involvement in an Equal Rights Amendment Referendum." In David G. Bromley and Anson Shupe (eds.), NEW CHRISTIAN POLITICS. Macon, Georgia: Mercer University Press, 1984, pp. 213-233.

A 1978 Nevada-based study.

1415. Sabagh, Georges, and David Lopez. "Religiosity and Fertility: The Case of Chicanos." SOCIAL FORCES 59,2 (1980): 431-439.

1973 interview data from Mexican-American Catholic women (aged 35-44) in Los Angeles.

1416. Scherer, Ross P. "A New Typology for Organizations: Market, Bureaucracy, Clan and Mission, with Application to American Denominations." JSSR 27,4 (1988): 475-498.

Arrays data from previous studies on various denominations, pertaining to the percentage of members still belonging to the denomination of their parents, and data on pastors' attitudes toward church organization and mission.

1417. Schoenherr, Richard A., and Annemette Sorensen. "Social Change in Religious Organizations: Consequences of Clergy Decline in the U.S. Catholic Church." SA 43,1 (1982): 23-52.

Estimation of population parameters for entrance, exit, and growth rates and for the age distribution of U.S. diocesan priests from 1966-73. Three series of population projections are made to the year 2000. A significant decline is expected.

1418. Schoenherr, Richard A., Lawrence A. Young, and José Pérez Vilarino. "Demographic Transitions in Religious Organizations: A Comparative Study of Priest Decline in Roman Catholic Dioceses." JSSR 27,4 (1988): 499-523.

Examines 1966-84 trends for an American and a Spanish diocese.

1419. Stack, Steven, and Mary J. Kanavy. "The Effect of Religion on Forcible Rape: A Structural Analysis." JSSR 22,1 (1983): 67-74.

Ecological data on the 50 states, from F.B.I. reports for 1970. Catholic percentage of state populations is inversely related to reported forcible rape rates.

   * Stryker, Robin. "Religio-ethnic Effects on Attainments in the Early Career." Cited above as item 520.

1420. Szafran, Robert F., Robert W. Peterson, and Richard A. Schoenherr. "Ethnicity and Status Attainment: The Case of the Roman Catholic Clergy." SOCIOLOGICAL QUARTERLY 21 (1980): 41-51.

1970 N.O.R.C. study of U.S. Catholic priests. Ethnicity effects are generally nil.

1421. Tamney, Joseph B., Ronald Burton, and Stephen Johnson. "Christianity,

Social Class, and the Catholic Bishops' Economic Policy." SA 49 (1988): 78-96.

Data from a Muncie, Indiana, random sample. Support for economic restructuring may be found among non-fundamentalist Catholics and fundamentalist Protestants.

1422. Terian, Sarah M.K. THE OTHER SIDE OF GOOD SAMARITANISM: THE HELPING ETHIC IN JUDEO-CHRISTIAN IDEOLOGY AND PRACTICE. Unpublished Ph.D. dissertation, University of Notre Dame, 1984. [DA 45:6 A, p. 1886]

Extensive literature review on doctrines pertaining to charitable works. Interviews of 20 respondents from each of representative denominations of the Jewish, Catholic, and Protestant traditions; respondents were responsible for charitable works in a midwestern U.S. city. Focus on views about recipients of help.

1423. Thorn, William J., and Bruce Garrison. "Institutional Stress: Jour-nalistic Norms in the Catholic Press." RRR 25,1 (1983): 49-62.

Examines the incongruency between views of the Catholic press held by bishops and by editors.

1424. Varacalli, Joseph A. TOWARD THE ESTABLISHMENT OF LIBERAL CATHOLICISM IN AMERICA. Washington: University Press of America, 1983.

Analysis of the American Catholic Bicentennial,'Liberty and Justice for All,' using Weber's concept of rationalization, the dispersion-of-charisma framework of Edward Shils, and Peter Berger's sociology of knowledge.

1425. Varacalli, Joseph A. "The Changing Nature of the 'Italian Problem' in the Catholic Church of the United States." FAITH AND REASON 12,1 (1986): 38-73.

A historical and sociological investigation of the relationship between the southern Italian immigrant and American Catholicism.

1426. Varacalli, Joseph A. "The Resurrection of 'Catholic Sociologies': Toward a Catholic Center." SOCIAL JUSTICE REVIEW 78,5-6 (1987): 100-106.

Investigates the birth and eventual decline of the 'Catholic sociology movement' in the United States.

1427. Varacalli, Joseph A. "The State of the American Catholic Laity: Propositions and Proposals." FAITH AND REASON 13,2 (1987): 126-166.

Examines the conflict between 'orthodox' and 'heterodox' factions within American Catholicism.

1428. Varacalli, Joseph A. "To Empower Catholics: The Catholic League for Religious and Civil Rights as a 'Mediating Structure'." NASSAU REVIEW 5,4 (1988): 45-61.

Analyzes an association which was founded in 1973 and designed to be a Catholic counterpart of the Jewish Anti-Defamation League.

1429. Vera, Hernan. PROFESSIONALIZATION AND PROFESSIONALISM OF CATHOLIC PRIESTS. Gainsville: University Presses of Florida, 1982.

Analysis of data from the 1970 N.F.P.C.-sponsored survey of American Catholic priests.

1430. Verdieck, Mary J., Joseph J. Shields, and Dean R. Hoge. "Role Commitment Processes Revisited: American Catholic Priests 1970 and 1985." JSSR 27,4 (1988): 524-535.

Smaller U.S. probability sample of diocesan clergy, 1985, replicating the 1970 N.O.R.C. study.

1431. Wallace, Ruth A. "Catholic Women and the Creation of a New Social Reality." GENDER AND SOCIETY 2,1 (1988): 24-38.

Considers the post-Vatican II era; includes 1986 exploratory interviews.

1432. Welch, Michael R., and David C. Leege. "Religious Predictors of Catholic Parishioners' Sociopolitical Attitudes: Devotional Style, Closeness to God, Imagery, and Agentic/Communal Religious Identity." JSSR 27,4 (1988): 536-552.

Based on an American sample of Catholic parishioners.

1433. Wiener, Richard L., Thomas J. Kramer, and Miriam J. Nolan. "Ministerial Discernment: An Application of the Lens Model to the Study of Decision Making." RRR 29,1 (1987): 57-68.

Questionnaire data from a sample of nuns in a Southern U.S. province of an international order, selected from those working in education, health, community service, and diverse ministries.

1434. Willms, J. Douglas. "Catholic-school Effects on Academic Achievement: New Evidence from the High School and Beyond Follow-up Study." SOCIOLOGY OF EDUCATION 58,2 (1985): 98-114.

1982 follow-up of Coleman, Hoffer, and Kilgore [item 1356]: achievement test data from U.S. high-school seniors who participated in the 1980 study as sophomores. There were no pervasive Catholic-school effects.

1435. Yeaman, Patricia A. "Prophetic Voices: Differences between Men and Women." RRR 28,4 (1987): 367-376.

Study of the Association for the Rights of Catholics in the Church. Female members more than male members use inclusive language and see sexism and patriarchy as sinful.

# 11
## Roman Catholic: International Studies

*AFRICA*

* Aquina, Mary. "A Sociological Study of a Religious Congregation of African Sisters in Rhodesia." Cited above as item 949.

1436. Currin, Theresa E.V. THE INDIAN IN DURBAN: AN EXPLORATORY STUDY OF THE ROMAN CATHOLIC INDIAN MINORITY, WITH SPECIAL EMPHASIS ON THE SOCIOLOGICAL ASPECTS OF CONVERSION. Unpublished M.Soc.Sc. thesis, University of Natal, 1962.

1437. De Craemer, Willy. THE JAMAA AND THE CHURCH. A BANTU CATHOLIC MOVEMENT IN ZAIRE. New York: Oxford University Press, 1977.

1438. Haar, Gerrie ter. "Religion and Healing: The Case of Milingo." SC 34,4 (1987): 475-493.

Examines controversies which surrounded the healing ministry of Emmanuel Milingo, former archbishop of the Catholic archdiocese of Lusaka, 1970-82.

1439. Higgins, Edward. "Les rôles religieux dans le contexte multi-racial sud-africain: Le profil du ministère dans le calvinisme et le catholicisme." SC 19,1 (1972): 29-47.

Review of C.J. Alant's study of the Dutch Reformed pastor and J. Kiernan's study of the Catholic priest [item 1440]. Both roles are worship-centered in South Africa, rather detached from current events.

1440. Kiernan, James. FRAGMENTED PRIEST. Durban: Unity Publications, 1970.

1441. Laurentin, René. "A Statistical Survey of Christians in Africa." In Claude Geffré and Bertrand Luneau (eds.), THE CHURCHES OF AFRICA: FUTURE PROSPECTS (CONCILIUM 106). New York: Seabury, 1977, pp. 94-104.

1969-74 figures: adherents, clergy; breakdown by regions.

1442. Margarido, Alfredo. "L'Eglise Catholique en Afrique 'portugaise'." REVUE FRANÇAISE D'ETUDES POLITIQUES AFRICAINES 61 (1971): 87-112.

Overview, with membership data from 1960.

1443. Masson, Joseph. "Vocations to the Priesthood and Environment: An Enquiry into the Belgian Congo, Ruanda and Urundi." LUMEN VITAE 13 (1958): 120-145.

An ecological analysis.

1444. Verryn, Trevor D. "Anglican and Roman Catholic Priests in South Africa: Some Questionnaire Responses." SC 19,1 (1972): 93-99.

1970-71 survey of Anglican and Roman Catholic priests in South Africa. There is evidence of conflict between this-worldly and other-worldly stances.

1445. Vertraelen, F.J. AN AFRICAN CHURCH IN TRANSITION -- FROM MISSIONARY DEPENDENCY TO MUTUALITY IN MISSION (A CASE STUDY ON THE ROMAN-CATHOLIC CHURCH IN ZAMBIA), Parts 1 and 2. Leiden: Development Research Institute, 1975.


*AUSTRALIA AND NEW ZEALAND*

1446. Angus, Lawrence B. CONTINUITY AND CHANGE IN CATHOLIC SCHOOLING: AN ETHNOGRAPHY OF A CHRISTIAN BROTHERS COLLEGE IN AUSTRALIAN SOCIETY. London: Falmer, 1988.

1447. Day, Lincoln H. "Fertility Differentials among Catholics in Australia." MILBANK MEMORIAL FUND QUARTERLY 42,2 (1964): 57-83.

1954 data.

1448. König, Walter. "Das katholische Australien. Ein noch unbekanntes Land." STIMMEN DER ZEIT 146,10 (1950): 276-286.

1449. Lewins, Frank W. "Ethnicity as Process: Some Considerations of Italian Catholics." AUSTRALIAN AND NEW ZEALAND JOURNAL OF SOCIOLOGY 11,3 (1975): 15-17.

Case study of one Australian parish in which an 'Italian' identity emgerged.

1450. Lewins, Frank W. "Ethnic Diversity within Australian Catholicism: A Comparative and Theoretical Analysis." AUSTRALIAN AND NEW ZEALAND JOURNAL OF SOCIOLOGY 12,2 (1976): 126-135.

Rather than Catholicism playing a role in assimilation, the Catholic immigrant ethnic groups (Italian, Ukrainian, Polish, Croatian) retain ethnic identities.

1451. Lewins, Frank W. "Continuity and Change in a Religious Organization: Some Aspects of the Australian Catholic Church." JSSR 16,4 (1977): 371-382.

The Australian church is analyzed with a model, consisting of 'Rome,' 'the Australian hierarchy,' and 'the parish.' Its organizational nature is examined in terms of migration policy and official accounts of implementation, as well as the actual responses to situations involving migrants.

1452. Lewins, Frank W. THE MYTH OF THE UNIVERSAL CHURCH: CATHOLIC MIGRANTS IN AUSTRALIA. Canberra: Faculty of Arts, Australian National University, 1978.

1453. Lewins, Frank W. "Wholes and Parts: Some Aspects of the Relationship between the Australian Catholic Church and Migrants." In A. Black and P. Glasner (eds.), PRACTICE AND BELIEF [volume cited in item 91], pp. 74-85.

The various immigrant cultures differ sufficiently to call into question whether a Parsonian approach, which would look for a common integrating religion, can be applied usefully to Australian Catholicism.

  * Mol, J.J. (Hans) "A Collation of Data about Religion in Australia." Cited above as item 308.

1454. Ray, John J., and Dianne Doratis. "Religiocentrism and Ethnocentrism: Catholic and Protestant in Australian Schools." SA 32,3 (1971): 170-179.

Study of Australian fifth-form students in two Catholic and two public schools.

1455. Reidy, M.T.V., and L.C. White. "The Measurement of Traditionalism among Roman Catholic Priests: An Exploratory Study." BRITISH JOURNAL OF SOCIOLOGY 28,2 (1977): 226-241.

Survey of priests from the Wellington, New Zealand, Archdiocese.


*PACIFIC AND EAST ASIA*

1456. Anzai, Shin. "Le catholicisme dans un village isolé." SC 17,1 (1970): 153-156.

The integration of Christianity into the culture of a village such as the one studied, Nishiamuro (Japan), remains problematic insofar as religion is found tied or subordinated to relations of parentage because traditional beliefs passed on in the family result in a syncretism. By forcing a pluralism, however, Christianity may be a factor in modernization.

1457. Anzai, Shin. "Newly-adopted Religions and Social Change on the Ryukyu Islands (Japan) (with special reference to Catholicism)." SC 23,1 (1976): 57-70.

Examines the relation between social change, the decline of traditional religion, and the adoption of recently imported religions in Japan; analysis of a village in Okinawa after World War II.

1458. Doherty, John F. "The Image of the Priest: A Study in Stereotyping." PHILIPPINE SOCIOLOGICAL REVIEW 12,1-2 (1964): 70-76.

Analysis of projective essays written by 75 male Catholic university students in Manila.

* Gheddo, P. CATTOLICI E BUDDISTI NEL VIETNAM. IL RUOLO DELLE COMUNITA RELIGIOSE NELLA CONSTRUZIONE DELLE PACE. Cited above as item 142.

1459. Jim-chang im, Luke, and W.E. Biernatzki. CATHOLIC SOCIO-RELIGIOUS SURVEY OF KOREA, Part 2: RESULTS OF THE OPINION SURVEY. Seoul: Social Research Institute, Sogang University, 1972.

1460. Naito, Kanji. "Inheritance Practices on a Catholic Island: Youngest-son Inheritance (Ultimogeniture) on Kuroshima, Nagasaki Prefecture." SC 17,1 (1970): 21-36.

1461. Nguyen Ho Dinh. "Les communistes, les catholiques et les coopérateurs au Nord Vietnam." COMMUNAUTE 37 (1975): 153-182.

1462. Quec-Hung, Nguyen. "Church and Nation in Vietnam." In J.B. Metz and J.P. Jossua (eds.), CHRISTIANITY AND SOCIALISM. New York: Seabury, 1977, pp. 99-105.

1463. Spae, Joseph J. CATHOLICISM IN JAPAN. A SOCIOLOGICAL STUDY. Tokyo: ISR Press, 1964.

* Tamney, Joseph B. "Chinese Family Structure and the Continuation of Chinese Religions." Cited above as item 156.

## INDIA

* Deliège, Robert. "Arockyai Mary, gardienne du village chez les Parayars de l'Inde du Sud." Cited above as item 937.

* Houtart, François. "L'implantation portugaise au Kerala et ses effets sur l'organisation sociale et religieuse des Syriens et sur le système des castes." Cited above as item 791.

1464. Houtart, François, and Geneviève Lemercinier. "Religion and the Reproduction of Social Structures. Catholicism and the Structure of Caste in an Area of South India." In Gregory Baum (ed.), WORK AND RELIGION (CONCILIUM 131). New York: Seabury; Edinburgh: T. & T. Clark, 1980, pp. 33-42.

Examines the success since the sixteenth century of Catholic missions in Tamil-Nadu.

1465. Houtart, François, and Geneviève Lemercinier. GENESIS AND INSTITU-TIONALIZATION OF THE INDIAN CATHOLICISM. Louvain-la-Neuve: Centre de Recherches Socio-Religieuse, 1981.

1466. Houtart, François, and Geneviève Lemercinier. SIZE AND STRUCTURES OF THE CATHOLIC CHURCH IN INDIA. Louvain-la-Neuve: Centre de Recherches Socio-Religieuse, 1982.

1467. Lemercinier, Geneviève. "The Effect of the Caste System on Conversions to Christianity in Tamilnadu." SC 28,2-3 (1981): 237-268.

## SRI LANKA

* DeVallée, Thérèse. "Devotion to the Virgin Mary in Sri Lanka: Letters to Our Lady of Perpetual Succour." Cited above as item 938.

* Fernando, Charlie. "How Buddhists and Catholics of Sri Lanka see Each Other -- A Factor Analytic Approach." Cited above as item 161.

1468. Houtart, François. RELIGION AND IDEOLOGY IN SRI LANKA. Maryknoll, N.Y.: Orbis, 1980.

1469. Houtart, François, and Geneviève Lemercinier. "Modèles culturels socio-religieux des groupes élitiques catholiques à Sri Lanka." SC 20,2 (1973): 303-320.

1969 questionnaire data from Catholic élite members in Sri Lanka, subjected to factor analysis.

## EUROPE (GENERAL)

1470. Anzai, Shin. DIE RELIGIÖSE PRAXIS DER KATHOLIKEN IN ZUSAMMENHANG MIT EINIGEN SOZIALFAKTOREN IN MITTEL UND WESTEUROPA. INTERNATIONALES KATHOLISCHES INSTITUT FÜR KIRCHLICHE SOZIALFORSCHUNG, BERICHT NR. 70. Wien, 1961.

1471. Baan, Melchior A., and L. Grond. "Inventaire statistique de l'Ordre des Frères Mineurs dans le Nord-Ouest de l'Europe." SC 13,3 (1966): 257-275.

1960 data: Germany, Netherlands, France, Belgium, Austria.

1472. Houtart, François. "Social Problems of the Church in Europe." AMERICAN CATHOLIC SOCIOLOGICAL REVIEW 15,3 (1954): 230-243.

1473. Pope, Whitney, and Nick Danigelis. "Sociology's 'One Law'." SOCIAL FORCES 60,2 (1981): 495-516.

Examines 1919-1972 suicide rates of Catholic and Protestant countries in Europe.

1474. Zeegers, George H.L. "Einige Betrachtungen über Fragen der katholischen Diaspora in Nord-Europa." SC 2,3 (1954): 88-98.

Numbers and percentages of Catholics in England, Denmark, Iceland, Norway, Sweden, Finland; most data from 1950. Catholicism generally disappeared in these countries as a result of the Reformation, and reappeared through immigration.

## AUSTRIA

1475. Bodzenta, E. DIE KATHOLIKEN IN ÖSTERREICH: EIN RELIGIONSSOZIOLOGISCHER ÜBERBLICK. Wien: Herder, 1962.

1476. Dellepoort, J.J., and Linus Grond. "Stand und Bedarf an Priestern in Österreich." SC 4,3-4 (1957): 108-148.

Consideration of 1952 data.

1477. Lindner, Traugot, Leopold Lentner, and Adolf Holl. PRIESTERBILD UND BERUFSWAHLMOTIVE. ERGEBNISSE EINER SOZIAL-PSYCHOLOGISCHEN UNTERSUCHUNG BEI DEN WIENER MITTELSCHÜLERN. Wien: Herder Verlag, 1963.

1478. Suk, Walter. "Soziologische Untersuchungen deutscher Kirchengemeinden. Das Bild einer Großstadtpfarre." In Dietrich Goldschmidt, Franz Greiner, and Helmut Schelsky (eds.), SOZIOLOGIE DER KIRCHENGEMEINDE. Stuttgart: Ferdinand Enke, 1960, pp. 109-122.

Study of a Vienna parish.

1479. Zeegers, George H.L. "Österreich im Rahmen der weltweiten Priester-frage." SC 4,3-4 (1957): 101-107.

Overview, and 1952 data.

1480. Zulehner, Paul M., and S.R. Graupe. WIE PRIESTER HEUTE LEBEN. ERGEB-NISSE DER WIENER PRIESTERUNTERSUCHUNG 1967. Wien: Herder, 1970.


## BELGIUM

1481. Degand, André. "La défense de la propriété privée. Aux sources de la doctrine sociale de l'église." SC 34,2-3 (1987): 175-186.

Analysis of the social doctrine produced within Belgian Catholicism at the end of the nineteenth century. It was a response to the impover-ishment of subordinate social classes.

1482. Dobbelaere, Karel. "Une typologie de l'intégration à l'église." SC 15 (1968): 117-141.

Application of a typology to 1958-59 interview data from Heverlee, Belgium.

1483. Dobbelaere, Karel. "Organising Christian Values in Social Organisa-tions: The Case of Catholic Hospitals in Belgium." SOCIAL STUDIES: IRISH JOURNAL OF SOCIOLOGY 2,5 (1973): 475-483.

Questionnaire research among directors, managers, and religious superiors.

1484. Dobbelaere, Karel. "Professionalization and Secularization in the Belgian Catholic Pillar." JAPANESE JOURNAL OF RELIGIOUS STUDIES 6,1-2 (1979): 39-64.

Consideration of medical and educational institutions, 1950s and 1960s.

1485. Dobbelaere, Karel. "La dominante catholique." In Liliane Voyé et al. (eds.), LA BELGIQUE ET SES DIEUX: EGLISES, MOUVEMENTS RELIGIEUX ET LAIQUES. Louvain-la-Neuve: Cabay, 1985, pp. 193-220.

1486. Dobbelaere, Karel, M. Ghesquierre-Waelkens, and J. Lauwers. LA DIMENSION CHRETIENNE D'UNE INSTITUTION HOSPITALIERE. UNE ANALYSE SOCIOLOGIQUE DE SA LEGITIMATION: HUMANISATION, SECULARISATION ET CLOISONNEMENT. Brussels: Hospitalia, 1975.

1487. Estruch, Juan. "Catholics and the Institutional Church: Obedience versus Critical Distance." SC 17,3 (1970): 379-401.

Presents the obedience/critical distance continuum as a dimension of Belgian Catholic religiosity.

1488. Houtart, François. LES PAROISSES DE BRUXELLES 1803-1951, LEGISLATION, DELIMITATION, DEMOGRAPHIE, EQUIPEMENT. Louvain: Institut de Recherches Economiques et Sociales, 1955.

1489. Laloux, Joseph. "Pratique religieuse et appartenance sociale." SC 14,2 (1967): 105-116.

Sample survey in Seraing, Belgium.

1490. Mattez, M.T. "Les religieuses du diocese de Tournai. Etude sociologique de leur provenance." BULLETIN DE L'INSTITUT DE RECHERCHES ECONOMIQUES ET SOCIALES (Louvain) (1956): 649-698.

1491. Nesti, Arnaldo. "Eglises et modernité en Europe occidentale. Pour une analyse comparative." SC 34,2-3 (1987): 137-149.

Examines essential features of Catholicism in Belgium, Spain, and Italy during the nineteenth century. In Belgium, there was a compromise between the church and a 'liberal revolution.' For Spain and Italy, there was a conflict with the liberal movement, despite the abandonment of relations with the 'ancien régime.'

1492. Remy, Jean. "Le défi de la modernité: La stratégie de la hiérarchie catholique aux XIXe et XXe siècles et l'idée de chrétienté." SC 34, 2-3 (1987): 151-173.

The idea of Christianity has been a powerful resource for the Catholic Church's resistence against modernity.

1493. Remy, Jean, and L. Voye. "L'Eglise catholique de Belgique et la transaction avec la modernité." RECHERCHES SOCIOLOGIQUES 16,3 (1985): 11-30.


*FRANCE*

1494. Bessière, G., J. Piquet, J. Potel, and H. Vulliez. LES VOLETS DU

PRESBYTERE SONT OUVERTS. 2000 PRÊTRES RACONTENT. Paris: Desclée de Brouwer, 1985.

1495. Blanc de la Fontaine, M. "La population des paroisses de Lyon." CHRONIQUE SOCIAL DE LA FRANCE 63 (1955): 88-94.

1496. Brechon, Pierre, and Bernard Denni. "L'univers politique des catholiques pratiquants. Une enquête par questionnaire dans huit assemblées dominicales grenobloises." REVUE FRANÇAISE DE SOCIOLOGIE 24,3 (1983): 505-534.

1982 questionnaire data from adult French Catholics at eight masses in three parishes in the Grenoble area, pertaining to political preferences.

1497. Daniel, Yvan. ASPECTS DE LA PRATIQUE RELIGIEUSE A PARIS. Paris: Ed. Ouvrières, 1952.

1498. Delacroix, Simon. "Parish Inquiries in France." AMERICAN CATHOLIC SOCIOLOGICAL REVIEW 13,3 (1952): 169-173.

Review of the literature.

1499. Donegani, Jean-Marie. "L'appartenance au catholicisme français. Point de vue sociologique." REVUE FRANÇAISE DE SCIENCE POLITIQUE 34,2 (1984): 197-228.

Review of the literature on numbers of adherents and meanings of adherence.

1500. Gros, Lucien. LA PRATIQUE RELIGIEUSE DANS LE DIOCESE DE MARSEILLE. Paris: Ed. Ouvrières, 1954.

1501. Isambert, François-A. "Les ouvriers et l'Eglise catholique." REVUE FRANÇAISE DE SOCIOLOGIE 15,4 (1974): 529-551.

Questionnaire data from French workers.

1502. Isambert, François-A., and Jean-Paul Terrenoire. ATLAS DE LA PRATIQUE RELIGIEUSE DES CATHOLIQUES EN FRANCE. FNSP-CNRS, 1980.

1503. Lambert, Yves. DIEU CHANGE EN BRETAGNE: LA RELIGION A LIMERZEL DE 1900 A NOS JOURS. Paris: Les Editions du Cerf, 1985.

Longitudinal community study of a small-town parish.

1504. Lambert, Yves. "From Parish to Transcendent Humanism in France." In J.A. Beckford and T. Luckmann (eds.), THE CHANGING FACE OF RELIGION [volume cited in item 549], pp. 49-63.

1505. Le Bras, Gabriel. "Description de la France catholique." NOUVELLE REVUE THEOLOGIQUE 70 (1948): 835-845.

Account of the author's project on the historical sociology of the dechristianization of France.

1506. Le Bras, Gabriel. "Mesure de la réalité social du catholicisme en France." CAHIERS INTERNATIONAUX DE SOCIOLOGIE 8 (1950): 3-39.

Review of research techniques and of post-World War II studies.

1507. Le Bras, Gabriel. "La sociologie du catholicisme en France." LUMEN VITAE 6 (1951): 24-42.

1508. Le Bras, Gabriel. "Pour une sociologie historique du catholicisme en France." CAHIERS INTERNATIONAUX DE SOCIOLOGIE 16 (1954): 14-34.

Suggestions for the development of an historical sociology of Catholicism, especially in France.

1509. Le Bras, Gabriel. ETUDES DE SOCIOLOGIE RELIGIEUSE. Tomes 1 and 2. Paris: Presses Universitaires de France, 1956.

1510. Le Bras, Gabriel. "Masstäbe für die Vitalität des Katholizismus in Frankreich." In Friedrich Fürstenberg (ed.), RELIGIONSSOZIOLOGIE. SOZIOLOGISCHE TEXTE, 19. Berlin: Luchterhand, Neuwied, 1964, 1970, pp. 203-227. Translated from G. Le Bras [item 1509], pp. 587-603, 608-612.

Based on data from the 1940s.

1511. Le Bras, Gabriel. "L'image du clerc." ARCHIVES DE SOCIOLOGIE DES RELIGIONS 23 (1967): 23-36.

A historical discussion of images held of the Catholic priest in France.

1512. Maître, Jacques. "Catholicisme français contemporain. Variété et limites de ses dénombrements." ARCHIVES DE SOCIOLOGIE DES RELIGIONS 2 (1956): 27-38.

1513. Maître, Jacques. "Les sociologies du catholicisme français." CAHIERS INTERNATIONAUX DE SOCIOLOGIE 24 (1958): 104-124.

Review of the literature.

1514. Maître, Jacques, Emile Poulat, and Jean-Paul Terrenoire. "L'Eglise Catholique et la vie publique en France." ARCHIVES DE SOCIOLOGIE DES RELIGIONS 34 (1972): 49-99.

1515. Michelat, Guy, and Michel Simon. "Un état du catholicisme en France." ARCHIVES DE SCIENCES SOCIALES DES RELIGIONS 53,2 (1982): 193-204.

A review essay on item 1502.

1516. Morlet, Joël. "L'Eglise Catholique et la modernisation de l'agriculture en France." SC 34,2-3 (1987): 187-202.

Examines relations between the Catholic Church of France and the world of agriculture during the twentieth century. Social Catholicism and Catholic Action represented efforts by the church to regain its influence in rural society.

1517. Palard, Jacques. POUVOIR RELIGIEUX ET SPACE SOCIAL: LA DIOCESE DE BORDEAUX COMME ORGANISATION. Paris: Cerf, 1985.

1518. Pin, Emile. PRATIQUE RELIGIEUSE ET CLASSES SOCIALES DANS UNE PAROISSE URBAINE. SAINT-POTHIN A LYON. Paris: Editions Spes, 1956.

1519. Potel, Julien. MOINS DE BAPTÊMES EN FRANCE. POURQUOI? Paris: Cerf, 1974.

   1968 data, compared to earlier figures.

1520. Potel, Julien. DEMAIN, D'AUTRES PRÊTRES? Paris: Ed. du Centurion, 1977.

1521. Potel, Julien. LES PRÊTRES SECULIERS EN FRANCE. EVOLUTION DE 1965 A 1975. Paris: Centurion, 1977.

1522. Potel, Julien, Paul Huot-Pleuroux, and Jacques Maître. LE CLERGE FRANÇAIS. EVOLUTION DEMOGRAPHIQUE - NOUVELLES STRUCTURES DE FORMATION - IMAGES DE L'OPINION PUBLIQUE. Paris: Centurion, 1967.

1523. Poulat, Emile. "Le Catholicisme français et son personnel dirigeant." ARCHIVES DE SOCIOLOGIE DES RELIGIONS 19 (1965): 117-124.

   Historical discussion of the canonical structure of authority within French Catholicism.

1524. Poulat, Emile. EGLISE CONTRE BOURGEOISIE. INTRODUCTION AU DEVENIR DU CATHOLICISME ACTUEL. Paris: Casterman, 1977.

1525. Poulat, Emile. "La querelle de l'intégrisme en France." SC 32,4 (1985): 343-351.

   A semantic and genetic approach and a review of the current situation, to clarify conflicts between integral Catholics, social Catholics, and Christian democrats in France.

1526. Poulat, Emile. L'EGLISE, C'EST UN MONDE. L'ECCLESIOSPHERE. Paris: Editions du Cerf, 1986.

1527. Roche de Coppens, Peter. "The Worker-priest Movement: An Essay on the Emergence, Growth and Waning of the Worker-priests in France and of the Sociocultural Factors that Lay Behind It." REVISTA INTERNACIONAL DE SOCIOLOGIA 31,5-6 (1973): 215-238.

   Historical analytical account of the movement, 1942-54.

1528. Suaud, Charles. "Contributions à une sociologie de la vocation: Destin religieux et projet scolaire." REVUE FRANÇAISE DE SOCIOLOGIE 15,1 (1974): 75-112.

   Examines the process of recruitment into minor seminaries in rural western France.

1529. Suaud, Charles. "L'imposition de la vocation sacerdotale." ACTES DE

LA RECHERCHE EN SCIENCES SOCIALES 3 (1975): 2-17.

Examines 1920-1970 recruitment to the Roman Catholic priesthood in the Vendée region of France.

1530. Suaud, Charles. LA VOCATION. CONVERSION ET RECONVERSION DES PRÊTRES RURAUX. Paris: Editions de Minuit, 1978.

Study of minor seminarians in the Vendée, using 1920-70 data.

1531. Terrenoire, Jean-Paul. "Groupes socio-professionnels et pratiques cultuelles catholiques. Une analyse écologique quantitative sur des données françaises contemporaines." ARCHIVES DE SCIENCES SOCIALES DES RELIGIONS 37 (1974): 117-155.

Uses religious census data collected by French dioceses in the 1950s and 60s and presents the regional variations in church attendance for different occupational groups as well as the evolution of the gap between them.

1532. Vassort-Rousset, Brigitte. LES EVÊQUES DE FRANCE EN POLITIQUE. Paris: Editions du Cerf, 1986.

1979-80 interviews with a sample of French bishops.

1533. Verscheure, Jacques. "Recherches sur le prêtre: Problèmes méthodologiques." SC 16,4 (1969): 453-469.

Account of conducting research after 1965 in Lille, Cambrai, and Arras dioceses.


*GERMANY*

1534. Geller, Helmut. "Sozialstrukturelle Voraussetzungen für die Durchsetzung der Sozialform <Katholizismus> in Deutschland in der ersten Hälfte des 19. Jahrhunderts." In K. Gabriel and F.-X. Kaufmann (eds.), ZUR SOZIOLOGIE DES KATHOLIZISMUS [item 802], pp. 66-88.

1535. Greinacher, Norbert. "The Development of Applications to Leave the Church and the Transfer from One Church to Another, and Its Causes." SC 8,1 (1961): 61-72.

Based on official applications, 1917-58.

1536. Greinacher, Norbert, and Heinz T. Risse. BILANZ DES DEUTSCHEN KATHOLIZISMUS. Mainz: Mattias Grünwald Verlag, 1966.

1537. Keller, H.E. DIE SOZIOLOGISCHE HERKUNFT DER KATHOLISCHEN PFARRER IN DER DIÖZESE WÜRZBURG DER GEGENWART. Würzburg, 1939.

1538. Neundörfer, L. "Einige Grunddaten zur Struktur der katholischen Kirche in Deutschland." SOZIALE WELT 5 (1954): 197-207.

1539. Rovan, J. LE CATHOLICISME POLITIQUE EN ALLEMAGNE. Paris: Editions du Seuil, 1956.

1540. Scheler, Max. "Soziologische Neuorientierung und die Aufgabe der deutschen Katholiken nach dem Kriege." CHRISTENTUM UND GESELLSCHAFT. Vol. I: KONFESSIONEN. Leipzig, 1924.

1541. Zahn, Gordon C. "The German Catholic Press and Hitler's Wars." CROSS CURRENTS 10,4 (1960): 337-351.

Examines how the Catholic press encouraged cooperation with the military under Hitler.

1542. Zahn, Gordon C. GERMAN CATHOLICS AND HITLER'S WARS. New York: Sheed and Ward, 1962; Notre Dame: University of Notre Dame Press, 1989.


*WEST GERMANY*

1543. Bindereif, Elisabeth. "Berufspositionen und Berufsvorstellungen promovierter katholischer Laientheologen." In Günter Dux, Thomas Luckmann, and Joachim Matthes (eds.), INTERNATIONALES JAHRBUCH FÜR RELIGIONSSOZIOLOGIE 7. Opladen: Westdeutscher Verlag, 1971, pp. 212-251.

1969 interview data from lay holders of the Ph.D. in theology in West Germany.

1544. Fichter, Joseph H. SOZIOLOGIE DER PFARRGRUPPEN. UNTERSUCHUNGEN ZUR STRUKTUR UND DYNAMIK DER GRUPPEN EINER DEUTSCHEN PFARREI. Muenster: Aschendorf, 1958.

1954 study of a West German parish, focusing on lay organizations.

1545. Golomb, Egon. KIRCHE UND KATHOLIKEN IN DER BUNDESREPUBLIK. DATEN UND ANALYSEN. Aschaffenburg: Pattloch Verlag, 1974.

1546. Greinacher, Norbert. "Die Katholiken in der Bundesrepublik. Ihre religiöse und soziale Situation in Wandel der Gesellschaft." WORT UND WAHRHEIT 10 (1965): 598-614.

1547. Groner, Franz. "Statistik der katholischen Kirchengemeinden in Deutschland." In D. Goldschmidt, F. Greiner, and H. Schelsky (eds.), SOZIOLOGIE DER KIRCHENGEMEINDE [volume cited in item 1478], pp. 196-208.

1548. Menges, Walter. "Die katholische Kirche in Schleswig-Holstein. Entwicklung und heutige Situation." SC 2,3 (1954): 99-145.

Catholicism had virtually disappeared in the region as a result of the Reformation. Catholic immigrants came in small numbers in the late nineteenth century, and large numbers as displaced persons from the East after World War II.

1549. Menges, Walter. DIE ORDENSMÄNNER IN DER BUNDESREPUBLIK DEUTSCHLAND.

EINE EMPIRISCHE UNTERSUCHUNG. Köln: Wienland, 1969.

1550. Schmitz, Karl M. "Kirche im Feld sozialer Interaktion." In G. Dux, T. Luckmann, and J. Matthes (eds.), INTERNATIONALES JAHRBUCH FÜR RELIGIONSSOZIOLOGIE 7 [volume 1543], pp. 168-183.

1968 sample from a small city with industrial tendencies; inverse relationship between church participation and social participation.

1551. Siefer, G. (ed.) STERBEN DIE PRIESTER AUS? SOZIOLOGISCHE ÜBERLEGUN-GEN ZUR FUNKTIONSWANDEL EINES BERUFSSTANDES. Essen: Driewer, 1973.

Draws on a series of earlier studies.

## HUNGARY

1552. Káldi, Georg. "Die Kirche in Ungarn. Entwicklung und heutige Situa-tion der kirchlichen Verhältnisse in Ungarn." SC 4,2 (1956): 37-67.

Discusses the revival experienced by the Hungarian church from 1894 to 1944, as well as the persecution of the church in the decade following World War II. Features demographic data and comparisons with other denominations.

1553. Morel, Julius, and Emmerich András. "L'opinion des catholiques hongrois sur les reformes de l'Eglise." SC 15 (1968): 383-401.

Interview data from a national sample.

## ITALY

1554. Abbruzzese, Salvatore. "Religion et modernité: Le cas de <Comunione e Liberazione>." SC 36,1 (1989): 13-32.

Discusses developments within Italian Catholicism since World War II.

1555. Anfossi, Anna. "Funzioni della parrocchia e partizipazione dei parrocchiani alla vita religiosa in comuni agricoli della Sardegna." QUADERNI DI SOCIOLOGIE 16,2 (1967): 190-216.

Discusses the integrative function of the priests in a group of Sardinian communities.

1556. Anfossi, Giuseppe, and Sergio Zenatti. "Une istituzione ecclesiale in cambiamento." QUADERNI DI SOCIOLOGIA 24,3 (1975): 244-266.

Study of the theological seminary at Turin, 1966-72, highlighting the breakdown of institutional and ideological totalitarianism.

1557. Berzano, Luigi. "Ideologia e utopia nella Diocesi di Roma: Analisi di communità e gruppi ecclesiali non istituzionalizzati." CRITICA SOCIOLOGICA 32 (1974-75): 71-84.

Study of nine dissident Catholic groups in Rome, 1968-73.

1558. Boulard, Fernand. NELLE PARROCCHIE DI CAMPAGNA. Brescia: Morcelliana, 1948.

1559. Braga, G. "Tipologia delle sottostructure della parrocchie siciliana." SOCIOLOGIA RELIGIOSA 1 (1957): 119-138.

1560. Burgalassi, Silvano. "Il problema delle vocazioni religiosi e del clero secolare in une diocesi toscana." ORIENTAMENTI SOCIALI 10,14 (1954): 312-316.

1561. Burgalassi, Silvano. "La sociologia del cattolicismo in Italia." LETTURA DI SOCIOLOGIA RELIGIOSA (supplement to ORIENTAMENTI PASTORALI) 2,5-6 (1965): 132-247.

1562. Burgalassi, Silvano. PRETI IN CRISI? TENDENZE SOCIOLOGICHE DEL CLERO ITALIANO. Fossano: Esperienze, 1970.

1563. Burgalassi, Silvano. "Situazione e problemi del clero rurale italiano." PRESENZA PASTORALE 10-11 (1974): 875-880.

   * Carroll, Michael P. "Italian Catholicism: Making Direct Contact with the Sacred." Cited above as item 1352.

1564. Cipriani, Roberto. "'Diffused Religion' and New Values in Italy." In J.A. Beckford and T. Luckmann (eds.), THE CHANGING FACE OF RELIGION [volume cited in item 549], pp. 24-48.

1565. Contigualia, C. "Una tipica parrocchia siciliana, Totorici." STUDI SOCIALI 5 (1964): 414-428.

1566. De Rosa, Gabriele. "I Fratelli Cavanis e la società religiosa Veneziana nel clima della Restaurazione." RIVISTA DI SOCIOLOGIA 11, 1-3 (1973): 43-62.

   External forces undermined civil and religious structures in Venice at the end of the eighteenth century and the beginning of the nineteenth. The brothers Cavanis established an institute to re-establish the structures, supported by the Austrian emperor.

1567. Evans, Robert H. "Parish Priests, Political Power and Decision-making: An Italian Case." AMERICAN BEHAVIORAL SCIENTIST 17,6 (1974): 813-826.

   Case study of a village in southwest Padua, where the archpriest is both a religious and a political-patronage figure.

1568. Fasola-Bologna, Alfredo. "Il ruolo del sacerdote nelle aspettative della popolazione di una parrocchia romana." RIVISTA DI SOCIOLOGIA 6,15 (1968): 69-88.

   Based on 1966 interviews in the lower-middle-class parish of Saints Fabiano and Venanzia in Rome.

1569. Giuriati, Paolo. "Dinamica vocazionale in cifre. Il flusso delle entrate e uscite nel Seminario Maggiore di Padova dal 1950-51 al 1970-71." STUDIA PATAVINA 2 (1977): 245-310.

1570. Hazelrigg, Lawrence E. "Occupation and Religious Practice in Italy. The Thesis of 'Working-class Alienation'." JSSR 11,4 (1972): 335-346.

1963-64 national sample of male heads of households. Level of participation in religion correlates positively but very weakly with socioeconomic status.

1571. Martelli, S., with I. Colozzi. L'ARCIPELAGO CATTOLICO. ANALISI SOCIO-LOGICA DELL'ASSOCIAZIONISMO ECCLESIALE A BOLOGNA. Bologna: CIC-IPSSER, 1988.

1572. Montezemolo, Maria I. "Una ricerca pilota sui vescovi italiani." LA CRITICA SOCIOLOGICA 20 (1971): 61-81.

Interview data from 35 Italian bishops in different provinces.

* Nesti, Arnaldo. "Eglises et modernité en Europe occidentale. Pour une analyse comparative." Cited above as item 1491.

1573. Orsini, Gabriele. "Aspetti della secolarizzazione. (Il giorno del Signore e le vocazioni in Italia con particolare attenzione all' Abruzzo-Molise)." SOCIOLOGIA. RIVISTA DI SCIENZE SOCIALI (NS) 11,2-3 (1977): 151-180.

Historical-sociological examination of Sunday observance from ancient times onward, and some data on priest vocations in the 1970s, with reference to the problem of hyperproductivism (be it a Marxist or capitalist form of alienation).

1574. Parisi, Arturo. "Per un'interpretazione delle transformazioni in atto nella chiesa cattolica italiana." RASSEGNA ITALIANA DI SOCIOLOGIA 10,3 (1969): 377-410.

Observations on organizational elasticity in the Roman Catholic church, utilizing concepts of horizontal pluralism and vertical pluralism.

1575. Parisi, Arturo. LA MATRICE SOCIORELIGIOSA DEL DISSENSO CATTOLICO IN ITALIA. Bologna: Il Mulino, 1971.

* Poggi, Gianfranco. CATHOLIC ACTION IN ITALY: SOCIOLOGY OF A SPONSORED ORGANIZATION. Cited above as item 851.

1576. Poulat, Emile. CATHOLICISME, DEMOCRATIE ET SOCIALISME: LE MOUVEMENT CATHOLIQUE ET MGR. BEGNINI DE LA NAISSANCE DU SOCIALISME A LA VICTOIRE DU FASCISME. Tournai: Castermann, 1977.

1577. Tomasi, Luigi. LA CONTESTAZIONE RELIGIOSA GIOVANILE IN ITALIA (1968-78). Milano: Franco Angeli, 1981.

Summarizes various previous studies of Italian youth, reproducing tables of attitudes and practice.

1578. Valenzano, Paolo M., and Benevenuto Castellani. "L'evoluzione del clero italiano: Una propostadi riflessione." BOLLETINO DI STATISTICA E SOCIOLOGIA RELIGIOSA 4 (1974): 65-74.


## MALTA

1579. Houtart, François, and Benjamin Tonna. "The Implications of Change for the Church in Malta." SC 7 (1960): 461-474.

Provides a social context up to 1958.

1580. Vassallo, M. MEN IN BLACK. A REPORT ON MALTA'S DIOCESAN CLERGY. Malta: P.R.S. Publication, 1973.


## NETHERLANDS

1581. Baan, Melchior A. "Structural and Cultural Changes in the Dutch Franciscan Province." SC 13,3 (1966): 245-256.

Focus is on the period of 1853-1965.

1582. Bax, Mart. "Religious Infighting and the Formation of a Dominant Catholic Regime in Southern Dutch Society." SC 32,1 (1985): 57-72.

Describes and explains the growth of a clerical domination in the south of the Netherlands, focusing on the tensions inherent in the dual nature of the Catholic hierarchical structure in the context of the power relations within and between government changes.

1583. Coleman, John A. THE EVOLUTION OF DUTCH CATHOLICISM 1958-1974. Berkeley: University of California Press, 1978.

1584. Dellepoort, J. "Analyse sociographique et statistique des vocations sacerdotales aux pays-bas." In E. Collard et al. (eds.), VOCATION DE LA SOCIOLOGIE RELIGIEUSE - SOCIOLOGIE DES VOCATIONS. Tournai: Casterman, 1958, pp. 118-131.

1585. Goddijn, Walter. THE DEFERRED REVOLUTION: A SOCIAL EXPERIMENT IN CHURCH INNOVATION IN HOLLAND. Amsterdam: Elsevier, 1975.

1586. Hutjes, Jan M. "Dutch Catholics on Birth Control and Sexuality." SOCIOLOGIA NEERLANDICA 11,2 (1975): 144-158.

1969 survey of 1000 Dutch Catholic couples, where wives were aged under 50 years. Commitment to the church was inversely related to use of artificial contraception.

1587. Laeyendecker, Leo. "Soziologie des Katholizismus in den Niederlanden." In K. Gabriel and F.-X. Kaufmann (eds.), ZUR SOZIOLOGIE DES KATHOLIZ- ISMUS [item 802], pp. 166-200.

Long-term historical view, beginning with the twelfth century.

1588. Lechner, Frank J. "Catholicism and Social Change in the Netherlands: A Case of Radical Secularization?" JSSR 28,2 (1989): 136-147.

1589. Poeisz, Josef J. "Déterminants sociaux des inscriptions dans les séminaires et des ordinations de nouveaux prêtres aux Pays-Bas." SC 10,6 (1963): 491-524.

Data for 1853-1962.

1590. Poeisz, Josef J. "Gruppenisolierung, Kirchlichkeit und Religiosität: Das niederländische Beispiel." INTERNATIONALES JAHRBUCH FÜR RELIGIONS-SOZIOLOGIE 1. Opladen: Westdeutschen Verlag, 1965, pp. 113-148.

1591. Poeisz, Josef J. "The Parishes of the Dutch Church Province, 1-1-1966." SC 14,3 (1967): 203-231.

Detailed ecclesiastical data.

1592. Poeisz, Josef J. "The Priests of the Dutch Church Province, Number and Functions." SC 14,3 (1967): 233-253.

1965 data: numbers, ages, background, assignments.

1593. Steeman, Theodor M. "L'Eglise d'aujourd'hui. Une exploration de la Hollande catholique en 1966." SC 14 (1967): 165-202.

1594. Stoop, W. "Quatre enquêtes sur la signification de la vie religieuse parmi quatre groupes differents de religieux aux Pays-Bas." SC 18,1 (1971): 117-122.

Discusses 1966-1970 studies.

1595. Thurlings, Jan M.G. "The Case of Dutch Catholicism: A Contribution to the Theory of the Pluralistic Society." SOCIOLOGIA NEERLANDICA 7,2 (1971): 118-136. See also "Il caso del cattolicesimo olandese: Un contributo alla teoria della societa pluralistics." HUMANITAS 1973, No. 4, pp. 243-263.

Historical analysis since the seventeenth century, focusing on minority group identity.

1596. Thurlings, Jan M.G. "Identity and Pluralism. A Case-study." In H. Mol (ed.), IDENTITY AND RELIGION [volume cited in item 118], pp. 169-177.

Examines Dutch Catholicism in terms both of its minority status and the strength of its collective identity.

1597. Van Heek, F. "Roman Catholicism and Fertility in the Netherlands: Demographic Aspects of Minority Status." POPULATION STUDIES 10,2 (1956): 125-138.

Analyzes the then high fertility of the Dutch Catholic population.

1598. Van Hemert, Martien. "La pratique dans le cadre des modèles pastoreaux." SC 30,4 (1983): 457-475.

1599. Van Kemenade, Josephus A. "Roman Catholics and Their Schools." SOCIOLOGIA NEERLANDICA 7,1 (1971): 15-27.

Survey of Dutch Catholic educators and parents. Catholic opinion is tending toward a belief that separate schools are not necessary, but the opposite view is held by some 74% of the teachers and 75% of the parents.

1600. Vekemans, R. "La sociographie du catholicisme aux Pays-Bas." ARCHIVES DE SOCIOLOGIE DES RELIGIONS 1 (1957): 129-136.

1601. Weima, J. "Authoritarianism, Religious Conservatism, and Sociocentric Attitudes in Roman Catholic Groups." HUMAN RELATIONS 18,3 (1965): 231-240.

Notes the corresponding relation between authoritarianism and negative attitudes held by Dutch Catholics and Calvinists toward one another.


*NORWAY, SWEDEN*

1602. Jolson, Alfred J. "The Role of the Priest and Obstacles to Priestly Vocations in Oslo, Norway: A Research Note." SA 31,2 (1970): 115-117.

Study in an Oslo parish.

1603. Menges, Walter. "Die geistigen und religiösen Verhältnisse Schwedens und der schwedische Katholizismus." SC 4,5-6 (1957): 234-273.

1954 overview, with historical context.


*POLAND*

1604. Borowski, Karel H. "Secular and Religious Education in Poland." JOURNAL OF RELIGIOUS EDUCATION 70,1 (1975): 71-76.

1605. Majka, Josef. "The Character of Polish Catholicism." SC 15,3-4 (1968): 185-208.

1606. Majka, Josef. "Historical and Cultural Conditions of Polish Catholicism." THE CHRISTIAN IN THE WORLD 14 (1981): 24-38.

1607. Mariański, Janusz. "Dynamics of Changes in Rural Religiosity under Industrialization. The Case of Poland." SC 28,1 (1981): 63-78.

Discusses the shift to a selective religiosity, with a concomitant preference for a relatively deinstitutionalized religion.

1608. Michel, Patrick. "Le catholicisme polonais. Approches sociologiques." ARCHIVES DE SCIENCES SOCIALES DES RELIGIONS 49,1 (1980): 161-172.

Discusses the central position of Roman Catholicism in the national life of Poland.

1609. Piwowarski, Wladyslaw. "The Image of the Priest in the Eyes of Parishioners in Three Rural Parishes." SC 15,3-4 (1968): 235-249.

1610. Piwowarski, Wladyslaw. "Continuity and Change of Ritual in Polish Folk Piety." SC 29,2-3 (1982): 125-134.

Rituals have come to express nationalism; they have been secularized and also privatized (or familialized).

1611. Piwowarski, Wladyslaw. "Le catholicisme polonais, garant de l'identité nationale." CONCILIUM 206 (1986): 33-41.

1612. Strassberg, Barbara. "Changes in Religious Culture in post-World War II Poland." SA 48,4 (1988): 342-354.

Religious practice in Poland has maintained an anthropocentric focus and a non-dogmatic aspect that have proved less likely to be undermined by scientific thought and social change; rather, religion is deeply embedded in the culture as a broad socio-cultural Catholicism.

1613. Taras, Piotr. "Pratiques religieuses, contenu de foi et comportement moral. Resultats d'une enquête dans trois villes polonaises." SC 15 (1968): 251-259.

Survey of church attenders in three cities in 1964.

1614. Taras, Piotr. "Conditionnements sociaux des vocations sacerdotales en Pologne." SC 17,4 (1970): 545-552.

Interpretation of a 1962 survey.

1615. Zdaniewicz, Witold. "Le problème des vocations religieuses en Pologne." SC 15,2-3 (1968): 209-234.

Data for 1945-58, on members of male and female orders.

## SPAIN

1616. Abellán, José L. "Sociología del catolicismo español." SISTEMA 26 (1978): 39-57.

Uses Max Weber as a point of departure; comparison with Calvinism.

1617. Carrasco, Salvador. "El paso del 'catolicismo social catalan' al pluralismo de los catolicos en cataluna (1899-1951)." PERSPECTIVA SOCIAL 21 (1985): 111-132.

1618. Castillo, Juan J. "Modulaciones ideológicas del catolicismo social en España: De los circulos a los sindicatos." REVISTA ESPAÑOLA DE LA OPINION PUBLICA (Spain) 45 (1976): 37-75.

Depicts an early twentieth-century shift in church's labor strategy, from efforts to bring workers and employers together on common ground, to denominational unions which recognized a basic opposition of interests.

1619. Diaz-Mozaz, José M. "Les vocations en Espagne." SC 12,4-5 (1965): 303-311.

Features 1961 data.

1620. Duocastella, Rogelio. "Géographie de la pratique religieuse en Espagne." SC 12,4-5 (1965): 253-302.

Assemblage of data from previous studies.

1621. Duocastella, Rogelio. "La formation religieuse et sociale dans l'enseignement secondaire confessional en Espagne." LUMEN VITAE 24,4 (1969): 683-698.

1622. Duocastella, Rogelio, et al. ANALISIS SOCIOLOGICO DEL CATOLICISMO ESPAÑOL. Barcelona: Nova Terra, 1967.

1623. Frigolé Reixach, Joan. "Religión y politica en un pueblo murciano entre 1966-1976: La crisis del nacional catolicismo desde la perspectiva local." REVISTA ESPAÑOLA DE INVESTIGACIONES SOCIOLOGICAS 23 (1983): 77-126.

Analysis of a conflict between a local Marianist convent, at the Santuario de la Virgen, and local authorities, 1966-76. Local elites did not want to democratize control over the sanctuary.

1624. Gallagher, Charles F. RELIGION, CLASS, AND FAMILY IN SPAIN. American Universities Field Staff VIII, No. 4, September 1973.

1625. Gonzalez Seara, Luis, and Juan Diez Nicolas. "Progresismo y conservadurismo en el catolicismo español." ANALES DE SOCIOLOGIA 1 (1966): 56-67.

1626. Lizcano, Manuel. "Typologie et modes d'appartenance et de dissidence chrétiennes dans une société de tradition catholique, telle la société espagnole." SC 12,2 (1965): 245-251.

1627. Marcos Alonso, Jesus. "A Social and Psychological Typology of Religious Identification in Spanish Catholicism." SC 12,4-5 (1965): 217-243. See also "Hacia una tipología de la identificación religiosa en el catolicismo español." In R. Duocastella et al., ANALISIS SOCIOLOGICO DEL CATOLICISMO ESPAÑOL [item 1622], pp. 97-132.

General discussion and conceptualization.

1628. Moreno-Navarro, Isidoro. "Religiosité populaire andalouse et catholicisme." SC 33,4 (1986): 437-455.

Andalusia is the most anti-clerical part of Spain, having the lowest rates of Catholic practice. Yet popular religious lay organizations are strong. Popular religion appears to be an expression of Andalusian identity.

1629. Nebreda, Julián. "La crisis vocacional del Instituto Marista y su futuro en Andalucia." CUADERNOS DE REALIDADES SOCIALES 6 (1975): 59-107.

1630. Nesti, Arnaldo. "Introduction: Le Catholicisme espagnol dix ans après la mort de Franco." SC 33,4 (1986): 337-345.

Review of the situation of Catholicism in Spain during the nation's restructuring.

* Nesti, Arnaldo. "Eglises et modernité en Europe occidentale. Pour une analyse comparative." Cited above as item 1491.

1631. Pereda, Carlos, and Miguel Angel de Prada. "The Breakdown of Religious Debates in Spain in the 80's." SC 33,4 (1986): 347-362.

Catholicism in Spain is pluralist, ranging from Francoism to Liberation Theology.

1632. Ruiz Olabuénaga, José. "Ex-prêtres en Espagne." SC 17,4 (1970): 503-516.

Survey of 115 ex-priests and ex-seminarians in Spain; descriptive data and social-psychological typology.

1633. Ruiz Olabuénaga, José. LOS EX-SACERDOTES Y EX-SEMINARISTAS EN ESPAÑA. Cuernavaca: Cidoc, 1971.

* Schoenherr, Richard A., and José Pérez Vilarino. "Organizational Role Commitment in the Catholic Church in Spain and the USA." Cited above as item 1323.

* Schoenherr, Richard A., Lawrence A. Young, and José Pérez Vilarino. "Demographic Transitions in Religious Organizations: A Comparative Study of Priest Decline in Roman Catholic Dioceses." Cited above as item 1418.

1634. Urbina, Fernando. "Le catholicisme espagnol et le processus de modernisation au XIXe siècle." SC 34,2-3 (1987): 211-222.

Spain's bourgeois revolution early in the nineteenth century eliminated the privileges of the aristocracy and the church's medieval system, but the bourgeoisie, not as powerful as that of France, joined the wealth of the old agrarian ruling class. This consolidated a traditionalist Catholicism despite political changes.

1635. Vazquez, Jesús M. LOS RELIGIOSOS ESPAÑOLES, HOY (Estudio sociologico). Madrid: Organizacion Sala Ed., 1973.

1636. Vazquez, Jesús M. "Los religiosos españoles, hoy (Sintesis de conclusiones)." CUADERNOS DE REALIDADES SOCIALES 4 (1974): 133-159.

*SWITZERLAND*

1637. Altermatt, Urs. "Thesen zum Konzept der 'katholischen Subgesell-
schaft' am Beispiel des Schweizer Katholizismus." In K. Gabriel and
F.-X. Kaufmann (eds.), ZUR SOZIOLOGIE DES KATHOLIZISMUS [item 802],
pp. 145-165.

Focus on the past two centuries.

1638. Wagner, A. DIE SCHWEIZERISCHE PRIESTERFRAGE. UNTERSUCHUNG ZUM PROBLEM
DES PRIESTERNACHWUCHSES. St. Gallen: Schweizerische Pastoralsoziolo-
gisches Institut, 1968.


*YUGOSLAVIA*

1639. Vrcan, Srdjan. "Changing Functions of Religion in a Socialist
Society. The Case of Catholicism in Jugoslavia." SC 28,1 (1981): 43-
61.


*GREAT BRITAIN*

1640. Bressan, Vanni. "La participation sociale dans la vie d'une paroisse
urbaine." SC 9,3 (1962): 243-257.

Application of Fichter's typology of parishioners to a London parish.

1641. Brothers, Joan. CHURCH AND SCHOOL. A STUDY OF THE IMPACT OF EDUCA-
TION ON RELIGION. Liverpool: Liverpool University Press, 1964.

Interview data focusing on relationships of former Catholic grammer-
school pupils with formal organizations of the church. Conducted in
Liverpool.

1642. Bryman, Alan. "Professionalism and the Clergy: A Research Note."
RRR 26,3 (1985): 253-260.

1972-73 data from England (Anglican, Methodist, Roman Catholic) do not
allow a good 'fit' of the Hall professionalism scale.

1643. Chou, Ru-chi, and S. Brown. "A Comparison of the Size of Families of
Roman Catholics and non-Catholics in Great Britain." POPULATION
STUDIES 22,1 (1968): 51-60.

Both ideal and real family sizes are larger for Catholics than for
others in the U.K.

1644. Gay, John. "Some Aspects of the Social Geography of Religion in
England: The Roman Catholics and the Mormons." SOCIOLOGICAL YEARBOOK
OF RELIGION IN BRITAIN 1 (1968): 47-64.

Assesses distribution patterns of Mormons and Catholics in England
from 1851 to 1967.

1645. Goldstein, Reine. "La minorité catholique d'une petite ville industrielle anglaise." ARCHIVES DE SOCIOLOGIE DES RELIGIONS 9 (1960): 113-127.

Based on 1957 research conducted in Durham County.

1646. Goldstein, Reine. "Types de comportement religieux et cadres sociaux dans deux paroisses catholiques anglaises." REVUE FRANÇAIS DE SOCIOLOGIE 6,1 (1965): 58-67.

Questionnaire data on religious practices in a Westfield parish.

1647. Hornsby-Smith, Michael P. CATHOLIC EDUCATION: THE UNOBTRUSIVE PARTNER. SOCIOLOGICAL STUDIES OF THE CATHOLIC SCHOOL SYSTEM IN ENGLAND AND WALES. London: Sheed and Ward, 1978.

Review of studies, mostly in Great Britain, 1960s and 1970s; representation of much quantitative information.

1648. Hornsby-Smith, Michael P. "Catholic Accounts: Problems of Institutional Involvement." In G. Nigel Gilbert and Peter Abell (eds.), ACCOUNTS AND ACTION. SURREY CONFERENCES ON SOCIOLOGICAL THEORY AND METHOD. Aldershot: Gower, 1983, pp. 132-152.

Discusses the problem of interviewing respondents who may be marginal to the institution to which they 'belong.' 1974-77 interviews with British Catholics: clergy and involved laity, practicing Catholics, dormant Catholics.

1649. Hornsby-Smith, Michael P. "The Immigrant Background of Roman Catholics in England and Wales: A Research Note." NEW COMMUNITY 13,1 (1986): 79-85.

Estimates from 1981 census information.

1650. Hornsby-Smith, Michael P. ROMAN CATHOLICS IN ENGLAND: STUDIES IN SOCIAL STRUCTURE SINCE THE SECOND WORLD WAR. Cambridge: Cambridge University Press, 1987.

Focus on the Catholics of England and Wales, 1973-83. Based on several separate collections of data.

1651. Hornsby-Smith, Michael P. "Into the Mainstream: Recent Transformations in British Catholicism." In Thomas M. Gannon (ed.), WORLD CATHOLICISM IN TRANSITION. New York: Macmillan; London: Collier Macmillan, 1988, pp. 218-231.

Reviews recent transformation in British Catholicism as a result of postwar social change and in the light of the Second Vatican Council.

1652. Hornsby-Smith, Michael P. THE CHANGING PARISH. A STUDY OF PARISHES, PRIESTS AND PRACTITIONERS AFTER VATICAN II. London: Routledge, 1989.

1653. Hornsby-Smith, Michael P., and Kathryn A. Turcan. "Are Northern Catholics Different?" CLERGY REVIEW 66,7 (1981): 231-241.

1978 survey of Roman Catholics in England, broken down by region, focusing on beliefs, practices, and attitudes.

1654. Hornsby-Smith, Michael P., Raymond M. Lee, and Peter A. Reilly. "Social and Religious Change in Four English Roman Catholic Parishes." SOCIOLOGY 18,3 (1984): 353-365.

Social mobility and its effects seem minimal; attitudes toward contraception and liturgical changes suggest a change in attitudes toward religious authority.

1655. Hornsby-Smith, Michael P., Raymond M. Lee, and Kathryn A. Turcan. "A Typology of English Catholics." SOCIOLOGICAL REVIEW 30,3 (1982): 433-459.

1978 national survey of Catholics aged 15 and over. Ten types are identified.

1656. Hornsby-Smith, Michael P., Kathryn A. Turcan, and Lynda T. Rajan. "Patterns of Religious Commitment, Intermarriage and Marital Breakdown among English Catholics." ARCHIVES DE SCIENCES SOCIALES DES RELIGIONS 64,1 (1987): 137-155.

Presents evidence which indicates the collapse of a distinct Catholic subculture in England and Wales in the post-war years.

1657. Hornsby-Smith, Michael P., Michael Procter, Lynda T. Rajan, and Jennifer Brown. "A Typology of Progressive Catholics: A Study of the Delegates to the National Pastoral Congress." JSSR 26,2 (1987): 234-248.

Data from a survey of delegates to the 1980 National Pastoral Congress of English Catholics; no simple unidimensional scale of progressivism.

1658. Murray, C. "The Moral and Religious Beliefs of Catholic Adolescents: Scale Development and Structure." JSSR 17,4 (1978): 439-447.

A study of Catholic adolescents in U.K. secondary schools. The structure of their moral beliefs is well defined by two components, termed moral conservatism and moral liberalism.

1659. O'Toole, Roger. "Refugees from the National Myth: The English Catholic Odyssey." In R. O'Toole (ed.), SOCIOLOGICAL STUDIES IN ROMAN CATHOLICISM [item 821], pp. 85-105.

Discusses English Catholicism's transition from a small, indigenous, rural, upper-class sect to a populous, proletarian, urban church.

1660. Ranson, Stewart, Alan Bryman, and Bob Hinings. CLERGY, MINISTERS, AND PRIESTS. Boston: Routledge and Kegan Paul, 1977.

1972-73 questionnaire research on Church of England, Roman Catholic, and Methodist clergy in Great Britain.

1661. Spencer, A.E.C.W. "The Structure and Organization of the Catholic Church in England." In J.D. Halloran and Joan Brothers (eds.), USES OF SOCIOLOGY. London: Sheed and Ward, 1966, pp. 92-125.

Overview; description of a loosening of discipline.

1662. Spencer, A.E.C.W. "The Demography and Sociography of the Roman Catholic Community of England and Wales." In L. Bright and S. Clements (eds.), THE COMMITTED CHURCH. London: Darton, Longman and Todd, 1966, pp. 60-85.

1663. Spencer, A.E.C.W. "The Catholic Community as a British Melting Pot." NEW COMMUNITY 2,2 (1973): 125-131.

1664. Ward, Conor K. "Some Aspects of the Social Structure of a Roman Catholic Parish." SOCIOLOGICAL REVIEW 6,1 (1958): 75-93.

Interview data from a Liverpool parish.

1665. Ward, Conor K. PRIESTS AND PEOPLE. A STUDY IN THE SOCIOLOGY OF RELIGION. Liverpool: Liverpool University Press, 1961.

Based on participant observation and interviews with a representative sample of parishioners, in a parish in Liverpool, 1957.

## NORTHERN IRELAND

1666. Burton, F.P. THE SOCIAL MEANING OF CATHOLICISM IN NORTHERN IRELAND. Unpublished Ph.D. dissertation, London School of Economics, 1976.

1667. McCallister, Ian. "Religious Commitment and Social Attitudes in Ireland." RRR 25,1 (1983): 3-20.

1973 data from males in Northern Ireland and the Irish Republic.

1668. Macourt, Malcolm. "The Nature of Religion in Ireland." SOCIOLOGICAL YEARBOOK OF RELIGION IN BRITAIN 7 (1974): 26-45.

Emphasizes the importance of social, cultural, and political dimensions for understanding divisions in Irish society.

## IRELAND

1669. Hannigan, John A. "Containing the Luciferine Spark: The Catholic Church and Recent Movements for Social Change in the Republic of Ireland." In Roger O'Toole (ed.), SOCIOLOGICAL STUDIES IN ROMAN CATHOLICISM [item 821], pp. 71-84.

Focuses on the role played by the church in two recent national referenda in the Irish Republic - the 1983 constitutional referendum on abortion and the 1986 referendum on divorce.

1670. Hynes, Eugene. "Family and Religious Change in a Peripheral Capitalist Society: Mid-nineteenth-century Ireland." In D.L. Thomas (ed.), THE RELIGION AND FAMILY CONNECTION [volume cited in item 414], pp. 161-174.

Argues that the family-economy structure promoted a puritannical version of Catholicism.

1671. Hynes, Eugene. "Nineteenth-century Irish Catholicism, Farmers' Ideology, and National Religion: Explorations in Cultural Explanation." In Roger O'Toole (ed.), SOCIOLOGICAL STUDIES IN ROMAN CATHOLICISM [item 821], pp. 45-69.

Argues that Romanization of the Irish population was promoted by the compatibility of interests between clergy and tenant farmers, a convergence central also to the forging of an indissoluble bond between Catholicism and national identity.

1672. Inglis, Tom. "Legalism and Irish Catholicism." SOCIAL STUDIES. IRISH JOURNAL OF SOCIOLOGY 7,1 (1982-83): 33-41.

Assesses the symptoms of the Catholic Church's apparently progressive loss of power in Irish society.

1673. Inglis, Tom. MORAL MONOPOLY: THE CATHOLIC CHURCH IN MODERN IRISH SOCIETY. Dublin: Gill and Macmillan, 1987.

1674. Lennon, James, et al. "Survey of Brothers." SOCIAL STUDIES. IRISH JOURNAL OF SOCIOLOGY 1,2 (1972): 201-223.

1675. Lennon, James, et al. "Survey of Orders of Sisters." SOCIAL STUDIES. IRISH JOURNAL OF SOCIOLOGY. 1,2 (1972): 181-200.

1676. Lennon, James, et al. "A Survey of Male Religious Orders." SOCIAL STUDIES. IRISH JOURNAL OF SOCIOLOGY 1,2 (1972): 159-180.

1677. Lennon, James, et al. "Survey of Diocesan Clergy." SOCIAL STUDIES. IRISH JOURNAL OF SOCIOLOGY 1,2 (1972): 144-158.

1678. Lennon, James, et al. "Survey of Catholic Clergy and Religious Personnel." SOCIAL STUDIES. IRISH JOURNAL OF SOCIOLOGY. 1,2 (1972): 137-143.

   * McCallister, Ian. "Religious Commitment and Social Attitudes in Ireland." Cited above as item 1667.

   * Macourt, Malcolm. "The Nature of Religion in Ireland." Cited above as item 1668.

1679. Newman, Jeremiah. "The Priests of Ireland: A Socio-religious Survey. 1: Numbers and Distribution. 2: Patterns of Vocations." IRISH ECCLESIASTICAL RECORD 98,1 (1962): 1-27; 98,2 (1962): 65-91.

Secular and regular clergy, ratio of clergy to laity, distribution of clergy in the nation, 1956-60; some data 1871-1961; current data for 1961.

1680. Newman, Jeremiah, Liam Ryan, and Conor K. Ward. "Attitudes of Young People towards Vocations (Part of a study commissioned by the Irish hierarchy)." SOCIAL STUDIES. IRISH JOURNAL OF SOCIOLOGY 1,5 (1972): 531-550.

1681. Streib, Gordon F. "Attitudes of the Irish toward Changes in the Catholic Church." SC 20,1 (1973): 49-71.

Survey conducted in Dublin, showing differences in the acceptance of religious changes.

## NORTH AMERICA

1682. Burch, Thomas K. "The Fertility of North American Catholics: A Comparative Overview." DEMOGRAPHY 3 (1966): 174-187.

Canadian census data, 1931, 1941, and 1951-61; Official Catholic Directory (U.S.A.) data, 1951-61; U.S. Census data, 1960, etc.; comparisons by ethnic groups.

* Cuneo, Michael W. LE CONSERVATISME CATHOLIQUE NORD-AMERICAIN. Cited above as item 872.

1683. Cuneo, Michael W. "Soldiers of Orthodoxy: Revivalist Catholicism in North America." STUDIES IN RELIGION/SCIENCES RELIGIEUSES 17,3 (1988): 347-363.

An assessment of the vocabulary of dissent associated with a revitalization movement within contemporary North American Catholicism.

1684. Johnson, Byron R., Dennis M. Doyle, and Michael H. Barnes. "Are there Two Catholicisms?" SA 49,4 (1989): 430-439.

## CANADA

1685. Barnes, Samuel H. "Quebec Catholicism and Social Change." REVIEW OF POLITICS 23,1 (1961): 52-76.

Based on a study conducted in 1955-56.

1686. Bélanger, Paul. LES ASSOCIATIONS PAROISSIALES ET LA CONCEPTION DE LA PAROISSE A SAINT-JEROME-DE-L'AUVERGNE. Unpublished M.A. thesis, L'Université Laval, 1963.

1687. Bergeron, Cécile. COMMUNAUTES RELIGIEUSES ET EDUCATION. Unpublished M.A. thesis, Université de Sherbrooke, 1970-71.

Socio-historical study of the participation of religious orders and congregations in the social and educational development of Quebec, 1950-60.

1688. Beyer, Peter. "The Mission of Quebec Ultramontanism: A Luhmannian Perspective." SA 46 (1985): 37-48.

1689. Beyer, Peter. "The Evolution of Roman Catholicism in Quebec: A

Luhmannian Neo-functionalist Interpretation." In Roger O'Toole (ed.), SOCIOLOGICAL STUDIES IN ROMAN CATHOLICISM [item 821], pp. 1-26.

By laying the foundations of modernity in Quebec, the church unintentionally became the chief architect of its own irrelevance.

1690. Crysdale, Stewart. "The Sociology of the Social Gospel: Quest for a Modern Ideology." In S. Crysdale and L. Wheatcroft (eds.), RELIGION IN CANADIAN SOCIETY [volume cited in item 316], pp. 423-433. Also in Richard Allen (ed.), THE SOCIAL GOSPEL IN CANADA. Ottawa: National Museums of Canada, 1975, pp. 263-285.

* Cuneo, Michael W. LE CONSERVATISME CATHOLIQUE NORD-AMERICAIN. Cited above as item 872.

* Cuneo, Michael W. "Soldiers of Orthodoxy: Revivalist Catholicism in North America." Cited above as item 1683.

1691. Cuneo, Michael W. "Keepers of the Faith: Lay Militants, Abortion, and the Battle for Canadian Catholicism." In Roger O'Toole (ed.), SOCIOLOGICAL STUDIES IN ROMAN CATHOLICISM [item 821], pp. 127-142.

Argues that the abortion issue is a symbolic line of fracture separating Canadian Catholics of strikingly different faith commitments.

1692. Cuneo, Michael W. CATHOLICS AGAINST THE CHURCH: ANTI-ABORTION PROTEST IN TORONTO, 1969-1985. Toronto: University of Toronto Press, 1989.

Examines the organizational and ideological ramifications of anti-abortion protest for Canadian Catholicism.

1693. Denault, Bernard, and Benoît Lévesque. ELEMENTS POUR UNE SOCIOLOGIE DES COMMUNAUTES RELIGIEUSES AU QUEBEC. Sherbrooke: Université de Sherbrooke; Montréal: Les Presses de l'Université de Montréal, 1975.

General sociography of religious communities in Quebec, 1837-1970. Consideration of them as a utopian emigration, 1837-1876.

1694. Dumont-Johnson, Micheline. "Les communautés religieuses et la condition féminine." RECHERCHES SOCIOGRAPHIQUES 19,1 (1978): 79-102.

Discusses female religious communities, 1840-1950, as a first manifestation of Quebecois feminism.

1695. Falardeau, Jean-Charles. "The Parish as an Institutional Type." CANADIAN JOURNAL OF ECONOMICS AND POLITICAL SCIENCE 15,3 (1949): 365-371.

Discusses changes in traditional parochial organization in rural French Canada in the context of industrializing and socially heterogeneous cities.

* Fee, Joan L., Andrew M. Greeley, William C. McCready, and Theresa A. Sullivan. YOUNG CATHOLICS. Cited above as item 939.

1696. Gaudet, Robert. "Canadian Priest in Profile." AMERICA 126,10 (1972):

258-260.

Early 1970s survey of English-speaking priests.

1697. Germain-Brodeur, Elisabeth. LE CLERGE CATHOLIQUE DU CANADA. Québec: Centre de Recherches en Sociologie Religieuse, 1969-1971, 1973.

Study of some variables: language, age, function.

   * Greeley, Andrew M. THE RELIGIOUS IMAGINATION. Cited above as item 1376.

1698. Hamelin, Louis-Edmond. "Contribution aux recherches sociales au Québec par une étude des variations régionales du nombre de vocations sacerdotales." CAHIERS DE GEOGRAPHIE DE QUEBEC 2,3 (1957): 5-36.

1699. Hamelin, Louis-Edmond. "Evolution numérique séculaire du clergé catholique dans le Québec." RECHERCHES SOCIOGRAPHIQUES 2,2 (1961): 189-242.

Study, using quantitative indices of growth and number, of the evolution of the active clergy in Quebec.

1700. Horrigan, J.P. OCCUPATIONAL RECRUITMENT: PREDICTING INTELLECTUAL INTEREST IN THE ROMAN CATHOLIC PRIESTHOOD. Unpublished M.A. thesis, University of Guelph, 1971.

1701. Horrigan, J.P., and Kenneth Westhues. "A Model for the Study of Occupational Choice of the Roman Catholic Priesthood." SA 32,4 (1971): 229-237.

1970 data from male high-school students in southern Ontario.

1702. Hunsberger, Bruce. "Background Religious Denomination, Parental Emphasis, and the Religious Orientation of University Students." JSSR 15,3 (1976): 251-255.

Mennonite university students (University of Manitoba) were in greater agreement with parental religious teachings than were United Church of Canada students, with Roman Catholic students being intermediate.

1703. Légaré, Jacques. "Les religieuses du Canada: Leur évolution numérique entre 1965 et 1980." RECHERCHES SOCIOGRAPHIQUES 10,1 (1969): 7-21.

Projections based on studies by Lessard and Montminy [item 1704] on the demography of Canadian orders and congregations.

1704. Lessard, Marc-Andre, and Jean-Paul Montminy. "Le recensement des religieuses du Canada." DONUM DEI 11 (1966): 259-386; RECHERCHES SOCIOGRAPHIQUES 8,1 (1967): 15-47.

Examines the demographic and geographic situation of members of orders and congregations in Canada: age, family origin, occupation, academic qualification, etc.

1705. MacInnes, Daniel W. CLERICS, FISHERMEN, FARMERS AND WORKERS: THE

ANTIGONISH MOVEMENT AND IDENTITY IN EASTERN NOVA SCOTIA, 1928-1939. Unpublished Ph.D. dissertation, McMaster University, 1978.

1706. Mifflen, Francis J. THE ANTIGONISH MOVEMENT: A REVITALIZATION MOVE-MENT IN EASTERN NOVA SCOTIA. Unpublished Ph.D. dissertation, Boston College, 1974. [DA 35:10 A, p. 6823]

Examines the institutionalization and subsequent upward mobility of the movement.

1707. Miner, Horace. SAINT-DENIS, A FRENCH-CANADIAN PARISH. Chicago: University of Chicago Press, 1939, 1963.

Field study.

1708. Moreux, Colette. FIN D'UNE RELIGION? MONOGRAPHIE D'UNE PAROISSE CANADIENNE-FRANÇAISE. Montréal: Presses de l'Université de Montréal, 1969.

1709. Moreux, Colette. "Idéologies religieuses et pouvoir: L'example du catholicisme québécois." CAHIERS INTERNATIONAUX DE SOCIOLOGIE 25,64 (1978): 35-62.

The institutional church is seeking to retain a measure of influence over its flock by replacing authoritarianism with egalitarian phrase-ology. This is tantamount to an ideological suicide with a view to regaining on another plane what is lost in the process.

1710. Newson, Janice A. THE ROMAN CATHOLIC CLERICAL EXODUS: A STUDY OF ROLE-ADAPTATION AND ORGANIZATIONAL CHANGE. Unpublished Ph.D. disser-tation, University of Toronto, 1976.

Comparison of 36 resignees and 37 non-resignees from the Archdiocese of Toronto.

1711. Northover, Wallace E. RELIGIOUS DISAFFECTION AND PERCEIVED VALUE DISCREPANCY AMONG ROMAN CATHOLICS. Unpublished Ph.D. dissertation, York University, 1972. [National Library of Canada, Canadian Theses on Microfilm #11438]

Questionnaire data from samples of Toronto practicing Catholics, priests, and disaffiliates: Allport's extrinsic/intrinsic religiosity scale, Rokeach's dogmatism scale, Hunt's belief survey, Rokeach's value survey, dimensions of religiosity. Religion was most important for working class, then (from high to low) lower/poor, middle, upper, academicians. Little internal unity among Catholics.

1712. Northover, Wallace E. "Variations in Belief among Roman Catholics." In Stewart Crysdale and Christopher Beattie (eds.), SOCIOLOGY CANADA: READINGS, first edition. Toronto: Butterworth, 1974.

1713. O'Toole, Roger. "Some Good Purpose: Notes on Religion and Political Culture in Canada." ANNUAL REVIEW OF THE SOCIAL SCIENCES OF RELIGION 6 (1982): 177-217. Reprinted in S.D. Berkowitz (ed.), MODELS AND MYTHS IN CANADIAN SOCIOLOGY. Toronto: Butterworth, 1984, pp. 75-109.

Explores the role of Catholic and Protestant traditions in the creation of Canadian political culture and the formation of a Canadian national identity.

1714. O'Toole, Roger. RELIGION: CLASSIC SOCIOLOGICAL APPROACHES. Toronto: McGraw-Hill Ryerson, 1984.

Contains a postscript on the sociology of religion in Canada, with specific reference to Canadian Catholicism.

1715. O'Toole, Roger. "Society, the Sacred and the Secular: Sociological Observations on the Changing Role of Religion in Canadian Culture." CANADIAN ISSUES/THEMES CANADIENS 7 (1985): 99-117.

Emphasizes the role of religious factors in the shaping of the Canadian nation, and assesses the utility of secularization theories in the interpretation of contemporary religious and political developments.

1716. Porter, John. THE VERTICAL MOSAIC. Toronto: University of Toronto Press, 1965, pp. 98-103, 511-519.

Examines the relationship between religious affiliation and income level; compares the social characteristics of Anglican and Roman Catholic church leaders.

1717. Ralston, Helen. "The Typologies of Weber and Troeltsch. A Case Study of a Catholic Religious Group in Atlantic Canada." ARCHIVES DE SCIENCES SOCIALES DES RELIGIONS 50,1 (1980): 111-127.

Discusses the theological and sociocultural impetuses behind the formation of sect-like groups within contemporary Catholicism.

1718. Reny, Paul, and Jean-Paul Rouleau. LE FRERE ET LA RELIGIEUSE VUS PAR LES ETUDIANTS DU NIVEAU COLLEGIAL. Québec: Centre de Recherches en Sociologie Religieuse, Université Laval, 1975.

1719. Rouleau, Jean-Paul. LE PRÊTRE, LE FRERE ET LA RELIGIEUSE VUS PAR DES ETUDIANTS DE COLLEGES. Québec: Centre de Recherches en Sociologie Religieuse, Université Laval, 1971.

1720. Routhier, François, and Paul Stryckman. LES ETUDIANTS DES GRANDS SEMINAIRES DE LA VIE SACERDOTALE. Partially published by Routhier as "Les séminaristes d'aujourd'hui seront-ils les prêtres de demain?" in LE PRÊTRE, HIER, D'AUJOURD'HUI, DEMAIN. Montréal: Editions Fides, 1970, pp. 322-333.

1721. Routhier, François, and Grégoire Tremblay. LE PROFIL SOCIOLOGIQUE DU SEMINARISTE QUEBECOIS. Laval: Université Laval, Centre de Recherches en Sociologie Religieuse, 1968.

Study of the origin and evolution of the vocation, and the perception of the priesthood and of the priest by seminarians.

1722. Sacouman, Robert J. "Underdevelopment and the Structural Origins of

Antigonish Movement Co-operatives in Eastern Nova Scotia." ACADIENSIS
7 (1977): 66-85.

Argues that the structural effects of uneven underdevelopment in eastern Nova Scotia provided the basis for the movement.

1723. Stryckman, Paul. "Note de recherche: Le clergé séculier du Québec."
RECHERCHES SOCIOLOGIQUES 10,1 (1969): 116-122.

1724. Stryckman, Paul. LES PRÊTRES DU QUEBEC D'AUJOURD'HUI. Québec: Centre
de Recherches en Sociologie Religieuse, Université Laval, 1970.

Study of pastoral change after Vatican II and of social change in
Quebec after 1966: opinions of Catholic priests, attitudes, new pastoral practices.

1725. Stryckman, Paul. LES PRÊTRES DU QUEBEC D'AUJOURD'HUI, Vol. II.
Québec: Centre de Recherches en Sociologie Religieuse, Université
Laval, 1973.

1726. Stryckman, Paul. "Validation empirique d'une typologie des pratiques
du prêtre pasteur." CAHIERS DU CENTRE DE RECHERCHES EN SOCIOLOGIE
RELIGIEUSE 2 (1978): 57-89.

The study confirms the utility of the instrumental-expressive dimension for interpreting pastoral activities, but raises questions about
that of the hierarchy-functionality dimension. It also indicates that
the activities are more relevant to an intra-church perspective than
one oriented toward the wider society.

1727. Stryckman, Paul, and Robert Gaudet. PRIESTS IN CANADA, 1971: A REPORT
ON ENGLISH-SPEAKING CLERGY. Québec: Centre de Recherches en Sociologie Religieuse, Université Laval, 1971.

Application of the sacro-hierarchic and prophetic-diaconal typology to
changes in the ideology and pastoral practice of English-speaking
Canadian priests to discover how they define themselves in belief and
action. Focus is on change in the post-conciliar church, and on the
use of a three-fold typology: traditional clergy, questioning clergy,
and redefined clergy.

1728. Stryckman, Paul, and Robert Gaudet. "Priests under Stress." In S.
Crysdale and L. Wheatcroft (eds.), RELIGION IN CANADIAN SOCIETY
[volume cited in item 316], pp. 336-345.

Examines pastoral and ideological tensions experienced by Canadian
Catholic priests in the aftermath of the Second Vatican Council.

1729. Sylvain, P. "Projet d'une histoire de l'Eglise catholique du Québec."
RECHERCHES SOCIOGRAPHIQUES 15,1 (1974): 113-118.

1730. Turcotte, Paul-André. "Education catholique et nationalisme dans
l'enseignement secondaire québécois." SC 31,4 (1984): 365-377.

Two kinds of Quebec nationalism emerged respectively from the classic
humanities Catholic schools of the upper-class and the working-class

Catholic schools of the teaching brothers.

1731. Vaillancourt, Jean-Guy. "Les groupes socio-politiques progressistes
dans le Catholicisme Québécois contemporain." LES MOUVEMENTS RELI-
GIEUX AUJOURD'HUI. THEORIES ET PRATIQUES. LES CAHIERS DE RECHERCHES
EN SCIENCES DE LA RELIGION 5 (1984): 261-282.

1732. Wallace, Ruth A. "A Model of Change of Religious Affiliation." JSSR
14,4 (1975): 345-355.

Data on 357 inquirers enrolled in a course of instruction on the
tenets of Roman Catholicism, 1958-65. Predisposing factors hypothesized: deficit of social awards, deficit of consistency of life
experiences, deficit of religious solidarity, personal influence.
High rates of affiliation change occurred among inquirers with two or
more deficits who were engaged or married to a Catholic.

1733. Wener, Normand. LES CATHOLIQUES PRATIQUANTS ET L'EGLISE DE MONTREAL.
Montréal: Action Catholique de Montréal, 1968.

Independent variables: age and occupation. Dependent variables:
church membership (idea of church, perception of the conditions of
membership, grounds for belonging, quality and norms of interaction),
perception of church's expectations (of religion and of life).

1734. Westhues, Kenneth. "Public vs. Sectarian Legitimation: The Separate
Schools of the Catholic Church." CANADIAN REVIEW OF SOCIOLOGY AND
ANTHROPOLOGY 13,2 (1976): 137-151.

1973-74 study of primary and secondary schools in Canada (excluding
Quebec). Catholic school success depends on public funding, cultural
support, and religious commitment - all which vary geographically.

1735. Westhues, Kenneth. "The Adaptation of the Roman Catholic Church in
Canadian Society." In S. Crysdale and L. Wheatcroft (eds.), RELIGION
IN CANADIAN SOCIETY [volume cited in item 316], pp. 290-306.

Examines the evolving relationship between Canadian Catholicism and
Canadian political culture.

   * Westhues, Kenneth. "Stars and Stripes, the Maple Leaf, and the Papal
Coat of Arms." Cited above as item 1341.

1736. Westhues, Kenneth. "Nationalisme et catholicisme canadien." CONCILIUM
131 (1978): 61-68.

1737. Westhues, Kenneth. "The Option for (and against) the Poor." GRAIL
3,1 (1987): 23-38.

A critical appraisal of recent public policy statements issued by the
Canadian Catholic bishops.

1738. Alonso, Isidoro.  LA IGLESIA EN AMERICA LATINA: ESTRUCTURAS ECCLESIAS-
TICAS.  Frigurgo-Bogotá: FERES, 1964.

1739. Alonso, Isidoro.  "Les statistiques religieuses en Amérique latine."
SC 14,5-6 (1967): 365-398.

    Data from 1945-65.

1740. Dealy, Glen C.  THE PUBLIC MAN: AN INTERPRETATION OF LATIN AMERICAN
AND OTHER CATHOLIC COUNTRIES.  Amherst, Massachusetts: University of
Massachusetts Press, 1977.

1741. Floridi, Alexis U., and Annette E. Stiefbold.  THE UNCERTAIN ALLIANCE:
THE CATHOLIC CHURCH AND LABOR IN LATIN AMERICA.  Washington: Center
for Advanced International Studies, University of Miami, 1973.

1742. Godoy, H.H.  "La iglesia y la integración de la América Latina."
ANUARIO DE SOCIOLOGIA DE LOS PUEBLOS IBERICOS 3 (1967): 160-180.

1743. Hewitt, Warren E.  "Liberation Theology as Social Science: Contributions and Limitations."  In Roger O'Toole (ed.), SOCIOLOGICAL STUDIES
IN ROMAN CATHOLICISM [item 821], pp. 143-165.

    An iconoclastic assessment of Liberation Theology and 'Basic Christian
    Communities' in Latin America.

1744. Houtart, François.  "Les effets du changement social sur la religion
catholique en Amérique Latine."  ARCHIVES DE SOCIOLOGIE DES RELIGIONS
12 (1961): 63-73.

    Based on 1958-1961 field work in Latin America.

1745. Houtart, François.  "Die Wirkungen des sozialen Wandels auf die
katholische Religion in Lateinamerika."  In D. Goldschmidt and J.
Matthes (eds.), PROBLEME DER RELIGIONSSOZIOLOGIE.  KÖLNER ZEITSCHRIFT
FÜR SOZIOLOGIE UND SOZIALPSYCHOLOGIE, SONDERHEFT 6.  Köln and Opladen:
Westdeutscher Verlag, 1962, pp. 166-178.

    Overview, from colonial times onward.

1746. Houtart, François.  LA IGLESIA LATINO-AMERICANA A LA HORA DEL
CONCILIO.  Fribourg and Bogotá: FERES, 1962.  See also L'EGLISE
LATINO-AMERICAINE A L'HEURE DU CONCILE.  Fribourg and Bogotá: FERES,
1963; and THE LATIN-AMERICAN CHURCH AND THE COUNCIL.  Fribourg:
FERES, 1963.

1747. Houtart, François, and Emile Pin.  THE CHURCH AND THE LATIN AMERICAN
REVOLUTION.  New York: Sheed and Ward, 1965.

1748. Lalive d'Epinay, Christian.  "L'esprit de la champ oecuméniques de
pasteurs sud-américains."  SC 14,5-6 (1967): 423-437.

    1965-66 questionnaire data from South American Protestant pastors in

Chile and seminarians in Argentina, focusing on attitudes toward 11 denominations.

1749. Lalive d'Epinay, Christian. "Sociologie du catholicisme et problématique de développement en Amérique Latine." CULTURES ET DEVELOPPE-MENT 4,4 (1972): 845-855.

Review of the literature, especially item 1774.

1750. Levine, Daniel H. RELIGION AND POLITICS IN LATIN AMERICA: THE CATHO-LIC CHURCH IN VENEZUELA AND COLUMBIA. Princeton: Princeton University Press, 1981.

1751. McNamara, Patrick H. "Conscience, Catholicism and Social Change in Latin America." SOCIAL RESEARCH 46,2 (1979): 329-349.

1752. Maduro, Otto. "Extracción de plusvalia, represion de la sexualidad y catolicismo en latinoaméricana." EXPRESAMENTE (Caracas) 4 (1978): 33-39.

1753. Maduro, Otto. "La democratie chrétienne et l'option de libération des opprimes dans le catholicisme latino-américain." CONCILIUM 213 (1987): 111-125.

1754. Mutchler, David. "Adaptations of the Roman Catholic Church to Latin American Development: The Meaning of Internal Church Conflict." SOCIAL RESEARCH 36,2 (1969): 231-252.

Review of the literature and identification of opposed elitist groups within the church.

1755. Mutchler, David. THE CHURCH AS A POLITICAL FACTOR IN LATIN AMERICA WITH PARTICULAR REFERENCE TO COLOMBIA AND CHILE. New York: Praeger, 1971.

1756. Perez Ramirez, Gustavo. "Les attentes vis-à-vis de la déclaration pontificale sur la régulation des naissances en Amérique Latine en 1967." SC 15,6 (1968): 443-452.

Opinions of clergy and laity on contraception in Brazil, Chile, Colombia, Mexico, and Venezuela, prior to the encyclical *Humanae Vitae*. Background variables are considered.

1757. Perez Ramirez, Gustavo, and Yván Labelle. EL PROBLEMA SACERDOTAL EN AMERICA LATINA. ESTUDIOS SOCIO-RELIGIOSOS LATINO-AMERICANOS 16. Fribourg and Bogotá: FERES, 1964.

Presents characteristics of seminarians: geographical, family, and socio-cultural origins. Considers the influence of each variable on the priest problem in Latin America.

1758. Perez Ramirez, Gustavo, F. Escobar, O. Maldonado, and L. Leñero. POBLACION, IGLESIA Y CULTURA. SISTEMAS EN CONFLICTO. México: FERESAL, 1970.

215

1759. Pin, Emile. ELEMENTOS PARA UNA SOCIOLOGIA DEL CATOLICISMO LATINO-AMERICANO. Bogotá: FERES, 1963.

1760. Pin, Emile. "Catholicisme et changement social en Amerique Latine." REVUE DE L'ACTION POPULAIRE 178 (1964): 595-610.

1761. Poblete Barth, Renato. "Vocations - Problems and Promise." In John J. Considine (ed.), THE RELIGIOUS DIMENSION IN THE NEW LATIN AMERICA. Notre Dame: Fides, 1966, pp. 148-158.

1762. Poblete Barth, Renato. "From Medellín to Puebla: Notes for Reflection." JOURNAL OF INTERAMERICAN STUDIES AND WORLD AFFAIRS 21,1 (1979): 31-44.

1763. Ribeiro de Oliveira, Pedro A. CATOLICISMO POPULAR NA AMERICA LATINA. Rio de Janeiro: CERIS, 1970.

1764. Stycos, J. Mayone. HUMAN FERTILITY IN LATIN AMERICA. Ithaca: Cornell University Press, 1968, chapter 11.

1765. Tobias, C.L. DOMINANT-SUBORDINATE RELATIONS IN THE JESUIT MISSION COMMUNITIES (REDUCCIONES) OF COLONIAL ARGENTINA AND PARAGUAY. Unpublished Ph.D. dissertation, University of Chicago, 1977. [DA 38:5 A, p. 3069]

Archival information on the bases and forms of control by the Jesuits, 1609-1767.

1766. Turner, Frederick C. "El protestantismo y el cambio social en Latinoamerica." No. 18 de LA COLECCION DE REIMPRESSIONES. Asuncion: Centro Paraguayo de Estudios Sociologicos, 1967. Also in REVISTA PARAGUAYA DE SOCIOLOGIA 7/17 (1970): 5-27.

Analysis using data from the late 1960s.

1767. Turner, Frederick C. "Catholicism and Nationalism in Latin America." SC 18,4 (1971): 593-607.

Individual nations are used as units of analysis.

1768. Turner, Frederick C. CATHOLICISM AND POLITICAL DEVELOPMENT IN LATIN AMERICA. Chapel Hill: University of North Carolina Press, 1971.

1769. Turner, Frederick C. "Catholicism and Nationalism in Latin America." AMERICAN BEHAVIORAL SCIENTIST 17,6 (1974): 845-864.

Use of admittedly crude measures of the strengths of Catholicism and nationalism in the Latin American nations, shows a positive correlation between them. An adaptation of Catholicism appears to be a feasible stratagem for advancing humanist concerns in the process of social development.

1770. Vallier, Ivan. "Religious Elites in Latin America: Catholicism, Leadership and Social Change." AMERICA LATINA 8,4 (1965): 93-115.

General analysis, with a typology of élites - politician, papist, pastor, pluralist.

1771. Vallier, Ivan. "Roman Catholic Elites in Latin America." In Seymour M. Lipset and Aldo Solari (eds.), ELITES IN LATIN AMERICA. New York: Oxford University Press, 1967, pp. 190-232.

Overview and typology.

1772. Vallier, Ivan. "Church 'Development' in Latin America: A Five Country Comparison." JOURNAL OF DEVELOPING AREAS 1 (1967): 461-476. See also "El 'desarollo' de la Iglesia en América Latina: Una comparación en cinco países." REVISTA PARAGUAYA DE SOCIOLOGIA 7/17 (1970): 28-46.

A study of the national church systems of Argentina, Brazil, Chile, Colombia, and Mexico, with consideration of the following elements: autonomy, ideology of change, episcopal unity on change-oriented goals, capacity to acquire strategic resources.

1773. Vallier, Ivan. "Extraction, Insulation, and Re-entry." In Henry A. Landsberger (ed.), THE CHURCH AND SOCIAL CHANGE IN LATIN AMERICA. Notre Dame: University of Notre Dame Press, 1970.

Latin American Catholicism is analyzed according to the following three stages: 1) The church is based on a traditional and static power structure; 2) As the power structure changes the church withdraws; and 3) With the advent of a new secular power structure, the church re-enters the world as a cultural-pastoral influence.

1774. Vallier, Ivan. CATHOLICISM, SOCIAL CONTROL, AND MODERNIZATION IN LATIN AMERICA. Englewood Cliffs, N.J.: Prentice-Hall, 1970.

Presents a five-stage model for the evolution of church strategy: 1) Monopoly power structure; church attempts to be part of the monopoly; 2) Secular oligarchy; church takes sides, joining a party; 3) Power instability; after a failure, church recruits a following on the basis of cultural advantages; 4) Under democratization, the church becomes concerned with social causes; and 5) Totally secular society, neither favoring nor opposing religion; church adopts a cultural-pastoral model.


*MEXICO*

1775. Eckstein, Susana. "La ley férrea de la oligarquía y las relationes inter-organizacionales: Las nexos entra la Iglesia y el Estado en Mexico." REVISTA MEXICANA DE SOCIOLOGIA 37,2 (1975): 327-348.

Interview, documentary, and participant-observation data from low-income communities in Mexico City. R. Michels' 'iron law of oligarchy' is used to explain linkages between church and state officials, in a society which formally separates their offices.

1776. Estrada, Isaac. "Notre Dame de Guadeloupe, expression du processus de métissage au Mexique." SC 33,1 (1986): 23-55.

217

Interpretation of the sixteenth-century apparitions.

1777. Labelle, Yvan, et al. CUERNAVACA: MENTALIDAD RELIGIOSA POPULAR. Cuernavaca: CIDOC, 1969.

Sex and age correlated with idea of God, idea of Christ, idea of the saints. The religious mentality is a popular translation of the catechism of the Council of Trent.

1778. Lafaye, Jacques. QUETZALCOATL ET GUADALUPE. LA FORMATION DE LA CONSCIENCE NATIONALE AU MEXIQUE. Paris: Gallimard, 1974.

1779. Meyer, Jean. "Pour une sociologie des catholicismes mexicains." CAHIERS DE SOCIOLOGIE ECONOMIQUE 12 (1965): 82-103.

Discusses types of Catholicism and their interaction with secular society.

1780. Ramos, Rutilo, Isidoro Alonso, and Domingo Garre. LA IGLESIA EN MEXICO: ESTRUCTURAS ECLESIASTICAS. Fribourg: FERES, 1963.

1781. Sicard, Emile. "Amérique Latine: L'Eglise et le développement des pays latino-américains, les classes sociales, situation présente du Mexique." ANNEE SOCIOLOGIQUE 21 (1970): 313-332.

Review of the literature.

1782. Stryckman, Paul. "Religious Knowledge and Attitudes in Mexico City." SC 14,5-6 (1967): 469-482.

1962 samples in the Federal District of Mexico, focusing on doctrinal knowledge and attitudes about religion.

## ARGENTINA

1783. Amato, Enrique L. LA IGLESIA EN ARGENTINA. ESTUDIOS SOCIO-RELIGIOSOS LATINO-AMERICANOS 5. Brussels and Bogotá: FERES, 1965.

1784. Amato, Enrique L., and François Houtart. "La demographie paroissia de Buenos Aires." In C.I.S.R., PAROISSES URBAINES, PAROISSES RURALES. Paris: Casterman, 1958, pp. 70-73.

1785. Büntig, Aldo J. "Hipótesis para una interpretación del catolicismo popular en la Argentina." CENTRO DE INVESTIGACION Y ACCION SOCIAL 171 (1968): 7-39.

1786. Büntig, Aldo J. EL CATOLICISMO POPULAR EN LA ARGENTINA. Buenos Aires: Ed. Bonum, 1969.

1787. Büntig, Aldo J. RELIGION-ENAJENACION EN UNE SOCIEDAD DEPENDIENTE: ANALISIS INTERDISCIPLINAR DE GRUPOS DE 'CATOLICOS NORMALES' ARGENTINOS. Buenos Aires: Ed. Guadalupe, 1973, 1974.

1788. Rosato, N. EXPECTATIVAS SOCIALES Y SACERDOCIO. INVESTIGACION SOCIOLO-

GICA DE LA IMAGEN DEL SACERDOTE EN BUENOS AIRES. Buenos Aires: Ecoisyr, 1971.

## BOLIVIA, ECUADOR, PERU, URUGUAY, VENEZUELA

1789. Alonso, Isidoro, et al. LA IGLESIA EN VENEZUELA Y ECUADOR. ESTUDIOS SOCIO-RELIGIOSOS LATINO-AMERICANOS 3. Fribourg and Bogotá: FERES, 1962.

1790. Alonso, Isidoro, et al. LA IGLESIA EN PERU Y BOLIVIA. ESTUDIOS SOCIO-RELIGIOSOS LATINO-AMERICANOS 3 (II). Fribourg and Bogotá: FERES, 1962.

1791. Arnold, Pierre. "Pélerinages et processions comme formes de pouvoir symbolique des classes subalternes: Deux cas péruviens." SC 32,1 (1985): 45-56.

Consideration of an Andean sanctuary and an Afro-Peruvian procession.

* Centro de Estudios Cristianos. ASPECTOS RELIGIOSOS DE LA SOCIEDAD URUGUAYA. Cited above as item 398.

1792. Cosper, Ronald. "Attendance at Mass and Fertility in Caracas." SA 36,1 (1975): 43-56.

Unlike in Europe and the U.S.A., an inverse relationship is indicated.

1793. Navarro, Juan C. "Too Weak for Change: Past and Present in the Venezuelan Church." In T.M. Gannon (ed.), WORLD CATHOLICISM IN TRANSITION [volume cited in item 1651], pp. 297-307.

Depicts a national church marked by a precarious and chaotic past that is finally at peace with the prevailing political system and at the same time relatively backward in most pastoral and organizational respects.

1794. Offutt, J. James. PARISH STYLES: LIBERATION AND DEVELOPMENT. Unpublished Ph.D. dissertation, University of Notre Dame, 1976. [DA 37:3 A, p. 1809]

1972 interview data from three communities in southern Peru, focusing on the formation of change-related consciousness.

1795. Ponce Garcia, J., and O. Uzin Fernandes. EL CLERO EN BOLIVIA, 1968. Cuernavaca, México: Centro Intercultural de Documentación, 1970.

1796. Rama, Carlos M. LA RELIGION EN EL URUGUAY. Montevideo: Ediciones Nuestra Tiempo, 1964.

In the rural areas, races are differentiated by degree of Europeanized orthodoxy of beliefs. Upper classes, especially males, are non-supportive of religion.

1797. Romero, Catalina. "Cambios en la relación iglesia-sociedad en el

Peru: 1958–1978." DEBATE EN SOCIOLOGIA 7 (1982): 115–141.

## BRAZIL

1798. Adriance, Madeleine. "Opting for the Poor: A Social-historical Analysis of the Changing Brazilian Catholic Church." SA 46,2 (1985): 131–146.

A Gramscian approach to political-economic and religious-institutional conditions in Brazil that provided the context for the emergence of the option for the poor. Based on documentation from published sources and field research.

1799. Adriance, Madeleine. OPTING FOR THE POOR: BRAZILIAN CATHOLICISM IN TRANSITION. Kansas City: Sheed and Ward, 1986.

Study of the base community phenomenon, using interviews and participant observation.

1800. Adriance, Madeleine. "Brazil and Chile: Seeds of Change in the Latin American Church." In T.M. Gannon (ed.), WORLD CATHOLICISM IN TRANSITION [volume cited in item 1651], pp. 283–296.

Discusses paradoxes related to the institutionalization of the 'preferential option for the poor' in the Chilean and Brazilian churches.

1801. Antoniazzi, Alberto. "Várias interpretações do catolicismo popular no Brasil." REVISTA ECLESIASTICA BRASILEIRA 36,141 (1976): 82–94.

1802. Bruneau, Thomas C. "Obstacles to Change in the Church: Lessons from Four Brazilian Dioceses." JOURNAL OF INTERAMERICAN STUDIES AND WORLD AFFAIRS 15,4 (1973): 395–414.

1968 accounts of the state of affairs in the dioceses of Crateus, Itabira, Recife, and Salvador.

1803. Bruneau, Thomas C. THE POLITICAL TRANSFORMATION OF THE BRAZILIAN CATHOLIC CHURCH. Cambridge: Cambridge University Press, 1973.

1804. Bruneau, Thomas C. "Basic Christian Communities in Latin America. Their Nature and Significance (especially in Brazil)." In Daniel H. Levine (ed.), CHURCHES AND POLITICS IN LATIN AMERICA. Beverly Hills, California: Sage, 1979, pp. 225–237.

General description and account.

1805. Bruneau, Thomas C. THE CHURCH IN BRAZIL: THE POLITICS OF RELIGION. Austin: University of Texas Press, 1982.

1806. Busjan, Callistus. "Priests and the Rising Generation of Priests in the Opinion of Brazilians." SC 8,4 (1961): 317–326.

1956 poll of 7–12 year old students, high-school students and adult laity.

1807. Cabral, Clóvis. "O Negro no Brasil: Relações com a Igreja e a formação dos movimentos negros urbanos." CADERNOS CENTRO DE ESTUDOS E AÇÃO SOCIAL 112 (1987): 30-36.

1808. Da Silva, J. Fábio Barbosa. JOAZEIRO: A NOVA JERUSALEM. Unpublished tese for the Mestre em Ciências Sociais, Universidade de São Paulo, 1960.

1809. Da Silva, J. Fábio Barbosa. "Organização social de Juàzeiro e tensões entre litoral e interior." SOCIOLOGIA (São Paulo) 24,2 (1962): 181-194.

The early twentieth-century social movement and counter-movement associated with Padre Cicero is examined in the context of conflicting regional systems.

1810. De Azevedo, Thales. "Catholicism in Brazil. A Personal Evaluation." THOUGHT 28/109 (1953): 253-274.

Overview, 1889-1950; census data, 1940 and 1950.

1811. De Azevedo, Thales. O CATOLICISMO NO BRASIL. UM CAMPO PARA A PESQUISA SOCIAL. Rio de Janeiro: Ministério da Educação e Cultura, Serviçe de Documentação, 1955.

1812. De Azevedo, Thales. "Popular Catholicism in Brazil. Typology and Functions." In Raymond S. Sayers (ed.), PORTUGAL AND BRAZIL IN TRANSITION. Minneapolis, 1968, pp. 175-178.

1965 interview data in Salvador, showing contrasts between popular and formal Catholicism.

1813. De Camargo, C.P. Ferreira. "Essai de typologie du catholicisme brésilien." SC 14,5-6 (1967): 399-422.

Typology based on research and reflection: traditional rural Catholicism, traditional urban Catholicism, internalized Catholicism.

1814. De Camargo, C.P. Ferreira. "Catolicismo e familia no Brasil contemporâneo." ESTUDOS CEBRAP (Centro Brasileiro de Análise e Planejamento, São Paulo) 12 (1975): 149-160.

Overview of the evolution of Catholic family ideology.

1815. Deelen, G.J. DIOCESE DE PONTA GROSSA, PARANA. Rio de Janeiro: Centro de Estatistica Religiosa e Investigações Sociais, 1965.

1816. Deelen, G.J. KIRCHE AUF DEM WEG ZUM VOLKE. SOZIOLOGISCHE BETRACHTUNGEN ÜBER KIRCHLICHE BASISGEMEINDEN IN BRASILIEN. Mittingen: BKV Brasilienkundverlag, 1982.

1817. DeKadt, E.J. CATHOLIC RADICALS IN BRAZIL. London: Oxford University Press, 1970.

1818. De Medina, C.A., and Pedro A. Ribeiro de Oliveira. "A Igreja católica

no Brasil: Uma perspectiva sociológica." REVISTA ECLESIASTICA
BRASILEIRA 33,129 (1973): 72-91.

Overview, based on studies from the previous decade.

1819. De Oliveira, Gonzaga. A RADIODIFUSÃO CATOLICA NO BRASIL. Estudo
sociográfico. Rio de Janeiro: CERIS, 1968.

1820. De Souza Martins, H.H.T. "Catolicismo y clase obrera en Brasil. Los
años posteriores a 1964." CRISTIANISMO Y SOCIEDAD 24,90 (1986): 35-
64.

1821. Gregory, Alfonso. A IGREJA NO BRASIL. ESTUDIOS SOCIO-RELIGIOSOS
LATINO-AMERICANOS 2. Louvain and Bogotá: FERES, 1965.

1822. Gregory, Alfonso. ESTUDIO SOCIO-ECONOMICA E SOCIO-RELIGIOSO DA DIOCESE
DE CARAVELAS. Rio de Janeiro: CERIS, 1966.

1823. Gutwirth, Jacques. "Aspects du catholicisme au Brésil." ARCHIVES DE
SCIENCES SOCIALES DES RELIGIONS 44,2 (1977): 175-180.

A review of literature from the 1970s dealing with the role played by
Catholicism in Brazilian culture.

1824. Hewitt, Warren E. "Strategies for Social Change Employed by Communi-
dades de Base (CEBs) in the Archdiocese of São Paulo." JSSR 25,1
(1986): 16-30.

1984 interview, questionnaire, and participant-observation data.

1825. Hewitt, Warren E. "Basic Christian Communities of the Middle-classes
in the Archdiocese of São Paulo." SA 48,2 (1987): 158-166.

1984 interview, questionnaire, and participant-observation data,
comparing lower and middle-class base communities.

1826. Hewitt, Warren E. "Origins and Prospects of the Option for the Poor
in Brazilian Catholicism." JSSR 28,2 (1989): 120-135.

1827. Hoonaert, Eduardo. "O padre Católico, visto, pelos indigenas do
Brasil e do Maranhão." REVISTA ECLESIASTICA BRASILEIRA 36,142 (1976):
347-364.

1828. Mainwaring, Scott. "A Igreja Católica e o movimento popular em Nova
Iguaçu: 1974-85." RELIGIÃO E SOCIEDADE 12,3 (1985): 74-101.

Discusses base communities as a significant social force.

1829. Pereira de Queiroz, Maria I. "O catolicismo rústico no Brasil." In
M.I. Pereira de Queiroz, O CAMPESINATO BRASILEIRO. Petrópolis:
Vozes, 1973, pp. 72-99.

1830. Pereira de Queiroz, Maria I. "Messies, thaumaturges et 'dualité
catholique' au Brésil." REVUE INTERNATIONALE DES SCIENCES SOCIALES
29,2 (1977): 323-337.

1831. Perez, Gustavo, Alfonso Gregory, and François Lepargneur. O PROBLEMA SACERDOTAL NO BRASIL. Brussels: FERES, 1965; Rio de Janeiro: CERIS, 1965.

1832. Ribeiro de Oliveira, Pedro A. CATOLICISMO POPULAR NO BRASIL. Rio de Janeiro: CERIS, Estudos Socio-Religiosos 9, 1970.

1833. Ribeiro de Oliveira, Pedro A. "Catolicismo popular e romanização do catolicismo brasileiro." REVISTA ECLESIASTICA BRASILEIRA 36,141 (1976): 131-141.

1834. Ribeiro de Oliveira, Pedro A. "Presença da Igreja Catolica no socie-dade brasileira." RELIGIÃO E SOCIEDADE 2 (1977): 111-113.

1835. Ribeiro de Oliveira, Pedro A. "The 'Romanization' of Catholicism and Agrarian Capitalism in Brazil." SC 26,2-3 (1979): 309-329.

Examines transformations within Catholicism associated with the establishment of capitalism in Brazil during the second half of the nineteenth century.

1836. Ribeiro de Oliveira, Pedro A. "Catholicisme populaire et hégémonie bourgeoise au Brésil." ARCHIVES DE SCIENCES SOCIALES DES RELIGIONS 47,1 (1979): 53-79.

Examines the political context of the historic conflict between 'popular' and 'clerical' Catholicism in Brazil.

1837. Ribeiro de Oliveira, Pedro A. RELIGIÃO E DOMINAÇÃO DE CLASSE: GÊNESE, ESTRUCTURA E FUNÇÃO DO CATOLICISMO ROMANIZADO NO BRASIL. Petrópolis: Vozes, 1985.

1838. Ribeiro de Oliveira, Pedro A. "Comunidade, igreja e poder - em busca de um conceito sociológico de 'igreja'." RELIGIÃO E SOCIEDADE 13,3 (1986): 42-60.

Conceptual consideration prompted by the phenomenon of the base communities in the Archdiocese of Victória.

1839. Rolim, Antonio. "Quelques aspects de la pratique dominicale au Brésil." SC 14,5-6 (1967): 457-468.

Presents church attendance rates for various localities in the mid-1960s.

1840. Rolim, Antonio, F. Cartaxo, and C.A. de Medina. RELIGIOSOS NO BRASIL, ESTUDO SOCIOGRAFICO. Rio de Janeiro: CERIS, 1968.

1841. Sanders, Thomas G. "Catholicism and Development: The Catholic Left in Brazil." In Kalman H. Silvert (ed.), CHURCHES AND STATES: THE RELI-GIOUS INSTITUTIONS AND MODERNIZATION. New York: American Universities Field Staff, 1967, pp. 81-100.

Overview and review of previous studies; twentieth-century focus.

1842. Schwartzman, Simon. "A política da Igreja e a educação: O sentido de um pacto." RELIGIÃO E SOCIEDADE 13,1 (1986): 110-127.

Review since 1934.

1843. Wanderley, Luiz E. EDUCAR PARA TRANSFORMAR: EDUCAÇÃO POPULAR - IGREJA CATOLICA - POLITICA NO MOVIMENTO DE EDUCAÇÃO DE BASE (MEB) - 1961-1965. Unpublished Ph.D. dissertation, Universidade de São Paulo, 1982.

1844. Willems, Emilio. "Religiöser Pluralismus und Klassenstruktur in Brasilien und Chile." In Joachim Matthes (ed.), INTERNATIONALES JAHR-BUCH FÜR RELIGIONSSOZIOLOGIE 1. Opladen: Westdeutscher Verlag, 1965, pp. 189-211. See also "Religious Pluralism and Class Structure: Brazil and Chile." In R. Robertson (ed.), SOCIOLOGY OF RELIGION [volume cited in item 573], pp. 195-217.

Protestant membership from 1916 for Chile, from 1890 to 1961 for Bra-zil; counts of hospitals, schools, and other institutions sponsored by Catholic, Protestant, and Spiritualist groups in Brazil, 1958.

## CHILE

* Adriance, Madeleine. "Brazil and Chile: Seeds of Change in the Latin American Church." Cited above as item 1800.

1845. Fichter, Joseph H. CAMBIO SOCIAL EN CHILE. UN ESTUDIO DE ACTITUDES. Santiago de Chile: Editorial Universidad Catolica, 1962.

1961 clergy and lay samples from Santiago.

1846. Galilea, C., Katherine Gilfeather, and J. Puga. LAS MUJERES QUE TRAVAJAN EN LA IGLESIA: LA EXPERIENCIA CHILEÑA. Santiago, Chile: Centro Bellarmino, 1976.

1847. Gilfeather, Katherine. "The Changing Role of Women in the Catholic Church in Chile." JSSR 16,1 (1977): 39-54.

Women in Chile have taken on responsibility for pastoral functions - administration and formation. They have developed a more modern post-conciliar view than have some bishops.

1848. Gilfeather, Katherine. RELIGIOSAS EN APOSTOLADOS MARGINALES. Santiago, Chile: Centro Bellarmino, 1978.

1849. Gilfeather, Katherine. "Women Religious, the Poor, and the Institu-tional Church in Chile." In D.H. Levine (ed.), CHURCHES AND POLITICS IN LATIN AMERICA [volume cited in item 1804], pp. 198-224. Also in JOURNAL OF INTERAMERICAN STUDIES AND WORLD AFFAIRS 21 (1979): 129-155.

Data from questionnaires and visitations in rural areas.

1850. Lopez Fernandez, Francisco. "Lutte pour l'hégémonie et production de sens dans l'Eglise catholique chilienne (1970-1973)." SC 26,2-3 (1979): 285-308.

Analysis of an apparently religious conflict during the period of Popular Unity among the Catholic hierarchy, the Christian Democrats, and the Christians for Socialism. Contrasting discursive forms point to underlying origins of the conflict.

1851. Poblete Barth, Renato. "La foi chez les étudiants des collèges catholiques." SC 14,5-6 (1967): 483-494.

Interview data from secondary-school students in Santiago and Valparaiso.

1852. Poblete Barth, Renato. "The Minor Seminaries in Chile." SC 14,5-6 (1967): 439-455.

Data on students and personnel, 1935-64.

1853. Poblete Barth, Renato. EL SACERDOTE CHILEÑO. ESTUDIO SOCIOLOGICO. Santiago: Centro Bellarmino, Departamento de Investigaciones Socioculturales, 1971.

1854. Poblete Barth, Renato. "Iglesia y cambio social en Chile." RAZON Y FE 188/908-909 (1973): 173-185.

1855. Poblete Barth, Renato. "El pluralismo en la Iglesia: El caso de Chile." PRO MUNDI VITA 45 (1973): 19-22.

Examines conflict in the Chilean church since 1930.

1856. Poblete Barth, Renato, and Ginés Garrido. LA IGLESIA EN CHILE. ESTUDIOS SOCIO-RELIGIOSOS LATINO-AMERICANOS 6. Fribourg and Bogotá: FERES, 1962.

1857. Smith, Brian H. THE CHURCH AND POLITICS IN CHILE. CHALLENGES TO MODERN CATHOLICISM. Princeton: Princeton University Press, 1982.

1858. Villela, Hugo G. "The Church and the Process of Democratization in Latin America." SC 26,2-3 (1979): 261-283.

Conceptualization, based on the Chilean case.

1859. Watzke, James N. "Paganization and Dechristianization, or the Crisis in Institutional Symbols." SC 16,1 (1969): 91-99.

1967 survey data from working-class people in Santiago.

1860. Zylberberg, Jacques. "Les catholicismes chiliens et le politique." CAHIERS DU CENTRE DE RECHERCHES EN SOCIOLOGIE RELIGIEUSE 2 (1978): 170-219.

The current institutional containment of religion in Chile, far from separating religion from politics, in the near term will only accelerate the reappearance of politicized religions and religious ideologies.

*COLOMBIA*

1861. Benoit, André.  EDUCACION COLOMBIANA. ASPECTOS DE SU FUNCION IDEO-
LOGICA.  Bogotá: FERES, 1968.

Secondary-school survey in Catholic, Protestant, and state schools.

1862. Benoit, André.  "Valeurs sociales transmises par l'enseignement
secondaire des églises et de l'état en Colombie."  SC 16,1 (1969):
29-49.

Secondary-school survey in Catholic, Protestant, and state schools.

1863. Jiminez Cadena, Gustavo.  SACERDOTE Y CAMBIO SOCIAL. ESTUDIO SOCIOLO-
GICO EN LOS ANDES COLOMBIANOS.  Bogotá: Ediciones Tercer Mundo, 1967.

Interview data from samples of clergy and laity in Cundimarca and
Boyaca states in central Colombia.

1864. Perez Ramirez, Gustavo, and Isaac Wust.  LA IGLESIA EN COLOMBIA.
Freiburg: FERES, 1961.

1865. Rodriguez Forero, Jaime.  EDUCACION CATOLICA Y SECULARIZACION EN
COLOMBIA.  Bogotá: Stella, 1970.  See also EDUCATION CATHOLIQUE ET
SECULARISATION EN COLUMBIE.  Cuernavaca: Cidoc, 1970.

1866. Schoultz, Lars.  "The Roman Catholic Church in Colombia: Revolution,
Reform and Reaction."  AMERICA LATINA 14,3-4 (1971): 90-108.

The institutional church has advocated reforms in the past, but not
social revolution.  This may change, as religion is being differentiated from the political institutionalization of Colombian society.

1867. Walker, Kenneth N.  "Determinants of Castro Support among Latin
American University Students."  BERKELEY JOURNAL OF SOCIOLOGY 9 (1964):
31-55.

Practicing Catholics were the least likely to support Castro.  Religious commitment was by far the most powerful predictor of Castro-
support or rejection.


*PARAGUAY*

1868. Banks, Lorenzo L.  "Notas para la comprension de la funcion socio-
historica de la Iglesia catolica apostolica romana en el Paraguay."
REVISTA PARAGUAYA DE SOCIOLOGIA 7/17 (1970): 123-132.

1869. Carron, Juan.  "El cambio social y el clero en el Paraguay."  REVISTA
PARAGUAYA DE SOCIOLOGIA 4 (1967): 129-132.

1870. Chartain, François.  L'EGLISE ET LES PARTIES DANS LA VIE POLITIQUE DU
PARAGUAY DEPUIS L'INDEPENDENCE.  Unpublished Ph.D. dissertation,
University of Paris, 1972.

1871. Hicks, Frederick. "Politics, Power, and the Role of the Village Priest in Paraguay." JOURNAL OF INTER-AMERICAN STUDIES 9,2 (1967): 273–282.

Based on 1965 field work in Capiatá.

1872. Westhues, Kenneth. "The Established Church as an Agent of Change." SA 34,2 (1973): 106–123.

The arrival in Paraguay of missionary clergy, with democratic and modernizing ideas, served to make the national church more critical of the established regime.

1873. Westhues, Kenneth. "Curses versus Blows: Tactics in Church-state Conflict." SA 36,1 (1975): 1–16.

Applies an open-systems-model approach to the conflict between the Paraguayan church and the Stroessner government after the late 1960s.


## GUATEMALA

1874. Adams, Richard N. "El renacimiento de la Iglesia guatemalteca." REVISTA PARAGUAYA DE SOCIOLOGIA 9/24 (1972): 7–37.

Covers events from the 1930s onward.

1875. Holleran, Mary P. CHURCH AND STATE IN GUATEMALA. New York: Columbia University Press, 1949.

1876. Sierra Pop, Oscar R. "Iglesia y conflicto social en Guatemala." ESTUDIOS SOCIALES CENTROAMERICANOS 11 (1982): 59–91.

1877. Sierra Pop, Oscar R. "The Church and Social Conflicts in Guatemala." SC 30,2–3 (1983): 317–348.

Focus on the period of 1954–1982.


## NICARAGUA

1878. Avila, Raphaël. "Religion et société politique au Nicaragua après la révolution sandiniste." SC 30,2–3 (1983): 233–259.

1879. Crahan, Margaret E. "Cuba and Nicaragua: Religion and Revolution." In T.M. Gannon (ed.), WORLD CATHOLICISM IN TRANSITION [volume cited in item 1651], pp. 265–282.

Argues that the church in neither country is monolithically in favor of the status quo or of radical change.

   * Greil, Arthur L., and David Kowalewski. "Church-state Relations in Russia and Nicaragua: Early Revolutionary Years." Cited above as item 780.

1880. Guzman Garcia, Luis, and Maria Puente de Guzman. "Formation des classes, luttes populaires et discours religieux au Nicaragua." SC 30,2-3 (1983): 211-231.

Historical survey from the 1850s onward.

1881. Opazo Bernales, Andres. "Les conditions sociales du surgissement d'une Eglise populaire." SC 30,2-3 (1983): 175-209.

Focuses on the 1970s.

1882. Samandu, Luis, and Ruud Jansen. "Nicaragua: Dictadura somicista, movimiento popular e Iglesia 1968-1979." ESTUDIOS SOCIALES CENTRO-AMERICANOS 11 (1982): 249-271.


## OTHER CENTRAL AMERICAN AND CARIBBEAN

1883. Alonso, Isidoro, and Ginés Garrido. LA IGLESIA EN AMERICA CENTRAL Y EL CARIBE. ESTUDIOS SOCIO-RELIGIOSOS LATINO-AMERICANOS 4. Fribourg and Bogotá: FERES, 1962.

1884. Caceres Prendes, Jorge. "Radicalización politica y pastoral popular en El Salvador: 1969-1979." ESTUDIOS SOCIALES CENTROAMERICANOS 11 (1982): 93-153.

1885. Caceres Prendes, Jorge. "Revolutionary Struggle and Church Commitment: The Case of El Salvador." SC 30,2-3 (1983): 261-298.

Focuses on the period of 1969-1980.

   * Crahan, Margaret E. "Cuba and Nicaragua: Religion and Revolution." Cited above as item 1879.

1886. Dohen, Dorothy. "Religious Practice and Marital Patterns in Puerto Rico." AMERICAN CATHOLIC SOCIOLOGICAL REVIEW 20,3 (1959): 203-218.

Based on a census of Catholic families in Ponce.

1887. Dohen, Dorothy. TWO STUDIES OF PUERTO RICO. RELIGION DATA. THE BACK-GROUND OF CONSENSUAL UNION. Cuernavaca: CIDOC, 1966.

1888. Fernandez Vasquez, Rodrigo. "Costa Rica: Interpretacion histórica sobre reforma social y acción eclesiástica: 1940-1982." ESTUDIOS SOCIALES CENTROAMERICANOS 11 (1982): 221-247. See also "Essai d'interprétation historique de la reforme sociale et de l'action ecclésiale au Costa Rica." SC 30,2-3 (1983): 299-316.

Examines the impact of social, economic, and political processes on church action between 1940 and 1982.

1889. Lietz, Paul S. "The Role of the Catholic Church in Caribbean Life." In A. Curtis Wilgus (ed.), THE CARIBBEAN: ITS CULTURE. Gainesville: University of Florida Press, 1955, pp. 149-157.

A general discussion, with special focus on church-state relations in the Caribbean area.

1890. Opazo, Andres, and David Smith. "Decadencia populista, protesta popular y comunidades de base en Panama." ESTUDIOS SOCIALES CENTRO-AMERICANOS 11 (1982): 249-271.

1891. Picard Ami, M.A. LOS COLEGIOS CATOLICOS EN LA ARQUIDIOCESIS DE PANAMA. Panamá: Centro de Investigaciones Socio-Religiosas de la Arquidiocesis de Panama, 1971.

1892. Souffrant, Claude. "Un catholicisme de résignation en Haïti. Sociologie d'un recueil de cantiques religieux." SC 17,3 (1970): 425-438.

Analysis of RECUEIL DE CANTIQUES CREOLES, a popular book published in Port-au-Prince by La Phalange Press in 1954, reveals attitudes which are likely to perpetuate underdevelopment.

1893. Thébaud, Frantz. "Katholizismus, Vaudou und Ideologie im soziokulturellen Entwicklungsprozess der Republik Haiti." In R. König (ed.), ASPEKTE DER ENTWICKLUNGSSOZIOLOGIE [volume cited in item 41], pp. 122-135.

Voodoo had been a focal force in the Haitian independence movement, but today it is a mystical escape for the poor and a means of intimidation for the powerful.

1894. White, Robert A. STRUCTURAL FACTORS IN RURAL DEVELOPMENT: THE CHURCH AND THE PEASANT IN HONDURAS. Unpublished Ph.D. dissertation, Cornell University, 1977. [DA 38:9 A, p. 5731]

A 1968-75 inquiry into the organization of campesinos in the Christian Social Movement.

# 12
## Anglican

*CHURCH OF ENGLAND*

1895. Aldridge, Alan. "Slaves to No Sect: The Anglican Clergy and Liturgical Change." SOCIOLOGICAL REVIEW 34,2 (1986): 357-380.

Questionnaire data from the parochial clergy of one English diocese show approval of the 1980 Alternative Service Book and an absence of sect-like attitudes.

1896. Aldridge, Alan. "In the Absence of the Minister: Structures of Subordination in the Role of Deaconess in the Church of England." SOCIOLOGY 21,3 (1987): 377-392.

Interview data from deaconesses in the Nottingham area.

1897. Ball, Peter. "Dimensions in Neopentecostal Identity in the Church of England." EUROPEAN JOURNAL OF SOCIAL PSYCHOLOGY 11 (1981): 349-363.

1898. Bedouelle, G. L'EGLISE D'ANGLETERRE ET LA SOCIETE POLITIQUE CONTEMPORAINE. Paris: Pichon et Durand-Auzias, 1968.

1899. Bentley, James. "The Bishops, 1860-1960: An Elite in Decline." SOCIOLOGICAL YEARBOOK OF RELIGION IN BRITAIN 5 (1972): 161-183.

Argues that the class alignment of individual bishops largely was responsible for the rapid decline in quality of the Church of England's episcopate at the beginning of the present century.

1900. Bocock, Robert J. "The Role of the Anglican Clergyman." SC 17,4 (1970): 533-544.

By virtue of its progressive adaptation to its cultural environment, the Church of England has perhaps forfeited some of its capacity to provide a critique of English society.

1901. Bocock, Robert J. "Anglo-Catholic Socialism: A Study of a Protest Movement within a Church." SC 20,1 (1973): 31-48.

Focus is on the late-nineteenth, early-twentieth century.

1902. Bocock, Robert J. RITUAL IN INDUSTRIAL SOCIETY. London: Allen and Unwin, 1974.

1903. Bryman, Alan. "Sociology of Religion and Sociology of Elites. Elite and Sous-elite in the Church of England." ARCHIVES DE SCIENCES SOCIALES DES RELIGIONS 19,38 (1974): 109-121.

Identifies some of the differing social and career experiences of those men who were diocesan bishops and archdeacons in 1968.

   * Bryman, Alan. "Professionalism and the Clergy: A Research Note." Cited above as item 1642.

1904. Bryman, Alan, and C. Robin Hinings. "Participation, Reform and Ecumenism: The View of Laity and Clergy." SOCIOLOGICAL YEARBOOK OF RELIGION IN BRITAIN 7 (1974): 13-25.

Based on questionnaire data in an urban Church of England diocese; concludes that the laity are more conservative than the clergy in attitudes toward reform and organic union.

1905. Coxon, Anthony P.M. A SOCIOLOGICAL STUDY OF THE SOCIAL RECRUITMENT, SELECTION, AND PROFESSIONAL SOCIALIZATION OF ANGLICAN ORDINANDS. Unpublished Ph.D. thesis, University of Leeds, 1965.

1906. Coxon, Anthony P.M. "Patterns of Occupational Recruitment: The Anglican Ministry." SOCIOLOGY 1,1 (1967): 73-80.

Discusses the increasing trend toward choosing at a later age the ministry as an occupation.

1907. Daniel, Michael. "Catholic, Evangelical and Liberal in the Anglican Priesthood." SOCIOLOGICAL YEARBOOK OF RELIGION IN BRITAIN 1 (1968): 115-123.

Discusses varying rates of professional prestige among clergy of the Church of England.

1908. Francis, Leslie J. RURAL ANGLICANISM: A FUTURE FOR YOUNG CHRISTIANS? London: Collins, 1985.

1909. Francis, Leslie J. PARTNERSHIP IN RURAL EDUCATION: CHURCH SCHOOLS AND TEACHER ATTITUDES. London: Collins, 1986.

1910. Goodridge, R.M. "The Religious Condition of the West Country in 1851." SC 14 (1967): 285-296.

Attendance data from the 1851 ecclesiastical census, organized into maps.

1911. Hill, Michael. THE RELIGIOUS ORDER IN A SOCIOLOGICAL CONTEXT: A STUDY OF VIRTUOSO RELIGION AND ITS LEGITIMATION IN THE NINETEENTH-CENTURY CHURCH OF ENGLAND. Unpublished Ph.D. thesis, University of London, 1971.

\* Hill, Michael. THE RELIGIOUS ORDER. Cited above as item 972.

1912. Homan, Roger. "Church Membership and the Liturgy." FAITH AND WORSHIP 9 (1980): 19-24.

Membership rolls, 1975 and 1980, in the archdeaconry of Chichester, England. Liturgical change adoption is correlated with membership loss.

1913. Homan, Roger. "Liturgical Change and the Clerisy in Crisis." FAITH AND WORSHIP 13 (1982): 10-17.

Discusses occasions during which the clergy find 'sanctuary.'

1914. Jones, W. Rowland. "Sociology and the Church of England." SOCIOLOGICAL REVIEW 17,2 (1925): 131-135.

Discusses the divergence but possible rapprochement between sociology as a philosophy and the Church of England.

1915. Lehman, Edward C., Jr. "The Local/Cosmopolitan Dichotomy and Acceptance of Women Clergy: A Replication." JSSR 25,4 (1986): 461-482.

Refinement of the local/cosmopolitan dichotomy: structural, cultural, ecclesiological localism. The refinement is useful in interpreting data from lay members of the Church of England, 1983-84, and three other denominations, on the acceptance of female clergy.

1916. Martin, Bernice. "Adolescent Interaction in an Anglican Church." SC 14,1 (1967): 33-51.

1950s participant-observation study in Lancashire, focusing on group formation and the impact of school groups.

1917. Morgan, D.H.J. "The Social and Educational Background of Anglican Bishops - Continuities and Changes." BRITISH JOURNAL OF SOCIOLOGY 20, 3 (1969): 295-310.

Discovers considerable continuity, 1860-1960.

1918. Musgrove, Frank. "Late-entrants to the Anglican Ministry: A Move into Marginality." SOCIOLOGICAL REVIEW 23,4 (1975): 841-866.

Contrary to common belief, entrants found the step a move into greater social involvement and greater meaning. Based on 12 interviews conducted in 1974 in the industrial Midlands.

1919. Nason-Clark, Nancy. CLERICAL ATTITUDES TOWARDS APPROPRIATE ROLES FOR WOMEN IN CHURCH AND SOCIETY: AN EMPIRICAL INVESTIGATION OF ANGLICAN, METHODIST AND BAPTIST CLERGY IN SOUTHERN ENGLAND. Unpublished Ph.D. thesis, London School of Economics and Political Science, 1984.

1920. Nason-Clark, Nancy. "Ordaining Women as Priests: Religious vs. Sexist Explanations for Clerical Attitudes." SA 48,3 (1987): 259-273.

Data from a clerical sample in England, showing religion as a channel for conservative sex role ideology.

* Ranson, Stewart, Alan Bryman, and Bob Hinings. CLERGY, MINISTERS, AND PRIESTS. Cited above as item 1660.

1921. Simey, Thomas S. "The Church of England and English Society." SC 11, 3-4 (1964): 5-12.

1922. Swatos, William H., Jr. INTO DENOMINATIONALISM: THE ANGLICAN METAMOR-PHOSIS. Storrs, Connecticut: Society for the Scientific Study of Religion, 1979.

Use of church/sect typology in studying the history of organizational change in the Church of England and its sister churches in Scotland and America, seventeenth and eighteenth centuries.

1923. Towler, Robert. "Puritan and Antipuritan. Types of Vocation to the Ordained Ministry." SOCIOLOGICAL YEARBOOK OF RELIGION IN BRITAIN 2 (1969): 109-122.

Based on interviews with 80 Church of England ordinands.

1924. Towler, Robert. "The Changing Status of the Ministry." CRUCIBLE (May 1968): 73-78. Reprinted with changes as "The Social Status of the Anglican Minister," in R. Robertson (ed.), SOCIOLOGY OF RELIGION [volume cited in item 573], pp. 443-450.

Discusses the loss of social prestige during the twentieth century.

1925. Towler, Robert, and Anthony P.M. Coxon. THE FATE OF THE ANGLICAN CLERGY. A SOCIOLOGICAL STUDY. London: Macmillan, 1979.

Based mainly on data from studies conducted in the 1960s.


CHURCH OF IRELAND

* McCallister, Ian. "Religious Commitment and Social Attitudes in Ireland." Cited above as item 1667.

* Macourt, Malcolm. "The Nature of Religion in Ireland." Cited above as item 1668.


ANGLICAN CHURCH OF CANADA

1926. Bibby, Reginald W. ANGLITRENDS. A PROFILE AND PROGNOSIS. Toronto: Incorporated Synod of the Diocese of Toronto, 1986.

Based on 1985 questionnaire data from a sample of the Diocese of Toronto.

1927. Bibby, Reginald W. FRAGMENTED GODS: THE POVERTY AND POTENTIAL OF RELIGION IN CANADA. Toronto: Irwin, 1987.

Documents the declining internal integrity and doctrinal coherence of most of Canada's major Christian denominations; a synthesis of six major studies conducted over a twenty-year period.

1928. Campbell, Douglas F. "The Anglican and United Churches in Church Union Dialogue, 1943-75." STUDIES IN RELIGION/SCIENCES RELIGIEUSES 17,3 (1988): 303-314.

Study of an unsuccessful Canadian dialogue; shows the difficulties posed for church unions by quasi-ethnic allegiances.

1929. Harvey, Andrew, and Ron Smith. SPIRITUALITY IN THE ANGLICAN CHURCH OF CANADA: A SURVEY ANALYSIS. Halifax, Nova Scotia: Institute of Public Affairs, 1980.

1930. Herman, Nancy J. "Conflict in the Church: A Social Network Analysis of an Anglican Congregation." JSSR 23,1 (1984): 60-74.

1931. Kaill, Robert C. "Ecumenism, Clergy Influence and Liberalism: An Investigation into the Sources of Lay Support for Church Union." CANADIAN REVIEW OF SOCIOLOGY AND ANTHROPOLOGY 8,3 (1971): 142-163.

Attempts to identify the characteristics which predisposed church members to adopt positive or negative attitudes towards the proposed union between the Anglican Church of Canada and the United Church of Canada.

1932. MacRae, Peter H. THE ANGLICAN CHURCH AND THE ECUMENICAL MOVEMENT IN NEW BRUNSWICK. Unpublished M.A. thesis, University of New Brunswick, 1969.

1933. Pickering, W.S.F. "The Church in a Changing Society." In BULLETIN OF THE COUNCIL FOR SOCIAL SERVICE, Anglican Church of Canada, No. 187 (September 1963).

What is the extent of the following of the Anglican inner-city churches, and what kinds of people make up the congregations?

1934. Pickering, W.S.F., and J.L. Blanchard. TAKEN FOR GRANTED. A SURVEY OF THE PARISH CLERGY OF THE ANGLICAN CHURCH OF CANADA. General Synod of the Anglican Church of Canada, 1967.

Study of social background, attitudes, and needs of Anglican Church of Canada clergy employed full-time in pastoral work.

1935. Pickering, W.S.F., and J.E.W. Jackson. "A Brief Sociological Examination of Local United and Anglican Churches." CANADIAN JOURNAL OF THEOLOGY 14,4 (1968): 249-261.

A comparison of the social characteristics of two adjacent Anglican and United churches in Winnipeg, and evaluation of the findings in relation to the problems of institutional union.

   * Porter, John. THE VERTICAL MOSAIC. Cited above as item 1716.

1936. Stevens, Lesley. "Different Voice/Different Voices: Anglican Women in

Ministry."  RRR 30,3 (1989): 262-275.

Questionnaire data from women ordained in the Anglican Church of Canada.


*EPISCOPAL (U.S.A.)*

* Allinsmith, Wesley, and Beverly Allinsmith.  "Religious Affiliation and Politico-economic Attitude."  Cited above as item 404.

1937. Betts, George H.  THE BELIEFS OF 700 MINISTERS.  New York: Abingdon Press, 1929.

1938. Bonn, Robert L., and Ruth T. Doyle.  "Secularly Employed Clergymen: A Study in Occupational Role Recomposition."  JSSR 13,3 (1974): 325-343.

1970 survey of nonstipendary clergy in the U.S.A.

1939. Broughton, Walter, and Edgar W. Mills, Jr.  "Resource Inequality and Accumulative Advantage: Stratification in the Ministry."  SOCIAL FORCES 58,4 (1980): 1289-1301.

1969 data from 21 denominations, show resources accumulate with seniority in the ministry.  The trend appears in the total sample and within seven denominations, including Episcopal.

* Finke, Roger, and Rodney Stark.  "How the Upstart Sects Won America: 1776-1850."  Cited above as item 1369.

1940. Glock, Charles Y., and Benjamin B. Ringer.  "Church Policy and the Attitudes of Ministers and Parishioners on Social Issues."  AMERICAN SOCIOLOGICAL REVIEW 21,2 (1956): 148-156.  Reprinted as Chapter 12 in C.Y. Glock and R. Stark, RELIGION AND SOCIETY IN TENSION  [item 1118].

Examines the relationship between official church policy on a number of social, economic, and political issues, and prevailing opinion among members and among clergy.  Clergy tend to be closer to official positions.

* Glock, Charles Y., and Rodney Stark.  RELIGION AND SOCIETY IN TENSION. Cited above as item 1118.

* Glock, Charles Y., and Rodney Stark.  CHRISTIAN BELIEFS AND ANTI-SEMITISM.  Cited above as item 1119.

1941. Glock, Charles Y., Benjamin B. Ringer, and Earl R. Babbie.  TO COMFORT AND TO CHALLENGE: A DILEMMA OF THE CONTEMPORARY CHURCH.  Berkeley: University of California Press, 1967.

* Gockel, Galen L.  "Income and Religious Affiliation: A Regression Analysis."  Cited above as item 437.

1942. Hadden, Jeffrey K. THE GATHERING STORM IN THE CHURCHES. A SOCIOLOGIST LOOKS AT THE WIDENING GAP BETWEEN CLERGY AND LAYMEN. Garden City, New York: Doubleday, 1969.

1965 questionnaire data from U.S. clergy in six denominations, focusing on beliefs and attitudes toward the civil rights movement.

1943. Hammond, Phillip, Albert Gedicks, Edward Lawler, and Louise Allen Turner. "Clergy Authority and Friendship with Parishioners." PACIFIC SOCIOLOGICAL REVIEW 15 (1972): 185-201.

Based on 1969 data from Wisconsin clergy in four denominations. High and Low church perspectives, puritannical outlooks, and friendships with parishioners are the principal variables.

1944. Hartley, Shirley F., and Mary G. Taylor. "Religious Beliefs of Clergy Wives." RRR 19,1 (1977): 63-72.

1970 survey of U.S. clergy wives in six denominations. Focus is on beliefs and amount of education.

1945. Hoge, Dean R., and John E. Dyble. "The Influence of Assimilation on American Protestant Ministers' Beliefs, 1928-1978." JSSR 20,1 (1981): 64-77.

Replication of the survey of Chicago Protestant clergy conducted by Betts in 1928. There is evidence of a liberalization of theological beliefs.

  * Hoge, Dean R., Esther Heffernan, Eugene F. Hemrick, Hart M. Nelsen, James P. O'Connor, Paul J. Philibert, and Andrew D. Thompson. "Desired Outcomes of Religious Education and Youth Ministry in Six Denominations." Cited above as item 1387.

  * Homola, Michael, Dean Knudsen, and Harvey Marshall. "Religion and Socio-economic Achievement." Cited above as item 463.

  * Homola, Michael, Dean Knudsen, and Harvey Marshall. "Status Attainment and Religion: A Re-evaluation." Cited above as item 464.

  * Jeffries, Vincent, and Clarence E. Tygart. "More on Clergy and Social Issues." Cited above as item 1266.

  * Laumann, Edward O. "The Social Structure of Religious and Ethnoreligious Groups in a Metropolitan Community." Cited above as item 469.

  * Lazerwitz, Bernard. "Religion and Social Structure in the United States." Cited above as item 471.

1946. Lenski, Gerhard. "Social Correlates of Religious Interest." AMERICAN SOCIOLOGICAL REVIEW 18 (1953): 533-544.

1941 interview survey data from Indianapolis, Indiana; white Protestant households of couples who had been married 1927-29. Table 10 gives religious interest by denomination.

1947. Lindenthal, Jacob J. "Entrance into the Ministry at Two Points in Life: Some Findings." JSSR 7,2 (1968): 284-285.

A study of 72 seminarians at the Berkeley Divinity School, 1965-66.

1948. Longino, Charles F., Jr., and Jeffrey K. Hadden. "Dimensionality of Belief among Mainstream Protestant Clergy." SOCIAL FORCES 55,1 (1976): 30-42.

1965 survey data from U.S. clergy from six denominations, suggesting the usefulness of using a common belief scale across denominations.

1949. Maddock, Richard, Charles T. Kenny, and Morris M. Middleton. "Preference for Personality versus Role-activity Variables in the Choice of a Pastor." JSSR 12,4 (1973): 449-452.

Questionnaire data from 70 active Episcopalians; their preferences were based on personality descriptions.

* Maranell, Gary M. RESPONSES TO RELIGION. STUDIES IN THE SOCIAL PSYCHOLOGY OF RELIGIOUS BELIEF. Cited above as item 1294.

* Mayer, Albert J., and Harry Sharp. "Religious Preference and Worldly Success." Cited above as item 484.

1950. Mitchell, Robert E. MINISTER-PARISHIONER RELATIONS. Unpublished Ph.D. dissertation, Columbia University, 1962. [DA 26:3, p. 1820]

1960 U.S. sample of clergy from eight Protestant denominations.

1951. Mitchell, Robert E. "Polity, Church Attractiveness, and Ministers' Careers." JSSR 5,2 (1966): 241-258.

Focuses on the materialist basis of career decisions.

* Mueller, Charles W. "Evidence on the Relationship between Religion and Educational Attainment." Cited above as item 490.

1952. Newman, William M. "Role Conflict in the Ministry and the Role of the Seminary: A Pilot Study." SA 32,4 (1971): 238-248.

Role definitions were found to be consistent both during and after the seminary years. Role conflicts among the clergy were found likely to continue.

* Norr, James L. "Religion and Nation Building: The American Case." Cited above as item 1304.

* Perrin, Robin D. "American Religion in the Post-aquarian Age: Values and Demographic Factors in Church Growth and Decline." Cited above as item 1409.

* Philibert, Paul J., and Dean R. Hoge. "Teachers, Pedagogy and the

Process of Religious Education." Cited above as item 1413.

1953. Quinley, Harold E. THE PROPHETIC CLERGY. SOCIAL ACTIVISM AMONG PROTESTANT MINISTERS. New York: Wiley, 1974.

1968 California sample of clergy in nine denominations.

1954. Ringer, Benjamin B. THE PARISHIONER AND HIS CHURCH: A STUDY IN THE SOCIOLOGY OF RELIGION. Unpublished Ph.D. dissertation, Columbia University, 1956.

1955. Ringer, Benjamin B., and Charles Y. Glock. "The Political Role of the Church as Defined by Its Parishioners." PUBLIC OPINION QUARTERLY 18,4 (1954-55): 337-347.

U.S. probability sample of parishioners, contacted by clergy.

1956. Roof, Wade Clark. "Traditional Religion in Contemporary Society: A Theory of Local-cosmopolitan Plausibility." AMERICAN SOCIOLOGICAL REVIEW 41,2 (1976): 195-208.

Analysis of a North Carolina sample of Episcopalians shows that the local/cosmopolitan dichotomy explains multidimensional religiosity patterns and provides a parsimonious interpretation for the effects of education and community size.

1957. Roof, Wade Clark. COMMUNITY AND COMMITMENT. RELIGIOUS PLAUSIBILITY IN A LIBERAL PROTESTANT CHURCH. New York: Elsevier, 1978.

1968 questionnaire data from a sample of North Carolina Episcopal Diocese lay members.

 * Roof, Wade Clark. "Socioeconomic Differentials among White Socio-religious Groups in the United States." Cited above as item 501.

1958. Roof, Wade Clark, and Richard B. Perkins. "On Conceptualizing Salience in Religious Commitment." JSSR 14,2 (1975): 111-128.

Data from a North Carolina sample of Episcopalians support a linear, additive model of salience in religious commitment, rather than a specification model.

 * Scherer, Ross P. "A New Typology for Organizations: Market, Bureau-cracy, Clan and Mission, with Application to American Denominations." Cited above as item 1416.

1959. Smith, Luke. "The Clergy: Authority Structure, Ideology, Migration." AMERICAN SOCIOLOGICAL REVIEW 18,3 (1953): 242-248.

Based on 24 interviews, 12 of Episcopal and 12 of Congregational clergy. Institutionalized control of workers by clients tends to increase worker migration, to change the services performed for the clients, and to result in an effort toward control by professionaliza-tion of the workers.

 * Sorensen, Andrew A. "Need for Power among Alcoholic and Nonalcoholic

Clergy." Cited above as item 1330.

* Sorensen, Andrew A. ALCOHOLIC PRIESTS: A SOCIOLOGICAL STUDY. Cited above as item 1331.

1960. Stark, Rodney, Bruce D. Foster, Charles Y. Glock, and Harold E. Quinley. WAYWARD SHEPHERDS: PREJUDICE AND THE PROTESTANT CLERGY. New York: Harper and Row, 1971.

1968 questionnaire data from a sample of California ministers. Focus is on anti-semitism.

1961. Steed, Mary Lou. "Church Schism and Secession: A Necessary Sequence?" RRR 27,4 (1986): 344-355.

Analyzes the formation of secessionist congregations within the Episcopal Church following a schism predicated on the issues of women's ordination and revision of the Book of Common Prayer.

* Steinberg, Stephen. "The Changing Religious Composition of American Higher Education." Cited above as item 518.

* Swatos, William H., Jr. INTO DENOMINATIONALISM: THE ANGLICAN METAMOR-PHOSIS. Cited above as item 1922.

1962. Van Roy, Ralph F., Frank D. Bean, and James R. Wood. "Social Mobility and Doctrinal Orthodoxy." JSSR 12,4 (1973): 427-439.

Interview data from 12 congregations representing six denominations in Indianapolis, Indiana.

1963. Warren, Bruce L. THE RELATIONSHIPS BETWEEN RELIGIOUS PREFERENCE AND SOCIO-ECONOMIC ACHIEVEMENT OF AMERICAN MEN. Unpublished Ph.D. dissertation, University of Michigan, 1970. [DA 31:12, p. 6743-A]

* Warren, Bruce L. "Socioeconomic Achievement and Religion: The American Case." Cited above as item 522.


*AFRICA, AUSTRALIA, LATIN AMERICA*

1964. Barrett, David B. "The Meaning of Money in an Anglican Diocese of East Africa: Masasi." SC 16,1 (1969): 77-90.

Discusses cross-cultural difficulties of supporting churches with contributions of money.

* Lalive d'Epinay, Christian. "L'esprit et la champ oecuméniques de pasteurs sud-americains." Cited above as item 1748.

* Mol, J.J. (Hans) "A Collation of Data about Religion in Australia." Cited above as item 308.

* Verryn, Trevor D. "Anglican and Roman Catholic Priests in South Africa: Some Questionnaire Responses." Cited above as item 1444.

# PART IV
# CHRISTIAN: REFORMATION TRADITIONS

# 13
## Protestant: General and Historical Studies

*REFORMATION*

1965. Birnbaum, Norman. SOCIAL STRUCTURE AND THE GERMAN REFORMATION. New York: Arno Press, 1980.

1966. Mendes Sargo, David-Emmanuel. "Martin Luther, Thomas Müntzer and the Birth of the Modern State: Reflections on the Status of Lutheran Reform in the Historical Sociology of Protestantism." SC 36,1 (1989): 105-131.

1967. Sánchez Cano, José. "La sociología de la religión y el fenómeno religioso. Ernst Troeltsch y la reforma protestante." REVISTA DE ESTUDIOS POLITICOS 205 (1976): 139-161.

1968. Schöffler, Herbert. WIRKUNGEN DER REFORMATION. RELIGIONSSOZIOLOGISCHE FOLGERUNGEN FÜR ENGLAND UND DEUTSCHLAND. Frankfurt: Klostermann, 1948, 1960.

1969. Swanson, Guy E. RELIGION AND REGIME. A SOCIOLOGICAL ACCOUNT OF THE REFORMATION. Ann Arbor, Michigan: University of Michigan Press, 1967.

*EUROPE*

1970. Dhooghe, Jos. "Le protestantisme en Belgique." RECHERCHES SOCIOLO-GIQUES 16,3 (1985): 311-332.

General description of the United Protestant Church of Belgium, formed in 1978 by a merger of three mainline denominations, and four other important groups - Evangelicals, Baptists, Darbyists, and Pentecostals.

1971. Gustafsson, Berndt. "The State of Sociology of Protestantism in Scandinavia." SC 12,6 (1965): 359-366.

1972. Luckmann, Thomas. "Four Protestant Parishes in Germany: A Study in the Sociology of Religion." SOCIAL RESEARCH 26,4 (1959): 423-488.

1973. Luckmann, Thomas. "Vier protestantische Kirchengemeinden. Bericht über eine vergleichende Untersuchung." In D. Goldschmidt, F. Greiner, and H. Schelsky (eds.), SOZIOLOGIE DER KIRCHENGEMEINDE [volume cited in item 1478], pp. 132-144.

Based on 1953-54 field work in four congregations in different settings in Germany.

* Pope, Whitney, and Nick Danigelis. "Sociology's 'One Law'." Cited above as item 1473.

1974. Vogt, Edvard. "The Sociology of Protestantism in Norway." SC 13,5-6 (1966): 439-441.

1975. Willaime, Jean-Paul. LES EX-PASTEURS, LES DEPARTS DE PASTEURS DE 1950 A 1975. Bulletin No. 2 de L'Association des Publications de la Faculté de Théologie Protestante. Strasbourg: Centre de Sociologie du Protestantisme, 1979.

1976. Willaime, Jean-Paul. "Protestantisme, théologie et société. Regard sociologique sur quelques évolutions théologiques dans le protestantisme français." SC 32,2-3 (1985): 175-201.

Study of post-World War II theological movements among French Protestants.

1977. Williams, C.R. "The Welsh Religious Revival, 1904-05." BRITISH JOURNAL OF SOCIOLOGY 3,3 (1952): 242-259.

Historical background and account.


## CANADA

* Bibby, Reginald W. FRAGMENTED GODS. Cited above as item 1927.

1978. Fallding, Harold. "Mainline Protestantism in Canada and the United States of America: An Overview." CANADIAN JOURNAL OF SOCIOLOGY 3 (1978): 141-160. Reprinted in Patrick H. McNamara (ed.), RELIGION: NORTH AMERICAN STYLE, second edition. Belmont, California: Wadsworth, 1984, pp. 71-88.


## U.S.A.

* Abel, Theodore. PROTESTANT HOME MISSIONS TO CATHOLIC IMMIGRANTS. Cited above as item 1013.

* Alston, Jon P. "Occupational Placement and Mobility of Protestants and Catholics, 1953-1964." Cited above as item 1091.

* Alwin, Duane F. "Religion and Parental Child-rearing Orientations: Evidence of a Catholic-Protestant Convergence." Cited above as item 1348.

* Anderson, Charles H. "Religious Communality among White Protestants, Catholics and Mormons." Cited above as item 1093.

1979. Anderson, Susan. SEX DIFFERENTIALS IN PROTESTANT LOCAL CHURCH LEADER-SHIP AND PARTICIPATION. Unpublished Ph.D. dissertation, Indiana University, 1977. [DA 38:4 A, p. 2354]

Examination of lay leadership in 58 Protestant churches in Indianapolis, Indiana.

* Burchinal, Lee G., and William F. Kenkel. "Religious Identification and Occupational Status of Iowa Grooms, 1953-7." Cited above as item 1098.

* Cantril, Hadley. "Education and Economic Compositions of Religious Groups: An Analysis of Poll Data." Cited above as item 1018.

1980. Carroll, Jackson W. "Structural Effects of Professional Schools on Professional Socialization: The Case of Protestant Clergymen." SOCIAL FORCES 50,1 (1971): 61-74.

1965 sample of U.S. Protestant clergy; kinds of seminary are related to theological orientation.

1981. Catton, William R. "Exploring Techniques for Measuring Human Values." AMERICAN SOCIOLOGICAL REVIEW 19,1 (1954): 49-55.

Content analysis of responses of 18 ministers.

* Christopherson, Victor A., and James Walters. "Responses of Protes-tants, Catholics, and Jews concerning Marriage and Family Life." Cited above as item 419.

1982. Coates, Charles H., and Robert C. Kistler. "Role Dilemmas of Protes-tant Clergymen in a Metropolitan Community." RRR 6 (1965): 147-152.

Based on 1962 questionnaire research conducted in the Washington, D.C. metropolitan area. Discusses conflicts between the vocational demands of pastoral service and the realistic demands of administrative service.

* Crespi, Irving. "Occupational Status and Religion." Cited above as item 1100.

* DeJong, Gordon F., and Joseph E. Faulkner. "The Church, Individual Religiosity, and Social Justice." Cited above as item 1101.

* Dundon, Mary C. "The Christian Character of Certain Liberal Arts Colleges with a Focus on the Academic Arena." Cited above as item 1225.

* Fallding, Harold. "Mainline Protestantism in Canada and the United States of America: An Overview." Cited above as item 1978.

* Featherman, David L. "The Socioeconomic Achievement of White Religio-

ethnic Subgroups. Social and Psychological Explanations." Cited above as item 428.

* Fox, William S., and Elton F. Jackson. "Protestant-Catholic Differences in Educational Achievement and Persistence in School." Cited above as item 1233.

* Gaede, Stan. "Religious Affiliation, Social Mobility, and the Problem of Causality: A Methodological Critique of Catholic-Protestant Socioeconomic Achievement Studies." Cited above as item 1234.

* Glenn, Norval D., and Ruth Hyland. "Religious Preference and Worldly Success: Some Evidence from National Surveys." Cited above as item 1117.

* Glock, Charles Y., and Rodney Stark. RELIGION AND SOCIETY IN TENSION. Cited above as item 1118.

* Glock, Charles Y., and Rodney Stark. CHRISTIAN BELIEFS AND ANTI-SEMITISM. Cited above as item 1119.

* Goldstein, Sidney. "Socioeconomic Differentials among Religious Groups in the U.S." Cited above as item 441.

* Greeley, Andrew M. "The Religious Behavior of Graduate Students." Cited above as item 1128.

* Greeley, Andrew M. "The 'Religious Factor' and Academic Careers: Another Communication." Cited above as item 446.

* Herberg, Will. PROTESTANT-CATHOLIC-JEW. Cited above as item 454.

1983. Hoge, Dean R., John E. Dyble, and David T. Polk. "Organizational and Situational Influences on Vocational Commitment of Protestant Ministers." RRR 23,2 (1981): 133-149.

Based on a 1978 survey of clergy from seven Protestant denominations in the Chicago metropolitan area. Subjective feelings of challenge and skill utilization were the main determinants of vocational commitment.

1984. Houghland, James G., Jr., and James R. Wood. "Control in Organizations and the Commitment of Members." SOCIAL FORCES 59,1 (1980): 85-105.

Data from 58 churches in Indianapolis, Indiana.

* Jackson, Elton F., William S. Fox, and Harry J. Crockett, Jr. "Religion and Occupational Achievement." Cited above as item 1265.

* Kelly, James R. "The Spirit of Ecumenism: How Wide, How Deep, How Mindful of Truth?" Cited above as item 466.

1985. Koller, Norman B., and Joseph D. Retzer. "The Sounds of Silence

Revisited." SA 41,2 (1980): 155-161. Reprinted in Jeffrey K. Hadden and Theodore E. Long (eds.), RELIGION AND RELIGIOSITY IN AMERICA. STUDIES IN HONOR OF JOSEPH H. FICHTER. New York: Crossroads, 1983, pp. 89-98.

1978 survey of Protestant clergy in two counties in southwestern North Carolina. In contrast to the case a decade earlier, conservatives were found to be as likely as liberals to give sermons on social issues.

* Lazerwitz, Bernard. "Religion and Social Structure in the United States." Cited above as item 471.

* Lazerwitz, Bernard. "Contrasting the Effects of Generation, Class, Sex, and Age on Group Identification in the Jewish and Protestant Communities." Cited above as item 472.

* Lenski, Gerhard. THE RELIGIOUS FACTOR. Cited above as item 1152.

* Lipset, Seymour M., and Reinhard Bendix. SOCIAL MOBILITY IN INDUSTRIAL SOCIETY. Cited above as item 1073.

* Mack, Raymond W., Raymond J. Murphy, and Seymour Yellin. "The Protestant Ethic, Level of Aspiration, and Social Mobility: An Empirical Test." Cited above as item 1075.

* Mayer, Albert J., and Harry Sharp. "Religious Preference and Worldly Success." Cited above as item 484.

1986. Means, Richard L. "Protestantism and American Sociology: Problems of Analysis." SA 27,3 (1966): 128-137.

Discusses problems involved in using the category 'Protestant' as an indicator of identity; reviews 161 research publications.

1987. Miller, Robert M. "A Note on the Relation between the Protestant Churches and the Revival of the Ku Klux Klan." JOURNAL OF SOUTHERN HISTORY 22,3 (1956): 355-368.

Focuses on American Protestantism's critique of the Ku Klux Klan in the 1920s.

* Mitchell, Robert E. MINISTER-PARISHIONER RELATIONS. Cited above as item 1950.

* Mueller, Charles W. "Evidence on the Relationship between Religion and Educational Attainment." Cited above as item 490.

* Mueller, Charles W., and Weldon T. Johnson. "Socioeconomic Status and Religious Participation." Cited above as item 491.

* Nelsen, Hart M. "Religious Conformity in an Age of Disbelief: Contextual Effects of Time, Denomination, and Family Processes upon Church Decline and Apostasy." Cited above as item 1405.

247

* Nelsen, Hart M., and Lynda Dickson. "Attitudes of Black Catholics and Protestants. Evidence for Religious Identity." Cited above as item 1302.

1988. Nelsen, Hart M., and Robert F. Everett. "Impact of Church Size on Clergy Role and Career." RRR 18,1 (1976): 62-72.

1972 U.S. sample of clergy, subsample from member denominations of the National Council of Churches. Focus is on correlates of satisfaction and plans to either change or remain in careers.

* Nelson, Joel I., and Charles Simpkins. "Family Size and College Aspirations: A Note on Catholic-Protestant Differences." Cited above as item 1303.

* Organic, Harold N. RELIGIOUS AFFILIATION AND SOCIAL MOBILITY IN CONTEMPORARY AMERICAN SOCIETY: A NATIONAL STUDY. Cited above as item 1173.

* Peck, Gary R. "Black Radical Consciousness and the Black Christian Experience: Toward a Critical Sociology of Afro-American Religion." Cited above as item 1407.

* Rhodes, A. Lewis, and Charles B. Nam. "The Religious Context of Educational Expectations." Cited above as item 499.

* Roof, Wade Clark. "Socioeconomic Differentials among White Socioreligious Groups in the United States." Cited above as item 501.

* Schuman, Howard. "The Religious Factor in Detroit: Review, Replication, and Reanalysis." Cited above as item 1324.

1989. Smith, James O., and Gideon Sjoberg. "Origins and Career Patterns of Leading Protestant Clergymen." SOCIAL FORCES 39,4 (1961): 290-296.

Study of 297 U.S. Protestant clergy drawn from the listings in WHO'S WHO IN AMERICA. Data on background variables are reported.

* Steinberg, Stephen. "The Changing Religious Composition of American Higher Education." Cited above as item 518.

* Stryker, Robin. "Religio-ethnic Effects on Attainments in the Early Career." Cited above as item 520.

* Wagner, Helmut R., Kathryn Doyle, and Victor Fisher. "Religious Background and Higher Education." Cited above as item 1088.

* Weller, Neil J. RELIGION AND SOCIAL MOBILITY IN INDUSTRIAL SOCIETY. Cited above as item 1191.

* Zelan, Joseph. "Religious Apostasy, Higher Education, and Occupational Choice." Cited above as item 526.

1990. Chaunu, P.  "Pour une sociologie du protestantisme latinoaméricain. Problèmes de methode."  CAHIERS DE SOCIOLOGIE ECONOMIQUE 12 (1965): 5-18.

1991. Damboriena, Prudencio.  "Protestantisme Latino-américain: 1958." NOUVELLE REVUE THEOLOGIQUE 80 (1958): 944-965, 1062-1076.

Based on analysis of Protestant church publications.

1992. Damboriena, Prudencio.  EL PROTESTANTISMO EN AMERICA LATINA. Tomo I. Freiburg:  FERES, 1962.

1993. Damboriena, Prudencio, and Enrique Dussell.  EL PROTESTANTISMO EN AMERICA LATINA.  Friburgo-Bogotá: FERES, 1963.

* Lalive d'Epinay, Christian.  "L'esprit et la champ oecuméniques de pasteurs sud-américains."  Cited above as item 1748.

1994. Lalive d'Epinay, Christian.  "Toward a Typology of Latin American Protestantism."  RRR 10,1 (1968): 4-11.

Exposes certain traits which are fundamental for the study of Protestantism in Latin America and which challenge the applicability of some traditional sociological concepts.

1995. Taylor, Clyde W., and Wade T. Coggins.  PROTESTANT MISSIONS IN LATIN AMERICA: A STATISTICAL SURVEY.  Washington:  Evangelical Foreign Missions Association, 1961.


*MEXICO*

1996. Bastian, Jean-Pierre.  "Protestantismo y politica in México."  REVISTA MEXICANA DE SOCIOLOGIA 43,E (1981): 1947-1966.

A historical review dating from the late-nineteenth century.  Protestantism was allowed entry by liberals, partly in order to weaken the Catholic Church.  It became identified with American corporate interests, however, and itself weakened in the 1940s.

1997. Bastian, Jean-Pierre.  PROTESTANTISMO Y SOCIEDAD EN MEXICO.  México City: CUPSA, 1983.

1998. Bastian, Jean-Pierre.  "Dissidence religieuse dans le milieu rural mexicain."  SC 32,2-3 (1985): 245-260.

Protestant sects have spread in Mexico, especially in the rural south, mainly because they have incorporated healing practices which are consonant with the indigenous magico-religious symbol system.

1999. Carrasco Malhue, Pedro.  PROTESTANTISMO Y CAMPO RELIGIOSO EN UN PUEBLO DEL ESTADO DE OAXACA.  Tesis Licenciatura en Sociología de la Religión, Instituto Internacional de Estudios Superiores, México, D.F., 1983.

2000. Bastide, Roger. "Nicht-katholische Religionen und die ökonomische und soziale Entwicklung in Brasilien." In Joachim Matthes (ed.), INTERNATIONALES JAHRBUCH FÜR RELIGIONSSOZIOLOGIE 6. Opladen: Westdeutscher Verlag, 1970, pp. 83-98.

2001. Borges Costa, Esdras. RELIGIÃO E DESENVOLVIMENTO ECONOMICO NO NORDESTE DO BRASIL (IGREJAS PROTESTANTES). The Hague: Federação Internacional dos Institutos de Pesquinas Sociais e Socio-Religiosas, 1968; Louvain: Institute of Social Studies, 1968.

2002. Borges Costa, Esdras. "Protestantisme et développement au Nord-Est du Brésil." SC 16,1 (1969): 51-61.

Although divided into various denominations, the Protestantism of the Natal area in Brazil is in fact one single movement. Characteristics are an emphasis on conversion, a model of morality and set of typical attitudes, and strong local group cohesion. The dominant trend sustains rather than challenges traditional structures of power, but divergencies are beginning to arise.

2003. Cesar, Waldo. PARA UMA SOCIOLOGIA DO PROTESTANISMO BRASILEIRO. Petrópolis: Vozes, 1973.

2004. Lalive d'Epinay, Christian. RELIGION, DYNAMIQUE SOCIALE ET DEPENDANCE. LES MOUVEMENTS PROTESTANTS EN ARGENTINE ET AU CHILI. Paris and La Haye: Mouton, 1975.

2005. Nelson, Reed E. "Organizational Homogeneity, Growth, and Conflict in Brazilian Protestantism:" SA 48,4 (1988): 319-327.

Identifies three kinds of Brazilian Protestant church, based respectively upon rational-legal, clientelist, and patriarchal types of authority.

2006. Villeroy, Magdelaine. "Enquête sur les Eglises protestantes dans le Brésil en crise des années 1962-1963." CAHIERS DE SOCIOLOGIE ECONOMIQUE 12 (1965): 19-80.

Basic membership data for Protestant denominations circa 1961, showing much growth from 1959. General description, and discussion of ecumenism.

2007. Willems, Emilio. "Protestantism as a Factor of Culture Change in Brazil." ECONOMIC DEVELOPMENT AND CULTURAL CHANGE 3 (1955): 321-333.

Converts to Protestant faiths have broken secular as well as religious traditions. They have turned out to be more secularized, literate, and to have a broader outlook upon life. They also have participated selectively in certain sectors of the economy.

2008. Willems, Emilio. "Protestantismus und Klassenstruktur in Chile." KÖLNER ZEITSCHRIFT FÜR SOZIOLOGIE UND SOZIALPSYCHOLOGIE 12,4 (1960):

652-671.

Examines the internal class tensions and schools of three Protestant church groups: European immigrant, traditional North American, and Pentecostal.

2009. Willems, Emilio. "Culture Change and the Rise of Protestantism in Brazil and Chile." In S.N. Eisenstadt (ed.), THE PROTESTANT WORK ETHIC AND MODERNIZATION. New York: Basic, 1963.

Low socio-economic status creates a desire for an expression of equality among the lower classes, a desire met by Protestant religions in Brazil and Chile. The converts maintain different values and a different relationship to society, thus resulting in increased literacy and other changes conducive to upward mobility.

2010. Willems, Emilio. "Protestantism and Culture Change in Brazil and Chile." In W.V. D'Antonio and F.B. Pike (eds.), RELIGION, REVOLUTION, AND REFORM. New York: Praeger, 1964, pp. 91-108.

Overview, using data for the period 1890 to 1959.

* Willems, Emilio. "Religiöser Pluralismus und Klassenstruktur in Brasilien und Chile." Cited above as item 1844.

2011. Willems, Emilio. FOLLOWERS OF THE NEW FAITH: CULTURE CHANGE AND THE RISE OF PROTESTANTISM IN BRAZIL AND CHILE. Nashville, Tennessee: Vanderbilt University Press, 1967.

Lower-class immigrants from the countryside favor brands of fundamentalism which are compatible with rural supernaturalism. Protestant sects instill discipline and teach literacy, thereby making the immigrants economically dependable.


## ARGENTINA

2012. Lalive d'Epinay, Chistian. "Les églises du transplant: Le Protestantisme d'immigration en Argentine." SC 18,2 (1971): 213-229.

Results of a study of 11 'immigrant churches' in Argentina. The determining factor in their emergence was not the immigrant status of their members but rather ecclesiastical tradition.

2013. Lalive d'Epinay, Christian. PENETRATION CULTURELLE ET PRESSE RELIGIEUSE. LE CAS D'UNE REVUE PROTESTANTE ARGENTINE. SONDEOS 80. Cuernavaca: CIDOC, 1971.

2014. Lalive d'Epinay, Christian. "Elites protestantes, politique et procès du développement. Le cas de l'Argentine." REVUE FRANÇAISE DE SOCIOLOGIE 15,4 (1974): 553-569.

Questionnaire data from 341 leaders of five Protestant churches. A typology of churches (ethnic minority, U.S.-affiliate, etc.) is related to levels and kinds of political activity.

* Lalive d'Epinay, Christian. RELIGION, DYNAMIQUE SOCIALE ET DEPENDANCE. Cited above as item 2004.

## COLOMBIA, GUATEMALA, NICARAGUA, URUGUAY

2015. Bastian, Jean-Pierre. "Religión popular protestante y comportamiento politico en América Central. Clientela religiosa y estado patron en Guatemala y Nicaragua." CRISTIANISMO Y SOCIEDAD 24,88 (1986): 41-56.

   * Benoit, André. EDUCACION COLOMBIANA. ASPECTOS DE SU FUNCION IDEOLOGI-CA. Cited above as item 1861.

   * Benoit, André. "Valeurs sociales transmises par l'enseignement secondaire des églises et de l'état en Colombie." Cited above as item 1862.

   * Centro de Estudios Cristianos. ASPECTOS RELIGIOSOS DE LA SOCIEDAD URUGUAYA. Cited above as item 398.

2016. Roberts, Bryan. "Protestant Groups and Coping with Urban Life in Guatemala City." AMERICAN JOURNAL OF SOCIOLOGY 73,6 (1968): 753-767.

   Protestant sectarian groups in Guatemala City recruit individuals who have aspirations for social and economic improvement but who lack a network of secular relationships in the city.

## ASIA

   * Tamney, Joseph B. "Chinese Family Structure and the Continuation of Chinese Religion." Cited above as item 156.

2017. Wiebe, Paul D. "Protestant Missions in India: A Sociological Review." JOURNAL OF ASIAN AND AFRICAN STUDIES 5 (1970): 293-301.

   General account of the Christian population of India, based on previous studies, generally reflecting the 1960s.

# 14
## Lutheran

*GERMANY, HUNGARY*

2018. Dahm, Karl-Wilhelm. PFARRER UND POLITIK. SOZIALE POSITION UND
POLITISCHE MENTALITÄT DES DEUTSCHEN EVANGELISCHEN PFARRERSTANDES
ZWISCHEN 1918 UND 1933. BAND 29 DER DORTMUNDER SCHRIFTEN ZUR SOZIAL-
FORSCHUNG. Köln und Opladen: Westdeutscher Verlag, 1965.

* Greinacher, Norbert. "The Development of Applications to Leave the
  Church and the Transfer from One Church to Another, and Its Causes."
  Cited above as item 1535.

* Karady, Victor. "Juifs et Luthériens dans le système scolaire
  hongrois." Cited above as item 337.


*WEST GERMANY*

2019. Bormann, Günther. "Studien zu Berufsbild und Berufswirklichkeit
evangelischer Pfarrer in Württemberg." SC 13,2 (1966): 95-138.

Background data (fathers' occupations in particular), 1700-1961.

2020. Bormann, Günther. "Studien zu Berufsbild und Berufswirklichkeit
evangelischer Pfarrer in Württemberg: Tendenzen der Berufseinstellung
und des Berufsverhaltens." In J. Matthes (ed.), ESSAYS ON RESEARCH IN
THE SOCIOLOGY OF RELIGION 4 [volume cited in item 121], pp. 158-209.

Interviews with members of the clergy reveal varying conceptions of
the ministerial role, some more grounded than others in Lutheran
theology.

2021. Bormann, Günther. "L'organisation sociale de l'Eglise évangélique du
Wurtemberg." SC 16,2 (1969): 185-225.

Data on the Wurtemberg Landeskirche, 1815-1964.

2022. Daiber, Karl F. "Que devient l'Eglise Evangelique d'Allemagne?" SC
32,2-3 (1985): 229-232.

Reflections on a West German survey which reported that some 1.5

million people had left the Evangelical Church during the previous decade.

2023. Köster, Reinhard. DIE KIRCHENTREUEN. ERFAHRUNGEN UND ERGEBNISSE EINER SOZIOLOGISCHEN UNTERSUCHUNG IN EINER GROSSTADTISCHEN EVANGELISCHEN KIRCHENGEMEINDE. Stuttgart: Ferdinand Enke Verlag, 1959.

2024. Köster, Reinhard. "Die Kirchentreuen. Bericht über eine Untersuchung in einer evangelisch-lutherischen Gemeinde Nord-deutschlands." In D. Goldschmidt, F. Greiner, and H. Schelsky (eds.), SOZIOLOGIE DER KIRCHEN-GEMEINDE [volume cited in item 1478], pp. 144-153.

1956 study in Hamburg.

2025. Wurzbacher, Gerard, et al. DER PFARRER IN DER MODERNEN GESELLSCHAFT. SOZIOLOGISCHE STUDIEN ZUR BERUFSSITUATION DES EVANGELISCHEN PFARRERS. Hamburg: Furche Verlag, 1960.

2026. Zieger, Paul. "Statistik der Evangelischen Kirche in Deutschland." In D. Goldschmidt, F. Greiner, and H. Schelsky (eds.), SOZIOLOGIE DER KIRCHENGEMEINDE [volume cited in item 1478], pp. 208-238.


*FINLAND*

2027. Huotari, Voitto. "Finnish Revivalism as an Expression of Popular Piety." SC 29,2-3 (1982): 113-123.

More so than other European Lutheran churches, the Finnish has small revival groups supplementing the central organization.

2028. Lampinen, Tapio. "The Content of the Parochial Sermons in the Evangelical Luthern Church of Finland as Indicators of the Openness and Closeness of the Church as System." SC 27,4 (1980): 417-435.

1975 data; factor analysis of sermon contents.


*SWEDEN*

2029. Gustafsson, Berndt. "Staatskirche und Entkirchlichung in Schweden." In D. Goldschmidt and J. Matthes (eds.), PROBLEME DER RELIGIONSSOZI-OLOGIE [volume cited in item 1745], pp. 158-165. See also "The Established Church and the Decline in Church Attendance in Sweden." In Norman Birnbaum and G. Lenzer (eds.), SOCIOLOGY AND RELIGION: A BOOK OF READINGS. Englewood Cliffs, N.J.: Prentice-Hall, 1969, pp. 360-365.

Historical analysis of a general ambivalence about the state church.

2030. Gustafsson, Göran. "Popular Religion in Sweden." SC 29,2-3 (1982): 103-112.

Sweden by all accounts is not a religious nation, but most of the people belong to the established church and ritualize important moments with religious ceremonial. This would seem to indicate the existence of a kind of popular religion.

2031. Pettersson, Thorleif. "Swedish Church Statistics. Unique Data for Sociological Research." SC 35,1 (1988): 15-31.

Statistics have been collected since 1686.

2032. Stendahl, Brita. THE FORCE OF TRADITION: A CASE STUDY OF WOMEN PRIESTS IN SWEDEN. Philadelphia: Fortress, 1985.

## CANADA, AUSTRALIA

2033. Dewitt, Robert L. THE LUTHERAN CHURCH IN FREDERICKTON. Unpublished M.A. thesis, University of New Brunswick, 1965.

Describes the different functions which the church serves for immigrant and native-Canadian members respectively.

* Mol, J.J. (Hans) "A Collation of Data about Religion in Australia." Cited above as item 308.

## LATIN AMERICA

2034. Bideau, Alain, and Sergio O. Nadalin. "Study of Birth Rates in a Lutheran Evangelical Community in Curtiba (Brazil) from 1866 to 1939." POPULATION 43,6 (1988): 1035-1064.

* Lalive d'Epinay, Christian. "L'esprit et la champ oecuméniques de pasteurs sud-américains." Cited above as item 1748.

## U.S.A. (GENERAL)

* Allinsmith, Wesley, and Beverly Allinsmith. "Religious Affiliation and Politico-economic Attitude." Cited above as item 404.

* Betts, George H. THE BELIEFS OF 700 MINISTERS. Cited above as item 1937.

2035. Bradfield, Cecil D., and R. Ann Myers. "Clergy and Funeral Directors: An Exploration in Role Conflict." RRR 21,3 (1980): 343-350.

Data from a sample of U.S. Lutheran clergy.

2036. Demerath, Nicholas J., III. SOCIAL CLASS IN AMERICAN PROTESTANTISM. Chicago: Rand McNally, 1965.

1957 non-South U.S. sample of five denominations; the Lutheran sample does not include the Missouri and Wisconsin synods.

2037. Frerking, Kenneth. "Religious Participation of Lutheran Students." RRR 6 (1965): 153-162.

1962 questionnaire research among a sample of 178 Lutheran (Missouri Synod) students at Ohio State University.

2038. Frerking, Kenneth. SOCIAL AND RELIGIOUS ATTITUDES AMONG LUTHERAN STUDENTS. Unpublished Ph.D. dissertation, University of Missouri, Columbia, 1970. [DA 31:5 A, p. 2493]

Data from surveys of Lutheran students, focusing on pacifism, racial prejudice, welfare; evaluation of Christianity, institutional church, new morality; political anomie.

2039. Glock, Charles Y., and Philip Roos. "Parishioners' Views of How Ministers Spend Their Time." RRR 2 (1961): 170-175.

Based on the secondary analysis of 2729 questionnaires received in 1956 from a sample of the membership of 12 urban Lutheran congregations located primarily in the east and mid-west.

* Gockel, Galen L. "Income and Religious Affiliation: A Regression Analysis." Cited above as item 437.

* Hoge, Dean R., and John E. Dyble. "The Influence of Assimilation on American Protestant Ministers' Beliefs, 1928-1978." Cited above as item 1945.

2040. Johnson, Arthur L., Milo L. Brekke, Merton P. Strommen, and Ralph C. Underwager. "Age Differences and Dimensions of Religious Behavior." JOURNAL OF SOCIAL ISSUES 30,3 (1974): 43-67.

U.S. national sample of Lutherans; six age groups. Significant differences in religiosity across the age groups were found, with the 19-23 group most heterogeneous in belief, attitudes, and life style. There was some intra-stratum solidarity, but it was overshadowed by lineage solidarity.

2041. Johnstone, Ronald L. THE EFFECTIVENESS OF LUTHERAN ELEMENTARY AND SECONDARY SCHOOLS AS AGENCIES OF CHRISTIAN EDUCATION. St. Louis: Concordia, 1966.

2042. Johnstone, Ronald L. "The Public Image of Lutheran Pastors." LUTHER-AN QUARTERLY 24 (1972): 397-409.

1970 N.O.R.C. (U.S.) sample survey.

* Johnstone, Ronald L. "Public Images of Protestant Ministers and Catholic Priests: An Empirical Study of Anti-clericalism in the U.S." Cited above as item 1267.

2043. Kersten, Lawrence K. THE LUTHERAN ETHIC: THE IMPACT OF RELIGION ON LAYMEN AND CLERGY. Detroit: Wayne State University Press, 1970.

2044. Kloetzli, Walter. THE CITY CHURCH: DEATH OR RENEWAL. Philadelphia: The Muhlenberg Press, 1961.

* Kourvetaris, George A., and Betty A. Dobratz. "An Empirical Test of

Gordon's Ethclass Hypothesis among Three Ethnoreligious Groups."
Cited above as item 771.

* Laumann, Edward O. "The Social Structure of Religious and Ethno-
religious Groups in a Metropolitan Community." Cited above as item
469.

2045. Layne, Norman R., Jr., and Jack O. Balswick. ASCENSION AT THE CROSS-
ROADS: A CASE STUDY OF A CHURCH CAUGHT IN THE TURBULENCE OF RAPID
SOCIAL CHANGE. Athens, Georgia: Institute of Community and Area
Development and the Department of Sociology, 1973.

2046. Layne, Norman R., Jr., and Jack O. Balswick. "Church Generation: A
Neglected Research Issue." SA 38,3 (1977): 258-265.

Study of a Lutheran congregation in a medium-sized city in the southeastern U.S.A. Generations are analyzed by age and by time of entry
into the congregation.

* Lazerwitz, Bernard. "Religion and Social Structure in the United
States." Cited above as item 471.

* Lee, Gary R., and Robert W. Clyde. "Religion, Socioeconomic Status,
and Anomie." Cited above as item 1288.

* Lenski, Gerhard. "Social Correlates of Religious Interest." Cited
above as item 1946.

* Lutterman, Kenneth G. GIVING TO CHURCHES: A SOCIOLOGICAL STUDY OF THE
CONTRIBUTIONS TO EIGHT CATHOLIC AND LUTHERAN CHURCHES. Cited above as
item 1155.

* Maranell, Gary M. RESPONSES TO RELIGION. STUDIES IN THE SOCIAL
PSYCHOLOGY OF RELIGIOUS BELIEF. Cited above as item 1294.

2047. Maurer, Heinrich H. "The Political Attitudes of the Lutheran Parish
in America - A Study in Religious Sectionalism." AMERICAN JOURNAL OF
SOCIOLOGY 33 (1928): 568-585.

2048. Maurer, Heinrich H. "The Lutheran Community and American Society: A
Study in Religion as a Condition of Social Accommodation." AMERICAN
JOURNAL OF SOCIOLOGY 34 (1928): 282-295.

Case study of Christianity rationalizing the relationship between in
and out groups, and thereby providing a framework for the integration
of groups within society.

* Mayer, Albert J., and Harry Sharp. "Religious Preference and Worldly
Success." Cited above as item 484.

2049. Mol, J.J. (Hans) THE BREAKING OF TRADITIONS: THEOLOGICAL CONVICTIONS
IN COLONIAL AMERICA. Berkeley: Glendessary, 1968.

A study of German Lutheran and Dutch Reformed clergy in the American colonies (eighteenth century).

* Mueller, Charles W. "Evidence on the Relationship between Religion and Educational Attainment." Cited above as item 490.

2050. Mueller, Samuel A. "Changes in the Social Status of Lutheranism in Ninety Chicago Suburbs, 1950-1960." SA 27,3 (1966): 138-145.

Ranking of towns and observation of Lutherans moving among them in varying numbers.

* Nelsen, Hart M. "Religious Conformity in an Age of Disbelief: Contextual Effects of Time, Denomination, and Family Processes upon Church Decline and Apostasy." Cited above as item 1405.

* Norr, James L. "Religion and Nation Building: The American Case." Cited above as item 1304.

* Perrin, Robin D. "American Religion in the Post-aquarian Age: Values and Demographic Factors in Church Growth and Decline." Cited above as item 1409.

* Roof, Wade Clark. "Socioeconomic Differentials among White Socioreligious Groups in the United States." Cited above as item 501.

2051. Stange, Douglas C. "Al Smith and the Republican Party at Prayer: The Lutheran Vote - 1928." REVIEW OF POLITICS 32,3 (1970): 347-364.

Examination of the 1928 U.S. presidential election returns and some other election returns in heavily Lutheran counties. Review of the controversy among Lutherans over the campaign of a Roman Catholic for president.

* Steinberg, Stephen. "The Changing Religious Composition of American Higher Education." Cited above as item 518.

2052. Strommen, Merton P., Milo L. Brekke, Ralph C. Underwager, and Arthur L. Johnson. A STUDY OF GENERATIONS. Minneapolis: Augsburgh Publishing, 1972.

* Stryker, Robin. "Religio-ethnic Effects on Attainments in the Early Career." Cited above as item 520.


*UNITED LUTHERAN CHURCH IN AMERICA*

2053. Bossard, James H.S., and Harold C. Letts. "Mixed Marriages Involving Lutherans: A Research Report." MARRIAGE AND FAMILY LIVING 18,4 (1956): 308-311.

Questionnaire data from pastors.

2054. Hook, Wade F. A SOCIOLOGICAL ANALYSIS OF LAY LEADERSHIP IN THE LUTHERAN CHURCHES OF NORTH AND SOUTH CAROLINA (United Lutheran Church in America). Unpublished Ph.D. dissertation, Duke University, 1957.

2055. Hook, Wade F. "The Lutheran Church in the Carolinas Sociologically Interpreted." LUTHERAN QUARTERLY 11 (1959): 60-67.

Interprets nineteenth-century intra-church separations as constructive conflicts.

* Mitchell, Robert E. MINISTER-PARISHIONER RELATIONS. Cited above as item 1950.

* Mitchell, Robert E. "Polity, Church Attractiveness, and Ministers' Careers." Cited above as item 1951.


## LUTHERAN CHURCH IN AMERICA

2056. Berg, Philip L. "Professionalism and Lutheran Seminaries." LUTHERAN QUARTERLY 20 (1968): 406-441.

1962-63 survey of Protestant seminarians; American Lutheran Church and Lutheran Church in America subsamples; value orientation and professionalism scores.

* Broughton, Walter, and Edgar W. Mills, Jr. "Resource Inequality and Accumulative Advantage: Stratification in the Ministry." Cited above as item 1939.

2057. Hart, Stephen. "Christian Faith and Nuclear Weapons: Rank-and-file Opinions." JSSR 26,1 (1987): 38-62.

During a two-year period of debate, about one quarter of respondents became more wary of nuclear weapons, and one eighth more accepting of them.

* Hartley, Shirley F., and Mary G. Taylor. "Religious Beliefs of Clergy Wives." Cited above as item 1944.

2058. Heenan, Edward F. "Ideological and Structural Conflict in a Suburban Congregation: An Empirical Test of Dahrendorf's Conflict Model." SA 33,3 (1972): 177-187.

Based on study of a midwestern American congregation.

2059. Hook, Wade F. "Religious Regionalism: The Case of Lutherans in the South." RRR 27,1 (1985): 77-85.

Data related to membership, giving, and sex roles show divergence of Southern Lutherans from patterns found in the rest of the U.S. Data pertinent to ethnic membership and clergy dropout suggest conformity to national patterns.

2060. Johnson, Roger A. (ed.) VIEW FROM THE PEWS. CHRISTIAN BELIEFS AND ATTITUDES. Philadelphia: Fortress, 1983.

Various contributors - both sociologists and theologians - focusing on

1979 questionnaire data collected from lay members and pastors.

2061. Murphy, Steven E. "A Note on Clergy-laity Differences among Lutherans." JSSR 11,2 (1972): 177-179.

Northern Illinois sample of 77 clergy and 136 lay leaders. Clergy tended to give more liberal responses than did laity on a variety of social and political issues.

* Quinley, Harold E. THE PROPHETIC CLERGY. SOCIAL ACTIVISM AMONG PROTESTANT MINISTERS. Cited above as item 1953.

2062. Royle, Marjorie H. "Women Pastors. What happens after Placement?" RRR 24,2 (1982): 116-127.

Based on a 1976 sample of female clergy in four denominations ordained since 1970, and a comparable sample of male clergy. Few differences were found in either membership or financial trends between female-pastored and male-pastored churches.

* Scherer, Ross P. "A New Typology for Organizations: Market, Bureaucracy, Clan and Mission, with Application to American Denominations." Cited above as item 1416.

* Stark, Rodney, Bruce D. Foster, Charles Y. Glock, and Harold E. Quinley. WAYWARD SHEPHERDS: PREJUDICE AND THE PROTESTANT CLERGY. Cited above as item 1960.

* Terian, Sarah M.K. THE OTHER SIDE OF GOOD SAMARITANISM: THE HELPING ETHIC IN JUDEO-CHRISTIAN IDEOLOGY AND PRACTICE. Cited above as item 1422.


*AMERICAN LUTHERAN CHURCH*

* Berg, Philip L. "Professionalism and Lutheran Seminarians." Cited above as item 2056.

* Broughton, Walter, and Edgar W. Mills, Jr. "Resource Inequality and Accumulative Advantage: Stratification in the Ministry." Cited above as item 1939.

* Glock, Charles Y., and Rodney Stark. RELIGION AND SOCIETY IN TENSION. Cited above as item 1118.

* Glock, Charles Y., and Rodney Stark. CHRISTIAN BELIEFS AND ANTI-SEMITISM. Cited above as item 1119.

* Hadden, Jeffrey K. THE GATHERING STORM IN THE CHURCHES. A SOCIOLOGIST LOOKS AT THE WIDENING GAP BETWEEN CLERGY AND LAYMEN. Cited above as item 1942.

* Hammond, Phillip, Albert Gedicks, Edward Lawler, and Louise Allen Turner. "Clergy Authority and Friendship with Parishioners." Cited

above as item 1943.

* Longino, Charles F., Jr., and Jeffrey K. Hadden. "Dimensionality of Belief among Mainstream Protestant Clergy." Cited above as item 1948.

* Petersen, James C., and Gary R. Lee. "Religious Affiliation and Social Participation: Differences between Lutherans and Catholics." Cited above as item 1308.

* Quinley, Harold E. THE PROPHETIC CLERGY. SOCIAL ACTIVISM AMONG PROTESTANT MINISTERS. Cited above as item 1953.


## LUTHERAN CHURCH - MISSOURI SYNOD

2063. Cross, William M. "Perceived Influences on Occupational Choice of Seminarians." CONCORDIA THEOLOGICAL QUARTERLY 44,1 (1980): 3-16.

    1976-77 questionnaire data from students in Concordia Seminary, St. Louis; Seminex; and Concordia Seminary, Springfield.

2064. Graebner, Alan. UNCERTAIN SAINTS: THE LAITY OF THE LUTHERAN CHURCH - MISSOURI SYNOD, 1900-1970. Westport, Connecticut: Greenwood, 1976.

2065. Hofman, John E. "The Language Transition in Some Lutheran Denominations." In Joshua A. Fishman et al. (eds.), LANGUAGE LOYALTY IN THE UNITED STATES. The Hague: Mouton, 1966, pp. 139-155. Also in Joshua A. Fishman (ed.), READINGS IN THE SOCIOLOGY OF LANGUAGE. The Hague: Mouton, 1968, pp. 620-638.

    Data from 1917 onward.

2066. Johnson, Jeff G. AN ANALYSIS AND DESCRIPTION OF ROLE EXPECTATIONS FOR MINISTERS OF THE SOUTHERN CALIFORNIA DISTRICT OF THE LUTHERAN CHURCH - MISSOURI SYNOD. Unpublished Ph.D. dissertation, University of Southern California, 1961. [DA 22:12, p. 4431]

    Questionnaire data from ministers, parochial school teachers, lay leaders, congregation members, and District Committee members in the Southern California District.

2067. Maurer, Heinrich H. "Studies in the Sociology of Religion, III. The Problems of a National Church before 1860." AMERICAN JOURNAL OF SOCIOLOGY 30 (1925): 534-550. See also "Studies in the Sociology of Religion, IV. The Problems of Group Consciousness; Founding the Missouri Synod." AMERICAN JOURNAL OF SOCIOLOGY 30 (1925): 665-682; and "Studies in the Sociology of Religion, V. The Fellowship Law of a Fundamentalist Group. The Missouri Synod." AMERICAN JOURNAL OF SOCIOLOGY 31 (1925): 39-57.

2068. Mueller, Daniel J. "Effects and Effectiveness of Parochial Elementary Schools. An Empirical Study." RRR 9,1 (1967): 48-51.

2069. Nauss, Allen H. "The Relation of Pastoral Mobility to Effectiveness."

RRR 15,2 (1974): 80–86.

1970 sample of pastors ordained one to six, eight, 16, 24, 32 and 40 years prior to 1970.

2070. Nauss, Allen H., and Harry G. Coiner. "The First Parish Placement: Stayers and Movers." RRR 12,2 (1971): 95–101.

Survey of the 1963 and 1964 graduating classes of the denomination's two principal seminaries, focusing on placements as of 1968.

2071. Scherer, Ross P. MINISTERS OF THE LUTHERAN CHURCH - MISSOURI SYNOD: ORIGINS, TRAINING, CAREERS, LIVES, PLACES, PLANS OF WORK AND REFERENCE. Unpublished Ph.D. dissertation, University of Chicago, 1963.

2072. Scherer, Ross P. "The Lutheran Ministry." INFORMATION SERVICE (Department of Research, National Council of Churches of Christ in the United States of America) 42,9 (1963): 1–8.

1959 questionnaire data (social origins, education, career, etc.) from Missouri Synod clergy in the U.S.A.

   * Scherer, Ross P. "A New Typology for Organizations: Market, Bureaucracy, Clan and Mission, with Application to American Denominations." Cited above as item 1416.

2073. Schmidt, Alvin J. "Rural-urban Differences in the Decision to Enter the Ministry." JSSR 8,1 (1969): 166.

Study of Lutheran seminarians at Concordia Theological Seminary, Springfield, Illinois. Rural seminarians chose the ministry at an earlier age and with an apparently stronger charismatic self-concept than did their urban counterparts.

2074. Sommerfeld, Richard E. ROLE CONCEPTIONS OF LUTHERAN MINISTERS IN THE ST. LOUIS AREA. Unpublished Ph.D. dissertation, Washington University, 1957. [DA 17:4, p. 915]

Interview data from St. Louis-area ministers.

   * Van Roy, Ralph F., Frank D. Bean, and James R. Wood. "Social Mobility and Doctrinal Orthodoxy." Cited above as item 1962.


*NORWEGIAN LUTHERAN CHURCH IN AMERICA*

   * Hofman, John E. "The Language Transition in Some Lutheran Denominations." Cited above as item 2065.

# 15
## Calvinist

*CALVINIST (GENERAL)*

2075. Blasi, Anthony J., and Michael W. Cuneo. ISSUES IN THE SOCIOLOGY OF RELIGION: A BIBLIOGRAPHY. New York: Garland, 1986, pp. 224-234.

A bibliography of the literature engendered by Max Weber's 'Protestant ethic' thesis.

2076. Jacobson, David. "Protestantism, Authoritarianism and Democracy: A Comparison of the Netherlands, the United States and South Africa." RELIGION 17,3 (1987): 275-301.

Comparable forms of Calvinism developed in the Netherlands, the United States and South Africa. The three societies, however, fashioned very different political systems.

2077. Leites, Edmund. THE PURITAN CONSCIENCE AND MODERN SEXUALITY. New Haven: Yale University Press, 1986.

2078. MacKinnon, Malcolm H. "Part I: Calvinism and the Infallible Assurance of Grace: The Weber Thesis Reconsidered. Part II: Weber's Exploration of Calvinism: The Undiscovered Provenance of Capitalism." BRITISH JOURNAL OF SOCIOLOGY 39,2 (1988): 143-210.

Critique of Weber's 'Protestant ethic' thesis, on the ground that covenant theology overshadowed Calvin's predestinarianism.

2079. Rotenberg, Mordechai. DAMNATION AND DEVIANCE: THE PROTESTANT ETHIC AND THE SPIRIT OF FAILURE. New York: Free Press, 1978.

2080. Séguy, Jean. "Le centre et les marges." ARCHIVES DE SCIENCES SOCIALES DES RELIGIONS 38 (1974): 123-131.

A general discussion of Winstanley and the Diggers.

2081. Swatos, William H., Jr. "Charismatic Calvinism: Forging a Missing Link." In R.M. Glassman and W.H. Swatos, Jr. (eds.), CHARISMA, HISTORY, AND SOCIAL STRUCTURE [volume cited in item 720], pp. 73-81.

Because Calvinist doctrine was attached to an authority structure, it became a world view as well as a theology.

*NETHERLANDS*

2082. Brunt, L. "The 'Kleine Luyden' as a Disturbing Factor in the Emancipation of the Orthodox Calvinists (Gereformeerden) in the Netherlands." SOCIOLOGIA NEERLANDICA 8,2 (1972): 89-102.

Overview, with some 1970-71 local data from a Netherlands district. Part of the orthodox Calvinists, little people (kleine luyden) of lower socioeconomic status, appear not to be 'emancipated' - i.e., are still subject to stereotyping and discrimination.

2083. Vogler, Conrad C. BESIDE THE STILL WATER: A COMPARATIVE STUDY OF THE MAINTENANCE OF THE DISTINCTIVE RELIGIOUS IDENTITY OF THE CHRISTIAN REFORMED CHURCH IN EAST PALMYRIA, NEW YORK AND ABCOUDE, NETHERLANDS. Unpublished Ph.D. dissertation, State University of New York at Buffalo, 1971. [DA 32:3 A, p. 1653]

   * Weima, J. "Authoritarianism, Religious Conservatism, and Sociocentric Attitudes in Roman Catholic Groups." Cited above as item 1601.


*SOUTH AFRICA*

2084. Alant, C.J. "The Relevance of Socio-economic Groups in the Analysis of the Nederduitse Gereformeerde Kerk in South Africa." SC 19,1 (1972): 21-28.

1965 and 1969 surveys in the Transvaal indicate that class differences are straining the unity of the church.

2085. Beckers, G. RELIGIÖSE FAKTORE IN DER ENTWICKLUNG DER SÜDAFRICANISCHEN RASSENFRAGE: EIN BEITRAG ZUR ROLLE DES KAVINISMUS IN KOLONIALEN SITUATION. München: Fink-Verlag, 1969.

   * Higgins, Edward. "Les rôles religieux dans le contexte multi-racial sud-africain: Le profil du ministère dans le calvinisme et le catholicisme." Cited above as item 1439.

2086. Jubber, Ken. "The Prodigal Church: South Africa's Dutch Reformed Church and the Apartheid Policy." SC 32,2-3 (1985): 273-285.

In contrast to black Reformed churches in South Africa, white Reformed ones historically have supported apartheid.

2087. Loubser, Jan J. "Calvinism, Equality, and Inclusion: The Case of Afrikaner Calvinism." In S.N. Eisenstadt (ed.), THE PROTESTANT WORK ETHIC AND MODERNIZATION [volume cited as item 2009], pp. 367-383.

2088. Moodie, T. Dunbar. "The Dutch Reformed Churches as Vehicles of Political Legitimation in South Africa." SOCIAL DYNAMICS 1,2 (1975): 158-166.

Focuses on the decline of the legitimating function.

2089. Ngcokovane, Cecil M. RELIGIOUS AND MORAL LEGITIMATIONS OF APARTHEID IN NEDERDUITSE GEREFORMEERDE KERK, NATIONALIST PARTY AND BROEDERBOND, 1948 -PRESENT. Unpublished Ph.D. dissertation, Emory University, 1986. [DA 47:11 A, p. 4110]

2090. Russell, Margo. "Religion as a Social Possession – Afrikaner Reaction to the Conversion of. Bushmen to Their Church." ARCHIVES DE SCIENCES SOCIALES DES RELIGIONS 44,1 (1977): 59-73.

Argues that it is unhelpful oversimplification to dismiss as mere racism the Afrikaner resistance to the conversion of the Bushmen.

2091. Stokes, Randall G. "Afrikaner Calvinism and Economic Action: The Weberian Thesis in South Africa." AMERICAN JOURNAL OF SOCIOLOGY 81,1 (1975): 62-81.

Operant or everyday religion, as opposed to theological tradition, had a conservative impact on economic action, in contrast to the European case.

2092. Tiryakian, Edward A. "Apartheid and Religion." THEOLOGY TODAY 14,3 (October 1963): 385-400.

2093. Wallis, Roy, and Steve Bruce. "The Threatened Elect: Presbyterians in Ulster and South Africa." Chapter 10 in SOCIOLOGICAL THEORY, RELIGION AND COLLECTIVE ACTION. Belfast, Northern Ireland: The Queen's University, 1986.

A comparative socio-historical analysis.

*FRANCE*

2094. Scoville, Warren C. "The Economic Status of Huguenots." In W.C. Scoville, THE PERSECUTION OF HUGUENOTS AND FRENCH ECONOMIC DEVELOPMENT. Berkeley: University of California Press, 1960.

Attitudes are the mediating variable between religion and economic behavior, and hence status. Religion may also result in persecution, under which resort to economic success may be a route to security.

*AUSTRALIA*

2095. Black, Alan W. "The Impact of Theological Orientation and of Breadth of Perspective on Church Members' Attitudes and Behaviors: Roof, Mol and Kaill Revisited." JSSR 24,1 (1985): 87-100.

1979 survey of members of Presbyterian, Uniting, and Congregational churches in New South Wales, Australia.

* Mol, J.J. (Hans) "A Collation of Data about Religion in Australia." Cited above as item 308.

2096. Bruce, Steve. "The Persistence of Religion: Conservative Protestantism in the United Kingdom." SOCIOLOGICAL REVIEW 31,3 (1983): 453-470.

   Focuses on Scottish and Ulster Presbyterianism, 1950s to 1980s.

   * Goodridge, R.M. "The Religious Condition of the West Country in 1851." Cited above as item 1910.

   * Lehman, Edward C., Jr. "The Local/Cosmopolitan Dichotomy and Acceptance of Women Clergy: A Replication." Cited above as item 1915.

2097. Little, David. RELIGION, ORDER, AND LAW. A STUDY IN PRE-REVOLUTIONARY ENGLAND. Chicago: University of Chicago Press, 1969, 1984.

2098. Maxwell-Arnot, Madeleine. "Social Change and the Church of Scotland." SOCIOLOGICAL YEARBOOK OF RELIGION IN BRITAIN 7 (1974): 91-110.

   The Church of Scotland is examined as a case study in institutional adaptation.

2099. Spencer, Malcolm. "Social Contribution of Congregational and Kindred Churches." SOCIOLOGICAL REVIEW 35,3-4 (1943): 57-68.

   An insider's presentation of his church's ethic.

2100. Zaret, David. THE HEAVENLY CONTRACT: IDEOLOGY AND ORGANIZATION IN PRE-REVOLUTIONARY PURITANISM. Chicago: University of Chicago Press, 1985.

## *NORTHERN IRELAND*

   * Bruce, Steve. "The Persistence of Religion: Conservative Protestantism in the United Kingdom." Cited above as item 2096.

2101. Bruce, Steve. GOD SAVE ULSTER! THE RELIGION AND POLITICS OF PAISLEY-ISM. New York: Oxford University Press, 1987.

   * McCallister, Ian. "Religious Commitment and Social Attitudes in Ireland." Cited above as item 1667.

2102. Taylor, David F. "The Lord's Battle: Paisleyism in Northern Ireland." In Rodney Stark (ed.), RELIGIOUS MOVEMENTS: GENESIS, EXODUS, AND NUMBERS. New York: Paragon House, 1985, pp. 241-278.

   An ethnographic portrayal of the Democratic Unionist Party and the Free Presbyterian Church; the latter is compared with American fundamentalism.

   * Wallis, Roy, and Steve Bruce. "The Threatened Elect: Presbyterians in Ulster and South Africa." Cited above as item 2093.

*IRELAND (PRESBYTERIAN)*

* McCallister, Ian. "Religious Commitment and Social Attitudes in Ireland." Cited above as item 1667.

* Macourt, Malcolm. "The Nature of Religion in Ireland." Cited above as item 1668.

*LATIN AMERICA (PRESBYTERIAN, CHRISTIAN AND MISSIONARY ALLIANCE)*

* Lalive d'Epinay, Christian. "L'esprit et le champ oecuméniques de pasteurs sud-américains." Cited above as item 1748.

*PURITAN (U.S.A.)*

2103. Baltzell, E. Digby. PURITAN BOSTON AND QUAKER PHILADELPHIA. New York: Free Press, 1979; Boston: Beacon, 1982.

2104. Erikson, Kai T. WAYWARD PURITANS. A STUDY IN THE SOCIOLOGY OF DEVIANCE. New York: Wiley, 1966.

Historical sociology, focusing on the Massachusetts Bay Colony.

2105. Heimert, Alan. "Puritanism, the Wilderness, and the Frontier." NEW ENGLAND QUARTERLY 26 (1953): 361-382.

Examination of seventeenth-century writings.

2106. Michaelsen, Robert S. "Changes in the Puritan Concept of Calling or Vocation." NEW ENGLAND QUARTERLY 26 (1953): 315-336.

Examination of Puritan writings on the doctrine of the 'calling.'

2107. Tiryakian, Edward A. "Neither Marx nor Durkheim...Perhaps Weber." AMERICAN JOURNAL OF SOCIOLOGY 81,1 (1975): 1-33.

Search for a heuristic model toward the understanding of American culture.

2108. Tiryakian, Edward A. "Puritan America in the Modern World: Mission Impossible?" SA 43,4 (1982): 351-368.

Argues that the collapse of the Calvinist religious-mundane dichotomy has resulted in an ethic of service and mission.

*CONGREGATIONALIST (U.S.A.)*

* Allinsmith, Wesley, and Beverly Allinsmith. "Religious Affiliation and Politico-economic Attitude." Cited above as item 404.

2109. Berry, Benjamin D., Jr. "The Plymouth Congregational Church of Louisville, Kentucky." PHYLON 42,3 (1981): 224-232.

Social history of a middle/upper-class black congregation which left
the emotional black tradition and joined the Congregationalist
denomination.

* Betts, George H. THE BELIEFS OF 700 MINISTERS. Cited above as item
  1937.

* Demerath, Nicholas J., III. SOCIAL CLASS IN AMERICAN PROTESTANTISM.
  Cited above as item 2036.

* Finke, Roger, and Rodney Stark. "How the Upstart Sects Won America:
  1776-1850." Cited above as item 1369.

2110. Fukuyama, Yoshio. "The Major Dimensions of Church Membership." RRR
  2 (1961): 154-161.

  Class differences among each church's members is smaller than in the
  general population. In a study of Congregational churches, positive
  relationships between class and cultic and cognitive dimensions of
  religious involvement occurred, inverse relationships with creedal
  (orthodoxy) and devotional dimensions. "Different social classes differ not so much in the degree to which they are religiously oriented
  but in the manner in which they give expression to their religious
  propensities." (p. 159)

* Glock, Charles Y., and Rodney Stark. RELIGION AND SOCIETY IN TENSION.
  Cited above as item 1118.

* Glock, Charles Y., and Rodney Stark. CHRISTIAN BELIEFS AND ANTI-
  SEMITISM. Cited above as item 1119.

2111. Goode, Erich. "Class Styles of Religious Sociation." THE BRITISH
  JOURNAL OF SOCIOLOGY 19,1 (1968): 1-16.

  1957 questionnaire data from northern U.S. church members; Congregational subsample.

2112. Goode, Erich. SOCIAL CLASS AND CHURCH PARTICIPATION. New York: Arno,
  1980.

  Two data bases are used in the study - a general survey carried out in
  Appalachia in 1959, and a 1956-59 questionnaire study of the members
  of metropolitan Congregationalist churches in various localities
  throughout the U.S.A.

2113. Hammond, Phillip E. THE ROLE OF IDEOLOGY IN CHURCH PARTICIPATION.
  New York: Arno Press, 1980.

  1956 questionnaire data from a survey of American church members.

* Laumann, Edward O. "The Social Structure of Religious and Ethnoreligious Groups in a Metropolitan Community." Cited above as item 469.

* Mitchell, Robert E. MINISTER-PARISHIONER RELATIONS. Cited above as
  item 1950.

* Mitchell, Robert E. "Polity, Church Attractiveness, and Ministers' Careers." Cited above as item 1951.

2114. Nash, Dennison, and Peter L. Berger. "Church Commitment in an American Suburb: An Analysis of the Decision to Join." ARCHIVES DE SOCIOLOGIE DES RELIGIONS 13 (1962): 105-120.

A study of joiners of three Congregational churches in a suburban community adjacent to Hartford, Connecticut.

2115. Nash, Dennison, and Peter L. Berger. "The Child, the Family, and the Religious Revival in Suburbia." JSSR 2,1 (1962): 85-93.

1960 data from three churches in a Hartford, Connecticut, suburb.

* Norr, James L. "Religion and Nation Building: The American Case." Cited above as item 1304.

2116. Pangborn, Cyrus R. FREE CHURCHES AND SOCIAL CHANGE. A CRITICAL STUDY OF THE COUNCIL FOR SOCIAL ACTION OF THE CONGREGATIONAL CHURCHES OF THE UNITED STATES. Unpublished Ph.D. dissertation, Columbia University, 1951. [DA 11:4, p. 1125]

* Patrick, John W. "Personal Faith and the Fear of Death among Divergent Religious Populations." Cited above as item 180.

* Roof, Wade Clark. "Socioeconomic Differentials among White Socioreligious Groups in the United States." Cited above as item 501.

* Smith, Luke. "The Clergy: Authority Structure, Ideology, Migration." Cited above as item 1959.

* Steinberg, Stephen. "The Changing Religious Composition of American Higher Education." Cited above as item 518.


## PRESBYTERIAN (U.S.A.)

* Allinsmith, Wesley, and Beverly Allinsmith. "Religious Affiliation and Politico-economic Attitude." Cited above as item 404.

* Demerath, Nicholas J., III. SOCIAL CLASS IN AMERICAN PROTESTANTISM. Cited above as item 2036.

2117. Dornbusch, Sanford M., and Roger Irle. "The Failure of Presbyterian Union." AMERICAN JOURNAL OF SOCIOLOGY 64,4 (1959): 352-356.

Doctrinal rather than social issues prevented an attempt at union.

2118. Earle, Clifford J. "How Presbyterians Think about Civil Rights." SOCIAL PROGRESS 59 (1969): 5-35.

* Finke, Roger, and Rodney Stark. "How the Upstart Sects Won America: 1776-1850." Cited above as item 1369.

* Gockel, Galen L. "Income and Religious Affiliation: A Regression Analysis." Cited above as item 437.

2119. Hadden, Jeffrey K., and Charles F. Longino, Jr. GIDEON'S GANG: A CASE STUDY OF THE CHURCH IN SOCIAL ACTION. Philadelphia: Pilgrim Press from the United Church Press, 1974.

A case study from Dayton, Ohio.

2120. Hargrove, Barbara W. "Local Congregations and Social Change." SA 30,1 (1969): 13-22.

Discusses local variations in support for social activism.

2121. Hoge, Dean R., and Jeffrey L. Faue. "Sources of Conflict over Priorities of the Protestant Church." SOCIAL FORCES 52,2 (1973): 178-194.

Conflicts are greatest over the type and importance of church missions and outreach; there is little conflict over congregational life, religious education, or spiritual nurture. Based on surveys of lay people, ministers, and seminary seniors.

* Hoge, Dean R., Esther Heffernan, Eugene F. Hemrick, Hart M. Nelsen, James P. O'Connor, Paul J. Philibert, and Andrew D. Thompson. "Desired Outcomes of Religious Education and Youth Ministry in Six Denominations." Cited above as item 1387.

2122. Ingram, Larry C. "Sectarian Colleges and Academic Freedom." RRR 27,4 (1986): 300-314.

Examination of official policies of six undergraduate colleges - two affiliated with the Tennessee Baptist Convention (Southern Baptist), one with the United Presbyterian Church, one with the Presbyterian Church in the U.S., and two with the Churches of Christ. In the text of the article, the two Presbyterian colleges are simply labeled 'Presbyterian.'

* Laumann, Edward O. "The Social Structure of Religious and Ethno-religious Groups in a Metropolitan Community." Cited above as item 469.

* Lazerwitz, Bernard. "Religion and Social Structure in the United States." Cited above as item 471.

2123. Lee, Robert, and Russell Galloway. THE SCHIZOPHRENIC CHURCH: CONFLICT OVER COMMUNITY ORGANIZATION. Philadelphia: Westminster, 1969.

* Lenski, Gerhard. "Social Correlates of Religious Interest." Cited above as item 1946.

* Maranell, Gary M. RESPONSES TO RELIGION. STUDIES IN THE SOCIAL PSYCHOLOGY OF RELIGIOUS BELIEF. Cited above as item 1294.

* Mitchell, Robert E. "Polity, Church Attractiveness, and Ministers' Careers." Cited above as item 1951.

270

* Mueller, Charles W. "Evidence on the Relationship between Religion and Educational Attainment." Cited above as item 490.

2124. Nelsen, Hart M. "Sectarianism, World View and Anomie." SOCIAL FORCES 51,2 (1972): 226-233.

Sectarianism derives not from economic deprivation but rather from a world view formed by individuals who are from the lower classes and rural areas and who have low levels of reading. (All data from Southern Appalachian Presbyterians.)

* Norr, James L. "Religion and Nation Building: The American Case." Cited above as item 1304.

* Perrin, Robin D. "American Religion in the Post-aquarian Age: Values and Demographic Factors in Church Growth and Decline." Cited above as item 1409.

2125. Perry, Everett L., and Dean R. Hoge. "Faith Priorities of Pastor and Laity as a Factor in the Growth or Decline of Presbyterian Congregations." RRR 22,3 (1981): 221-232.

Faith and theological priorities did not correlate strongly with congregational growth patterns.

* Philibert, Paul J., and Dean R. Hoge. "Teachers, Pedagogy and the Process of Religious Education." Cited above as item 1413.

* Roof, Wade Clark. "Socioeconomic Differentials among White Socioreligious Groups in the United States." Cited above as item 501.

* Scherer, Ross P. "A New Typology for Organizations: Market, Bureaucracy, Clan and Mission, with Application to American Denominations." Cited above as item 1416.

* Spaulding, Kent E. "The Theology of the Pew." Cited above as item 832.

* Steinberg, Stephen. "The Changing Religious Composition of American Higher Education." Cited above as item 518.

* Terian, Sarah M.K. THE OTHER SIDE OF GOOD SAMARITANISM: THE HELPING ETHIC IN JUDEO-CHRISTIAN IDEOLOGY AND PRACTICE. Cited above as item 1422.

* Warren, Bruce L. "Socioeconomic Achievement and Religion: The American Case." Cited above as item 522.


UNITED PRESBYTERIAN CHURCH (U.S.A.)

* Broughton, Walter, and Edgar W. Mills, Jr. "Resource Inequality and Accumulative Advantage: Stratification in the Ministry." Cited above as item 1939.

* Demerath, Nicholas J., III. SOCIAL CLASS IN AMERICAN PROTESTANTISM.
Cited above as item 2036.

2126. Hadaway, Christopher K. "Conservatism and Social Strength in a
Liberal Denomination." RRR 21,3 (1980): 302-314.

A 1975 survey of 681 United Presbyterian churches reveals that conservatism is mostly unrelated to their growth patterns.

* Hadden, Jeffrey K. THE GATHERING STORM IN THE CHURCHES. A SOCIOLOGIST
LOOKS AT THE WIDENING GAP BETWEEN CLERGY AND LAYMEN. Cited above as
item 1942.

* Hartley, Shirley F., and Mary G. Taylor. "Religious Beliefs of Clergy
Wives." Cited above as item 1944.

2127. Hoge, Dean R. "Theological Views of America among Protestants." SA
37,2 (1976): 127-139.

Based on a 1973 sample of United Presbyterian clergy and lay people.

* Hoge, Dean R., and John E. Dyble. "The Influence of Assimilation on
American Protestant Ministers' Beliefs, 1928-1978." Cited above as
item 1945.

2128. Hoge, Dean R., Everett L. Perry, and Gerald L. Klever. "Theology as a
Source of Disagreement about Protestant Church Goals and Priorities."
RRR 19,2 (1978): 116-138.

Survey data from Presbyterian ministers and laity show general agreement that highest priority should be given to congregational 'nurture'
goals such as preaching, fellowship, religious education, spiritual
guidance, and counseling. Disagreement arises over the importance and
proper forms of mission and outreach outside the membership. The main
disagreement concerns the relative emphases that should be accorded
evangelism and social involvement.

2129. Lehman, Edward C., Jr. WOMEN CLERGY. BREAKING THROUGH GENDER BARRIERS.
New Brunswick, N.J.: Transaction Books, 1985.

* Longino, Charles F., Jr., and Jeffrey K. Hadden. "Dimensionality of
Belief among Mainstream Protestant Clergy." Cited above as item
1948.

2130. McGaw, Douglas B. CONGREGATION AND RELIGIOUS COMMITMENT: A COMPARA-
TIVE STUDY OF RELIGIOUS MEANING AND BELONGING. Unpublished Ph.D.
dissertation, University of Massachusetts, 1977. [DA 38:6 A, p. 3743]

Participant-observation, interview, and questionnaire data from two
New England congregations, one charismatic and one mainstream.

2131. McGaw, Douglas B. "Commitment and Religious Community: A Comparison
of a Charismatic and a Mainline Congregation." JSSR 18,2 (1979): 146-
163.

The charismatic congregation has stronger commitment; it is more effective at providing meaning and belonging to its members through stronger closure, strictness, consensus on authority, and cohesion.

2132. McGaw, Douglas B. "Meaning and Belonging in a Charismatic Congregation: An Investigation into Sources of Neo-pentecostal Success." RRR 21,3 (1980): 284-301.

Belonging is found to be as important as meaning.

2133. McGaw, Douglas B., and Elliott Wright. A TALE OF TWO CONGREGATIONS. COMMITMENT AND SOCIAL STRUCTURE IN A CHARISMATIC AND MAINLINE CONGREGATION. Hartford: Hartford Seminary Foundation, 1981.

2134. Mills, Edgar W. "Career Change in the Protestant Ministry." MINISTRY STUDIES 3,1 (1969): 5-21.

1964 interviews with active or former clergy, who had moved since January 1958.

 * Mitchell, Robert E. "Polity, Church Attractiveness, and Ministers' Careers." Cited above as item 1951.

2135. Nelsen, Hart M., and Raytha L. Yokley. "Civil Rights Attitudes of Rural and Urban Presbyterians." RURAL SOCIOLOGY 35,2 (1970): 161-174.

1967 questionnaire data from ministers and elders from 151 presbyteries.

2136. Nelsen, Hart M., and Raytha L. Yokley. "Presbyterians, Civil Rights and Church Pronouncements." RRR 12,1 (1970): 43-50.

Analyzes the civil rights attitudes of a sample of elders.

 * Quinley, Harold E. THE PROPHETIC CLERGY. SOCIAL ACTIVISM AMONG PROTESTANT MINISTERS. Cited above as item 1953.

2137. Roof, Wade Clark, Dean R. Hoge, John E. Dyble, and C. Kirk Hadaway. "Factors Producing Growth or Decline in United Presbyterian Congregations." In Dean R. Hoge and David A. Roozen (eds.), UNDERSTANDING CHURCH GROWTH AND DECLINE 1950-78. New York: Pilgrim Press, 1979, pp. 198-223.

National data on congregations for 1968-74, focusing on growth and decline of congregations; purpose sampling design.

 * Royle, Marjorie H. "Women Pastors. What happens after Placement?" Cited above as item 2062.

 * Stark, Rodney, Bruce D. Foster, Charles Y. Glock, and Harold E. Quinley. WAYWARD SHEPHERDS: PREJUDICE AND THE PROTESTANT CLERGY. Cited above as item 1960.

2138. Taylor, Mary G. AUTHORITY AND COMPLIANCE IN A NORMATIVE ORGANIZATION: A STUDY OF THE SAN FRANCISCO PRESBYTERY. Unpublished Ph.D. dissertation, University of California, Berkeley, 1969. [DA 31:4 A, p. 1910]

Focuses on specific involvements in social action programs in the San Francisco Presbytery.

2139. Taylor, Mary G.  "Two Models of Social Reform Action in a Normative Organization."  SA 36,2 (1975): 161-167.

The denominational model used corporate power, expert reform leaders, and dedication to structural change and standardized action.  The congregational model stressed ad hoc voluntary groups, lay participation, individual change, and a 'cafeteria' approach to reform.

2140. Warner, R. Stephen.  "Visits to a Growing Evangelical and a Declining Liberal Church in 1978."  SA 44,3 (1983): 243-254.

Focuses on theological differences, other factors having been controlled.


## REFORMED CHURCH IN AMERICA

2141. Bouma, Gary D.  "The Real Reason One Conservative Church Grew."  RRR 20,2 (1979): 127-137.

Compares the growth rate of the Christian Reformed Church with that of the Reformed Church in America.  The higher growth rate of the CRC is explained by immigration patterns and high fertility rates.  Moreover, the high level of commitment demanded by the CRC promotes retention of membership.

   * Lenski, Gerhard.  "Social Correlates of Religious Interest."  Cited above as item 1946.

2142. Luidens, Donald.  ORGANIZATIONAL GOALS, POWER, AND EFFECTIVENESS: DESIRES AND PERCEPTIONS IN A PROTESTANT DENOMINATION; AN EMPIRICAL STUDY IN THE SOCIAL PSYCHOLOGY OF FORMAL ORGANIZATIONS.  Unpublished Ph.D. dissertation, Rutgers University, 1978.  [DA 39:2 A, p. 1115]

A systems study, using questionnaire data from laity, clergy, governing boards, and national staff.

2143. Luidens, Donald.  "Comments on Hoge's 'Free Will Behavior Index'."  RRR 20,2 (1979): 214-218.

2144. Luidens, Donald.  "Bureaucratic Control in a Protestant Denomination."  JSSR 21,2 (1982): 163-175.

2145. Luidens, Donald, and Roger J. Nemeth.  "'Public' and 'Private' Protestantism Reconsidered: Introducing the 'Loyalists'."  JSSR 26,4 (1987): 450-464.

The private party, interested in personal salvation, and the public party, interested in social ethics, are familiar.  The loyalists are interested in the denomination, its tradition, and its congregations.

2146. Nemeth, Roger J., and Donald Luidens.  "The New Christian Right and

Mainline Protestantism: The Case of the Reformed Church in America."
SA 49,4 (1989): 343-352.

1986 Reformed Church in America sample; questionnaire data.

## CHRISTIAN REFORMED CHURCH (U.S.A.)

2147. Bouma, Donald H. "Religious Mixed Marriages: Denominational Consequences in the Christian Reformed Church." MARRIAGE AND FAMILY LIVING
25,4 (1963): 428-432.

The denomination opposes religiously mixed marriages, but grows
because of them. Study focuses on a two-year period.

* Bouma, Gary D. "The Real Reason One Conservative Church Grew." Cited
above as item 2141.

2148. Bouma, Gary D. "Keeping the Faithful: Patterns of Membership Retention in the Christian Reformed Church." SA 41,3 (1980): 259-264.

People leave the Christian Reformed Church because they find its
community too demanding, constricting, and intolerant. Those who stay
cite commitment to its conservative Calvinist theology and worship as
their primary reasons; they also mention the positive importance of
the church community to them.

2149. Bouma, Gary D. HOW THE SAINTS PERSEVERE: SOCIAL FACTORS IN THE
VITALITY OF THE CHRISTIAN REFORMED CHURCH. Clayton, Victoria, Australia: Monash University, Department of Anthropology and Sociology,
1984.

Includes items 2141 and 2148 as well as related material.

2150. Huizenga, Bartel N. "Home Missions and Tension Management in the
Christian Reformed Church." Unpublished M.A. thesis, University of
New Mexico, 1970.

* Vogler, Conrad C. BESIDE THE STILL WATER. Cited above as item 2083.

## DUTCH REFORMED, GERMAN REFORMED (U.S.A.)

* Mol, J.J. (Hans) THE BREAKING OF TRADITIONS: THEOLOGICAL CONVICTIONS
IN COLONIAL AMERICA. Cited above as item 2049.

* Norr, James L. "Religion and Nation Building: The American Case."
Cited above as item 1304.

# 16
## Anabaptist

*ANABAPTIST (GENERAL AND HISTORICAL)*

2151. Driedger, Leo. "The Anabaptist Identification Ladder: Plain-urbane Continuity in Diversity." MENNONITE QUARTERLY REVIEW 51 (1977): 278-291.

Discusses processes of boundary maintenance in the context of the following: Old Order Amish, Old Colony Mennonites, and urban Mennonites.

2152. Kniss, Fred. "Toward a Theory of Ideological Change: The Case of the Radical Reformation." SA 49,1 (1988): 29-38.

Argues that ideology as an independent variable cannot be neglected; application of theories of ideological change to early Anabaptist history.

* Lewy, Guenter. RELIGION AND REVOLUTION. Cited above as item 34.

2153. Peachey, Paul. DIE SOZIALE HERKUNFT DER SCHWEIZER TAUFER IN DER REFORMATIONSZEIT. Karlsruhe: Heinrich Schneider, 1954.

Discusses the history, as well as the social and occupational structure, of the sixteenth-century Swiss Anabaptists. (Appendix contains detailed data on the occupations of Taufer individuals.)

2154. Rammstedt, Otthein. SEKTE UND SOZIALE BEWEGUNG. SOZIOLOGISCHE ANALYSE DER TÄUFER IN MÜNSTER (1534-1535). DORTMUNDER SCHRIFTEN ZUR SOZIAL-FORSCHUNG, BD. 34. Köln and Opladen: Westdeutscher Verlag, 1966.

2155. Séguy, Jean. "Problèmes historiques et sociologiques de l'anabaptisme." ARCHIVES DE SOCIOLOGIE DES RELIGIONS 7 (1959): 105-115.

2156. Séguy, Jean. "Religion et réussite agricole. La vie professionnelle des anabaptists français du XVIIe au XIXe siècle." ARCHIVES DE SOCIOLOGIE DES RELIGIONS 28 (1969): 93-130.

2157. Séguy, Jean. LES ASSEMBLEES ANABAPTISTES-MENNONITES DE FRANCE. Paris et La Haye: Mouton, 1977.

2158. Barclay, Harold B.  "The Plain People of Oregon."  RRR 8 (1967): 140–165.

An analysis of the survival mechanisms employed in Oregon by the following groups:  Church of God in Christ (Mennonite), Old Order Amish, Unaffiliated Conservative Amish Mennonites, and Old German Baptist Brethren.

2159. Billings, Thomas A.  THE OLD ORDER AMISH VS. THE COMPULSORY SCHOOL ATTENDANCE LAWS: AN ANALYSIS OF CONFLICT.  Unpublished Ph.D. dissertation, University of Oregon, 1961.

2160. Buck, Roy C.  "Boundary Maintenance Revisited: Tourist Experience in an Old Amish Community."  RURAL SOCIOLOGY 43,2 (1978): 221–234.

1976 participant-observation study in Lancaster County, Pennsylvania, of both the Amish and tourists.

2161. Ediger, Marlow.  "Amish Adaptations to Modern Society: Technical, Medical and Legal."  SOCIOLOGY AND SOCIAL RESEARCH 70,4 (1986): 286.

Observations in rural Iowa and Ohio.

2162. Hostetler, John A.  THE AMISH FAMILY IN MIFFLIN COUNTY, PENNSYLVANIA. Unpublished M.S. thesis, Pennsylvania State College, 1951.

2163. Hostetler, John A.  "Old World Extinction and New World Survival of the Amish: A Study of Group Maintenance and Dissolution."  RURAL SOCIOLOGY 20,3–4 (1955): 212–219.

Historical review, from Swiss origins in the 1690s to twentieth-century U.S.A.

2164. Huntington, A.G.E.  THE OLD ORDER AMISH IN OHIO.  Unpublished Ph.D. dissertation, Yale University, 1957.

2165. Kollmorgen, Walter M.  "The Agricultural Stability of the Old Order Amish and the Old Order Mennonites of Lancaster County, Pennsylvania." AMERICAN JOURNAL OF SOCIOLOGY 49,3 (1943): 233–241.

Argues that their conviction of worldly isolation is largely responsible for their stability.

2166. Olshan, Marc A.  "Family Life: An Old Order Amish Manifesto."  In D.L. Thomas (ed.), THE RELIGION AND FAMILY CONNECTION [volume cited in item 414], pp. 143–160.

Content analysis of letters, 1971–81, appearing in an Amish publication.

2167. Quinlan, Patrick T.  "Solidarity among the Amish."  AMERICAN JOURNAL OF ECONOMICS AND SOCIOLOGY 6,4 (1947): 561–563.

A general description of Amish in the U.S.A.

2168. Schwieder, Elmer, and Dorothy Schwieder. A PECULIAR PEOPLE: IOWA'S OLD ORDER AMISH. Davenport: Iowa State University Press, 1975.

2169. Smith, Elmer L. A STUDY OF ACCULTURATION IN AN AMISH COMMUNITY. Unpublished Ph.D. dissertation, Syracuse University, 1955. [DA 16:1526]

Examination of contemporary Amish in the light of the history of Amish values.

2170. Smith, Elmer L. "Personality Differences between Amish and Non-Amish Children." RURAL SOCIOLOGY 23,4 (1958): 371-376.

Personality inventory instrument administered to seventh and eighth-graders in two rural schools in southeastern Pennsylvania.


*HUTTERITE*

2171. Bennett, John W. HUTTERIAN BRETHREN. Stanford, California: Stanford University Press, 1967.

Pages 34-52 are a discussion of basic Hutterian beliefs and their relationship to social structure.

2172. Bennett, John W. "The Hutterites: A Communal Sect." In J.W. Bennett, PLAINS PEOPLE: ADAPTIVE STRATEGY AND AGRARIAN LIFE IN THE GREAT PLAINS. Chicago: Aldine, 1969. Reprinted in J.L. Elliott (ed.), IMMIGRANT GROUPS [volume cited in item 314], pp. 15-32; and in S. Crysdale and L. Wheatcroft (eds.), RELIGION IN CANADIAN SOCIETY [volume cited in item 316], pp. 256-267.

Discusses the history, beliefs, social organization, and environmental relations of the Hutterite colonies in the 'Jasper' region of Saskatchewan.

2173. Boldt, Edward D. CONVENTIONALITY AND ACQUIESCENCE IN A COMMUNAL SOCIETY. Unpublished Ph.D. dissertation, University of Alberta, 1969.

Mennonites but not Hutterites had a greater tendency to acquiesce than subjects from a 'worldly' control group, and the hypothesis that Gemeinschaft reduces deviance through the production of acquiescent personalities is challenged.

2174. Conkin, P.K. TWO PATHS TO UTOPIA: THE HUTTERITES AND THE LLANO COLONY. Lincoln: University of Nebraska Press, 1964.

2175. Deets, Lee E. THE HUTTERITES: A STUDY IN SOCIAL COHESION. Gettysburg, Pennsylvania: Times and News Publishing, 1939.

2176. Desroche, Henri. "Les communautés huttériennes." ARCHIVES INTERNATIONALES DE LA SOCIOLOGIE DE LA COOPERATION ET DU DEVELOPPEMENT 1 (1953): 13-21.

2177. Desroche, Henri. "Mesures des fraternités huttériennes en 1950." ARCHIVES INTERNATIONALES DE LA SOCIOLOGIE DE LA COOPERATION ET DU

DEVELOPPEMENT 2 (1954): 63-66.

2178. Frideres, James S. "The Death of Hutterite Culture." PHYLON 33,3 (1972): 260-265. See also Karl A. Peter, "The Death of Hutterite Culture: A Rejoinder." PHYLON 40 (1979): 189-194.

The policies of some Canadian provinces apparently are undermining Hutterian distinctiveness.

2179. Hostetler, John A. HUTTERITE SOCIETY. Baltimore: John Hopkins University Press, 1974.

2180. Mackie, Marlene M. "Defection from Hutterite Colonies." In Robert M. Pike and Elia Zureik (eds.), SOCIALIZATION AND VALUES IN CANADIAN SOCIETY, volume 2. Toronto: McClelland and Stewart, 1975, pp. 291-316.

1965 interview data from Hutterite defectors living in Canada and the U.S.A.; background data, reasons for defection, adjustment.

2181. Peter, Karl A. "The Certainty of Salvation: Ritualization of Religion and Economic Rationality among Hutterites." COMPARATIVE STUDIES IN SOCIETY AND HISTORY 25,2 (1983): 222-240.

The ideal interests of the Hutterites became traditionalized while their material interests underwent a process of rationalization.

2182. Peter, Karl A. THE DYNAMICS OF HUTTERITE SOCIETY. Edmonton: University of Alberta Press, 1987.

2183. Peter, Karl A., Edward D. Boldt, Ian Whitaker, and Lance W. Roberts. "The Dynamics of Religious Defection among Hutterites." JSSR 21,4 (1982): 327-337.

Some recent Hutterite defectors have been attracted to the personalized individualism of evangelical Protestantism.

2184. Pickering, W.S.F. "Hutterites and Problems of Persistence and Social Control in Religious Communities." ARCHIVES DE SCIENCES SOCIALES DES RELIGIONS 44,1 (1977): 75-92.

A functionalist approach which assesses the prospects for future success of the Hutterites.


*MENNONITE (RUSSIA, FRANCE)*

2185. Francis, E.K. "The Russian Mennonites: From Religious to Ethnic Group." AMERICAN JOURNAL OF SOCIOLOGY 54,2 (1948): 101-107.

Historical sociology of those Mennonites whose Dutch ancestors migrated to Germany and then Russia, before coming to North America, all the while preserving their ethnic identity.

2186. Froese, Leonhard. DAS PÄDAGOGISCHE KULTURSYSTEM DER MENNONITISCHEN

SIEDLUNGSGRUPPE IN RUSSLAND. Unpublished Ph.D. dissertation, University of Göttingen, 1949.

2187. Raphaël, Freddy, and J. Mathias. "Représentation de la pérennité et du changement chez les Mennonites de l'est de la France." REVUE DES SCIENCES SOCIALES DE LA FRANCE DE L'EST 13 (1984): 249-266.

* Séguy, Jean. LES ASSEMBLEES ANABAPTISTES-MENNONITES DE FRANCE. Cited above as item 2157.


## MENNONITE (LATIN AMERICA)

2188. Driedger, Leo. "From Mexico to British Honduras." MENNONITE LIFE 13,4 (1958): 160-166.

A colony which had moved from Manitoba and Saskatchewan to Chihuahua and Durango states, Mexico, 1921-24, was moving to British Honduras in 1958, with a few families going to Honduras. The Mennonites involved were Kleine Gemeinde and Old Colony.

2189. Fretz, J. Winfield. MENNONITE COLONIZATION IN MEXICO. Akron, Pennsylvania: Mennonite Central Committee, 1945.

2190. Fretz, J. Winfield. PILGRIMS IN PARAGUAY. Scottdale, Pennsylvania: Herald Press, 1953.

2191. Hack, D.H. DIE KOLONISATION DER MENNONITEN IM PARAGUAYISCHEN CHACO. Unpublished Ph.D. dissertation, University of Amsterdam, 1961.

2192. Kliewer, Fritz. "Die Mennoniten in Brasilien." STADEN-JAHRBUCH 5 (1957): 233-246.

Overview of the religion and its Brazilian settlements, beginning in 1930.

2193. Krause, Annemarie E. MENNONITE SETTLEMENTS IN THE PARAGUAYAN CHACO. Unpublished Ph.D. dissertation, University of Chicago, 1952.

2194. Sotero Giando, Rodolfo. RESULTADOS DE LA COLONIZACION EXTRANJERA EN MEXICO; LA COLONIZACION MENONITA EN CHIHUAHUA. Unpublished Ph.D. dissertation, University of Mexico (Mexico City), 1956.


## MENNONITE (NORTH AMERICA)

2195. Anderson, Alan, and Leo Driedger. "The Mennonite Family: Culture and Kin in Rural Saskatchewan." In K. Ishwaran (ed.), CANADIAN FAMILIES: ETHNIC VARIATIONS. Toronto: McGraw-Hill Ryerson, 1980, pp. 161-180.

Longitudinal community study, 1955-77 by Driedger; 1969-71 sample survey of 18 group settlements in north-central Saskatchewan, including two Mennonite, by Anderson. Focus is on strength of identity, church attendance, language and custom retention.

\* Barclay, Harold B.  "The Plain People of Oregon."  Cited above as item 2158.

2196. Barclay, Harold B.  "The Protestant Ethic versus the Spirit of Capitalism."  RRR 10,3 (1969): 151-158.

The Holdeman Mennonites, as indicated by the group at Linden, Alberta, encourage individual private enterprise, yet stifle the evolution of any complex, corporate system out of such enterprise.

2197. Bergen, John, and David Friesen.  "Changing Attitudes of Mennonite University Students."  MENNONITE LIFE 23,4 (1968): 169-172.

What do Mennonite university students believe and how do they view their Mennonite background?

\* Boldt, Edward D.  CONVENTIONALITY AND ACQUIESCENCE IN A COMMUNAL SOCIETY.  Cited above as item 2173.

2198. Chesebro, Scott E.  THE MENNONITE URBAN COMMUNE: A HERMENEUTIC-DIALECTICAL UNDERSTANDING OF ITS ANABAPTIST IDEOLOGY AND PRACTICE.  Unpublished Ph.D. dissertation, University of Notre Dame, 1982.  [DA 43:6 A, p. 2125]

Study of the Fellowship of Hope commune.

2199. Driedger, Leo.  A SECT IN MODERN SOCIETY. THE OLD COLONY MENNONITES OF SASKATCHEWAN.  Unpublished M.A. thesis, University of Chicago, 1955.

2200. Driedger, Leo.  "Development in Higher Education among Mennonites in Manitoba."  MANITOBA JOURNAL OF EDUCATIONAL RESEARCH 3 (1967): 24-34.

2201. Driedger, Leo.  "A Perspective on Canadian Mennonite Urbanization."  MENNONITE LIFE 23,4 (1968): 147-151.

Suggests that new forms of community may be emerging among urban Mennonites in Canada.

2202. Driedger, Leo.  "Urbanization of Mennonites in Canada."  In Henry Poettcker and Rudy Regehr (eds.), CALL TO FAITHFULNESS: ESSAYS IN CANADIAN MENNONITE STUDIES.  Altona, Manitoba: D.W. Friesen, 1972, pp. 143-155.

Discusses social changes from rural to urban patterns, and their effect on community solidarity.

2203. Driedger, Leo.  "Native Rebellion and Mennonite Invasion: A Focus on Two Canadian River Valleys."  MENNONITE QUARTERLY REVIEW 46,3 (1972): 290-300.

Examines the Mennonite settlements of the Red River Valley (1869-74) and the Saskatchewan River Valley (1884-95).

2204. Driedger, Leo.  "Canadian Mennonite Urbanism: Ethnic Villagers or Metropolitan Remnant?"  MENNONITE QUARTERLY REVIEW 49,3 (1975): 226-241.

1961-71 census data; Winnipeg student data on ethnic identity strength
and social distance.

2205. Driedger, Leo. "Mennonite Change: The Old Colony Revisited, 1955-
1977." MENNONITE LIFE 32,4 (1977): 4-12.

A follow-up study to item 2199.

2206. Driedger, Leo. "Fifty Years of Mennonite Identity in Winnipeg: A
Sacred Canopy in a Changing Laboratory." In Harry Loewen (ed.),
MENNONITE IMAGES: HISTORICAL, CULTURAL, AND LITERARY ESSAYS DEALING
WITH MENNONITE ISSUES. Winnipeg: Hyperion Press, 1980.

2207. Driedger, Leo. "Individual Freedom vs. Community Control: An Adaptation of Erikson's Ontogeny of Ritualization." JSSR 21,3 (1982): 226-
242.

Use of a modified version of Erik Erikson's six-stage ontogeny of
ritualization, to interpret the case of Johann Driedger, who tested
the boundaries of an Old Colony Mennonite community.

2208. Driedger, Leo. "Community Change: From Ethnic Enclaves to Social
Networks." MENNONITE QUARTERLY REVIEW 60,3 (1986): 374-386.

2209. Driedger, Leo. MENNONITE IDENTITY IN CONFLICT. Lewiston, New York:
Edwin Mellen Press, 1988.

2210. Driedger, Leo, and J. Howard Kauffman. "Urbanization of Mennonites:
Canadian and American Comparisons." MENNONITE QUARTERLY REVIEW 56,3
(1982): 269-290.

1972 questionnaire data from a five-Mennonite denomination survey,
Canada and the U.S.A.

2211. Driedger, Leo, and Jacob Peters. "Ethnic Identity among Mennonite and
Other Students of German Heritage." In S. Crysdale and L. Wheatcroft
(eds.), RELIGION IN CANADIAN SOCIETY [volume cited in item 316], pp.
449-461.

Abridged from MENNONITE QUARTERLY REVIEW 47,3 (1973). Sample of ethnic
German students at the University of Manitoba, circa 1972.

2212. Driedger, Leo, Raymond Currie, and Rick Linden. "Dualistic and Wholis-
tic Views of God and the World: Consequences for Social Action." RRR
24,3 (1983): 225-244.

Study of Canadian Mennonites reveals that 'wholists,' in comparison
with 'dualists,' are more this-worldly and more liberal with regard to
personal morality, community control, and minority rights.

2213. Driedger, Leo, J. Winfield Fretz, and Donovan E. Smucker. "A Tale of
Two Strategies: Mennonites in Chicago and Winnipeg." MENNONITE QUAR-
TERLY REVIEW 52,4 (1978): 294-311.

Profile of Mennonite churches in Chicago, 1893-1940; comparisons with
Winnipeg; note on Chicago Mennonites in 1977.

2214. Driedger, Leo, Roy Vogt, and Mavis Reimer. "Mennonite Intermarriage: National, Regional and Intergenerational Trends." MENNONITE QUARTERLY REVIEW 57,2 (1983): 132-144.

Based on 1921-81 Canadian census data; 1977 Mennonite church survey data (Canada).

2215. Francis, E.K. IN SEARCH OF UTOPIA. THE MENNONITES IN MANITOBA. Altona, Manitoba: D.W. Friesen, 1955; Glencoe, Illinois: Free Press, 1955.

2216. Fretz, J. Winfield. MENNONITE MUTUAL AID. Unpublished Ph.D. dissertation, University of Chicago, 1941.

2217. Gaede, Stan. "A Causal Model of Belief-orthodoxy: Proposal and Empirical Test." SA 37,3 (1976): 205-217.

Based on data from five Mennonite denominations in North America. Age, education, and primary and secondary interaction (communal involvement) are all significant predictors of belief-orthodoxy.

2218. Gaede, Stan. "Religious Participation, Socioeconomic Status, and Belief-orthodoxy." JSSR 16,3 (1977): 245-253.

Secondary analysis of data from male, non-student North American Mennonites from five denominations. The relationship between socioeconomic status and religious participation may be due to educational rather than economic factors. Zero-order correlation between orthodoxy of belief and religious participation is probably not spurious. Belief-orthodoxy acts as a suppressor of the education/religious participation relationship.

2219. Hamm, Peter M. CONTINUITY AND CHANGE AMONG CANADIAN MENNONITE BRETHREN. Waterloo, Ontario: Wilfrid Laurier University Press, 1987.

1972 survey data: Mennonite Brethren subsample, and a review of denominational literature.

2220. Harder, Leland D. THE QUEST FOR EQUILIBRIUM IN AN ESTABLISHED SECT: A STUDY OF SOCIAL CHANGE IN THE GENERAL CONFERENCE MENNONITE CHURCH. Unpublished Ph.D. dissertation, Northwestern University, 1962. [DA 23:9, p. 3516]

Historical sociology, from the organization of the General Conference denomination in 1860.

2221. Hilty, Dale M., Rick L. Morgan, and Joan E. Burns. "King and Hunt Revisited: Dimensions of Religious Involvement." JSSR 23,3 (1984): 252-266.

Dimensions of religiosity different from those found by King and Hunt emerged in a Mennonite sample.

2222. Hostetler, John A. THE SOCIOLOGY OF MENNONITE EVANGELISM. Scottdale, Pennsylvania: Herald Press, 1954.

Sample of converts to the Mennonite Church, and of people who had left the church, 1942-51. Additional interviews and field work in Minnesota, Iowa, Indiana, Pennsylvania, Chicago.

2223. Hostetler, John A. "Religious Mobility in a Sect Group: The Mennonite Church." RURAL SOCIOLOGY 19,3 (1954): 245-255.

1942-51 data from pastors of 135 churches, and questionnaire responses from converts and ex-members.

* Hunsberger, Bruce. "Background Religious Denomination, Parental Emphasis, and the Religious Orientation of University Students." Cited above as item 1702.

2224. Just, L. Roy. AN ANALYSIS OF THE SOCIAL DISTANCE REACTION OF STUDENTS FROM THE THREE MAJOR AMERICAN MENNONITE GROUPS. Unpublished Ph.D. dissertation, University of Southern California, 1953.

2225. Kauffman, J. Howard. "Interpersonal Relations in Traditional and Emergent Families among Midwest Mennonites." MARRIAGE AND FAMILY LIVING 23,3 (1961): 247-252.

Questionnaire data from 149 midwestern U.S. Mennonite families.

2226. Kauffman, J. Howard. "Report of Mennonite Sociological Research." MENNONITE QUARTERLY REVIEW 37,2 (1963): 126-131.

Bibliographic report, dissertations, 1928-62.

2227. Kauffman, J. Howard. "Boundary Maintenance and Cultural Assimilation of Contemporary Mennonites." MENNONITE QUARTERLY REVIEW 51,3 (1977): 227-240.

1972 questionnaire data from a survey of five Mennonite denominations (Canada and U.S.A.)

2228. Kauffman, J. Howard. "Social Correlates of Spiritual Maturity among North American Mennonites." SA 40,1 (1979): 27-42.

Data from a 1972 survey of five Mennonite denominations in North America show scores on a spiritual maturity scale correlating positively with age, socio-economic status, rural residence, and sex (females higher).

2229. Kauffman, J. Howard. "Dilemmas of Christian Pacifism within a Historic Peace Church." SA 49,4 (1989): 368-385.

Data from a 1972 survey of five Mennonite denominations in North America.

2230. Kauffman, J. Howard, and Leland Harder. ANABAPTISTS FOUR CENTURIES LATER. Scottdale, Pennsylvania: Herald Press, 1975.

Based on the same data as reported for item 2229.

2231. Kaufman, Edmund G. THE DEVELOPMENT OF THE MISSIONARY AND PHILANTHROPIC

INTEREST AMONG MENNONITES OF NORTH AMERICA. Berne, Indiana: Mennonite Book Concern, 1931.

2232. Kollmorgen, Walter M. "The Agricultural Stability of the Old Order Amish and the Old Order Mennonites of Lancaster County, Pennsylvania." AMERICAN JOURNAL OF SOCIOLOGY 49,3 (1943): 233-241.

Their stability is due to their religious belief in isolation from the world.

2233. Kurokawa, Minako. "Beyond Community Integration and Stability: A Comparative Study of Oriental and Mennonite Children." JOURNAL OF SOCIAL ISSUES 25,1 (1969): 195-213.

Comparison of oriental children in the U.S.A. and Canadian Mennonite children. The author hypothesizes that the extensive social control of these children leaves little room for overt antisocial activities but that the children are not free of covert symptoms of maladjustment. Cultural conflict is said to be related to mental disturbance.

2234. Kurokawa, Minako. "Psycho-social Roles of Mennonite Children in a Changing Society." CANADIAN REVIEW OF SOCIOLOGY AND ANTHROPOLOGY 6,1 (1969): 15-35. Reprinted as "Mennonite Children in Waterloo County," in J.L. Elliott (ed.), IMMIGRANT GROUPS [volume cited in item 314], pp. 33-46.

The focus is on the extent to which a Mennonite identity adversely affects children in their interactions with the larger society.

2235. Lester, Geoffrey A. THE DISTRIBUTION OF RELIGIOUS GROUPS IN ALBERTA, 1961. Unpublished M.A. thesis, University of Alberta, 1966.

An introductory statement of the shape and meaning of Alberta's religious areal patterns in 1961, and related distributions. Alberta was settled by people with a variety of religious backgrounds, and this variety has been expressed ecologically. Religion has been a very potent force in the migration of certain groups into Alberta, notably the Mormons and Mennonites.

2236. Letkeman, Peter. "Mennonites in Vancouver - a Survey." MENNONITE LIFE 23,4 (1968): 160-164.

Examines behavioral patterns of Mennonites in Vancouver.

* Maranell, Gary M. RESPONSES TO RELIGION. STUDIES IN THE SOCIAL PSYCHOLOGY OF RELIGIOUS BELIEF. Cited above as item 1294.

2237. Miller, D. Paul. AN ANALYSIS OF COMMUNITY ADJUSTMENT: A CASE STUDY OF JANSEN, NEBRASKA. Unpublished Ph.D. dissertation, University of Nebraska, 1955.

2238. Pannabecker, Samuel F. THE DEVELOPMENT OF THE GENERAL CONFERENCE OF THE MENNONITE CHURCH OF NORTH AMERICA IN THE AMERICAN ENVIRONMENT. Unpublished Ph.D. dissertation, Yale University, 1944.

2239. Peachey, Paul. "Identity Crisis among American Mennonites." MENNONITE QUARTERLY REVIEW 42,4 (1968): 243-259.

General discussion of the dilemmas brought about by ethnic accultura-tion to American society.

2240. Peters, Frank C. A COMPARISON OF ATTITUDES AND VALUES EXPRESSED BY MENNONITE AND NON-MENNONITE COLLEGE STUDENTS. Unpublished Ph.D. dissertation, University of Kansas, 1959.

2241. Redekop, Calvin. THE SECTARIAN BLACK AND WHITE WORLD (OLD COLONY MENNONITES). Unpublished Ph.D. dissertation, University of Chicago, 1959.

2242. Redekop, Calvin. THE OLD COLONY MENNONITES: DILEMMAS OF MINORITY LIFE. Baltimore: John Hopkins University Press, 1969.

2243. Redekop, Calvin. "A New Look at Sect Development." JSSR 13,3 (1974): 345-352.

What sects become in time is not simply a function of their initial characteristics but the product of an ongoing process of interaction with their environments. The histories of the Old Colony Mennonites and the Mormons are illustrative.

2244. Rushby, William F., and John C. Trush. "Mennonites and Social Compas-sion: The Rokeach Hypothesis Reconsidered." RRR 15,1 (1973): 16-28.

Socially compassionate views and their opposite reflect conventional-ity more than religiosity. Data from a Mennonite college student sample.

2245. Smucker, Joseph. "Religious Community and Individualism: Conceptual Adaptations by One Group of Mennonites." JSSR 25,3 (1986): 273-291.

A study of rural-to-urban migrants in an Ontario city.

2246. Thielman, George T. THE CANADIAN MENNONITES. A STUDY OF AN ETHNIC GROUP IN RELATION TO THE STATE AND COMMUNITY WITH EMPHASIS ON FACTORS CONTRIBUTING TO SUCCESS OR FAILURE OF ITS ADJUSTMENT TO CANADIAN WAYS OF LIVING. Unpublished Ph.D. dissertation, Western Reserve University, 1955.

2247. Urry, James. "Who are the Mennonites?" ARCHIVES EUROPEENNES DE SOCIOLOGIE 24,2 (1983): 241-262.

Historical review. Identity maintenance in Canada is difficult and requires re-invention.

2248. Watts, Clayton R. STUDY OF MENNONITE COMMUNITIES IN WESTERN ONTARIO. Unpublished Ph.D. dissertation, Washington University, 1942.

2249. Wiesel, Barbara B. "From Separation to Evangelism: A Case Study of Social and Cultural Change among the Franconia Conference Mennonites, 1945-1975." RRR 18,3 (1977): 254-263.

# 17
# Baptist

* Goodridge, R.M. "The Religious Condition of the West Country in 1851." Cited above as item 1910.

* Lehman, Edward C., Jr. "The Local/Cosmopolitan Dichotomy and Acceptance of Women Clergy: A Replication." Cited above as item 1915.

* Nason-Clark, Nancy. CLERICAL ATTITUDES TOWARDS APPROPRIATE ROLES FOR WOMEN IN CHURCH AND SOCIETY: AN EMPIRICAL INVESTIGATION OF ANGLICAN, METHODIST AND BAPTIST CLERGY IN SOUTHERN ENGLAND. Cited above as item 1919.

*EUROPE*

2250. Dienel, Peter. "Zwischen Sekte und Kirche. Bericht aus einer Untersuchung freikirchlicher Gemeinden." In D. Goldschmidt, F. Greiner, and H. Schelsky (eds.), SOZIOLOGIE DER KIRCHENGEMEINDE [volume cited in item 1478], pp. 171-179.

2251. Karg, Siegfried. "Initiationsriten und Übergangsriten in der Baptistenkirche. Empirische Ergebnisse." SCHWEIZERISCHE ZEITSCHRIFT FÜR SOZIOLOGIE 11,3 (1985): 581-594.

   Survey data on European Baptists. Infant dedication serves as a functional substitute for infant baptism; most baptisms occur in adolescence. Graduation from religious education is an important rite of passage.

2252. King, Arthur. "Religion and Rights: A Dissenting Minority as a Social Movement in Romania." SC 28,1 (1981): 113-119.

   A protest movement against the Communist Party of Romania, focusing on freedom of religion, was largely Baptist.

*SOVIET UNION*

2253. Klibanov, A.I., and L.N. Mitrokhin. "The Schism in Contemporary Baptism." SC 21,2 (1974): 133-151.

2254. Kowalewski, David. "Religious Protest Outcomes: The Soviet Baptist Case." RRR 22,2 (1980): 198-206.

A study of 40 protest demonstrations reveals that dissident religious groups can attain some degree of control over their political fate by confronting the regime in areas of its weakest ideological and coercive strength and by mobilizing members from many localities.

2255. Zlobin, N.S. "Le baptisme contemporain et son idéologie." ARCHIVES DE SOCIOLOGIE DES RELIGIONS 20 (1965): 97-121.

Laments the threat posed by the Baptist faith to Marxist orthodoxy in the Soviet Union.

*AUSTRALIA, INDIA*

* Mol, J.J. (Hans) "A Collation of Data about Religion in Australia." Cited above as item 308.

2256. Pruett, Gordon E. "Christianity, History, and Culture in Nagaland." CONTRIBUTIONS TO INDIAN SOCIOLOGY 8 (1974): 51-65.

Based on limited 1972 field work and on historical inquiry.

*CANADA*

2257. Christy, Richard D. HIDDEN FACTORS IN RELIGIOUS CONFLICT: A SOCIOLOGICAL ANALYSIS. Unpublished M.A. thesis, University of Waterloo, 1969.

2258. Clark, S.D. "The Religious Sect in Canadian Politics." AMERICAN JOURNAL OF SOCIOLOGY 51,3 (1945): 207-216. Reprinted in S.D. Clark, THE DEVELOPING CANADIAN COMMUNITY. Toronto: University of Toronto Press, 1962, pp. 131-146.

The major contribution of Protestant religion in Canada to the growth of liberal principles has originated not from the philosophies and activities of the mainline churches but the sects out of which the Protestant churches developed. Discussion is confined to the Baptists in Nova Scotia, the Methodists in Upper Canada, and the Bible Prophecy movement led by William Aberhart in Alberta.

2259. Luft, Murray C. "Religious Secularization: A Study of a Contemporary Baptist Church." Unpublished M.A. thesis, University of Calgary, 1969.

2260. Schindeler, Fred, and David Hoffman. "Theological and Political Conservatism: Variations in Attitudes among Clergymen of One Denomination." CANADIAN JOURNAL OF POLITICAL SCIENCE 1,4 (1968): 429-441.

Based on questionnaire data from ordained clergymen of the Baptist Convention of Ontario and Quebec.

## U.S.A. (GENERAL)

* Allinsmith, Wesley, and Beverly Allinsmith. "Religious Affiliation and Politico-economic Attitude." Cited above as item 404.

* Betts, George H. THE BELIEFS OF 700 MINISTERS. Cited above as item 1937.

2261. Davidson, James D. "Patterns of Belief at the Denominational and Congregational Levels." RRR 13,3 (1972): 197-205.

1968 questionnaire data from working-class and middle-class congregations (Baptist and Methodist) in an Indiana community.

2262. Davidson, James D. "Socio-economic Status and Ten Dimensions of Religious Commitment." SOCIOLOGY AND SOCIAL RESEARCH 61 (1977): 462-485.

Data from working-class and middle-class Methodist and Baptist congregations. Analysis focused on relationships between socio-economic status and dimensions of religiosity. Results suggest that deprivation and privilege may not have as much effect as people's group affiliations on religious belief and action.

* Finke, Roger, and Rodney Stark. "How the Upstart Sects Won America, 1776-1850." Cited above as item 1369.

* Gockel, Galen L. "Income and Religious Affiliation: A Regression Analysis." Cited above as item 437.

2263. Greeley, Andrew M., and William C. McCready. ETHNICITY IN THE UNITED STATES. A PRELIMINARY RECONNAISSANCE. New York: Wiley, 1974.

In a W.A.S.P. sample, Baptists and fundamentalists were less likely to vote, campaign, or engage in civic activity than other Protestants.

* Homola, Michael, Dean Knudsen, and Harvey Marshall. "Religion and Socio-economic Achievement." Cited above as item 463.

* Homola, Michael, Dean Knudsen, and Harvey Marshall. "Status Attainment and Religion: A Re-evaluation." Cited above as item 464.

2264. Johnson, Benton. "Theology and Party Preference among Protestant Clergymen." AMERICAN SOCIOLOGICAL REVIEW 31,2 (1966): 200-208.

2265. Johnson, Benton. "Theology and the Position of Pastors on Public Issues." AMERICAN SOCIOLOGICAL REVIEW 32,3 (1967): 433-442.

1962 survey of clergy of The Methodist Church and five Baptist conferences in Oregon. North American Baptist data were merged with General Conference Baptist. Theologically liberal and neo-orthodox respondents were more likely to take politically liberal stands. Theology is a good predictor, but not necessarily the determinant.

* Klemmack, David L., and Jerry D. Cardwell. "Interfaith Comparison of Multidimensional Measures of Religiosity." Cited above as item 1278.

2266. Knudten, Richard D. "The Religion of the Indiana Baptist Prisoner." RRR 19,1 (1977): 16-31, 42.

Baptist prisoners in an Indiana maximum security prison were orthodox in areas of religious belief, requisites for salvation, and barriers to salvation, while less orthodox in religious belief in God and Jesus, ritual practices, devotionalism, experience, and knowledge.

2267. Larson, Donald E. SOME SOCIOLOGICAL ASPECTS OF CHURCH RELOCATION: A STUDY OF A MIDDLE-CLASS PARISH. Unpublished M.A. thesis, Indiana University, Bloomington, 1959.

* Lazerwitz, Bernard. "Religion and Social Structure in the United States." Cited above as item 471.

* Lenski, Gerhard. "Social Correlates of Religious Interest." Cited above as item 1946.

* McMurray, Martha. "Religion and Women's Sex Role Traditionalism." Cited above as item 483.

* Maranell, Gary M. RESPONSES TO RELIGION. STUDIES IN THE SOCIAL PSYCHOLOGY OF RELIGIOUS BELIEF. Cited above as item 1294.

* Mayer, Albert J., and Harry Sharp. "Religious Preference and Worldly Success." Cited above as item 484.

2268. Moberg, David O. "A Sociologist's Interpretation of the Recent Rapid Growth of the Baptist General Conference." BETHEL SEMINARY QUARTERLY 7,4 (1959): 19-24.

2269. Moberg, David O. "Evaluation of Reasons for Conference Growth." BETHEL SEMINARY QUARTERLY 8,3 (1960): 58-66.

2270. Nelsen, Hart M., and Raymond H. Potvin. "Toward Disestablishment: New Patterns of Social Class, Denomination and Religiosity among Youth?" RRR 22,2 (1980): 137-154.

1975 U.S.A. Gallup sample of Protestant adolescents (aged 13-18). Focus is on the interaction of socioeconomic status, religious denomination, and religiosity.

2271. Nelson, John J., and Harry H. Hiller. "Norms of Verbalization and the Decision-making Process in Religious Organizations." JSSR 20,2 (1981): 173-180.

Analysis of decisions in three churches.

* Norr, James L. "Religion and Nation Building: The American Case." Cited above as item 1304.

* Perrin, Robin D. "American Religion in the Post-aquarian Age: Values and Demographic Factors in Church Growth and Decline." Cited above as item 1409.

* Rhodes, A. Lewis, and Charles B. Nam. "The Religious Context of Educational Expectations." Cited above as item 499.

* Roof, Wade Clark. "Socioeconomic Differentials among White Socio-religious Groups in the United States." Cited above as item 501.

2272. Scalf, John H., Michael J. Miller, and Charles W. Thomas. "Goal Specificity, Organizational Structure, and Participant Commitment in Churches." SA 34,3 (1973): 169-184.

Most formal churches had specific goals, bureaucracy, and members committed to the local church and traditional ideology. Communal churches had diffuse goals, little bureaucracy, and members committed to the denomination and non-traditional ideology.

* Steinberg, Stephen. "The Changing Religious Composition of American Higher Education." Cited above as item 518.

* Warren, Bruce L. THE RELATIONSHIPS BETWEEN RELIGIOUS PREFERENCES AND SOCIO-ECONOMIC ACHIEVEMENT OF AMERICAN MEN. Cited above as item 1963.

* Warren, Bruce L. "Socioeconomic Achievement and Religion: The American Case." Cited above as item 522.


## AMERICAN BAPTIST CONVENTION

2273. Brown, Robert L. ATTITUDES OF MINISTERS AND LAY LEADERS OF THE AMERICAN BAPTIST CONVENTION OF THE STATE OF WASHINGTON ON SELECTED SOCIAL ISSUES. Unpublished Ph.D. dissertation, University of Southern California, 1962. [DA 23:3, p. 1102]

Interview data on attitudes toward liquor traffic, social welfare measures, likelihood of war, church-state relations, law enforcement, overseas relief programs, and relations with Jews. Clergy were more liberal than were lay leaders.

2274. Brown, Robert L. "Attitudes among Local Baptist Church Leaders in Washington State." SOCIOLOGY AND SOCIAL RESEARCH 47,3 (1963): 322-330.

Questionnaire data from American Baptist clergy and lay officers in Washington State. Clergy were not more liberal than lay officers.

2275. Campolo, Anthony. A DENOMINATION LOOKS AT ITSELF. Valley Forge, Pennsylvania: Judson, 1971.

* Demerath, Nicholas J., III. SOCIAL CLASS IN AMERICAN PROTESTANTISM. Cited above as item 2036.

* Glock, Charles Y., and Rodney Stark. RELIGION AND SOCIETY IN TENSION. Cited above as item 1118.

* Glock, Charles Y., and Rodney Stark. CHRISTIAN BELIEFS AND ANTI-SEMITISM. Cited above as item 1119.

* Hadden, Jeffrey K. THE GATHERING STORM IN THE CHURCHES. A SOCIOLOGIST LOOKS AT THE WIDENING GAP BETWEEN CLERGY AND LAYMEN. Cited above as item 1942.

* Hammond, Phillip, Albert Gedicks, Edward Lawler, and Louise Allen Turner. "Clergy Authority and Friendship with Parishioners." Cited above as item 1943.

2276. Harrison, Paul M. AUTHORITY AND POWER IN THE FREE CHURCH TRADITION: A SOCIAL CASE STUDY OF THE AMERICAN BAPTIST CONVENTION. Princeton: Princeton University Press, 1959.

Although it began as a lower-class sect, the Baptist movement has taken on higher-status members who have exerted increasing influence towards modernization. Not only has much of Baptist fundamentalism been subdued, but its principle of local autonomy for each parish has been subverted. Bureaucratization has quietly gained sway at the national level.

* Hartley, Shirley F., and Mary G. Taylor. "Religious Beliefs of Clergy Wives." Cited above as item 1944.

2277. Hine, Leland D. "Are American Baptists Declining? Chicago Baptists, 1931-1955." FOUNDATIONS 3 (1960): 144-156.

Discusses difficulties involved in assessing church membership data; losses seem to have been overstated.

* Hoge, Dean R., and John E. Dyble. "The Influence of Assimilation on American Protestant Ministers' Beliefs, 1928-1978." Cited above as item 1945.

2278. Hood, Ralph W. "Normative and Motivational Determinants of Reported Religious Experience in Two Baptist Samples." RRR 13,3 (1972): 192-196.

Intrinsically religiously-oriented subjects were more likely than extrinsically religiously-oriented to report religious experiences. Southern Baptists were more likely to report them than were American Baptists.

* Jeffries, Vincent, and Clarence E. Tygart. "More on Clergy and Social Issues." Cited above as item 1266.

* Johnson, Benton. "Theology and the Position of Pastors on Public

Issues." Cited above as item 2265.

2279. Lehman, Edward C., Jr. PROJECT SWIM: A STUDY OF WOMEN IN MINISTRY. Valley Forge, Pennsylvania: The Ministers Council, American Baptist Churches, 1979.

2280. Lehman, Edward C., Jr. "Patterns of Lay Resistance to Women in Ministry." SA 41,4 (1980): 317-338.

1977-78 survey, using a national sample. Two clusters of factors differently influence resistance to female ministers: one affects the tendency to stereotype, the other the willingness to discriminate.

2281. Lehman, Edward C., Jr. "Organizational Resistance to Women in Ministry." SA 42,2 (1981): 101-118.

Officials are more concerned with the impact of clergy placements on congregation viability than they are influenced by sex role socialization or sex stratification attitudes. Their concerns may either hinder or facilitate the placement of female clergy.

  * Longino, Charles F., Jr., and Jeffrey K. Hadden. "Dimensionality of Belief among Mainstream Protestant Clergy." Cited above as item 1948.

2282. Longino, Charles F., Jr., and Gay C. Kitson. "Parish Clergy and the Aged: Examining Stereotypes." JOURNAL OF GERONTOLOGY 31,3 (1976): 340-345.

1965 sample of American Baptist Convention clergy, focusing on the relative extent to which respondents enjoyed ministering to the aged.

  * Mitchell, Robert E. MINISTER-PARISHIONER RELATIONS. Cited above as item 1950.

  * Mitchell, Robert E. "Polity, Church Attractiveness, and Ministers' Careers." Cited above as item 1951.

  * Quinley, Harold E. THE PROPHETIC CLERGY. SOCIAL ACTIVISM AMONG PROTESTANT MINISTERS. Cited above as item 1953.

  * Scherer, Ross P. "A New Typology for Organizations: Market, Bureaucracy, Clan and Mission, with Application to American Denominations." Cited above as item 1416.

  * Stark, Rodney, Bruce D. Foster, Charles Y. Glock, and Harold E. Quinley. WAYWARD SHEPHERDS: PREJUDICE AND THE PROTESTANT CLERGY. Cited above as item 1960.


SOUTHERN BAPTIST (U.S.A.)

2283. Boling, T. Edwin. "Southern Baptists in the North." RRR 8 (1967): 95-100.

Based on a sample drawn from the membership of 11 Southern Baptist

295

churches in the metropolitan area of Columbus, Ohio.

2284. Boling, T. Edwin. "Southern Baptist Migrants and Converts: A Study of Southern Religion in the Urban North." SA 33,3 (1972): 188-199.

Sample from Columbus, Ohio, congregations (1963 and 1969). Over a period of time, the Southern Baptists are maintaining a sectarian stance that appeals to persons with rural backgrounds.

2285. Boling, T. Edwin. "Social Factors in Church Extension: Southern Baptists in the North." FOUNDATIONS 18,2 (1975): 146-152.

Discusses rural religion as a means of maintaining rural identity in an urban context.

2286. Dever, John P. PREJUDICE AND RELIGIOUS TYPES: A FOCUSED STUDY OF SOUTHERN BAPTISTS (A REPLICATION). Unpublished M.A. thesis, University of Louisville, 1969.

2287. Eighmy, John L. THE SOCIAL CONSCIOUSNESS OF SOUTHERN BAPTISTS, 1900 TO THE PRESENT AS REFLECTED IN THEIR ORGANIZED LIFE. Unpublished Ph.D. dissertation, University of Missouri, 1959. [DA 20:7, p. 2770]

2288. Eighmy, John L. CHURCHES IN CULTURAL CAPTIVITY. Knoxville: University of Tennessee Press, 1972.

2289. Elifson, Kirk W. "Religious Behavior among Urban Southern Baptists: A Causal Inquiry." SA 37,1 (1976): 32-44.

Adult urban sample in 17 Southern and near-Southern states. Factor analysis to produce dimensions of religiosity; causal model using the measures, among other variables. The model served as a better predictor for the female subsample.

2290. Feagin, Joe R. "Prejudice and Religious Types: A Focused Study of Southern Fundamentalists." JSSR 4,1 (1964): 3-13.

286 respondents from five mid-Southern cities. Southern Baptists varied in religiosity along an intrinsic/extrinsic spectrum. Generally, the extrinsic score correlated with prejudice. Controlling for education, orthodoxy did not correlate with the extrinsic/intrinsic dimension; orthodoxy did correlate with prejudice.

* Glock, Charles Y., and Rodney Stark. RELIGION AND SOCIETY IN TENSION. Cited above as item 1118.

* Glock, Charles Y., and Rodney Stark. CHRISTIAN BELIEFS AND ANTI-SEMITISM. Cited above as item 1119.

2291. Guth, James L. "Southern Baptist Clergy: Vanguard of the Christian Right?" In Robert C. Liebman and Robert Wuthnow (eds.), THE NEW CHRISTIAN RIGHT. Hawthorne, New York: Aldine, 1983, pp. 117-130.

1980 sample of Southern Baptist pastors in the U.S. Support for the Moral Majority political program was inconsistent.

2292. Guth, James L. "The Politics of Preachers: Southern Baptist Ministers and Christian Right Activism." In D.G. Bromley and A. Shupe (eds.), NEW CHRISTIAN POLITICS [volume cited in item 1414], pp. 235-249.

1980-81 sample of Southern Baptist ministers in the U.S. Support for the New Christian Right was inconsistent.

2293. Herb, Terry R. "Organizational Effectiveness in the Southern Baptist Convention: A Further Study." LOUISIANA STATE UNIVERSITY JOURNAL OF SOCIOLOGY 3 (1973): 97-109.

   * Hoge, Dean R., and Gregory H. Petrillo. "Development of Religious Thinking in Adolescence: A Test of Goldman's Theories." Cited above as item 1258.

   * Hoge, Dean R., and Gregory H. Petrillo. "Determinants of Church Participation and Attitudes among High School Youth." Cited above as item 1259.

   * Hoge, Dean R., Esther Heffernan, Eugene F. Hemrick, Hart M. Nelsen, James P. O'Connor, Paul J. Philibert, and Andrew D. Thompson. "Desired Outcomes of Religious Education and Youth Ministry in Six Denominations." Cited above as item 1387.

   * Hood, Ralph W. "Normative and Motivational Determinants of Reported Religious Experience in Two Baptist Samples." Cited above as item 2278.

2294. Ingram, Larry C. "Notes on Pastoral Power in the Congregational Tradition." JSSR 19,1 (1980): 40-48.

Participant-observation study of two Southern Baptist churches. The pastors exerted considerable power.

2295. Ingram, Larry C. "Leadership, Democracy, and Religion: Role Ambiguity among Pastors in Southern Baptist Churches." JSSR 20,2 (1981): 119-129.

Focuses on the socialization process whereby clergy develop an authoritarian self-image, and on the interplay between religious understanding and democratic organization.

2296. Ingram, Larry C. "Underlife in a Baptist Church." RRR 24,2 (1982): 138-152.

A study of secondary adjustment; that is, the type of conduct wherein a person seeks clandestine rewards whilst appearing sincerely engaged in a role.

   * Ingram, Larry C. "Sectarian Colleges and Academic Freedom." Cited above as item 2122.

   * Johnson, Benton. "Theology and the Position of Pastors on Public Issues." Cited above as item 2265.

2297. Jones, Phillip B. "An Examination of the Statistical Growth of the Southern Baptist Convention." In D.R. Hoge and D.A. Roozen (eds.), UNDERSTANDING CHURCH GROWTH AND DECLINE 1950-78 [volume cited in item 2137], pp. 160-178.

1900-76 data taken from the yearly handbook issues of the QUARTERLY REVIEW: A SURVEY OF SOUTHERN BAPTIST PROGRESS, published by the Sunday School Board of the Southern Baptist Convention.

2298. Kahoe, Richard D. "Intrinsic Religion and Authoritarianism: A Differentiated Relationship." JSSR 16,2 (1977): 179-183.

Only two factors, 'conventionalism' and 'superstition and stereotypy' accounted for the previously reported relationship between authoritarianism and intrinsic religion; both factors are salient for 'sincerely but traditionally religious Baptists.'

2299. McClerren, Beryl F. THE SOUTHERN BAPTIST STATE NEWSPAPERS AND THE RELIGIOUS ISSUE DURING THE PRESIDENTIAL CAMPAIGNS OF 1928 and 1960. Unpublished Ph.D. dissertation, Southern Illinois University, 1963.

* Patrick, John W. "Personal Faith and the Fear of Death among Divergent Religious Populations." Cited above as item 180.

* Philibert, Paul J., and Dean R. Hoge. "Teachers, Pedagogy and the Process of Religious Education." Cited above as item 1413.

* Quinley, Harold E. THE PROPHETIC CLERGY. SOCIAL ACTIVISM AMONG PROTESTANT MINISTERS. Cited above as item 1953.

2300. Rochte, Frederick C. DEPARTURE FROM THE PASTORATE: A STUDY OF SOUTHERN BAPTIST MINISTERS. Unpublished M.A. thesis, Wake Forest University, 1967.

2301. Roof, Wade Clark. "The Local-cosmopolitan Orientation and Traditional Religious Commitment." SA 33,1 (1972): 1-15.

The local/cosmopolitan dimension is proposed as a predictor of traditional religiosity. The hypothesis is tested and substantiated with exploratory data from a sample of Southern Baptists - 150 respondents from Chapel Hill and Carrboro, North Carolina.

* Scherer, Ross P. "A New Typology for Organizations: Market, Bureaucracy, Clan and Mission, with Application to American Denominations." Cited above as item 1416.

* Stark, Rodney, Bruce D. Foster, Charles Y. Glock, and Harold E. Quinley. WAYWARD SHEPHERDS: PREJUDICE AND THE PROTESTANT CLERGY. Cited above as item 1960.

2302. Stott, Gerald N. "Familial Influence on Religious Involvement." In D.L. Thomas (ed.), THE RELIGION AND FAMILY CONNECTION [volume cited in item 414], pp. 258-271.

Questionnaire survey in the St. Louis metropolitan area.

2303. Strickland, Bonnie R., and Sallie Cone Weddell. "Religious Orientation, Racial Prejudice, and Dogmatism: A Study of Baptists and
Unitarians." JSSR 11,4 (1972): 395-399.

The Unitarians were more extrinsic in religious orientation, less
dogmatic, and less prejudiced against racial minorities, than were the
Baptists.

2304. Thompson, Robert C. "A Research Note on the Diversity among American
Protestants: A Southern Baptist Example." RRR 15,2 (1974): 87-92.

Examines the degree of orthodoxy among three different diploma or
degree groups graduating from the Southwestern Baptist Theological
Seminary in Fort Worth. Findings suggest future polarization within
the membership, ministry, and hierarchy of the Southern Baptist Convention.

    * Van Roy, Ralph F., Frank D. Bean, and James R. Wood. "Social Mobility
    and Doctrinal Orthodoxy." Cited above as item 1962.

2305. Wimberley, Ronald C. "Mobility in Ministerial Career Patterns:
Exploration." JSSR 10,3 (1971): 249-253.

Sample of pastors: 40 percent upwardly mobile; slightly over 25 percent stable; remainder split between erratic mobility, downward
mobility, and immobility. Further analysis by congregation variables
and personal characteristics.

2306. Wimberley, Ronald C. "Toward the Measurement of Commitment Strength."
SA 35,3 (1974): 211-215.

Suggests that strength of commitment be measured apart from the underlying commitment positions. Data from 812 questionnaire respondents
(Southern Baptist adults in Texas).

# 18
## Methodist

*GENERAL*

2307. Currie, Robert. METHODISM DIVIDED: A STUDY IN THE SOCIOLOGY OF ECUMENICALISM. London: Faber and Faber, 1968.

2308. Jones, Larry A. CHRISTIAN MORALISM: A SOCIOLOGICAL ANALYSIS. Unpublished Ph.D. dissertation, University of Chicago, 1975.

2309. Smith, James A., Jr. "Methodist Episcopacy: From the General to the Specific." RRR 7 (1966): 163-166.

Discusses the manner in which the diffuse and unstructured 'original' charisma of Francis Asbury has become increasingly routinized.


*GREAT BRITAIN*

2310. Archer, Antony. "Remaining in the State in which God has Called You: An Evangelical Revival." ARCHIVES DE SCIENCES SOCIALES DES RELIGIONS 20/40 (1975): 67-78.

A study of a revival group connected with a Methodist circuit in a country district in the North East of England (participant observation and informal interviewing, 1973).

2311. Baxter, John. "The Great Yorkshire Revival 1792-6: A Study of Mass Revival among the Methodists." SOCIOLOGICAL YEARBOOK OF RELIGION IN BRITAIN 7 (1974): 46-76.

Investigates a wide range of historical evidence related to the revival.

   * Bryman, Alan. "Professionalism and the Clergy: A Research Note." Cited above as item 1642.

2312. Burton, Lewis. "Social Class in the Local Church: A Study of Two Methodist Churches in the Midlands." SOCIOLOGICAL YEARBOOK OF RELIGION IN BRITAIN 8 (1975): 15-29.

Argues that social class within the local congregation depends on what outlook a church may have to its neighborhood and where it is located.

2313. Chamberlayne, John H.  "From Sect to Church in British Methodism."
BRITISH JOURNAL OF SOCIOLOGY 15,2 (1964): 139-149.

General account, beginning with the eighteenth century.

2314. Field, Clive D.  METHODISM IN METROPOLITAN LONDON, 1850-1920: A SOCIAL
AND SOCIOLOGICAL STUDY.  Unpublished Ph.D. thesis, Oxford University,
1975.

2315. Field, Clive D.  "The Social Structure of English Methodism: Eighteenth
-Twentieth Centuries."  BRITISH JOURNAL OF SOCIOLOGY 28,2 (1977): 199-
225.

Document sources suggest that early Methodists were artisans rather
than unskilled laborers.  Victorian Wesleyans were not always a
bourgeois force.  Nineteenth-century Primitive Methodists were manual
workers, but not always poorest grade.  By 1932 the social gulf between
the several branches of the church had disappeared.

2316. Fry, Peter.  "Two Religious Movements: Protestantism and Umbanda."  In
John D. Wirth and R.L. Jones (eds.), MANCHESTER AND SÃO PAULO: PROBLEMS
OF RAPID URBAN GROWTH.  Stanford: Stanford University Press, 1978,
pp. 177-202.

Focus is on nineteenth-century Manchester and twentieth-century São
Paulo.

  * Goodridge, R.M.  "The Religious Condition of the West Country in 1851."
Cited above as item 1910.

  * Hill, Michael.  THE RELIGIOUS ORDER.  Cited above as item 972.

2317. Hill, Michael.  "Methodism as a Religious Order: A Question of Categories."  SOCIOLOGICAL YEARBOOK OF RELIGION IN BRITAIN 6 (1973): 91-99.

Argues that early Methodism shared characteristics of both the religious order and the religious sect.

2318. Hill, Michael, and Peter Wakeford.  "Disembodied Ecumenicalism: A
Survey of the Members of Four Methodist Churches in or near London."
SOCIOLOGICAL YEARBOOK OF RELIGION IN BRITAIN 2 (1969): 19-46.

Investigates attitudes of Methodists in an area south of London toward
ecumenicalism in general and toward the Church of England in particular.

  * Lehman, Edward C., Jr.  "The Local/Cosmopolitan Dichotomy and Acceptance of Women Clergy: A Replication."  Cited above as item 1915.

2319. Moore, Robert.  "The Political Effects of Village Methodism."
SOCIOLOGICAL YEARBOOK OF RELIGION IN BRITAIN 6 (1973): 156-182.

A critical reassessment of Halévy's argument that early Methodism
served to avert social revolution in England.

\* Nason-Clark, Nancy. CLERICAL ATTITUDES TOWARDS APPROPRIATE ROLES FOR WOMEN IN CHURCH AND SOCIETY: AN EMPIRICAL INVESTIGATION OF ANGLICAN, METHODIST AND BAPTIST CLERGY IN SOUTHERN ENGLAND. Cited above as item 1919.

2320. Pagden, Frank. "An Analysis of the Effectiveness of Methodist Churches of Varying Sizes and Types in the Liverpool District." SOCIOLOGICAL YEARBOOK OF RELIGION IN BRITAIN 1 (1968): 124-134.

Concludes that Methodism in Liverpool works best in suburban areas with congregations of between 200 and 280 members.

\* Ranson, Stewart, Alan Bryman, and Bob Hinings. CLERGY, MINISTERS, AND PRIESTS. Cited above as item 1660.

2321. Turner, Bryan S. "Institutional Persistence and Ecumenicalism in Northern Methodism." SOCIOLOGICAL YEARBOOK OF RELIGION IN BRITAIN 2 (1969): 47-57.

Concludes that institutional persistence, the lay rejection of ecumenicalism, and the ambiguities of the Methodist minister's role are factors which militate against union with Anglicanism.

2322. Turner, Bryan S. "Belief, Ritual and Experience: The Case of Methodism." SC 18,2 (1971): 187-201.

The experiential dimension of religiosity seems central.

2323. Turner, Bryan S., and Michael Hill. "Methodism and the Pietist Definition of Politics: Historical Development and Contemporary Evidence." SOCIOLOGICAL YEARBOOK OF RELIGION IN BRITAIN 8 (1975): 159-180.

Depiction of the historical continuities within Methodist political thought, its distinctiveness when compared with the positions adopted by other denominations, as well as its links with the attitudes of wider Nonconformity.


*CANADA, AUSTRALIA*

2324. Clark, S.D. CHURCH AND SECT IN CANADA. Toronto: University of Toronto Press, 1948.

Socio-historical study of Canadian Methodism reveals growing pressures of high-status laity for modernization and growing disaffection of the lower classes from the church. Church form of religion is preferred by the upper classes, sect form by the lower classes.

\* Clark, S.D. "The Religious Sect in Canadian Politics." Cited above as item 2258.

2325. Dempsey, Kenneth C. "Conflict in Minister/Lay Relations." SOCIOLOGICAL YEARBOOK OF RELIGION IN BRITAIN 2 (1969): 58-74.

Progress report on an ongoing study of tension and conflict in minister/lay relations in an Australian Methodist Church.

* Mol, J.J. (Hans) "A Collation of Data about Religion in Australia."
  Cited above as item 308.

## LATIN AMERICA

2326. Bastian, Jean-Pierre. "Metodismo y clase obrera en México (1878–1910)." CHRISTUS 52,603–604 (1987): 36–50.

* Lalive d'Epinay, Christian. "L'esprit et le champ oecuméniques de pasteurs sud-américains." Cited above as item 1748.

2327. Saunders, John V.D. "Organização social de uma congregação protetante no Estado da Guanabara." SOCIOLOGIA 22 (1960): 415–449; 23 (1961): 37–66, 155–173.

A study of Methodism in Brazil.

## AFRICAN METHODIST EPISCOPAL CHURCH

2328. Beck, Carolyn S. "Our Own Vine and Fig Tree: The Authority of History and Kinship in Mother Bethel." RRR 29,4 (1988): 369–384.

Ethnography of Mother Bethel (Philadelphia, Pennsylvania).

2329. Johnson, Walton R. WORSHIP AND FREEDOM. A BLACK AMERICAN CHURCH IN ZAMBIA. New York: Holmes and Meier, 1978.

## U.S.A. (GENERAL)

2330. Allen, John L. THE METHODIST BOARD OF TEMPERANCE AS AN INSTRUMENT OF CHURCH POLICY. Unpublished Ph.D. dissertation, Yale University, 1957.

* Allinsmith, Wesley, and Beverly Allinsmith. "Religious Affiliation and Politico-economic Attitude." Cited above as item 404.

* Betts, George H. THE BELIEFS OF 700 MINISTERS. Cited above as item 1937.

2331. Brewer, Earl D.C. METHODISM IN CHANGING AMERICAN SOCIETY. Unpublished Ph.D. dissertation, University of North Carolina, 1950.

2332. Brewer, Earl D.C. "Sect and Church in Methodism." SOCIAL FORCES 30 (1952): 400–408. Reprinted in L. Schneider (ed.), RELIGION, CULTURE AND SOCIETY [volume cited in item 307], pp. 471–482.

Interpretation of the history of American Methodism as a shift from a sect-like to a church-like form.

2333. Brewer, Earl D.C. "Attitudes toward Inclusive Practices in the Methodist Church in the Southeast." RRR 6 (1965): 82–89.

2334. Culver, Dwight. NEGRO SEGREGATION IN THE METHODIST CHURCH. New Haven: Yale University Press, 1953.

* Davidson, James D. "Patterns of Belief at the Denominational and Congregational Levels." Cited above as item 2261.

* Davidson, James D. "Socio-economic Status and Ten Dimensions of Religious Commitment." Cited above as item 2262.

2335. Decker, Carmer C. THE RELATIONSHIP OF ESCHATOLOGICAL EMPHASIS TO ECONOMIC STATUS OF TWO METHODIST CHURCHES IN BLOOMINGTON. Unpublished M.A. thesis, Indiana University, Bloomington, 1947.

* Finke, Roger, and Rodney Stark. "How the Upstart Sects Won America: 1776-1850." Cited above as item 1369.

* Glock, Charles Y., and Rodney Stark. RELIGION AND SOCIETY IN TENSION. Cited above as item 1118.

* Glock, Charles Y., and Rodney Stark. CHRISTIAN BELIEFS AND ANTI-SEMITISM. Cited above as item 1119.

* Gockel, Galen L. "Income and Religious Affiliation: A Regression Analysis." Cited above as item 437.

* Hadden, Jeffrey K. THE GATHERING STORM IN THE CHURCHES. A SOCIOLOGIST LOOKS AT THE WIDENING GAP BETWEEN CLERGY AND LAYMEN. Cited above as item 1942.

* Hoge, Dean R., and Gregory H. Petrillo. "Determinants of Church Participation and Attitudes among High School Youth." Cited above as item 1259.

* Homola, Michael, Dean Knudsen, and Harvey Marshall. "Religion and Socio-economic Achievement." Cited above as item 463.

* Homola, Michael, Dean Knudsen, and Harvey Marshall. "Status Attainment and Religion: A Re-evaluation." Cited above as item 464.

2336. Hougland, James G., Jr., James R. Wood, and Samuel A. Mueller. "Organizational 'Goal Submergence': The Methodist Church and the Failure of the Temperance Movement." SOCIOLOGY AND SOCIAL RESEARCH 58,4 (1974): 408-416.

'Goal submergence' is the change of organizational goals by executives who seek to provide different incentives for various elements in the organization. Content analysis of episcopal addresses are used to illustrate the concept.

* Johnstone, Ronald L. "Public Images of Protestant Ministers and Catholic Priests: An Empirical Study of Anti-clericalism in the U.S." Cited above as item 1267.

* Jones, Larry A. "Empirical Evidence on Moral Contextualism." Cited above as item 1268.

* Klemmack, David L., and Jerry D. Cardwell. "Interfaith Comparison of Multidimensional Measures of Religiosity." Cited above as item 1278.

* Lazerwitz, Bernard. "Religion and Social Structure in the United States." Cited above as item 471.

* Lenski, Gerhard. "Social Correlates of Religious Interest." Cited above as item 1946.

* Longino, Charles F., Jr., and Jeffrey K. Hadden. "Dimensionality of Belief among Mainstream Protestant Clergy." Cited above as item 1948.

* Maranell, Gary M. RESPONSES TO RELIGION. STUDIES IN THE SOCIAL PSYCHOLOGY OF RELIGIOUS BELIEF. Cited above as item 1294.

* Mayer, Albert J., and Harry Sharp. "Religious Preference and Worldly Success." Cited above as item 484.

* Mitchell, Robert E. MINISTER-PARISHIONER RELATIONS. Cited above as item 1950.

* Mitchell, Robert E. "Polity, Church Attractiveness, and Ministers' Careers." Cited above as item 1951.

* Mueller, Charles W. "Evidence on the Relationship between Religion and Educational Attainment." Cited above as item 490.

* Nelsen, Hart M. "Religious Conformity in an Age of Disbelief: Contextual Effects of Time, Denomination, and Family Processes upon Church Decline and Apostasy." Cited above as item 1405.

* Norr, James L. "Religion and Nation Building: The American Case." Cited above as item 1304.

2337. Nottingham, Elizabeth K. METHODISM AND THE FRONTIER: INDIANA PROVING GROUND. New York: Columbia University Press, 1941.

* Perrin, Robin D. "American Religion in the Post-aquarian Age: Values and Demographic Factors in Church Growth and Decline." Cited above as item 1409.

* Photiadis, John D., and John F. Schnabel. "Religion: A Persistent Institution in a Changing Appalachia." Cited above as item 1311.

* Roof, Wade Clark. "Socioeconomic Differentials among White Socioreligious Groups in the United States." Cited above as item 501.

2338. Rymph, Raymond C., and Jeffrey K. Hadden. "The Persistence of Regionalism in Racial Attitudes of Methodist Clergy." SOCIAL FORCES 49,1

(1970): 41-50.

The merger of the northern and southern branches of the Methodist church in 1939 has not resulted in a convergence of racial attitudes among clergy; both groups of clergy have become more liberal about racial issues. (1965 questionnaire data from a sample of clergy.)

* Scherer, Ross P. "A New Typology for Organizations: Market, Bureaucracy, Clan and Mission, with Application to American Denominations." Cited above as item 1416.

* Spaulding, Kent E. "The Theology of the Pew." Cited above as item 832.

* Steinberg, Stephen. "The Changing Religious Composition of American Higher Education." Cited above as item 518.

* Stryker, Robin. "Religio-ethnic Effects on Attainments in the Early Career." Cited above as item 520.

* Van Roy, Ralph F., Frank D. Bean, and James R. Wood. "Social Mobility and Doctrinal Orthodoxy." Cited above as item 1962.

* Warren, Bruce L. THE RELATIONSHIPS BETWEEN RELIGIOUS PREFERENCE AND SOCIO-ECONOMIC ACHIEVEMENT OF AMERICAN MEN. Cited above as item 1963.

* Warren, Bruce L. "Socioeconomic Achievement and Religion: The American Case." Cited above as item 522.


THE METHODIST CHURCH (U.S.A.)

* Johnson, Benton. "Theology and Party Preference among Protestant Clergymen." Cited above as item 2264.

* Johnson, Benton. "Theology and the Position of Pastors on Public Issues." Cited above as item 2265.

2339. Turbeville, Gus. "Religious Schism in The Methodist Church: A Sociological Analysis of the Pine Grove Case." RURAL SOCIOLOGY 14,1 (1949): 29-50.

Focus on a 1939 conflict in the Pine Grove Methodist Church in the village of Turbeville, South Carolina, associated with local divisions and the controversy accompanying the uniting of three Methodist denominations into The Methodist Church.


UNITED METHODIST CHURCH (U.S.A.)

2340. Bell, Bill D. "Church Participation and the Family Life Cycle." RRR 13,1 (1971): 57-64.

Age and religiosity are stronger predictors of church participation than is life-cycle status. 1970 survey of 60 male members from a Manhattan, Kansas, congregation.

2341. Blanchard, Dallas A. SOME SOCIAL AND ORIENTATIVE CORRELATES OF CAREER CHANGE AND CONTINUITY AS REVEALED AMONG UNITED METHODIST PASTORS OF THE ALABAMA-WEST FLORIDA CONFERENCE, 1960-1970. Unpublished Ph.D. dissertation, Boston University, 1972. [DA 33:12 A, p. 7010]

2342. Blanchard, Dallas A. "Seminary Effects on Professional Role Orientations." RRR 22,4 (1981): 346-361.

1970 questionnaire data from pastors and former pastors in the Alabama-West Florida Conference of the United Methodist Church. Graduate school seminaries produced pastors more change-oriented, while the religious community produced persons more oriented toward the local parish; the vocational school graduates occupied an intermediate position. Non-graduates are found to be strikingly similar to religious community graduates.

 * Broughton, Walter, and Edgar W. Mills, Jr. "Resource Inequality and Accumulative Advantage: Stratification in the Ministry." Cited above as item 1939.

2343. Gibbs, James O., and Phyllis A. Ewer. "The External Adaptation of Religious Organizations: Church Response to Social Issues." SA 30,4 (1969): 223-234.

Data from 209 churches indicate that membership size and educational composition are related to responses to social issues. Certain personnel and leadership resources are key factors.

2344. Glass, J. Conrad, Jr. "Premarital Sexual Standards among Church Youth Leaders: An Exploratory Study." JSSR 11,4 (1972): 361-367.

Exploratory study concerning premarital sexual standards of teenage United Methodist church leaders from eastern North Carolina.

2345. Hale, Harry, Jr., Morton King, and Doris Moreland Jones. NEW WITNESSES: UNITED METHODIST CLERGYWOMEN. Nashville: Board of Higher Education and Ministry, United Methodist Church, 1980.

 * Hartley, Shirley F., and Mary G. Taylor. "Religious Beliefs of Clergy Wives." Cited above as item 1944.

2346. Hartman, Warren J. MEMBERSHIP TRENDS: A STUDY OF DECLINE AND GROWTH IN THE UNITED METHODIST CHURCH 1949-1975. Nashville: Discipleship Resources, 1976.

 * Hoge, Dean R., and John E. Dyble. "The Influence of Assimilation on American Protestant Ministers' Beliefs, 1928-1978." Cited above as item 1945.

 * Hoge, Dean R., and Gregory H. Petrillo. "Development of Religious Thinking in Adolescence: A Test of Goldman's Theories." Cited above

as item 1258.

* Hoge, Dean R., Esther Heffernan, Eugene F. Hemrick, Hart M. Nelsen, James P. O'Connor, Paul J. Philibert, and Andrew D. Thompson. "Desired Outcomes of Religious Education and Youth Ministry in Six Denominations." Cited above as item 1387.

* Jeffries, Vincent, and Clarence E. Tygart. "More on Clergy and Social Issues." Cited above as item 1266.

2347. Leiffer, Murray H. THE DISTRICT SUPERINTENDANT IN THE UNITED METHOD-IST CHURCH. Evanston, Illinois: Bureau of Social Religious Research, Garrett Theological Seminary, 1971.

* Philibert, Paul J., and Dean R. Hoge. "Teachers, Pedagogy and the Process of Religious Education." Cited above as item 1413.

2348. Prestwood, Charles M., Jr. SOCIAL IDEAS OF METHODIST MINISTERS IN ALABAMA SINCE UNIFICATION. Unpublished Ph.D. dissertation, Boston University, 1960. [DA 21:5, p. 1273]

* Quinley, Harold E. THE PROPHETIC CLERGY. SOCIAL ACTIVISM AMONG PROTES-TANT MINISTERS. Cited above as item 1953.

2349. Rankin, Robert P. RELIGIOUS IDEALS AND CHURCH ADMINISTRATION: A SOCI-OLOGICAL STUDY OF METHODISM. Unpublished Ph.D. dissertation, University of California at Berkeley, 1958.

* Royle, Marjorie H. "Women Pastors. What Happens after Placement?" Cited above as item 2062.

2350. Schreckengost, George E. "The Effect of Latent Racist, Ethnic and Sexual Biases on Placement." RRR 28,4 (1987): 351-366.

Survey of pastors and laity in the East Ohio Conference of the United Methodist Church, 1983. Factor analysis produced factors which pre-dicted little of the variation of acceptance of the idea of female or minority pastors. Pastors underestimated the level of acceptance by laity.

* Spaulding, Kent E. "The Theology of the Pew." Cited above as item 832.

* Stark, Rodney, Bruce D. Foster, Charles Y. Glock, and Harold E. Quinley. WAYWARD SHEPHERDS: PREJUDICE AND THE PROTESTANT CLERGY. Cited above as item 1960.

2351. Wood, James R., and Mayer N. Zald. "Aspects of Racial Integration in the Methodist Church: Sources of Resistance to Organizational Policy." SOCIAL FORCES 45,2 (1966): 255-265.

A study of the national church's attempt to initiate policies of racial integration. Some congregations responded by decreasing their

'race-relations giving'; local and conference-level leaders accommo-
dated the opponents of integration.

# 19
## Holiness and Pentecostal

*HOLINESS RELIGION (GENERAL)*

2352. Dann, Norman K.   CONCURRENT SOCIAL MOVEMENTS: A STUDY OF THE INTER-
RELATIONSHIPS BETWEEN POPULIST POLITICS AND HOLINESS RELIGION.
Unpublished Ph.D. dissertation, Syracuse University, 1974.   [DA 36:10
A, p. 7005]

2353. Dann, Norman K.   "Spatial Diffusion of a Religious Movement."   JSSR
15,4 (1976): 351-360.

The spread and strength of the Holiness movement was influenced by
population migration, the reaction to national crises, and reactions
to contemporary and related movements.

2354. Holt, John B.   "Holiness Religion: Cultural Shock and Social Reorganization."   AMERICAN SOCIOLOGICAL REVIEW 5 (1940): 740-747.   Abridged
version in J.M. Yinger (ed.), RELIGION, SOCIETY, AND THE INDIVIDUAL
[volume cited in item 684], pp. 463-470.

Differences of social status result in different psychological needs
and therefore different religious forms.

2355. Johnson, Benton.   A FRAMEWORK FOR THE ANALYSIS OF RELIGIOUS ACTION
WITH SPECIAL REFERENCE TO HOLINESS AND NON-HOLINESS GROUPS.   Unpublished Ph.D. dissertation, Harvard University, 1953.

2356. Johnson, Benton.   "Do Holiness Sects Socialize in Dominant Values?"
SOCIAL FORCES 39 (1961): 309-316.

Some sects help lower-class people rise socially by imparting to them
economically helpful values.

2357. Jones, Dean C.   IDEOLOGICAL CONFLICT AND RELATED BUFFERING MECHANISMS
IN A VOLUNTARY ORGANIZATION.   Unpublished Ph.D. dissertation, University of Washington, 1971.   [DA 32:3 A, p. 1644]

Features questionnaire data from two Holiness churches.

2358. Kroll-Smith, J. Stephen.   "The Testimony as Performance: The Relationship of an Expressive Event to the Belief System of a Holiness Sect."

JSSR 19,1 (1980): 16-25.

The step-by-step structure of the fundamentalist theology, the lack of formal passage rites between steps, and a belief in spiritual growth through a series of private transformative experiences, create the need for some identity work. Testimony is shown to address this need. A study of the Church of God in Christ.

2359. Warburton, T. Rennie. A COMPARATIVE STUDY OF MINORITY RELIGIOUS GROUPS: WITH SPECIAL REFERENCE TO HOLINESS AND RELATED MOVEMENTS IN BRITAIN IN THE PAST 50 YEARS. Unpublished Ph.D. thesis, University of London, 1966.

2360. Warburton, T. Rennie. "Holiness Religion. An Anomaly of Sectarian Typologies." JSSR 8,1 (1969): 130-139.

The Holiness religions differ from Pentecostal in having fewer sectarian tendencies. The highly sujective nature of Holiness religious experience has few implications for separatism and enables many Holiness movements to remain interdenominational.

2361. Wood, William W. CULTURE AND PERSONALITY ASPECTS OF THE PENTECOSTAL HOLINESS RELIGION. The Hague: Mouton, 1965.


*HOLINESS (CHURCH OF GOD - ANDERSON, INDIANA)*

2362. Clear, Val. "The Church of God: A Study in Social Adaptation." RRR 2 (1961): 129-133.

Examines those historical adaptations which have moved the church closer to the dominant Protestant pattern in the U.S.A.

* Hoge, Dean R., Esther Heffernan, Eugene F. Hemrick, Hart M. Nelsen, James P. O'Connor, Paul J. Philibert, and Andrew D. Thompson. "Desired Outcomes of Religious Education and Youth Ministry in Six Denominations." Cited above as item 1387.

* Perrin, Robin D. "American Religion in the Post-aquarian Age: Values and Demographic Factors in Church Growth and Decline." Cited above as item 1409.

* Philibert, Paul J., and Dean R. Hoge. "Teachers, Pedagogy and the Process of Religious Education." Cited above as item 1413.


*HOLINESS (FATHER DIVINE)*

2363. Burnham, Kenneth E. GOD COMES TO AMERICA: FATHER DIVINE AND THE PEACE MISSION MOVEMENT. Boston: Lambeth, 1979.

2364. Mayne, F. Blair. "Beliefs and Practices of the Cult of Father Divine." JOURNAL OF EDUCATIONAL SOCIOLOGY 10,5 (1935): 296-306.

General description.

* Lenski, Gerhard. "Social Correlates of Religious Interest." Cited above as item 1946.

* Maranell, Gary M. RESPONSES TO RELIGION. STUDIES IN THE SOCIAL PSYCHOLOGY OF RELIGIOUS BELIEF. Cited above as item 1294.

* Perrin, Robin D. "American Religion in the Post-aquarian Age: Values and Demographic Factors in Church Growth and Decline." Cited above as item 1409.

2365. Pinto, Leonard J., and Kenneth E. Crow. "The Effects of Size on Other Structural Attributes of Congregations within the Same Denomination." JSSR 21,4 (1982): 304-316.

Not size of the denomination but size of congregations and of the communities in which they are located should influence the prevalence of sect-like attributes, according to the Troeltsch/Weber conceptual-izations. 1970-77 data give strong support for the view that small congregations in the Church of the Nazarene correlate with sectness and moderate support for the view that small communities do so.

2366. Reed, H.W. THE GROWTH OF A CONTEMPORARY SECT-TYPE AS REFLECTED IN THE DEVELOPMENT OF THE CHURCH OF THE NAZARENE. Unpublished Ph.D. disser-tation, University of Southern California, 1943.

2367. Schwartz, Norman B. "Protestantism, Community Organization and Social Status: Different Responses to Missions in a Guatemalan Town." CULTURES ET DEVELOPPEMENT 4,3 (1972): 585-600.

Based on 1960-61 and 1970 field work in northern El Petén, in a town where slash-and-burn cultivation is common. The Protestants are Nazarene and a later group having less strict membership requirements. Most conversion decisions were made in the 1940s, with a 3-1 Catholic-Protestant ratio persisting.

2368. Ward, David A. "Toward a Normative Explanation of 'Old Fashioned Revivals'." QUALITATIVE SOCIOLOGY 3,1 (1980): 3-22.

The sinner and the revival culture must first interact, and definitions of self and others must be forged. Second, structural facilities must be available for learning the Christian role. Third, opportunity structures must present themselves to afford the expression of appro-priate behaviors. Fourth, the status passage from salvation to sanc-tification is an orderly one, requiring salvation before sanctification.


*PENTECOSTAL (GENERAL)*

2369. Allen, Gillian, and Roy Wallis. "Pentecostalists as a Medical Minor-ity." In Roy Wallis and Peter Morley (eds.), MARGINAL MEDICINE. New York: Free Press, 1976, pp. 110-137.

\* Ball, Peter. "Dimensions in Neopentecostal Identity in the Church of England." Cited above as item 1897.

2370. Bloch-Hoell, Nils. THE PENTECOSTAL MOVEMENT. London: Allen and Unwin, 1964.

2371. Choi, Syn-Duk. "A Comparative Study of Two New Religious Movements in the Republic of Korea: The Unification Church and the Full Gospel Central Church." In J.A. Beckford (ed.), NEW RELIGIOUS MOVEMENTS AND RAPID SOCIAL CHANGE [volume cited in item 50], pp. 113-145.

Includes 1978 questionnaire data from eight large congregations of the Full Gospel Central Church (Korean-based affiliate of the Assemblies of God).

2372. Cohn, Werner. "Personality, Pentecostalism and Glossolalia: A Research Note on Some Unsuccessful Research." CANADIAN REVIEW OF SOCIOLOGY AND ANTHROPOLOGY 5,1 (1968): 36-39.

Concern is with the relationship between psychological factors and membership in Pentecostal groups, as well as the experimental production of glossolalia (speaking in tongues).

2373. Darrand, Tom C., and Anson Shupe. METAPHORS OF SOCIAL CONTROL IN A PENTECOSTAL SECT. New York: Edwin Mellen Press, 1983.

A study of Latter Rain, a deinstitutionalized form of Pentecostalism. Based on participant observation by one of the authors as a member (1969-76), and as a non-member (1977-81), mostly in Oakland, California.

2374. Elinson, Howard. "The Implications of Pentecostal Religion for Intellectualism, Politics, and Race Relations." AMERICAN JOURNAL OF SOCIOLOGY 70,4 (1965): 403-415.

The teachings of A.A. Allen are examined. Strict scripturalism and belief in miraculous healing delimit the relevance of science; eschatological teachings encourage withdrawal from politics; biblical literalism and evaluation of persons on spiritual grounds result in opposition to racial segregation. The movement is a response at the individual level to illness, poverty, and status deprivation.

2375. Freemesser, George F., and Howard B. Kaplan. "Self-attitudes and Deviant Behavior: The Case of the Charismatic Religious Movement." JOURNAL OF YOUTH AND ADOLESCENCE 5,1 (1976): 1-10.

A comparison of charismatic or neo-Pentecostal youths with traditional members of three urban Protestant churches.

2376. Gerlach, Luther P. "Pentecostalism: Revolution or Counter-revolution?" In I.I. Zaretsky and M.P. Leone (eds.), RELIGIOUS MOVEMENTS IN CONTEMPORARY AMERICA [volume cited in item 87], pp. 669-699.

Comparative study of U.S. and Haitian phenomena, with occasional references to African parallels.

2377. Gerlach, Luther P., and Virginia H. Hine. "Five Factors Crucial to

the Growth and Spread of a Modern Religious Movement."  JSSR 7,1
(1968): 23-40.

Factors affecting the growth of a movement differ from those contributing to its origin.  The growth factors reflect organization and
interaction.

2378.  Hine, Virginia H.  "Pentecostal Glossolalia: Toward a Functional
Interpretation."  JSSR 8,2 (1969): 211-226.

Data from case histories and questionnaires in four countries.  Explanations of glossolalia as symptomatic of pathology, suggestibility,
hypnosis, social disorganization, and social deprivation are found inadequate.  Concepts of it as learned conduct and as part of a process
of personality reorganization are found more useful.

2379.  Hine, Virginia H.  "Bridge Burners: Commitment and Participation in a
Religious Movement."  SA 31,2 (1970): 61-66.

The experiential source of commitment is comprised of a subjective
experience in which the self-image changes and some cognitive restructuring occurs, and an overt act which sets the individual apart from
the larger society in some significant way.

2380.  Hine, Virginia H.  "The Deprivation and Disorganization Theories of
Social Movements."  In I.I. Zaretsky and M.P. Leone (eds.), RELIGIOUS
MOVEMENTS IN CONTEMPORARY AMERICA [volume cited in item 87], pp. 646-
661.

Based on a study of the Pentecostal movement in the U.S.A., Mexico,
Haiti, and Colombia.  Quantitative data reported from interviews in
the U.S.

2381.  Hollenweger, Walter J.  ENTHUSIASTISCHES CHRISTENTUMS. DIE PFINGSTBE-
WEGUNG IN GESCHICHTE UND GEGENWART.  Wuppertal: Theologischer Verlag
Brockhaus, 1969.  See also THE PENTECOSTALS. THE CHARISMATIC MOVEMENT
IN THE CHURCHES.  Minneapolis: Augsburg, 1972.

2382.  Homan, Roger.  "Interpersonal Communication in Pentecostal Meetings."
SOCIOLOGICAL REVIEW 26,3 (1978): 499-518.

A study of linguistic behavior in Pentecostal meetings, based on four
years of observation in England and Wales, Canada, and the United
States.  Focus is on the indirectness of interpersonal transactions.

2383.  Homan, Roger.  "Crises in the Definition of Reality."  SOCIOLOGY 15,2
(1981): 210-224.

Data from observation and interviews in 66 assemblies in England and
Wales, Canada, and the United States.  Crises in definition occur when
definitions are contested, or when sacred definitions resemble profane
realities.

2384.  Kaplan, Berton H.  "The Structure of Adaptive Sentiments in Lower
Class Religious Groups in Appalachia."  JOURNAL OF SOCIAL ISSUES 21,1
(1965): 126-141.

Participation-observation study of a Free Will Baptist congregation of deprived people in a remote mountain community in western South Carolina. Members coped with hardship by projecting rewards in an afterlife and by means of devices of psychological withdrawal from the everyday world.

* McGaw, Douglas B. CONGREGATION AND RELIGIOUS COMMITMENT: A COMPARATIVE STUDY OF RELIGIOUS MEANING AND BELONGING. Cited above as item 2130.

* McGaw, Douglas B. "Commitment and Religious Community: A Comparison of a Charismatic and a Mainline Congregation." Cited above as item 2131.

* McGaw, Douglas B. "Meaning and Belonging in a Charismatic Congregation: An Investigation into Sources of Neo-pentecostal Success." Cited above as item 2132.

* McGaw, Douglas B., and Elliott Wright. A TALE OF TWO CONGREGATIONS. COMMITMENT AND SOCIAL STRUCTURE IN A CHARISMATIC AND MAINLINE CONGREGATION. Cited above as item 2133.

2385. McGuire, Meredith B. RITUAL HEALING IN SUBURBAN AMERICA. New Brunswick, N.J.: Rutgers University Press, 1988, pp. 38-78.

Description of healing practices, based on participant observation in Essex County, New Jersey.

2386. Maynard, Jeanine. EXPLORING THE IDEOLOGY OF NEO-PENTECOSTALS AND THEIR ATTITUDES TOWARDS CONCERN FOR SOCIAL STATUS. Unpublished M.A. thesis, University of Massachusetts, Amherst, 1974.

2387. Mehl, Roger. "Approche sociologique des mouvements charismatiques." BULLETIN DE LA SOCIETE D'HISTOIRE DU PROTESTANTISME FRANÇAIS 120,4 (1974): 555-573.

2388. Poloma, Margaret M. THE CHARISMATIC MOVEMENT: IS THERE A NEW PENTECOST? Boston: Twayne, 1982.

2389. Poloma, Margaret M. "Pentecostals and Politics in North and Central America." In J.K. Hadden and A. Shupe (eds.), PROPHETIC RELIGIONS AND POLITICS [volume cited in item 197], pp. 329-352.

General overview.

2390. Richardson, James T., and M.T. Vincent Reidy. "Neo-pentecostalism in Ireland: A Comparison with the American Experience." SOCIAL STUDIES. IRISH JOURNAL OF SOCIOLOGY 5, 3-4 (1977): 243-261.

2391. Richardson, James T., and M.T. Vincent Reidy. "Form and Fluidity in Two Contemporary Glossolalic Movements." ANNUAL REVIEW OF THE SOCIAL SCIENCES OF RELIGION 4 (1980): 183-220.

A comparison of the neo-Pentecostal and Jesus movements.

2392. Robbins, Thomas. "Government Regulatory Powers and Church Autonomy:

Deviant Groups as Test Cases." JSSR 24,3 (1985): 237-252.

Current legal conflicts over church autonomy reflect an incompatibility of two contemporary tendencies: 1. the functional diversification of constitutionally protected religious organizations, and 2. the expanding regulatory mandate of the state to enforce public accountability of organizations for harmful or fraudulent practices.

2393. Rose, Susan D. "Women Warriors: The Negotiation of Gender in a Charismatic Community." SA 48,3 (1987): 245-258.

Ethnographic study of an independent charismatic fellowship in upstate New York, 1982-83. The ideology called for male supremacy, but power was in fact exerted in a more egalitarian fashion.

2394. Samarin, William J. "Making Sense of Glossolalic Nonsense." SOCIAL RESEARCH 46,1 (1979): 88-105.

Based on field data and questionnaires. An understanding of the folk linguistics of the United States in general helps in understanding both glossolalists and those who comment on them.

2395. Schwartz, Gary. SECTS, IDEOLOGIES AND SOCIAL STATUS. Chicago: University of Chicago Press, 1970.

2396. Séguy, Jean. "Situation socio-historique du Pentecôtisme." LUMIERE ET VIE 24,125 (1975): 33-58.

Discusses the movement's prehistory and American origins.

2397. Smidt, Corwin. "'Praise the Lord' Politics: A Comparative Analysis of the Social Characteristics and Political Views of American Evangelical and Charismatic Christians." SA 50,1 (1989): 53-72.

1978-79 U.S. Gallup survey data suggest that evangelicals and charismatics are unlikely to unite politically.

2398. Von Hoffman, Nicholas, and Sally W. Cassidy. "Interviewing Negro Pentecostals." AMERICAN JOURNAL OF SOCIOLOGY 62,2 (1956): 195-197.

2399. Walker, Andrew G. "Pentecostal Power: The 'Charismatic Renewal Movement' and the Politics of Pentecostal Experience." In E. Barker (ed.), OF GODS AND MEN [volume cited in item 64], pp. 89-108.

General account.

2400. Wilson, Bryan R. "Role Conflicts and Status Contradictions of the Pentecostal Minister." AMERICAN JOURNAL OF SOCIOLOGY 64,5 (1959): 494-504.

A conflict stems from retaining sectarian ideology while recruiting unsectarian members.

2401. Wilson, Bryan R. SECTS AND SOCIETY: A SOCIOLOGICAL STUDY OF ELIM TABERNACLE, CHRISTIAN SCIENCE, AND CHRISTADELPHIANS. Berkeley: University of California Press, 1961.

2402. Wilson, Bryan R. "The Pentecostal Minister." In B.R. Wilson (ed.), PATTERNS OF SECTARIANISM. London: Heinemann, 1967.

2403. Wilson, Bryan R. RELIGIOUS SECTS. A SOCIOLOGICAL STUDY. New York: McGraw-Hill, 1970, pp. 66-92.

General description.

2404. Wilson, John, and Harvey K. Clow. "Themes of Power and Control in a Pentecostal Assembly." JSSR 20,3 (1981): 241-250.

Theories which stress the compensatory functions of Pentecostalism have little to say about its most distinctive feature - Spirit posses-sion. A replication theory of religious ritual, emphasizing an expressive role, can interpret this phenomenon better. Themes of power and control are most prominent; these resonate with Pentecostals' social situation, particularly their attitude toward work.

* Wood, William W. CULTURE AND PERSONALITY ASPECTS OF THE PENTECOSTAL HOLINESS RELIGION. Cited above as item 2361.


PENTECOSTAL (ITALY, FRANCE)

2405. Di Bella, Maria P. "Maladie et guérison dans les groupes pentecôtiste de l'Italie méridionale." SC 34,4 (1987): 465-474.

Malady and healing are occasioned by a conversion from the wicked world to the good and by an incorporation into the religious body.

2406. Williams, P. "Pour une approche de phénomène pentecôtiste chez Les Tsiganes." ETUDES TSIGANES 2 (1984): 49-51.

A study of Pentecostalism among Gypsies in France.


PENTECOSTAL (GREAT BRITAIN)

2407. Calley, Malcolm J.C. "Pentecostal Sects among West Indian Migrants." RACE 3,2 (1962): 55-64.

Information on the New Testament Church of God, the Church of God in Christ, and the Church of God of Prophecy, in 1961; schisms discussed. General description.

2408. Calley, Malcolm J.C. GOD'S PEOPLE: WEST INDIAN PENTECOSTAL SECTS IN ENGLAND. New York: Oxford University Press, 1965.

2409. Hill, Clifford. "Immigrant Sect Development in Britain: A Case of Status Deprivation?" SC 18,2 (1971): 231-236.

Anomie caused by racial prejudice and a consequent lowered status is more important than economic deprivation.

2410. Kiev, Ari. "Psychotherapeutic Aspects of Pentecostal Sects among West Indian Immigrants to England." BRITISH JOURNAL OF SOCIOLOGY 15,2

(1964): 129-138.

The sect provides a community experience, a cathartic ritual, and an ideology which places less emphasis on this life than on the life hereafter.

2411. Walker, Andrew G. "From Revival to Restoration: The Emergence of Britain's New Classical Pentecostalism." SC 32,2-3 (1985): 261-271.

Interprets Pentecostal sectarianism as a defense against modernity and secularization.

2412. Walker, Andrew G. RESTORING THE KINGDOM: THE RADICAL CHRISTIANITY OF THE HOUSE CHURCH MOVEMENT. London: Hodder and Stoughton, 1985.

2413. Walker, Andrew G., and James S. Atherton. "An Easter Pentecostal Convention: The Successful Management of a 'Time of Blessing'." SOCIOLOGICAL REVIEW 19,3 (1971): 367-387.

Research undertaken at an urban location in northern England.

## PENTECOSTAL (GENERAL LATIN AMERICAN)

* Lalive d'Epinay, Christian. "L'esprit et la champ oecuméniques de pasteurs sud-américains." Cited above as item 1748.

2414. Ribeiro de Oliveira, Pedro A. "Movimientos carismaticos na America Latina. Uma visão sociologica." CADERNOS ISER (Instituto Superior de Estudos da Religião, São Paulo) 5 (1975): 36-48.

## PENTECOSTAL (BRAZIL)

2415. De Souza, Muniz. A EXPERIÊNCIA DA SALVAÇÃO. PENTECOSTAIS EM SÃO PAULO. São Paulo: Livraria Duas Cidades, 1969.

2416. Howe, Gary N. "Capitalism and Religion at the Periphery: Pentecostalism and Umbanda in Brazil." In Stephen D. Glazier (ed.), PERSPECTIVES ON PENTECOSTALISM: CASE STUDIES FROM THE CARIBBEAN AND LATIN AMERICA. Washington: University Press of America, 1980, pp. 125-141.

2417. Nelson, Reed E. "Análise organizacional de uma igreja Brasileira: A Congregação Cristã no Brasil." REVISTA ECLESIASTICA BRASILEIRA 44 (1984): 544-558.

2418. Nelson, Reed E. "Funções organizacionais do culto numa igreja anarquista." RELIGIÃO E SOCIEDADE 12,1 (1985): 112-126.

2419. Novaes, Regina. OS ESCOLHIDOS DE DEUS. PENTECOSTAIS, TRABALHADORES E CIDADANIA. CADERNOS DO ISER Nº 19. Rio de Janeiro: Instituto de Estudos da Religião, 1985.

1976-77 field work on a congregation of the Assembléia de Deus in a municipio of Pernambuco.

2420. Rolim, Francisco Cartaxo. "Pentecôtisme et société au Brésil." SC 26,2-3 (1979): 345-372.

Identifies the capitalist class structure as the infrastructure of Pentecostalism in Brazil.

2421. Rolim, Francisco Cartaxo. PENTECOSTAIS NO BRASIL. UMA INTERPRETAÇÃO SOCIO-RELIGIOSA. Petrópolis: Vozes, 1985.

Review of data from diverse sources; new data from four municipios of Grande Rio.

2422. Willems, Emilio. "Validation of Authority in Pentecostal Sects of Chile and Brazil." JSSR 6,2 (1967): 253-258.

Comparison of one Brazilian and two Chilean Pentecostal sects. Opposing the class system in which they rank low, the sects seek to shape their own structure after an egalitarian model in which the criteria of conventional ranking are rejected. However, compromise with authoritarian principles seems common. The comparisons suggest that the closer a sect comes to the egalitarian model the more its leaders validate their authority by seeking supernatural sanctions for their decisions.

## PENTECOSTAL (CHILE)

2423. Damboriena, Prudencio. "Une secte protestante très active au Chili: Les Pentecôtistes." CHRIST AU MONDE 3 (1958): 103-115.

2424. Lalive d'Epinay, Christian. "Changements sociaux et développement d'une secte. Le pentecôtisme au Chile." ARCHIVES DE SOCIOLOGIE DES RELIGIONS 12 (1967): 65-90.

Examines an array of social and cultural factors which have made Pentecostalism an increasingly attractive religious option in Chilean society.

2425. Lalive d'Epinay, Christian. "La 'conquista' pentecostal en Chile." MENSAJE (July 1968): 1-8. See also "Pentecostal 'Conquista' in Chile." ECUMENICAL REVIEW 20 (1968): 16-32; and "The Pentecostal 'Conquest' of Chile: Rudiments of a Better Understanding." In D.E. Cutler (ed.), THE RELIGIOUS SITUATION [volume cited in item 1009], pp. 179-193.

General discussion.

2426. Lalive d'Epinay, Christian. EL REFUGIO DE LAS MASAS: ESTUDIO SOCIO-LOGICO DEL PROTESTANTISMO CHILEÑO. Santiago: Ed. Pacífico, 1968. See also HAVEN OF THE MASSES: A STUDY OF THE PENTECOSTAL MOVEMENT IN CHILE. London: Butterworth, 1969.

2427. Lalive d'Epinay, Christian. "Régimes politiques et millénarisme dans un société dépendante. Réflexions à propos du Pentecôtisme au Chili." CONCILIUM 181 (1983): 87-104.

2428. Rajana, E.W.  A SOCIOLOGICAL STUDY OF NEW RELIGIOUS MOVEMENTS: CHILEAN
PENTECOSTALISM AND JAPANESE NEW RELIGION.  Unpublished Ph.D. dissertation, London School of Economics, 1974.

2429. Tennekes, Johannes.  "Le mouvement pentecôtiste chilien et la politique."  SC 25,1 (1978): 55-80.

Survey of Chilean Pentecostals, 1971.  The leaders sympathized with
the right while the mass of the Pentecostal faithful supported the
left.

 * Willems, Emilio.  "Validation of Authority in Pentecostal Sects of
Chile and Brazil."  Cited above as item 2422.


*PENTECOSTAL (COLOMBIA, MEXICO, PUERTO RICO)*

2430. Flora, Cornelia Butler.  "Social Dislocation and Pentecostalism: A
Multi-variate Analysis."  SA 34,4 (1973): 296-307.

Respondents from Palmira in the Cauca Valley of Colombia.  Individuals
of low socio-economic status who have experienced personal social
dislocation in terms of migration and employment are more likely than
others to become Pentecostals.  Primary ties are also important.

2431. Flora, Cornelia Butler.  PENTECOSTALISM IN COLOMBIA: BAPTISM BY FIRE
AND SPIRIT.  Rutherford, N.J.: Fairleigh Dickinson University Press,
1976.

1966-68 observations and interviews, including the collection of
historical information.

2432. Goodman, Felicitas D.  "Prognosis: A New Religion?"  In I.I. Zaretsky
and M.P. Leone (eds.), RELIGIOUS MOVEMENTS IN CONTEMPORARY AMERICA
[volume cited in item 87], pp. 244-254.

Based on 1969 research in an Apostolic church in the Yucutan (Mexico).

2433. Goodman, Felicitas D., Jeanette H. Henney, and Esther Pressel.  TRANCE,
HEALING, AND HALLUCINATION: THREE FIELD STUDIES IN RELIGIOUS EXPERIENCE.
New York: Wiley-Interscience, 1974.

Study of an Apostolic church in Mexico.

2434. LaRuffa, Anthony L.  "Culture Change and Pentecostalism in Puerto Rico."
SOCIAL AND ECONOMIC STUDIES 18,3 (1969): 273-281.

Based on 1963-64 field work.

2435. Poblete Barth, Renato.  SECTARISMO PORTORRIQUEÑO. BUSQUEDA DE COMUNI-
DAD Y EXPANSION PENTECOSTAL.  Cuernavaca: CIDOC, Sonderos No. 55, 1969.

Study of the proliferation of Pentecostal groups among Puerto Ricans
in New York City.

2436. Abell, Troy D. THE HOLINESS-PENTECOSTAL EXPERIENCE IN SOUTHERN APPALACHIA. Unpublished Ph.D. dissertation, Purdue University, 1974. [DA 36:2 A, p. 956]

1973-74 field study among two congregations, as well as two control groups. Focus is on knowledge systems, perceptions of self as agent of change, and glossolalic experience.

* Garrison, Vivian. "Sectarianism and Psychosocial Adjustment: A Controlled Comparison of Puerto Rican Pentecostals and Catholics." Cited above as item 1238.

2437. Goldsmith, Peter. "Revivalism and the Advent of Cash Economy on the Georgia Coast." RRR 29,4 (1988): 385-397.

The ostensive otherworldliness of African-American Pentecostalism may militate against challenges to the status quo in the here-and-now, yet on the ideological level it withholds validation of dominant precepts by seeking meaning in the sphere of sacred relations and by attributing circumstances and events to forces beyond the control of individuals.

2438. Hawley, Florence. "The Keresan Holy Rollers: An Adaptation to American Individualism." SOCIAL FORCES 26,3 (1948): 272-280.

Study of a small Holy Roller group in a Catholic Pueblo (Keresan) community in New Mexico (after 1932).

2439. Lawless, Elaine J. GOD'S PECULIAR PEOPLE: WOMEN'S VOICES AND FOLK TRADITION IN A PENTECOSTAL CHURCH. Lexington: University Press of Kentucky, 1988.

* Lenski, Gerhard. "Social Correlates of Religious Interest." Cited above as item 1946.

2440. Paris, Arthur E. BLACK PENTECOSTALISM. SOUTHERN RELIGION IN AN URBAN WORLD. Amherst, Massachusetts: University of Massachusetts Press, 1982.

Based on 1971-73 participant observation in Boston, Massachusetts.

2441. Parsons, Anne. "The Pentecostal Immigrants." JSSR 4,2 (1965): 183-197.

Study of the Chiesa Evangelica Italiana, in New York City.

* Poblete Barth, Renato. SECTARISMO PORTORRIQUEÑO. BUSQUEDA DE COMUNIDAD Y EXPANSION PENTECOSTAL. Cited above as item 2435.

* Poloma, Margaret M. THE CHARISMATIC MOVEMENT: IS THERE A NEW PENTECOST? Cited above as item 2388.

2442. Shopshire, James M. A SOCIO-HISTORICAL CHARCTERIZATION OF THE BLACK PENTECOSTAL MOVEMENT IN AMERICA. Unpublished Ph.D. dissertation,

Northwestern University, 1975. [DA 36:11 A, p. 7488]

Interpretations from a church/sect perspective.

2443. Simpson, George E. "Black Pentecostalism in the United States."
PHYLON 35,2 (1974): 203-211.

An overview.

2444. Williams, Melvin D. COMMUNITY IN A BLACK PENTECOSTAL CHURCH. AN
ANTHROPOLOGICAL STUDY. Pittsburgh: University of Pittsburgh Press,
1974.

Anthropological study of a church in Pittsburgh, Pennsylvania.

## PENTECOSTAL CHURCH OF GOD IN AMERICA

2445. Young, Frank W. SOCIOCULTURAL ANALYSIS OF A CALIFORNIA PENTECOSTAL
CHURCH. Unpublished M.A. thesis, Cornell University, 1954.

2446. Young, Frank W. "Adaptation and Pattern Integration of a California
Sect." RRR 1,4 (1960): 137-150. Reprinted in Richard D. Knudten
(ed.), THE SOCIOLOGY OF RELIGION. AN ANTHOLOGY. New York: Appleton-
Century-Crofts, 1967, pp. 136-146.

Examines the gradual shift of a local congregation from a sectarian
to a denominational type of religion.

## UNITED PENTECOSTAL CHURCH (U.S.A.)

2447. Dearman, Marion V. DO HOLINESS SECTS SOCIALIZE IN DOMINANT VALUES?:
AN EMPIRICAL INQUIRY. Unpublished Ph.D. dissertation, University of
Oregon, 1972. [DA 33:9 A, p. 5296]

Interview data from congregations in six Oregon cities.

2448. Dearman, Marion V. "Christ and Conformity: A Study of Pentecostal
Values." JSSR 13,4 (1974): 437-453.

The United Pentecostal Church apparently does socialize members in
some central American values; based on interviews conducted in
Oregon.

## ASSEMBLY OF GOD (U.S.A.)

* Hammond, Phillip E., Albert Gedicks, Edward Lawler, and Louise Allen
Turner. "Clergy Authority and Friendship with Parishioners." Cited
above as item 1943.

* Maranell, Gary M. RESPONSES TO RELIGION. STUDIES IN THE SOCIAL
PSYCHOLOGY OF RELIGIOUS BELIEF. Cited above as item 1294.

* Perrin, Robin D. "American Religion in the Post-aquarian Age: Values

and Demographic Factors in Church Growth and Decline." Cited above as item 1409.

2449. Poloma, Margaret M. THE ASSEMBLIES OF GOD AT THE CROSSROADS. CHARISMA AND INSTITUTIONAL DILEMMAS. Knoxville: University of Tennessee Press, 1989.

## FULL GOSPEL BUSINESSMEN'S FELLOWSHIP INTERNATIONAL

2450. Bradfield, Cecil D. AN INVESTIGATION OF NEO-PENTECOSTALISM. Unpublished Ph.D. dissertation, American University, 1975. [DA 36:6 A, p. 4031]

Observation, review of movement literature, and questionnaire data on a Virginia chapter.

2451. Bradfield, Cecil D. "Our Kind of People: The Consequences of Neo-pentecostalism for Social Participation." VIRGINIA SOCIAL SCIENCE JOURNAL 13 (1978): 1-12.

2452. Bradfield, Cecil D. NEO-PENTECOSTALISM: A SOCIOLOGICAL ASSESSMENT. Washington: University Press of America, 1979.

1972-74 participant-observation and questionnaire research on a chapter of the group in western Virginia.

## SNAKE HANDLING

2453. Gerrard, Nathan L. "The Serpent-handling Religions of West Virginia." TRANSACTION 5,6 (1968): 22-28.

Religious serpent-handling is a safety valve for many of the frustrations of life in Appalachia.

2454. La Barre, Weston. THEY SHALL TAKE UP SERPENTS: PSYCHOLOGY OF THE SOUTHERN SNAKE-HANDLING CULT. Minneapolis: University of Minnesota Press, 1962.

2455. Morland, J. Kenneth. MILLWAYS OF KENT. Chapel Hill: University of North Carolina Press, 1958.

Study of a community in South Carolina.

# 20
## Independent Protestant Traditions

*WALDENSIAN*

2456. Lalive d'Epinay, Christian. "L'héritage et la dynamique externe du changement." ARCHIVES DE SCIENCES SOCIALES DES RELIGIONS 36 (1973): 35-70.

An analysis of the Waldensian community (Iris) in Chile and Argentina; based on participant observation and interviews.

*MORAVIAN*

2457. Bemmann, Herbert. DIE SOZIOLOGISCHE STRUKTUR DES HERRNHUTERTUMS. Unpublished Ph.D. dissertation, University of Heidelberg, 1921.

2458. Binöder, Carl. ZUR SOZIOLOGISCHEN BEDEUTUNG DER HERRNHUTER BRUDER-GEMEINE. Unpublished Ph.D. dissertation, University of Erlangen, 1956.

2459. Gollin, Gillian Lindt. MORAVIANS IN TWO WORLDS. A STUDY OF CHANGING COMMUNITIES. New York: Columbia University Press, 1967.

Historical sociology of the Moravians in Europe and America.

2460. Gollin, Gillian Lindt. "The Religious Factor in Social Change. Max Weber and the Moravian Paradox." ARCHIVES DE SOCIOLOGIE DES RELIGIONS 12,23 (1967): 91-97.

A comparative analysis of Herrnhut, the major Moravian settlement in Europe, and Bethlehem, the major American settlement.

2461. Roucek, Joseph S. "The Moravian Brethren in America." SOCIAL STUDIES 43 (1959): 58-61.

2462. Steiner, Jesse F. "Daytona: The Changing Status of Religious Conflict." In J.F. Steiner, THE AMERICAN COMMUNITY IN ACTION: CASE STUDIES OF AMERICAN COMMUNITIES. New York: Holt, 1928, pp. 264-278.

Discussion focuses on the nineteenth and twentieth centuries. Conflict between Moravians and Methodists subsided, only to be replaced by one between progressives and conservatives.

2463. Gillin, John L. THE DUNKERS: A SOCIOLOGICAL INTERPRETATION. Unpublished Ph.D. dissertation, Columbia University, 1906.

A study of the Church of the Brethren (Dunkers).

* Lenski, Gerhard. "Social Correlates of Religious Interest." Cited above as item 1946.

* Mol, J.J. (Hans) "A Collation of Data about Religion in Australia." Cited above as item 308.

* Photiadis, John D., and John F. Schnabel. "Religion: A Persistent Institution in a Changing Appalachia." Cited above as item 1311.

2464. Pletsch, Donald J. ECUMENISM IN TWO PROTESTANT CHURCHES IN ONTARIO. Unpublished M.Sc. thesis, University of Guelph, 1966.

A study of attitudes toward ecumenism among members of the Evangelical United Brethren Church.

* Scherer, Ross P. "A New Typology for Organizations: Market, Bureaucracy, Clan and Mission, with Application to American Denominations." Cited above as item 1416.

2465. Wilson, Bryan R. "The Exclusive Brethren: A Case Study in the Evolution of a Sectarian Ideology." In B.R. Wilson (ed.), PATTERNS OF SECTARIANISM [volume cited in item 2402], pp. 287-342.


*QUAKER*

* Baltzell, E. Digby. PURITAN BOSTON AND QUAKER PHILADELPHIA. Cited above as item 2103.

* Burnham, Kenneth E., John F. Connors III, and Richard C. Leonard. "Religious Affiliation, Church Attendance, Religious Education and Student Attitudes toward Race." Cited above as item 416.

2466. Child, John. "Quaker Employers and Industrial Relations." SOCIOLOGICAL REVIEW 12,3 (1964): 293-315.

After the 1920s in Great Britain, Quaker employers substituted a managerial theory for the Quaker ethic of industrial democracy.

2467. Doherty, Robert W. "Religion and Society: The Hicksite Separation of 1827." AMERICAN QUARTERLY 17,1 (1965): 63-80.

Analysis of the early nineteenth-century schism from church/sect and stratification perspectives.

2468. Doherty, Robert W. THE HICKSITE SEPARATION: A SOCIOLOGICAL ANALYSIS OF RELIGIOUS SCHISM IN EARLY NINETEENTH CENTURY AMERICA. New Brunswick, N.J.: Rutgers University Press, 1967.

2469. Hare, A. Paul. "Group Decisions by Consensus: Reaching Unity in the Society of Friends." SOCIOLOGICAL INQUIRY 43,1 (1973): 75-84.

Data from a Quaker committee's minutes. Traditionally, Quakers decide by reaching a 'sense of the meeting' rather than by a vote. Analysis in terms of Parsons' functional requisites - pattern maintenance, adaptation, integration, goal-attainment.

2470. Isichei, Elizabeth Allo. "From Sect to Denomination in English Quakerism, with Special Reference to the Nineteenth Century." BRITISH JOURNAL OF SOCIOLOGY 15,3 (1964): 207-222. See also "From Sect to Denomination among English Quakers." In B.R. Wilson (ed.), PATTERNS OF SECTARIANISM [volume cited in item 2402], pp. 161-181.

Suggests modification of the sect-to-denomination hypothesis.

2471. Isichei, Elizabeth Allo. "Organisation and Power in the Society of Friends." ARCHIVES DE SOCIOLOGIE DES RELIGIONS 10,19 (1965): 31-49.

Discusses the development within English Quakerism of an informal but tacitly accepted concentration of power, in apparent violation of the sect's democratic ideals.

2472. Kent, Stephen A. "Relative Deprivation and Resource Mobilization: A Study of Early Quakerism." BRITISH JOURNAL OF SOCIOLOGY 33,4 (1982): 529-544.

Resource mobilization and relative deprivation theories can be complementary rather than contradictory. Early Quakerism in England is used to illustrate the point.

2473. Kent, Stephen A. "Psychological and Mystical Interpretations of Early Quakerism: William James and Rufus Jones." RELIGION 17,3 (1987): 251-274.

Critique of discussions of early Quakerism by William James and Rufus Jones. By refuting their interpretations, the article argues that interpretations of Quakerism should be based upon historically grounded, social-psychological frameworks.

* Lenski, Gerhard. "Social Correlates of Religious Interest." Cited above as item 1946.

* Naveskar, Balwant. CAPITALISTS WITHOUT CAPITALISM: THE JAINS OF INDIA AND THE QUAKERS OF THE WEST. Cited above as item 219.

* Norr, James L. "Religion and Nation Building: The American Case." Cited above as item 1304.

2474. Ross, Jack C. TRADITIONALISM AND CHARISMA IN A RELIGIOUS GROUP: MEMBERSHIP CAREERS AND ROLE CONTINGENCIES OF QUAKERS. Unpublished Ph.D. dissertation, University of Minnesota, 1964. [DA 26:1, p. 531]

Questionnaire data from a small sample, and some participant observation, in a midwestern American setting.

2475. Ross, Jack C. "The Establishment Process in a Middle Class Sect."
SC 16,4 (1969): 500-507.

A midwestern U.S. Quaker Meeting was studied as an established introversionist sect with a highly educated membership. Establishment was
achieved in a short time due to the operation of internal institutions.

2476. Shideler, Emerson. AN EXPERIMENT IN SPIRITUAL ECCLESIOLOGY. Unpublished Ph.D. dissertation, University of Chicago, 1948.


*PIETIST*

2477. Gutwirth, Jacques. "Piétistes juifs et protestants. Une analyse
comparative/Jewish and Protestant Pietists. A Comparative Analysis."
ARCHIVES DE SCIENCES SOCIALES DE RELIGION 20,40 (1975): 53-66.

2478. Kaser, G. "L'eveil du sentiment national. Rôle du piétisme dans la
naissance du patriotisme." ARCHIVES DE SOCIOLOGIE DES RELIGIONS 22
(1966): 59-80.

2479. Lundby, Knut. "Closed Circles. An Essay on Culture and Pietism in
Norway." SC 35,1 (1988): 57-66.

2480. Stromberg, Peter G. SYMBOLS OF COMMUNITY: THE CULTURAL SYSTEM OF A
SWEDISH CHURCH. Tucson: University of Arizona Press, 1986.

Study of the Swedish Mission Covenant.

2481. Taggart, Morris. "Ecumenical Attitudes in the Evangelical Covenant
Church of America." RRR 9 (1967): 36-44.


*SALVATION ARMY*

2482. Milligan, J.E. THE PERSISTENCE OF THE SALVATION ARMY: A CHALLENGE TO
THE "SOCIOLOGY OF SECTARIANISM." Unpublished Ph.D. dissertation,
University of Glasgow, 1982. [DA 44:4 C, p. 788, #8/3498c]

Avoids using the church/sect typology, and applies the social-
construction-of-reality approach.

* Mol, J.J. (Hans) "A Collation of Data about Religion in Australia."
Cited above as item 308.

2483. Nieves, Alvar. CORRELATES OF CLERGY COMMITMENT: THE SALVATION ARMY
OFFICERS, AN ILLUSTRATIVE CASE STUDY. Unpublished Ph.D. dissertation,
Virginia Polytechnic Institute and State University, 1977.

2484. Robertson, Roland. "The Salvation Army: The Persistence of Sectarianism." In B.R. Wilson (ed.), PATTERNS OF SECTARIANISM [volume cited in
item 2402], pp. 49-105.

Examines the perdurance of the Salvation Army as an established sect.

ADVENTIST (IRVINGITE, MILLERITE)

2485. Allan, Graham. "A Theory of Millennialism: The Irvingite Movement as an Illustration." BRITISH JOURNAL OF SOCIOLOGY 25,3 (1974): 296-311.

The Irvingite movement activated the European millennial tradition in response to growing doubt and relativism within the British middle class during the 1830s.

2486. Barkun, Michael. CRUCIBLE OF THE MILLENNIUM: THE BURNED-OVER DISTRICT OF NEW YORK IN THE 1840s. Syracuse: Syracuse University Press, 1986.

Argues that Millerism and other religions of crisis in the region were responses to environmental and sociocultural disaster.

2487. Jones, Robert K. "The Catholic Apostolic Church: A Study in Diffused Commitment." SOCIOLOGICAL YEARBOOK OF RELIGION IN BRITAIN 5 (1972): 137-160.

Application of Smelser's theory of collective behavior to account for the emergence and development of the Irvingite movement in nineteenth-century Scotland.


ADVENTIST (JEHOVAH'S WITNESSES)

2488. Aguirre, B.E., and Jon P. Alston. "Organizational Change and Religious Commitment. Jehovah's Witnesses and Seventh-day Adventists in Cuba, 1938-1965." PACIFIC SOCIOLOGICAL REVIEW 23,2 (1980): 171-190.

Examines the fluctuating rates of membership activity and commitment in relation to changes in congregational sizes for the two movements.

2489. Alston, Jon P., and B.E. Aguirre. "Congregational Size and the Decline of Sectarian Commitment: The Case of Jehovah's Witnesses in South and North America." SA 40,1 (1979): 63-70.

Commitment levels for the period of 1950-76 were highest in smaller congregations.

2490. Beckford, James A. A SOCIOLOGICAL STUDY OF JEHOVAH'S WITNESSES IN BRITAIN. Unpublished Ph.D. thesis, University of Reading, 1972.

2491. Beckford, James A. "The Embryonic Stage of a Religious Sect's Development: The Jehovah's Witnesses." SOCIOLOGICAL YEARBOOK OF RELIGION IN BRITAIN 5 (1972): 11-32.

Argues that an idiosyncratic combination of circumstances favored the emergence and development of the Jehovah's Witnesses.

2492. Beckford, James A. "Organization, Ideology and Recruitment: The Structure of the Watch Tower Movement." SOCIOLOGICAL REVIEW 23,4 (1975): 893-909.

Historical review suggests a 'legitimation of praxis' model is more appropriate than a 'routinization of charisma' model for interpreting the fortunes of the movement.

2493. Beckford, James A. "Two Contrasting Types of Sectarian Organization." In R. Wallis (ed.), SECTARIANISM [volume cited in item 82], pp. 70-85.

Comparison of the Jehovah's Witnesses, and the United Family (Unification Church) in Great Britain.

2494. Beckford, James A. THE TRUMPET OF PROPHECY. A SOCIOLOGICAL STUDY OF JEHOVAH'S WITNESSES. Oxford: Basil Blackwell, 1975; New York: Halsted Press, 1975.

2495. Beckford, James A. "New Wine in New Bottles: A Departure from Church-sect Conceptual Tradition." SC 23,1 (1976): 71-85.

Church/sect conceptualizations did not prove to be useful in studying the Jehovah's Witnesses in Great Britain. Three theoretical orientations proved to be applicable: frustration/compensation, world-view construction, social integration.

2496. Beckford, James A. "Structural Dependence in Religious Organizations: From 'Skid-row' to Watch Tower." JSSR 15,2 (1976): 169-175.

Far from being discrepant, the goals at the periphery of the Jehovah's Witnesses accord with those of its organizational center.

2497. Beckford, James A. "Introduction. The Watchtower Movement World-wide." SC 24,1 (1977): 5-31.

Introduction of the topic of a thematic issue of SOCIAL COMPASS.

2498. Cohn, Werner. "Jehovah's Witnesses as a Proletarian Movement." THE AMERICAN SCHOLAR 24,3 (1955): 281-298.

The proletarian condition leads to a desire to secede from the wider society; the Witnesses exemplify this.

2499. Cooper, Lee R. "'Publish' or Perish: Negro Jehovah's Witness Adaptation to the Ghetto." In I.I. Zaretsky and M.P. Leone (eds.), RELIGIOUS MOVEMENTS IN CONTEMPORARY AMERICA [volume cited in item 87], pp. 700-721.

1968-69 participant-observation data from a black Jehovah's Witnesses congregation in North Philadelphia.

2500. Cross, Sholto. THE WATCH TOWER MOVEMENT IN SOUTH CENTRAL AFRICA, 1908-1945. Unpublished Ph.D. thesis, Oxford University, 1973.

2501. Cross, Sholto. "Social History and Millennial Movements: The Watch Tower in South Central Africa." SC 24,1 (1977): 83-95.

2502. Dericquebourg, Régis. "Les Témoins de Jéhovah dans le Nord de la France: Implantation et expansion." SC 24,1 (1977): 71-82.

The movement spread among mine workers, especially Polish immigrants.

2503. Dobbelaere, Karel, and Bryan R. Wilson. "Jehovah's Witnesses in a Catholic Country." ARCHIVES DE SCIENCES SOCIALES DES RELIGIONS 50,1 (1980): 89-110.

Based on questionnaire and interview data on nine Belgian congregations.

2504. Dye, Elsa. SECTARIAN PROTESTANTISM: ANOTHER DIMENSION - THE CASE OF THE JEHOVAH'S WITNESSES. Unpublished M.A. thesis, San Diego State College, 1968.

2505. Hébert, G. LES TEMOINS DE JEHOVAH. Montréal: Les Editions Bellarmin, 1960.

2506. Jubber, Ken. "The Persecution of Jehovah's Witnesses in Southern Africa." SC 24,1 (1977): 121-134.

The Witnesses' political neutrality provoked considerable persecution.

* Lalive d'Epinay, Christian. "L'esprit et la champ oecuméniques de pasteurs sud-américains." Cited above as item 1748.

2507. Leman, Johan. "Jehovah's Witnesses and Immigration in Continental Western Europe." SC 26,1 (1979): 41-72.

Study of the Witnesses in Belgium. The immigrant members seemed concerned about securing their future.

2508. Long, Norman. "Rural Entrepreneurship and Religious Commitment in Zambia." In J. Matthes (ed.), INTERNATIONALES JAHRBUCH FÜR RELIGIONS-SOZIOLOGIE 6 [volume cited in item 2000], pp. 142-157.

Based on 1963-64 field work.

2509. Maesen, William A., and Lawrence La Fave. "The Jehovah's Witnesses Today: A Study by Participant Observation." PROCEEDINGS OF THE SOUTHWESTERN SOCIOLOGICAL SOCIETY 9 (1960): 102-104.

2510. Montague, Havor. "The Pessimistic Sect's Influence on the Mental Health of Its Members: The Case of Jehovah's Witnesses." SC 24,1 (1977): 135-147.

Advanced age and socio-economic status are more important predictors of mental illness among Jehovah's Witnesses than anything inherent in the religion itself.

2511. Munters, Quirinus J. "Recruitment as a Vocation: The Case of Jehovah's Witnesses." SOCIOLOGIA NEERLANDICA 7,2 (1971): 88-100.

Questionnaire data from Jehovah's Witnesses in Utrecht, the Netherlands, 1965-69.

2512. Munters, Quirinus J. "Recrutement et candidats en puissance." SC 24,1 (1977): 59-69.

Based on research undertaken in the Netherlands. The Witnesses distinguish between promoting their message and, once coming upon promising

331

candidates, recruiting new members.

* Perrin, Robin D. "American Religion in the Post-aquarian Age: Values and Demographic Factors in Church Growth and Decline." Cited above as item 1409.

2513. Rogerson, Alan T. MILLIONS NOW LIVING WILL NEVER DIE. London: Constable, 1969.

2514. Rogerson, Alan T. A SOCIOLOGICAL ANALYSIS OF THE ORIGINS AND DEVELOPMENT OF THE JEHOVAH'S WITNESSES AND THEIR SCHISMATIC GROUPS. Unpublished Ph.D. dissertation, Oxford University, 1972.

2515. Rogerson, Alan T. "Témoins de Jéhovah et Etudiants de la Bible. Qui est schismatique?" SC 24,1 (1977): 33-43.

Analysis of schisms after Russell's death: the Pastoral Bible Institute was introversionist; the Laymen's Home Missionary Movement emphasized the doctrines of a charismatic leader; Rutherford's Watch Tower Society emphasized evangelization and structure; the Dawn Bible Student Association moved away from sectarianism toward a denominational stance. During the period of 1919-32, Rutherford transformed the Watch Tower Society into the Jehovah's Witnesses.

2516. Séguy, Jean. "Messianisme et échec social: Les Témoins de Jéhovah." ARCHIVES DE SOCIOLOGIE DES RELIGIONS 21 (1966): 89-99.

Suggests that new adherents to the movement are likely to be recruited from the ranks of the socially marginalized.

2517. Singelenberg, Richard. "'It Separated the Wheat from the Chaff': The '1975' Prophecy and Its Impact among Dutch Jehovah's Witnesses." SA 50,1 (1989): 23-40.

Examines trends in Witnesses' activity levels in the Netherlands before and after an apparently disconfirmed millennial prophecy, as a possible test of cognitive balance theory.

2518. Stroup, Herbert H. THE JEHOVAH'S WITNESSES. New York: Russell, 1967 (reprint of 1945 original).

2519. White, T. A PEOPLE FOR HIS NAME. New York: Vantage, 1967.

2520. Wilson, Bryan R. "Jehovah's Witnesses in Africa." NEW SOCIETY 25/562 (1973): 73-75.

Examines why political attacks against the Witnesses are so often popular.

2521. Wilson, Bryan R. "Jehovah's Witnesses in Kenya." JOURNAL OF RELIGION IN AFRICA 5,2 (1973): 128-149.

Discussion focuses on the 1960s and early 1970s; points out the tribal origins of adherents.

2522. Wilson, Bryan R. "Aspects of Kinship and the Rise of Jehovah's

Witnesses in Japan." SC 24,1 (1977): 97-120.

The reinforcement of kinship bonds, the operation of a wider community functioning almost as an extended clan, and the involvement in a pattern of rationally-organized activity that has few western cultural-style characteristics, appear to help explain the success of the Jehovah's Witnesses in Japan.

2523. Zygmunt, Joseph F. JEHOVAH'S WITNESSES. A STUDY OF SYMBOLIC AND STRUCTURAL ELEMENTS IN THE DEVELOPMENT AND INSTITUTIONALIZATION OF A SECTARIAN MOVEMENT. Unpublished Ph.D. dissertation, University of Chicago, 1967.

2524. Zygmunt, Joseph F. "Prophetic Failure and Chiliastic Identity: The Case of Jehovah's Witnesses." AMERICAN JOURNAL OF SOCIOLOGY 75,6 (1970): 926-948.

Longitudinal analysis of the impact of the group's millenarian orientation upon its developmental career.

2525. Zygmunt, Joseph F. "Jehovah's Witnesses in the U.S.A.: 1942-1976." SC 24,1 (1977): 45-57.

There have been important changes of style, including a re-emphasis of eschatological predictions, but no abandonment of a sectarian stance toward the world.

* Zylberberg, Jacques. "Nationalisation et dénationalisation: Le cas des collectivités sacrales excentriques." Cited above as item 539.

## SEVENTH-DAY ADVENTIST

* Aguirre, B.E., and Jon P. Alston. "Organizational Change and Religious Commitment. Jehovah's Witnesses and Seventh-day Adventists in Cuba, 1938-1965." Cited above as item 2488.

2526. Bull, Malcolm. "The Seventh-day Adventists: Heretics of American Civil Religion." SA 50,2 (1989): 177-187.

Focus is on the group in the U.S.A., 1850s and thereafter.

2527. Dudley, Roger L. "Alienation from Religion in Adolescents from Fundamentalist Religious Homes." JSSR 17,4 (1978): 389-398.

A study of 400 American high-school students. Authoritarian image of parents as well as image of parental inconsistency of profession and action attenuate the religious commitment of respondents, especially on the practice dimension.

2528. Dudley, Roger L., and Des Cummings, Jr. "Factors Related to Pastoral Morale in the Seventh-day Adventist Church." RRR 24,2 (1982): 127-137.

Survey of pastoral morale among 172 pastors in the U.S. and Canada. Most were generally happy in their work, but a substantial minority had low morale experiences. Low morale correlated with quality of pastor-spouse relationships. Pastors wanted to be relieved of administrative trivia, to have more continuing education, and an egalitarian relationship with conference administrators.

2529. Dudley, Roger L., and Des Cummings, Jr. "A Study of Factors Relating to Church Growth in the North American Division of Seventh Day Adventists." RRR 24,4 (1983): 322-333.

1980 survey from 249 pastors and 8211 members in the U.S.A. (excluding Alaska and Hawaii) and Canada.

2530. Dudley, Roger L., and Margaret G. Dudley. "Transmission of Religious Values from Parents to Adolescents." RRR 28,1 (1986): 3-15.

Presents correlations between youths' values and those of their fathers and of their mothers. Significant differences occurred between generations, but significant correlations as well. Mothers were most traditional, followed by fathers and then by youths. Respondents (712 total: 218 triads and 29 dyads) from 21 randomly selected congregations in the U.S.A.

2531. Jackson, L.F. "Seventh-day Adventists in New Zealand: Towards a Demographic History." In Peter H. Ballis (ed.), IN AND OUT OF THE WORLD. SEVENTH-DAY ADVENTISTS IN NEW ZEALAND. Palmerston North: Dunmore Press, 1985.

* Lalive d'Epinay, Christian. "L'esprit et la champ oecuméniques de pasteurs sud-américains." Cited above as item 1748.

2532. Lewellen, Ted C. "Deviant Religion and Cultural Evolution: The Aymara Case." JSSR 18,3 (1979): 243-251.

Among the Aymara of Peru, a once ostracized and persecuted religious minority, Seventh-day Adventism assumed leadership as the community economy changed from subsistence agriculture to a money system. A 'Weberian' explanation is rejected. The deviant religion was not a cause of the money economy but an important factor in developments.

* Maranell, Gary M. RESPONSES TO RELIGION. STUDIES IN THE SOCIAL PSY-CHOLOGY OF RELIGIOUS BELIEF. Cited above as item 1294.

* Mol, J.J. (Hans) "A Collation of Data about Religion in Australia." Cited above as item 308.

* Perrin, Robin D. "American Religion in the Post-aquarian Age: Values and Demographic Factors in Church Growth and Decline." Cited above as item 1409.

2533. Theobald, Robin. "Seventh-day Adventists and the Millennium." SOCI-OLOGICAL YEARBOOK OF RELIGION IN BRITAIN 7 (1974): 111-131.

Examines the unique cultural conditions which facilitated the rise of the Seventh-day Adventist movement.

2534. Theobald, Robin. "The Role of Charisma in the Development of Social

Movements: Ellen G. White and the Emergence of Seventh-day Adventism."
ARCHIVES DE SCIENCES SOCIALES DES RELIGIONS 49,1 (1980): 83-100.

Discusses how the charismatic authority of Ellen G. White became
routinized in a complex bureaucratic structure, even while the found-
ress of Seventh-day Adventism was still alive.

2535. Theobald, Robin. "The Politicization of a Religious Movement: British
Adventism under the Impact of West Indian Immigration." BRITISH
JOURNAL OF SOCIOLOGY 32,2 (1981): 202-223.

Assesses the impact (including an organizational split) of black
immigrant recruits to the religion in Britain.

2536. Topalov, Anne-Marie. "Religion et santé: Le cas de la diététique des
Adventistes du 7e jour." SC 34,4 (1987): 509-514.

Discusses the importance of health concerns in the evolution of the
church.


*ADVENTIST (CHRISTADELPHIAN)*

* Wilson, Bryan R. SECTS AND SOCIETY: A SOCIOLOGICAL STUDY OF ELIM
TABERNACLE, CHRISTIAN SCIENCE, AND CHRISTADELPHIANS. Cited above as
item 2401.


*CHRISTIAN SCIENCE*

2537. Braden, Charles S. CHRISTIAN SCIENCE TO-DAY. Dallas: Southern
Methodist University Press, 1958.

2538. Demarest, Janice L. "A Sociolinguistic Study of Christian Science Oral
Testimonies." WORKING PAPERS IN SOCIOLINGUISTICS No. 26. Austin:
Southwest Educational Development Laboratory, 1975.

2539. DeNood, Neal B. THE DIFFUSION OF A SYSTEM OF BELIEF. Unpublished
Ph.D. dissertation, Harvard University, 1937.

* Ebaugh, Helen Rose Fuchs, and Sharron Lee Vaughn. "Ideology and Recruitment in Religious Groups." Cited above as item 890.

* Ebaugh, Helen Rose Fuchs, Kathe Richman, and Janet Saltzman Chafetz.
"Life Crises among the Religiously Committed: Do Sectarian Differences
Matter?" Cited above as item 889.

2540. England, R.W. "Some Aspects of Christian Science as Reflected in
Letters of Testimony." AMERICAN JOURNAL OF SOCIOLOGY 59,5 (1954):
448-453.

Description of the relationship between Christian Science's concern
with physical health and its membership, dynamics, and appeal.

* Lenski, Gerhard. "Social Correlates of Religious Interest." Cited

above as item 1946.

2541. Nudelman, Arthur E. "Dimensions of Religiosity: A Factor-analytic View of Protestants, Catholics and Christian Scientists." RRR 13,1 (1971): 42-56.

Data from 1967 interviews with midwestern U.S. college students, all Christian Scientists. Two principal factors emerged in factor analysis - devotion and participation, duplicating findings by Stark and Glock on Protestants and Roman Catholics.

2542. Nudelman, Arthur E. "Christian Science and Secular Science: Adaptation on the College Scene." JSSR 11,3 (1972): 271-276.

Data from a 1967 survey by interviews with Christian Science students at a midwestern U.S. university. While Christian Science students were less likely than others to major in the behavioral and life sciences, they were no less likely to major in the physical sciences, and more likely than others to major in engineering.

2543. Nudelman, Arthur E. "The Maintenance of Christian Science in Scientific Society." In R. Wallis and P. Morely (eds.), MARGINAL MEDICINE [volume cited in item 2369], pp. 42-60.

2544. Nudelman, Arthur E., and Barbara E. Nudelman. "Health and Illness Behavior of Christian Scientists." SOCIAL SCIENCE AND MEDICINE 6,2 (1972): 253-262.

Interview data from undergraduate Christian Scientists attending a large midwestern U.S. university.

2545. Pfautz, Harold W. CHRISTIAN SCIENCE. THE SOCIOLOGY OF A SOCIAL MOVEMENT AND RELIGIOUS GROUP. Unpublished Ph.D. dissertation, University of Chicago, 1954.

2546. Pfautz, Harold W. "Christian Science: A Case Study of the Social Psychological Aspect of Secularization." SOCIAL FORCES 34,3 (1956): 246-251.

Content analysis of published letters of testimony, 1890-1950. The proportion of purposeful-rational letters, as opposed to affective ones, increased.

2547. Pfautz, Harold W. "A Case Study of an Urban Religious Movement: Christian Science." In Ernest W. Burgess and Donald J. Bogue (eds.), CONTRIBUTIONS TO URBAN SOCIOLOGY. Chicago: University of Chicago Press, 1964, pp. 284-303.

History of Christian Science, conceptualizing it as a social movement. Uses secondary sources.

2548. Thorner, Isidor. CHRISTIAN SCIENCE AND ASCETIC PROTESTANTISM: A STUDY IN THE SOCIOLOGY OF RELIGION, PERSONALITY TYPE AND SOCIAL STRUCTURE. Cambridge: Harvard University Press, 1951.

2549. Wardwell, Walter I. "Christian Science Healing." JSSR 4,2 (1964-65): 175-181. See also David E. Sleeper, "Christian Science Healing: Comment." JSSR 5,2 (1965-66): 296-297; and W.I. Wardwell, "Reply to D.E. Sleeper." JSSR 5,2 (1965-66): 298.

Review of the healing methods and teachings of Christian Science.

2550. Wilson, Bryan R. "The Origins of Christian Science: A Survey." HILBERT JOURNAL 57 (1959): 161-170.

* Wilson, Bryan R. SECTS AND SOCIETY: A SOCIOLOGICAL STUDY OF ELIM TABERNACLE, CHRISTIAN SCIENCE, AND CHRISTADELPHIANS. Cited above as item 2401.


COMMUNITARIAN

2551. Barthel, Diane L. AMANA: FROM PIETIST SECT TO AMERICAN COMMUNITY. Lincoln: University of Nebraska Press, 1984.

2552. Mikkelsen, Michael A. THE BISHOP HILL COLONY. A RELIGIOUS COMMUNIST SETTLEMENT IN HENRY COUNTY, ILLINOIS. Baltimore: Johns Hopkins University Press, 1892.

A study of the Erik Janssonist movement.

2553. Nelson, Charles H. "The Erik Janssonist Movement of Pre-industrial Sweden." SA 38,3 (1977): 209-225.

Study of a nineteenth-century sect which left Sweden because of persecution and settled in western Illinois, sparking a Swedish national debate about religious liberty. Both material conditions and religious distinctiveness gave the movement a protest character.

2554. Treece, James W., Jr. "Theories on Religious Communal Development." SC 18,1 (1971): 85-100.

Description of the Bethany Fellowship, followed by a general comparison with four other communal groups - Koinonia Farm in Sumter County, Georgia; Hutterites; St. Julian's in Sussex, England; and Mayeem Kareem kibbutz in Israel.

2555. Whitworth, John. GOD'S BLUEPRINTS: A SOCIOLOGICAL STUDY OF THREE UTOPIAN SECTS. London: Routledge and Kegan Paul, 1975.

Examination of the Shakers, the Oneida Community, and the Society of Brothers (or Bruderhof).

2556. Zablocki, Benjamin D. THE JOYFUL COMMUNITY. Baltimore: Penguin, 1971; Chicago: University of Chicago Press, 1980.

Study of the Society of Brothers (or Bruderhof).

2557. Adams, Robert L., and John Mogey. "Marriage, Membership and Mobility in Church and Sect." SA 28,4 (1967): 205-214.

Data from marriage records for 1943-65 in five Disciples of Christ congregations in Nashville, Tennessee. Theology and gender (husband's denomination) more than class determine selection of denomination in cases of religiously mixed marriage.

* Demerath, Nicholas J., III. SOCIAL CLASS IN AMERICAN PROTESTANTISM. Cited above as item 2036.

2558. Ethridge, F. Maurice, and Joe R. Feagin. "Varieties of 'Fundamentalism': A Conceptual and Empirical Analysis of Two Protestant Denominations." SOCIOLOGICAL QUARTERLY 20,1 (1979): 37-48.

1972 questionnaire data from lay leaders in Texas in the Churches of Christ and Disciples of Christ denominations. The fundamentalists in the two churches have different kinds of fundamentalism, and different demographic variables correlate with the two fundamentalisms. The authors advocate denomination-specific fundamentalism scales.

* Glock, Charles Y., and Rodney Stark. RELIGION AND SOCIETY IN TENSION. Cited above as item 1118.

* Glock, Charles Y., and Rodney Stark. CHRISTIAN BELIEFS AND ANTI-SEMITISM. Cited above as item 1119.

* Hartley, Shirley F., and Mary G. Taylor. "Religious Beliefs of Clergy Wives." Cited above as item 1944.

* Lenski, Gerhard. "Social Correlates of Religious Interest." Cited above as item 1946.

* Maranell, Gary M. RESPONSES TO RELIGION. STUDIES IN THE SOCIAL PSYCHOLOGY OF RELIGIOUS BELIEF. Cited above as item 1294.

* Norr, James L. "Religion and Nation Building: The American Case." Cited above as item 1304.

* Perrin, Robin D. "American Religion in the Post-aquarian Age: Values and Demographic Factors in Church Growth and Decline." Cited above as item 1409.

* Royle, Marjorie H. "Women Pastors. What Happens after Placement?" Cited above as item 2062.

* Scherer, Ross P. "A New Typology for Organizations: Market, Bureaucracy, Clan and Mission, with Application to American Denominations." Cited above as item 1416.

* Van Roy, Ralph F., Frank D. Bean, and James R. Wood. "Social Mobility and Doctrinal Orthodoxy." Cited above as item 1962.

2559. Whitley, Oliver R. "The Sect-to-Denomination Process in an American Religious Movement: The Disciples of Christ." SOUTHWESTERN SOCIAL SCIENCE QUARTERLY 36,3 (1955): 275-281.

Descriptive hypothesis.

## CHURCHES OF CHRIST

2560. Banowsky, William S. THE MIRROR OF A MOVEMENT. Dallas: Christian Publishing Co., 1965.

* Ethridge, F. Maurice, and Joe R. Feagin. "Varieties of 'Fundamentalism': A Conceptual and Empirical Analysis of Two Protestant Denominations." Cited above as item 2558.

2561. Garrison, Charles E. "The Effect of Participation in Congregational Structures on Church Attendance." RRR 18,1 (1976): 36-43.

1973 survey of church members among students at Milligan College in Tennessee. Having held a position in a church organization correlated positively with church attendance.

2562. Gaustad, Edwin S. "Churches of Christ in America." In D.R. Cutler (ed.), THE RELIGIOUS SITUATION [volume cited in item 1009], pp. 1013-1033.

* Ingram, Larry C. "Sectarian Colleges and Academic Freedom." Cited above as item 2122.

* Laumann, Edward O. "The Social Structure of Religious and Ethno-religious Groups in a Metropolitan Community." Cited above as item 469.

* Maranell, Gary M. RESPONSES TO RELIGION. STUDIES IN THE SOCIAL PSYCHOLOGY OF RELIGIOUS BELIEF. Cited above as item 1294.

* Mol, J.J. (Hans) "A Collation of Data about Religion in Australia." Cited above as item 308.

2563. Money, Royce L. CHURCH-STATE RELATIONS IN THE CHURCHES OF CHRIST SINCE 1945: A STUDY IN RELIGION AND POLITICS. Unpublished Ph.D. dissertation, Baylor University, 1975. [DA 36:9 A, p. 6156]

Questionnaires, interviews with church leaders, and a review of denominational literature, focusing on politics (e.g., anti-Catholicism, anti-Communism, and American nationalism).

2564. Woodroof, J. Timothy. RELIGIOSITY AND REFERENCE GROUPS: TOWARDS A MODEL OF ADOLESCENT SEXUALITY. Unpublished Ph.D. dissertation, University of Nebraska, 1984. [DA 45:9 A, p. 3002]

College freshman questionnaire study.

2565. Woodroof, J. Timothy. "Premarital Sexual Behavior and Religious

Adolescents." JSSR 24,4 (1985): 343-366.

Questionnaire data from freshmen attending eight colleges affiliated with the Churches of Christ. Religious practice frequency and orthodoxy both correlate negatively with premarital sexual activity.

2566. Woodroof, J. Timothy. "Reference Groups, Religiosity, and Premarital Sexual Behavior." JSSR 25,4 (1986): 436-460.

Questionnaire data from students at eight colleges affiliated with the Churches of Christ. Both peers' and parents' religious practice and attitudes about sexual conduct are influential on the respondents, but peers are by far the more important reference group.

## MAINLINE MERGER (UNITED CHURCH OF CANADA)

* Bibby, Reginald W. FRAGMENTED GODS: THE POVERTY AND POTENTIAL OF RELIGION IN CANADA. Cited above as item 1927.

2567. Black, Alan W. "Church Union in Canada and Australia: A Comparative Analysis." AUSTRALIAN-CANADIAN STUDIES 1 (1983): 44-56.

Examines the formation of the United Church of Canada (1925) and the Uniting Church in Australia (1977).

* Campbell, Douglas F. "The Anglican and United Churches in Church Union Dialogue, 1943-75." Cited above as item 1928.

2568. Crysdale, Stewart. THE CHANGING CHURCH IN CANADA: BELIEFS AND SOCIAL ATTITUDES OF UNITED CHURCH PEOPLE. Toronto: United Church of Canada Publishing House, 1965.

The beliefs and social attitudes of members and adherents of the United Church of Canada in relation to their level of urbanism as a life style, to their region, size of community, level of education, frequency of church attendance, age, and other possibly influential factors. Two problems are central. One is consensus in beliefs. The other is how to implement beliefs in such major issues as civil liberty and public responsibility for economic planning and social welfare.

* Hunsberger, Bruce. "Background Religious Denomination, Parental Emphasis, and the Religious Orientation of University Students." Cited above as item 1702.

* Kaill, Robert C. "Ecumenism, Clergy Influence and Liberalism: An Investigation into the Sources of Lay Support for Church Union." Cited above as item 1931.

2569. Lovelace, Arthur B. THE ROLE OF THE UNITED CHURCH IN SOCIAL POLITICS. Unpublished M.A. thesis, McGill University, 1936.

2570. Mair, Nathan H. "The Quebec Protestant Churches and the Question of Nationalism." SC 31,4 (1984): 379-390.

The clergy were more open to Quebec nationalism than were the laity.

* Pickering, W.S.F., and J.E.W. Jackson. "A Brief Sociological Examination of Local United and Anglican Churches." Cited above as item 1935.

* Pletsch, Donald J. ECUMENISM IN TWO PROTESTANT CHURCHES IN ONTARIO. Cited above as item 2464.

2571. Stone, David R. A STUDY OF ROLE PERCEPTIONS AS INDICES OF SOCIAL DISTANCE BETWEEN UNITED CHURCH OF CANADA CLERGYMEN AND UNITED CHURCH UNDERGRADUATES. Unpublished M.A. thesis, Wayne State University, 1968.

A survey of how well two groups perceive each other's activities, attitudes, and aspirations.

## MAINLINE MERGER (UNITED CHURCH OF CHRIST)

2572. Bass, Dorothy C., and Kenneth B. Smith (eds.) THE UNITED CHURCH OF CHRIST: STUDIES IN IDENTITY AND POLITY. Chicago: Exploration Press of the Chicago Theological Seminary, 1987.

* Broughton, Walter, and Edgar W. Mills, Jr. "Resource Inequality and Accumulative Advantage: Stratification in the Ministry." Cited above as item 1939.

2573. Campbell, Thomas C., and Yoshio Fukuyama. THE FRAGMENTED LAYMAN: AN EMPIRICAL STUDY OF LAY ATTITUDES. Philadelphia: Pilgrim Press, 1971.

2574. Cooper, Charles W., Jr. "United Church of Christ Pastors: A Demographic and Psychographic Description." RRR 13,3 (1972): 212-218.

U.S.A. random sample, 1970.

2575. Fukuyama, Yoshio. "Parishioners' Attitudes towards Issues in the Civil Rights Movement." SA 29,2 (1968): 94-103.

Based on a 1964-65 sample. White and black respondents differed in perception of clergy roles as well as in support of the civil rights movement.

2576. Fukuyama, Yoshio. THE MINISTRY IN TRANSITION. A CASE STUDY OF THEOLOGICAL EDUCATION. University Park, Pennsylvania: Pennsylvania State University Press, 1972.

1967 survey of a sample of UCC clergy, one subset ordained 1962-66 and the other 1952-61; another survey of UCC theology students.

* Gockel, Galen L. "Income and Religious Affiliation: A Regression Analysis." Cited above as item 437.

* Hoge, Dean R., and John E. Dyble. "The Influence of Assimilation on American Protestant Ministers' Beliefs, 1928-1978." Cited above as item 1945.

* Jeffries, Vincent, and Clarence E. Tygart. "More on Clergy and Social Issues." Cited above as item 1266.

2577. Jud, Gerald J., Edgar W. Mills, Jr., and Genevieve Walters Burch. EX-PASTORS: WHY MEN LEAVE THE PARISH MINISTRY. Philadelphia: Pilgrim Press, 1970.

2578. McKinney, William J., Jr. "Performance of United Church of Christ Congregations in Massachusetts and in Pennsylvania." In D.R. Hoge and D.A. Roozen (eds.), UNDERSTANDING CHURCH GROWTH AND DECLINE 1950-78 [volume cited in item 2137], pp. 224-247.

1976 Church Membership Inventory data from the Massachusetts and Central Pennsylvania conferences.

2579. McKinney, William J., Jr., and Dean R. Hoge. "Community and Congregational Factors in the Growth and Decline of Protestant Churches." JSSR 22,1 (1983): 51-66.

Study of 3247 UCC congregations' growth or decline between 1970 and 1978. Larger churches declined more, city churches markedly. New churches grew most, as did churches of young people.

* Maranell, Gary M. RESPONSES TO RELIGION. STUDIES IN THE SOCIAL PSYCHOLOGY OF RELIGIOUS BELIEF. Cited above as item 1294.

2580. Newman, William M. "The United Church of Christ Merger: A Case Study in Organizational Structure, Policy and Ideology." In Deborah I. Offenbacher and Constance H. Poster (eds.), SOCIAL PROBLEMS AND SOCIAL POLICY. New York: Appleton-Century-Crofts, 1970, pp. 137-145.

* Perrin, Robin D. "American Religion in the Post-aquarian Age: Values and Demographic Factors in Church Growth and Decline." Cited above as item 1409.

* Quinley, Harold E. THE PROPHETIC CLERGY. SOCIAL ACTIVISM AMONG PROTESTANT MINISTERS. Cited above as item 1953.

* Scherer, Ross P. "A New Typology for Organizations: Market, Bureaucracy, Clan and Mission, with Application to American Denominations." Cited above as item 1416.

* Stark, Rodney, Bruce D. Foster, Charles Y. Glock, and Harold E. Quinley. WAYWARD SHEPHERDS: PREJUDICE AND THE PROTESTANT CLERGY. Cited above as item 1960.

* Van Roy, Ralph F., Frank D. Bean, and James R. Wood. "Social Mobility and Doctrinal Orthodoxy." Cited above as item 1962.

2581. Walters Burch, Genevieve. "The Ex-pastor's Message to the Church as an Occupational System." SC 17,4 (1970): 517-532.

1967 survey of former UCC clergy indicates strains and problems associated with the following systems: professional training, hiring, work and reward, support, family and personality.

## MAINLINE MERGER (UNITING CHURCH IN AUSTRALIA)

* Black, Alan W. "Church Union in Canada and Australia: A Comparative Analysis." Cited above as item 2567.

2582. Black, Alan W. "The Sociology of Ecumenism: Initial Observations on the Formation of the Uniting Church in Australia." In A. Black and P. Glasner (eds.), PRACTICE AND BELIEF [volume cited in item 91], pp. 86-107.

* Black, Alan W. "The Impact of Theological Orientation and of Breadth of Perspective on Church Members' Attitudes and Behaviors: Roof, Mol and Kaill Revisited." Cited above as item 2095.

2583. Black, Alan W. "Some Aspects of Religion and Law. The Case of Church Union in Australia." RELIGION 16,3 (1986): 225-247.

## JESUS MOVEMENT (MISCELLANEOUS)

2584. Adams, Robert L., and Robert J. Fox. "Mainlining Jesus: The New Trip." SOCIETY 9,4 (1972): 50-56.

Observation and interview data from Gethsemane Chapel, a commune located in Orange County, California.

2585. Balswick, Jack. "The Jesus People Movement: A Generational Interpretation." JOURNAL OF SOCIAL ISSUES 30,3 (1974): 23-42.

Based on 1971 participant observation in a California group of Jesus People. The Jesus People, as members of a distinctive age stratum, have many of the attributes of the counterculture: subjectivism, informality, spontaneity, new forms and media of communication. They also share attributes of fundamentalist and Pentecostal Christianity: scriptural inerrancy, emphasis on the Holy Spirit, and commitment to 'one way' to God.

2586. Balswick, Jack. "The Jesus People Movement: A Sociological Analysis." In P.H. McNamara (ed.), RELIGION AMERICAN STYLE [volume cited in item 1275], pp. 359-366.

2587. Borowski, Karol H. ATTEMPTING AN ALTERNATIVE SOCIETY. A SOCIOLOGICAL STUDY OF A SELECTED COMMUNAL-REVITALIZATION MOVEMENT IN THE UNITED STATES. Norwood, Pennsylvania: Norwood Editions, 1984.

Participant-observation and interview study of Renaissance, a communal group which specialized in popular music. Data were gathered in western Massachusetts during the period of 1973-82.

2588. Borowski, Karol H. "The Renaissance Movement in the U.S.A. Today: An Account of Alternative Religion in Popular Media." SC 34,1(1987): 33-40.

Pop music enhanced communication concerning the alternative religion and also provided a basis for its internal solidarity.

* Castiglione, Miriam. I NEOPENTECOSTALI IN ITALIA. DAL JESUS MOVEMENT AI BAMBINI DI DIO. Cited above as item 881.

2589. Ellwood, Robert S. ONE WAY: THE JESUS MOVEMENT AND ITS MEANING. Englewood Cliffs: Prentice-Hall, 1973.

Includes observations from the early 1970s in the Los Angeles area.

2590. Enroth, Ronald M., Edward E. Ericson, Jr., and C. Breckinridge Peters. THE JESUS PEOPLE: OLD-TIME RELIGION IN THE AGE OF AQUARIUS. Grand Rapids, Michigan: Eerdmans Publishing, 1972; THE STORY OF THE JESUS PEOPLE. Exeter: Paternoster, 1972.

A description of the movement on the basis of observations in California.

2591. Gordon, David F. "The Jesus People: An Identity Synthesis Interpretation." URBAN LIFE AND CULTURE 3,2 (1974): 159-179.

Based on participant observation and interviews in an inner-city Jesus commune, 1971-72. Discusses types of identity modification and religious career.

2592. Gordon, David F. "Identity and Social Commitment." In H. Mol (ed.), IDENTITY AND RELIGION [volume cited in item 118], pp. 229-241.

Comparison of two Jesus People groups in a midwestern U.S. city - one communal and one not.

2593. Gordon, David F. "The Role of the Local Social Context in Social Movement Accommodation: A Case Study of Two Jesus People Groups." JSSR 23,4 (1984): 381-395.

Suburban and urban environments are important factors in shaping religious movement organizations.

2594. Gordon, David F. "Dying to Self: Self-control through Self-abandonment." SA 45,1 (1984): 41-56.

1973-75 study of two groups, focusing on individual self-transformations within them.

2595. Gregg, Roy G. GETTING IT ON WITH JESUS: A STUDY OF ADULT SOCIALIZATION. Unpublished Ph.D. dissertation, University of Southern California, 1973. [DA 34:7 A, p. 4427]

Field observation and interviews in a Jesus commune called Mansion Messiah, located in a large western U.S. state. The commune approximated the 'total institution' model.

2596. Harder, Mary W. THE CHILDREN OF CHRIST COMMUNE: A STUDY OF A FUNDAMENTALIST COMMUNAL SECT. Unpublished Ph.D. dissertation, University of Nevada, Reno, 1973. [DA 33:12 A, p. 7036]

Description of a fundamentalist communal sect which was part of the
Jesus Movement.

2597. Harder, Mary W. "Sex Roles in the Jesus Movement." SC 21,3 (1974):
345-353.

Discusses the subservience of women in a Jesus commune.

2598. Harder, Mary W., James T. Richardson, and Robert B. Simmonds. "Jesus
People." PSYCHOLOGY TODAY 6,7 (Dec. 1972): 45-50, 110, 112-113.

Participant-observation and statistical description of a Jesus People
commune, written at a popular level.

2599. Harder, Mary W., James T. Richardson, and Robert Simmonds. "Life
Style: Courtship, Marriage and Family in Changing Jesus Movement Organization." INTERNATIONAL REVIEW OF MODERN SOCIOLOGY 6,1 (1976): 155-
172.

Study of the oldest and best organized segment of the Jesus movement,
the 'Christ Organization' (pseudonym), having about 1000 members
throughout the U.S.A. Based on interview and participant-observation
data from a four-year period. Discusses the gradual liberalization
of life style.

2600. Harper, Charles L. "Cults and Communities: The Community Interfaces
of Three Marginal Religious Movements." JSSR 21,1 (1982): 26-38.

Study of the Unification Church, Scientology, and a youth evangelical
group, Assembly, in Omaha, Nebraska. The first, seeking to transform
society, precipitates conflicts in Omaha. The second, seeking legitimacy for a client-centered activity, engages in pre-emptive aggression.
The third, seeking personal transformation, has no problem with such
conflict, but has a difficulty proving itself relevant to the
surrounding community.

2601. Heinz, Donald J. JESUS IN BERKELEY. Unpublished Ph.D. dissertation,
Graduate Theological Union, Berkeley, 1976. [DA 37:4 A, p. 2245]

Ethnography of a Jesus group in Berkeley, California, which split in
1975 into a coalition of neo-evangelical ministries and a tightly-
structured family church.

2602. Heinz, Donald J. "The Christian World Liberation Front." In C.Y.
Glock and R.N. Bellah (eds.), THE NEW RELIGIOUS CONSCIOUSNESS [volume
cited in item 75], pp. 143-161.

Based on a field study conducted in Berkeley, California, during the
early 1970s.

2603. Jacobson, Cardell K., and Thomas J. Pilarzyk. "Croissance, développement et fin d'une secte conversioniste: Les Jesus People de Milwaukee."
SC 21,3 (1974): 255-268.

The sect failed to routinize the affective and instrumental roles of
its charismatic leader and also to socialize its new converts. The
latter failure arose from a contradiction between boundary-expansion

and boundary-maintenance.

2604. Jorstad, Erling. THAT NEW-TIME RELIGION: THE JESUS REVIVAL IN AMERICA. Minneapolis: Augsburg, 1972.

2605. Mauss, Armand L., and Donald W. Petersen. "Les 'Jesus Freaks' et le retour à la respectabilité." SC 21,3 (1974): 283-301.

At the time of the study, 1971-73, the Jesus movement was in the process of routinization; it was a way station to respectability for a cohort of stigmatized youth.

2606. Petersen, Donald W., and Armand L. Mauss. "The Cross and the Commune. An Interpretation of the Jesus People." In C.Y. Glock (ed.), RELIGION IN SOCIOLOGICAL PERSPECTIVE [volume cited in item 189], pp. 261-279. Also in Robert R. Evans (ed.), SOCIAL MOVEMENTS. Chicago: Rand McNally, 1973, pp. 150-170.

Based on 1971-72 interviews in Spokane, Washington; Seattle, Washington; and Idaho.

* Pin, Emile. "En guise d'introduction: Comment se sauver de l'anomie et de l'aliénation. Jesus People et Catholiques Pentecostaux." Cited above as item 920.

2607. Richardson, James T. "Causes and Consequences of the Jesus Movement in America." SOCIAL STUDIES. IRISH JOURNAL OF SOCIOLOGY 2,5 (1973): 457-473.

Application of Smelser's collective behavior model: structural conduciveness, structural strain, spread of a generalized belief, precipitating factors, mobilization of participants for action.

2608. Richardson, James T. "The Jesus Movement: An Assessment." LISTENING: JOURNAL OF RELIGION AND CULTURE 9,3 (1974): 20-42.

Description of a commune; analysis drawn from item 2607.

2609. Richardson, James T., and Rex Davis. "Experimental Fundamentalism: Revisions of Orthodoxy in the Jesus Movement." JOURNAL OF THE AMERICAN ACADEMY OF RELIGION 51,3 (1983): 397-425. Also in William Shaffir and L. Greenspan (eds.), IDENTIFICATION AND THE REVIVAL OF ORTHODOXY. The Hague: Mouton, 1983.

Examines the belief structure of the Jesus movement in general, and in particular that of the Children of God.

* Richardson, James T., and M.T. Vincent Reidy. "Form and Fluidity in Two Contemporary Glossolalic Movements." Cited above as item 2391.

2610. Richardson, James T., and Mary W. Stewart. "Conversion Process Models and the Jesus Movement." AMERICAN BEHAVIORAL SCIENTIST 20,6 (1977): 819-838.

Develops a model from previous models of conversion, taking into account the degree of congruence of a group with the potential convert's predispositions and the strength of affective ties with members of the group.

2611. Richardson, James T., Mary W. Harder, and Robert B. Simmonds. "Thought Reform and the Jesus Movement." YOUTH AND SOCIETY 4,2 (1972): 185-202.

Based on extensive survey and participant-observation research of a Jesus movement group. Application of the 'brainwashing' model.

2612. Richardson, James T., Robert B. Simmonds, and Mary W. Stewart. "The Evolution of a Jesus Movement Organization." JOURNAL OF VOLUNTARY ACTION RESEARCH 8,3-4 (1979): 93-111.

Examination of 'Christ Communal Organization' as an organization - goals, leadership, material support system, living arrangements, training, evangelization methods.

2613. Richardson, James T., Mary W. Stewart, and Robert B. Simmonds. ORGAN- IZED MIRACLES. A STUDY OF A CONTEMPORARY, YOUTH COMMUNAL, FUNDAMENTAL- IST ORGANIZATION. New Brunswick, N.J.: Transaction, 1979.

1971-77 observation data and use of three personality instruments on 'Christ Communal Organization,' pseudonym for a group which began in Southern California.

   * Robbins, Thomas. CONTEMPORARY 'POST-DRUG' CULTS: A COMPARISON OF TWO GROUPS. Cited above as item 102.

2614. Simmonds, Robert B. THE PEOPLE OF THE JESUS MOVEMENT: A PERSONALITY ASSESSMENT OF MEMBERS OF A FUNDAMENTALIST RELIGIOUS COMMUNITY. Un- published Ph.D. dissertation, University of Nevada, Reno, 1977. [DA 38:2 B, p. 969]

Use of a questionnaire, three personality tests, and other instruments on a fundamentalist communal sect which was part of the Jesus movement.

2615. Simmonds, Robert B. "Conversion or Addiction?: Consequences of Join- ing a Jesus Movement Group." AMERICAN BEHAVIORAL SCIENTIST 20,6 (1977): 909-924.

Personality assessment data on a western U.S. Jesus People group. Conversion is seen as less a transformation of self than a shift in 'addiction.'

2616. Simmonds, Robert B., James T. Richardson, and Mary W. Harder. "Organ- izational Aspects of a Jesus Movement Community." SC 21,3 (1974): 269-281.

Description of an agricultural Jesus People commune.

2617. Simmonds, Robert B., James T. Richardson, and Mary W. Harder. "A Jesus Movement Group: An Adjective Check List Assessment." JSSR 15,4 (1976): 323-337.

Application of a personality test to members of a Jesus People commune suggests many maladapted personalities; however, the proper interpre-

347

tation of the 'maladaptiveness' requires some reconsideration.

2618. Stones, Christopher R. "The Jesus People: Changes in Security and Life-style as a Function of Nonconformist Religious Influence." JOURNAL OF SOCIAL PSYCHOLOGY 97 (1977): 127-133.

A study of Jesus movement members in Johannesburg, South Africa.

2619. Stones, Christopher R. "The Jesus People in South Africa. A Personal Encounter." ODYSSEY 1,5 (1977): 28-32.

2620. Stones, Christopher R. "The Jesus People: Fundamentalism and Changes in Factors Associated with Conservatism." JSSR 17,2 (1978): 155-158.

A study of English-speaking members of the Jesus movement in Johannesburg, South Africa. Conversion made the respondents more biblically fundamentalistic, less ecclesiastically fundamentalistic, less conservative, less militaristic, less antihedonistic.

2621. Streiker, Lowell D. THE JESUS TRIP: ADVENT OF THE JESUS FREAKS. Nashville: Abingdon Press, 1971.

* Tipton, Steven M. GETTING SAVED FROM THE SIXTIES. Cited above as item 208.

JESUS MOVEMENT (CHILDREN OF GOD [OR FAMILY OF LOVE])

* Bromley, David G., and Anson D. Shupe, Jr. STRANGE GODS. THE GREAT AMERICAN CULT SCARE. Cited above as item 66.

* Castiglione, Miriam. I NEOPENTECOSTALI IN ITALIA. DAL JESUS MOVEMENT AI BAMBINI DI DIO. Cited above as item 881.

2622. Davis, Rex, and James T. Richardson. "The Organization and Functioning of the Children of God." SA 37,4 (1976): 321-339.

Examines the group's early history and its international organizational structure.

2623. Kuner, Wolfgang. YOU GOTTA BE A BABY ODER HAPPINESS FLUTSCH FLUTSCH. EINE UNTERSUCHUNG ZU CHARAKTER, GENESE UND SOZIALEN URSACHEN EINER DEN SOGENANNTEN <JUGENDRELIGIONEN> ZUGEORDNETEN SOZIALEN BEWEGUNG, DER KINDER GOTTES (FAMILIE DER LIEBE). Tübingen, Unpublished M.A.-Arbeit, 1979.

* Kuner, Wolfgang. SOZIOGENESE DER MITGLIEDSCHAFT IN DREI NEUEN RELI-GIÖSEN BEWEGUNGEN. Cited above as item 63.

* Kuner, Wolfgang. "New Religious Movements and Mental Health." Cited above as item 64.

* Richardson, James T., and Rex Davis. "Experiential Fundamentalism: Revisions of Orthodoxy in the Jesus Movement." Cited above as item 2609.

2624. Wallis, Roy. "Observations on the Children of God." SOCIOLOGICAL REVIEW 24,4 (1976): 807-829.

Interviews, documents, and limited participant observation suggest beliefs of leader and members are as important as organizational dynamics.

2625. Wallis, Roy. "Recruiting Christian Manpower." SOCIETY 15,4 (1978): 72-74.

Report on the use of the sexual attractiveness of young female members to recruit new disciples and allies for the Children of God.

2626. Wallis, Roy. SALVATION AND PROTEST. New York: St. Martin's, 1979.

2627. Wallis, Roy. "Yesterday's Children: Cultural and Structural Change in a New Religious Movement." In Bryan R. Wilson (ed.), THE SOCIAL IMPACT OF NEW RELIGIOUS MOVEMENTS. New York: Rose of Sharon Press, 1981, pp. 97-133.

Historical sociology of the movement.

2628. Wallis, Roy. "The Social Construction of Charisma." SC 29,1 (1982): 25-39. Reprinted as Chapter 6 in R. Wallis and S. Bruce, SOCIOLOGICAL THEORY, RELIGION AND COLLECTIVE ACTION [volume cited in item 110].

Argues that charisma is not an inherent property of an individual, but rather is a property of a situationally generated social relationship. Illustrative case of David Berg (or Moses David), founder of the Children of God.

2629. Wallis, Roy. "Charisma, Commitment and Control in a New Religious Movement." In Roy Wallis (ed.), MILLENNIALISM AND CHARISMA. Belfast: The Queen's University of Belfast, 1982, pp. 73-140.

2630. Wallis, Roy. "Hostages to Fortune: Thoughts on the Future of Scientology and the Children of God." In D.G. Bromley and P.E. Hammond (eds.), THE FUTURE OF NEW RELIGIOUS MOVEMENTS [volume cited in item 94], pp. 80-90.

General observations.

 * Wright, Stuart A. LEAVING CULTS: THE DYNAMICS OF DEFECTION. Cited above as item 97.


## AFRICAN INDEPENDENT (MISCELLANEOUS)

2631. Barrett, David B. "Two Hundred Independent Church Movements in East Africa." SC 15,2 (1968): 101-116.

Includes basic information on churches in 34 tribes, four nations, and seven 'chains.'

2632. Barrett, David B. "L'évolution des mouvements religieux dissidents en Afrique (1862-1967)." ARCHIVES DE SOCIOLOGIE DES RELIGIONS 25 (1968):

349

111-140.

An extract of item 2633.

2633. Barrett, David B.  SCHISM AND RENEWAL IN AFRICA: AN ANALYSIS OF SIX THOUSAND CONTEMPORARY RELIGIOUS MOVEMENTS.  Nairobi: Oxford University Press, 1968.

2634. Bernard, Guy.  "Diversité des nouvelles églises congolaises."  CAHIERS D'ETUDES AFRICAINES 10/38 (1970): 203-227.

Textual analysis of the constitution of L'Eglise des Dignes (Zaire).

2635. Dubb, Allie A.  COMMUNITY OF THE SAVED: AN AFRICAN REVIVALIST CHURCH IN THE EAST CAPE.  South Africa: Witwatersrand University Press, 1976.

2636. Janosik, Robert J.  "Religion and Political Involvement: A Study of Black African Sects."  JSSR 13,2 (1974): 161-175.

Attempts to explain why religious sects among the Kikuyu tribe are more politicized than are sects among the Zulu.

2637. Wright, Beryl.  "The Sect that Became an Order: The Order of Ethiopia." SOCIOLOGICAL YEARBOOK OF RELIGION IN BRITAIN 5 (1972): 60-71.

Presents the history of the Order of Ethiopia in the Church of the Province of South Africa (Anglican Church) as a case study for a sociological theory of schism.

## AFRICAN INDEPENDENT (APOSTOLIC CHURCH OF JOHN MARANKE)

2638. Aquina, Mary.  "The People of the Spirit: An Independent Church in Rhodesia."  AFRICA 37 (1967): 203-219.

2639. Jules-Rosette, Bennetta.  "Bapostolo Ritual: An African Response to Christianity."  CANADIAN JOURNAL OF AFRICAN STUDIES 9,1 (1975): 89-102.

General description.

2640. Jules-Rosette, Bennetta.  "Song and Spirit: The Use of Song in the Management of Ritual Settings."  AFRICA 45,2 (1975): 150-166.

2641. Jules-Rosette, Bennetta.  AFRICAN APOSTLES. RITUAL AND CONVERSION IN THE CHURCH OF JOHN MARANKE.  Ithaca, New York: Cornell University Press, 1975.

Participant-observation study.

2642. Jules-Rosette, Bennetta.  "Ceremonial Trance Behavior in an African Church: Private Experience and Public Expression."  JSSR 19,1 (1980): 1-16.

2643. Asch, Susan. L'EGLISE DU PROPHETE KIMBANGU. DE SES ORIGINES A SON ROLE ACTUEL AU ZAIRE. Paris: Karthala, 1983.

2644. Bernard, Guy. "Les églises congolaises et la construction nationale." In SOCIOLOGIE DE LA 'CONSTRUCTION NATIONALE' DANS LES NOUVEAUX ETATS. Brussels: Institut de Sociologie, 1968, pp. 55-61.

Proceedings of a 1965 conference.

2645. Bernard, Guy. "Eglises noires et formes de connaissance." REVUE TUNISIENNE DE SCIENCES SOCIALES 11,36-39 (1974): 339-346.

Discusses the variable forms of consciousness among the new churches, with particular attention accorded L'Eglise de Jésus-Christ sur Terre par le Prophète Kimbangu.

2646. Desroche, Henri, and Paul Raymaekers. "Départ d'un prophète--Arrivée d'une église: Textes et recherches sur la mort de Simon Kimbangu et sur sa survivance." ARCHIVES DE SCIENCES SOCIALES DES RELIGIONS 42 (1976): 117-162.

Presents documents and studies relating to the death in 1951, after 30 years spent in prison, of the Congolese prophet Simon Kimbangu, and his survival in the church bearing his name.

*JAPANESE INDEPENDENT (MUKYOKAI)*

2647. Caldarola, Carlo. CHRISTIANITY: THE JAPANESE WAY. Leiden: E.J. Brill, 1979.

*RUSSIAN ORIGIN (DOUKHOBOR)*

2648. Hawthorn, H.B. "A Test of Simmel on the Secret Society: The Doukhobors of British Columbia." AMERICAN JOURNAL OF SOCIOLOGY 62,1 (1956): 1-7.

A test of some of Simmel's statements on the operation of a secret society by reference to the Sons of Freedom sect of the British Columbia Doukhobors.

2649. Herbison, Hugh. "Doukhobor Religion." Chapter 4 in H.B. Hawthorn (ed.), THE DOUKHOBORS OF BRITISH COLUMBIA. Vancouver: University of British Columbia Press and J.M. Dent Ltd., 1955. Reprinted in B.R. Blishen et al. (eds.), CANADIAN SOCIETY. SOCIOLOGICAL PERSPECTIVES, third edition. Toronto: Macmillan, 1971, pp. 336-354.

Doukhobor religion has three bases: group mysticism, perfectionist ideology, and an internal church-state fusion. Also noted are the religion's lack of adaptability and its lack of techniques for releasing feelings of sin and guilt.

2650. Hirabayashi, Gordon K. THE RUSSIAN DOUKHOBORS OF BRITISH COLUMBIA: A

STUDY OF SOCIAL ADJUSTMENT AND CONFLICT. Unpublished Ph.D. dissertation, University of Washington, 1952.

An attempt to investigate and analyze the processes of adjustment and the attendant conflicts that have been experienced by a primitive religious sect. The Doukhobors' problem can be seen as that of a primary group facing a secondary group situation.

## RUSSIAN ORIGIN (MOLOKAN)

2651. Lane, Christel O. "Social-political Accommodation and Religious Decline: The Case of the Molokan Sect in Soviet Society." COMPARATIVE STUDIES IN SOCIETY AND HISTORY 17,2 (1975): 221-237.

The strength of the Molokan sect rested in part on its ability to give expression to political dissent against the Tsars. By adjusting to the Soviet system, it lost that capacity and hence has declined, almost to the point of extinction.

2652. Young, Pauline V. "The Russian Molokan Community in Los Angeles." AMERICAN JOURNAL OF SOCIOLOGY 35 (1929): 393-402.

Discusses pressures of urbanism and assimilation upon a strongly ethnocentric group.

## BRITISH INDEPENDENT (OXFORD GROUP MOVEMENT)

2653. Eister, Allan W. "The Oxford Group Movement: A Typological Analysis." SOCIOLOGY AND SOCIAL RESEARCH 34 (1949): 116-124.

Analysis of group members' acritical attitude toward religious experience.

2654. Eister, Allan W. DRAWING-ROOM CONVERSION: A SOCIOLOGICAL ACCOUNT OF THE OXFORD GROUP MOVEMENT. Durham: Duke University Press, 1950.

## BRITISH INDEPENDENT (NEW TESTAMENT CHURCH OF GOD, LEVELLERS)

2655. Hill, Clifford. "From Church to Sect: West Indian Religious Sect Development in Britain." JSSR 10,2 (1971): 114-123.

West Indian black immigrants in England largely forsake their traditional church affiliations, with many joining sects of a Pentecostal character. The largest of these, the New Testament Church of God, is used as a case study.

2656. Leites, Edmund. "Conscience, Leisure, and Learning: Locke and the Levellers." SA 39,1 (1978): 36-61.

The Leveller (Rainborough) view held that poor people may morally judge for themselves. Locke maintained that a studied self-discipline is necessary for moral judgment; the poor do not have the leisure time to develop it. Yet Locke did not promote a social reformation which would permit all to develop the skills of moral judgment.

## AMERICAN INDEPENDENT (MISCELLANEOUS)

2657. Gerth, Hans H. "Midwestern Sectarian Community." SOCIAL RESEARCH 11,3 (1944): 354-362.

A study of the Apostolic Christian Church (Peoria, Illinois).

2658. Sobel, B.Z. HEBREW CHRISTIANITY: THE THIRTEENTH TRIBE. New York: Wiley, 1974.

2659. Walker, Paul R. THE INFLUENCE OF THE CHRISTIAN CHURCH IN AMERICA ON PEACE AND WAR, 1914-1935. Unpublished M.A. thesis, Clark University, 1936.

## AMERICAN INDEPENDENT (JEWS FOR JESUS)

2660. La Magdeleine, Dan. JEWS FOR JESUS: ORGANIZATIONAL STRUCTURE AND SUPPORTERS. Unpublished M.A. thesis, Graduate Theological Union, Berkeley, 1977.

2661. Lipson, Juliene G. JEWS FOR JESUS: AN ANTHROPOLOGICAL STUDY. Unpublished Ph.D. dissertation, University of California, San Francisco, 1978. [DA 40:2 A, p. 940]

Focus on a small Hebrew Christian group which evolved out of the early 1970s Jesus movement.

## AMERICAN INDEPENDENT (POLISH NATIONAL CATHOLIC CHURCH)

2662. Les, Barbara A. "The Changes of the Character and Function of the Parish of the Polish National Church." In PNCC STUDIES (Scranton, Pennsylvania) 1980, pp. 37-49.

2663. Wierzbicki, Zbigniew T. "The Polish Schism in the United States of America." POLISH SOCIOLOGICAL BULLETIN 4/48 (1979): 47-56.

Studies the emergence of the Polish National Catholic Church at the turn of the twentieth century.

# 21

## Protestant: Theological and Ideological Alignments

*LIBERAL PROTESTANT (MISCELLANEOUS)*

2664. Berger, Peter L. "American Religion: Conservative Upsurge, Liberal Prospects." In Robert S. Michaelson and Wade Clark Roof (eds.), LIBERAL PROTESTANTISM. REALITIES AND POSSIBILITIES. New York: Pilgrim Press, 1986, pp. 19-36.

An overview of developments in the U.S.A. throughout the 1970s and 80s.

2665. Cavanaugh, Michael A. "Liberalism and Rationalism in Modern Theology: The Sociological Hypothesis." RRR 29,1 (1987): 25-43.

Liberal and rationalist mutations of theological culture are selected initially from a universal modern crisis in rationalist orthodoxies. Thereafter, social processes and structures of communication further select and consolidate rationalism and liberalism into, respectively, peripheral and central media of communication.

2666. Dempsey, Kenneth C. "Secularization and the Protestant Parish Minister." AUSTRALIAN AND NEW ZEALAND JOURNAL OF SOCIOLOGY 9,3 (1973): 46-50.

General observations on conservative and liberal responses to secularization.

2667. Hammond, Phillip E. "The Extravasation of the Sacred and the Crisis in Liberal Protestantism." In R.S. Michaelson and W. Clark Roof (eds.), LIBERAL PROTESTANTISM [volume cited in item 2664], pp. 51-64.

Discussion of American trends framed in terms of a disestablishment process.

2668. Johnson, Benton. "Liberal Protestantism: End of the Road?" ANNALS OF THE AMERICAN ACADEMY OF POLITICAL AND SOCIAL SCIENCE 480 (1985): 39-52.

Reviews the major eras of mainline Protestantism in the U.S.A., followed by proposals and rationale for its reinvigoration.

2669. Johnson, Benton. "Winning Lost Sheep: A Recovery Course for Liberal Protestantism." In R.S. Michaelson and W. Clark Roof (eds.), LIBERAL

355

PROTESTANTISM [volume cited in item 2664], pp. 220-234.

2670. McKinney, William J., Jr., and Wade Clark Roof. "Liberal Protestantism: A Sociodemographic Perspective." In R.S. Michaelson and W. Clark
Roof (eds.), LIBERAL PROTESTANTISM [volume cited in item 2664], pp.
37-50.

1972-84 N.O.R.C. (U.S.) data.

2671. Pratt, Henry J. "Organizational Stress and Adaptation to Changing
Political Status. The Case of the National Council of Churches of
Christ in the United States." AMERICAN BEHAVIORAL SCIENTIST 17,6
(1974): 865-883.

The National Council of Churches turned to U.S. domestic and foreign
policy concerns as the member denominations lost political influence.
To avoid losing the members because of controversies, it emphasized
meaningful incentives outside of the political realm.

2672. Reagin, Ewell. "A Study of the Southern Christian Leadership Conference." RRR 9 (1968): 88-96.

2673. Schoenfeld, Eugen. "Image of Man: The Effect of Religion on Trust. A
Research Note." RRR 20,1 (1978): 61-67.

1973 N.O.R.C. (U.S.) data. The image people have of others is rooted
in a complex array of life experiences encompassing religious conduct
and theology. Membership in liberal churches is associated with trust
and in conservative churches with distrust. Increased church attendance, irrespective of denomination, tends to increase one's sense of
trust.


LIBERAL PROTESTANT (SOCIAL GOSPEL)

2674. Hadden, Jeffrey K., Charles F. Longino, Jr., and Myer S. Reed, Jr.
"Further Reflections on the Development of Sociology and the Social
Gospel in America." SA 35,4 (1974): 282-286.

A critique of item 2675, which had attempted to link the origins of
American sociology to the Social Gospel Movement.

2675. Morgan, J. Graham. "The Development of Sociology and the Social Gospel in America." SA 30,1 (1969): 42-53.

Parallels between late nineteenth-century sociology and the tenets of
the Social Gospel Movement made sociology an acceptable course in many
American denominational colleges. This contributed to the discipline's
rapid growth in the U.S.

2676. Swatos, William H., Jr. "The Faith of the Fathers: On the Christianity of Early American Sociology." SA 44,1 (1983): 33-52.

The reformist component of early American sociology paralleled but did
not stem from reformist trends within American Protestantism.

2677. Swatos, William H., Jr. FAITH OF THE FATHERS. SCIENCE, RELIGION, AND REFORM IN THE DEVELOPMENT OF EARLY AMERICAN SOCIOLOGY. Bristol, Indiana: Wyndham Hall Press, 1984.

2678. Yinger, J. Milton. RELIGION IN THE STRUGGLE FOR POWER. Durham: Duke University Press, 1946.

## LIBERAL PROTESTANT (UNITARIAN)

2679. Demerath, Nicholas J., III, and Victor Thiessen. "On Spitting against the Wind: Organizational Precariousness and American Irreligion." AMERICAN JOURNAL OF SOCIOLOGY 71,6 (1966): 674-687.

Analysis of a small-town (Sauk City, Wisconsin) free-thought movement of immigrant Germans, and its decline from 1852 to the present. It joined the Unitarian Universalist Fellowship in 1955.

* Maranell, Gary M. RESPONSES TO RELIGION. STUDIES IN THE SOCIAL PSYCHOLOGY OF RELIGIOUS BELIEF. Cited above as item 1294.

2680. Miller, Robert L. "The Religious Value System of Unitarian Universalists." RRR 17,3 (1976): 189-208.

Survey based on 1974 mailing lists. Frequency of church attendance, salience, and economic class have almost no influence on value patterns. The value system differed from those of Christians, Jews, and those claiming no religion. The distinctive Unitarian Universalist paradigm of values gave high ranking to terminal values (self-respect, wisdom, inner harmony, mature love, a world of beauty, an exciting life) and instrumental values (loving, independent, intellectual, imaginative, logical). This suggests an orientation toward competence, personal realization, self-fulfillment, self-actualization.

* Norr, James L. "Religion and Nation Building: The American Case." Cited above as item 1304.

* Strickland, Bonnie R., and Sallie Cone Weddell. "Religious Orientation, Racial Prejudice, and Dogmatism: A Study of Baptists and Unitarians." Cited above as item 2303.

2681. Sykes, Richard E. MASSACHUSETTS UNITARIANISM AND SOCIAL CHANGE: A RELIGIOUS SOCIAL SYSTEM IN TRANSITION, 1780-1870. Unpublished Ph.D. dissertation, University of Minnesota, 1966. [DA 28:9 A, p. 3588]

The explosive growth of the Unitarian movement ceased after three decades.

2682. Sykes, Richard E. "The Changing Class Structure of Unitarian Parishes in Massachusetts, 1780-1800." RRR 12,1 (1970): 26-34.

The upper-class appeal of Unitarianism limited its growth potential.

2683. Tapp, Robert B. "Dimensions of Religiosity in a Post-traditional Group." JSSR 10,1 (1971): 41-47.

Factor analysis of questionnaire data from 12,146 Unitarian Universalists in the U.S. and Canada. A large first factor was made up of theological values, institutional values, and personal moral values. A second contained items reflecting social morality. Other dimensions are proposed as well.

2684. Tapp, Robert B. RELIGION AMONG THE UNITARIAN UNIVERSALISTS. CONVERTS IN STEPFATHER'S HOUSE. New York: Seminar Press, 1973.

*LIBERAL PROTESTANT (YMCA)*

2685. Zald, Mayer N. ORGANIZATIONAL CHANGE: THE POLITICAL ECONOMY OF YMCA. Chicago: University of Chicago Press, 1970.

2686. Zald, Mayer N., and Patricia Denton. "From Evangelism to General Service: The Transformation of the YMCA." ADMINISTRATIVE SCIENCE QUARTERLY 8,2 (1963): 214-234.

Analysis of an organizational character leading to a successful transformation. Broadly-stated goals and unrestricted clientele encourage a wide diversification of programs and target populations. Federated structure leads to decentralized decision-making and control by local elites.

*FUNDAMENTALIST PROTESTANT*

2687. Acock, Alan C., Charles Wright, and Kay McKensie. "Predicting Intolerance: The Impact of Parents' Own Tolerance vs. Social Class and Religious Fundamentalism." DEVIANT BEHAVIOR 3,1 (1981): 65-84.

Data from a sample of subscribers to a Los Angeles area medical plan, prior to 1975. Examines fundamentalism as a mechanism for transmitting intolerance of deviance.

* Alexander, Daniel. "Is Fundamentalism an Integrism?" Cited above as item 546.

2688. Ammerman, Nancy T. "Comment: Operationalizing Evangelicalism: An Amendment." SA 43,2 (1982): 170-171.

Biblical literalism distinguishes fundamentalists from evangelicals; the difference is one which concerns social phenomena as well as theologies.

2689. Ammerman, Nancy T. BIBLE BELIEVERS. FUNDAMENTALISTS IN THE MODERN WORLD. New Brunswick, N.J.: Rutgers University Press, 1987.

Based on participant observation in a large suburban fundamentalist congregation in the northeastern U.S.A.

2690. Berg, Philip L. "Self-identified Fundamentalism among Protestant Seminarians: A Study of Persistence and Change in Value-orientations." RRR 12,2 (1971): 88-94.

Survey of 1164 students from seven Protestant seminaries. Persisting
fundamentalists, as compared to ex-fundamentalists and others, more
often held a charismatic concept of the ministry, were more devotion-
alist, were slightly more inclined to base their career decisions on a
religious experience, were somewhat less ethicalist, and were less
concerned with mastery of technical skills.

2691. Burton, Ronald, Stephen Johnson, and Joseph B. Tamney. "Education and
Fundamentalism." RRR 30,4 (1989): 344-359.

Based on 1989 telephone interviews conducted in the Muncie, Indiana,
area.

2692. Caplan, Lionel. CLASS AND CULTURE IN URBAN INDIA. FUNDAMENTALISM IN A
CHRISTIAN COMMUNITY. New York: Oxford University Press, 1988.

Study of a community in Madras, India.

2693. Chi, S. Kenneth, and Sharon K. Houseknecht. "Protestant Fundamentalism and Marital Success: A Comparative Approach." SOCIOLOGY AND
SOCIAL RESEARCH 69,3 (1985): 351-375.

1972-80 N.O.R.C. (U.S.) data. Fundamentalist Protestants have a higher
marital dissolution rate than other Protestants or Catholics. Religious congruence of spouses and conversion do not explain this pattern.

2694. DeJong, Gordon F. "Religious Fundamentalism, Socio-economic Status,
and Fertility Attitudes in the Southern Appalachians." DEMOGRAPHY 2
(1965): 540-548.

1958 survey data from 190 South Appalachian counties (U.S.). Fundamentalism positively correlates with support of high fertility.

2695. DeJong, Gordon F., and Thomas R. Ford. "Religious Fundamentalism and
Denominational Preference in the Southern Appalachian Region." JSSR
5,1 (1965): 24-33.

1958 survey in 190 counties in seven states, comprising the Southern
Appalachian Mountain region. The denominational composition of the
population has a high proportion of groups whose orientation is
fundamentalist. Members of sect-type groups are most fundamentalist.
Fundamentalism is inversely correlated with socio-economic status.
Differences between denominational groups persist even when socio-
economic status is controlled.

* Ethridge, F. Maurice, and Joe R. Feagin. "Varieties of 'Fundamentalism': A Conceptual and Empirical Analysis of Two Protestant Denominations." Cited above as item 2558.

2696. Ford, Thomas R. "Status, Residence, and Fundamentalist Religious
Beliefs in the Southern Appalachians." SOCIAL FORCES 39 (1960): 41-49.

190 county, seven state region; 1958 sample of households. Test of
hypothesis of an inverse relationship between fundamentalist belief
and urbanization, education, and socio-economic status. Generally,
the hypothesis is supported.

* Greeley, Andrew M., and William C. McCready. ETHNICITY IN THE UNITED
  STATES. A PRELIMINARY RECONNAISSANCE. Cited above as item 2263.

2697. Hendricks, John S. RELIGIOUS AND POLITICAL FUNDAMENTALISM: THE LINK
      BETWEEN ALIENATION AND IDEOLOGY. Unpublished Ph.D. dissertation,
      University of Michigan, 1977. [DA 38:11 A, p. 6909]

      1974 southeastern Michigan sample of church members in five conserva-
      tive Protestant denominations. The most economically threatened
      respondents focused most on an individual relationship to Christ and
      were most likely to reject differing Christian views. The ideologi-
      cally sophisticated fundamentalists opposed the social gospel. The
      most committed were the least politically active.

2698. Hood, Ralph W., and Ronald J. Morris. "Boundary Maintenance, Social-
      political Views, and Presidential Preference among High and Low
      Fundamentalists." RRR 27,2 (1985): 134-145.

      Questionnaire data from students at the University of Tennessee at
      Chattanooga, at the time of the 1984 U.S. presidential election. Data
      indicate a selective relevance of religious fundamentalism with politi-
      cal issues rather than a general correlation between religious funda-
      mentalism and conservatism.

2699. Hudson, Charles. "The Structure of a Fundamentalist Christian Belief-
      system." In Samuel S. Hill (ed.), RELIGION AND THE SOLID SOUTH.
      Nashville: Abingdon, 1972, pp. 122-142.

      Describes the coherence of the fundamentalist symbol system.

2700. Jackson, Audrey R. "A Model for Determining Information Diffusion in
      a Family Planning Program." JOURNAL OF MARRIAGE AND THE FAMILY 34,3
      (1972): 503-513.

      Based on a 1966-67 study of white female residents of low-income areas
      in Nashville, Tennessee. Fundamentalism is a control variable in the
      study.

2701. Jelen, Ted G. "Fundamentalism, Feminism, and Attitudes toward Porno-
      graphy." RRR 28,2 (1986): 97-103.

      1982-83 N.O.R.C. (U.S.) data. Both fundamentalists and feminists seek
      the legal suppression of sexually-explicit materials, the former
      because they believe it leads to the breakdown of morals, the latter
      because they believe it leads to the exploitation of women.

2702. Jelen, Ted G. "The Effects of Religious Separatism on White Protes-
      tants in the 1984 Presidential Election." SA 48,1 (1987): 30-46.

      1985 N.O.R.C. (U.S.) data. Both evangelicals and fundamentalists
      embrace personally conservative positions on moral issues; the funda-
      mentalists are more likely to seek the legal enforcement of their
      values. However, the evangelicals were somewhat more likely to use
      moral or social issues as criteria for their 1984 presidential vote
      choice.

2703. Lamar, Ralph E.  FUNDAMENTALISM AND SELECTED SOCIAL FACTORS IN THE
SOUTHERN APPALACHIAN REGION.  Unpublished M.A. thesis, University of
Kentucky, 1962.

Lamar developed a four-item fundamentalism scale;  it is printed in
SOCIAL SCIENCE QUARTERLY 51 (1970): 678, in a footnote to an article
by Anthony Orum.

2704. Lechner, Frank J.  "Forms of Fundamentalism. A Comparative Perspective
on Cultural Revitalization in Modern Societies."  SOCIALE WETENSCHAP-
PEN  25,4 (1982): 322-336.

2705. Lechner, Frank J.  "Modernity and Its Discontents."  In Jeffrey C.
Alexander (ed.), NEOFUNCTIONALISM.  Beverly Hills, California: Sage,
1985, pp. 157-176.

Presents a typology of revitalization syndromes.

2706. Lechner, Frank J.  "Fundamentalism and Sociocultural Revitalization in
America: A Sociological Interpretation."  SA 46,3 (1985): 243-260.

Applying concepts from neo-Parsonian action theory to revitalization
movements and Awakenings, the author proposes a conception of fundamentalism.  Various revitalization episodes in American history had
fundamentalist aspects but also entailed unintended modernizing
consequences.  Outlining some of the factors accounting for the re-
emergence of ostensibly anti-modern fundamentalism, he argues that it
is in fact a quintessentially modern phenomenon.

  * McMurray, Martha.  "Religion and Women's Sex Role Traditionalism."
Cited above as item 483.

2707. Maranell, Gary M.  "Regional Patterns of Fundamentalistic Attitude
Configuration."  KANSAS JOURNAL OF SOCIOLOGY 4 (1968): 159-174.

2708. Mathisen, James A.  "Thomas O'Dea's Dilemmas of Institutionalization:
A Case Study and Re-evaluation after Twenty-five Years."  SA 47,4
(1987): 302-318.

Historical examination of the Moody Bible Institute of Chicago.  The
five dilemmas of institutionalization outlined by O'Dea provide some
descriptive insight but do not satisfy the author's quest for a
middle-range theory.

2709. Miller, Wesley E.  "The New Christian Right and Fundamentalist Discon-
tent: The Politics of Lifestyle Concern Hypothesis Revisited."
SOCIOLOGICAL FOCUS 18,4 (1985): 325-336.  See also Steve Bruce,
"Comment," 20,3 (1987): 242-246; and W.E. Miller, "Reply," 20,3 (1987):
247-249.

Quantitative content analysis of fundamentalist publications, 1955-80,
suggests that increasing feelings of life-style concern brought on by
life-style threats cannot account for the rise of the New Christian Right.

2710. Moberg, David O.  "Fundamentalists and Evangelicals in Society."  In

David F. Wells and John D. Woodbridge (eds.), THE EVANGELICALS. WHAT THEY BELIEVE, WHO THEY ARE, WHERE THEY ARE CHANGING. Nashville: Abingdon, 1975, pp. 143-169.

2711. Monoghan, Robert R.  "Three Faces of the True Believer: Motivations for Attending a Fundamentalist Church."  JSSR 6,2 (1967): 236-245.

Survey in an independent fundamentalist church in a midwestern industrial metropolis, U.S.A.  Factor analysis produced three distinct member orientations:  that of the authority-seeker, who wants strong guidance from the minister; the comfort-seeker, who wants fear of death, damnation, illness, and old age assuaged; and the social participator, who enjoys the friendly social interaction.

* Nelsen, Hart M., and Raymond H. Potvin.  "Toward Disestablishment: New Patterns of Social Class, Denomination and Religiosity among Youth?"  Cited above as item 2270.

2712. Ness, Robert C.  "The Impact of Indigenous Healing Activity: An Empirical Study of Two Fundamentalist Churches."  SOCIAL SCIENCE AND MEDICINE 14B,3 (1980): 167-180.

Field study in a Newfoundland coastal community; finds an inverse relationship between religious involvement and symptoms of emotional stress.

2713. Peek, Charles W., and Sharon Brown.  "Sex Prejudice among White Protestants: Like or Unlike Ethnic Prejudice?"  SOCIAL FORCES 59,1 (1980): 169-185.  See also Brian Powell and Lala Carr Steelman, "Fundamentalism and Sexism: A Reanalysis of Peek and Brown."  SOCIAL FORCES 60,4 (1982): 1154-1158; and C.W. Peek, "Deficient Methods or Different Data? Another Interpretation of Divergent Findings on Fundamentalism and Political Sexism: Response to Powell and Steelman."  SOCIAL FORCES 60,4 (1982): 1159-1167.

1974-75 N.O.R.C. (U.S.) data.  The fundamentalist opposition to female participation in politics seems based more on biblical statements than on women's social status.

2714. Perry, Everett L.  "Socio-economic Factors and American Fundamentalism."  RRR 1,2 (1959): 57-61.

2715. Peshkin, Alan.  THE TOTAL WORLD OF A FUNDAMENTALIST CHRISTIAN SCHOOL.  Chicago: University of Chicago Press, 1986.

Ethnographic study, U.S.A., mostly 1979-80.

2716. Quinney, Richard.  "Political Conservatism, Alienation, and Fatalism: Contingencies of Social Status and Religious Fundamentalism."  SOCIOMETRY 27,3 (1964): 372-381.

Sample survey of a Southern Appalachian region.  Political conservatism is related to high school status and low religious fundamentalism. Political alienation is associated with low social status and high religious fundamentalism, as is fatalism.

2717. Reinhardt, Robert M. RELIGION AND POLITICS: THE POLITICAL BEHAVIOR OF WEST VIRGINIA PROTESTANT FUNDAMENTALIST SECTARIANS. Unpublished Ph.D. dissertation, University of West Virginia, 1974. [DA 35:4 A, p. 2359]

West Virginia mail survey of sect-type and church-type clergy and laity, using level of attachment to the religious body as a variable.

2718. Richardson, James T. "New Forms of Deviancy in a Fundamentalist Church: A Case Study." RRR 16,2 (1975): 134-141.

Controversy in a fundamentalist church over fiscal policy is discussed in terms of labelling theory, boundary maintenance, moral entrepreneurship, and degradation ceremonies.

2719. Roof, Wade Clark. "The New Fundamentalism: Rebirth of Political Religion in America." In J.K. Hadden and A. Shupe (eds.), PROPHETIC RELIGIONS AND POLITICS [volume cited in item 197], pp. 18-34.

Historical overview.

2720. Stempien, Richard, and Sarah Coleman. "Processes of Persuasion: The Case of Creation Science." RRR 27,2 (1985): 169-177.

In the reactivated confrontation between evolutionism and creationism in the U.S., a content analysis of debates shows that some of the apparent success of the creationists in influencing public opinion is a result of differences in the form rather than the content of the arguments.

2721. Tamney, Joseph B., and Stephen D. Johnson. "Consequential Religiosity in Modern Society." RRR 26,4 (1985): 360-378.

1981 sample from Muncie, Indiana. Religious influence was greatest on family life, least on political life, moderate on work life. Of various measures, fundamentalism had the greatest impact on consequential religiosity.

2722. Tamney, Joseph B., and Stephen D. Johnson. "Fundamentalism and Self-actualization." RRR 30,3 (1989): 276-286.

Questionnaire data from a 1981 random sample of Muncie, Indiana, residents; no relationship between fundamentalism and commitment to self-actualization.

2723. Weigert, Andrew J. "Christian Eschatological Identities and the Nuclear Context." JSSR 27,2 (1988): 175-191.

Socially-constructed time is an important aspect of both community and individual self-understanding. Eschatology refers to the ultimate time frame. Within recent decades of nuclear build-up, the plausibility attached to liberal versus fundamentalist types of Christian eschatology has undergone a historical shift from the former to the latter.

2724. Wilcox, W. Clyde. THE NEW CHRISTIAN RIGHT AND THE WHITE FUNDAMENTALIST: AN ANALYSIS OF A POTENTIAL POLITICAL MOVEMENT. Unpublished Ph.D.

dissertation, Ohio State University, 1984. [DA 45:6 A, p. 1859]

1980 National Election Study data, and a mail survey of the Ohio Moral Majority; comparison with a movement from the 1960s.

2725. Wilcox, W. Clyde. "Evangelicals and Fundamentalists in the New Christian Right: Religious Differences in the Ohio Moral Majority." JSSR 25,3 (1986): 355-363.

1982 survey of the Ohio Moral Majority. Fundamentalists are more likely than evangelicals to be consistently conservative and to perceive a strong connection between their religious and political beliefs. Evangelicals are more politically active and sophisticated.


EVANGELICAL (U.S.A.)

* Ammerman, Nancy T. "Comment: Operationalizing Evangelicalism: An Amendment." Cited above as item 2688.

2726. Bedell, Kenneth B. "Young Evangelicals in the 19th and 20th Centuries." RRR 30,3 (1989): 255-261.

Content analysis of a nineteenth-century journal; comparison with the content analysis of SOJOURNERS and THE OTHER SIDE by James D. Hunter.

* Betts, George H. THE BELIEFS OF 700 MINISTERS. Cited above as item 1937.

* Boling, T. Edwin. "Sectarian Protestants, Churchly Postestants and Roman Catholics: A Comparison in a Mid-American City." Cited above as item 1210.

2727. Fleming, J.J., and G.W. Marks. "Mobilizing for Jesus: Evangelicals and the 1980 Election in the United States." LA REVUE TOCQUEVILLE 3,1 (1980): 195-208.

2728. Golding, Gordon. "L'évangélisme: Un intégrisme protestant américain?" SC 32,4 (1985): 363-371.

American evangelicalism has often been presented in Europe as a counterpart of conservative and traditionalist movements in the Catholic Church. The comparison is tempting.

2729. Hammond, Phillip E. "An Approach to the Political Meaning of Evangelicalism in Present-day America." ANNUAL REVIEW IN THE SOCIAL SCIENCES OF RELIGION 5 (1981): 187-202.

Application of Tocqueville's analysis of the Second Great Awakening, to the evangelical revival of the 1970s.

2730. Hammond, Phillip E., and James D. Hunter. "On Maintaining Plausibility: The Worldview of Evangelical College Students." JSSR 23,3 (1984): 221-238.

Data from over 2000 students from ten colleges, ranging from secular-public to exclusively Christian. While more evangelical students are found at the evangelical campuses, the religious outlook of those at less evangelical campuses appears not threatened but stronger. The plausibility of minority religious viewpoints is relatively easily maintained.

2731. Hunter, James D. "The New Class and the Young Evangelicals." RRR 22, 2 (1980): 155-169. See also Boyd Reese, "Comment," 24,3 (1983): 261-267; and J.D. Hunter, "Reply," 24,3 (1983): 267-276.

Recent social science literature documents the emergence of a 'new class' of knowledge workers having left-liberal class interests and class ideology. Within theologically-conservative American Protestantism, the young evangelicals appear to be a structural, political, and ideological parallel.

2732. Hunter, James D. "Subjectivization and the New Evangelical Theodicy." JSSR 21,1 (1982): 39-47.

Based on content analysis of evangelical literature. Subjectivism characterizes modern culture; it is not so much vanity as an endless preoccupation with hitherto undiscovered complexities of the self. No longer does conservative Protestant theodicy deal only with suffering, grief, and death. It now copes with the musings of modern intra-subjectivity: 'psychological balance,' 'emotional maturity,' 'self-actualization,' etc.

2733. Hunter, James D. "Operationalizing Evangelicalism: A Review, Critique and Proposal." SA 42,4 (1982): 363-372.

Central to evangelicalism is belief in biblical inerrancy, the divinity of Jesus, and salvation through faith in Jesus Christ. See also item 2688.

2734. Hunter, James D. AMERICAN EVANGELICALISM. CONSERVATIVE RELIGION AND THE QUANDARY OF MODERNITY. New Brunswick, N.J.: Rutgers University Press, 1983.

Analysis of primary and secondary historical data, 1979 Gallup (U.S.) data, and content analysis of evangelical publications.

2735. Hunter, James D. "Religion and Political Civility: The Coming Generation of American Evangelicals." JSSR 23,4 (1984): 364-380.

1982 survey of students at nine evangelical liberal arts colleges and seminaries in the U.S.A. The respondents were mobilized against the proposed Equal Rights Amendment, homosexual teachers in public schools, and abortion liberalization. Most did not identify with the Moral Majority.

2736. Hunter, James D. EVANGELICALISM: THE COMING GENERATION. Chicago: University of Chicago Press, 1987.

1982 student surveys of nine denominational colleges and seven Evangelical seminaries; use of other data bases as well, including a 1985 survey of denominational college faculty.

2737. Jacobs, Anton K. EVANGELICALISM AND CAPITALISM: A CRITICAL STUDY OF THE DOCTRINE OF ATONEMENT IN THE HISTORY OF AMERICAN RELIGION. Unpublished Ph.D. dissertation, University of Notre Dame, 1985. [DA 46:5 A, p. 1312]

Focus is on Jonathan Edwards and Carl F.H. Henry.

* Jelen, Ted G. "The Effects of Religious Separatism on White Protestants in the 1984 Presidential Election." Cited above as item 2702.

2738. Lorentzen, Louise J. "Evangelical Life Style Concerns Expressed in Political Action." SA 41,2 (1980): 144-154. Reprinted in J.K. Hadden and T.E. Long (eds.), RELIGION AND RELIGIOSITY IN AMERICA [volume cited in item 1985], pp. 99-117.

Study of a 1978 state Democratic Party nomination convention in Virginia.

2739. Moberg, David O. THE GREAT REVERSAL: EVANGELISM VERSUS SOCIAL CONCERN. Philadelphia: Lippincott, 1972.

* Moberg, David O. "Fundamentalists and Evangelicals in Society." Cited above as item 2710.

2740. Rose, Susan D. CHRISTIAN SCHOOLS IN SECULAR SOCIETY. Unpublished Ph.D. dissertation, Cornell University, 1984. [DA 45:10 A, p. 3215]

Ethnographic case studies of two schools; surveys of all Evangelical Christian schools in three counties in New York State and in Lynchburg, Virginia; and a preliminary study of charismatic students as they moved from Christian to public high school. Some schools isolated students from society, others attempted to instill values in confrontation with society.

2741. Rose, Susan D. KEEPING THEM OUT OF THE HANDS OF SATAN. EVANGELICAL SCHOOLING IN AMERICA. New York: Routledge, 1988.

2742. Rothenberg, Stuart, and Frank Newport. THE EVANGELICAL VOTER. RELIGION AND POLITICS IN AMERICA. Washington: Free Congress Research and Education Foundation, 1984.

1983 U.S. telephone survey, screening out non-evangelical respondents.

* Smidt, Corwin. "'Praise the Lord' Politics: A Comparative Analysis of the Social Characteristics and Political Views of American Evangelical and Charismatic Christians." Cited above as item 2397.

2743. Warner, R. Stephen. "Theoretical Barriers to the Understanding of Evangelical Christianity." SA 40,1 (1979): 1-9.

The assumption that evangelicalism is in essence the religion of the disinherited, the conservative, or the atavistic stands in the way of understanding its resurgence in mainline and middle-class churches.

* Warner, R. Stephen. "Visits to a Growing Evangelical and a Declining

Liberal Church in 1978." Cited above as item 2140.

* Wilcox, W. Clyde. "Evangelicals and Fundamentalists in the New Christian Right: Religious Differences in the Ohio Moral Majority." Cited above as item 2725.

2744. Wulf, Jean, David Prentice, Donna Hansum, Archie Ferrar, and Bernard Spilka. "Religiosity and Sexual Attitudes and Behavior among Evangelical Christian Singles." RRR 26,2 (1984): 119-131.

Survey of participants in an evangelical singles program. Liberalism in sexual matters was evident for some kinds of conduct, conservatism for others. Intrinsic religiosity scores were negatively correlated with sexual liberalism while extrinsic scores were positively correlated with it. Those sexually active tended to be older and divorced.

## EVANGELICAL (FRANCE, LATIN AMERICA)

2745. Baubérot, Jean, and Jean-Paul Willaime. "Le courant évangélique français: Un 'intégrisme protestant'?" SC 32,4 (1985): 393-411.

Discusses the revival of French evangelicalism and how the evangelical phenomenon is different from integrism.

2746. Brinkerhoff, Merlin B., and Reginald W. Bibby. "Circulation of the Saints in South America: A Comparative Study." JSSR 24,1 (1985): 39-55.

Evangelical church growth in Bolivia, Brazil, and Peru is at the expense of the Roman Catholic Church. The diversification of religious offerings by the Catholics, especially the introduction of charismatic Catholicism, may well make evangelicals' inroads in the future more difficult. The prospect of forming a self-sustaining evangelical pool similar to those found in Canada and the United States is rather dim.

2747. O'Connor, Mary. "Two Kinds of Religious Movements among the Mayo Indians of Sonora, Mexico." JSSR 18,3 (1979): 260-268.

1977-78 field work on a nativist movement and an evangelical Protestant movement.

2748. Turner, Paul R. "Religious Conversion and Community Development." JSSR 18,3 (1979): 252-260.

Examines the mass conversion of Tzeltal Indians in Oxchuc, Chiapas (Mexico), from folk Catholicism to evangelical Protestantism during the late 1940s and early 1950s.

## EVANGELICAL (BILLY GRAHAM CRUSADE)

2749. Alston, Jon P. "The Popularity of Billy Graham, 1963-1969." JSSR 12, 2 (1973): 227-230.

Gallup poll data, U.S.A.

2750. Altheide, David L., and John M. Johnson. "Counting Souls: A Study of
Counseling at Evangelical Crusades." PACIFIC SOCIOLOGICAL REVIEW 20,3
(1977): 323-348.

Observations and interviews at a May 1974 crusade in Phoenix, Arizona.
The task of counseling prospective converts has organizational and
practical considerations. It involves introducing people to God and
Bible, leading them to commitment and understanding, collecting information about them, and then 'counting' their souls among the reborn.

2751. Apel, William D. "The Lost World of Billy Graham." RRR 20,2 (1979):
138-149.

The theological history behind Billy Graham is important for understanding his movement.

2752. Clelland, Donald A., Thomas C. Hood, C.M. Lipsey, and Ronald C.
Wimberley. "In the Company of the Converted: Characteristics of a
Billy Graham Crusade Audience." SA 35,1 (1974): 45-56.

Crusade attenders are more educated and affluent and of higher occupational prestige than average area residents. They attend church more
and are more conservative in religious beliefs. Revivalism seems to
reaffirm a threatened life style. Based on a 1970 study in Knoxville,
Tennessee.

2753. Ingram, Larry C. "Evangelism as Frame Intrusion: Observations on
Witnessing in Public Places." JSSR 28,1 (1989): 17-26.

1969-70 participant-observation data from California.

2754. Johnson, Norris R., David A. Choate, and William Bunis. "Attendance
at a Billy Graham Crusade: A Resource Mobilization Approach." SA 45,4
(1984): 383-392.

Attendance at a crusade in Cincinnati, Ohio, was a function of the
extent to which local churches made efforts to mobilize their congregations.

2755. Whitam, Frederick L. ADOLESCENCE AND MASS PERSUASION: A STUDY OF
TEEN-AGE DECISION-MAKING AT A BILLY GRAHAM CRUSADE. Unpublished Ph.D.
dissertation, Indiana University, 1965. [DA 27:2 A, p. 542]

2756. Whitam, Frederick L. "Revivalism as Institutionalized Behavior: An
Analysis of the Social Base of a Billy Graham Crusade." SOCIAL
SCIENCE QUARTERLY 49,1 (1986): 115-127.

A 1963 questionnaire study on people who had filled out 'decision
cards' at a 1957 crusade in New York City.

2757. Wimberley, Ronald C., et al. "Conversion in a Billy Graham Crusade."
In M.D. Pugh (ed.), COLLECTIVE BEHAVIOR: A SOURCE BOOK. St. Paul,
Minnesota: West, 1980, pp. 278-285.

2758. Bruce, Steve. "Research Note: Identifying Conservative Protestantism."
SA 44,1 (1983): 65-70.

Because of scholarly disagreement over the meaning and scope of such
terms as 'evangelical,' 'fundamentalist,' and 'conservative,' a
definition of conservative Protestantism is made, based on the different epistemologies which underlie the various modern Christian
traditions.

* Dempsey, Kenneth C. "Secularization and the Protestant Parish Minister." Cited above as item 2666.

2759. Wallis, Roy, and Steve Bruce. "Sketch for a Theory of Conservative
Protestant Politics." SC 32,2-3 (1985): 145-161.

The impact of conservative Protestantism on politics is high in Northern Ireland and South Africa, moderate in the U.S., the Netherlands,
and Scandinavia, and low in Canada, Austria, New Zealand, England, and
Scotland. Different models of this impact can be described in terms
of a) the initial formation of a socio-religious culture, b) later
changes within this culture from immigration, secularization, and
church-state accommodations, and c) the structure of the politics and
media of the environing society.

2760. Wallis, Roy, and Steve Bruce. "A Comparative Analysis of Conservative
Protestant Politics." Chapter 9 in SOCIOLOGICAL THEORY, RELIGION AND
COLLECTIVE ACTION. Belfast: The Queen's University, 1986.

International comparisons.


CONSERVATIVE (CANADA, AUSTRALIA)

2761. Bibby, Reginald W. "Why Conservative Churches Really are Growing:
Kelley Revisited." JSSR 17,2 (1978): 129-137.

1975 Canadian national sample. The conservative churches grew because
of birth and religious socialization, switching from one Christian
church to another, and higher levels of participation. See also item
2780.

2762. Bibby, Reginald W., and Merlin B. Brinkerhoff. "The Circulation of
the Saints: A Study of People who Join Conservative Churches." JSSR
12,3 (1973): 273-283.

Study of membership additions, 1966-70, in 20 evangelical churches in
a western Canadian city. New members generally came from other
evangelical churches.

2763. Bibby, Reginald W., and Merlin B. Brinkerhoff. "Circulation of the
Saints Revisited: A Longitudinal Look at Conservative Church Growth."
JSSR 22,3 (1983): 253-262.

Replication of item 2762. Study of membership additions, 1976-80, in

20 evangelical churches in a western Canadian city. New members generally came from other evangelical churches.

* Black, Alan W. "The Impact of Theological Orientation and of Breadth of Perspective on Church Members' Attitudes and Behaviors: Roof, Mol and Kaill Revisited." Cited above as item 2095.

## CONSERVATIVE (U.S.A.)

* Bouma, Gary D. "The Real Reason One Conservative Church Grew." Cited above as item 2141.

2764. Bruce, Steve. ONE NATION UNDER GOD? Belfast, Northern Ireland: The Queen's University (Department of Social Studies), 1983.

An outside view of American phenomena.

2765. Bruce, Steve. FIRM IN THE FAITH. Brookfield, Vermont: Gower, 1984.

2766. Bruce, Steve. THE RISE AND FALL OF THE NEW CHRISTIAN RIGHT. CONSERVATIVE PROTESTANT POLITICS IN AMERICA 1978-1988. New York: Oxford University Press, 1989.

2767. Ebaugh, Helen Rose Fuchs, and C. Allen Haney. "Church Attendance and Attitudes toward Abortion: Differentials in Liberal and Conservative Churches." JSSR 17,4 (1978): 407-413.

Based on 1976 U.S. survey data; church attendance is shown positively related to disapproval of legalized abortion for members of conservative churches. No relation exists between church attendance and attitudes toward abortion for members of liberal churches.

2768. Ezcurra, Ana Maria. "Neoconservative and Ideological Struggle toward Central America in the U.S.A." SC 30,2-3 (1983): 349-362.

Study of the political and economic connections between the Institute on Religion and Democracy and the neo-conservative establishment.

* Hadaway, Christopher K. "Conservatism and Social Strength in a Liberal Denomination." Cited above as item 2126.

2769. Hadden, Jeffrey K. "Televangelism and the New Christian Right." In J.K. Hadden and T.E. Long (eds.), RELIGION AND RELIGIOSITY IN AMERICA [volume cited in item 1985], pp. 114-127.

2770. Hadden, Jeffrey K. "Televangelism and the Mobilization of a New Christian Right Family Policy." In W.V. D'Antonio and J. Aldous (eds.), FAMILIES AND RELIGIONS [volume cited in item 421], pp. 247-266.

2771. Hadden, Jeffrey K. "Religious Broadcasting and the Mobilization of the New Christian Right." JSSR 26,1 (1987): 1-24.

The charismatic leaders of religious broadcasting are the principal actors in an important social movement. The ideology of the movement is based on the view that the U.S.A. is a 'New Israel.' The movement's resources and techniques grew out of nineteenth-century urban revivalism. In dismissing the movement as backward, many have underestimated its complexity, strength, and potential.

2772. Hammond, Phillip E. "In Search of a Protestant Twentieth Century: American Religion and Power since 1900." RRR 24,4 (1983): 281-294.

Changes in American Protestantism, 1880-1920, broke the link between mainline denominations and the exercise of power, and brought about a failure of nerve in the foreign missions. Although conservative Protestantism sounds as if it were at war with modernism, in fact its quarrel is with the diminished political role played by religion.

2773. Hammond, Phillip E. "The Curious Path of Conservative Protestantism." THE ANNALS OF THE AMERICAN ACADEMY OF POLITICAL AND SOCIAL SCIENCE 480 (1985): 53-62.

History of the emergence of liberal and conservative wings in American Protestantism. The recent reinvigoration of the conservative movement is a national event more than a theological development.

2774. Heinz, Donald J. "Clashing Symbols: The New Christian Right as Countermythology." ARCHIVES DE SCIENCES SOCIALES DES RELIGIONS 59,1 (1985): 153-173.

Argues that the New Christian Right can best be interpreted as an emerging coalition of social movements engaged in a contest over the meaning of America's story.

2775. Hill, Samuel S. "NRPR: The New Religious-political Right in America." In E. Barker (ed.), OF GODS AND MEN [volume cited in item 64], pp. 109-126.

2776. Hunter, James D. "Conservative Protestantism." In Phillip E. Hammond (ed.), THE SACRED IN A SECULAR AGE. Berkeley: University of California Press, 1985, pp. 150-166.

Considerations framed within the context of the secularization question.

2777. Hunter, James D. "Conservative Protestantism on the American Scene." SC 32,2-3 (1985): 233-243.

Conservative Protestantism in the U.S. thrives by making selective adaptations to modern conditions.

2778. Johnson, Stephen D., and Joseph B. Tamney. "The Christian Right and the 1984 Presidential Election." RRR 27,2 (1985): 124-133.

1984 interview data from intended voters in Muncie, Indiana. Although religious factors had more of an influence on Reagan's election in 1984 than in 1980, moderate, not high, Christian Rightists supported Reagan; the Moral Majority had a negative impact since there were more anti-Moral Majority voters who voted for Mondale than pro-Moral Majority voters who voted for Reagan.

371

2779. Johnson, Stephen D., Joseph B. Tamney, and Sandy Halebsky. "Christianity, Social Traditionalism, and Economic Conservatism." SOCIOLOGICAL FOCUS 19,3 (1986): 299-314.

Interview data from a Muncie, Indiana, sample.

2780. Kelley, Dean M. WHY CONSERVATIVE CHURCHES ARE GROWING. A STUDY IN THE SOCIOLOGY OF RELIGION. New York: Harper and Row, 1972.

2781. Kelley, Dean M. "Why Conservative Churches are Still Growing." JSSR 17,2 (1978): 165-172.

Membership data continue to show that the conservative churches are growing, largely because they do a better job of making life meaningful in ultimate terms.

2782. Kitay, Philip M. RADICALISM AND CONSERVATISM TOWARD CONVENTIONAL RELIGION. (Teachers College, Columbia University, Publication No. 919.) New York: Columbia University Press, 1947.

2783. Miller, Wesley E. "The New Christian Right and Its Preexistent Network: A Resource Mobilization Explanation." HUMANITY AND SOCIETY 10,2 (1986): 179-195.

Changes in U.S. campaign-financing laws made useful fundraising techniques of previously existing groups - the old Right and the fundamentalist church growth movement.

2784. Moen, Matthew C. "Status Politics and the Political Agenda of the Christian Right." SOCIOLOGICAL QUARTERLY 29,3 (1988): 429-438.

Participant observation as a congressional aide in Washington, and interviews with legislative directors of the National Christian Action Coalition, the Christian Voice, and the Moral Majority. Status politics fails to explain adequately the moral, nonsymbolic, and 'offensive' dimensions of the Christian Right.

2785. Mueller, Carol. "In Search of a Constituency for the 'New Religious Right'." PUBLIC OPINION QUARTERLY 47,2 (1983): 213-229.

1972-80 N.O.R.C. (U.S.) data. There is no conservative trend on feminist issues. Differences between the religiously involved and others existed from the beginning. The New Religious Right has failed to create a mass constituency or a new 'moral majority.'

2786. Nawn, Joanne Young. THE CHRISTIAN WOMEN'S NATIONAL CONCERNS AND THE NEW RELIGIOUS RIGHT IN THE DALLAS-FORT WORTH METROPOLEX: AN EMPIRICAL ASSESSMENT. Unpublished M.A. thesis, University of Texas, Arlington, 1982.

* Nemeth, Roger J., and Donald A. Luidens. "The New Christian Right and Mainline Protestantism: The Case of the Reformed Church in America." Cited above as item 2146.

* Schoenfeld, Eugen. "Image of Man: The Effect of Religion on Trust. A

Research Note." Cited above as item 2673.

2787. Shupe, Anson D., and John Heinerman. "Mormonism and the New Christian Right: An Emerging Coalition?" RRR 27,2 (1985): 146-157.

After a history of hostilities, there is an alliance between Mormons and the New Christian right, including rapprochement between Moral Majority founder Rev. Jerry Falwell and the right-wing, largely Mormon, Freeman Institute. Both can be tied to the John Birch Society. Such a coalition makes strategic sense from a social movements perspective.

2788. Smidt, Corwin, and James M. Penning. "Religious Commitment, Political Conservatism, and Political and Social Tolerance in the United States: A Longitudinal Analysis." SA 43,3 (1982): 231-246.

1974, 1977, and 1980 N.O.R.C. (U.S.) data. Religious commitment is negatively related to political tolerance. Political tolerance and liberal political identity are separate dimensions, as are political intolerance and both religious and political conservatism. The impact of religious commitment on political tolerance varies by issue.

2789. Stacey, William A., and Anson D. Shupe. "Religious Values and Religiosity in the Textbook Adoption Controversy in Texas, 1981." RRR 25, 4 (1984): 321-333.

1981 survey in the Dallas/Fort Worth metropolitan area. Examines transcripts of testimony before the Texas school textbook authorities. The evidence suggests a lack of consensus in the public over the value positions promoted by conservative Christians.

2790. Symington, Thomas A. RELIGIOUS LIBERALS AND CONSERVATIVES. (Teachers College Contributions to Education, No. 64.) New York: Columbia University Press, 1935.

2791. Wald, Kenneth D., Dennis E. Owen, and Samuel S. Hill. "Evangelical Politics and Status Issues." JSSR 28,1 (1989): 1-16.

1986-87 questionnaire data from the Gainesville, Florida, SMSA.

2792. Wallis, Roy, and Steve Bruce. "The New Christian Right in America." Chapter 11 in SOCIOLOGICAL THEORY, RELIGION AND COLLECTIVE ACTION. Belfast, Northern Ireland: The Queen's University, 1986.

2793. White, O. Kendall, Jr. "A Review and Commentary on the Prospects of a Mormon New Christian Right Coalition." RRR 28,2 (1986): 180-188.

Proponents of the emergence of a coalition have a more compelling case than those who deny it.

2794. Wilcox, W. Clyde. "America's Radical Right Revisited. A Comparison of the Activists in Christian Right Organizations from the 1960s and the 1980s." SA 48,1 (1987): 46-57.

In 1982 the Ohio Moral Majority resembled comparable organizations from twenty years earlier; activists in such organizations are higher SES Republicans.

373

2795. Woodrum, Eric. "Moral Conservatism and the 1984 Presidential Election." JSSR 27,2 (1988): 192-210.

1984 Raleigh, North Carolina, survey specifying the importance of moral conservatism in electoral preferences.

2796. Woodrum, Eric. "Determinants of Moral Attitudes." JSSR 27,4 (1988): 553-573.

1984 Raleigh, North Carolina, sample.

2797. Wuthnow, Robert. "Religious Commitment and Conservatism: In Search of an Elusive Relationship." In C.Y. Glock (ed.), RELIGION IN SOCIOLOGICAL PERSPECTIVE [volume cited in item 189], pp. 117-132.

A review of quantitative studies from the previous decade.


## MORAL MAJORITY

2798. Brinkerhoff, Merlin B., Jeffrey C. Jacob, and Marlene M. MacKie. "Mormonism and the Moral Majority make Strange Bedfellows?: An Exploratory Critique." RRR 28,3 (1987): 236-251.

Questionnaire data from students at four universities in the U.S.A. and Canada. There is a value congruence between Mormons and conservative Christians, but there is still considerable social distance between the two.

2799. Cable, Sherry. "Professionalization in Social Movement Organization: A Case Study of Pennsylvanians for Biblical Morality." SOCIOLOGICAL FOCUS 17,4 (1984): 287-304.

Interview and observation data on the Pennsylvania chapter of the Moral Majority, Inc.

2800. Gannon, Thomas M. "The New Christian Right in America as a Social and Political Force." ARCHIVES DE SCIENCES SOCIALES DES RELIGIONS 52 (1981): 69-83.

An overview of the Moral Majority and associated groups; assessment of the movement's political potential.

   * Guth, James L. "Southern Baptist Clergy: Vanguard of the Christian Right?" Cited above as item 2291.

   * Hammond, Phillip E., and James D. Hunter. "On Maintaining Plausibility: The Worldview of Evangelical College Students." Cited above as item 2730.

2801. Harper, Charles L., and Kevin Leicht. "Religious Awakenings and Status Politics: Sources of Support for the New Religious Right." SA 45,4 (1984): 339-353.

Questionnaire data from United Church of Christ, Disciples of Christ, and Assembly of God church members in Nebraska, show that support for the program of the Moral Majority is more strongly related to religious and cultural variables than to threatened statuses.

2802. Johnson, Stephen D., and Joseph B. Tamney. "Support for the Moral Majority: A Test of a Model." JSSR 23,2 (1984): 183-196.

Based on 1982 interview data from Muncie, Indiana. A Christian right orientation, cultural ethnocentrism, and authoritarianism had a major impact on Moral Majority support. Education, age, and the viewing of religious television had a secondary influence.

* Johnson, Stephen D., and Joseph B. Tamney. "The Christian Right and the 1984 Presidential Election." Cited above as item 2778.

2803. Johnson, Stephen D., and Joseph B. Tamney. "Mobilizing Support for the Moral Majority." PSYCHOLOGICAL REPORTS 56 (1985): 987-994.

1983 telephone interview data from a Muncie, Indiana, sample; only modest support for the Moral Majority.

2804. Liebman, Robert C. "Mobilizing the Moral Majority." In R.C. Liebman and R. Wuthnow (eds.), THE NEW CHRISTIAN RIGHT [volume cited in item 2291], pp. 49-73.

Historical documentation.

2805. Schwartz, Anthony, and James McBride. "The Moral Majority in the U.S.A. as a New Religious Movement." In E. Barker (ed.), OF GODS AND MEN [volume cited in item 64], pp. 127-146.

Overview.

2806. Shupe, Anson D., and William A. Stacey. BORN AGAIN POLITICS AND THE MORAL MAJORITY: WHAT SOCIAL SURVEYS REALLY SHOW. New York: Edwin Mellen Press, 1982.

1981 questionnaire sample in the Dallas-Fort Worth metropolitan area.

2807. Shupe, Anson D., and William A. Stacey. "The Moral Majority Constituency." In R.C. Liebman and R. Wuthnow (eds.), THE NEW CHRISTIAN RIGHT [volume cited in item 2291], pp. 103-116.

1981 questionnaire sample in the Dallas-Fort Worth metropolitan area.

2808. Shupe, Anson D., and William A. Stacey. "Public and Clergy Sentiments toward the Moral Majority: Evidence from the Dallas-Fort Worth Metroplex." In D.G. Bromley and A.D. Shupe (eds.), NEW CHRISTIAN POLITICS [volume cited in item 1414], pp. 91-100.

A 1981 questionnaire sample in the Dallas-Fort Worth metropolitan area, and a telephone sample of Christian clergy listed in the Dallas and Fort Worth telephone directory Yellow Pages.

2809. Simpson, John H. "Moral Issues and Status Politics." In R.C. Liebman and R. Wuthnow (eds.), THE NEW CHRISTIAN RIGHT [volume cited in item 2291], pp. 187-205.

Analysis of data from the General Social Survey (U.S.A.) for 1977.

2810. Simpson, John H. "Support for the Moral Majority and Its Sociomoral Platform." In D.G. Bromley and A.D. Shupe (eds.), NEW CHRISTIAN POLITICS [volume cited in item 1414], pp. 65-68.

Part of an analysis of 1977 data from the General Social Survey (U.S.).

2811. Simpson, John H., and Henry MacLeod. "The Politics of Morality in Canada." In R. Stark (ed.), RELIGIOUS MOVEMENTS [volume cited in item 2102], pp. 221-240.

Examines the demographic and cultural conditions which make unlikely the formation of a Canadian equivalent to the Moral Majority.

2812. Tamney, Joseph B., and Stephen D. Johnson. "The Moral Majority in Middletown." JSSR 22,2 (1983): 145-157.

Data based on interviews in Muncie, Indiana. Moral Majority support had three independent sources: 1) persuasion via religious television, 2) cultural fundamentalist attitude stressing continuation of the status quo, and 3) advocacy of the Christian right perspective.

* Wilcox, W. Clyde. THE NEW CHRISTIAN RIGHT AND THE WHITE FUNDAMENTAL-ISTS: AN ANALYSIS OF A POTENTIAL POLITICAL MOVEMENT. Cited above as item 2724.

* Wilcox, W. Clyde. "Evangelicals and Fundamentalists in the New Christian Right: Religious Differences in the Ohio Moral Majority." Cited above as item 2725.

* Wilcox, W. Clyde. "America's Radical Right Revisited. A Comparison of the Activists in Christian Right Organizations from the 1960s and the 1980s." Cited above as item 2794.

2813. Wilcox, W. Clyde. "Seeing the Connection: Religion and Politics in the Ohio Moral Majority." RRR 30,1 (1988): 47-58.

1982 survey of the Ohio Moral Majority. The subjective connection between religious and political beliefs is high. The strength of the connection varies with issue, especially for female respondents. The strength of the connection has a different impact for fundamentalists and evangelicals respectively.

2814. Yinger, J. Milton, and Stephen J. Cutler. "The Moral Majority viewed Sociologically." SOCIOLOGICAL FOCUS 15,4 (1982): 289-306. Reprinted in D.G. Bromley and A.D. Shupe (eds.), NEW CHRISTIAN POLITICS [volume cited in item 1414], pp. 69-90.

1973-80 N.O.R.C. (U.S.) surveys. Support for the Moral Majority position declined somewhat over the seven years. Religiosity, age, and education explain much of the variance in indications of support for the Moral Majority position.

# PART V
# INDEPENDENT TRADITIONS

# 22
# Mormon

*WORKS, 1937-1949*

2815. Anderson, Nels. "The Mormon Family." AMERICAN SOCIOLOGICAL REVIEW 2,5 (1937): 601-608.

Focuses on the size of families in Utah, with the attendant economic burden. Change in this respect and others is most evident in the urban areas.

2816. Anderson, Nels. DESERT SAINTS: THE MORMON FRONTIER IN UTAH. Chicago: University of Chicago Press, 1942.

2817. Bock, Ruth C. THE CHURCH OF JESUS CHRIST OF LATTER-DAY SAINTS IN THE HAWAIIAN ISLANDS. Unpublished M.A. thesis, University of Hawaii, 1941.

2818. Christensen, Harold T. "Mormon Fertility: A Survey of Student Opinion." AMERICAN JOURNAL OF SOCIOLOGY 53,4 (1948): 270-275.

Mormon fertility is responsive to general trends toward practice of birth control and smaller families.

2819. DeHart, William A. "Fertility of Mormons in Utah and Adjacent States." AMERICAN SOCIOLOGICAL REVIEW 6,6 (1941): 818-829.

Using county data from parts of Idaho, Utah, Wyoming, and Nevada, proportion Mormon and fertility rates correlate.

2820. Done, G. Byron. A STUDY OF MORMON-GENTILE INTERMARRIAGE IN LOS ANGELES. Unpublished M.A. thesis, University of Southern California, 1937.

2821. Done, G. Byron. THE PARTICIPATION OF LATTER-DAY SAINTS IN THE COMMUNITY LIFE OF LOS ANGELES. Unpublished Ph.D. dissertation, University of Southern California, 1939.

2822. Durham, G. Homer. "Administrative Organization of the Mormon Church." POLITICAL SCIENCE QUARTERLY 57,1 (1942): 51-71.

Overview of the presidency of the Mormon church.

2823. Hulett, J.E., Jr. THE SOCIAL AND PSYCHOLOGICAL ASPECTS OF THE MORMON FAMILY. Unpublished Ph.D. dissertation, University of Wisconsin, Madison, 1939.

2824. Hulett, J.E., Jr. "Social Role and Personal Security in Mormon Polygamy." AMERICAN JOURNAL OF SOCIOLOGY 45 (1940): 452-553.

Persons from monogamous backgrounds adjust with difficulty to polygamous family life, particularly in regard to the perception of familial roles.

2825. Hulett, J.E., Jr. "The Social Role of the Mormon Polygamous Male." AMERICAN SOCIOLOGICAL REVIEW 8,3 (1946): 279-287.

The dominant position of the Mormon polygamous male in the family group favored his ego-security, but the non-normative nature of polygamy from the viewpoint of American society undermined it.

2826. Rose, Arnold M. "The Mormon Church and Utah Politics: An Abstract of a Statistical Study." AMERICAN SOCIOLOGICAL REVIEW 7,6 [Part 2] (1942): 853-854.

The Church of Jesus Christ of Latter-day Saints was unable during the late 1930s to sway the Utah electorate its way.

2827. Tappan, Paul W. MORMON-GENTILE CONFLICT: A STUDY OF THE INFLUENCES OF PUBLIC OPINION ON IN-GROUP VERSUS OUT-GROUP INTERACTION WITH SPECIAL REFERENCE TO POLYGAMY. Unpublished Ph.D. dissertation, University of Wisconsin, 1939.

2828. West, Roy A. "The Mormon Village Family." SOCIOLOGY AND SOCIAL RESEARCH 23,4 (1939): 353-359.

Based on interviews of 400 families and on church records; Cache County, Utah.

2829. Young, Kimball. "Variations in Personality Manifestations in Mormon Polygynous Families." In Quinn McNemar and Maud A. Sherill (eds.), STUDIES IN PERSONALITY CONTRIBUTED IN HONOR OF LEWIS M. TERMAN. New York: McGraw-Hill, 1942. Reprinted as "Sex Roles in Polygynous Mormon Families," in Theodore M. Newcomb et al. (eds.), READINGS IN SOCIAL PSYCHOLOGY. New York: Henry Holt, 1947, pp. 373-383.

125 records of men and their families, who lived under Mormon polygyny. Qualitative data collected 1935-39; cases go back to the 1860s.


*WORKS, 1950-1959*

2830. Arrington, Leonard J. "Property among the Mormons." RURAL SOCIOLOGY 16,4 (1951): 339-353.

Upon settling in Utah in 1847, the Mormons did not absolutize property rights in the manner of the rest of the United States, but rather followed the principle of stewardship.

2831. Bolino, August C. "Brigham Young an Entrepreneur." AMERICAN JOURNAL OF ECONOMICS AND SOCIOLOGY 18,2 (1959): 181-192.

Examines the economic activities of the Mormon leader.

2832. Christopherson, Victor A. FAMILY LIFE AND FAMILY LIFE EDUCATION IN THE MORMON CHURCH FROM EARLY TIMES TO THE PRESENT DAY. Unpublished Ph.D. dissertation, Columbia University, 1954.

2833. Christopherson, Victor A. "An Investigation of Patriarchal Authority in the Mormon Family." MARRIAGE AND FAMILY LIVING 18,4 (1956): 328-333.

Based on interviews with Mormon couples who were parents of at least two children, and whose parents had also been Mormons. Patriarchal authority was still seen as a divine endowment, but family patriarchs were religious figureheads rather than controllers of family affairs. Shared control typified most family matters. There was some cross-generational decrease of patriarchal authority.

2834. Dean, William H. THE MORMONS OF EL DORADO STAKE AND THE VALLEY CITY WARD: A STUDY IN SOCIAL NORMS AND THEIR EFFECTIVENESS. Unpublished Ph.D. dissertation, Washington University, Saint Louis, 1954.

2835. Follett, E.J.N. A STUDY OF INTERFAITH MARRIAGES AMONG MORMONS IN BERKELEY, CALIFORNIA. Unpublished M.A. thesis, University of California at Berkeley, 1959.

2836. Morsa, J. "Les Mormons." REVUE DE L'INSTITUT DE SOCIOLOGIE 4 (1953): 607-616.

2837. Nelson, Lowry. "Education and the Changing Size of Mormon Families." RURAL SOCIOLOGY 17,4 (1952): 335-342.

Data from two Utah villages; 1925 and 1950.

2838. Nelson, Lowry. THE MORMON VILLAGE: A PATTERN AND TECHNIQUE OF LAND SETTLEMENT. Salt Lake City: University of Utah Press, 1952.

2839. O'Dea, Thomas F. MORMON VALUES: THE SIGNIFICANCE OF A RELIGIOUS OUT-LOOK FOR SOCIAL ACTION. Unpublished Ph.D. dissertation, Harvard University, 1953.

2840. O'Dea, Thomas F. "Mormonism and the Avoidance of Sectarian Stagnation: A Study of Church, Sect, and Incipient Nationality." AMERICAN JOURNAL OF SOCIOLOGY 60 (1954): 285-293. Reprinted in T.F. O'Dea, SOCIOLOGY AND THE STUDY OF RELIGION [volume cited in item 1077], pp. 116-130.

Case study analyzing factors which prevented the development of sectarianism and contributed instead toward the development of a religious community.

2841. O'Dea, Thomas F. "Geographical Position and Mormon Behavior." RURAL SOCIOLOGY 19,4 (1954): 358-364. Reprinted as "The Effects of Geographical Position on Belief and Behavior in a Rural Mormon Village," in T.F. O'Dea, SOCIOLOGY AND THE STUDY OF RELIGION [volume cited in item 1077], pp. 131-140.

Based on 1950-51 field work in a community in northwestern New Mexico, along the Little Colorado River. Isolation and peripheral location helped deepen and make important the New Mexico community's ties to the wider Mormon universe.

2842. O'Dea, Thomas F. "Mormonism and the American Experience of Time." WESTERN HUMANITIES REVIEW 8,3 (1954): 181-190. Reprinted in T.F. O'Dea, SOCIOLOGY AND THE STUDY OF RELIGION [volume cited in item 1077], pp. 141-152.

Time as a process over which humans are gaining mastery, is an American view which Mormonism has incorporated into its system.

2843. O'Dea, Thomas F. THE MORMONS. Chicago: University of Chicago Press, 1957.

The 'church' form of Mormonism is related to the upper class, the 'sect' form to the lower.

2844. Smith, Wilford E. A COMPARATIVE STUDY OF INDULGENCE OF MORMON AND NON-MORMON STUDENTS IN CERTAIN SOCIAL PRACTICES WHICH ARE AUTHORITA-TIVELY CONDEMNED BY THE CHURCH OF JESUS CHRIST OF LATTER-DAY SAINTS. Unpublished Ph.D. dissertation, University of Washington, 1952.

2845. Smith, Wilford E. "The Urban Threat to Mormon Norms." RURAL SOCIOLO-GY 24,4 (1959): 355-361.

1956-57 data from urban (Phoenix, Los Angeles, Salt Lake City) and rural (Arizona) Mormon stakes, based on assessments of Mormons made by bishops.

2846. Vogt, Evon Z., and Thomas F. O'Dea. "A Comparative Study of the Role of Values in Social Action in Two Southwestern Communities." AMERICAN SOCIOLOGICAL REVIEW 18,6 (1953): 645-654. Reprinted in T.F. O'Dea, SOCIOLOGY AND THE STUDY OF RELIGION [volume cited in item 1077], pp. 99-115.

Field research in western New Mexico, in which two communities, one Mormon and one 'Texas,' responded to similar problems in quite different ways. Value systems are cited as explanations for the differences.

2847. Young, Kimball. "ISN'T ONE WIFE ENOUGH?" THE STORY OF MORMON POLYGAMY. New York: Henry Holt, 1954.


*WORKS, 1960-1969*

* Anderson, Charles H. "Religious Communality among White Protestants, Catholics and Mormons." Cited above as item 1093.

2848. Brinkerhoff, David B. A STUDY OF THE RELATIONSHIP BETWEEN TYPES OF

382

RELIGIOUS ORIENTATION AND DEGREE OF RELIGIOUS INVOLVEMENT OF LDS
CHURCH MEMBERS IN THE PROVO COMMUNITY. Unpublished M.S. thesis,
Brigham Young University, 1968.

2849. Christensen, Harold T., and Kenneth L. Cannon. "Temple versus Nontemple
Marriages in Utah: Some Demographic Considerations." SOCIAL SCIENCE
39,1 (1964): 26-33.

A study of 1905-51 marriages in the Salt Lake City area.

2850. Christensen, James W. THE CONSTRUCTION OF A MORMON IDEOLOGICAL COMMIT-
MENT SCALE. Unpublished M.S. thesis, University of Utah, 1966.

2851. Christensen, John R. "Contemporary Mormons' Attitudes toward Polygynous Practices." MARRIAGE AND FAMILY LIVING 25 (1963): 167-170.

1962 interview data from married people in a rural community in
central Utah.

2852. Davies, J. Kenneth. "The Mormon Church: Its Middle-class Propensities." RRR 4 (1963): 84-95.

Based on 1957 questionnaire research on Mormons in the continental
U.S.A.

   * Gay, John. "Some Aspects of the Social Geography of Religion in
England: The Roman Catholics and the Mormons." Cited above as item
1644.

   * Gockel, Galen L. "Income and Religious Affiliation: A Regression
Analysis." Cited above as item 437.

2853. Hill, Reuben. "L'appartenance religieuse chez les Mormons." SC 12,3
(1965): 171-176.

General account.

2854. Kunz, Phillip R. "Mormon and Non-Mormon Divorce Patterns." JOURNAL
OF MARRIAGE AND THE FAMILY 26,2 (1964): 211-213.

Questionnaire data from introductory sociology students in two western
U.S. universities, reporting parents' marital status.

   * Lalive d'Epinay, Christian. "L'esprit et la champ oecuméniques de
pasteurs sud-américains." Cited above as item 1748.

   * Lester, Geoffrey A. THE DISTRIBUTION OF RELIGIOUS GROUPS IN ALBERTA,
1961. Cited above as item 2235.

2855. Madsen, Gary E. A COMPARISON OF THE DIRECT AND INDIRECT METHODS OF
RELIGIOUS MEASUREMENT. Unpublished M.A. thesis, University of Utah,
1968.

2856. Mauss, Armand L. "Mormonism and Secular Attitudes toward Negroes."
PACIFIC SOCIOLOGICAL REVIEW 9,2 (1966): 91-99.

Questionnaire data from three northern-California wards.

2857. Mauss, Armand L. "Mormon Semitism and Anti-semitism." SA 29,1 (1968): 11-27.

San Francisco Bay Area sample of Mormons, compared with a general Bay Area sample. Mormons are less likely than others to hold secular anti-Jewish beliefs.

2858. O'Dea, Thomas F. "The Mormons - Strong Voice in the West." INFORMATION, THE CATHOLIC CHURCH IN AMERICAN LIFE (March 1961): 15-20.

2859. O'Dea, Thomas F. "Mormonism Today." DESERT. MAGAZINE OF THE SOUTHWEST 26 (1963): 23-27.

2860. Vallier, Ivan. "Church, Society and Labor Resources: An Intradenominational Comparison." AMERICAN JOURNAL OF SOCIOLOGY 68,1 (1962): 21-33.

Labor resources available to a religious body are related to its external situation in society.


*WORKS, 1970-1979*

2861. Albrecht, Stan L., Bruce A. Chadwick, and David S. Alcorn. "Religiosity and Deviance: Application of an Attitude-behavior Contingent Consistency Model." JSSR 16,3 (1977): 263-274.

Data from Mormon teenagers in southern Idaho, central Utah, and suburban Los Angeles, California. Good prediction of deviance was obtained when religious indicators were combined with measures of peer and family relationships. Religious variables were more strongly related to victimless than to victim deviance.

2862. Arrington, Leonard J. "The Latter-day Saints and Public Education." SOUTHWESTERN JOURNAL OF THE SOCIOLOGY OF EDUCATION 7 (1977): 9-25.

2863. Bahr, Stephen J., and Howard M. Bahr. "Religion and Family Roles: A Comparison of Catholic, Mormon and Protestant Families." In Phillip R. Kunz (ed.), THE MORMON FAMILY. Provo, Utah: Family Research Center, Brigham Young University, 1977, pp. 45-61.

2864. Bellah, Robert N. "American Society and the Mormon Community." In T.G. Madsen (ed.), REFLECTIONS ON MORMONISM: JUDAEO-CHRISTIAN PARALLELS. Salt Lake City: Bookcraft, 1978, pp. 1-12.

2865. Brinkerhoff, Merlin B. "Religion and Goal Orientations: Does Denomination Make a Difference?" SA 39,3 (1978): 203-218.

Data from sixth, ninth, and twelfth-grade students from largely Mormon schools in central Utah. Mormon doctrine on women's roles increased the relationship between gender and goals, and belief in large families decreased the effect of family size on goals. Denominational identity and religious involvement serve as important statistical control variables allowing these relationships to appear.

2866. Buckle, Robert. "Mormons in Britain. A Survey." SOCIOLOGICAL YEAR-
BOOK OF RELIGION IN BRITAIN 4 (1971): 160-179.

Based upon a full sample of the active members of the Hereford city
church branch.

2867. Bunker, Gary L., and Martin A. Johnson. "Ethnicity and Resistance to
Compensatory Education. A Comparison of Mormon and Non-Mormon Attitudes." RRR 16,2 (1975): 74-82.

High school and college student surveys show that Mormons as compared
to others in U.S. culture are not significantly different in their
secular racial attitudes.

2868. Bunker, Gary L., Harry Coffey, and Martin A. Johnson. "Mormons and
Social Distance: A Multidimensional Analysis." ETHNICITY 4,4 (1977):
352-369.

Brigham Young University and Biola College (La Mirada, California)
student subjects, responded to social distance instruments. Social
distance proved to have dimensions. Current ecclesiastical doctrines
of the Mormon church about Semitic identification and the ordination
of blacks had some carry over into social distance, as was evidenced
by comparisons between the BYU Mormon respondents and Biola College
evangelicals.

2869. Christensen, Harold T., and Kenneth L. Cannon. "The Fundamentalist
Emphasis at Brigham Young University: 1935-1973." JSSR 17,1 (1978):
53-57.

Notes the increasing theological conservatism of BYU students.

2870. Clark, John. PERCEIVED STATUS OF THE GENERAL AUTHORITIES OF THE
CHURCH OF LATTER-DAY SAINTS. Unpublished M.A. thesis, University of
Utah, 1973.

2871. Davies, Douglas J. "Aspects of Latter-day Saints Eschatology."
SOCIOLOGICAL YEARBOOK OF RELIGION IN BRITAIN 6 (1973): 122-135.

Traces the change in orientation of the Mormon church to the world,
with specific reference to Mormon eschatological doctrines.

2872. Duke, James T., and D. Wayne Brown, Jr. "Three Paths to Spiritual
Well-being among the Mormons: Conversion, Obedience, and Repentance."
In David O. Moberg (ed.), SPIRITUAL WELL-BEING. SOCIOLOGICAL PERSPEC-
TIVES. Washington: University Press of America, 1979, pp. 173-189.

Includes data from interviews conducted in Provo, Utah.

2873. Hastings, Donald W., Charles H. Reynolds, and Ray R. Canning. "Mormonism and Birth Planning: The Discrepancy between Church Authorities'
Teachings and Lay Attitudes." POPULATION STUDIES 26,1 (1972): 19-28.

Historical overview and review of published studies, 1941-68.

2874. Leone, Mark P. "The Economic Basis for the Evolution of Mormon

Religion." In I.I. Zaretsky and M.P. Leone (eds.), RELIGIOUS MOVEMENTS IN CONTEMPORARY AMERICA [volume cited in item 87], pp. 722-766.

Case study of the adaptive modification of Mormon culture in east-central Arizona, along the drainage of the Little Colorado River, from the time of its settlement in the 1870s.

2875. Lyon, Joseph L., Melville R. Klauber, John W. Gardner, and Charles R. Smart. "Cancer Incidence in Mormons and Non-Mormons in Utah 1966-1970." NEW ENGLAND JOURNAL OF MEDICINE 294,3 (1976): 129-133.

Mormon abstention from tobacco and alcohol is associated with lower cancer rates.

2876. Mauss, Armand L. "Moderation in All Things: Political and Social Outlook of Modern Urban Mormons." DIALOGUE 7,3 (1972): 57-69.

2877. Mauss, Armand L. "Saints, Cities, and Secularism: Religious Attitudes and Behavior of Modern Urban Mormons." DIALOGUE 7 (1972): 8-27.

2878. Mauss, Armand L. MORMONS AND MINORITIES. Richmond, California: University of California Press, 1974.

Questionnaire data (three sets from the 1960s) from the east San Francisco Bay area, San Francisco, and Salt Lake City, to determine whether specific Mormon beliefs about Jews, Blacks, and native Americans correlate with corresponding positive and negative prejudices.

2879. Mauss, Armand L. "Shall the Youth of Zion Falter? Mormon Youth and Sex: A Two-city Comparison." DIALOGUE 10,2 (1976): 82-84.

2880. O'Dea, Thomas F. "The Mormons: Church and People." In Edward H. Spicer and Raymond H. Thompson (eds.), PLURAL SOCIETY IN THE SOUTHWEST. New York: Interbrook, 1972, pp. 115-165.

Overview and historical background.

2881. O'Dea, Thomas F. "Sources of Strain in Mormon History Reconsidered." In Marvin S. Hill and James B. Allen (eds.), MORMONISM AND AMERICAN CULTURE. New York: Harper and Row, 1972, pp. 147-166.

Consideration of developments after 1957.

2882. Payne, David E. SOCIAL DETERMINANTS OF LEADERSHIP IN THE MORMON MISSIONARY SYSTEM. Unpublished M.A. thesis, University of North Carolina, Chapel Hill, 1970.

2883. Payne, David E. "Socioeconomic Status and Leadership Selection in the Mormon Missionary System." RRR 13,2 (1972): 118-125.

Similarity in socio-economic status between selector and selectee is important.

* Redekop, Calvin. "A New Look at Sect Development." Cited above as item 2243.

* Richardson, James T., and Sandie Wightman Fox. "Religion and Voting on Abortion Reform: A Follow-up Study." Cited above as item 1314.

2884. Seggar, John F., and Reed H. Blake. "Post-joining Nonparticipation: An Exploratory Study of Convert Inactivity." RRR 11 (1970): 204-209.

The study's nonparticipants tended to: 1) no longer perceive the doctrine, worship services, and organizational structure of the church as attractive as formerly; 2) have difficulty adhering to the church's financial and dietary demands; 3) possess dissimilar beliefs about central doctrinal tenents; and 4) have experienced economic problems since joining.

2885. Spicer, Judith C., and Susan O. Gustavus. "Mormon Fertility through Half a Century: A Test of the Americanization Hypothesis." SOCIAL BIOLOGY 21,1 (1974): 70-76.

1920-70 data.

2886. Thornton, Arland. "Religion and Fertility: The Case of Mormonism." JOURNAL OF MARRIAGE AND THE FAMILY 41,1 (1979): 131-142.

Census data comparing Utah and the remainder of the U.S., and census data from Canada, show continuing higher birth rates for Mormons, which cannot be accounted for by factors other than religion.

2887. Vernon, Glenn M., and Charles E. Waddell. "Dying as Social Behavior: Mormon Behavior through Half a Century." OMEGA 5,3 (1974): 199-206.

Mortality rates, Utah, 1920-70, compared to U.S. rates.

2888. Warenski, Marilyn. PATRIARCHS AND POLITICS: THE PLIGHT OF THE MORMON WOMAN. New York: McGraw-Hill, 1978.

2889. Weigert, Andrew J., and Darwin L. Thomas. "Parental Support, Control, and Adolescent Religiosity: An Extension of Previous Research." JSSR 11,4 (1970): 389-393.

Previous research has found that parental control and support are jointly related to religiosity among urban Catholic adolescents. The present research yielded substantially the same findings among a sample of Mormon adolescents in a university town in the western U.S.

2890. White, O. Kendall, Jr. "Mormonism's Anti-black Policy and Prospects for Change." JOURNAL OF RELIGIOUS THOUGHT 29,2 (1972): 39-60.

Overview.

2891. White, O. Kendall, Jr. "Overt and Covert Politics: The Mormon Church's Anti-ERA Campaign in Virginia." VIRGINIA SOCIAL SCIENCE JOURNAL 19 (1974): 11-16.

2892. White, O. Kendall, Jr. "Mormonism in America and Canada: Accommodation to the Nation-state." CANADIAN JOURNAL OF SOCIOLOGY 3 (1978): 161-181.

2893. Wright, Paul A. THE GROWTH AND DISTRIBUTION OF THE MORMON AND NON-
MORMON POPULATIONS IN SALT LAKE CITY. Unpublished Ph.D. dissertation,
University of Chicago, 1970.

*WORKS, 1980-1989*

2894. Albrecht, Stan L., and Howard M. Bahr. "Patterns of Religious Disaffiliation: A Study of Lifelong Mormons, Mormon Converts, and
Former Mormons." JSSR 22,4 (1983): 366-379.

Based on 1980 and 1981 Utah surveys. Former Mormons tend to drop out
of religion altogether.

2895. Albrecht, Stan L., and Tim B. Heaton. "Secularization, Higher Education, and Religiosity." RRR 26,1 (1984): 43-58.

1981 U.S. Mormon sample, as well as previously published U.S. data on
all religions. Nationally, there is a negative relationship between
education and religiosity, but within denominations a positive relationship between education and church attendance. Within Mormons,
there is a positive relationship between education and other measures
of religiosity as well.

2896. Albrecht, Stan L., Marie Cornwall, and Perry H. Cunningham. "Religious
Leave-taking. Disengagement and Disaffiliation among Mormons." In D.G.
Bromley (ed.), FALLING FROM THE FAITH [volume cited in item 1363], pp.
62-80.

U.S. Mormon sample drawn some time before 1985; questionnaire data;
a second questionnaire data base from Utah adults, 1980-81.

2897. Bahr, Howard M. "Religious Contrasts in Family Role Definitions and
Performance: Utah Mormons, Catholics, Protestants, and Others." JSSR
21,3 (1982): 200-217.

Based on a 1974 Utah survey. Mormons differ from others more in attitudes about family than in family behavior. They are less tolerant
of nontraditional role definitions and evince more family centeredness
in their attitudes. Apparent differences in role enactment are
differences between those with a religious preference and those without one rather than a denominational set of differences.

2898. Bahr, Howard M., and Stan L. Albrecht. "Strangers Once More: Patterns
of Disaffiliation from Mormonism." JSSR 28,2 (1989): 180-200.

Based on 1980 and 1981 Utah mail surveys.

2899. Bean, Lee L., Geraldine Mineau, and Douglas Anderton. "Residence and
Religious Effects on Declining Family Size: An Historical Analysis of
the Utah Population." RRR 25,2 (1983): 91-101.

Data from Utah genealogical archives, tracing a decline in fertility
rates.

* Brinkerhoff, Merlin B., Jeffrey C. Jacob, and Marlene M. MacKie.

388

"Mormonism and the Moral Majority make Strange Bedfellows?: An Exploratory Critique." Cited above as item 2798.

2900. Cornwall, Marie. PERSONAL COMMUNITIES: THE SOCIAL AND NORMATIVE BASES OF RELIGION. Unpublished Ph.D. dissertation, University of Minnesota, 1985. [DA 46:7 A, p. 2078]

U.S. Mormon questionnaire sample data.

2901. Cornwall, Marie. "The Social Bases of Religion: A Study of Factors Influencing Religious Belief and Commitment." RRR 29,1 (1987): 44-56.

Religious socialization is important not only because it provides the individual with a world view, but because it channels individuals into personal communities that sustain a particular world view through the adult years.

2902. Cornwall, Marie. "The Influence of Three Agents of Religious Socialization: Family, Church, and Peers." In D.L. Thomas (ed.), THE RELIGION AND FAMILY CONNECTION [volume cited in item 414], pp. 207-231.

Based on a U.S. sample of Mormon adults. Family influence is not direct but rather is mediated.

2903. Cornwall, Marie, Stan L. Albrecht, Perry H. Cunningham, and Brian L. Pitcher. "The Dimensions of Religiosity: A Conceptual Model with an Empirical Test." RRR 27,3 (1986): 226-244.

Six dimensions are derived by cross-classifying three general components (belief, commitment, behavior) with two modes of religiosity (personal and institutional).

2904. Crapo, Richley H. "Grass-roots Deviance from Official Doctrine: A Study of Latter-day Saint (Mormon) Folk-beliefs." JSSR 26,4 (1987): 465-485.

Beliefs held by Mormons at the local level often deviate from official doctrines, without the people being aware of the deviations.

2905. Duke, James T., and Barry L. Johnson. "Spiritual Well-being and the Consequential Dimension of Religiosity." RRR 26,1 (1984): 59-72.

Based on a national survey of Mormon households. Factor analysis of responses to items suggests religiosity factors as well as consequences of religion, one of which is termed 'Beatitudes,' and another 'spiritual well-being.' 'Beatitudes' seems to contribute toward marital satisfaction and global happiness. 'Spiritual well-being' is closely related to extrinsic religiosity.

2906. Foster, Lawrence. RELIGION AND SEXUALITY: THE SHAKERS, THE MORMONS, AND THE ONEIDA COMMUNITY. Urbana: University of Illinois Press, 1984.

2907. Gilette, Alain. LES MORMONS, THEOCRATES DU DESERT. Paris: Desclée de Brouwer, 1982.

2908. Hampshire, Annette P., and James A. Beckford. "Religious Sects and

389

the Concept of Deviance: The Moonies and the Mormons." BRITISH JOURNAL OF SOCIOLOGY 34,2 (1983): 208-229.

Discusses limitations of the deviance-amplification and sect-to-denomination models of conflict between new religions and their host societies.

2909. Heaton, Tim B. "How does Religion Influence Fertility?: The Case of Mormons." JSSR 25,2 (1986): 248-258.

1981 survey of U.S. and Canadian adult Mormons. Socioeconomic status has no simple relationship with fertility; acceptance of Mormon theology upon marriage, contact with other Mormons as a reference group, and socialization in the Mormon culture have positive effects on it.

2910. Heaton, Tim B. "Four C's of the Mormon Family: Chastity, Conjugality, Children, and Chauvinism." In D.L. Thomas (ed.), THE RELIGION AND FAMILY CONNECTION [volume cited in item 414], pp. 107-124.

Review of previously published survey data.

2911. Heaton, Tim B. "Religious Influence on Mormon Fertility: Cross-national Comparisons." RRR 30,4 (1989): 401-411.

1981-84 questionnaire data: U.S.A., Great Britain, Mexico, Japan.

2912. Heaton, Tim B., and Sandra Calkins. "Family Size and Contraceptive Use among Mormons: 1965-1975." RRR 25,2 (1983): 102-113.

Analysis of data from Mormons included in the 1965, 1970, and 1975 National Fertility Surveys (U.S.). Mormons are at least as likely to have ever used birth control as white Protestants. They are less likely to be current users than are Catholics or Protestants. Half delay use until after a first child and 25% until after a second. They use modern methods. The more devout Mormons have distinctive patterns of timing contraception use. Pro-family rather than anti-birth control beliefs seem related to high Mormon fertility.

2913. Heeren, John, Donald B. Lindsey, and Marylee Mason. "The Mormon Concept of Mother in Heaven: A Sociological Account of Its Origins and Development." JSSR 23,4 (1984): 396-411.

The belief is required by the Mormon anthropomorphic concept of God. The belief has served social-psychological purposes in the past. It has been a point of pride for some Mormon feminists, but is unlikely to contribute to any change in Mormon teaching on women's roles.

2914. Johnson, Barry L., Susan Eberley, James T. Duke, and Deborah Hunt Sartain. "Wives' Employment Status and Marital Happiness of Religious Couples." RRR 29,3 (1988): 259-270.

U.S. survey of Mormon parents. Husbands were most satisfied when wives worked full time, less so when wives were not employed, least so when wives were employed part time. Among wives, homemakers were most satisfied, full-time employed wives less so, part-time employed least so.

2915. Mauss, Armand L. "The Fading of the Pharaoh's Curse: The Decline and Fall of the Priesthood Ban against Blacks in the Mormon Church." DIALOGUE 14,3 (1981): 10-45.

2916. Mauss, Armand L. "Sociological Perspectives on the Mormon Subculture." ANNUAL REVIEW OF SOCIOLOGY 10 (1984): 437-460.

Review of the twentieth-century literature.

* Perrin, Robin D. "American Religion in the Post-aquarian Age: Values and Demographic Factors in Church Growth and Decline." Cited above as item 1409.

* Richardson, James T. "The 'Old Right' in Action: Mormon and Catholic Involvement in an Equal Rights Amendment Referendum." Cited above as item 1414.

2917. Shepherd, Gary, and Gordon Shepherd. "Mormon Commitment Rhetoric." JSSR 23,2 (1984): 129-139.

Content analysis of Mormon leaders' 'commitment rhetoric' shows changes over time. 'Transcendence' is the most consistently salient category.

2918. Shepherd, Gary, and Gordon Shepherd. "Modes of Leader Rhetoric in the Institutional Development of Mormonism." SA 47,2 (1986): 125-136.

Indicates variation in the expressive modes of official religious rhetoric by Mormon leaders during a 150 year span.

2919. Shepherd, Gordon, and Gary Shepherd. "Mormonism in Secular Society: Changing Patterns in Official Ecclesiastical Rhetoric." RRR 26,1 (1984): 28-42.

Content analysis of adresses delivered by ecclesiastical authorities at Mormon General Conference sessions. Indicates changes in the relative emphasis given to general themes - utopianism, the supernatural, eschatology, personal morality, family life, doctrinal distinctiveness.

2920. Shepherd, Gordon, and Gary Shepherd. A KINGDOM TRANSFORMED. THEMES IN THE DEVELOPMENT OF MORMONISM. Salt Lake City: University of Utah Press, 1984.

Content analysis of addresses at Mormon General Conferences.

* Shupe, Anson D., and John Heinerman. "Mormonism and the New Christian Right: An Emerging Coalition?" Cited above as item 2787.

2921. Stark, Rodney. "The Rise of a New World Faith." RRR 26,1 (1984): 18-27.

Observations on Mormon growth in numbers and sophistication. The author calls for academics to respect this denomination's accomplishments.

&ast; Stott, Gerald N. "Familial Influence on Religious Involvement."
Cited above as item 2302.

2922. Thomas, Darwin L. "Family in the Mormon Experience." In W.V. D'Antonio
and J. Aldous (eds.), FAMILIES AND RELIGIONS [volume cited in item
421], pp. 267-288.

Overview, including previously published data from several studies.

2923. Thomas, Darwin L. "Future Prospects for Religion and Family Studies:
The Mormon Case." In D.L. Thomas (ed.), THE RELIGION AND FAMILY
CONNECTION [volume cited in item 414], pp. 357-382.

1985 U.S. sample of adult Mormons; analysis using well-being as the
dependent variable.

2924. Toney, Michael B., Carol McKewen Stinner, and Stephan Kan. "Mormon
and Non-Mormon Migration In and Out of Utah." RRR 25,2 (1983): 114-
126.

Two 1975 surveys of Utah adults and graduating high-school seniors,
respectively. Mormons are more likely than others to in-migrate to
Utah, and less likely to out-migrate from the state.

2925. White, O. Kendall, Jr. "Boundary Maintenance, Blacks, and the Mormon
Priesthood." JOURNAL OF RELIGIOUS THOUGHT 37,2 (1980): 30-44.

Examines the nineteenth-century origins of the prohibition of a black
priesthood.

2926. White, O. Kendall, Jr. "Mormon Resistance and Accommodation: From
Communitarian Socialism to Corporate Capitalism." In Scott B. Cummings
(ed.), SELF-HELP IN URBAN AMERICA: PATTERNS OF MINORITY ECONOMIC
DEVELOPMENT. Port Washington, N.Y.: Kennikat, 1980, pp. 89-112, 219-
221.

Discussion covers the breadth of Mormon history.

2927. White, O. Kendall, Jr. "'Mormons for ERA': An Internal Social Movement." JOURNAL FOR ETHNIC STUDIES 13,1 (1985): 29-50.

Use of the resource mobilization model to account for the origin and
development of Mormons for ERA, as an internal social movement organization. The movement organization arose in response to the church's
campaign against the Equal Rights Amendment proposal, with a noted
confrontation generating interest and support for the emerging
organization.

&ast; White, O. Kendall, Jr. "A Review and Commentary on the Prospects of
a Mormon New Christian Right Coalition." Cited above as item 2793.

2928. White, O. Kendall, Jr., and Daryl White. "Abandoning an Unpopular
Policy: An Analysis of the Decision Granting the Mormon Priesthood to
Blacks." SA 41,3 (1980): 231-245. See also Armand L. Mauss, "Comment,"
42,3 (1981): 277-282; and O.K. White, Jr., and D. White, "Reply," 42,3
(1981): 283-288.

White and White see the decision admitting blacks to the Mormon priest-hood as an adaptation to environmental pressures, the logical outcome of organizational practices, and the resolution of internal contra-dictions. The comment and reply focus on whether the article marshals evidence sufficient enough to warrant its conclusions.

2929. White, O. Kendall, Jr., and Daryl White. "A Critique of Leone's and Dogin's Application of Bellah's Evolutionary Model to Mormonism." RRR 23,1 (1981): 39-53.

While Bellah's model has a Protestant bias, the authors mostly criti-cize Mark Leone and Janet Dolgin's use of the model to interpret contemporary Mormonism. Nineteenth-century Mormonism more closely approximated Bellah's modern religion at the symbolic and action levels than does contemporary Mormonism, and Mormonism has never resembled it at the organizational level.

2930. Wyatt, Gary. "Mormon Polygyny in the Nineteenth Century: A Theoreti-cal Analysis." JOURNAL OF COMPARATIVE FAMILY STUDIES 20,1 (1989): 13-20.

## AARONIC ORDER

2931. Baer, Hans A. THE LEVITES OF UTAH: THE DEVELOPMENT OF AND CONVERSION TO A SMALL MILLENARIAN SECT. Unpublished Ph.D. dissertation, Univer-sity of Utah, 1976. [DA 37:1 A, p. 418]

Interpretation of the Aaronic Order as a 1930s and 1940s revitaliza-tion movement in a Mormon context, attempting to renew a *Gemeinschaft* ethic.

2932. Baer, Hans A. "A Field Perspective of Religious Conversion: The Levites of Utah." RRR 19,3 (1978): 279-294.

The Aaronic Order, or Levites, resembles Mormons in some respects and evangelical Christians in others. This article presents an inductive study of the Levite conversion experience, based on the analysis of the conversion of 35 individuals.

2933. Baer, Hans A. RECREATING UTOPIA IN THE DESERT. A SECTARIAN CHALLENGE TO MODERN MORMONISM. Albany: State University of New York Press, 1988.

Based on 1973-75 participation observation and interviews.

## MORRISITES

2934. Anderson, C. Leroy. FOR CHRIST WILL COME TOMORROW: THE SAGA OF THE MORRISITES. Logan, Utah: Utah State University Press, 1981.

2935. Halford, L.J., C. Leroy Anderson, and R.E. Clark. "Prophecy Fails Again and Again: The Morrisites." FREE INQUIRY IN CREATIVE SOCIOLOGY 9,1 (1981): 5-10.

# 23
## New Religions

*est*

2936. Abraham, Gary A. "The Protestant Ethic and the Spirit of Utilitarian-
ism: The Case of EST." THEORY AND SOCIETY 12,6 (1983): 739-773.

Presents parallels between the Protestant Ethic and the human potential movement, illustrated with the case of est.

2937. Stone, Donald. THE PERSONAL AND SOCIAL SIGNIFICANCE OF EST AND THE
HUMAN POTENTIAL MOVEMENT. Unpublished Ph.D. dissertation, University
of California, Berkeley, 1981.

2938. Stone, Donald. "The Charismatic Authority of Werner Erhard." In R.
Wallis (ed.), MILLENNIALISM AND CHARISMA [volume cited in item 2629],
pp. 141-175.

Discusses the leadership career of the founder of est.

  * Tipton, Steven M. GETTING SAVED FROM THE SIXTIES. Cited above as
item 208.

2939. Tipton, Steven M. "Making the World Work: Ideas of Social Responsibility in the Human Potential Movement." In E. Barker (ed.), OF GODS
AND MEN [volume cited in item 64], pp. 265-282.

Based on 1975-78 interviews with est graduates in the San Francisco
Bay area, and subsequent field work.


*HUMAN POTENTIAL MOVEMENT*

2940. Stone, Donald. "The Human Potential Movement." In C.Y. Glock and
R.N. Bellah (eds.), THE NEW RELIGIOUS CONSCIOUSNESS [volume cited in
item 75], pp. 93-115.

Overview, illustrated by specific reference to groups in the San
Francisco Bay area.

  * Stone, Donald. THE PERSONAL AND SOCIAL SIGNIFICANCE OF EST AND THE
HUMAN POTENTIAL MOVEMENT. Cited above as item 2937.

2941. Wallis, Roy. "The Dynamics of Change in the Human Potential Movement." In R. Stark (ed.), RELIGIOUS MOVEMENTS [volume cited in item 2102], pp. 129-156. Reprinted as Chapter 7 in R. Wallis and S. Bruce, SOCIOLOGICAL THEORY, RELIGION AND COLLECTIVE ACTION. Belfast, Northern Ireland: The Queen's University, 1986.

Descriptive overview.

2942. Westley, Frances R. THE COMPLEX FORMS OF THE RELIGIOUS LIFE. A DURKHEIMIAN VIEW OF NEW RELIGIOUS MOVEMENTS. Chico, California: Scholars Press, 1983.

Based on 1973-78 field studies and interviews focusing on Shakti, Silva Mind Control, Psychosynthesis, Arica, est, and Scientology, in the Montreal area.

## NEW THOUGHT

2943. Braden, Charles S. SPIRITS IN REBELLION: THE RISE AND DEVELOPMENT OF NEW THOUGHT. Dallas: Southern Methodist University Press, 1963.

2944. Griswold, Alfred W. "New Thought: A Cult of Success." AMERICAN JOURNAL OF SOCIOLOGY 40,3 (1934): 309-318.

The New Thought movement stresses economic success and provides esoteric methods for its achievement.

## OCCULT

2945. Adorno, Theodor W. "Theses against Occultism." TELOS 19 (1974): 7-12.

2946. Adorno, Theodor W. "The Stars Down to Earth: The Los Angeles TIMES Astrology Column." TELOS 19 (1974): 13-90.

2947. Bainbridge, William Sims, and Rodney Stark. "Friendship, Religion, and the Occult: A Network Study." RRR 22,4 (1981): 313-327.

1979 student survey at the University of Washington, Seattle. Analysis focuses on attitude concordances across close friend pairs. Objectively important ideological positions and questions of social policy are not salient for personal relationships. Objectively trivial habits and tastes often are salient. Religious attitudes and beliefs are salient only when they are promoted by social movements and vigorous formal organizations.

2948. Ben-Yehuda, Nachman. DEVIANCE AND MORAL BOUNDARIES: WITCHCRAFT, THE OCCULT, SCIENCE FICTION, DEVIANT SCIENCES AND SCIENTISTS. Chicago: University of Chicago Press, 1985.

2949. Campbell, Colin, and Shirley McIver. "Cultural Sources of Support for Contemporary Occultism." SC 34,1 (1987): 41-60.

Conceptualizing occult subculture as cognitive deviance is inadequate.

There are continuities between orthodox and occult cultures.

2950. Emmons, Charles F., and Jeff Sobal. "Paranormal Beliefs: Testing the Marginality Hypothesis." SOCIOLOGICAL FOCUS 14,1 (1981): 49-56.

1978 Gallup Poll data show unmarried females more likely than others to believe in paranormal phenomena, but that there is no correlation between such belief and age, low education levels, being black, or being unemployed. Marginality does not seem to be a viable explanation for belief in the paranormal.

2951. Emmons, Charles F., and Jeff Sobal. "Paranormal Beliefs: Functional Alternatives to Mainstream Religion." RRR 22,4 (1981): 301-312.

1978 U.S. Gallup data show that those having no religious preference, or for whom religious beliefs are unimportant, are more likely to believe in nonreligious and less likely to believe in paranormal phenomena.

2952. Hartman, Patricia A. "Social Dimensions of Occult Participation: The Gnostica Study." BRITISH JOURNAL OF SOCIOLOGY 27,2 (1976): 169-183.

Random sample of the readership of the occult magazine, GNOSTICA: young middle class.

2953. Jorgensen, Danny L. TAROT DIVINATION IN THE VALLEY OF THE SUN: AN EXISTENTIAL SOCIOLOGY OF THE ESOTERIC AND OCCULT. Unpublished Ph.D. dissertation, Ohio State University, 1979. [DA 40:1 A, p. 470]

1975-78 participant-observation study in a southwestern U.S. urban center.

2954. Lemieux, Raymond. "Occultisme et religion. La commerce avec l'autre en société industrielle." STUDIES IN RELIGION/SCIENCES RELIGIEUSES 5,2 (1975): 134-151.

Programmatic statement.

2955. Lynch, Frederick R. "Toward a Theory of Conversion and Commitment to the Occult." AMERICAN BEHAVIORAL SCIENTIST 20,6 (1977): 887-907.

Participant observation in an occult church in California, which fused ancient Egyptian and mystical Hebrew symbols. Prior interest in relevant topics and involvement in the group as a community are the important factors in conversion. The drama involved in such conversion to the occult had diminished prior to the time of the study because social pressures against it had diminished in the locality.

2956. Lynch, Frederick R. "'Occult Establishment' or 'Deviant Religion'? The Rise and Fall of a Modern Church of Magic." JSSR 18,3 (1979): 281-298.

Study of an occult church which consisted of 30 to 40 people devoted to the learning principles and practices in the 'Egyptian Kabbalistic Tradition,' a fusion of ancient Egyptian and mystical Hebrew traditions. The members are similar to those in several other occult and new religious groups, seeking a deeper, more mystical, and more complex understanding of their individual identities within the context of mass society. They also gain a sense of community from their participation in collective ritual.

2957. Nederman, Cary J., and James W. Goulding. "Popular Occultism and Critical Social Theory: Exploring Some Themes in Adorno's Critique of Astrology and the Occult." SA 42,4 (1982): 325-332.

Popular occultism fosters pseudo-individualism and a metaphysic of the 'dopes' which serve to stifle self-reflection. It achieves what traditional organized religion cannot: the complete internalization of domination. As a distortion of consciousness which conceals material conditions, it legitimates the irrational contradictions of industrial society.

2958. Scott, Gini Graham. CULT AND COUNTERCULT. A STUDY OF A SPIRITUAL GROWTH GROUP AND A WITCHCRAFT ORDER. Westport, Connecticut: Greenwood Press, 1980.

A comparison of two occult groups, one adhering to mainstream middle-class values and the other countercultural. Based on 1974-76 participant observation in both groups.

2959. Tiryakian, Edward A. (ed.) ON THE MARGIN OF THE VISIBLE: SOCIOLOGY, THE ESOTERIC AND THE OCCULT. New York: Wiley-Interscience, 1974.

2960. Truzzi, Marcello. "Towards a Sociology of the Occult: Notes on Modern Witchcraft." In I.I. Zaretsky and M.P. Leone (eds.), RELIGIOUS MOVEMENTS IN CONTEMPORARY AMERICA [volume cited in item 87], pp. 628-645.

Survey of witchcraft activities in the United States.

2961. Whitehead, Harriet. "Reasonably Fantastic: Some Perspectives on Scientology, Science Fiction, and Occultism." In I.I. Zaretsky and M.P. Leone (eds.), RELIGIOUS MOVEMENTS IN CONTEMPORARY AMERICA [volume cited in item 87], pp. 547-587.

Situates phenomena within a historical and cultural context.


*PEOPLE'S TEMPLE (JONESTOWN)*

2962. Baechler, Jean. "Mourir à Jonestown." ARCHIVES EUROPEENES DE SOCIOLOGIE 20,2 (1979): 173-210.

Review of the history of the tragedy, the individual problems of James Jones, and the thought processes which could have led his followers into suicide.

   * Bromley, David G., and Anson D. Shupe, Jr. STRANGE GODS. THE GREAT AMERICAN CULT SCARE. Cited above as item 66.

2963. Chidester, David. SALVATION AND SUICIDE: AN INTERPRETATION OF JIM

JONES, THE PEOPLE'S TEMPLE, AND JONESTOWN. Bloomington: Indiana
University Press, 1988.

2964. Coser, Rose, and Lewis Coser. "Jonestown -- The Case of a Greedy
Institution." SOCIALE WETENSCHAPPEN 22,2 (1979): 100-107.

2965. Gutwirth, Jacques. "Le suicide-massacre de Guyana et son contexte."
ARCHIVES DE SCIENCES SOCIALES DES RELIGIONS 47,2 (1979): 167-187.

A review of journalistic accounts of the Jonestown catastrophe.

2966. Hall, John R. "The Apocalypse at Jonestown." In T. Robbins and
D. Anthony (eds.), IN GODS WE TRUST [volume cited in item 451], pp.
171-190.

2967. Hall, John R. GONE FROM THE PROMISED LAND: JONESTOWN IN AMERICAN
CULTURAL HISTORY. New Brunswick, N.J.: Transaction, 1987.

2968. Hall, John R. "The Impact of Apostates on the Trajectory of Religious
Movements. The Case of People's Temple." In D.G. Bromley (ed.), FALL-
ING FROM THE FAITH [volume cited in item 1363], pp. 229-250.

2969. Hall, John R. "Collective Welfare as Resource Mobilization in People's
Temple: A Case Study of a Poor People's Religious Social Movement."
SA 49 (1988): 64-77.

People's Temple exemplifies resource-related organizational tensions
in a poor people's movement. Its communal and world-transforming
orientation was grafted onto conventional fund-raising techniques in
ways that exacerbated conflict with external critics. Internally it
became a charismatic bureaucracy that absorbed those for whom it
lessened social alienation.

2970. Johnson, Doyle P. "Dilemmas of Charismatic Leadership: The Case of
the People's Temple." SA 40,4 (1979): 315-323.

The inherent precariousness of charismatic authority can be countered
by recruiting from the ranks of the societally disprivileged and
fostering among new members total dependency upon the group.

2971. Jorgensen, Danny L. "The Social Construction and Interpretation of
Deviance: Jonestown and the Mass Media." DEVIANT BEHAVIOR 1,3-4
(1980): 309-332.

Media reaction to the November 1978 events was selective and stylized.

2972. Levi, Ken (ed.) VIOLENCE AND RELIGIOUS COMMITMENT: IMPLICATIONS OF
JIM JONES'S PEOPLE'S TEMPLE MOVEMENT. University Park: Pennsylvania
State University Press, 1982.

2973. Pozzi, Enrico. "Sécularisation et déboires du sacré: Le suicide
collectif de Jonestown." CAHIERS INTERNATIONAUX DE SOCIOLOGIE 29,72
(1982): 131-144.

Use of U.S. Dept. of Justice data on the 1978 victims at Jonestown:

68 percent female, 80 percent black, etc.

2974. Richardson, James T. "People's Temple and Jonestown: A Corrective Comparison and Critique." JSSR 19,3 (1980): 239-255.

The Jonestown/People's Temple movement does not resemble the other new religious movements in social location and time of inception, kinds of member, organization, social control technique and outside contact, resocialization techniques, ideology, general orientation, ritual.

* Robbins, Thomas. "Religious Mass Suicide before Jonestown: The Russian Old Believers." Cited above as item 784.

2975. Weightman, Judith M. MAKING SENSE OF THE JONESTOWN SUICIDES: A SOCIOLOGICAL HISTORY OF PEOPLE'S TEMPLE. New York: Edwin Mellen Press, 1983.


SATANISM

2976. Alfred, H. Randall. "The Church of Satan." In C.Y. Glock and R.N. Bellah (eds.), THE NEW RELIGIOUS CONSCIOUSNESS [volume cited in item 75], pp. 180-202.

Based on 1968-73 field work in San Francisco.

2977. Bainbridge, William Sims. SATAN'S POWER: A DEVIANT PSYCHOTHERAPY CULT. Berkeley: University of California Press, 1978.

Ethnography of a group which began in Great Britain in 1963, moved to Mexico, and then to the U.S. Data collection continued into 1975.

2978. Raphaël, Freddy. "Conditionnements socio-politiques et socio-psychologiques du Satanisme." REVUE DES SCIENCES RELIGIEUSES 50,2 (1976): 112-156.

Overview of post-medieval phenomena.

2979. Rhodes, H.T.F. THE SATANIC MASS: A SOCIOLOGICAL AND CRIMINOLOGICAL STUDY. New York: Citadel Press, 1955.


SCIENTOLOGY

2980. Bainbridge, William Sims. THE SCIENTOLOGY GAME. Unpublished M.A. thesis, Boston University, 1970.

2981. Bainbridge, William Sims. "Science and Religion: The Case of Scientology." In D.G. Bromley and P.E. Hammond (eds.), THE FUTURE OF NEW RELIGIOUS MOVEMENTS [volume cited in item 94], pp. 59-79.

2982. Bainbridge, William Sims, and Rodney Stark. "Scientology: To be Perfectly Clear." SA 41,2 (1980): 128-136.

The cult may be forced to evolve more fully into a true religion that promises supernatural rather than natural rewards.

* Bromley, David G., and Anson D. Shupe, Jr. STRANGE GODS. THE GREAT AMERICAN CULT SCARE. Cited above as item 66.

2983. Chagnon, Roland. LA SCIENTOLOGIE: UNE NOUVELLE RELIGION DE LA PUIS-SANCE. Montréal: Hurtubise HMH, 1985.

Focus on the church in Montreal; includes data from a 1982 question-naire.

2984. Chagnon, Roland. "Religion et santé: Le cas de l'Eglise de Scientol-ogie." SC 34,4 (1987): 495-507.

Review of the teachings of Dianetics and Scientology; descriptions of Scientology in Montreal.

* Harper, Charles L. "Cults and Communities: The Community Interfaces of Three Marginal Religious Movements." Cited above as item 2600.

2985. Stark, Rodney, and William Sims Bainbridge. THE FUTURE OF RELIGION. SECULARIZATION, REVIVAL AND CULT FORMATION. Berkeley: University of California Press, 1985, chapter 12.

Revision of item 2982.

2986. Straus, Roger A. "Scientology 'Ethics': Deviance, Identity and Social Control in a Cult-like Social World." SYMBOLIC INTERACTION 9,1 (1986): 67-82.

Based largely on 1968-70 experience and 1972 field notes.

2987. Wallis, Roy. "The Sectarianism of Scientology." SOCIOLOGICAL YEAR-BOOK OF RELIGION IN BRITAIN 6 (1973): 136-155.

Argues that Scientology qualifies as a sect (that is, a minority group organized around a belief-system regarded by its adherents as a unique and privileged mode of access to the truth or salvation).

2988. Wallis, Roy. A SOCIOLOGICAL ANALYSIS OF A QUASI-RELIGIOUS SECT. Un-published Ph.D. thesis, Oxford University, 1974.

2989. Wallis, Roy. "Scientology: Therapeutic Cult to Religious Sect." SOCIOLOGY 9,1 (1975): 89-100.

Application of a typology, with 'cult' characterized by epistemologi-cal individualism and 'sect' by epistemological authoritarianism.

2990. Wallis, Roy. "Societal Reaction to Scientology: A Study of the Sociology of Deviant Religion." In R. Wallis (ed.), SECTARIANISM [vol-ume cited in item 82], pp. 86-116.

International review.

2991. Wallis, Roy. THE ROAD TO TOTAL FREEDOM. New York: Columbia Univer-sity Press, 1977.

* Wallis, Roy. "Hostages to Fortune: Thoughts on the Future of Scien-tology and the Children of God." Cited above as item 2630.

2992. Weldon, John. "A Sampling of the New Religions: Four Groups Described."
INTERNATIONAL REVIEW OF MISSIONS 67,268 (1978): 407-426.

* Whitehead, Harriet. "Reasonably Fantastic: Some Perspectives on
Scientology, Science Fiction, and Occultism." Cited above as item
2961.

## SPIRITUALISM (GENERAL)

2993. Castelli, Y. LE SPIRITISME. Paris: Presses Universitaires de France,
1954.

2994. Skultans, Vieda. INTIMACY AND RITUAL. A STUDY OF SPIRITUALISM, MEDIUMS
AND GROUPS. London: Routledge and Kegan Paul, 1974.

## SPIRITUALISM (AUSTRALIA, PHILIPPINES)

2995. Locke, Ralph G. "Who am I in the City of Mammon? The Self, Doubt and
Certainty in a Spiritualist Cult." In A. Black and P. Glasner (eds.),
PRACTICE AND BELIEF [volume cited in item 91], pp. 108-133.

Focus is on The Sanctuary, in Fremantle, the port city for Perth,
Western Australia.

2996. Schlegel, Stuart A. "The Upi Espiritistas: A Case Study in Cultural
Adjustment." JSSR 4,2 (1965): 198-212.

Examines the formation and growth of a local Filipino cult, with
special emphasis accorded the cult's integration of religious belief
and medical practice.

## SPIRITUALISM (GHANA)

2997. Baeta, C. PROPHETISM IN GHANA: A STUDY OF SOME 'SPIRITUAL' CHURCHES.
London: S.C.M., 1962.

2998. Wyllie, Robert W. SPIRITISM IN GHANA: A STUDY OF NEW RELIGIOUS MOVE-
MENTS. Chico, California: Scholars Press, 1982.

## SPIRITUALISM (GREAT BRITAIN)

2999. Martin, Bernice. "The Spiritualist Meeting." SOCIOLOGICAL YEARBOOK
OF RELIGION IN BRITAIN 3 (1970): 146-161.

Description of the main features of the Spiritualist religious service;
its most appropriate analogues are to be found not in the religious
institutions of modern Christian cultures but in shamanism, spirit
possession, and divination.

3000. Nelson, Geoffrey K. "The Analysis of a Cult: Spiritualism." SC 15,6
(1968): 469-481.

Conceptualization of 'cult'; historical data.

3001. Nelson, Geoffrey K. "The Spiritualist Movement: A Need for the Redefinition of the Concept of the Cult." JSSR 8,1 (1969): 152-160.

The need for a refined concept of cult emerged after a study of
Spiritualism. A proposed definition has a basic criterion - religious
movements which make a fundamental break with the religious tradition
of the culture - and two subordinate criteria - seekers of mystical,
psychic, or ecstatic experiences, and a concern with problems of
individuals.

3002. Nelson, Geoffrey K. SPIRITUALISM AND SOCIETY. London: Routledge and
Kegan Paul, 1969.

General survey, focusing on Great Britain.

3003. Nelson, Geoffrey K. "The Membership of a Cult: The Spiritualist
National Union." RRR 13,3 (1972): 170-177.

Survey of members of a central England district of the Spiritualist
National Union, 1968. They wish to understand 'psychic gifts,' are
dissatisfied with Christianity, seek meaning, are influenced by
parents and friends, and seek healing and comfort in grief. They tend
to be middle class, occupationally mobile, and widowed.

3004. Nelson, Geoffrey K. "Modern Spiritualist Conception of Ultimate
Reality." ULTIMATE REALITY AND MEANING 11,2 (1988): 102-114.

Examines the intellectual provenance of modern Spiritualism, as well
as the role of the medium.

SPIRITUALISM (BRAZIL)

3005. Bastide, Roger. "Le spiritisme au Brésil." ARCHIVES DE SOCIOLOGIE
DES RELIGIONS 12,24 (1967): 3-16.

Discusses the social sources of Spiritualism's appeal in Brazil since
its arrival there in 1853.

* Bastide, Roger. "Nicht-katholische Religionen und die ökonomische
und soziale Entwicklung in Brasilien." Cited above as item 2000.

3006. De Camargo, C.P. Ferreira. ASPECTOS SOCIOLOGICOS DEL ESPIRITISMO EM
SÃO PAULO. Freiburg and Bogotá: FERES, 1961.

3007. De Camargo, C.P. Ferreira. KARDECISMO E UMBANDA: UNA INTERPRETAÇÃO
SOCIOLOGICA. São Paulo: Livraria Pioneira Editora, 1961.

3008. De Camargo, C.P. Ferreira. CATOLICOS, PROTESTANTES, ESPIRITAS.
Petrópolis: Vozes, 1973.

3009. De Camargo, C.P. Ferreira, and J. Labbens. "Aspects socio-culturele
du spiritisme au Brésil." SC 7 (1960): 407-430.

Discusses the factors in five cultural areas behind the growth of Umbanda (white magic), Quimbanda (black magic), and Kardecism.

3010. Kloppenburg, Boaventura. "Der brasilianische Spiritismus als religiöse Gefahr." SC 5,5-6 (1958): 237-255.

Discusses organizational histories of Kardecism, Umbanda, and other groups, and also their beliefs and methods of growth; provides 1940 and 1950 membership data, by city.

3011. Kloppenburg, Boaventura. O ESPIRITISMO NO BRASIL. Petrópolis: Ed. Vozes, 1960, 1964.

3012. Negrão, Lisias N. "Messianismo e espiritismo." CADERNOS (Brazil) 8 (1975): 329-357.

* Willems, Emilio. "Religiöser Pluralismus und Klassenstruktur in Brasilien und Chile." Cited above as item 1844.

3013. Xidieh, Osvaldo E. "Elementos mágicos no folk paulista: O intermediario." SOCIOLOGIA (São Paulo) 7 (1945): 11-29.

Continuation of a study of folk beliefs, under the direction of Roger Bastide. See also O.E. Xidieh, "Elementos mágicos no folk mogiano." SOCIOLOGIA 5 (1943): 116-133.

## SPIRITUALISM (MEXICO)

3014. Finkler, Kaja. "Dissident Sectarian Movements, the Catholic Church, and Social Class in Mexico." COMPARATIVE STUDIES IN SOCIETY AND HISTORY 25,2 (1983): 277-305.

Background, and 1977-79 field data from Mexico City, supplemented by interviews.

3015. Finkler, Kaja. SPIRITUALIST HEALERS IN MEXICO: SUCCESSES AND FAILURES OF ALTERNATIVE THERAPEUTICS. New York: Bergen and Garvey, 1985.

3016. Finkler, Kaja. "Spiritualist Healing Outcomes and the Status Quo: A Micro and Macro Analysis." SC 34,4 (1987): 381-395.

Brief depiction of Mexican Spiritualist therapeutic practices and beliefs; the ways in which Spiritualists fit into the larger society; and reasons why people participate in Spiritualism. Paradoxically, while Spiritualist healing is embedded in a religious movement that arose in response to social change, its current healing techniques and ideologies perpetuate the social order.

## SPIRITUALISM (PUERTO RICO)

3017. Harwood, Alan. RX: SPIRITIST AS NEEDED. A STUDY OF A PUERTO RICAN COMMUNITY MENTAL HEALTH RESOURCE. New York: Wiley, 1977.

3018. Koss, Joan D. "Terapeutica del sistema de une secta en Puerto Rico." REVISTA DE CIENCIAS SOCIALES 14,2 (1970): 259-278.

Based on field work conducted in Puerto Rico and Philadelphia, 1961-67.

3019. Koss, Joan D. "El porqué de los cultos religiosos: El caso del Espiritismo en Puerto Rico." REVISTA DE CIENCIAS SOCIALES 16,1 (1972): 61-72.

Maintains that such cults flourish when cosmologies are in conflict and people are living in deprived conditions.

3020. Rogler, Lloyd H., and August B. Hollingshead. "The Puerto Rican Spiritualist as a Psychiatrist." AMERICAN JOURNAL OF SOCIOLOGY 67,1 (1961): 17-21.


SPIRITUALISM (U.S.A.)

3021. Baer, Hans A. THE BLACK SPIRITUAL MOVEMENT: A RELIGIOUS RESPONSE TO RACISM. Knoxville: University of Tennessee Press, 1984.

3022. Baer, Hans A. "The Metropolitan Spiritual Churches of Christ: The Socio-religious Evolution of the Largest of the Black Spiritual Associations." RRR 30,2 (1988): 140-150.

Historical sociological analysis, showing the founding of the church in one congregation and its growth. There is a trend toward becoming more mainstream Protestant and de-emphasizing spiritualist and thaumaturgical traditions.

3023. Haywood, Carol L. "The Authority and Empowerment of Women among Spiritualist Groups." JSSR 22,2 (1983): 157-166.

Participant observation, 1978-82, in four Spiritualist groups in New England and Indiana, uncovered some institutional patterns apparently amenable to the exercise of authority by women.

3024. Richard, Michel R., and Albert Adato. "The Medium and Her Message: A Study of Spiritualism at Lily Dale, New York." RRR 22,2 (1980): 186-197.

Field study at Lily Dale, New York, 1974. The authors argue that Spiritualism is a sect rather than a cult.


SYNANON

3025. Naranjo, Betty Ann. BIOBEHAVIORAL BELONGING: THE REORGANIZATION OF BEHAVIOR AND THE RECONSTRUCTION OF SOCIAL REALITY DURING RITES OF PASSAGE AT SYNANON. Unpublished Ph.D. dissertation, University of California, Irvine, 1979. [DA 39:10 A, p. 6206]

Participant-observation study in Santa Monica, California, 1974-76.

3026. Ofshe, Richard. "The Social Development of the Synanon Cult: The

Managerial Strategy of Organizational Transformation." SA 41,2 (1980): 109-127.

Review of the developmental history of Synanon Foundation, from its inception in 1958 as an Alcoholics Anonymous alternative through its three transformations into a therapeutic community, an alternative society, and finally a religion. The transformations were strategies by management to expand, solidify, and consolidate control of the group.

## THEOSOPHY

3027. Campbell, Bruce F. WISDOM OF THE SOUL: A CONTEMPORARY THEOSOPHICAL CULT. Unpublished Ph.D. dissertation, University of California, Santa Barbara, 1977. [DA 38:4 A, p. 2201]

Participant observation in southern California, 1973-74, in a group (pseudonym: Wisdom of the Soul) founded in the theosophical tradition but having no conscious relationship with Theosophy. Focus is on the tension between the experiential and spontaneous on the one hand and roles and routinization on the other.

* Tiryakian, Edward A. (ed.) ON THE MARGIN OF THE VISIBLE: SOCIOLOGY, THE ESOTERIC AND THE OCCULT. Cited above as item 2959.

## TRANSCENDENTAL MEDITATION

3028. Bainbridge, William Sims, and Daniel H. Jackson. "The Rise and Decline of Transcendental Meditation." In B.R. Wilson (ed.), THE SOCIAL IMPACT OF NEW RELIGIOUS MOVEMENTS [volume cited in item 2627], pp. 135-158.

Secondary analysis of statistics; review of primary literature.

3029. Fagerstrom, Mary F. A DESCRIPTIVE STUDY OF BEGINNING TRANSCENDENTAL MEDITATION. Unpublished M.A. thesis, University of Washington, 1973.

3030. Johnston, Hank. "The Marketed Social Movement: A Case Study of the Rapid Growth of TM." PACIFIC SOCIOLOGICAL REVIEW 23,3 (1980): 333-354.

The success of Transcendental Meditation rests upon its recruitment and organizational strategy, modeled upon that of a large-scale consumer products firm.

3031. McCutchan, Robert. "The Social and the Celestial: Mary Douglas and Transcendental Meditation." PRINCETON JOURNAL OF THE ARTS AND SCIENCES 50,2 (1977): 130-163.

3032. Macioti, Maria I. TEORIA E TECHNICA DELLA PACE INTERIORE. SAGGIO SULLA 'MEDITAZIONE TRANSCENDENTALE.' Napoli: Liguori, 1980.

3033. Phelan, Michael. "Transcendental Meditation. A Revitalization of the American Civil Religion." ARCHIVES DE SCIENCES SOCIALES DES RELIGIONS 48,1 (1979): 5-20.

Argues that the success of TM was due to its reintegration of cultural values within the American belief system.

\* Stark, Rodney, and William Sims Bainbridge. THE FUTURE OF RELIGION. SECULARIZATION, REVIVAL AND CULT FORMATION. Cited above as item 2985.

3034. Woodrum, Eric. "The Development of the Transcendental Meditation Movement." ZETETIC SCHOLAR 1,2 (1977): 38-48.

3035. Woodrum, Eric. "Religious Organizational Change: An Analysis Based on the TM Movement." RRR 24,2 (1982): 89-103.

During the spiritual-mystical period (1959-65), the movement attracted a few salvation-oriented persons with a variant of Hinduism. The counterculture period (1965-69) brought growth, with youths seeking world transformation and this-worldly bliss. In the secularized, popular religious period (1970 onward), it has been marketed as a scientifically validated technique for worldly benefits. Within the secular movement there is a hidden religious group.


UFO CULT

3036. Balch, Robert W. "Bo and Peep: A Case Study of the Origins of Messianic Leadership." In R. Wallis (ed.), MILLENNIALISM AND CHARISMA [volume cited in item 2629], pp. 13-72.

3037. Balch, Robert W. "Looking behind the Scenes in a Religious Cult: Implications for the Study of Conversion." SA 41,2 (1980): 137-143. Also in P.H. McNamara (ed.), RELIGION: NORTH AMERICAN STYLE, 2nd. ed. [volume cited in item 1978], pp. 309-316.

Religious conversion is commonly understood to involve dramatic transformations in personality. This participant-observation study concludes that apparently dramatic changes may result from the rapid learning of roles.

3038. Balch, Robert W. "'When the Light Goes Out, Darkness Comes': A Study of Defection from a Totalistic Cult." In R. Stark (ed.), RELIGIOUS MOVEMENTS [volume cited in item 2102], pp. 11-63.

3039. Balch, Robert W., and David Taylor. "Seekers and Saucers: The Role of the Cultic Milieu in Joining a UFO Cult." AMERICAN BEHAVIORAL SCIENTIST 20,6 (1977): 839-860. Also in James T. Richardson (ed.), CONVERSION CAREERS: IN AND OUT OF THE NEW RELIGIONS. Beverly Hills: Sage, 1977, pp. 43-64.

Defines the 'seeker' as one who is socially oriented to the quest for personal growth, and for whom affective ties with the group are unnecessary for conversion.

3040. Lewison, Thea S., and Robert W. Balch. "Bo and Peep: The Tale of a Modern Religious Odyssey." ZEITSCHRIFT FÜR MENSCHENKUNDE 44 (1980): 369-392.

3041. Ambrose, Kenneth P. "Function of the Family in the Process of Commitment within the Unification Movement." In Gene G. James (ed.), THE FAMILY AND THE UNIFICATION CHURCH. New York: Rose of Sharon Press, 1983, pp. 23-34.

3042. Anthony, Dick, and Thomas Robbins. "The Effect of Detente on the Growth of New Religions: Reverend Moon and the Unification Church." In J. Needleman and G. Barker (eds.), UNDERSTANDING THE NEW RELIGIONS [volume cited in item 105], pp. 80-100.

Interview material.

3043. Barker, Eileen. "Living the Divine Principle: Inside the Reverend Sun Myung Moon's Unification Church in Britain." ARCHIVES DE SCIENCES SOCIALES DES RELIGIONS 45,1 (1978): 75-93.

Attempts to show how a theological belief ('The Divine Principle') contributes to the continuance of the Unification Church in Britain.

3044. Barker, Eileen. "Whose Service is Perfect Freedom: The Concept of Spiritual Well-being in Relation to the Reverend Moon's Unification Church." In D.O. Moberg (ed.), SPIRITUAL WELL-BEING [volume cited in item 2872], pp. 153-171.

3045. Barker, Eileen. "Free to Choose? Some Thoughts on the Unification Church and Other Religious Movements." CLERGY REVIEW 65,10 (1980): 365-368; and 65,11 (1980): 392-398.

3046. Barker, Eileen. "Who'd be a Moonie?" In B.R. Wilson (ed.), THE SOCIAL IMPACT OF NEW RELIGIOUS MOVEMENTS [volume cited in item 2627], pp. 59-96.

1978 survey of members in Great Britain, seminarians in New York State, and other members in the U.S.; 1979 survey of people who attended workshops in Great Britain.

3047. Barker, Eileen. "Doing Love: Tensions in the Ideal Family." In G.G. James (ed.), THE FAMILY AND THE UNIFICATION CHURCH [volume cited in item 3041], pp. 35-52.

3048. Barker, Eileen. "The Ones who Got Away: People who Attend Unification Church Workshops and do not Become Members." In E. Barker (ed.), OF GODS AND MEN [volume cited in item 64], pp. 309-336. Reprinted in R. Stark (ed.), RELIGIOUS MOVEMENTS [volume cited in item 2102], pp. 65-93.

3049. Barker, Eileen. THE MAKING OF A MOONIE. BRAINWASHING OR CHOICE? Oxford: Basil Blackwell, 1984.

Use of both participant observation and questionnaires.

3050. Barker, Eileen. "Quo Vadis? The Unification Church." In D.G. Bromley and P.E. Hammond (eds.), THE FUTURE OF NEW RELIGIOUS MOVEMENTS [volume cited in item 94], pp. 141-152.

3051. Barker, Eileen. "Defection from the Unification Church. Some Statistics and Distinctions." In D.G. Bromley (ed.), FALLING FROM THE FAITH [volume cited in item 1363], pp. 166-184.

Various cohorts, mostly in Great Britain, followed from 1976-85.

   * Beckford, James A. "Two Contrasting Types of Sectarian Organization." Cited above as item 2493.

3052. Beckford, James A. "British Moonies on the Wane." PSYCHOLOGY TODAY, British edition (August 1977): 22-23.

3053. Beckford, James A. "Through the Looking-glass and Out the Other Side -- Withdrawal from Reverend Moon's Unification Church." ARCHIVES DE SCIENCES SOCIALES DES RELIGIONS 45,1 (1978): 95-116.

Discusses the kinds of devices by which members and ex-members of the Unification Church account verbally for their experiences of affiliation, participation, and withdrawal.

3054. Beckford, James A. "Talking of Apostasy, or Telling Tales and 'Telling' Tales." In G.N. Gilbert and P. Abell (eds.), ACCOUNTS AND ACTION [volume cited in item 1648], pp. 77-97.

Based on interviews with people leaving the church.

3055. Beckford, James A. "The Moral Career of the ex-Moonie." Chapter 5 in J.A. Beckford, CULT CONTROVERSIES: THE SOCIAL RESPONSE TO THE NEW RELIGIOUS MOVEMENTS. London: Tavistock, 1985.

Based on interviews conducted in Great Britain.

   * Berger, Alan L. "Hasidism and Moonism: Charisma in the Counterculture." Cited above as item 530.

3056. Bromley, David G. "Financing the Millennium: The Economic Structure of the Unificationist Movement." JSSR 24,3 (1985): 253-274.

The church's economic structure is consistent with the characteristics of a world-transforming movement. It is most unusual in its creation of a corporate conglomerate to underwrite its theological agenda.

3057. Bromley, David G. "Deprogramming as a Mode of Exit from New Religious Movements. The Case of the Unificationist Movement." In D.G. Bromley (ed.), FALLING FROM THE FAITH [volume cited in item 1363], pp. 185-204.

Examination of 397 cases of coercive deprogramming which took place from 1973 to 1986.

3058. Bromley, David G. "Economic Structure and Charismatic Leadership in the Unificationist Movement." In James T. Richardson (ed.), MONEY AND POWER IN THE NEW RELIGIONS. New York: Edwin Mellen Press, 1988.

3059. Bromley, David G., and Anson D. Shupe, Jr. "Just a Few Years Seem like a Lifetime: A Role Theory Approach to Participation in Religious Movements." In Louis Kriesberg (ed.), RESEARCH IN SOCIAL MOVEMENTS, CONFLICT, AND CHANGE, volume 2. Greenwich, Connecticut: JAI Press, 1979, pp. 159-185.

1977 interview data from movement proselytizers in several Texas cities.

3060. Bromley, David G., and Anson D. Shupe, Jr. 'MOONIES' IN AMERICA. CULT, CHURCH, AND CRUSADE. Beverly Hills, California: Sage, 1979.

3061. Bromley, David G., and Anson D. Shupe, Jr. "Emerging Foci in Participant Observation: Research as an Emerging Process." In William B. Shaffir, Allan Turowetz, and Robert A. Stebbins (eds.), FIELDWORK EXPERIENCE: QUALITATIVE APPROACHES TO SOCIAL RESEARCH. New York: St. Martin's Press, 1980, pp. 191-203.

1976-78 interview, field observation, and primary literature data on the conflict between the church and the anti-cult organization, the International Foundation for Individual Freedom.

   * Bromley, David G., and Anson D. Shupe, Jr. STRANGE GODS. THE GREAT AMERICAN CULT SCARE. Cited above as item 66.

3062. Bromley, David G., and Anson D. Shupe, Jr. "The Archetypal Cult: Conflict and the Social Contruction of Deviance." In G.G. James (ed.), THE FAMILY AND THE UNIFICATION CHURCH [volume cited in item 3041], pp. 1-22.

3063. Bromley, David G., Bruce C. Busching, and Anson D. Shupe, Jr. "The Unification Church and the American Family: Strain, Conflict and Control." In E. Barker (ed.), NEW RELIGIOUS MOVEMENTS [volume cited in item 96], pp. 302-311.

3064. Bromley, David G., Anson D. Shupe, Jr., and J.C. Ventimiglia. "Atrocity Tales, the Unification Church and the Social Construction of Evil." JOURNAL OF COMMUNICATION 29,3 (1979): 42-53.

Atrocity tales help deprogrammers and their supporters in the anti-cult movement to legitimate their otherwise illegal actions. The study focuses on tales about the Unification Church.

3065. Choi, Syn-Duk. "Korea's Tong-il Movement." In Spencer J. Palmer (ed.), THE NEW RELIGIONS OF KOREA. TRANSACTIONS OF THE KOREA BRANCH OF THE ROYAL ASIATIC SOCIETY, Vol. 53. Seoul: Royal Asiatic Society, 1967, pp. 101-113.

Reports on an early form of the church.

   * Choi, Syn-Duk. "A Comparative Study of Two New Religious Movements in the Republic of Korea: The Unification Church and the Full Gospel Central Church." Cited above as item 2371.

3066. Fichter, Joseph H. "Family and Religion among the Moonies: A Descriptive Analysis." In W.V. D'Antonio and J. Aldous (eds.), FAMILIES AND RELIGIONS [volume cited in item 421], pp. 289-304.

3067. Fichter, Joseph H. AUTOBIOGRAPHIES OF CONVERSION. Lewiston, N.Y.: Edwin Mellen Press, 1986.

3068. Grace, James H. SEX AND MARRIAGE IN THE UNIFICATION MOVEMENT: A SOCIOLOGICAL STUDY. New York: Edwin Mellen Press, 1985.

* Hampshire, Annette P., and James A. Beckford. "Religious Sects and the Concept of Deviance: The Moonies and the Mormons." Cited above as item 2908.

3069. Hardin, Bert L., and Guenter Kehrer. "Identity and Commitment." In H. Mol (ed.), IDENTITY AND RELIGION [volume cited in item 118], pp. 83-96.

Based on observations in West Germany.

3070. Hardin, Bert L., and Guenter Kehrer. "Some Social Factors Affecting the Rejection of New Belief Systems." In E. Barker (ed.), NEW RELIGIOUS MOVEMENTS [volume cited in item 96], pp. 267-283.

Based on observations in West Germany.

3071. Hardin, Bert L., and Wolfgang Kuner. "Entstehung und Entwicklung der Vereinigungskirche in der Bundesrepublik Deutschland." In Guenter Kehrer (ed.), DAS ENSTEHEN EINER NEUEN RELIGION. München: Kösel-Verlag, 1981.

* Harper, Charles L. "Cults and Communities: The Community Interfaces of Three Marginal Religious Movements." Cited above as item 2600.

3072. Horowitz, Irving L. "Science, Sin and Scholarship." ATLANTIC 239,3 (March 1977): 98-102.

Critiques the acceptance by scholars of conference grants from the Unification Church.

3073. Horowitz, Irving L. (ed.) SCIENCE, SIN AND SCHOLARSHIP: THE POLITICS OF REVEREND MOON AND THE UNIFICATION CHURCH. Cambridge, Massachusetts: MIT Press, 1978.

3074. Horowitz, Irving L. "Religion and the Rise of the Rev. Moon." THE NATION 228,13 (April 7, 1979): 365-367.

Criticism of the Unification Church in terms of church-state relationships.

3075. Horowitz, Irving L. "The Politics of New Cults: Non-prophetic Observations on Science, Sin and Scholarship." In T. Robbins and D. Anthony (eds.), IN GODS WE TRUST [volume cited in item 451], pp. 161-170.

3076. Kilbourne, Brock K. "Equity or Exploitation?: The Case of the Unification Church." RRR 28,2 (1986): 143-150.

Questionnaire data from members of the Unification Church, the Presbyterian Church, and the Roman Catholic Church, in different places in
the western U.S. The Presbyterians reported a lesser sense of fair
exchange between themselves and their church than did either Catholics
or Unificationists.

* Kuner, Wolfgang. SOZIOGENESE DER MITGLIEDSCHAFT IN DREI NEUEN
RELIGIÖSEN BEWEGUNGEN. Cited above as item 63.

* Kuner, Wolfgang. "New Religious Movements and Mental Health." Cited
above as item 64.

3077. Lofland, John. DOOMSDAY CULT. A STUDY OF CONVERSION, PROSELYTIZATION,
AND MAINTENANCE OF FAITH, enlarged edition. New York: Irvington, 1977.

Participant-observation study of what was evidently an early mission
of the Unification Church in the San Francisco area.

3078. Lofland, John. "Social Movement Culture and the Unification Church."
In D.G. Bromley and P.E. Hammond (eds.), THE FUTURE OF NEW RELIGIOUS
MOVEMENTS [volume cited in item 94], pp. 91-108.

3079. Long, Theodore E., and Jeffrey K. Hadden. "Religious Conversion and
the Concept of Socialization: Integrating the Brainwashing and Drift
Models." JSSR 22,1 (1983): 1-14.

The Unification Church combined strong social incorporation of converts
with weak creation of new belief systems, a pattern which simultaneous-
ly fostered strong initial commitment and created blockages to long-
term affiliation.

3080. Mickler, M.I. A HISTORY OF THE UNIFICATION CHURCH IN THE BAY AREA:
1960-1974. Unpublished M.A. thesis, Graduate Theological Union,
Berkeley, California, 1980.

3081. Parsons, Arthur S. "Redemptory Intimacy: The Family Culture of the
Unification Church." COMMUNAL SOCIETIES 5 (1985): 137-175.

3082. Parsons, Arthur S. "Messianic Personalism: A Role Analysis of the
Unification Church." JSSR 25,2 (1986): 141-161.

Presents results of a participant-observation study. The Unification
Church synthesizes the seemingly opposed forms of personalism and
authoritarianism in a distinctly therapeutic religion.

3083. Parsons, Arthur S. "The Secular Contribution to Religious Innovation:
A Case Study of the Unification Church." SA 50,3 (1989): 209-227.

Although forcefully opposed to much of secular society, the Unification
Church has appropriated and even rationalized pivotal elements of the
contemporary secular culture of the emotions.

3084. Robbins, Thomas. "Even a Moonie has Civil Rights." THE NATION 224,8
(1977): 238-241.

412

If persecution of deviant religions on obscurantist grounds of 'mind control' is institutionalized, its application to political dissidents may be inevitable.

* Robbins, Thomas. "Government Regulatory Powers and Church Autonomy: Deviant Groups as Test Cases." Cited above as item 2392.

3085. Robbins, Thomas, Dick Anthony, Madeline Doucas, and Thomas Curtis. "The Last Civil Religion: Reverend Moon and the Unification Church." SA 37,2 (1976): 111-125.

Considers the Unification Church as a civil religious sect, substituting for the family as a socializing agency for civic and theistic values.

3086. Shupe, Anson D., and David G. Bromley. "The Moonies and the Anti-cultists: Movement and Countermovement in Conflict." SA 40,4 (1979): 325-334. Also in J.K. Hadden and T.E. Long (eds.), RELIGION AND RELIGIOSITY IN AMERICA [volume cited in item 1985], pp. 70-84.

The anti-cult movement's institutional origins in the family and (secondarily) in organized religion, as well as the controversial tactics it adopted (including deprogramming), are considered relative to specific aspects of the 'Moonies' and similar groups.

3087. Shupe, Anson D., and David G. Bromley. "Walking a Tightrope: Dilemmas of Participant Observation of Groups in Conflict." QUALITATIVE SOCIOLOGY 2,3 (1980): 3-21.

Discusses problems involved in participant-observation study of two groups in conflict - the Unification Church and the anti-cult movement. Problems included role definition and justification, pressures to 'go native,' public pressure to take a stand, evolving commitments, and gaining comparable information and insights.

3088. Shupe, Anson D., and David G. Bromley. "Reverse Missionizing: Sun Myung Moon's Unificationist Movement in the United States." FREE INQUIRY IN CREATIVE SOCIOLOGY 8 (1980): 197-203.

3089. Solomon, Trudy. "Integrating the 'Moonie' Experience: A Survey of Ex-members of the Unification Church." In T. Robbins and D. Anthony (eds.), IN GODS WE TRUST [volume cited in item 451], pp. 275-294.

Questionnaire data on 100 former members of the church.

3090. Taylor, David F. "Becoming New People: The Recruitment of Young Americans into the Unification Church." In R. Wallis (ed.), MILLEN-NIALISM AND CHARISMA [volume cited in item 2629], pp. 177-230.

3091. Wilson, Bryan R., and Karel Dobbelaere. "Unificationism - A Study of the Moonies in Belgium." BRITISH JOURNAL OF SOCIOLOGY 38 (1987): 184-198.

Field study and data from 21 interviews.

* Wright, Stuart A. LEAVING CULTS: THE DYNAMICS OF DEFECTION. Cited

above as item 97.

*MISCELLANEOUS*

3092. Ahern, Geoffrey. SUN AT MIDNIGHT: THE RUDOLPH STEINER MOVEMENT AND THE WESTERN ESOTERIC TRADITION. Wellingborough, U.K.: Aquarian Press, 1984.

A study of Anthroposophy.

3093. Bainbridge, William Sims. THE SPACEFLIGHT REVOLUTION. New York: Wiley-Interscience, 1976.

Study of an organization called Committee for the Future.

   * Chagnon, Roland. TROIS NOUVELLES RELIGIONS DE LA LUMIERE ET DU SON: LA SCIENCE DE LA SPIRITUALITE, ECKANKAR, LA MISSION DE LA LUMIERE DIVINE. Cited above as item 67.

3094. Champion, Françoise. "D'une alliance entre religion et utopie post 68: Le rapport à la société du groupe <Eveil à la conscience planétaire>." SC 36,1 (1989): 51-69.

Study of an eclectic commune in France.

3095. Gauthier, Madeleine. "Le problème de la définition sociologique de la gnose." Gnoses d'hier et d'aujourd'hui. LES CAHIERS DE RECHERCHES EN SCIENCES DE LA RELIGION 7 (1986): 231-255.

Examination of two modern gnostic groups in order to develop a definition of gnosticism. Gnosticism gives a primacy to interior vision, based on scientific data and much more. It has an underlying dualism of spirit and matter and a collapse of past, present, and future into a common presence.

3096. Hardacre, Helen. KUROZUMIKYO AND THE NEW RELIGIONS OF JAPAN. Princeton: Princeton University Press, 1986.

3097. Jabbour, Millard E. THE SECT OF TENSHO-KOTAI-JINGU-KYO: THE EMERGENCE AND CAREER OF A RELIGIOUS MOVEMENT. Unpublished M.A. thesis, University of Hawaii, 1958.

3098. Rigby, Andrew, and Bryan S. Turner. "Findhorn Community, Centre of Light: A Sociological Study of New Forms of Religion." SOCIOLOGICAL YEARBOOK OF RELIGION IN BRITAIN 5 (1972): 72-86.

Descriptive study of a non-Christian, de-institutionalized commune in Britain.

3099. Wallis, Roy. "The Aetherius Society: A Case Study in the Formation of a Mystagogic Congregation." SOCIOLOGICAL REVIEW 22,1 (1974): 27-45. Also in R. Wallis (ed.), SECTARIANISM [volume cited in item 82], pp. 17-34.

Historical sociology, beginning with the cult's origins in the 1950s.

# 24
## Little Traditions and
## Third-World Syncretisms

*AFRICANIST RELIGION IN BRAZIL*

3100. Bastide, Roger. "Estructuras sociales e religiões afro-brasileiras." ANHEMBI 26,4 (1957): 228-243.

3101. Bastide, Roger. LES RELIGIONS AFRICAINES AU BRESIL: VERS UNE SOCIOLOGIE DES INTERPENETRATIONS DE CIVILISATIONS. Paris: Presses Universitaires de France, 1960. See also THE AFRICAN RELIGIONS OF BRAZIL. TOWARD A SOCIOLOGY OF THE INTERPENETRATION OF CIVILIZATIONS, translated by Helen Sebba. Baltimore: Johns Hopkins University Press, 1978.

3102. Camara, Evandro M. "Afro-American Religious Syncretism in Brazil and the United States: A Weberian Perspective." SA 48,4 (1988): 299-318.

The character of Brazilian Catholicism aided the preservation of religious Africanisms via a structural parallelism between the two models, manifested in syncretism and greater accommodation on the part of the dominant church toward the minority ones. Evangelical Protestantism in the U.S., in contrast, proved inimical to the continuation of African religious practices due to structural incompatibility and to the resulting suppression of African cultural traits by Protestant clergymen.

3103. Cavalcanti, Maria Laura Viveiros de Castro. "Origens, para que a quero? Questões para uma investigação sobre a Umbanda." RELIGIÃO E SOCIEDADE 13,2 (1986): 84-101.

Review of the literature, covering many Africanist religious phenomena in Brazil, including Umbanda.

3104. Dantas, Beatriz Góis. "A organização econômica de um terreiro de Xangô." RELIGIÃO E SOCIEDADE 4 (1979): 181-191.

* De Camargo, C.P. Ferreira. KARDECISMO E UMBANDA. Cited above as item 3007.

3105. Pereira de Queiroz, Maria I. "Afro-Brazilian Cults and Religious Change in Brazil." In J.A. Beckford and T. Luckmann (eds.), THE

415

CHANGING FACE OF RELIGION [volume cited in item 549], pp. 64-108.

3106. Pierson, Donald. NEGROES IN BRAZIL. Chicago: University of Chicago Press, 1942.

3107. Ribeiro, René. CULTOS AFRO-BRASILEIROS DO RECIFE: UM ESTUDO DE AJUSTA-MENTO SOCIAL. Recife: Instituto Joaquim Nabuco, 1952.

3108. Ribeiro, René. "Novos aspectos do processo de reinterpretação nos cultos afrobrasileiros do Recife." ANAIS DO XXXI CONGRESSO INTERNA-CIONAL DE AMERICANISTAS, SÃO PAULO, 23 A 28 AGÔSTO DE 1954, Volume I. São Paulo: Editora Anhembi, 1955, pp. 473-491.

Documentation of the incorporation of strictly Brazilian lore into African rituals in Recife.

3109. Ribeiro, René. "Problemática pessôal e interpretação divinatoria nos cultos afro-brasileiros do Recife." REVISTA DO MUSEU PAULISTA 10 (1956/58): 225-242.

3110. Ribeiro, René. "Análises socio-psicológico de la posesión en los cultos afrobrasileños." ACTA NEUROPSIQUIATRICA ARGENTINA 5 (1959): 249-262.

3111. Rodrigues, Jose H. BRAZIL AND AFRICA. Berkeley: University of California Press, 1965.

The maintenance of different religious forms under a syncretism with a dominant religion was a resistance of slaves against their masters' culture. The dominant religion served largely to reinforce the ideo-logical validity of the masters' position.

3112. Simpson, George E. BLACK RELIGIONS IN THE NEW WORLD. New York: Columbia University Press, 1978.

3113. Valente, Waldemar. SINCRETISMO RELIGIOSO AFRO-BRAZILEIRO. São Paulo: 1955.

## UMBANDA

3114. Bastide, Roger. "The Birth of a Religion." Chapter 14 in R. Bastide, THE AFRICAN RELIGIONS OF BRAZIL [item 3101].

3115. Birman, Patricia. "Laços que nos unem: Ritual, familia e poder na Umbanda." RELIGIÃO E SOCIEDADE 8 (1982): 21-28.

3116. Brown, Diana. "Umbanda e classes sociais." RELIGIÃO E SOCIEDADE 1 (1977): 31-42.

3117. Da Matta e Silva, W. UMBANDA DO BRASIL. Rio de Janeiro: Livraria Freitas Bastos, 1969.

3118. Dann, Graham M.S. "Religion and Cultural Identity: The Case of

Umbanda." SA 40,3 (1979): 208-225.

Umbanda appeals to its adherents in terms of Brazilian national identity. Items of belief and ritual blend African, Amerindian, colonial Christian, and Kardecist (Spiritualist) elements. The syncretism gives Umbanda a unique indigenous character.

* De Camargo, C.P. Ferreira. KARDECISMO E UMBANDA. Cited above as item 3007.

* Fry, Peter. "Two Religious Movements: Protestantism and Umbanda." Cited above as item 2316.

* Goodman, Felicitas D., Jeanette H. Henney, and Esther Pressel. TRANCE, HEALING, AND HALLUCINATION: THREE FIELD STUDIES IN RELIGIOUS EXPERIENCE. Cited above as item 2433.

* Howe, Gary N. "Capitalism and Religion at the Periphery: Pentecostalism and Umbanda in Brazil." Cited above as item 2416.

3119. Kloppenburg, Boaventura. A UMBANDA NO BRASIL: ORIENTAÇÃO PARA OS CATOLICOS. Petrópolis: Editora Vozes Limitada, 1961.

3120. Negrão, Lisias N. "A Umbanda como expressão de religiosidade popular." RELIGIÃO E SOCIEDADE 4 (1979): 171-180.

3121. Ortiz, Renato. "Du syncrétisme à la synthèse: Umbanda, une religion brésilienne/From Syncretism to Synthesis: Umbanda, a Brazilian Religion." ARCHIVES DE SCIENCES SOCIALES DES RELIGIONS 20,40 (1975): 89-97.

Traces the origins and subsequent development of the Umbanda religion, and analyzes its present social and religious characteristics.

3122. Ortiz, Renato. "Umbanda, magie blanche. Quimbande, magie noire." ARCHIVES DE SCIENCES SOCIALES DES RELIGIONS 47,1 (1979): 135-146.

The doctrine of the Umbanda religion in Brazil is articulated around the two principles of Good (Umbanda) and Evil (Quimbanda).

3123. Ortiz, Renato. "Etica, poder e politica: Umbanda, um mito-ideologia." RELIGIÃO E SOCIEDADE 11,3 (1984): 36-54.

Reinterpretation of work originally published in 1978.

3124. Pechman, Tema. "Umbanda e politica no Rio de Janeiro." RELIGIÃO E SOCIEDADE 8 (1982): 37-44.

A study of a Brazilian spiritualist cult.

3125. Teixeira, A. O LIVRO DOS MEDIUNS DE UMBANDA. Rio de Janeiro: Editôra Eco, 1967.

3126. Bastide, Roger. O CANDOMBLE DA BAHIA, translated by Maria Isaura Pereira de Queiroz. São Paulo: Companhia Editora Nacional, 1961.

3127. Bastide, Roger. "Eglises baroques et candomblés en fête." ARCHIVES INTERNATIONALES DE LA SOCIOLOGIE DE LA COOPERATION ET DU DEVELOPPEMENT 40 (1976): 35-51.

3128. Birman, Patricia. "Identidade social e homosexualismo no Candomblé." RELIGIÃO E SOCIEDADE 12,1 (1985): 2-21.

3129. Costa, F. A PRATICA DO CANDOMBLE NO BRASIL. Rio de Janeiro: Editora Renes, 1974.

3130. Goldman, Marcio. "A construção ritual da pessoa: A possessão no Candomblé." RELIGIÃO E SOCIEDADE 12,1 (1985): 22-54.

Review of the literature; analysis based on a 1982-83 field study in Bahia.

3131. Herskovits, Melville J. "The Social Organization of the Afro-Brazilian Candomblé." PHYLON 17,2 (1956): 147-166.

Based on 1941-42 field research in Bahia.

*ANTONIENS*

3132. Jadin, Louis. "Le Congo et la secte des Antoniens." BULLETIN INSTITUT HISTORIQUE BELGE 33 (1961): 411-416.

3133. Jadin, Louis. "Les sectes religieuses secrètes des Antoniens au Congo (1703-1709)." CAHIERS DES RELIGIONS AFRICAINES 2/3 (1968): 109-120.

Suggests parallels with the modern Kimbanguist movement.

*JAMAA*

3134. De Craemer, Willy. ANALYSE SOCIOLOGIQUE DE LA JAMAA. Leopoldville: Centre de Recherches Sociologiques, 1965.

3135. De Craemer, Willy. "The Jamaa Movement in the Katanga and Kasai Regions of the Congo." RRR 10 (1968): 11-23.

3136. De Craemer, Willy. JAMAA AND ECCLESIA: A CHARISMATIC MOVEMENT IN THE CONGOLESE CATHOLIC CHURCH. Unpublished Ph.D. dissertation, Harvard University, 1974.

* De Craemer, Willy. THE JAMAA AND THE CHURCH. A BANTU CATHOLIC MOVEMENT IN ZAIRE. Cited above as item 1437.

3137. Fabian, Johannes. JAMAA: A CHARISMATIC MOVEMENT IN KATANGA. Evanston:

Northwestern University Press, 1971.

3138. Tanner, R.E.S. "The 'Jamaa' Movement in the Congo: A Sociological Comment on Some Religious Interpretations." HEYTHROP JOURNAL 9,2 (1968): 164-178.

Response to recent literature.

*BHILS*

3139. Ahuja, Ram. "Religion of the Bhils: A Sociological Analysis." SOCIOLOGICAL BULLETIN 14,1 (1965): 21-23.

1891, 1901, 1911, and 1921 religious identity data on the Bhils of south Rajasthan, compared to a survey by the author. Discusses the manner in which the Bhils, the third largest tribe in India, have retained their tribal religion.

3140. Bhuriya, Mahipal. "Tribal Religion in India: A Case Study of the Bhils." SC 33,2-3 (1986): 275-283.

Examines vestiges of the Bhil religion in the Jhabua district, 1970-85.

*CARGO CULTS*

3141. Jarvie, I.C. "Theories of Cargo Cults: A Critical Analysis." OCEANIA 34 (1963): 1-31, 108-136.

Review of the literature on cargo cults and parallel phenomena, 1892-1957.

3142. Jarvie, I.C. "On the Explanation of Cargo Cults." ARCHIVES EUROPEENES DE SOCIOLOGIE 7,2 (1966): 299-312.

Reflections stimulated by Peter Lawrence's ROAD BELONG CARGO (Manchester, 1965).

3143. Lanternari, Vittorio. THE RELIGIONS OF THE OPPRESSED. A STUDY OF MODERN MESSIANIC CULTS, translated by Lisa Sergio. New York: Knopf, 1963.

3144. Lawrence, Peter. "Die Cargo-bewegung im Südlichen Madang-distrikt von Neuguinea." In R. König (ed.), ASPEKTE DER ENTWICKLUNGS SOZIOLOGIE [volume cited in item 41], pp. 182-218.

   * Lewy, Guenter. RELIGION AND REVOLUTION. Cited above as item 34.

3145. Worsley, Peter. THE TRUMPET SHALL SOUND. A STUDY OF CARGO CULTS IN MELANESIA. London: MacGibbon and Kee, 1957.

3146. Thornton, Russell. "Demographic Antecedents of a Revitalization Movement: Population Change, Population Size and the 1890 Ghost Dance." AMERICAN SOCIOLOGICAL REVIEW 46,1 (1981): 88-96.

The 1890 Ghost Dance movement among native Americans occurred at the time of the native American population nadir and had the objective of returning deceased populations to life. Differential tribal participation suggests size of tribal population was an important factor.

3147. Thornton, Russell. "Demographic Antecedents of Tribal Participation in the 1870 Ghost Dance Movement." AMERICAN INDIAN CULTURE AND RESEARCH JOURNAL 6 (1982): 79-91.

3148. Thornton, Russell. WE SHALL LIVE AGAIN. THE 1870 AND 1890 GHOST DANCE MOVEMENTS AS DEMOGRAPHIC REVITALIZATION. Cambridge: Cambridge University Press, 1986.

*RASTAFARIAN*

3149. Barrett, Leonard E. SOUL FORCE: AFRICAN HERITAGE IN AFRO-AMERICAN RELIGION. New York: Doubleday, 1974.

A study of the movement in Jamaica.

3150. Barrett, Leonard E. THE RASTAFARIANS: SOUNDS OF CULTURAL DISSONANCE. Boston: Beacon, 1977.

3151. Cashmore, Ernest. RASTAMAN. THE RASTAFARIAN MOVEMENT IN ENGLAND. London: Allen and Unwin, 1979.

3152. Glazier, Stephen D. "Prophecy and Ecstasy: Religion and Politics in the Caribbean." In J.K. Hadden and A. Shupe (eds.), PROPHETIC RELIGIONS AND POLITICS [volume cited in item 197], pp. 430-447.

Overview of Ras Tafari, Vodun, and the Spiritual Baptists.

 * Henry, Paget. "Indigenous Religions and the Transformation of Peripheral Societies." Cited above as item 575.

3153. Kitzinger, Sheila. "The Rastafari Brethren of Jamaica." COMPARATIVE STUDIES IN SOCIETY AND HISTORY 9 (1966): 33-39.

Report of field work among peasant Jamaican Rastafarians.

3154. Kitzinger, Sheila. "Protest and Mysticism: The Rastafari Cult of Jamaica." JSSR 8,2 (1969): 240-262.

Detailed anthropological study in Jamaica, interpreting the institution and its symbol system in sociological and psychoanalytic terms.

3155. Simpson, George E. "Political Cultism in West Kingston, Jamaica." SOCIAL AND ECONOMIC STUDIES 4,2 (1955): 133-149.

Based on 1953 field work. Describes doctrine, meetings, and song lyrics; assesses the political significance of the movement.

3156. Simpson, George E. "The Ras Tafari Movement in Jamaica: A Study of Race and Class Conflict." SOCIAL FORCES 34,2 (1955): 167-170.

Descriptive account, based on field work.

3157. Simpson, George E. "The Ras Tafari Movement in its Millennial Aspect." In Sylvia L. Thrupp (ed.), MILLENNIAL DREAMS IN ACTION (Comparative Studies in Society and History, Supplement No. 2). The Hague: Mouton, 1962, pp. 160-165.

A deprivation-theory approach.

  * Watson, G. Llewellyn. "Social Structure and Social Movements: The Black Muslims in the U.S.A. and the Ras-Tafarians in Jamaica." Cited above as item 700.


## VOODOO

3158. Desmangles, Leslie G. GOD IN HAITIAN VODUN: A CASE IN CULTURAL SYMBIOSIS. Unpublished Ph.D. dissertation, Temple University, Philadelphia, 1975. [DA 36:6 A, p. 3780]

Argues that the phenomenon is a juxtaposition of Africanist and Catholic symbols, rather than a syncretism.

3159. Desmangles, Leslie G. "African Interpretations of the Christian Cross in Vodun." SA 38,1 (1977): 13-24.

The contact between Dahomean religions and European Catholicism in Haiti during the colonial period (1492-1804) resulted in a system of correspondences between the two. Vodunists do not interpret the cross in a context of Christian theology but rather in one of Dahomean mythology.

  * Gerlach, Luther P. "Pentecostalism: Revolution or Counter-revolution?" Cited above as item 2376.

  * Glazier, Stephen D. "Prophecy and Ecstasy: Religion and Politics in the Caribbean." Cited above as item 3152.

3160. Gräbner, Jürgen. "Vodou und Gesellschaft in Haiti." In J. Matthes (ed.), INTERNATIONALES JAHRBUCH FÜR RELIGIONSSOZIOLOGIE 6 [volume cited in item 2000], pp. 158-176.

Overview.

3161. LaGuerre, Michel S. NATIVISM IN HAITI: THE POLITICS OF VOODOO. Unpublished M.A. thesis, Roosevelt University, Chicago, 1973.

3162. LaGuerre, Michel S. "The Place of Voodoo in the Social Structure of Haiti." CARIBBEAN QUARTERLY 19,3 (1973): 36-50.

3163. Pierre, Roland. "Caribbean Religion: The Voodoo Case." SA 38,1 (1977): 25-36.

The components of Voodoo in the religion of the Antilles are explored in their religious dimensions. The Voodoo religion appears to be the expression of the racial and cultural resistance of an oppressed class of people within a hostile society.

* Thébaud, Frantz. "Katholizismus, Vaudou und Ideologie im soziokulturellen Entwicklungsprozess der Republik Haiti." Cited above as item 1893.

3164. Wilmeth, Marlyn W., and J. Richard Wilmeth. "Theatrical Elements in Voodoo: The Case for Diffusion." JSSR 16,1 (1977): 27-37.

Elements of the *commedia dell'arte* appear in Voodoo in Haiti. They can be seen in some places in Haiti but not in Africa.

## TONGHAK

3165. Chung, Chai Sik. "Religion and Cultural Identity - The Case of 'Eastern Learning'." In Joachim Matthes (ed.), INTERNATIONALES JAHRBUCH FÜR RELIGIONSSOZIOLOGIE 5. Opladen: Westdeutscher Verlag, 1969, pp. 118-132.

Overview of a religion founded in the 1860s in Korea.

3166. Hong, Suhn-Kyoung. "Tonghak in the Context of Korean Modernization." RRR 10 (1968): 43-51.

3167. Kang, Wi Jo. "Belief and Political Behavior in Ch'ondogyo." RRR 10 (1968): 38-43.

3168. Leverrier, Roger. "Arrière-plan socio-politique et caractéristiques des nouvelles religions au Corée. Le cas du Tong Hak." SC 25,2 (1978): 217-237.

The Tong-Hak movement began with the intention of bringing about a solution to the extremely difficult situation inside Korea: economic, political, and social disorder in the nineteenth century. The traditions had deteriorated, leaving people with no ideological or moral guide, and Western culture had begun to invade.

## MISCELLANEOUS

3169. Bureau, René. "Prophétismes Africains: Le Harrisme en Côte-d'Ivoire." ARCHIVES DE SCIENCES SOCIALES DES RELIGIONS 41 (1976): 47-53.

Analyzes the contents and meaning of the Harrist religion, a modern religious movement which claims William Harris, a native of Liberia, as its chief prophet.

3170. Chesneaux, Jean. "Le millénarisme des Taiping." ARCHIVES DE SOCIOLOGIE DES RELIGIONS 16 (1963): 122-124.

3171. Horowitz, Michael M., and Morton Klass. "The Martiniquan East Indian Cult of Maldevidan." SOCIAL AND ECONOMIC STUDIES 10,1 (1961): 93-100.

Maldevidan is a chief deity of the East Indians in Martinique, variously equated with Hindu and Christian figures - e.g., Vishnu, Christ, St. Michael.

3172. Kreuer, Werner. "Die Balokole-Bewegung in Uganda. Geschichte, kulturelle und wirtschaftliche Auswirkungen bei den Hirtennomaden Ankoles." SOCIOLOGIA INTERNATIONALIS 11,1-2 (1976): 103-115.

Overview of a revitalization movement of the Bahima tribe in the former kingdom of Ankole/Uganda, now southwest Uganda. 'Balokole' means 'Saved Ones.'

3173. Leacock, Seth, and Ruth Leacock. SPIRITS OF THE DEEP. A STUDY OF AN AFRO-BRAZILIAN CULT. Garden City, N.Y.: Anchor-Doubleday, 1975.

A study of the Batuque cult.

3174. Martel, Gilles. LE MESSIANISME DE LOUIS RIEL. Waterloo, Ontario: Wilfrid Laurier University Press, 1984.

A study of the Riel movement in Manitoba, Canada.

3175. Pereira de Queiroz, Maria I. "Die Fanatiker des 'Contestado'." STADEN-JAHRBUCH 5 (1957): 203-215.

A study of the Contestado movement, a 1912-16 religio-political movement of a messianic character in the highlands of Santa Catarina state, southern Brazil.

3176. Sirven, Pierre. "Les conséquences géographiques d'un nouveau syncrétisme religieux en Côte d'Ivoire: Le Kokambisme." CAHIERS D'OUTRE-MER 20/78 (1967): 127-136.

Brief history of Kokambism from its initial appearance in 1956; analysis of its negative impact upon nutrition.

3177. Suk-jay, Yim. "Introduction au Mouïsme. La religion populaire coréene." SC 25,2 (1978): 175-189.

Mouism was spread throughout Korea for a long time, and was transmitted across generations by the *moudang* families. From the arrival of Buddhism, the group suffered discrimination and sometimes persecution. The *moudang* retained their traditions despite this until recent times.

# 25

## Other Independent Traditions

*GNOSTIC (ANCIENT)*

3178. Green, Henry A. THE ECONOMIC AND SOCIAL ORIGINS OF GNOSTICISM. Atlanta: Scholars Press, 1985.

3179. Kippenberg, H.G. "Versuch einer soziologischen Verortung des antiken Gnostizismus." NUMEN 17 (1970): 211-232. See also Peter Munz, "Comment," 19,1 (1972): 41-51.

A sociology-of-knowledge approach.

3180. Mendelson, E. Michael. "Some Notes on a Sociological Approach to Gnosticism." In Ugo Bianchi (ed.), LE ORIGINI DELLO GNOSTICISMO (Numen Supplement No. 12). Leiden: E.J. Brill, 1967, pp. 668-676.

3181. Rudolph, Kurt. "Stand und Aufgaben in der Erforschung des Gnostizismus." SONDERHEFT DES WISSENSCHAFTLICHEN ZEITSCHRIFT DER FRIEDRICH SCHILLER-UNIVERSITÄT (Jena, 1963): 89-102.

3182. Rudolph, Kurt. "Randerscheinungen des Judentums und das Problem der Entstehung des Gnostizismus." KAIROS 9,2 (1967): 105-122.

Examines Jewish and Hellenistic influences upon Jewish, heathen, and Christian gnosticisms.

3183. Rudolph, Kurt. "Das Problem einer Soziologie und <sozialen Verortung> der Gnosis." KAIROS 19,1 (1977): 35-44.

Provides an overview and conceptual framework for analysis of the problem.

*FREEMASONRY*

3184. Jolicoeur, Pamela M., and Louis L. Knowles. "Fraternal Associations and Civil Religion: Scottish Rite Freemasonry." RRR 20,1 (1978): 3-22.

Content analysis of a Masonic publication, 1964-74. The Freemasons have as a major purpose the maintenance and propagation of civil religion.

3185. Wilson, John. "Voluntary Associations and Civil Religion: The Case of Freemasonry." RRR 22,2 (1980): 125-136.

Survey in a midwestern U.S. state. Members are generally from higher socioeconomic strata, though less so than in the past. Most members describe themselves as inactive and unfamiliar with lodge proceedings, yet they exhibit loyalty to the order and its ideals. This paradox is resolved with the help of ideas from Bellah's writings on civil religion.


*SWEDENBORG*

3186. Jones, Robert K. "The Swedenborgians: An Interactionist Analysis." SOCIOLOGICAL YEARBOOK OF RELIGION IN BRITAIN 7 (1974): 132-153.

Use of an interaction analysis to illustrate how movements such as the Swedenborgian may have quite distinct meanings for members and for outsiders.

3187. Williams-Hogan, Jane. A NEW CHURCH IN A DISINTERESTED WORLD: A STUDY OF THE FORMATION AND DEVELOPMENT OF THE GENERAL CONFERENCE OF THE NEW CHURCH IN GREAT BRITAIN. Unpublished Ph.D. dissertation, University of Pennsylvania, 1985. [DA 46:5 A, p. 1405]

The founding of the 'New Christian Church' in England, 1787, is examined in the framework of Weber's theory of charisma.


*SHAKERS*

3188. Bainbridge, William Sims. "Shaker Demographics 1840-1900: An Example of the Use of U.S. Census Enumeration Schedules." JSSR 21,4 (1982): 352-365.

Data from original manuscript schedules of the U.S. census for 22 Shaker colonies in 1840, 1860, 1880, and 1900. The main analysis focuses on changing age structures and sex ratio.

3189. Cuneo, Michael W. THE SHAKERS: A CASE STUDY IN THE DYNAMICS OF AN ESTABLISHED SECT. Unpublished M.A. thesis, University of St. Michael's College, Toronto, 1982.

Examines the persistence and eventual decline of the Shakers.

3190. Desroche, Henri. LES SHAKERS AMERICAINS. D'UN NEO-CHRISTIANISME A UN PRE-SOCIALISME. Paris: Ed. Minuit, 1955. See also THE AMERICAN SHAKERS. Amherst: University of Massachusetts Press, 1971.

* Foster, Lawrence. RELIGION AND SEXUALITY: THE SHAKERS, THE MORMONS, AND THE ONEIDA COMMUNITY. Cited above as item 2906.

3191. Stark, Werner. THE SOCIOLOGY OF RELIGION, Vol. II. SECTARIAN

RELIGION. New York: Fordham University Press, 1967.

3192. Whitworth, John M. "The Shakers - Ideological Change and Organizational Persistence." SOCIOLOGICAL YEARBOOK OF RELIGION IN BRITAIN 8 (1975): 78-102.

Analysis of the shifting relationship between Shaker theology and the sect's external social environment.

3193. Whitworth, John M. "Communitarian Groups in the World." In R. Wallis (ed.), SECTARIANISM [volume cited in item 82], pp. 117-137.

* Whitworth, John M. GOD'S BLUEPRINTS: A SOCIOLOGICAL STUDY OF THREE UTOPIAN SECTS. Cited above as item 2555.

* Wilson, Bryan R. RELIGIOUS SECTS. A SOCIOLOGICAL STUDY. Cited above as item 2403.

3194. Wilson, John. RELIGION IN AMERICAN SOCIETY. THE EFFECTIVE PRESENCE. Englewood Cliffs, N.J.: Prentice-Hall, 1978.


## ONEIDA

3195. Carden, Maren Lockwood. ONEIDA: UTOPIAN COMMUNITY TO MODERN CORPORATION. Baltimore: Johns Hopkins University Press, 1969.

3196. Desroche, Henri. "Oneida, puritaine et libertaire." ARCHIVES DE SCIENCES SOCIALES DES RELIGIONS 36 (1973): 3-34.

Documents the tenuous, and somewhat ironic, place of Fourierist utopian themes within the Oneida community.

* Foster, Lawrence. RELIGION AND SEXUALITY: THE SHAKERS, THE MORMONS, AND THE ONEIDA COMMUNITY. Cited above as item 2906.

3197. Mandelker, Ira L. RELIGION, SOCIETY, AND UTOPIA IN NINETEENTH-CENTURY AMERICA. Amherst: University of Massachusetts Press, 1984.

Studies the Oneida community by locating it within a general societal context.

* Whitworth, John M. GOD'S BLUEPRINTS: A SOCIOLOGICAL STUDY OF THREE UTOPIAN SECTS. Cited above as item 2555.


## BAHA'I

3198. Archer, Mary E. GLOBAL COMMUNITY: CASE STUDY OF THE HOUSTON BAHA'IS. Unpublished M.A. thesis, University of Houston, 1977.

3199. Balch, Robert W., Gwenn Farnsworth, and Sue Wilkins. "When the Bombs Drop. Reactions to Disconfirmed Prophecy in a Millennial Sect." SOCIOLOGICAL PERSPECTIVES 26,2 (1983): 137-158.

1980 participant-observation study of a sect based in Missoula,
Montana, expecting an imminent nuclear war.

3200. Berger, Peter L.  FROM SECT TO CHURCH: A SOCIOLOGICAL INTERPRETATION
OF THE BAHA'I MOVEMENT.  Unpublished Ph.D. dissertation, New School
for Social Research, 1954.

3201. Berger, Peter L.  "Motif messianique et processus social dans le
Bahaisme."  ARCHIVES DE SOCIOLOGIE DES RELIGIONS 4 (1957): 93-107.

* Ebaugh, Helen Rose Fuchs, Kathe Richman, and Janet Saltzman Chafetz.
"Life Crises among the Religiously Committed: Do Sectarian Differences
Matter?"  Cited above as item 889.

* Ebaugh, Helen Rose Fuchs, and Sharron Lee Vaughn.  "Ideology and Recruitment in Religious Groups."  Cited above as item 890.

3202. Keene, James J.  "Baha'i World Faith: Redefinition of Religion."  JSSR
6,2 (1967): 221-235.  See also Agehananda Bharati, "Comment," 7,2
(1968): 281.

Factor analysis of 35 religious behaviors of 112 Baha'is.

3203. Ruff, Ivan J.  "Baha'i - The Invisible Community."  NEW SOCIETY 29/623
(1974): 665-668.

General description of the religion in Great Britain.

3204. Smith, Peter.  "Millenarianism in the Babi and Baha'i Religions."  In
R. Wallis (ed.), MILLENNIALISM AND CHARISMA [volume cited in item
2629], pp. 231-283.

* Smith, Peter.  BABI AND BAHA'I RELIGIONS: FROM MESSIANIC SHI'ISM TO A
WORLD RELIGION.  Cited above as item 676.


*MONOTHEISM AND POLYTHEISM*

3205. Lemert, Charles C.  "Cultural Multiplexity and Religious Polytheism."
SC 21,3 (1974): 241-253.

A sociology-of-knowledge approach.  Monotheism should be seen in the
light of a simpler pre-modern world, and a form of polytheism should
be expected in the modern complex world.

3206. Sheils, Dean.  "An Evolutionary Explanation of Supportive Monotheism:
A Comparative Study."  INTERNATIONAL JOURNAL OF COMPARATIVE SOCIOLOGY
15,1-2 (1974): 47-56.

Data from the ETHNOGRAPHIC ATLAS of Murdock show correlations of
various societies' attributes with 'supportive monotheism' (one deity
interested in creation and supporting moral codes).

3207. Underhill, Ralph.  "Economic and Political Antecedents of Monotheism:
A Cross-cultural Study."  AMERICAN JOURNAL OF SOCIOLOGY 80,4 (1975):

427

841-861.  See also Guy E. Swanson, "Comment," 80,4 (1975): 862-869;
R. Underhill, "Reply," 82,2 (1976): 418-421;  and G.E. Swanson, "Reply,"
82,2 (1976): 421-423.

Economic complexity and political complexity of societies are independently related to belief in monotheism.  Contrary to Swanson and
Durkheim, the findings are more consistent with Marx and Engels.

# AUTHOR INDEX
(Numbers refer to items)

## A

Abaza, M. 545
Abbott, M.M. 1037
Abbruzzese, S. 1554
Abel, T. 1013
Abell, T.D. 2436
Abellán, J. 1616
Abraham, G.A. 2936
Abramson, H.J. 1090, 1197, 1198, 1199
Ackerman, S.E. 909
Ackermann, W. 277
Acock, A.C. 2687
Adams, B.N. 1
Adams, R.N. 1874
Adams, R.L. 2557, 2584
Adato, A. 3024
Adorno, T.W. 2945, 2946
Adriance, M. 1798, 1799, 1800
Agena, M. 184
Aggarwal, P.C. 2
Aguirre, B.E. 2488, 2489
Ahern, G. 3092
Ahluwalis, G.S. 227
Ahmad, A. 649
Ahmad, I. 650
Ahuja, R. 3139
Akahoshi, H. 137
Alant, C.J. 2084
Alatas, S.H. 632
Alba, R.D. 1200, 1201, 1347
Albrecht, S.L. 2861, 2894, 2895, 2896, 2898, 2903
Alcorn, D.S. 2861
Aldridge, A. 1895, 1896
Alexander, D. 546
Alfred, H.R. 2976

Alidoost-Khaybari, Y. 710
Allan, G. 2485
Allen, G. 2369
Allen, J.L. 2330
Allen, M.R. 3
Allinsmith, B. 404
Allinsmith, W. 404
Aloisi, M.F. 999
Alonso, I. 1738, 1739, 1780, 1789, 1790, 1883
Alston, J.P. 1091, 1202, 2488, 2489, 2749
Alston, L.T. 1202
Altermatt, U. 1637
Altheide, D.L. 2750
Alvirez, D. 1203
Alwin, D.F. 1348
Amato, E.L. 1783, 1784
Ambroise, Y. 4, 5
Ambrose, K.P. 3041
Ames, M.M. 159
Ammentorp, W. 1092
Ammerman, N.T. 2688, 2689
Anderson, A. 2195
Anderson, C.H. 1093
Anderson, C.L. 2934, 2935
Anderson, N. 2815, 2816
Anderson, S. 1979
Anderton, D. 2899
Andezian, S. 679
András, E. 1553
Anfossi, A. 1555
Anfossi, G. 1556
Angus, L.B. 1446
Anthony, D. 99, 3042, 3085
Antoniazzi, A. 1801
Anzai, S. 1456, 1457, 1470
Apel, W.D. 2751

Apostal, R.A. 1204
Appadurai, A. 6
Aquina, M. 949, 2638
Arbuckle, G. 950
Archer, A. 2310
Archer, M. 3198
Arjomand, S.A. 547, 548, 549,
711, 712, 713, 714, 715, 716
Armstrong, P.F. 65
Arnold, P. 1791
Arrington, L.J. 2830, 2862
Asch, S. 2643
Assad, M.M. 763
Atherton, J.S. 2413
Attal, R. 300, 301
Augustine, D. 1014
Austruy, J. 550, 614
Aviad, J. 369
Avila, R. 1878
Awada, H. 717
Ayalon, H. 391
Azaria, R. 260

B

Baan, M.A. 1471, 1581
Babb, L.A. 7
Babbie, E.R. 189, 1941
Baccouche, H. 551
Bachi, R. 323, 370
Baechler, J. 2962
Baer, H.A. 2931, 2932, 2933,
3021, 3022
Baeta, C. 2997
Bahr, H.M. 2863, 2894, 2897,
2898
Bahr, S.J. 2863
Bainbridge, W.S. 2947, 2977, 2980,
2981, 2982, 2985, 3028, 3093,
3188
Balch, R.W. 3036, 3037, 3038,
3039, 3040, 3199
Balic, S. 552
Ball, P. 1897
Ballard, C. 228
Ballard, R. 228
Balswick, J. 814, 2045, 2046,
2585, 2586
Baltzell, E.D. 2103
Banks, L.L. 1868
Bannan, R.S. 405

Banowsky, W.S. 2560
Barclay, H.B. 680, 2158, 2196
Bardis, P. 230, 406
Barker, E. 3043, 3044, 3045, 3046,
3047, 3048, 3049, 3050, 3051
Barkun, M. 2486
Bar-Lev, M. 382
Barnes, M.H. 1684
Barnes, S.H. 1685
Baron, R.R. 261
Barrett, D.B. 1964, 2631, 2632, 2633
Barrett, J.E. 1012
Barrett, L.E. 3149, 3150
Barron, M.L. 407
Barthel, D.L. 2551
Bass, D.C. 2572
Bastenier, A. 682
Bastian, J.-P. 1996, 1997, 1998, 2015,
2326
Bastide, R. 681, 2000, 3005, 3100,
3101, 3114, 3126, 3127
Bataillon, M. 951
Batiuk, M.E. 878
Batra, S.M. 8, 9
Baubérot, J. 2745
Bauer, J. 262, 310, 540
Bax, M. 1582
Baxter, J. 2311
Bayyumi, M.A.M. 615
Bean, F.D. 1962
Bean, L.L. 2899
Bechert, H. 121, 201
Beck, C.S. 2328
Becker, T. 1205
Beckers, G. 2085
Beckford, J.A. 2490, 2491, 2492, 2493,
2494, 2495, 2496, 2497, 2908, 3052,
3053, 3054, 3055
Bedell, K.B. 2726
Bedouelle, G. 1898
Bel, A. 627
Bélanger, P. 1686
Bell, B.D. 2340
Bell, R. 1281
Bellah, R.N. 222, 553, 554, 2864
Bemmann, H. 2457
Bendix, R. 1073
Bennett, J.W. 2171, 2172
Benoit, A. 1861, 1862
Ben-Rafael, E. 391
Bensimon, D. 324, 325
Bentley, J. 1899

Ben-Yehuda, N.  2948
Berg, B.  434
Berg, P.L.  2056, 2690
Bergen, J.  2197
Berger, A.L.  530
Berger, M.  616
Berger, P.L.  231, 2114, 2115,
  2664, 3200, 3201
Bergeron, C.  1687
Bergmann, H.  705
Bergmann, W.  726
Bernard, G.  2634, 2644, 2645
Bernard, R.  1038
Berque, J.  555, 556
Berry, B.D.  2109
Berzano, L.  1557
Besanceney, P.H.  1094
Bessière, G.  1494
Betts, G.H.  1937
Beyer, P.  1688, 1689
Beynon, E.D.  689
Bharadwaj, L.  77
Bharati, A.  10
Bhuriya, M.  3140
Bibby, R.W.  1926, 1927, 2746, 2761,
  2762, 2763
Bideau, A.  2034
Biernatzki, W.E.  1459
Billette, A.  1095
Billings, T.A.  2159
Bindereif, E.  1543
Binöder, C.  2458
Birman, P.  3115, 3128
Birnbaum, N.  1965
Black, A.W.  2095, 2567, 2582, 2583
Blackburn, R.T.  1257
Blacker, C.  190
Blake, J.  1096, 1349
Blake, R.H.  2884
Blanc de la Fontaine, M.  1495
Blanchard, D.A.  2341, 2342
Blanchard, J.L.  1934
Blasi, A.J.  727, 728, 793, 1206,
  1207, 1208, 2075
Blass, J.H.  408
Blau, J.L.  409, 410
Blazowich, A.  952
Bloch-Hoell, N.  2370
Bock, G.E.  411
Bock, R.C.  2817
Bocock, R.J.  702, 1900, 1901,
  1902
Bode, J.G.  1209

Bodzenta, E.  1475
Bogan, R.V.  853
Bok, W.  263, 326
Boldt, E.D.  2173, 2183
Boling, T.E.  1210, 2283, 2284, 2285
Bolino, A.C.  2831
Bonmariage, J.  831
Bonn, R.L.  1938
Boorman, S.A.  1344
Bopegamage, A.  130
Bord, R.J.  879, 880
Borges Costa, E.  2001, 2002
Bormann, G.  2019, 2020, 2021
Borowski, K.H.  1604, 2587, 2588
Bosk, C.L.  531, 532
Bossard, J.H.S.  2053
Bouhdiba, A.  557
Boulard, F.  1558
Bouma, D.H.  2147
Bouma, G.D.  2141, 2148, 2149
Bouvier, L.F.  1211, 1212, 1213, 1214
Bowdern, T.S.  1015, 1016, 1017
Bowman, J.F.  1039
Braden, C.S.  2537, 2943
Bradfield, C.D.  2035, 2450, 2451, 2452
Braga, G.  1559
Braswell, G.W.  718
Braude, L.  412, 413
Brechon, P.  1496
Breckenridge, C.A.  6
Breckwoldt, R.  79
Breiger, R.L.  1344
Brekke, M.L.  2040
Brenner, R.R.  264
Bressan, V.  1640
Bressler, M.  1097
Brewer, E.D.C.  2331, 2332, 2333
Briefs, G.  794
Brinkerhoff, D.B.  2848
Brinkerhoff, M.B.  2746, 2762, 2763,
  2798, 2865
Brodbar-Nemzer, J.  414
Brohm, J.F.  138
Bromley, D.G.  66, 80, 795, 3056, 3057,
  3058, 3059, 3060, 3061, 3062, 3063,
  3064, 3086, 3087, 3088
Bronsztejin, S.  327, 328
Brothers, J.  1641
Brotz, H.  351
Broughton, W.  1939
Brown, D.  3116
Brown, D.W.  2872
Brown, J.  1657

Brown, R.L. 2273, 2274
Brown, S. 1643
Browne, J.P. 953, 1350
Brownstein, H.H. 415
Bruce, S. 110, 2093, 2096, 2101, 2758, 2759, 2760, 2764, 2765, 2766, 2792
Bruneau, T.C. 1802, 1803, 1804, 1805
Brunetta, G. 954, 1351
Brunt, L. 2082
Bryk, A.S. 1396
Bryman, A. 1642, 1660, 1903, 1904
Buck, R.C. 2160
Buckle, R. 2866
Buetow, H.A. 1215
Bukouski, A.F. 1040
Bull, M. 2526
Bumpass, L. 1342
Bunis, W. 2754
Bunker, G.L. 2867, 2868
Büntig, A.J. 1785, 1786, 1787
Burch, G.W. 2577
Burch, T.K. 1175, 1682
Burchinal, L.G. 1098
Bureau, R. 3169
Burgalassi, S. 1560, 1561, 1562, 1563
Burnham, K.E. 416, 2363
Burns, J.E. 2221
Burns, M.S. 1041
Burns, W.H. 690
Burton, F.P. 1666
Burton, L. 2312
Burton, R. 1421, 2691
Busching, B.C. 3063
Busjan, C. 1806

C

Cable, S. 2799
Cabral, C. 1807
Caceres Prendes, J. 1884, 1885
Caillat, C. 217
Calabro, W.V. 955
Caldarola, C. 2647
Calkins, S. 2912
Calley, M.J.C. 2407, 2408
Camara, E.M. 3102
Campbell, B.F. 3027
Campbell, C. 2949
Campbell, D.F. 1928

Campbell, T.C. 2573
Campolo, A. 2275
Camps, A. 651, 652
Canning, R.R. 2873
Cannon, K.L. 2849, 2869
Cantril, H. 1018
Capitanchik, D.B. 371
Caplan, L. 2692
Caporale, R. 1000, 1001, 1002
Carden, M.L. 3195
Cardwell, J.D. 1278
Carey, S. 81, 111
Carli, R. 956
Carlin, J.E. 417
Carrasco, S. 1617
Carrasco Malhue, P. 1999
Carré, O. 558
Carrier, H. 1099
Carroll, J.W. 1980
Carroll, M.P. 933, 934, 935, 1352
Carron, J. 1869
Carstairs, G.M. 11
Cartaxo, F. 1840
Carter, L.F. 106
Casanova, A. 1003
Cashmore, E. 3151
Cassidy, S.W. 2398
Castellani, B. 1578
Castelli, J. 1371
Castelli, Y. 2993
Castiglione, M. 881
Castillo, J.J. 1618
Catton, W.R. 1981
Causse, A. 232
Cavalcanti, M.L.V. 3103
Cavan, R.S. 418
Cavanaugh, M.A. 2665
Cavanaugh, M.J. 1358
Cayrac-Blanchard, F. 633
Centro de Estudios Cristianos 398
Cesar, W. 2003
Cestello, B.D. 1042
Chadwick, B.A. 1353, 2861
Chafetz, J.S. 889
Chagnon, R. 67, 882, 2983, 2984
Chakravarti, U. 126
Chamberlayne, J.H. 2313
Champion, F. 3094
Chapman, S.H. 1019
Charârâ, W. 673
Charnay, J.-P. 559, 560, 561, 562
Chartain, F. 1870
Charuty, G. 883

Chaudhuri, B.  12
Chaunu, P.  1990
Chelhod, J.  563, 564
Ch'en, K.  131
Chesebro, S.E.  2198
Chesneaux, J.  3170
Chi, S.K.  2693
Chidester, D.  2963
Child, J.  2466
Choate, D.A.  2754
Choi, S.-D.  2371, 3065
Chopra, S.  653
Chou, R.  1643
Chouraqui, A.  302
Christensen, H.T.  2818, 2849, 2869
Christiansen, J.R.  2850
Christiansen, J.W.  2851
Christina, M.  1020
Christopherson, V.A.  419, 2832, 2833
Christy, R.D.  2257
Chung, C.S.  3165
Cieslak, M.J.  1354
Cipriani, R.  1564
Cizon, F.A.  1043
Clark, J.  2870
Clark, R.E.  2935
Clark, S.D.  2258, 2324
Clarke, P.B.  703, 704
Clasby, M.  1170
Clear, V.  2362
Clelland, D.A.  2752
Clément, J.-F.  623
Clemente, F.  1216
Clow, H.K.  2404
Clyde, R.W.  1288
Coakley, J.J.  1149
Coates, C.H.  1982
Coffey, H.  2868
Coggins, W.T.  1995
Cohen, M.  329, 884, 885
Cohen, P.S.  372
Cohen, S.M.  420, 452
Cohen, S.A.  352
Cohn, W.  2372, 2498
Coiner, H.G.  2070
Coleman, J.A.  1355, 1356, 1380
Coleman, J.S.  1583
Coleman, S.  2720
Collins, D.F.  1217
Condominas, G.  139
Conkin, P.K.  2174
Connelly, J.T.  886
Connors, J.F.  416

Contigualia, C.  1565
Coogan, T.  1025
Cooper, C.W.  2574
Cooper, L.R.  2499
Cornwall, M.  2896, 2900, 2901, 2902, 2903
Coser, L.  957, 2964
Coser, R.  2964
Cosper, R.  1792
Costa, F.  3129
Cote, P.  887, 929
Coughlin, R.J.  140
Cousin, B.  936
Coxon, A.P.M.  1905, 1906, 1925
Crahan, M.E.  1879
Crapo, R.H.  2904
Creevey, L.E.  628
Crespi, F.  956
Crespi, I.  1100
Crockett, H.J.  1265
Cross, R.D.  1044
Cross, S.  2500, 2501
Cross, W.M.  2063
Crow, K.E.  2365
Cruise O'Brien, D.B.  706, 707, 708
Cryns, A.G.  1218
Crysdale, S.  1690, 2568
Culligan, M.J.  958
Culver, D.  2334
Cummings, D.  2528, 2529
Cuneo, M.W.  872, 1683, 1691, 1692, 2075, 3189
Cunningham, P.H.  2896, 2903
Curcione, N.R.  959, 1219
Currie, R.  2307
Currin, T.E.V.  1436
Curtis, J.H.  1045
Curtis, T.  3085
Cutler, S.J.  2814


D

Dahm, C.W.  1220
Dahm, K.-W.  2018
Daiber, K.F.  2022
Da Matta e Silva, W.  3117
Damboriena, P.  1991, 1992, 1993, 2423
Damrell, J.  114
Daner, F.J.  82, 83
Daniel, M.  1907
Daniel, Y.  1497
Danigelis, N.  1473

Dann, G.M.S. 796, 797, 3118
Dann, N.K. 2352, 2353
Dantas, B.G. 3104
D'Antonio, W.V. 1164, 1357, 1358, 1359
Darian, J.C. 127
Darrand, T.C. 2373
Dashefsky, A. 373, 421, 422, 510
Da Silva, J.F.B. 1808, 1809
Dassetto, F. 682
Dator, J.A. 191
Datta, J.M. 13, 14
Datunashvili, I.I. 683
Davidson, J.D. 1359, 2261, 2262
Davies, D.J. 2871
Davies, J.K. 2852
Davis, E. 617
Davis, R. 2609, 2622
Day, L.H. 1447
Dealy, G.C. 1740
Dean, W.H. 2834
Dearman, M.V. 2447, 2448
De Azevedo, T. 1810, 1811, 1812
De Bonte, W. 960
De Camargo, C.P.F. 1813, 1814, 3006, 3007, 3008, 3009
Decker, C.C. 2335
De Craemer, W. 1437, 3134, 3135, 3136
Deelen, G.J. 1815, 1816
Deets, L.E. 2175
Degand, A. 1481
Degive, C. 888
DeHart, W.A. 2819
DeJong, G.F. 1101, 2694, 2695
De Jong, J.A. 1360
DeKadt, E.J. 1817
Delacroix, S. 1498
Del Grande, M.V. 1102
Deliège, R. 937
Dellacava, F.A. 1221, 1222
Della Fave, L.R. 1361
Della Pergola, S. 330
Dellepoort, J.J. 1476, 1584
Deluz, C. 798
Demarest, J.L. 2538
De Medina, C.A. 1818
Demerath, N.J. 2036, 2679
Dempsey, K.C. 2325, 2666
Denault, B. 1693
Denhardt, R.B. 1223
Denni, B. 1496
DeNood, N.B. 2539

Denton, P. 2686
De Oliveira, G. 1819
Dericquebourg, R. 2502
Derks, F. 68
De Rosa, G. 1566
Deshen, S.A. 374, 375
Desmangles, L.G. 3158, 3159
De Souza, M. 2415
De Souza Martins, H.H.T. 1820
Desroche, H. 2176, 2177, 2646, 3190, 3196
DeVallée, T. 938
Dever, J.P. 2286
Dewey, G.J. 1103
Dewitt, R.L. 2033
Dhooghe, J. 1970
Diaz Mozaz, J.M. 1619
Di Bella, M.P. 2405
Dickson, L. 1302
Dienel, P. 2250
Dinges, W.D. 873, 874, 875, 876
Ditzler, J.R. 1204
Dixon, R.C. 1224
Dobbelaere, K. 1482, 1483, 1484, 1485, 1486, 2503, 3091
Dobratz, B.A. 771
Dobretsberger, J. 565
Dohen, D. 1104, 1886, 1887
Doherty, J.F. 1458
Doherty, R.W. 2467, 2468
Done, G.B. 2820, 2821
Donegani, J.-M. 1499
Donovan, D.C. 1360
Donovan, J.D. 799, 1046, 1047, 1105, 1106
Donus, R.B. 761
Don-Yehiya, E. 385, 386
Doratis, D. 1454
Dornbusch, S.M. 2117
Doucas, M. 3085
Dougherty, D. 1107, 1108
Doutreloux, A. 888
Downton, J.V. 69, 70
Doyle, D.M. 1684
Doyle, K. 1088
Doyle, R.T. 1938
Driedger, L. 311, 2151, 2188, 2195, 2199, 2200, 2201, 2202, 2203, 2204, 2205, 2206, 2207, 2208, 2209, 2210, 2211, 2212, 2213, 2214
Dubb, A.A. 2635
Dudley, C.J. 961
Dudley, M.G. 2530

Dudley, R.L.  2527, 2528, 2529, 2530
Dukar, A.G.  423
Duke, J.T.  2872, 2905, 2914
Dulfano, M.J.  399
Dulong, R.  1004
Dumont, L.  15
Dumont-Johnson, M.  1694
Dundon, M.C.  1225
Dunn, S.P.  331
Duocastella, R.  1620, 1621, 1622
DuPertuis, L.  71, 72
Durán, K.  566
Durham, G.H.  2822
Dussell, E.  1993
Duvignaud, J.  629
Dyble, J.E.  1945, 1983, 2137
Dye, E.  2504

E

Earle, C.J.  2118
Ebaugh, H.R.F.  889, 890, 1226, 1227, 1362, 1363, 1364, 2767
Eberhard, W.  654
Eberley, S.  2914
Eccel, A.C.  567, 568
Eckstein, S.  1775
Ediger, M.  2161
Edwards, H.  691
Ehrentraut, A.  223
Eighmy, J.L.  2287, 2288
Eister, A.W.  655, 2653, 2654
Elazar, D.J.  424, 425, 544
Elifson, K.W.  2289
Elinson, H.  2374
Ellickson, J.  656
Ellspermann, C.  1048
Ellwood, R.S.  2589
Emmons, C.F.  2950, 2951
Endres, M.E.  1005
England, R.W.  2540
Engleman, U.Z.  332, 426, 427
Ennis, J.G.  1228
Enroth, R.M.  2590
Ericson, E.E.  2590
Erickson, K.T.  2104
Escobar, F.  1758
Estrada, I.  1776
Estruch, J.  1487
Ethridge, F.M.  2558
Etzioni, A.  376

Etzioni-Halevy, E.  265, 377
Evans, R.H.  1567
Everett, R.F.  1988
Evers, H.-D.  141, 160
Ewer, P.A.  2343
Ezcurra, A.M.  2768

F

Faase, T.P.  962, 963, 964, 965
Fabian, J.  3137
Facey, P.W.  1056
Fagerstrom, M.F.  3029
Fahey, F.J.  785, 788, 789, 790, 1049
Falardeau, J.-C.  1695
Fallding, H.  1978
Faouzi, A.  610
Farnsworth, G.  3199
Fasola-Bologna, A.  1568
Fathi, A.  569
Faue, J.L.  2121
Faulkner, J.E.  879, 880, 1101
Fauset, A.  684
Fay, L.F.  1109, 1229, 1230
Feagin, J.R.  1110, 2290, 2558
Featherman, D.L.  428
Fecher, C.J.  966
Fedele, M.  800
Fee, J.L.  939, 1231
Feitelson, D.  304
Femminella, F.X.  1111
Ference, T.P.  854, 1240, 1241, 1316
Ferguson, D.W.  233
Fernandez Vasquez, R.  1888
Fernando, C.  161
Fernando, T.  162
Fichter, J.H.  801, 855, 856, 857, 858, 891, 892, 1050, 1051, 1052, 1053, 1054, 1055, 1056, 1112, 1113, 1114, 1115, 1232, 1365, 1366, 1367, 1368, 1544, 1845, 3066, 3067
Field, C.D.  2314, 2315
Finke, R.  1369
Finkelstein, L.  266
Finkler, K.  3014, 3015, 3016
Fireside, H.  776, 777
Fischoff, E.  234
Fisher, V.  1088
Fishman, A.  267, 268
Fiske, A.M.  132
Fistié, P.  634
Fitch, B.  1092

Fleming, J.J.   2727
Fletcher, J.E.   433
Fletcher, W.C.   778, 779
Flora, C.B.   2430, 2431
Floridi, A.U.   1741
Fogarty, J.C.   1370
Foley, A.S.   1057
Follett, E.J.N.   2835
Foote, R.L.   312
Ford, T.R.   2695, 2696
Foss, D.A.   73
Fosselman, D.H.   1058, 1059
Foster, B.D.   1960
Foster, L.   2906
Fox, J.T.   1116
Fox, R.J.   2584
Fox, S.W.   1314
Fox, W.S.   1233, 1265
Francis, E.K.   967, 2185, 2215
Francis, L.J.   1908, 1909
Franda, M.F.   16
Freedman, M.   353
Freemesser, G.F.   2375
Freiberg, J.W.   210, 211
Frerking, K.   2037, 2038
Fretz, J.W.   2189, 2190, 2213, 2216
Freund, W.S.   570
Frideres, J.S.   313, 2178
Friedman, N.L.   429
Friesen, D.   2197
Frigolé Reixach, J.   1623
Froese, L.   2186
Fry, P.   2316
Fukuyama, Y.   2110, 2573, 2575, 2576
Funk, A.   729
Furman, F.K.   430, 431


G

Gaborieau, M.   657, 658, 659, 660, 661
Gabovitch, B.   378
Gabriel, K.   802
Gadille, J.   940
Gaede, S.   1234, 2217, 2218
Gager, J.G.   730
Galilea, C.   1846
Gallagher, C.F.   1624
Galloway, R.   2123
Gallup, G.   1371
Gandhi, R.S.   17, 218, 571

Gannon, T.M.   968, 969, 1235, 1236, 1237, 1372, 2800
Gans, H.J.   432
Gardet, L.   572
Garre, D.   1780
Garrido, G.   1856, 1883
Garrison, B.   1423
Garrison, C.E.   2561
Garrison, V.   1238
Gaudet, R.   1696, 1727, 1728
Gaustad, E.S.   2562
Gauthier, M.   3095
Gay, J.   1644
Gedicks, A.   1943
Geller, H.   1534
Gellner, D.   18
Gellner, E.   573, 611, 624, 625
Gendarme, R.   612
Gephart, J.C.   433
Gerlach, L.P.   2376, 2377
Germain-Brodeur, E.   1697
Gerrard, N.L.   2453
Gerry, K.M.   1385
Gershuny, T.   306
Gerth, H.H.   2657
Gessner, J.C.   1239
Gheddo, P.   142
Ghesquierre-Waelkens, M.   1486
Gibbs, J.O.   2343
Gilette, A.   2907
Gilfeather, K.   1846, 1847, 1848, 1849
Gillard, J.T.   1021
Gillin, J.L.   2463
Gillis, A.R.   314
Gilsenan, M.   618, 619, 620
Ginsberg, M.   333
Giuriati, P.   1569
Gladstone, J.W.   19
Glanz, D.   379
Glass, J.C.   2344
Glassner, B.   434
Glazer, N.   435, 436
Glazier, S.D.   3152
Glenn, N.D.   1117
Glick, S.   115
Glock, C.Y.   1118, 1119, 1940, 1941, 1955, 1960, 2039
Gockel, G.L.   437
Goddijn, H.P.M.   970, 1006
Goddijn, W.   1006, 1585
Godoy, H.H.   1742
Golding, G.   2728
Goldman, M.   3130

Goldmann, L. 932
Goldner, F.H. 854, 1240, 1241, 1316
Golds, J. 1188
Goldscheider, C. 438, 439, 442, 1196
Goldsmith, P. 2437
Goldstein, J.E. 313
Goldstein, R. 1645, 1646
Goldstein, S. 440, 441, 442
Gollin, G.L. 2459, 2460
Golomb, E. 1545
Gombrich, R. 163
Gonzáles de Zarate, R.M. 192
Gonzalez Nieves, R.O. 1373, 1374
Gonzalez Seara, L. 1625
Goode, E. 2111, 2112
Goodman, F.D. 2432, 2433
Goodridge, R.M. 1910
Gordon, D.F. 2591, 2592, 2593, 2594
Gordon, L. 443
Göricke, F. 765
Gottwald, N.K. 235, 236
Gould, J. 444
Goulding, J.W. 2957
Goussidis, A. 767
Gräbner, J. 3160
Grace, J.H. 3068
Grady, L.A. 1120
Graebner, A. 2064
Granet, M. 212
Graupe, S.R. 1480
Greeley, A.M. 445, 446, 803, 939, 1121, 1122, 1123, 1124, 1125, 1126, 1127, 1128, 1129, 1130, 1131, 1132, 1133, 1134, 1135, 1136, 1181, 1189, 1242, 1243, 1244, 1245, 1246, 1247, 1248, 1249, 1250, 1251, 1322, 1375, 1376, 1377, 1378, 1380, 2263
Green, H.A. 3178
Greenwold, S.M. 133, 134
Greer, S. 1137
Gregg, R.G. 2595
Gregory, A. 1821, 1822, 1831
Greil, A.L. 780
Greinacher, N. 1535, 1536, 1546
Grichting, W.L. 1138, 1139
Griffin, J.J. 1252
Griffin, R.J. 893
Griswold, A.W. 2944
Groat, H.T. 1253
Grond, L. 1471, 1476

Groner, F. 1547
Gros, L. 1500
Grumelli, A. 804
Grunewald, T. 279
Gundlach, G. 971
Gupta, K.P. 20, 112
Gustafsson, B. 1971, 2029
Gustafsson, G. 2030
Gustavus, S.O. 2885
Guth, J.L. 2291, 2292
Guttmann, J. 237, 269
Gutwirth, J. 315, 533, 534, 535, 1823, 2477, 2965
Guzman Garcia, L. 1880

H

Haar, G. 1438
Hack, D.H. 2191
Hadaway, C.K. 2126, 2137
Haddad, J. 674
Haddad, Y. 685
Hadden, J.K. 1942, 1948, 2119, 2338, 2674, 2769, 2770, 2771, 3079
Hadj-sadok, M. 613
Hadot, J. 731
Hadzimichali, N. 768
Haerle, R.K. 1140
Hagan, R.A. 107
Hagopian, E.C. 626
Hale, H. 2345
Halebsky, S. 2779
Halevi, H.S. 334
Halevy, Z. 265
Halford, L.J. 2935
Hall, D.T. 1254
Hall, J.R. 2966, 2967, 2968, 2969
Halvorson, P.L. 492
Hamelin, L.-E. 1698, 1699
Hamès, C. 574, 686
Hamm, P.M. 2219
Hammond, J.A. 894
Hammond, P.E. 1943, 2113, 2667, 2729, 2730, 2772, 2773
Hampshire, A.P. 2908
Haney, C.A. 2767
Hanna, M.T. 1255
Hannigan, J.A. 1669
Hardacre, H. 3096
Harder, L.D. 2220, 2230
Harder, M.W. 2596, 2597, 2598, 2599, 2611, 2616, 2617

Hardin, B.L.  3069, 3070, 3071
Hare, A.P.  2469
Hargrove, B.W.  2120
Harper, C.L.  895, 2600, 2801
Harper, E.B.  21
Harrison, M.I.  379, 447, 476,
  477, 896, 897, 898, 899, 900,
  901
Harrison, P.M.  2276
Hart, S.  2057
Harte, T.C.  1022
Harte, T.J.  1060
Hartley, S.F.  1944
Hartman, M.  380
Hartman, P.A.  2952
Hartman, W.J.  2346
Harvey, A.  1929
Harwood, A.  3017
Hasegawa, C.  175
Hashimoto, H.  193
Hassenger, R.  1141, 1142, 1143,
  1144, 1145
Hastings, D.W.  2873
Hawley, F.  2438
Hawthorn, H.B.  2648
Haywood, C.L.  3023
Hazelrigg, L.E.  1570
Heaton, T.B.  2895, 2909, 2910,
  2911, 2912
Hébert, G.  2505
Heenan, E.F.  2058
Heeren, J.  2913
Heesterman, J.C.  22
Hégy, P.  805, 806, 902
Heilman, S.C.  448, 449, 450, 451,
  452
Heimer, D.D.  1256
Heimert, A.  2105
Heinerman, J.  2787
Heinz, D.J.  2601, 2602, 2774
Heirich, M.  903
Helmreich, W.B.  453
Hendricks, J.S.  2697
Henlein, G.A.  1257
Henney, J.H.  2433
Henry, P.  575
Herb, T.R.  2293
Herberg, W.  454, 455
Herbison, H.  2649
Herman, N.J.  1930
Hermassi, E.  576
Herskovits, M.J.  3131
Hertel, B.R.  23, 24

Hewitt, W.E.  1743, 1824, 1825, 1826
Heyer, F.  765
Hiatt, L.R.  103
Hicks, F.  1871
Hicks, T.H.  1379
Higgins, E.  1439
Hill, C.  2409, 2655
Hill, M.  972, 1911, 2317, 2318, 2323
Hill, R.  2853
Hill, S.S.  2775, 2791
Hiller, H.H.  2271
Hillery, G.A.  116, 961, 973, 1361
Hilty, D.M.  2221
Himmelfarb, H.S.  456, 457, 458, 459,
  460, 461, 462
Hine, L.D.  2277
Hine, V.H.  2377, 2378, 2379, 2380
Hinings, B.  1660
Hinings, C.R.  1904
Hirabayashi, G.K.  2650
Hirikoshi, H.  635
Hoben, A.  766
Hoc, J.M.N.-H.  807
Hoffer, T.  1355, 1356, 1380
Hoffman, D.  2260
Hofman, J.E.  2065
Hoge, D.R.  1224, 1258, 1259, 1359,
  1381, 1382, 1383, 1384, 1385, 1386,
  1387, 1403, 1413, 1430, 1945, 1983,
  2121, 2125, 2127, 2128, 2137, 2579
Holl, A.  1477
Hollenweger, W.J.  2381
Holleran, M.P.  1875
Hollingshead, A.B.  3020
Holmes, B.  84
Holstein, M.A.  238
Holt, J.B.  2354
Holtzapple, V.R.  194
Homan, R.  1912, 1913, 2382, 2383
Homola, M.  463, 464
Hong, L.K.  213, 1146
Hong, S.-K.  3166
Honigsheim, P.  808
Hood, R.W.  2278, 2698
Hood, T.C.  2752
Hook, W.F.  2054, 2055, 2059
Hoonaert, E.  1827
Horinouchi, I.  176
Hornsby-Smith, M.P.  1647, 1648, 1649,
  1650, 1651, 1652, 1653, 1654, 1655,
  1656, 1657
Horowitz, I.L.  270, 400, 3072, 3073,
  3074, 3075

Horowitz, M.M.  3171
Horrigan, J.P.  1700, 1701
Hostetler, J.A.  2162, 2163, 2179,
  2222, 2223
Hostie, R.  974, 975
Houghland, J.G.  1984, 2336
Hourmant, L.  195
Houseknecht, S.K.  2693
Houtart, F.  25, 26, 128, 135, 164,
  202, 271, 791, 809, 810, 1007,
  1061, 1062, 1063, 1064, 1464,
  1465, 1466, 1468, 1469, 1472,
  1488, 1579, 1744, 1745, 1746,
  1747, 1784
Howe, G.N.  2416
Hudson, C.  2699
Hudson, J.W.  443
Hughes, J.E.  846
Huizenga, B.N.  2150
Hulett, J.E.  2823, 2824, 2825
Humphreys, C.  1260
Hunsberger, B.  1702
Hunt, C.L.  811
Hunt, J.G.  1261, 1262, 1263, 1264
Hunt, L.L.  1261, 1262, 1263, 1264
Hunter, J.D.  2730, 2731, 2732,
  2733, 2734, 2735, 2736, 2776,
  2777
Huntington, A.G.E.  2164
Huotari, V.  2027
Hutjes, J.M.  1586
Hyland, R.  1117
Hynes, E.  1065
Hynes, Eu.  1670, 1671


I

Ibrahim, S.E.  621, 622
Imse, T.P.  812
Indradeva, S.  27
Inglis, T.  1672, 1673
Ingram, L.C.  2122, 2294, 2295,
  2296, 2753
Iqbal, S.M.  577
Irle, R.  2117
Isambert, F.-A.  813, 1501, 1502
Isichei, E.A.  2470, 2471


J

Jabbour, M.E.  3097

Jacks, I.  465
Jackson, A.R.  2700
Jackson, D.H.  3028
Jackson, E.F.  1233, 1265
Jackson, L.F.  2531
Jacob, J.C.  2798
Jacobs, A.K.  2737
Jacobs, N.  719
Jacobson, C.K.  2603
Jacobson, D.  2076
Jadin, L.  3132, 3133
Jaeckels, R.  1066
Jain, S.P.  28
Jai Singh, H.  662
James, W.R.  1147
Jammes, J.-M.  1067
Janosik, R.J.  2636
Jansen, R.  1882
Janson, E.  1028
Jarvie, I.C.  3141, 3142
Jeffrey, R.  29
Jeffries, V.  1266
Jelen, T.G.  2701, 2702
Jensen, G.F.  1388
Jim-chang im, L.  1459
Jiminez Cadena, G.  1863
Jioultsis, B.  769
Joffe, N.F.  335
Johnson, A.L.  2040
Johnson, B.L.  2905, 2914
Johnson, B.  2264, 2265, 2355, 2356,
  2668, 2669
Johnson, B.R.  1684
Johnson, C.L.  904
Johnson, D.P.  2970
Johnson, G.  85, 86
Johnson, J.G.  2066
Johnson, J.M.  2750
Johnson, M.A.  2867, 2868
Johnson, N.R.  2754
Johnson, R.A.  2060
Johnson, S.D.  1421, 2691, 2721, 2722,
  2778, 2779, 2802, 2803, 2812
Johnson, W.R.  2329
Johnson, W.T.  491
Johnston, H.  3030
Johnstone, R.L.  1267, 2041, 2042
Jolicoeur, P.M.  3184
Jolson, A.J.  1602
Jones, D.C.  2357
Jones, D.M.  2345
Jones, E.F.  1343
Jones, L.A.  1268, 2308

Jones, P.B. 2297
Jones, R.K. 2487, 3186
Jones, W.R. 1914
Jorgensen, D.L. 2953, 2971
Jorstad, E. 2604
Jubber, K. 2086, 2506
Jud, G.J. 2577
Judah, J.S. 87, 88
Judge, E.A. 732
Juergensmeyer, M. 105
Jules-Rosette, B. 2639, 2640,
  2641, 2642
Just, L.R. 2224
Juyal, B.N. 30


K

Kahoe, R.D. 2298
Kaill, R.C. 1931
Kaiser, M.A. 1269
Kalansuriya, A.D.P. 165
Káldi, G. 1552
Kallen, E. 316, 317, 318
Kan, S. 2924
Kanavy, M.J. 1419
Kane, J.J. 1023, 1068, 1069
Kang, W.J. 3167
Kantowsky, D. 31
Kanwar, M.A. 663
Kaplan, B.H. 2384
Kaplan, H.B. 2375
Kaplan, H.M. 692
Karady, V. 336, 337
Karcher, B.C. 814
Karg, S. 2251
Kaser, G. 2478
Kashima, T. 177
Katz, E. 381
Kauffman, J.H. 2210, 2225, 2226,
  2227, 2228, 2229, 2230
Kauffmann, M. 859
Kaufman, E.G. 2231
Kaufmann, F.-X. 802
Kayal, P.M. 762
Keane, R.C. 905
Kedourie, E. 578
Kee, H.C. 733
Keene, J.J. 3202
Kehrer, G. 3069, 3070
Keller, H.E. 1537
Kelley, D.M. 2780, 2781
Kelly, G.A. 1024, 1025

Kelly, H.E. 1270
Kelly, J.R. 466, 1271, 1272, 1273,
  1274, 1275, 1276, 1277, 1389, 1390,
  1391, 1392, 1393
Kenkel, W.F. 1098
Kennedy, R.D. 1070
Kennedy, R.E. 221
Kenny, C.T. 1949
Kent, S.A. 2472, 2473
Kersten, L.K. 2043
Kessler, C.S. 636
Kessler, R.C. 1201
Keyes, C.F. 143
Khalsa, K.S. 74
Kiernan, J. 1440
Kiev, A. 2410
Kilbourne, B.K. 3076
Kilgore, S.B. 1356
Kim, G. 1394
Kimbrough, S.T. 239
Kimmel, M.S. 720
King, A. 2252
King, M. 2345
Kippenberg, H.G. 240, 3179
Kistler, R.C. 1982
Kitay, P.M. 2782
Kitson, G.C. 2282
Kitzinger, S. 3153, 3154
Klass, M. 3171
Klemmack, D.L. 1278
Klever, G.L. 2128
Klibanov, A.I. 2253
Kliewer, F. 2192
Kloetzli, W. 2044
Kloppenburg, B. 3010, 3011, 3119
Knisely, E.C. 1253
Kniss, F. 2152
Knowles, L.L. 3184
Knudsen, D. 463, 464
Knudten, R.D. 2266
Kohls, M. 303
Kokosalakis, N. 770
Koller, D.B. 1279
Koller, N.B. 1985
Kollmorgen, W.M. 2165
Kolm, S.C. 122
König, W. 1448
Konstantinov, D. 781
Kosa, J. 1071, 1148, 1184
Koss, J.D. 3018, 3019
Köster, R. 2023, 2024
Kotre, J.N. 1280
Kourvetaris, G.A. 771

440

Koval, J. 1281
Kowalewski, D. 780, 2254
Krajzman, M. 338
Kramer, J.R. 467
Kramer, T.J. 1433
Kratcoski, P.C. 1282
Krause, A.E. 2193
Krausz, E. 272, 354, 355, 356, 357,
  358, 359, 382
Kreissig, H. 734
Kreuer, W. 3172
Krishna, G. 664, 665
Kroll-Smith, J.S. 2358
Kuner, W. 63, 64, 2623, 3071
Kunz, P.R. 2854
Kurokawa, M. 2233, 2234
Kurtz, L.R. 944, 945, 946
Kurz, J.T. 987
Kyrtatas, D. 735


L

La Barre, W. 2454
Labbens, J. 3009
Labelle, Y. 1757, 1777
Ladrière, P. 339, 1008
Laeyendecker, L. 1587
La Fave, L. 2509
Lafaye, J. 1778
LaGuerre, M.S. 3161, 3162
Lalive d'Epinay, C. 1748, 1749,
  1994, 2004, 2012, 2013, 2014,
  2424, 2425, 2426, 2427, 2456
Lally, J.J. 1283
Laloux, J. 976, 1489
La Magdeleine, D. 2660
LaMagdeleine, D.R. 1395
Lamanna, R.A. 1149
Lamar, R.E. 2703
Lambert, Y. 1503, 1504
Lampe, P. 736
Lampe, P.E. 1284, 1285, 1286,
  1287
Lampinen, T. 2028
Lane, C.O. 782, 2651
Lane, R. 906, 907, 1150, 1151
Lang, G. 241
Langrod, G. 815
Lanternari, V. 3143
Larkin, R.W. 73
Larson, D.E. 2267
Larson, R.F. 1072

LaRuffa, A.L. 2434
Lasker, A.A. 468
Latkin, C.A. 107
Laub, F. 737
Laue, J.H. 693
Laumann, E.O. 469
Laurentin, R. 908, 1441
Lautman, F. 325
Lauwers, J. 1486
La Velle, M. 1374
Lavender, A. 273, 470
Lawler, E. 1943
Lawless, E.J. 2439
Lawrence, P. 3144
Layne, N.R. 2045, 2046
Lazar, M.M. 319
Lazerwitz, B. 274, 373, 395, 447, 471,
  472, 473, 474, 475, 476, 477
Leacock, R. 3173
Leacock, S. 3173
Le Bras, G. 977, 1505, 1506, 1507,
  1508, 1509, 1510, 1511
Lechner, F.J. 1588, 2704, 2705, 2706
Lee, G.R. 1288, 1308
Lee, R.L. 909
Lee, R. 2123
Lee, R.M. 1654, 1655
Lee, V.E. 1396
Leege, D.C. 1397, 1432
Légaré, J. 1703
Lehman, E.C. 1915, 2129, 2279, 2280,
  2281
Leicht, K. 2801
Leiffer, M.H. 2347
Leites, E. 2077, 2656
Leman, J. 2507
Lemercinier, G. 26, 32, 33, 128, 271,
  579, 1464, 1465, 1466, 1467, 1469
Lemert, C.C. 3205
Lemieux, R. 2954
Leñero, L. 1758
Lennon, J. 1674, 1675, 1676, 1677,
  1678
Lenski, G. 1152, 1946
Lentner, L. 1477
Leonard, R.C. 416
Leone, M.P. 2874
Lepargneur, F. 1831
Lerner, N. 401
Les, B.A. 2662
Lessard, M.-A. 1704
Lestchinsky, J. 340
Lester, G.A. 2235

Letkeman, P.  2236
Letts, H.C.  2053
Levasseur, M.  89
Leventman, S.  467
Leverrier, R.  3168
Lévesque, B.  1693
Levi, K.  2972
Levine, B.C.  478
Levine, D.H.  1750
Levine, I.M.  421
Levitte, G.  341
Levy, R.  580
Lewellen, T.C.  2532
Lewins, F.W.  1449, 1450, 1451, 1452, 1453
Lewison, T.S.  3040
Lewy, G.  34, 144, 581
Liebman, C.S.  383, 384, 385, 386, 479, 480, 481
Liebman, R.C.  2804
Liénard, G.  847
Lienhardt, P.  630
Lietz, P.S.  1889
Light, D.W.  1153
Linblade, Z.G.  1289
Lincoln, C.E.  694, 695
Linden, R.  2212
Lindenthal, J.J.  1947
Lindholm, C.  666
Lindner, T.  1477
Lindsey, D.B.  2913
Ling, T.O.  145
Lipman, V.D.  360, 361, 362
Lipset, S.M.  1073
Lipsey, C.M.  2752
Lipson, J.G.  2661
Little, D.  2097
Littman, R.A.  107
Liu, W.T.  1074, 1154, 1164
Lizcano, M.  1626
Loar, R.M.  462
Locke, R.G.  2995
Loewe, R.  275
Lofland, J.  3077, 3078
Long, N.  2508
Long, T.E.  3079
Longino, C.F.  1948, 2119, 2282, 2674
Lopes, P.  941
Lopez, D.  1415
Lopez Fernandez, F.  1850
Lopez Pulido, A.  1398
Lorentzen, L.J.  2738

Loubser, J.J.  2087
Lovelace, A.B.  2569
Lovell, T.  931
Lowi, T.  482
Löwy, M.  276
Luckmann, T.  1972, 1973
Luft, M.C.  2259
Luidens, D.  2142, 2143, 2144, 2145, 2146
Lukes, T.J.  1350
Lummis, A.T.  685
Lundby, K.  2479
Lurje, M.  242
Lutterman, K.G.  1155
Lynch, F.R.  2955, 2956
Lynch, O.M.  35
Lyng, S.G.  946
Lyon, J.L.  2875


M

McAuley, E.N.  1399
McBride, J.  2805
McCallister, I.  1667
McCarrick, T.E.  1156
McCarthy, M.L.  848
McClerren, B.F.  2299
McCourt, K.  1251
McCready, W.C.  939, 1251, 2263
McCutchan, R.  3031
MacDonald, M.Y.  738
McEnery, J.N.  1295, 1296
McGaw, D.B.  2130, 2131, 2132, 2133
McGee, M.  100
McGuire, M.B.  910, 911, 912, 913, 914, 2385
MacInnes, D.W.  1705
Macioti, M.I.  915, 3032
McIver, S.  2949
Mack, R.W.  1075
McKensie, K.  2687
Mackie, M.M.  2180, 2798
McKinney, W.J.  2578, 2579, 2670
MacKinnon, M.H.  2078
MacLeod, H.  2811
McMurray, M.  483
McNamara, P.H.  1157, 1158, 1290, 1291, 1400, 1751
McNamara, R.J.  1120, 1159, 1160, 1161, 1162
MacNeil, P.J.  1208
Macourt, M.  1668

McPherson, W.  193
MacRae, P.H.  1932
McSweeney, B.  816, 817
Madan, T.N.  36, 229
Maddock, R.  1949
Madigan, F.C.  1163
Madsen, G.E.  2855
Maduro, O.  1752, 1753
Maesen, W.A.  696, 2509
Mahar, P.M.  37, 38, 39
Maher, J.A.  1292
Mainwaring, S.  1828
Maiolo, J.R.  1164
Mair, N.H.  2570
Maître, J.  1512, 1513, 1514, 1522
Majka, J.  1605, 1606
Malak, S.J.  1293
Malalgoda, K.  166
Malamat, A.  243
Maldonado, O.  1758
Malherbe, A.J.  739
Malina, B.J.  740
Maloney, D.J.  1165
Mamiya, L.H.  697
Mandelker, I.L.  3197
Mang, W.  1026
Maniha, J.K.  901
Mantzaridis, G.  772
Maranell, G.M.  1294, 2707
Marcos Alonso, J.  1627
Marcum, J.P.  1401
Margarido, A.  1442
Mariański, J.  1607
Marks, G.W.  2727
Marliere, M.  146
Marshall, H.  463, 464
Martel, G.  3174
Martelli, S.  1571
Marthelot, P.  582
Martin, B.  1916, 2999
Martin, B.G.  631
Martindale, D.  244
Mason, M.  2913
Masson, J.  1443
Mathias, J.  2187
Mathieson, M.  1399
Mathisen, J.A.  2708
Matras, J.  370, 387
Mattez, M.T.  978, 1490
Maurer, H.H.  2047, 2048, 2067
Mauroof, M.  667
Mauss, A.L.  2605, 2606, 2856,
    2857, 2876, 2877, 2878, 2879,

2915, 2916
Maxwell-Arnot, M.  2098
May, H.G.  245
Mayer, A.J.  484
Mayer, E.  485, 486, 487
Mayer, J.E.  488
Maynard, J.  2386
Mayne, F.B.  2364
Means, R.L.  1986
Mechanic, D.  489
Meeks, W.A.  741
Mehl, R.  2387
Mehok, W.J.  979, 980
Meisel, T.  402
Memmi, A.  277
Mendelson, E.M.  147, 148, 149, 3180
Mendes Sargo, D.-E.  1966
Mendlovitz, S.H.  417
Menges, W.  1548, 1549, 1603
Messer, J.  75
Meyer, J.  1779
Michael, S.M.  40
Michaelsen, R.S.  2106
Michel, P.  1608
Michelat, G.  1515
Mickey, T.J.  1402
Mickler, M.I.  3080
Middleton, M.M.  1949
Mies, M.  41
Mifflen, F.J.  1706
Mihanovich, C.  1027, 1028
Mikkelsen, M.A.  2552
Miller, D.P.  2237
Miller, M.J.  2272
Miller, R.L.  2680
Miller, R.M.  1987
Miller, W.E.  2709, 2783
Millett, D.  773
Milligan, J.E.  2482
Mills, E.W.  1939, 2134, 2577
Mineau, G.  2899
Miner, H.  1707
Mintz, J.S.  637
Mirsky, N.B.  278
Mishra, S.N.  42, 43
Mitchell, R.E.  1950, 1951
Mitrokhin, L.N.  2253
Moberg, D.O.  1295, 1296, 1403, 2268,
    2269, 2710, 2739
Moen, M.C.  2784
Mogey, J.  2557
Mol, J.J. (Hans)  308, 2049
Moles, A.A.  279

Molloy, S. 214
Momin, A.R. 668
Money, R.L. 2563
Monoghan, R.R. 2711
Monson, R.G. 425
Montague, H. 2510
Montague, J. 583
Monteil, V. 698, 709
Montezemolo, M.I. 1572
Montminy, J.-P. 930, 1704
Moodie, T.D. 2088
Moore, J. 860, 916
Moore, M.J. 1297
Moore, R. 2319
Moran, R. 861
More, D.R. 246
Morel, J. 1553
Moreno-Navarro, I. 1628
Moreux, C. 1708, 1709
Morgan, D.H.J. 1917
Morgan, J.G. 2675
Morgan, R.L. 2221
Morioka, K. 150, 224
Morland, J.K. 2455
Morlet, J. 818, 1516
Moroto, A. 185
Morris, R.J. 2698
Morrow, P.C. 116
Morsa, J. 2836
Mosès, S. 339
Moulin, L. 981
Mueller, C. 2785
Mueller, C.W. 490, 491
Mueller, D.J. 2068
Mueller, S.A. 2050, 2336
Mulder, J.A.N. 151
Müller-Armack, A. 757
Mullins, M.R. 178, 179
Munick, J. 1298
Munters, Q.J. 2511, 2512
Murphy, R.J. 1075
Murphy, R. 1166, 1167
Murphy, S.E. 2061
Murray, C. 1658
Murvar, V. 783
Musetto, A.P. 1299
Musgrove, F. 1918
Mutchler, D. 1754, 1755
Myers, R.A. 2035

N

Nadalin, S.O. 2034
Naito, K. 1460
Nam, C.B. 499
Nandy, S.K. 44
Naranjo, B.A. 3025
Nash, D. 2114, 2115
Nash, J.F. 1071
Nason-Clark, N. 1919, 1920
Nathan, N. 305
Nauss, A.H. 2069, 2070
Navarro, J.C. 1793
Naveskar, B. 219
Nawn, J.Y. 2786
Neal, A.G. 1253
Neal, M.A. 1168, 1169, 1170, 1300, 1301, 1404
Nebreda, J. 862, 1629
Nederman, C.J. 2957
Negrão, L.N. 3012, 3120
Neitz, M.J. 917, 918
Nelsen, H.M. 1302, 1405, 1988, 2124, 2135, 2136, 2270
Nelson, C.H. 2553
Nelson, G.K. 3000, 3001, 3002, 3003, 3004
Nelson, J.I. 1303
Nelson, J.J. 2271
Nelson, L. 2837, 2838
Nelson, R.E. 2005, 2417, 2418
Nemeth, R.J. 2145, 2146
Ness, R.C. 2712
Nesti, A. 1491, 1630
Neundörfer, L. 1538
Newman, J. 1679, 1680
Newman, W.M. 492, 1952, 2580
Newport, F. 2742
Newson, J.A. 1710
Neyrey, J.H. 740
Ngcokovane, C.M. 2089
Nguyen Ho Dinh 1461
Nicolas, J.D. 1625
Nieves, A. 2483
Noell, J. 1406
Nolan, M.J. 1433
Norr, J.L. 1304
Northover, W.E. 1711, 1712
Nottingham, E.K. 2337
Novaes, R. 2419
Nove, A. 342
Nudelman, A.E. 2541, 2542, 2543, 2544
Nudelman, B. 2544

Nuesse, C.J.  1029, 1076

O

Oakman, D.E.  742
Obeyesekere, G.  104, 123, 186
O'Brien, L.N.  90, 91
O'Brien, T.J.  1305
O'Connell, B.J.  1306
O'Connell, J.J.  982
O'Connor, M.  942, 2747
O'Dea, T.F.  493, 819, 1009, 1010,
  1077, 1078, 1171, 1172, 2839,
  2840, 2841, 2842, 2843, 2846,
  2858, 2859, 2880, 2881
Offutt, J.J.  1794
Ofshe, R.  3026
Oh, J.K.  196
Ohrenstein, R.A.  280
O'Kane, J.  1307
Olshan, M.A.  2166
O'Neill, R.  1208
Opazo Bernales, A.  1881, 1890
Organic, H.N.  1173
Orsini, G.  1573
Ortiz, R.  3121, 3122, 3123
Osborne, W.A.  1174
Osterrieth, A.  820
O'Toole, R.  821, 1659, 1713, 1714,
  1715
Owen, D.E.  2791

P

Pace, E.  108, 919
Pagden, F.  2320
Palard, J.  1517
Palazzolo, C.S.  1079
Palmer, S.J.  109
Pangborn, C.R.  2116
Pannabecker, S.F.  2238
Papaderos, A.  758
Parenti, M.J.  699
Paris, A.E.  2440
Parisi, A.  1574, 1575
Parsons, A.  2441
Parsons, A.S.  117, 3081, 3082,
  3083
Pathirana-Wimaladharma, K.  167
Patrick, J.W.  180
Pavan, G.  956

Payne, D.E.  2882, 2883
Peachey, P.  2153, 2239
Peacock, J.L.  638
Pechman, T.  3124
Peck, G.R.  1407
Peek, C.W.  2713
Penning, J.M.  1408, 2788
Pereda, C.  1631
Pereira de Queiroz, M.I.  1829, 1830,
  3105, 3175
Perez Ramirez, G.  1756, 1757, 1758,
  1831, 1864
Pérez Vilarino, J.  1323, 1418
Perkins, R.B.  1958
Perrin, R.D.  1409
Perry, E.L.  2125, 2128, 2714
Peshkin, A.  2715
Peter, K.A.  2181, 2182, 2183
Peters, C.B.  2590
Peters, F.C.  2240
Peters, J.  2211
Petersen, D.L.  247
Petersen, D.W.  2605, 2606
Petersen, J.C.  1308
Petersen, L.R.  1410, 1411, 1412
Petersen, N.R.  743
Peterson, R.W.  1309, 1310, 1420
Petrillo, G.H.  1258, 1259
Pettersson, T.  2031
Pfautz, H.W.  2545, 2546, 2547
Phelan, M.  3033
Philibert, P.J.  1413
Photiadis, J.D.  1311
Piazza, T.  494
Picard Ami, M.A.  1891
Pickering, W.S.F.  1933, 1934, 1935,
  2184
Pierre, R.  3163
Pierson, D.  3106
Piker, S.  152
Pilarzyk, T.J.  76, 77, 2603
Pillai, M.  45
Pin, E.  822, 823, 863, 920, 983, 1518,
  1747, 1759, 1760
Pinsker, S.  536
Pinsky, I.I.  495
Pinto, L.J.  2365
Piquet, J.  1494
Pitcher, B.L.  2903
Piwowarski, W.  1609, 1610, 1611
Pletsch, D.J.  2464
Poblete Barth, R.  864, 1761, 1762,
  1851, 1852, 1853, 1854, 1855, 1856,

2435
Poeisz, J.J.  1589, 1590, 1591, 1592
Poggi, G.  849, 850, 851
Poll, S.  537
Pollack, G.  496
Poloma, M.M.  2388, 2389, 2449
Polsky, H.W.  497
Ponce Garcia, J.  1795
Pope, W.  1473
Porter, J.  1716
Potel, J.  1494, 1519, 1520, 1521, 1522
Potvin, R.H.  1175, 1176, 1177, 1192, 1193, 1312, 1313, 1385, 2270
Potvin, R.  852
Poulat, E.  824, 825, 826, 827, 947, 1514, 1523, 1524, 1525, 1526, 1576
Pozzi, E.  2973
Pratt, H.J.  2671
Pressel, E.  2433
Preston, D.L.  204, 205, 206
Prestwood, C.M.  2348
Price, M.  78
Procter, M.  1657
Pruett, G.E.  2256
Puente de Guzman, M.  1880
Puga, J.  1846


Q

Quebedeaux, R.  921
Quec-Hung, N.  1462
Quinlan, P.T.  2167
Quinley, H.E.  1953, 1960
Quinney, R.  2716


R

Rabi, W.  281
Raboud, I.  877
Rachiele, L.D.  1184
Radosh, M.  1401
Rajan, L.T.  1656, 1657
Rajana, E.W.  2428
Ralston, H.  1717
Rama, C.M.  1796
Rammstedt, O.  2154
Ramos, R.  1780
Rankin, R.P.  2349

Ranson, S.  1660
Raphaël, F.  248, 249, 282, 283, 343, 2187, 2978
Ray, J.J.  1454
Raymaekers, P.  2646
Reagin, E.  2672
Redekop, C.  2241, 2242, 2243
Reed, H.W.  2366
Reed, M.S.  2674
Regan, D.  639, 640
Reidy, M.T.V.  1455, 2390, 2391
Reilly, P.A.  1654
Reimer, M.  2214
Reinhardt, R.M.  2717
Reiss, P.J.  1178, 1179
Reissman, L.  498
Reiterman, C.  1180
Remy, J.  828, 1492, 1493
Reny, P.  922, 1718
Retzer, J.D.  1985
Reynolds, C.H.  2873
Rhodes, A.L.  499
Rhodes, H.T.F.  2979
Ribeiro, R.  3107, 3108, 3109, 3110
Ribeiro de Oliveira, P.A.  923, 1763, 1818, 1832, 1833, 1834, 1835, 1836, 1837, 1838, 2414
Ribeyrol, M.  786
Richard, M.R.  3024
Richard, Y.  721, 722
Richardson, J.T.  1314, 1414, 2390, 2391, 2598, 2599, 2607, 2608, 2609, 2610, 2611, 2612, 2613, 2616, 2617, 2622, 2718, 2974
Richman, K.  889
Richter, P.J.  744
Rigali, L.J.  1315
Rigby, A.  3098
Ringer, B.B.  1940, 1941, 1954, 1955
Risse, H.T.  1536
Ritti, R.R.  854, 1240, 1241, 1316
Rivkin, E.  284
Robbins, R.  500
Robbins, T.  99, 101, 102, 784, 2392, 3042, 3084, 3085
Roberts, B.  2016
Roberts, L.W.  2183
Robertson, R.  2484
Robinsom, F.  669
Robinson, G.K.  1030
Robinson, I.E.  814
Roche, R.  1031
Roche de Coppens, P.  1527

Rochford, E.B.  92, 93, 94, 95
Rochte, F.C.  2300
Rodd, C.S.  250
Rodgers, S.  641
Rodinson, M.  584, 585, 586, 587, 588, 589, 590, 591
Rodrigues, J.H.  3111
Rodríguez Forero, J.  1865
Rogerson, A.T.  2513, 2514, 2515
Rogerson, J.W.  251
Rogler, L.H.  3020
Rolim, A.  1839, 1840
Rolim, F.C.  2420, 2421
Romero, C.  1797
Roof, W.C.  501, 1956, 1957, 1958, 2137, 2301, 2670, 2719
Roos, P.  2039
Rosato, N.  1788
Rose, A.  320
Rose, A.M.  2826
Rose, S.D.  2393, 2740, 2741
Rösel, J.A.  46
Rosen, B.C.  502
Rosenberg, L.  321
Rosenthal, E.  503
Rosenthal, E.I.J.  592
Rosenwaike, I.  403, 504
Ross, J.C.  2474, 2475
Rossi, A.S.  1080, 1182
Rossi, P.H.  1080, 1134, 1135, 1181, 1182
Rotenberg, M.  2079
Rothenberg, S.  2742
Roucek, J.S.  2461
Rouleau, J.-P.  922, 984, 1718, 1719
Rousseau, A.  847
Routhier, F.  1720, 1721
Rovan, J.  1539
Roy, P.  47
Royle, M.H.  2062
Rubin, N.  388
Rubinstein, J.  505
Rudavsky, D.  506
Rudolph, K.  3181, 3182, 3183
Rudy, Z.  285
Ruff, I.J.  3203
Ruiz Olabuénaga, J.  1632, 1633
Runciman, S.  759
Ruppin, S.A.  286, 287, 288
Rushby, W.F.  2244
Russell, M.  2090
Ryan, L.  1680

Ryan, M.D.  1317
Rymph, R.C.  2338

S

Sabagh, G.  1415
Sachchidananda  48
Sacouman, R.J.  1722
Saiedi, N.  593
Saldarini, A.J.  289
Salomone, J.J.  1223
Saloutos, T.  774
Samandu, L.  1882
Samaraweera, V.  670
Samarin, W.J.  2394
Sampson, S.F.  1183, 1318
Sánchez Cano, J.  792, 1967
Sandberg, N.C.  507
Sanders, T.G.  1841
Sangave, V.A.  220
SanGiovanni, L.F.  1319
Saniel, J.M.  225
Santy, H.  985
Sarachandra, E.R.  168
Saram, P.A.S.  169, 170
Sarkisyanz, M.  153, 154
Sartain, D.H.  2914
Saunders, J.V.D.  2327
Savramis, D.  760, 775
Scalf, J.H.  2272
Scarpati, R.  1011
Scarvagliere, G.  986
Schallert, E.J.  865
Scharf, B.R.  290
Scheler, M.  1540
Scherer, R.P.  1416, 2071, 2072
Scheuer, J.F.  1081
Schiff, G.S.  389
Schiffauer, W.  687
Schindeler, F.  2260
Schiper, I.  252
Schlegel, S.A.  2996
Schlesinger, B.  291
Schluchter, W.  253
Schmelz, U.  263
Schmidt, A.J.  2073
Schmidt, N.J.  508
Schmitz, K.M.  1550
Schnabel, J.F.  1311, 1320
Schnapper, D.  786
Schneider, B.  1254
Schneider, L.  1321

Schneiderman, L. 113
Schnepp, G.J. 987, 1032, 1033, 1034
Schoenfeld, E. 745, 2673
Schoenherr, R.A. 1310, 1322, 1323, 1417, 1418, 1420
Schöffler, H. 1968
Scholem, G. 344
Schommer, C.O. 1148, 1184
Schoultz, L. 1866
Schreckengost, G.E. 2350
Schreiber, A. 746
Schuman, H. 1324
Schuyler, J.B. 1082, 1083, 1084, 1085, 1086, 1185
Schwartz, A. 2805
Schwartz, D.F. 1325
Schwartz, G. 2395
Schwartz, N.B. 2367
Schwartzman, S. 1842
Schweigardt, E.H. 1326
Schwieder, E. 2168
Scorsone, S.R. 924
Scott, G.G. 2958
Scoville, W.C. 2094
Scroggs, R. 747
Seggar, J.F. 2884
Séguy, J. 925, 988, 2080, 2155, 2156, 2157, 2396, 2516
Seidler, J. 829, 1327, 1328
Seltzer, R. 675
Seneviratne, H.L. 171
Sengstock, M.C. 830
Servais, E. 831
Shadid, M. 675
Shaffir, W. 322, 390, 541, 542
Shaktir, M. 594
Shanabruch, C.H. 1329
Shapira, R. 377
Shapiro, H.M. 422, 509, 510
Shariati, A. 595
Sharma, A. 49, 50, 129
Sharma, S.L. 671
Sharma, U.M. 51, 52
Sharot, S. 292, 293, 294, 295, 363, 364, 365, 366, 367, 391, 511, 538
Sharp, H. 484
Sheils, D. 3206
Shepherd, G. 2917, 2918, 2919, 2920
Shideler, E. 2476
Shields, J.J. 1386, 1430
Shiels, M. 96

Shokeid, M. 392
Shopshire, J.M. 2442
Shupe, A.D. 66, 197, 795, 2373, 2787, 2789, 2806, 2807, 2808, 3059, 3060, 3061, 3062, 3063, 3064, 3086, 3087, 3088
Sicard, E. 1781
Sicking, T. 723
Siddique, S. 596
Siefer, G. 1551
Siegel, M.A. 433
Sierra, P. 1876, 1877
Silber, I.F. 203
Silbermann, A. 345
Simey, T.S. 1921
Simmonds, R.B. 2598, 2599, 2611, 2612, 2613, 2614, 2615, 2616, 2617
Simon, M. 1515
Simpkins, C. 1303
Simpson, G.E. 2443, 3112, 3155, 3156, 3157
Simpson, J.H. 2809, 2810, 2811
Simson, U. 597, 598
Singelenberg, R. 2517
Singer, M. 527, 528, 529, 543
Sinha, M. 118
Sirven, P. 3176
Sjoberg, G. 1989
Sklare, M. 512, 513, 514
Skocpol, T. 724
Skultans, V. 2994
Slotkin, J.S. 515
Smidt, C. 2397, 2788
Smith, A.D. 296
Smith, B.H. 1857
Smith, D. 1890
Smith, D.E. 172
Smith, E.L. 2169, 2170
Smith, J.A. 2309
Smith, J.O. 1989
Smith, K.B. 2572
Smith, L. 1959
Smith, P. 676, 3204
Smith, R. 1929
Smith, W.E. 2844, 2845
Smucker, D.E. 2213
Smucker, J. 2245
Smythe, H.H. 306
Snow, D.A. 198, 199, 200
Sobal, J. 2950, 2951
Sobel, B.Z. 2658
Sockeel-Richarté, P. 634
Solomon, G. 309

Solomon, T.  3089
Sombart, W.  297
Sommerfeld, R.E.  2074
Sorensen, A.A.  1330, 1331
Sorensen, A.  1417
Sotero Giando, R.  2194
Souffrant, C.  1892
Souryal, S.S.  677
Spae, J.J.  1463
Spaeth, J.L.  1186
Spaulding, K.E.  832
Spencer, A.E.C.W.  833, 1661, 1662, 1663
Spencer, M.  2099
Spencer, R.F.  181, 182
Spicer, J.C.  2885
Spiro, M.  155
Spitzer, A.  834
Srinivas, M.N.  53
Srinivasa Rao, G.S.S.  54
Srivastava, R.N.  671
Srole, L.  521
Stacey, W.A.  2789, 2806, 2807, 2808
Stack, S.  1419
Stackhouse, M.L.  55
Stamm, M.J.  1332
Stange, D.C.  2051
Stark, R.  748, 1118, 1119, 1369, 1960, 2921, 2947, 2982, 2985
Stark, W.  835, 836, 837, 3191
Stauth, G.  545
Steed, M.L.  1961
Steeman, T.M.  1593
Steinberg, B.  368, 516
Steinberg, S.  298, 517, 518, 519
Steiner, J.F.  2462
Stempien, R.  2720
Stendahl, B.  2032
Stern, H.  56
Stevens, L.  1936
Stewart, J.H.  866, 867, 868
Stewart, M.W.  2610, 2612, 2613
Stiefbold, A.E.  1741
Stinner, C.M.  2924
Stokes, R.G.  2091
Stone, D.R.  2571
Stone, D.  2937, 2938, 2940
Stones, C.R.  2618, 2619, 2620
Stoop, W.  1594
Stott, G.N.  2302
Stouffer, S.A.  1035
Strassberg, B.  1612

Straus, R.A.  2986
Streib, G.F.  1681
Streiker, L.D.  2621
Strenski, I.  124
Strickland, B.R.  2303
Strizower, S.  307
Stromberg, P.G.  2480
Strommen, M.P.  2040, 2052
Stroup, H.H.  2518
Struzzo, J.A.  1333
Stryckman, P.  1720, 1723, 1724, 1725, 1726, 1727, 1728, 1782
Stryker, R.  520
Stycos, J.M.  1764
Suaud, C.  1528, 1529, 1530
Subramaniam, K.  57
Suk, W.  1478
Suk-jay, Y.  3177
Sullivan, T.A.  939
Sundberg, N.D.  107
Sutter, J.  869
Swanson, G.E.  1969
Swatos, W.H.  1922, 2081, 2676, 2677
Sweetser, T.  1334
Sykes, R.E.  2681, 2682
Sylvain, P.  1729
Symington, T.A.  2790
Szafran, R.F.  1335, 1420


T

Tabory, E.  393, 394, 395
Taft, R.  309
Taggart, M.  2481
Tajima, P.J.  183
Takayama, K.P.  226, 1410, 1411, 1412
Talar, C.J.T.  948
Tambiah, S.J.  58, 125
Tamney, J.B.  156, 599, 642, 643, 644, 645, 646, 1421, 2691, 2721, 2722, 2778, 2779, 2802, 2803, 2812
Tanner, R.E.S.  3138
Tanoni, I.  943
Tapia, C.  346, 347
Tapp, R.B.  2683, 2684
Tappan, P.W.  2827
Taras, P.  1613, 1614
Tarleton, M.R.  1187
Tavakol, R.  720
Taylor, C.W.  1995
Taylor, D.F.  2102, 3039, 3090
Taylor, M.G.  1944, 2138, 2139

Teixeira, A. 3125
Tennekes, J. 2429
Terian, S.M.K. 1422
Terrenoire, J.-P. 1502, 1514, 1531
Thaiss, G. 725
Thapar, R. 59
Thébaud, F. 1893
Theissen, G. 749, 750, 751, 752, 753, 754
Theobald, R. 2533, 2534, 2535
Theophane, M. 254
Thielman, G.T. 2246
Thiessen, V. 2679
Thomas, C.W. 2272
Thomas, D.L. 842, 843, 844, 2889, 2922, 2923
Thomas, J.L. 1036, 1087
Thompson, J.R. 926
Thompson, M. 989
Thompson, R.C. 2304
Thorn, W.J. 1423
Thorner, I. 2548
Thornton, A. 2886
Thornton, R. 3146, 3147, 3148
Thurlings, J.M.G. 1595, 1596
Tibi, B. 600
Tint, H. 348
Tipton, S.M. 207, 208, 2939
Tiryakian, E.A. 2092, 2107, 2108, 2959
Tobey, A. 98
Tobias, C.L. 1765
Toffin, G. 136
Tomasi, L. 601, 1577
Toney, M.B. 2924
Tonna, B. 1579
Topalov, A.-M. 2536
Towler, R. 1923, 1924, 1925
Traina, F.J. 1336
Treece, J.W. 2554
Tremblay, G. 1721
Trent, J.W. 1188
Trozzolo, T.A. 1397
Trush, J.C. 2244
Truzzi, M. 2960
Turbeville, G. 2339
Turcan, K.A. 1653, 1655, 1656
Turcotte, P.-A. 1730
Turner, B.S. 602, 603, 604, 605, 2321, 2322, 2323, 3098
Turner, D.E. 870
Turner, F.C. 1766, 1767, 1768, 1769

Turner, L.A. 1943
Turner, P.R. 2748
Tygart, C.E. 1266


U

Underhill, R. 3207
Underwager, R.C. 2040
Urbina, F. 1634
Urry, J. 2247
Utrecht, E. 60, 647


V

Vaillancourt, J.-G. 838, 841, 1731
Vajda, G. 299
Valente, W. 3113
Valenzano, P.M. 1578
Vallier, I. 839, 840, 841, 1770, 1771, 1772, 1773, 1774, 2860
Van der Lans, J.M. 68
Van Dijck, C. 648
Van Heek, F. 1597.
Van Hemert, M. 1598
Van Kemenade, J.A. 1599
Van Roy, R.F. 1962
Varacalli, J.A. 1424, 1425, 1426, 1427, 1428
Vassallo, M. 1580
Vassort-Rousset, B. 1532
Vaughn, S.L. 890
Vazquez, J.M. 1635, 1636
Vekémans, R. 1600
Ventimiglia, J.C. 3064
Vera, H. 1429
Verdieck, M.J. 1386, 1430
Verdonk, A.L.T. 990
Vernon, G.M. 2887
Verryn, T.D. 1444
Verscheure, J. 1533
Vertraelen, F.J. 1445
Vetulani, A. 349
Villela, H.G. 1858
Villeroy, M. 2006
Vogler, C.C. 2083
Vogt, E. 1974
Vogt, E.Z. 2846
Vogt, R. 2214
Vollmer, H.M. 991
Von Deschwanden, L. 871
Von Hoffman, N. 2398

Voye, L. 1493
Vrcan, S. 1639
Vrga, D.J. 785, 787, 788, 789,
790
Vulliez, H. 1494

W

Waardenburg, J. 606, 607
Waddell, C.E. 2887
Wagner, A. 1638
Wagner, H.R. 1088
Wakeford, P. 2318
Wakin, E. 764
Wald, K.D. 2791
Walker, A.G. 927, 2399, 2411,
2412, 2413
Walker, K.N. 1867
Walker, P.R. 2659
Wall, D.F. 1337
Wallace, R.A. 1359, 1431, 1732
Wallis, R. 110, 2093, 2369, 2624,
2625, 2626, 2627, 2628, 2629,
2630, 2759, 2760, 2792, 2941,
2987, 2988, 2989, 2990, 2991,
3099
Walters, J. 419
Walters Burch, G. 2581
Wanderley, L.E. 1843
Warburton, T.R. 2359, 2360
Ward, C.D. 1012
Ward, C.K. 1664, 1665, 1680
Ward, D.A. 2368
Wardwell, W.I. 2549
Warenski, M. 2888
Warkov, S. 1189
Warner, R.S. 2140, 2743
Warner, W.L. 521
Warren, B.L. 522, 1963
Warrick, E. 1202
Watanabe, E. 187
Watson, F. 755
Watson, G.L. 700
Watt, W.M. 608
Watts, C.R. 2248
Watzke, J.N. 1338, 1859
Wax, M. 255
Weber, M. 61, 215, 256
Weddell, S.C. 2303
Wedge, R.B. 1190
Weibel, N. 688
Weigert, A.J. 842, 843, 844, 904,

992, 2723, 2889
Weightman, J.M. 2975
Weima, J. 1601
Weisbrod, A. 523
Weissbrod, L. 396, 397
Welch, M.R. 1397, 1432
Weldon, J. 2992
Weller, N.J. 1191
Weller, R.H. 1214
Wener, N. 1733
West, R.A. 2828
Westhues, K. 1339, 1340, 1341, 1701,
1734, 1735, 1736, 1737, 1872, 1873
Westley, F.R. 928, 2942
Westoff, C.F. 1097, 1176, 1177, 1192,
1193, 1342, 1343
Whitaker, I. 2183
Whitam, F.L. 2755, 2756
White, D. 2928, 2929
White, H.C. 1344
White, L.C. 1455
White, O.K. 2793, 2890, 2891, 2892,
2925, 2926, 2927, 2928, 2929
White, R.A. 1894
White, T. 2519
Whitehead, H. 2961
Whitehead, P.C. 314
Whitley, C.M. 993
Whitley, O.R. 2559
Whitworth, J. 96, 2555, 3192, 3193
Whyte, J. 845
Wichmann, A.A. 157, 158
Wicks, J.W. 1345
Wiebe, P.D. 2017
Wiefel, W. 756
Wiener, R.L. 1433
Wierzbicki, Z.T. 2663
Wiesel, B.B. 2249
Wilber, D.N. 672
Wilcox, W.C. 2724, 2725, 2794, 2813
Wiley, N. 1194
Wilkins, S. 3199
Willaime, J.-P. 1975, 1976, 2745
Willems, E. 1844, 2007, 2008, 2009,
2010, 2011, 2422
Williams, C.R. 1977
Williams, D. 994
Williams, M.D. 2444
Williams, P. 2406
Williams-Hogan, J. 3187
Willms, J.D. 1434
Willner, D. 303
Wilmeth, J.R. 3164

Wilmeth, M.W.   3164
Wilson, B.R.   2400, 2401, 2402,
   2403, 2465, 2503, 2520, 2521,
   2522, 2550, 3091
Wilson, H.A.   173
Wilson, Jim   62
Wilson, J.   2404, 3185, 3194
Wilson, R.R.   257
Wilson, S.R.   119, 120
Wimberley, R.C.   2305, 2306, 2752,
   2757
Winandy, D.H.   1195
Winter, J.A.   258
Wise, D.T.   209
Wittberg, P.   995, 996, 997, 998
Wood, J.R.   1962, 1984, 2336, 2351
Wood, W.W.   2361
Woodroof, J.T.   2564, 2565, 2566
Woodrum, E.   2795, 2796, 3034, 3035
Workman, R.L.   1345
Worsley, P.   3145
Wright, B.   2637
Wright, C.   2687
Wright, E.   2133
Wright, P.A.   2893
Wright, S.A.   97
Wrobel, P.   1346
Wulf, J.   2744
Wurzbacher, G.   2025
Wust, I.   1864
Wuthnow, R.   2797
Wyatt, G.   2930
Wyllie, R.W.   2998

                    X

Xidieh, O.E.   3013


                    Y

Yaari, A.   350
Yalman, N.   174, 678

Yama, E.K.   188
Yeaman, P.A.   1435
Yellin, S.   1075
Yinger, J.M.   2678, 2814
Yokley, R.L.   2135, 2136
York, A.   524
Yoshinaga, E.   184
Young, B.S.   846
Young, F.W.   2445, 2446
Young, K.   2829, 2847
Young, L.A.   1418
Young, P.V.   525, 2652
Young, T.R.   701


                    Z

Zablocki B.D.   2556
Zahn, G.C.   1089, 1541, 1542
Zald, M.N.   2351, 2685, 2686
Zaret, D.   2100
Zdaniewicz, W.   1615
Zeegers, G.H.L.   1474, 1479
Zeitlin, I.M.   259
Zelan, J.   526
Zenatti, S.   1556
Zieger, P.   2026
Zimmer, B.   1196
Zingerle, A.   216
Zlobin, N.S.   2255
Zobermann, N.   277
Zubaida, S.   609
Zulehner, P.M.   1480
Zurcher, L.A.   1321
Zygmunt, J.F.   2523, 2524, 2525
Zylberberg, J.   539, 929, 930, 1860

# SUBJECT INDEX
(Numbers refer to items)

## A

Adventist. *See* Christadelphian; Irvingite; Jehovah's Witnesses; Millerite; Seventh-day Adventist

Aetherius Society, 3099

African independent (Christian), 2631-2636. *See also* John Maranke, Apostolic Church of; Kimbangu; Order of Ethiopia

Africanist religion in Brazil, 3007, 3100-3113. *See also* Batuque cult; Candomblé; Umbanda

African Methodist Episcopal Church, 2328-2329

Amana, 2551

American Baptist Convention, 1118-1119, 1266, 1416, 1942-1945, 1948, 1950-1951, 1953, 1960, 2036, 2265, 2273-2282

American Lutheran Church, 1118-1119, 1308, 1939, 1942-1943, 1948, 1953, 2056

Amish, 2158-2170. *See also* Anabaptist; Mennonite

Anabaptist: general and historical studies, 34, 2151-2157. *See also* Amish; Hutterite; Mennonite

Ananda Marga, 63-64

Anglican: Church of England, 972, 1642, 1660, 1895-1925; Church of Ireland, 1667-1668; Anglican Church of Canada, 1716, 1926-1936; Episcopal (U.S.A.), 404, 437, 463-464, 469, 471, 484, 490, 501, 518, 522, 1118-1119, 1266, 1294, 1304, 1330-1331, 1369, 1387, 1409, 1416, 1922, 1937-1963; Africa, 1444, 1964; Australia, 308; Latin

America, 1748

Antigonish movement, 1705-1706, 1722

Antoniens, 3132-3133

Apostolic Christian Church (Peoria, Illinois), 2657

Assembly of God (U.S.A.), 1294, 1409, 1943, 2449

astrology, 2946, 2957

## B

Baha'i, 676, 889-890, 3198-3204

Balokole (Uganda), 3172

Baptist: Great Britain, 1910, 1915, 1919; Europe, 2250-2252; Soviet Union, 2253-2255; India, 2256; Australia, 308; Canada, 2257-2260; U.S.A. (general), 404, 437, 463-464, 471, 483-484, 499, 501, 518, 522, 1278, 1294, 1304, 1369, 1409, 1937, 1946, 1963, 2261-2272. *See also* American Baptist Convention; Southern Baptist (U.S.A.)

Batuque cult (Brazil), 3173

Benedictine, 952, 991, 993

Bethany Fellowship, 2554

Bhils (India), 3139-3140

Billy Graham Crusade, 2749-2757

Black Hebrew Nation, 527-529

Black Muslim, 689-701

Brethren, 308, 1311, 1416, 1946, 2463-2465

Bruderhof (Society of Brothers), 2555-2556

Buddhist: general studies, 121-125; India (Ancient), 25, 31, 61, 126-129; South Asia, 59, 130-136; Southeast Asia and Pacific, 137-158; Sri Lanka,

453

104, 141, 145, 159-174; Western, 137, 175-183; modern sects and movements (miscellaneous), 74, 184-188; Soka Gakkai, 189-200; Theravada, 201-203; Zen, 204-209

## C

Calvinist (general and international studies): general, 2075-2081; Netherlands, 1601, 2082-2083; South Africa, 1439, 2084-2093; France, 2094; Australia, 308, 2095; Great Britain, 1910, 1915, 2096-2100; Northern Ireland, 1667, 2093, 2096, 2101-2102; Ireland (Presbyterian), 1667-1668; Latin America (Presbyterian, Christian and Missionary Alliance), 1748. *See also* Paisleyism; Puritan (U.S.A.); Congregationalist (U.S.A.); Presbyterian (U.S.A.); United Presbyterian Church (U.S.A.); Reformed Church in America; Christian Reformed Church (U.S.A.); Dutch Reformed (U.S.A.); German Reformed (U.S.A.)
Candomblé, 3126-3131
Capuchin, 954, 956
cargo cults, 34, 3141-3145
Carmelite (female Discalced), 994
Catholic Action, 847-852
charismatic movement, Roman Catholic, 329, 539, 878-930
Children of God, 63-64, 66, 97, 881, 2609, 2622-2630. *See also* Jesus movement
Chowado, 188
Christadelphian, 2401
Christian, early, 25, 726-756
Christian Church in America, 2659
Christian Reformed Church (U.S.A.), 2083, 2141, 2147-2150
Christian Science, 889-890, 1946, 2401, 2537-2550
Churches of Christ, 308, 469, 1294, 2122, 2558, 2560-2566
Church of England. *See* Anglican
Church of God (Anderson, Indiana), 1387, 1409, 1413, 2362. *See also* Holiness religion
Church of Scotland (Calvinist), 2098
Claretian, 959
communitarian, Christian, 2551-2556
Confucian, 211-216
Congregationalist (U.S.A.), 180, 404, 469, 501, 518, 1118-1119, 1304, 1369, 1937, 1950-1951, 1959, 2036, 2109-2116
Conservative Protestant: general studies, 2666, 2758-2760; Canada, 2761-2763; Australia, 2095; United States, 2126, 2141, 2146, 2673, 2764-2797. *See also* Moral Majority
Contestado movement (Brazil), 3175
Coptic (Egyptian Christian), 763-764

## D

Daishi-Do, 184
Daughters of Wisdom, 988
Diggers, 2080
Disciples of Christ, 1118-1119, 1294, 1304, 1409, 1416, 1944, 1946, 1962, 2036, 2062, 2557-2559
Divine Light Mission, 65-78
Doukhobor, 2648-2650
Dutch Reformed (U.S.A.), 2049

## E

Episcopal (U.S.A.). *See* Anglican
Erik Janssonist movement, 2552-2553
est, 208, 2936-2939
Ethiopian Orthodox, 765-766
Evangelical Protestant: United States, 1210, 1937, 2140, 2397, 2688, 2702, 2710, 2725-2744; France, 2745; Latin America, 2746-2748. *See also* Billy Graham Crusade; Moral Majority
Evangelical United Brethren. *See* Brethren
Exclusive Brethren. *See* Brethren

## F

Family of Love. *See* Children of God
Father Divine, 2363-2364
Freemasonry, 3184-3185
Full Gospel Businessmen's Fellowship International, 2450-2452

Fundamentalist Protestant, 483,
546, 2263, 2270, 2558, 2687-2725.
*See also* Moral Majority


G

German Reformed (U.S.A.), 1304
Ghost Dance movements, 3146-3148
Gnostic (ancient), 3178-3183
Greek Orthodox, 308, 767-775


H

Hare Krishna, 79-97
Harrist religion (Ivory Coast),
3169
Hasidic, 315, 530-539
Healthy-Happy-Holy Organization,
74, 98
Hebrew, 25, 230-259
Hebrew Christianity, 2658
Hindu: general studies, 1-62;
Ananda Marga, 63-64; Divine Light
Mission, 65-78; Hare Krishna, 79-
97; Healthy-Happy-Holy Organiza-
tion, 74, 98; Meher Baba, 99-102;
Pattini, 103-104; Radhasoami, 72,
105; Rajneesh, 106-110; Rama-
krishna, 111-113; Vedanta, 96,
114; Yoga, 115-120
Holiness religion, 2352-2361. *See
also* Church of God (Anderson,
Indiana); Father Divine; Nazar-
ene, Church of the; Salvation
Army
Holy Family Missionaries, 990
Huguenots, 2094
human potential movement, 2937,
2940-2942. *See also* est;
Scientology
Huniyan, cult of, 186
Hutterite, 2171-2184. *See also*
Anabaptist


I

Irvingite, 2485, 2487
Islamic: general studies, 34, 545-
609; Algeria, 610-613; Egypt,
614-622; Morocco, 623-626; other
African studies, 627-631; Southeast
Asia and Pacific, 60, 632-648; South
Asia, 28, 36, 649-672; Middle East,
673-678; West, 679-688; Black Muslim,
689-701; Ismaili, 1, 702-704; Mouride,
705-709; Shi'ite, 710-725
Ismaili, 1, 702-704


J

Jain, 217-220
Jamaa, 1437, 3134-3138
Jansenist, 931-932
Jehovah's Witnesses, 539, 1409, 1748,
2488-2525
Jesuit. *See* Society of Jesus
Jesus movement, 102, 208, 881, 920,
2391, 2584-2621. *See also* Children of
God
Jewish: general studies, 260-299;
Africa, 300-303; Asia, 304-307;
Australia, 308-309; Canada, 310-322;
Europe, 323-350; Great Britain, 351-
368; Israel, 267, 369-397; Latin
America, 398-403; United States, 366,
404-526; Black Hebrew Nation, 527-529;
Hasidic, 315, 530-539; Lubavitcher,
540-543; Sephardic, 544
Jews for Jesus, 2660-2661
John Maranke, Apostolic Church of,
2638-2642
Jonestown. *See* People's Temple


K

Kimbangu, 2643-2646
Kokambism (Ivory Coast), 3176


L

Levellers, 2656
Liberal Protestant, 2664-2673. *See also*
Social Gospel; Unitarian; YMCA
Llano Colony, 2174
Lubavitcher, 540-543
Lutheran (general and international
studies): Germany, 1535, 2018; West
Germany, 2019-2026; Hungary, 337;
Finland, 2027-2028; Sweden, 2029-
2032; Australia, 308; Canada, 2033;

Latin America, 1748, 2034; U.S.A. (general), 404, 437, 469, 471, 484, 490, 501, 518, 520, 771, 1155, 1267, 1288, 1294, 1304, 1405, 1409, 1937, 1945-1946, 2035-2052. *See also* United Lutheran Church in America; Lutheran Church in America; American Lutheran Church; Missouri Synod (Lutheran); Norwegian Lutheran Church in America

Lutheran Church in America, 1416, 1422, 1939, 1944, 1953, 1960, 2056-2062

## M

magic. *See* occult, the
Maldevidan, cult of (Martinique), 3171
Mariology, 108, 933-943
Meher Baba, 99-102
Mennonite: Russia, 2185-2186; France, 2157, 2187; Latin America, 2188-2194; North America, 1294, 1702, 2158, 2173, 2195-2249. *See also* Amish; Anabaptist
Methodist: general studies, 2307-2309; Great Britain, 972, 1642, 1660, 1910, 1915, 1919, 2310-2323; Canada, 2258, 2324; Australia, 308, 2325; Latin America, 1748, 2326-2327; United States, 404, 437, 463-464, 471, 484, 490, 501, 518, 520, 522, 832, 1118-1119, 1259, 1267-1268, 1278, 1294, 1304, 1311, 1369, 1405, 1409, 1416, 1937, 1942, 1946, 1948, 1950-1951, 1962-1963, 2261-2262, 2330-2338. *See also* African Methodist Episcopal Church; The Methodist Church (U.S.A.); United Methodist Church (U.S.A.)
Metropolitan Spiritual Churches of Christ, 3021-3022
Millerite, 2486
Missionaries of the Society of Mary, 987-988
Missouri Synod (Lutheran), 1416, 1962, 2063-2074
modernist crisis (Roman Catholic), 944-948

Molokan, 2651-2652
monotheism, 3205-3207
Moral Majority, 2291, 2724-2725, 2730, 2778, 2794, 2798-2814
Moravian, 2457-2462
Mormon: works (1937-1949), 2815-2829; works (1950-1959), 2830-2847; works (1960-1969), 437, 1093, 1644, 1748, 2235, 2848-2860; works (1970-1979), 1314, 2243, 2861-2893; works (1980-1989), 1409, 1414, 2302, 2787, 2793, 2798, 2894-2930; Aaronic Order, 2931-2933; Morrisites, 2934-2935
Mouism (Korea), 3177
Mouride, 705-709
Mukyokai (Japanese Christian), 2647
Myochikai, 185

## N

National Council of Churches of Christ in the United States, 2671
National Federation of Priests' Councils (Roman Catholic), 866-868
Nazarene, Church of the, 1294, 1409, 1946, 2365-2368
New Christian Right (U.S.A.). *See* Moral Majority
new religions: miscellaneous, 67, 3092-3099. *See also* Children of God; est; human potential movement; People's Temple; Scientology; Synanon; Transcendental Meditation; Unification Church
New Testament Church of God, 2655
New Thought, 2943-2944
Nichiren Shoshu. *See* Soka Gokkai
Norwegian Lutheran Church in America, 2065

## O

occult, the, 2945-2961. *See also* Theosophy
Oneida community, 2555, 2906, 3195-3197
Order of Ethiopia, 2637
Orthodox (Christian): general studies, 757-760; Orthodox (U.S.A.), 469, 484, 761-762; Coptic, 763-764; Ethiopian Orthodox, 765-766; Greek Orthodox,

308, 767-775; Russian Orthodox, 776-784; Serbian Orthodox, 785-790; Syrian Orthodox, 773, 791; Ukrainian Orthodox, 773, 792
Oxford Group Movement, 2653-2654
Oxford Movement, 972


P

Paisleyism, 2093, 2096, 2101-2102
Parsi, 221
Pattini, 103-104
pentecostal: general studies, 1897, 2130-2133, 2361, 2369-2404; Italy, 2405; France, 2406; Great Britain, 2407-2413; Latin America (general), 1748, 2414; Brazil, 2415-2422; Chile, 2422-2429; Colombia, 2430-2431; Mexico, 2432-2433; Puerto Rico, 2434-2435; United States, 1238, 1946, 2388, 2435-2444. *See also* Pentecostal Church of God in America; United Pentecostal Church (U.S.A.); Assembly of God (U.S.A.); Full Gospel Businessmen's Fellowship International; Snake handling; New Testament Church of God
Pentecostal Church of God in America, 2445-2446
People's Temple, 66, 784, 2962-2975
pietist, 2477-2481
Polish National Catholic Church, 2662-2663
polytheism, 3205
Presbyterian (U.S.A.), 404, 437, 469, 471, 490, 501, 518, 522, 832, 1294, 1304, 1369, 1387, 1409, 1413, 1416, 1422, 1946, 1951, 2036, 2117-2125
Process, The, 2977
Protestant (general and historical studies): Europe, 1473, 1970-1977; Canada, 1927, 1978; United States, 419, 428, 441, 446, 454, 466, 471-472, 484, 490-491, 499, 501, 518, 520, 526, 1013, 1018, 1073, 1075, 1088, 1091, 1093, 1098, 1100-1101, 1117-1119, 1152, 1173,

1191, 1225, 1228, 1233-1234, 1265, 1302-1303, 1324, 1348, 1405, 1407, 1950, 1978-1989; Latin America (general), 1748, 1990-1995; Mexico, 1996-1999; Brazil and Chile, 1844, 2000-2011; Argentina, 2004, 2012-2014; Colombia, 1861-1862; Guatemala, 2015-2016; Nicaragua, 2015; Uruguay, 398; Asia, 156, 2017. *See also* Conservative Protestant; Evangelical Protestant; Fundamentalist Protestant; Liberal Protestant
Puritan (U.S.A.), 2103-2108


Q

Quaker, 219, 416, 1304, 1946, 2103, 2466-2476


R

Radhasoami, 72, 105
Rajneesh, 106-110
Ramakrishna, 111-113
Rastafarian, 575, 700, 3149-3157
Reformation (Protestant), 1965-1969
Reformed Church in America, 1946, 2141-2146
Riel movement (Canada), 3174
Rissho Kosei-kai, 187
Roman Catholic: general studies, 203, 723, 793-846; Catholic Action, 847-852; Catholic clergy, 853-871; Catholic Traditionalist, 872-877; charismatic movement, 329, 539, 878-930; Jansenist, 931-932; Mariology, 108, 933-943; modernist crisis, 944-948; religious orders and congregations, 116, 949-998; Second Vatican Council, 999-1012. *See also* Roman Catholic (International); Roman Catholic (U.S.A.)
Roman Catholic (International): Africa, 949, 1436-1445; Australia and New Zealand, 308, 1446-1455; Pacific and East Asia, 142, 156, 1456-1463; India, 791, 937, 1464-1467; Europe (general studies), 1470-1474; Austria, 1475-1480; Belgium, 1481-1493; France, 1494-1533; Germany, 1534-1542; West Germany, 1543-1551; Hungary, 1552-

1553; Italy, 851, 1352, 1491, 1554-1578; Malta, 1579-1580; Netherlands, 1581-1601; Norway, 1602; Sweden, 1603; Poland, 1604-1615; Spain, 1323, 1418, 1491, 1616-1636; Switzerland, 1637-1638; Yugoslavia, 1639; Great Britain, 1640-1665; Northern Ireland, 1666-1668; Ireland, 1669-1681; North America (general studies), 872, 1682-1684; Canada, 939, 1341, 1376, 1685-1737; Latin America (general studies), 1738-1774; Mexico, 1775-1782; Argentina, 1783-1788; Bolivia, 1790, 1795; Ecuador, 1789; Peru, 1790-1791, 1794, 1797; Uruguay, 398, 1796; Venezuela, 1789, 1792-1793; Brazil, 1798-1844; Chile, 1800, 1845-1860; Colombia, 1861-1867; Paraguay, 1868-1873; Guatemala, 1874-1877; Nicaragua, 780, 1878-1882; other Central American and Caribbean, 1879, 1883-1894
Roman Catholic (U.S.A.): works (1930-1949), 404, 1013-1036; works (1950-1959), 419, 454, 1037-1089; works (1960-1969), 405, 416, 437, 441, 469, 471, 484, 500, 526, 1090-1196; works (1970-1979), 428, 446, 466, 483, 491, 499, 501, 518-519, 522, 771, 910, 1197-1346; works (1980-1989), 463-464, 490, 520, 872, 939, 1347-1435
Russian Old Believers, 784
Russian Orthodox, 776-784

S

Salvation Army, 308, 2482-2484
Satanism, 2976-2979
science fiction, 2948, 2961
Scientology, 66, 2600, 2630, 2961, 2980-2992
Sephardic, 544
Serbian Orthodox, 785-790
Seventh-day Adventist, 308, 1294, 1409, 1748, 2488, 2526-2536
Shakers, 2403, 2555, 2906, 3188-3194

Shi'ite, 710-725
Shinto, 222-226
Sikh, 227-229
Sisters of Charity of St. Vincent de Paul, 955
Sisters of Providence, 976
Sisters of the Child Jesus of Fort Victoria, 949
snake handling, 2453-2455
Social Gospel, 2674-2678. *See also* Liberal Protestant
Society of Brothers. *See* Bruderhof
Society of Jesus, 951, 957, 962-965, 969, 971, 979, 980, 982, 991-992
Soka Gakkai, 189-200
Southern Baptist (U.S.A.), 180, 1118-1119, 1258-1259, 1387, 1413, 1416, 1953, 1960, 1962, 2122, 2265, 2278, 2283-2306
Southern Christian Leadership Conference, 2672
spiritualism: general studies, 2993-2994; Australia, 2995; Philippines, 2996; Ghana, 2997-2998; Great Britain, 2999-3004; Brazil, 1844, 2000, 3005-3013; Mexico, 3014-3016; Puerto Rico, 3017-3020; United States, 3021-3024
Sulpician, 953
Swedenborg, 3186-3187
Synanon, 3025-3026
Syrian Orthodox, 773, 791

T

Taiping, 3170
Taoist, 156, 210-216
The Methodist Church (U.S.A.), 2264-2265, 2339
Theosophy, 2959, 3027
Theravada Buddhist, 201-203
Tonghak (Korea), 3165-3168
Traditionalist, Roman Catholic, 872-877
Transcendental Meditation, 2985, 3028-3035
Trappist, 961, 973

U

UFO cult, 3036-3040
Ukrainian Orthodox, 773, 792
Umbanda, 2316, 2416, 2433, 3007,

3114-3125
Unification Church, 63-64, 66, 97,
  530, 2371, 2392, 2493, 2600,
  2908, 3041-3091
Unitarian, 1294, 1304, 2303, 2679-
  2684
United Brethren. *See* Brethren
United Church of Canada, 1702, 1927-
  1928, 1931, 1935, 2464, 2567-2571
United Church of Christ, 437, 1266,
  1294, 1409, 1416, 1939, 1945,
  1953, 1960, 1962, 2572-2581
United Lutheran Church in America,
  1950-1951, 2053-2055
United Methodist Church (U.S.A.),
  832, 1258, 1266, 1387, 1413,
  1939, 1944-1945, 1953, 1960,
  2062, 2340-2351
United Pentecostal Church (U.S.A.),
  2447-2448
United Presbyterian Church (U.S.A.),
  1939, 1942, 1944-1945, 1948,
  1951, 1953, 1960, 2036, 2062,
  2126-2140
Uniting Church in Australia, 2095,
  2567, 2582-2583

V

Vatican Council, Second, 999-1012
Vedanta, 96, 114
Vincentian, 958
Voodoo, 1893, 2376, 3152, 3158-3164

W

Waldensian, 2456
witchcraft, 2948, 2958, 2960

Y

YMCA, 2685-2686
Yoga, 115-120

Z

Zen Buddhist, 204-209